W9-COX-073

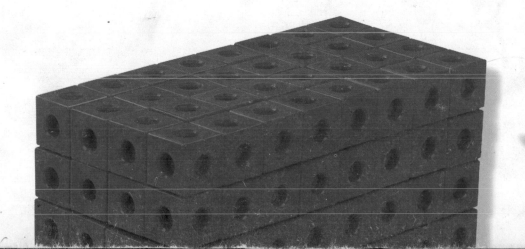

200,000

50,000

6,000

900

80

3

???,???

http://www.hbschool.com

200,000

50,000

6,000

900

80

3

???,???

MATH
ADVANTAGE

Harcourt Brace & Company

Orlando • Atlanta • Austin • Boston • San Francisco • Chicago • Dallas • New York • Toronto • London

http://www.hbschool.com

Requests for permission to make copies of any part of the work should be
mailed to: Permissions Department, Harcourt Brace & Company,
6277 Sea Harbor Drive, Orlando, Florida 32887-6777.

HARCOURT BRACE and Quill Design is a registered trademark of
Harcourt Brace & Company. MATH ADVANTAGE is a trademark of
Harcourt Brace & Company.

Printed in the United States of America

ISBN 0-15-305673-8

2 3 4 5 6 7 8 9 10 048 2000 99 98 97

▼▼ Senior Authors ▼▼

Grace M. Burton
Chair, Department of Curricular Studies
Professor, School of Education
University of North Carolina at Wilmington
Wilmington, North Carolina

Evan M. Maletsky
Professor of Mathematics
Montclair State University
Upper Montclair, New Jersey

▼▼ Authors ▼▼

George W. Bright
Professor of Mathematics Education
The University of North Carolina at Greensboro
Greensboro, North Carolina

Sonia M. Helton
Professor of Childhood Education
Coordinator, College of Education
University of South Florida
St. Petersburg, Florida

Loye Y. (Mickey) Hollis
Professor of Mathematics Education
*Director of Teacher Education and Undergradu-
  ate Programs*
University of Houston
Houston, Texas

Howard C. Johnson
Dean of the Graduate School
Associate Vice Chancellor for Academic Affairs
*Professor, Mathematics and Mathematics
  Education*
Syracuse University
Syracuse, New York

Joyce C. McLeod
Visiting Professor
Rollins College
Winter Park, Florida

Evelyn M. Neufeld
Professor, College of Education
San Jose State University
San Jose, California

Vicki Newman
Classroom Teacher
McGaugh Elementary School
Los Alamitos Unified School District
Seal Beach, California

Terence H. Perciante
Professor of Mathematics
Wheaton College
Wheaton, Illinois

Karen A. Schultz
*Associate Dean and Director of Graduate Studies
  and Research*
Research Professor, Mathematics Education
College of Education
Georgia State University
Atlanta, Georgia

Muriel Burger Thatcher
Independent Mathematics Consultant
Mathematical Encounters
Pine Knoll Shores, North Carolina

▼▼▼▼▼▼▼▼▼▼▼▼

Advisors

Anne R. Biggins
Speech-Language Pathologist
Fairfax County Public Schools
Fairfax, Virginia

Carolyn Gambrel
Learning Disabilities Teacher
Fairfax County Public Schools
Fairfax, Virginia

Asa G. Hilliard, III
*Fuller E. Callaway Professor of
  Urban Education*
Georgia State University
Atlanta, Georgia

Marsha W. Lilly
*Secondary Mathematics
  Coordinator*
Alief Independent School
  District
Alief, Texas

Clementine Sherman
*Director, Division of USI
  Mathematics and Science*
Dade County Public Schools
Miami, Florida

Judith Mayne Wallis
*Elementary Language Arts/So-
  cial Studies/Gifted Coordinator*
Alief Independent School
  District
Houston, Texas

CONTENTS

USING WHOLE NUMBERS AND DECIMALS — CHAPTERS 1–4

* **Algebra Readiness**

CHAPTER

4 ▶ Adding and Subtracting Decimals . . . 48

**Intervention
Lesson**
*Rounding
Decimals
H6–H7*

Assessment Checkpoint ✓ Chapters 1–4

MULTIPLY AND DIVIDE WHOLE NUMBERS   **CHAPTERS 5–8**

CHAPTER

5 ▶ Multiplying by One-Digit Numbers . . 68

**Intervention
Lesson**
*Multiplying by
One Digit
H8–H9*

* **Algebra Readiness**

Intervention Lesson
Estimating Products
H10–H11

Intervention Lesson
Recording Division
H12–H13

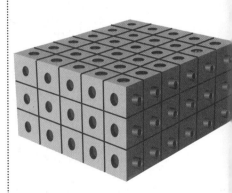

Extension Lesson
Using the Calculator to Divide
H34–H35

* Algebra Readiness

**Extension
Lesson**
*Interpreting
Histograms
H36–H37*

**Intervention
Lesson**
*Fractions: Parts of
a Whole
H14–H15*

* **Algebra Readiness**

Extension
Lesson
*Conduct a
Simulation
H38–H39*

DECIMAL OPERATIONS AND MEASUREMENTS   CHAPTERS 12–14

Intervention
Lesson
*Equivalent
Decimals
H16–H17*

* **Algebra Readiness**

Extension
Lesson
*Estimating
Quotients
H40–H41*

Intervention
Lesson
*Decimals and
Metric Measures
H18–H19*

CONCEPTS OF FRACTIONS   **CHAPTERS 15–18**

Intervention
Lesson
*Fractions: Part of
a Whole or Part
of a Group
H20–H21*

* **Algebra Readiness**

Intervention
Lesson
*Equivalent
Fractions
H22–H23*

Extension
Lesson
*Fractions as
Missing Addends
H42–H43*

Extension
Lesson
*Using Fraction
Circles to
Subtract
H44–H45*

* **Algebra Readiness**

Extension Lesson
Fractions in Music Notation
H46–H47

Extension Lesson
Renaming Mixed Numbers
H48–H49

* Algebra Readiness

Intervention
Lesson
*Customary
Units
H24–H25*

Extension
Lesson
*Exploring Division
of Fractions
H50–H51*

GEOMETRY CHAPTERS 23–26

* **Algebra Readiness**

xii

CHAPTER
24 ▶ Transformations, Congruence, and Symmetry **394**

CHAPTER
25 ▶ Circles **408**

**Intervention
Lesson**
*Classifying
Polygons
H26–H27*

**Intervention
Lesson**
*Point and Line
Symmetry
H28–H29*

**Extension
Lesson**
*Angles in Circle
Graphs
H52–H53*

* Algebra Readiness

RATIOS AND PERCENT   CHAPTERS 27–28

* **Algebra Readiness**

Extension Lesson
Finding Percent of a Number
H56–H57

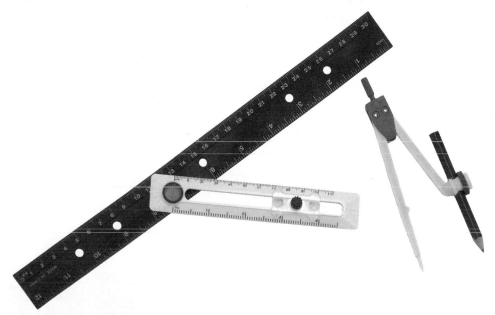

* Algebra Readiness

Welcome to MATH ADVANTAGE

As you work on math this year, use your book as a tool that makes learning easier—and more fun! Look for these things:

▶ **Team-Up Time** You'll work with a group of your classmates on activities that will help you become a good problem solver.

▶ **Why Learn This?** One way is answered for you at the beginning of every lesson. You can find other answers in all the ways you use math every day—at school, at home, and everywhere you go!

▶ **Word Power** Knowing the meanings of math words will help you solve problems and understand directions in your book and on your tests.

▶ **Remember** These boxes will remind you of math skills you've already learned that will help you in the new lesson.

▶ **Mixed Review** It's easy to forget how to do something when you haven't done it for a while. These sets of problems will help you keep your math skills sharp.

▶ **Math Fun** Games and activities you can do with classmates or family members will make learning math *fun*.

▶ **Technology Link** Computer and calculator activities will give you new ways to learn math and practice your math skills.

▶ **Links to Science, Social Studies, History, Language Arts, Health, and Physical Education** You'll learn how math is used in your other subjects.

▶ **Cultural Link** You'll find out how math is used in other cultures.

Math Advantage gives you "power tools" that will help you become a real mathematician!

The Authors

BE A GOOD PROBLEM SOLVER

Good problem solvers need to be good thinkers. They also need to know these strategies.

- Draw a Diagram
- Work Backward
- Use or Make a Table or Graph

- Act It Out
- Guess and Check
- Write a Number Sentence

- Make a Model
- Use a Formula
- Solve a Simpler Problem

- Make an Organized List

This plan can help you think through a problem.

☑ Understand the problem.

Ask yourself...	Then try this.
What is the problem about?	Retell the problem in your own words.
What is the question?	Say the question as a fill-in-the-blank sentence.
What information is given?	List the information given in the problem.

☑ Plan how to solve it.

Ask yourself...	Then try this.
What strategies might I use?	List some strategies you can use.
About what will the answer be?	Predict what your answer will be. Make an estimate if it will help.

☑ Solve it.

Ask yourself...	Then try this.
How can I solve the problem?	Follow your plan and show your solution.
How can I write my answer?	Write your answer in a complete sentence.

☑ Look Back and check your answer.

Ask yourself...	Then try this.
How can I tell if my answer is reasonable?	Compare your answer to your estimate. Check your answer by redoing your work. Match your answer to the question.
How else might I have solved the problem?	Try using another strategy to solve the problem.

You can be a good problem solver! Remember these important words—**Understand, Plan, Solve, Look Back.** Ask yourself questions as you think through the problem. Then be proud of your success!

CHAPTER 1

PLACE VALUE OF WHOLE NUMBERS

American Endangered Species Facts

A bald eagle can see better than you can. A human's eye retina contains 200,000 light sensitive cells per square millimeter. A bald eagle has 1,000,000 of these cells in the same retina area.

In 1800, 30 million buffalo roamed north America. By 1870 the buffalo population had fallen by 30%. By 1889, the herd was reduced to 1/20,000th of that population or about 1,000. Once protected, these survivors produced the present population of about 200,000.

The American burying beetle helps convert carion into nutrients in the food chain. This brightly marked insect grows to about 20 mm long (that's only 0.02 meter).

DID YOU KNOW . . .

The El Segundo butterfly lives in dunes near the Los Angeles International Airport. This lovely butterfly has a wing span of about 2.5 cm and a life span of 4-6 days.

Seven Special Numbers

Numbers are all around you—if you look in the right places. Work together to search for 7 special numbers. Look for numbers in books, magazines, newspapers, the Internet, and interviews with people.

Make a list of all the numbers you find. Then look for a theme that connects your seven numbers.

YOU WILL NEED: books, magazines, tagboard

Work in a group. Your job is to

- make a list of numbers and choose 7: a 1-digit number, a 2-digit number, and so forth up to a 7-digit number.

- explain each number's unit such as miles, feet, gallons, and so forth and tell where you found it.

- brainstorm ideas for themes and make a chart.

DID YOU

- ✓ choose 7 special numbers related to a theme?

- ✓ explain the numbers and where you found them?

- ✓ make a chart?

Animal Numbers

6	months that black bears sleep for hibernation	from High for Childr Jan. 1991
22	maximum life span of zebra (in years)	from The World Book
150	age of giant tortoise	from The Top Ten of Everything 1997
1804	year Lewis and Clark discovered a new woodpicker and a crow	from Kids Discover
14,000	miles flown by an Arctic Tern	from What Are
126,393	number of Labrador	
9,		

Using Numbers

You will learn to use numbers in different ways.	Why learn this? You can recognize different ways numbers are used every day.	**WORD POWER** cardinal ordinal nominal

Numbers can be expressed in different ways. **Cardinal** numbers tell how many. **Ordinal** numbers tell position or order. **Nominal** numbers name things. Look at how numbers are used in this poster.

- Which numbers in the poster are cardinal numbers? ordinal numbers? nominal numbers?

WELCOME TO THE 3RD ANNUAL **West Oaks Festival**

Game
Crafts Booth
Sports Events

15 Rides for $12.50

Food

150 T-Shirt Designs

When:
Saturday, September 5, 1998
12:00 noon - 8:30 P.M.
Where:
West Oaks School
567 East Fifth Avenue
Asbury, TX 65778
(4 miles east of Route 287)
Admission: $3.50
Call 555-2907
for more information.

Cardinal numbers can be expressed as measurements.

A. You can measure temperature in degrees.

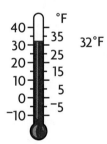

32°F

B. You can measure length in inches.

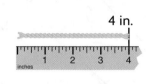

4 in.

C. You can measure capacity in cups.

1 cup

D. You can measure weight in pounds.

75 lb

- Name another example of a number expressed as a measurement.

Check Your Understanding 💡 CRITICAL THINKING

Tell whether each number is expressed as *cardinal*, *ordinal*, or *nominal*.

1. Sandy's phone number is (407) 555-3809.

2. Jason is 15th in line.

3. Mary put 2 cups of flour in the bowl.

4. Tim placed first in the sack race.

5. There were 5 puppies in the basket.

6. The number on Joe's football jersey is 72.

7. 72nd

8. twenty-six

9. 35 mm

10. 3295 Oak St.

PRACTICE

Tell whether the number in each picture is expressed as *cardinal*, *ordinal*, or *nominal*.

11.

12.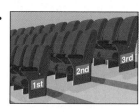

8 in.
×
10 in.

13.

1st 2nd 3rd

14.

452 M&M's

Tell whether each number is expressed as *cardinal*, *ordinal*, or *nominal*.

15. My phone number is (914) 555-2030.

16. Susan is tenth in line to use the computer.

17. It is 78° F outside today.

18. Bob lives at 319 Oak St.

19. Lee got 93 answers correct on the test.

20. Sofia won 2nd place in the essay contest.

21. A 10-lb box of paper was delivered to the class.

22. There are 25 students in our classroom.

Mixed Applications

For Problems 23–26, use the table.

23. What is the total number of tickets sold by the 3 winners?

24. If each ticket sold for $2, did Lauren make more than or less than $100?

25. If the second-place winner sold the same number of tickets on each of 4 days, how many tickets did she sell each day?

TICKET SALES CONTEST		
Winners	Name	Tickets Sold
1st Place	Lauren Krystal	48
2nd Place	Erin Clarke	36
3rd Place	Matt Fisher	34

26. **Write a problem** using the table.

Mixed Review

Write the letter of the unit used to measure the elapsed time. (taught in 4th grade)

a. days	b. hours	c. minutes

27. to be at school

28. to eat lunch

29. to travel from your house to school

30. to be on vacation out-of-town

Record how many hundreds, tens, and ones. (taught in 4th grade)

31. 237   **32.** 195   **33.** 463   **34.** 903

Benchmark Numbers

You will learn that using a benchmark number can help you make reasonable estimates.

Why learn this? You can estimate the number of objects by comparing them to a familiar number.

A **benchmark** is a point of reference. Benchmark numbers such as 5, 10, 25, 100, or 1,000 can help you determine whether an estimate is reasonable without counting.

EXAMPLES

A. Which estimate of the slices of bread in the tray is most reasonable, 50, 150, or 1,500?

Benchmark:
1 loaf has about **15** slices.

10 Loaves in a tray

So, the most reasonable estimate of slices of bread in the tray is 150.

B. Which estimate of the nickels in the full jar is most reasonable, 60, 300, or 3,000?

Benchmark:
50 nickels.

50 nickels

So, the most reasonable estimate of the nickels in the full jar is 300.

Talk About It

- In Example A, why is 50 not a reasonable estimate?
- Why is a benchmark of 50 easier to use than 15?
- What benchmark numbers would you use to estimate the number of students in your school?

Check Your Understanding

CRITICAL THINKING

Use the benchmark number to choose the more reasonable estimate.

1. pennies in the jar

50 pennies

100 or 1,000

2. pretzels in the bag

PRETZELS
Bulk Shop

15 or 75

3. windows on the building

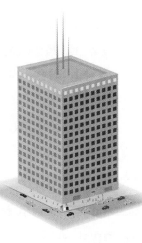

60 or 600

PRACTICE

Use the benchmark number to choose the more reasonable estimate.

4. seats in the audience

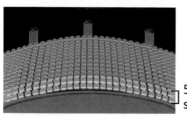

50 seats

500 or 5,000

5. soccer balls

10 or 100

6. paper clips

25 or 100

Write *yes* or *no* to tell whether the estimate is reasonable. Explain.

7. • 10 pans of cupcakes
• Each pan holds 12 cupcakes.
Estimate: There are about 25 cupcakes in the bakery.

8. • 20 sections in the gymnasium
• Each section seats 50 people.
Estimate: There are about 100 seats in the gymnasium.

9. • 18 packages of paper on the shelf
• 100 sheets of paper per package
Estimate: There are about 2,000 sheets of paper on the shelf.

10. • 8 pencils in a box
• 40 boxes at the school store
Estimate: There are about 100 pencils in the school store.

Mixed Applications

11. A group of students signed up to play on a basketball team. There will be about 10 students on each team. About 20 teams will be formed. Did more than or less than 100 students sign up?

12. Julia can hold 20 nickels in her hand at one time. Her piggy bank has enough nickels for her to hold 5 handfuls. About how much money does Julia have in nickels?

13. Angelo guessed there were 260 jelly beans in the jar. Ben guessed there were 325 jelly beans. There were actually 293 jelly beans. Whose guess was closer?

14. ✏️ **WRITE ABOUT IT** Explain when you would use a benchmark number.

Mixed Review

Write the number that is 1,000 more. (taught in 4th grade)

15. 3,046   **16.** 14,189   **17.** 29,504   **18.** 99,897

Use mental math to complete each equation. (taught in 4th grade)

19. $70 + 5 = 25 + \underline{\ ?\ }$ **20.** $\underline{\ ?\ } \times 10 = 8 \times 5$ **21.** $300 - \underline{\ ?\ } = 100 + 50$

MORE PRACTICE Student Handbook page H70

Place Value to Hundred Thousands

You will learn to understand the value of numbers to hundred thousands.

Why learn this? You can read and write large numbers, such as the distance from Earth to the moon.

Use the chart to see the value of 4 in each place-value position for the number 444,444.

THOUSANDS			ONES					
Hundreds	Tens	Ones	Hundreds	Tens	Ones			
					4 × 1	=	4	
				4 × 10		=	40	
			4 × 100			=	400	
		4 × 1,000				=	4,000	
	4 × 10,000					=	40,000	
4 × 100,000						=	400,000	
							444,444	

Talk About It

- How does the value of the 4 change as it moves from right to left?

- How does the expanded form of 444,444 show a pattern of zeros?

 **CRITICAL THINKING** How can you find the value of a digit when you know its place-value position?

REMEMBER:

Expanded form is a way to write numbers by showing the sum of the value of each digit.

567 = 500 + 60 + 7

Check Your Understanding

Write the value of the digit 8 in each number.

1. 1,486   **2.** 38,042

3. 854,369   **4.** 781,203

Write the value of the blue digit.

5. 560   **6.** 4,086

7. 13,859   **8.** 618,097

9. 47,092   **10.** 302,561

11. 712,583   **12.** 609,532

13. 507,146   **14.** 168,290

Science Link

The average distance from Earth to the moon is 238,857 mi. What is the value of the digit in the greatest place-value position of that number?

PRACTICE

Write the value of the blue digit.

15. 475,902   **16.** 695,337   **17.** 980,765   **18.** 871,253

19. 301,584   **20.** 820,426   **21.** 713,225   **22.** 214,607

Complete.

23. 765,910 = (_?_ × 100,000) + (_?_ × 10,000) + (_?_ × 1,000) + (_?_ × 100) + (_?_ × 10) + (_?_ × 1)

24. 802,054 = (_?_ × 100,000) + (_?_ × 10,000) + (_?_ × 1,000) + (_?_ × 100) + (_?_ × 10) + (_?_ × 1)

25. 642,703 = (6 × _?_) + (4 × _?_) + (2 × _?_) + (7 × _?_) + (_?_ × 10) + (3 × _?_)

Write the expanded numbers in standard form.

26. 200,000 + 50,000 + 6,000 + 900 + 80 + 3

27. 400,000 + 90,000 + 1,000 + 700 + 20 + 3

28. 700,000 + 0 + 4,000 + 200 + 30 + 5

29. 900,000 + 90,000 + 0 + 900 + 0 + 9

30. 800,000 + 0 + 0 + 800 + 80 + 0

Mixed Applications

31. The Earth's equator measures about 24,902 mi. Write the value of the digit 4 in this number.

32. I am a number greater than 149,998 but less than 150,000. What number am I?

33. The Butlers bought a house for $149,950. Two years later they sold their house for $155,275. How much more did their house sell for?

34. ✏️ **WRITE ABOUT IT** Explain how you know the value of the digit 7 in the number 742,126.

Mixed Review

Write *true* or *false* for each statement. (taught in 4th grade)

35. There are 100 pennies in $10.

36. There are 1,000 pennies in $10.

37. There are 10 dimes in $1.

38. There are 10 dimes in $10.

39. There are 100 dimes in $10.

40. There are 100 one-dollar bills in $10.

Write the greatest place-value position in which the digits differ. (taught in 4th grade)

41. 45 and 47   **42.** 68 and 78   **43.** 153 and 152   **44.** 694 and 964

MORE PRACTICE Student Handbook page H71

7

Place Value to Hundred Millions

You will learn to express numbers to hundred millions.	**Why learn this?** You can recognize and interpret large numbers, such as how many years ago dinosaurs existed on Earth.

In the year it was released, the film *Jurassic Park* by Universal Studios earned $868,132,005.

Look at the number on the place-value chart.

MILLIONS			THOUSANDS			ONES		
Hundreds	Tens	Ones	Hundreds	Tens	Ones	Hundreds	Tens	Ones
8	6	8	1	3	2	0	0	5

Large numbers are separated into periods, each containing three place-value positions. Commas separate the periods.

Standard Form: 868,132,005

Expanded Form: 800,000,000,+ 60,000,000 + 8,000,000 +100,000 + 30,000 + 2,000 + 0 + 0 + 5

Word Form: eight hundred sixty-eight *million*, one hundred thirty-two *thousand*, five

Talk About It

- Why is a comma used to separate periods when writing large numbers?

- What is alike about the periods?

- How do you use periods to help you read a number?

- How do you find the value of a digit?

Check Your Understanding

The film *Aladdin* by Buena Vista earned $302,698,051. Use this number to answer Exercises 1–4.

1. Write the number in expanded form.

2. Write the number in word form.

3. Write the name of the period that has the digits 698.

4. Write the place-value position of the digit 2.

Science Link

The Allosaurus was one of many dinosaurs that roamed Earth about 150 million years ago. How would you write that number in standard form?

Calculator Activities page H58

PRACTICE

Write the value of the blue digit.

5. 46,785,039   **6.** 39,806,527   **7.** 876,148,713

8. 268,432,116   **9.** 495,630,210   **10.** 780,904,652

Write two other forms for each number.

11. 65,200,108   **12.** 207,910,036   **13.** 148,000,965

14. 500,000,000 + 80,000,000 + 0 + 400,000 + 0 + 1,000 + 200 + 0 + 9

15. 600,000,000 + 60,000,000 + 8,000,000 + 0 + 0 + 6,000 + 800 + 0 + 8

16. seven hundred thirty million, eight hundred ninety-five thousand, fifteen

17. nine hundred million, six hundred fifty thousand, eight hundred seventy-five

Mixed Applications

For Problems 18–21, use the table.

18. Write the place-value position of the digit 7 in the earnings for *The Lion King*.

19. What is the difference in earnings between *Pocahontas* and *Apollo 13*?

20. Write the earnings for *Apollo 13* in expanded form.

21. ✏ **Write a problem** about place value, using the information in the table.

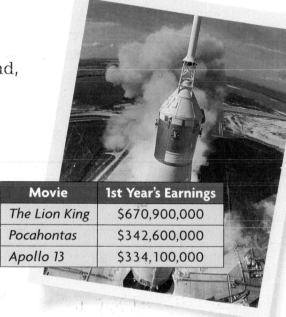

Movie	1st Year's Earnings
The Lion King	$670,900,000
Pocahontas	$342,600,000
Apollo 13	$334,100,000

Mixed Review

Write the number as you would say it with period names. (taught in 4th grade)

22. 5,147,216   5 _?_ , 147 _?_ , 216

23. 4,875,309   4 _?_ , 875 _?_ , 309

Write the next three numbers in the pattern. (taught in 4th grade)

24. 6, 9, 12, 15   **25.** 1, 2, 4, 7, 11

26. 40, 35, 30, 25   **27.** 4, 8, 12, 16

Technology Link

In *Mighty Math Number Heroes*, the game *Quizzo* challenges you to identify numbers.

PART 1 Comparing and Ordering

You will learn to compare and order whole numbers.

Why learn this? You can compare prices at the store or distances.

The Pacific Ocean and the Indian Ocean are two of the deepest on Earth. The average depth of the Indian Ocean is 12,598 ft. The average depth of the Pacific Ocean is 12,925 ft. Compare these two numbers to find which ocean has the greater average depth.

You can compare numbers by comparing the digits in each place-value position. Start at the left. Check each place until the digits are different.

PACIFIC OCEAN 12,925 ft

INDIAN OCEAN 12,598 ft

MODEL

▶ Step 1

Compare the ten thousands.

12,598 same number of
↓   ten thousands
12,925

▶ Step 2

Compare the thousands.

12,598 same number of
↓   thousands
12,925

▶ Step 3

Compare the hundreds.

12,598
↓   9 > 5
12,925

So, 12,925 > 12,598.

Since 12,925 > 12,598, the Pacific Ocean has the greater average depth.

You can order numbers by comparing them in the same way. Order these numbers from greatest to least. 24,785; 25,864; 22,678.

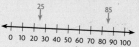

REMEMBER:

As you move to the right on a number line, the number gets larger. When you move to the left, the number gets smaller.

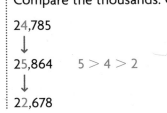

Read: 25 < 85, or 85 > 25

MODEL

▶ Step 1

Compare the ten thousands.

24,785
↓
25,864 same number of
↓   ten thousands
22,678

▶ Step 2

Compare the thousands. Order the digits.

24,785
↓
25,864   5 > 4 > 2
↓
22,678

▶ Step 3

Order the numbers.

So, 25,864 > 24,785 > 22,678.

- How would you order the numbers from least to greatest?

Check Your Understanding

Start at the left. Name the first place-value position where the numbers differ.

1. 1,733; 1,418
2. 25,670; 25,680
3. 178,452; 179,452

4. 9,678; 12,768
5. 807; 870
6. 205,769; 205,796

PRACTICE

Write <, >, or = for each ⬤.

7. 489 ⬤ 498
8. 5,650 ⬤ 5,650

9. 7,890 ⬤ 8,790
10. 13,420 ⬤ 13,402

11. 21,108 ⬤ 21,018
12. 187,418 ⬤ 187,418

Order from greatest to least.

13. 397; 379; 739
14. 5,217; 5,721; 7,521

15. 9,820; 8,902; 9,802
16. 16,295; 16,925; 19,625

17. 35,891; 31,581; 31,981
18. 418,652; 481,562; 418,562

Order from least to greatest.

19. 895; 590; 859
20. 4,210; 2,410; 4,120

21. 6,895; 6,598; 5,698
22. 49,086; 49,680; 48,690

23. 10,465; 10,645; 10,654
24. 235,289; 236,287; 236,178

Social Studies Link

Two of the highest mountains in the world are Aconcagua in South America at 22,834 ft and Mt. Everest in Asia at 29,028 ft. Which mountain is higher?

Mixed Applications

For Problems 25–30, use the table.

UNITED STATES NATIONAL PARKS		
Name	Location	Acres
Mammoth Cave	Kentucky	52,419
Bryce Canyon	Utah	35,835
Mesa Verde	Colorado	52,122
Kings Canyon	California	461,901
Mount Rainier	Washington	235,612

25. Which of these national parks covers the most acres?

26. Which national park is larger, Mammoth Cave or Mesa Verde?

27. How much larger is Kings Canyon National Park than Mount Rainier National Park?

28. What is the difference in the number of acres in the largest park and the number of acres in the smallest park?

29. List the national parks in order from the park with the fewest acres to the park with the most acres.

30. ✏️ **Write a problem** using the information in the table.

LESSON CONTINUES

PART 2 PROBLEM-SOLVING STRATEGY
Use a Table

THE PROBLEM Tammy's class is taking a 6-day field trip during Spring Break. The planning committee has recommended five trips. The principal asked that the committee narrow down the choices to the three trips with the least traveling distances. The parents asked that from those three, they choose the trip that costs the least. Which trip will they take?

REMEMBER:
- ☑ Understand
- ☑ Plan
- ☑ Solve
- ☑ Look Back

☑ Understand
- What are you asked to do?
- What information will you use?
- Is there information you will not use? If so, what?

☑ Plan
- What strategy can you use to solve the problem?

  You can *use a table* to analyze the data.

☑ Solve
- How can a table help you solve this problem?

The table organizes the data. Compare the distances. Find the 3 trips with the least distances. Then choose from those three, the one that costs the least.

	Trip 1	Trip 2	Trip 3	Trip 4	Trip 5
Place	New York City	Washington, D.C. area campout	Kennedy Space Center	Dude Ranch	Mountain Camping
Points of Interest	Museums Famous Landmarks	National Landmarks Smithsonian	Space Shuttle & Museum Space Camp	Horseback Riding Hikes	Hiking Rafting Canoeing
Traveling Distance	1,456 mi	1,198 mi	1,748 mi	1,308 mi	1,099 mi
Cost (per student)	$1,375	$325	$1,067	$410	$351

The three trips with least distances are: Trips 5, 2, and 4. So, the least costly of those three trips is Trip 2 to Washington, D.C. at $325 per student.

☑ Look Back
- How does the table help you find the answer?
- What other strategy could you use?

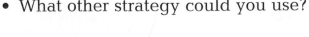

PRACTICE

Use a table to solve.

1. This table shows some capital cities in the United States and their populations. Which of these cities has the greatest population? the least population?

CAPITAL CITIES		
City	State	Population
Atlanta	Georgia	394,017
Juneau	Alaska	26,751
Phoenix	Arizona	983,392
Montpelier	Vermont	8,247
Santa Fe	New Mexico	55,859

2. This table shows five states in the United States and their areas in square miles. Which of these states has the greatest area? the least area?

U.S. STATES	
Name	Area (square miles)
New Jersey	8,722
Michigan	96,705
California	163,707
Delaware	2,489
Nevada	110,567

Mixed Applications

Solve.

CHOOSE A STRATEGY

- Act It Out   • Use a Table   • Find a Pattern   • Work Backward
- Make an Organized List   • Write a Number Sentence

3. The highest waterfall in the world is Angel Falls in Venezuela. How much higher is Angel Falls than Yosemite Upper Falls?

WATERFALLS	
Falls	Height (in ft)
Angel	3,212
Yosemite Upper	1,430

4. The Browns drove a total of 540 mi in 2 days. They drove twice as far on Tuesday as they did on Monday. How many miles did they drive on Monday? on Tuesday?

5. Elena's family is planning a vacation. They can go to either the beach or the mountains. They can either drive, fly, or take the train to their destination. Make a list of their choices.

6. Carmen spent $18 on a ticket to a theme park. She spent $6 for food during the day, and she bought a gift for $5. Carmen had $6 when she got home. How much money did she have when she left for the theme park?

7. The clock shows the time Melba arrived in Atlanta. Her airplane flight took 1 hour. She was at the airport for 45 minutes before her flight left. It took her 30 minutes to drive to the airport from her house. At what time did she leave her house?

MATH FUN!

COINS IN A ROW

PURPOSE To use place value to compare and order numbers

YOU WILL NEED 10 coins

Order the coins in a line, with oldest coins to the left and the newest coins to the right. How many years difference is there between the oldest and newest coins?

HOME NOTE Ask your parents when they were born. Do you have any coins older than your parents?

Biggest and Smallest Game

PURPOSE To make greatest and least possible numbers, using random digits

YOU WILL NEED 10 index cards, markers

Number each card with digits from 0 to 9. Take 3 cards for the first game. Arrange them so you have the greatest possible number. Write it on a separate sheet of paper.

Then rearrange the cards to create the least number. (You cannot start your number with zero.) Write the least number on your paper. Play by using 4 cards, 5 cards, up to 10 cards.

Greatest   Least
742

How Many Meals?

PURPOSE To use a benchmark to estimate a large number

YOU WILL NEED calculator

Will you have eaten 1 million meals by your 21st birthday? Estimate. Then check with a calculator.

Calculate how many meals you eat in a year. Start by estimating how many meals you eat in a day. Then multiply that by the number of days in a year. Now estimate how many meals you will have eaten in 21 years. Then use a calculator to find how many meals you will have eaten in 21 years.

A year has about 365 days.

✓ CHECK UNDERSTANDING

VOCABULARY

1. Numbers that tell how many are __?__ numbers.
   Numbers that tell position or order are __?__ numbers.
   Numbers that name things are __?__ numbers. (page 2)

2. A __?__ number is a point of reference. (page 4)

Tell whether each number is expressed as *cardinal, ordinal,* or *nominal.* (pages 2–3)

3. 23,968   4. (215) 555-9807   5. fifty-sixth   6. 35 ft

Use the benchmark number to choose the best estimate. (pages 4–5)

7. beans in the bag   8. cookies in a jar   9. people in a stadium

1,000 people

30 or 300   48 or 480   5,000 or 50,000

✓ CHECK SKILLS

Write two other forms for each number. (pages 6–9)

10. 13,092   11. 40,000 + 0 + 500 + 60 + 3

Write the value of the blue digit. (pages 6–9)

12. 406,213,893   13. 42,067   14. 973,536   15. 211,356,841

Write < , > , or = for each ●. (pages 10–11)

16. 489 ● 498   17. 5,650 ● 5,650   18. 7,890 ● 8,790

✓ CHECK PROBLEM SOLVING

Solve. (pages 12–13)

CHOOSE A STRATEGY

• Work Backward   • Use a Table   • Draw a Diagram

19. List the lakes from the least area to the greatest area.

Lakes	Area (sq mi)
Michigan	22,300
Erie	9,910
Superior	31,700
Huron	23,000

20. Each 1 of 4 walls in a room is 40 ft long. If stereo speakers are placed every 20 ft, how many speakers are in the room?

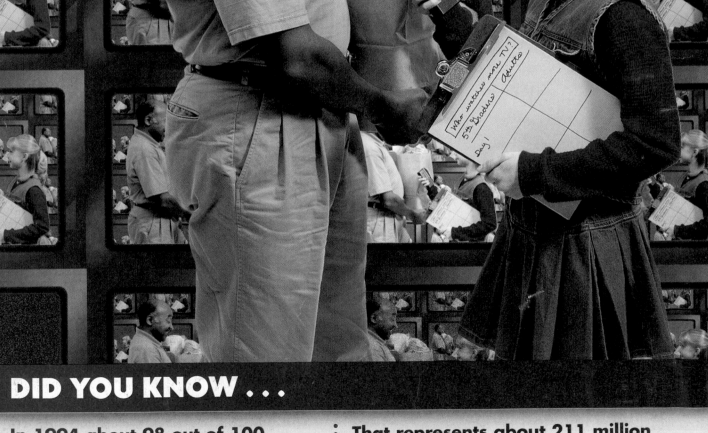

CHAPTER 2
ADDING AND SUBTRACTING WHOLE NUMBERS

DID YOU KNOW . . .

In 1994 about 98 out of 100 homes in the United States had television sets while only 94 out of 100 homes had telephone service!

That represents about 211 million television sets, with an average of a little more than 2 sets per home.

Tube Tracking

Have you ever wondered who watches more TV— fifth-graders or adults? Your class will find out by doing a 3-day survey. As a class, you can decide on dates to track and whether to count hours, half-hours, or minutes.

YOU WILL NEED: paper, pencils, calculators

Work with a group. Your job is to

- design and use a tracking sheet for 3 days.

- interview one adult whom you will track.

- record the times spent watching television by the adult and by yourself for 3 days.

- add viewing time in two categories: fifth- graders and adults.

- write a report that compares adult TV viewing time with that of fifth-graders.

DID YOU

- ☑ design a tracking sheet and conduct an interview?

- ☑ record TV-watching times daily?

- ☑ write a report that compares TV-watching habits of adults and fifth-graders?

In the 3 days, I wat
hours and mom watche
I think mom didn't watc
TV on Wednesday nigh
she has a class. On Tue
like to watch a show
My group (Kyle, Jam
me) watched 25 hours
Our parents watc
The kids watched 10
than the adults.
In our class, k
s. The par
The kid
more

Adding and Subtracting with Data

You will learn to recognize addition and subtraction as inverse operations.	**Why learn this?** You can add numbers such as scores in a game or how many hours you spend watching television.	**WORD POWER** inverse operations

The football coach keeps a table of the scoring statistics for the games played each season. Help him complete the table.

Add to find the final score for Game 2.

You can use *n* instead of ___?___ for a missing number.

$21 + 13 = n$, or
$$\begin{array}{r} 21 \\ +13 \\ \hline 34 \end{array}$$

So, the final score for Game 2 is 34.

Subtract to find the missing addend for the 2nd-half score in Game 3.

$10 + n = 28$, or
$$\begin{array}{r} 28 \\ -10 \\ \hline 18 \end{array}$$

So, the 2nd-half score for Game 3 is 18.

- Explain how to complete the table for Games 4 and 5.

Addition and subtraction are **inverse operations**. This means that one operation undoes the other operation. This inverse relationship allows you to check an addition problem by using subtraction. It also lets you check a subtraction problem by using addition.

EXAMPLES

A. Problem   Check

$$\begin{array}{r} 12 \\ +15 \\ \hline 27 \end{array} \qquad \begin{array}{r} 27 \\ -15 \\ \hline 12 \end{array}$$

B. Problem   Check

$$\begin{array}{r} 538 \\ -415 \\ \hline 123 \end{array} \qquad \begin{array}{r} 123 \\ +415 \\ \hline 538 \end{array}$$

- What number sentences can you write with the numbers 21, 63, and 84? How are the number sentences related?

Check Your Understanding  CRITICAL THINKING

Solve. Use the inverse operation to check each problem.

1. $$\begin{array}{r} 24 \\ +83 \end{array}$$
2. $$\begin{array}{r} 56 \\ -14 \end{array}$$
3. $$\begin{array}{r} 235 \\ +162 \end{array}$$
4. $$\begin{array}{r} 837 \\ -506 \end{array}$$

Social Studies Link

In 1928, the first regularly scheduled television programs were broadcast on station WGY in Schenectady, N.Y. For how many years have television programs been on the air?

PRACTICE

For Problems 5–8, use the data in the table.

5. How many total points were scored by the end of Game 3?

6. How many more points were scored in Game 5 than in Game 1?

7. How many points in all were scored during the 1998–99 season?

8. How many more points were scored in the 1998–99 season than the 279 points scored in the 1997–98 season?

GIRLS' BASKETBALL GAME SCORES 1998-99	
Game	Score
1	55
2	69
3	48
4	73
5	75

School Basketball Champs

Write the related number sentence. Find the sum or difference.

9. $85 - 32 = n$

10. $125 - 78 = n$

11. $140 - 96 = n$

12. $36 + n = 52$

13. $49 + n = 83$

14. $75 + n = 142$

15. $251 - 89 = n$

16. $76 + n = 164$

17. $n + 55 = 94$

Solve. Use the inverse operation to check each problem.

18. $\begin{array}{r} 16 \\ +25 \\ \hline \end{array}$

19. $\begin{array}{r} 49 \\ -32 \\ \hline \end{array}$

20. $\begin{array}{r} 37 \\ +26 \\ \hline \end{array}$

21. $\begin{array}{r} 125 \\ -\ 94 \\ \hline \end{array}$

Mixed Applications

22. Heather scored 28 points in the basketball game. She scored 16 points in the first half of the game. How many points did she score in the second half?

23. Antonio ran 118 yards in the first half of the football game. He ran 96 yards in the second half. What is the total number of yards that he ran in the football game?

24. A professional basketball team played 82 games one year. They won 51 games. How many games did they lose?

25. **Write a problem** using the numbers 14 and 25.

Mixed Review

Tell whether each number is expressed as *cardinal*, *ordinal*, or *nominal*. (pages 2–3)

26. 6 feet

27. 2nd

28. 118

29. (904) 555-1842

Write $<$, $>$, or $=$ for each ●. (pages 10–11)

30. 375 ● 357

31. 1,296 ● 1,296

32. 789 ● 798

33. 4,536 ● 4,563

MORE PRACTICE Student Handbook page H72

More About Subtracting

You will investigate how to use counters to model subtraction of whole numbers.

Why learn this? You will be able to find how much farther you must travel to reach a destination.

Jon and his family are going to the beach on vacation. They must travel 532 miles to get there. On Saturday they traveled 346 miles. How many miles are left to travel?

Explore

You can use subtraction to find how many miles are left to travel. Use color counters to model the subtraction.

MATERIALS: blue, red, green, and yellow counters; place-value mat

MODEL

Let ● = 1,000; ● = 100; ● = 10; ● = 1

▶ Step 1

Model the problem. Start by placing 5 red counters, 3 green counters, and 2 yellow counters on the place-value mat.

$$\begin{array}{r} 5\,3\,2 \\ -3\,4\,6 \end{array}$$

Hundreds	Tens	Ones

▶ Step 2

Look at the ones. Decide whether to regroup. Since 6 > 2, regroup 3 tens 2 ones as 2 tens 12 ones.

To subtract, take away 6 ones.

$$\begin{array}{r} {}^{2\ 12}5\,\cancel{3}\,\cancel{2} \\ -3\,4\,6 \\ \hline 6 \end{array}$$

Hundreds	Tens	Ones

▶ Step 3

Look at the tens. Since 4 > 2, regroup 5 hundreds 2 tens as 4 hundreds 12 tens. To subtract, take away 4 tens.

$$\begin{array}{r} {}^{4\ \ \,12}_{\ \,2\,12}\,\cancel{5}\,\cancel{3}\,\cancel{2} \\ -3\,4\,6 \\ \hline 8\,6 \end{array}$$

Hundreds	Tens	Ones

▶ Step 4

Look at the hundreds. 3 < 4

To subtract, take away 3 hundreds.

$$\begin{array}{r} {}^{4\ \ \,12}_{\ \,2\,12}\,\cancel{5}\,\cancel{3}\,\cancel{2} \\ -3\,4\,6 \\ \hline 1\,8\,6 \end{array}$$

Hundreds	Tens	Ones

Technology Link ▶
E-Lab • Activity 2 Available on CD-ROM
and the Internet at http://www.hbschool.com/elab

Record

Explain how you used the counters to find the difference.

Try This

Find the difference of 3,031 and 1,456. Make a model and record the subtraction for the model.

TALK ABOUT IT How is regrouping with counters different from regrouping with place-value blocks?

✏️ **WRITE ABOUT IT** Write a problem in which you take away to subtract. Explain how to solve the problem.

HANDS-ON PRACTICE

Draw the counters after regrouping. Find the difference.

1.
```
    1 13
  4 2̸ 3̸
 −2 1 5
```

Hundreds	Tens	Ones
●● ●●	● ●	○ ○ ○

2.
```
    4 11
  7 5̸ 1̸
 −5 3 9
```

Hundreds	Tens	Ones
●●● ●● ●●	● ● ●	○

Applying What You Learned

Find the difference. You may use counters.

3.	274 −165	4.	398 −159	5.	415 −231	6.	563 −356	7.	628 −147	8.	324 −163

9.	495 −276	10.	718 −325	11.	1,825 − 752	12.	4,395 −1,787	13.	6,211 −4,523	14.	9,532 −5,986

Mixed Applications

For Problems 15–17, use the map.

15. How many more miles is it from Boston to Pittsburgh than from Boston to Philadelphia?

16. How many more miles is it from Boston to Pittsburgh than from Boston to New York City and back to Boston?

17. If you drove round-trip from Boston to each of these cities, how many total miles would you travel?

18. Jerome's book has 238 pages. He has read 165 pages. How many more pages does he have to read?

19. ✏️ **WRITE ABOUT IT** Explain how to regroup to subtract 186 from 325.

Subtracting Across Zeros

You will learn to subtract with regrouping across zeros.	**Why learn this?** You can find how far you have to go to reach a goal, such as selling a large number of tickets.

The band members are selling tickets for the homecoming football game. Their goal is to sell 3,000 tickets. They have sold 1,740 tickets. How many more tickets must they sell to reach their goal?

MODEL

▶ **Step 1**

Subtract. $3{,}000 - 1{,}740 = n$

Subtract the ones. Look at the tens. Since $4 > 0$, regroup. There are 0 hundreds, so regroup 3 thousands as 2 thousands 10 hundreds.

```
  2  10
  3,0 0 0
-1,7 4 0
        0
```

▶ **Step 2**

Regroup 10 hundreds 0 tens as 9 hundreds 10 tens. Subtract the tens.

```
     9
  2 1010
  3,0 0 0
-1,7 4 0
     6 0
```

▶ **Step 3**

Subtract the hundreds and thousands.

```
     9
  2 1010
  3,0 0 0
-1,7 4 0
  1,2 6 0
```

So, the band members must sell 1,260 more tickets to reach their goal.

You can show regrouping in different ways.

EXAMPLES

A.
```
  3  9 910
  4,0 0 0
-1,8 6 3
  2,1 3 7
```
Regroup 400 tens as 399 tens 10 ones.

B.
```
  5 910
  6 0 0
-4 7 2
  1 2 8
```

C.
```
     2 9 911
  1 3,0 0 1
-1 2,5 6 7
        4 3 4
```

D.
```
  5 9  9 910
  6 0,0 0 0
-3 9,6 8 3
  2 0,3 1 7
```

Talk About It

• In Example C, why is the ones place regrouped to 11 instead of 10?

• How would you regroup 5,000 to subtract 16?

Check Your Understanding  CRITICAL THINKING

Show how you regrouped for each problem. Solve.

1.	**2.**	**3.**	**4.**	**5.**
300	506	8,004	12,000	30,005
−147	−284	−3,567	− 9,326	−18,690

PRACTICE

Show how you regrouped for each problem. Solve.

6. 400 −216	**7.** 2,005 −1,376	**8.** 6,000 −3,489	**9.** 14,000 − 8,713	**10.** 20,004 −12,562

Find the difference.

11. 300 −197	**12.** 800 − 76	**13.** 4,000 − 362	**14.** 1,002 − 543	**15.** 7,000 −2,895
16. 8,000 −2,560	**17.** 12,000 − 9,962	**18.** 18,000 − 4,021	**19.** 30,000 −23,918	**20.** 70,000 −55,739
21. 6,000 −4,773	**22.** 24,000 − 7,888	**23.** 13,000 − 7,095	**24.** 50,000 −27,688	**25.** 37,000 −19,408

Mixed Applications

26. The student council's goal is to sell 500 tickets to the dance. They sold 215 tickets during the week at school, and they sold 256 tickets at the door. How many more tickets do they need to sell to meet their goal?

27. There are 300 students in the marching band at Lakemont High School. Edgewater High School has 238 members in its marching band. How many more students are in the band at Lakemont?

28. During one professional football season, a leading player rushed 1,002 yards. His teammate rushed 875 yards. How many more yards did the leading player rush than his teammate?

29. ✏️ **Write a problem** about a football stadium that seats 63,000 people. Use subtraction.

Mixed Review

Find the sum. (taught in 4th grade)

30. $24 + 56 = n$ **31.** $216 + 37 = n$ **32.** $421 + 378 = n$

Write the value of the blue digit. (pages 6–9)

33. 40,756,125   **34.** 18,970,654   **35.** 36,085,213   **36.** 48,065,129

Choosing Addition or Subtraction

You will learn to choose addition or subtraction by analyzing the problem.

Why learn this? You will know whether to add or subtract to solve problems such as comparing the costs of two items.

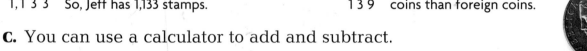

You can analyze a problem to decide which operation to use.

A. Jeff has 837 U.S. stamps and 296 foreign stamps in his stamp collection. How many stamps does Jeff have altogether?

Add if the problem asks you to *join groups*.

```
  1 1
  8 3 7
+ 2 9 6
-------
1,1 3 3    So, Jeff has 1,133 stamps.
```

B. Elissa has 304 U.S. coins and 165 foreign coins in her coin collection. How many more U.S. coins than foreign coins does Elissa have?

Subtract if the problem asks you to *take away* part of the group or to *compare* two groups.

```
  2 9 14
  3 0 4
- 1 6 5    So, Elissa has 139 more U.S.
-------
  1 3 9    coins than foreign coins.
```

C. You can use a calculator to add and subtract.

Add. 764 + 549 = n

Press: `=    1'313.`

Subtract. 403 − 289 = n

Press:  `=    114.`

- How is the relationship between the numbers in the problem and the answer different for addition and subtraction?

Check Your Understanding 💡 CRITICAL THINKING

Choose and name the operation. Solve.

1. Erica has 23 red ribbons and 12 green ribbons. How many ribbons does she have in all?

2. The store had 4,020 baseball cards and 1,839 were sold. How many does the store have left?

3. Jason has 56 antique cars and 123 new cars in his mini-car collection. How many more new cars are there?

4. Sue's class collected 337 shells. Bill's class collected 295 shells. How many shells were collected by the two classes?

Calculator Activities page H59

PRACTICE

Choose and name the operation. Solve.

5. Felipe scored 124 points in a bowling game, and Robert scored 98 points. How many more points did Felipe score?

6. Caroline bought a bicycle for $118 and a helmet for $24. How much did she spend for the two items?

7. Leslie collected 1,256 cards, and Robert collected 864 cars. What is the total number of cards the two friends collected?

8. There were 12,890 people at a gymnastics event on Friday. On Saturday 9,965 people attended. How many more people were there on Friday?

Mixed Applications

For Problems 9–10 and 13, use the table.

9. How many more total medals did the United States win than Russia?

10. Which country won 5 more silver medals than bronze medals?

11. The first modern Olympic Games in 1896 had athletes competing in 9 events. In 1996, athletes competed in 271 events. How many more events were there in 1996?

12. In the 1976 Olympics in Montreal, there were 1,247 women competitors. In 1996 in Atlanta 3,700 women competed in the Olympics. How many more women competed in 1996 than in 1976?

13. ✏️ **Write a problem** using the information in the table.

DAILY NEWS

SPORTS EXTRA

1996 OLYMPIC GAMES MEDALS TALLY

COUNTRY ►	GOLD	SILVER	BRONZE	TOTAL
U.S.A. ►	44	32	25	101
RUSSIA ►	26	21	16	63
GERMANY ►	20	18	27	65
CHINA ►	16	22	12	50

Mixed Review

Order from least to greatest. (pages 10–11)

14. 9,230; 9,203; 9,300

15. 12,486; 12,864; 12,468

For Problems 16–17, use the number 569,302,481. (pages 8–9)

16. Write the name of the period that has the digits 302.

17. Write the place-value position of the digit 9.

Social Studies Link

One of the first United States coins was called a *fugio*, or Franklin cent, named after Benjamin Franklin. It was made in 1787. How long ago was the Franklin cent made?

PART 1 Estimation and Column Addition

You will learn to estimate sums for three or more addends.	Why learn this? You can estimate the cost of several items to be sure you have enough money to buy them.	**WORD POWER** compatible numbers

The fifth-grade classes have started collecting aluminum cans for recycling. About how many cans have they collected so far?

Estimate the sum of 323, 408, 289, and 391.

You can estimate by rounding to the greatest place-value position.

$$
\begin{array}{rcl}
323 & \rightarrow & 300 \\
408 & \rightarrow & 400 \\
289 & \rightarrow & 300 \\
+391 & \rightarrow & 400 \\
\hline
& & 1,400
\end{array}
$$

So, to the nearest hundred, about 1,400 cans have been collected so far.

- How does rounding to the greatest place-value position make estimating easier?

_____

You can estimate another way by using **compatible numbers**. These are numbers that are easy to compute mentally.

Estimate. $48 + 51 + 85 + 16 = n$

$$
\begin{array}{l}
\left.\begin{array}{l} 48 \\ 51 \end{array}\right\} \rightarrow 48 + 51 \approx \quad 100 \\
\left.\begin{array}{l} 85 \\ +16 \end{array}\right\} \rightarrow 85 + 16 \approx \dfrac{+100}{200}
\end{array}
$$

≈ is the sign for "is approximately equal to."

So, the sum of $48 + 51 + 85 + 16$ is about 200.

Check Your Understanding  CRITICAL THINKING

Choose a method and estimate each sum.

	1.	2.	3.	4.	5.
	45	73	287	152	695
	63	30	164	348	301
	10	53	339	220	210
	+88	+46	+592	+181	+799

REMEMBER:

Rounding Rules
- Decide which digit is to be rounded.
- If the digit to its right is less than 5, the digit being rounded stays the same.
- If the digit to its right is 5 or more, the digit being rounded is increased by 1.

CANS COLLECTED				
Week	1	2	3	
Rm. 23	323			
Rm. 24	408			
Rm. 25	289			
Rm. 26	391			

PRACTICE

Choose a method and estimate each sum.

6.	7.	8.	9.	10.
18 27 32 +47	23 78 85 +11	34 92 47 +12	13 25 82 +91	52 65 73 +95

11.	12.	13.	14.	15.
179 226 481 +243	318 295 187 +206	479 618 735 +321	809 659 458 +575	940 768 832 +995

16.	17.	18.	19.	20.
905 642 756 +596	711 788 702 +704	299 103 111 +692	450 289 649 +198	1,006 2,972 3,112 +4,989

Mixed Applications

For Problems 21–24, use the table.

21. About how many magazine subscriptions were sold by all four grades?

22. The school's goal is to sell 1,000 subscriptions. About how many more subscriptions do they need to sell?

OAK RIDGE SCHOOL MAGAZINE SUBSCRIPTION SALES	
Grade	Number Sold
2nd	98
3rd	135
4th	196
5th	264

23. How many more subscriptions did the fifth grade sell than the fourth grade? the third grade sell than the second grade?

24. The school set a new goal for sales next year. The new goal is to sell 1,500 subscriptions. What might be the new goals for each grade?

25. Corey sold more subscriptions than Sandy but fewer than Sol. Christine sold the fewest subscriptions. Who sold the most?

26. Steve spent $4.89 for car wax, $1.98 for a sponge, and $3.59 for window cleaner. How much did he spend?

27. ▭➤ **Write a problem** that uses estimation and this data: Alana buys four items priced $9, $12, $25, and $18.

LESSON CONTINUES

PROBLEM-SOLVING
Estimate or Exact Answer?

THE PROBLEM Suppose you go to a pet store to purchase supplies for your new kitten. You take a $10.00 bill with you. You want to buy litter for $1.98, a collar for $3.89, and kitten treats for $2.79. Do you have enough money to pay for all three items? How much will you pay at the cash register. How much change will you receive?

REMEMBER:
- ☑ Understand
- ☑ Plan
- ☑ Solve
- ☑ Look Back

☑ Understand

- What are you asked to do?

- What information will you use?

- Is there information you will not use? If so, what?

☑ Plan

- How can you solve the problem?
  Estimate first. Then, find the exact amount of the items and the amount of change received.

☑ Solve

- Sometimes you need an exact answer to a problem. Sometimes an estimate will do. Look at each question to decide.

$1.98

$2.79

$3.89

Question 1	Question 2
Will you have enough money to pay for all 3 items?	How much will you pay at the cash register, and how much change will you receive?
To answer this question, you can estimate. Round to the next highest dollar.	To answer these questions, you need exact answers. Add to find the exact amount to pay at the cash register. Subtract that sum from $10.00 to find the amount of change you will receive.

Question 1:

$1.98 → $2.00
3.89 → 4.00
+ 2.79 → 3.00
$9.00

9 < 10, so $10.00 should be enough to pay for the three items.

Question 2:

$1.98 $10.00
3.89   − 8.66
+ 2.79 $ 1.34 change
$8.66

The exact cost of all three items is $8.66. You will receive $1.34 in change.

☑ Look Back

- How can you decide if your answer is reasonable?

- What other method could you use to solve the problem?

PRACTICE

Decide whether you need to estimate, find the exact answer, or both. Solve.

1. Mrs. Dunn has $10.00 with her at the grocery store. She chooses a roast for $5.89, potatoes for $1.79, and broccoli for $0.98. Does she have enough money to pay for all three items? How much will she pay at the cash register? How much change will she receive?

2. Michael received $40.00 for his birthday. He wants to buy headphones for $12.98, a microphone for $11.99, and a compact disc for $12.95. Does he have enough money to pay for all three items? How much will he pay? How much change will he receive?

3. Chet took $20.00 to spend at the theme park. He paid $8.95 for admission and $5.25 for lunch. Will he be able to spend $10.00 at the gift shop?

4. Ronnetta wants to buy a pattern for $3.95, material for $8.99, and buttons for $5.75. She has $20.00. How much will she spend on the items? How much change will she receive?

Mixed Applications

Solve.

CHOOSE A STRATEGY

• Use a Table   • Guess and Check   • Write a Number Sentence   • Work Backward

5. The table shows four Olympic winners in the Decathlon. Which of these winners earned the most points? Which earned the least points?

DECATHLON WINNERS		
Year	Name	Points
1984	Daley Thompson	8,798
1988	Christian Schenk	8,488
1992	Robert Zmelik	8,611
1996	Dan O'Brien	8,824

6. Pedro signed up for karate with a special offer. He paid $44.95 for two half-hour lessons and a uniform. The regular price for a half-hour lesson is $24.95, and a uniform is $9.95. Which is the better buy? If Pedro chose the better buy, how much did he save?

7. The Dunns arrived home at 10:30. It had taken them 30 minutes to get home from the football game, which lasted 2 hours and 30 minutes. It took 15 minutes for them to drive from their home to the stadium. At what time did the Dunns leave their house?

8. The softball coach has 42 students try out for her team, and the swimming coach has 26. The track coach has 12 more students try out than the swimming coach. If no student is on more than one team, how many students try out in all?

CULTURAL CONNECTION

Costa Rica—a Country with Two Coastlines

Andrés and his parents are moving to Costa Rica. Andrés' grandparents, who live in San José, wrote letters to the family. They explained that the small Central American country has two coastlines. The Pacific coastline is 745 miles long. The Atlantic Ocean side is 130 miles long. How much longer is the Pacific coastline than the Atlantic coastline?

CULTURAL LINK

Costa Rica is a country with strong influence from many different cultures around the world. Many Native Americans, Europeans, Africans, and Asians have settled and lived there throughout history. For at least 10,000 years, civilizations used Costa Rica as a land bridge between North and South America

A fishing village on the Atlantic Coast

Work Together

1. Costa Rica is a very narrow country. It is about 188 miles from Puerto Limón on the east coast to Puntarenas on the west coast. Cocos Island, located in the Pacific Ocean, is about 558 miles west of Puerto Limón. How far is Puntarenas from Cocos Island?

2. Andrés and his younger sister, Isabel, will go to American schools. Even though Costa Rica is a small country, there are more than 3,300 primary schools as well as 256 secondary schools. About how many more primary schools than secondary schools are there?

The beach near Corcovado National Park

3. Andrés' grandmother wrote that she had visited Corcovado National Park. She observed 14 hummingbirds, 6 scarlet macaws, 3 toucans, 2 laughing falcons, and 22 tanagers. About how many birds did she see?

4. Decide if you should add or subtract. Then solve the following problem. Chirripó Grande, 12,530 feet high, is the highest mountain peak in Costa Rica. Irazú, the second-highest peak, is 11,260 feet. How many feet higher is Chirripó Grande than Irazú?

✓ CHECK UNDERSTANDING

VOCABULARY

1. When one operation undoes the other operation, they are __?__ operations. (page 18)

2. Numbers that are easy to compute mentally are __?__ numbers. (page 26)

Draw the counters after regrouping. Find the difference. (pages 20–21)

3.
$$\begin{array}{r} \overset{3\ 11}{3\,4\,\cancel{1}} \\ -2\,1\,3 \\ \hline \end{array}$$

Hundreds	Tens	Ones

4.
$$\begin{array}{r} \overset{3\ 13}{8\,4\,\cancel{3}} \\ -5\,2\,8 \\ \hline \end{array}$$

Hundreds	Tens	Ones

✓ CHECK SKILLS

Solve. Use the inverse operation to check each problem. (pages 18–19)

5.
$$\begin{array}{r} 23 \\ +54 \\ \hline \end{array}$$

6.
$$\begin{array}{r} 48 \\ -15 \\ \hline \end{array}$$

7.
$$\begin{array}{r} 317 \\ +152 \\ \hline \end{array}$$

8.
$$\begin{array}{r} 956 \\ -435 \\ \hline \end{array}$$

Find the difference. (pages 22–23)

9.
$$\begin{array}{r} 4{,}000 \\ -1{,}230 \\ \hline \end{array}$$

10.
$$\begin{array}{r} 13{,}000 \\ -8{,}943 \\ \hline \end{array}$$

Choose a method and estimate each sum. (pages 26–27)

11.
$$\begin{array}{r} 289 \\ 156 \\ 392 \\ +235 \\ \hline \end{array}$$

12.
$$\begin{array}{r} 519 \\ 284 \\ 304 \\ +489 \\ \hline \end{array}$$

13.
$$\begin{array}{r} 199 \\ 418 \\ 526 \\ +311 \\ \hline \end{array}$$

Choose and name the operation. Solve. (pages 24–25)

14. Mary has $154 in savings. She spent $29 for a birthday gift. How much does Mary have left?

15. Jerry has 129 U.S. stamps and 317 foreign stamps. How many stamps does he have?

✓ CHECK PROBLEM SOLVING

Solve. (pages 28–29)

CHOOSE A STRATEGY
• Write a Number Sentence   • Act It Out   • Guess and Check

16. Stan ordered a T-shirt for $9.98, a belt for $5.25, and a cap for $6.79. He has $20.00. Does Stan have enough money to pay for the three items?

17. A pencil costs $0.98 and a package of paper costs $1.97. Kelly spent $9.82. How many pencils and packages of paper did she buy?

PLACE VALUE OF DECIMALS

DID YOU KNOW...

Tasty, crunchy salad sprouts can be grown from many grains or beans. The sprouts used in Chinese cooking come from mung beans, which are available in health food stores.

Team-Up Time

Speedy Sprouters

True or false? By the end of the week you can be eating salad sprouts you grew yourself. Your group will track the sprouting of the seeds. At the end of the week, you will compare two types of seeds to see which is the speedier sprouter.

YOU WILL NEED: 200 seeds (100 of each kind), 2 paper towels, 2 closeable plastic bags, 2 plates

Work with a group. Your job is to

- share the seeds among the groups.

- plant the seeds and record the number of each kind of seed that sprouts on each day for one week.

- make a decimal model that represents the number of seeds that sprouted out of each 100.

- report your results.

STEPS TO GROWING SPROUTS

Place seeds in moist paper towel.

Put the folded paper towel in a labeled plastic bag. Store in a warm, dark place.

Transfer sprouted seeds to a moist paper towel in a dish. Move them to a well-lit place. Change the towel daily.

DID YOU

☑ share the seeds and plant them?

☑ make a recording sheet for each day of the week and record the seeds that sprouted?

☑ make a model to represent how many seeds sprouted out of each 100 seeds?

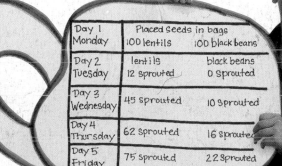

Day 1 Monday	Placed seeds in bags	
	100 lentils	100 black beans
Day 2 Tuesday	lentils 12 sprouted	black beans 0 sprouted
Day 3 Wednesday	45 sprouted	10 sprouted
Day 4 Thursday	62 sprouted	16 sprouted
Day 5 Friday	75 sprouted	22 sprouted

Using Tenths and Hundredths

You will learn to read and write decimal numbers in tenths and hundredths.

Why learn this? You can identify the value of each decimal place and relate decimals to measurement.

You can use base-ten blocks to model decimals.

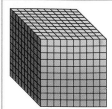
Let this model represent one whole, or 1.

Read: one

Write: 1, or 1.0

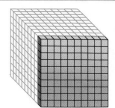
The whole is divided into 10 equal parts. Each part is $\frac{1}{10}$.

Read: one tenth

Write: $\frac{1}{10}$, or 0.1

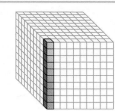
The whole is divided into 100 equal parts. Each part is $\frac{1}{100}$.

Read: one hundredth

Write: $\frac{1}{100}$, or 0.01

Science Link

Scientists use decimals when measuring plant growth. In the metric system, the decimeter is *one tenth* of a meter and the centimeter is *one hundredth* of a meter. One plant is 24 cm tall. How can you use a decimal to express this measurement in meters?

- In the models, what are the relationships of tenths and hundredths to the whole?

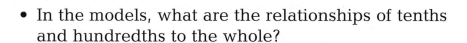

You can use a place-value chart to find the value of each digit. Show 1.45 on the place-value chart.

Ones	Tenths	Hundredths
1	4	5
$1 \times 1 = 1.0$	$4 \times 0.1 = 0.4$	$5 \times 0.01 = 0.05$

Standard Form: 1.45
Expanded Form: $1 + 0.4 + 0.05$
Written Form: one and forty-five hundredths

Talk About It

- Why do you use the word *and* to name the decimal point?

- How do you name the decimal part?

Check Your Understanding

CRITICAL THINKING

Write the decimal for each model.

1.
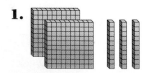

2.
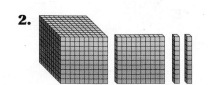

3.
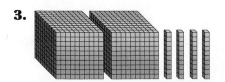

PRACTICE

Write the letter of the decimal that matches each model.

a. 1.21   **b.** 2.22   **c.** 2.12   **d.** 2.21

4.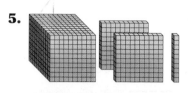

5.

6.

7.

Write the decimal for each.

8. three and six tenths   **9.** eighteen hundredths   **10.** one and six hundredths

11. $1 + 0.6$ **12.** $4 + 0 + 0.08$ **13.** $0.4 + 0.05$

Mixed Applications

For Problems 14–16, use the gymnast's score.

14. What is the value of the 5 in the gymnast's score?

15. Write the gymnast's score in written form.

16. ✏ **Write a problem** about the gymnast's score.

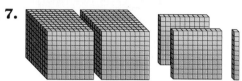

17. Mary is an Olympic gymnast. She practices gymnastics for 4 hours every day after school. On Saturday and Sunday she practices 6 hours each day. How many hours does Mary practice each week?

18. Brad left school at 3:20. He has practice at 4:30. It takes him 20 minutes to ride home, 15 minutes to eat a snack and get ready, and 25 minutes to ride to practice. What time will he arrive at practice?

Mixed Review

Write the value of the blue digit. (pages 6–7)

19. 123,985   **20.** 287,361   **21.** 475,932   **22.** 795,165

Order from greatest to least. (pages 10–11)

23. 5,479; 5,974; 4,597   **24.** 18,768; 18,678; 18,687

CCOPERATIVE
LEARNING

Thousandths

You will investigate decimal numbers to the thousandths.	Why learn this? You can record measurements that are accurate to the thousandth of a unit.	**WORD POWER** thousandths

Scientists sometimes use liters and milliliters to measure the volume of liquids. One milliliter equals one thousandth of a liter.

Base-ten blocks can help you think about **thousandths**.

Ones	Tenths	Hundredths	Thousandths
one 1.0, or 1	one tenth 0.1, or $\frac{1}{10}$	one hundredth 0.01, or $\frac{1}{100}$	one thousandth 0.001, or $\frac{1}{1000}$

Working in the science lab

• What part of a ones block is a thousandths block? What part of a liter is a milliliter?

Explore

Use base-ten blocks to show 7 milliliters.

MATERIALS: base-ten blocks

Record

Draw a picture of the base-ten blocks, and record the decimal number on a place-value chart. Write a number sentence to solve the problem.

Ones	Tenths	Hundredths	Thousandths
?	?	?	?

Standard Form: ?
Expanded Form: ?
Written Form: ?

Try This

Use base-ten blocks to model 1.342. Record by drawing the model and writing the decimal on a place-value chart.

 Link

E–Lab • Activity 3 Available on CD-ROM
and the Internet at http://www.hbschool.com/elab

 Calculator Activities page H69

TALK ABOUT IT How many places to the right of the decimal point do you place the thousandths digit?

▭▶ **WRITE ABOUT IT** Explain how you know that the thousandths block is $\frac{1}{1,000}$ of the ones block.

Technology **Link**

In *Mighty Math Calculating Crew*, the game *Nautical Number Line* challenges you to identify decimals on the number line.

HANDS-ON PRACTICE

Use base-ten blocks to model each number.
Record the number in a place-value chart.

1. 0.005　　**2.** 2.134　　**3.** 1.045　　**4.** 3.003

5. 1.067　　**6.** 0.123　　**7.** 2.065　　**8.** 3.206

Applying What You Learned

Write in standard form.

9. eight thousandths

10. three and six thousandths

11. fifty-four thousandths

12. one hundred thirty-two thousandths

13. two and ninety-five thousandths

14. eight and one hundred five thousandths

Write in expanded form.

15. 0.456　　　**16.** 0.037　　　**17.** 0.105　　　**18.** 0.068

Write in written form.

19. 0.002　　　**20.** 0.023　　　**21.** 0.405　　　**22.** 1.016

Mixed Applications

For Problems 23–24, use the calculator display.

23. Express the number in written form.

24. In what place-value position is the digit 3?

25. Talia needs 1,000 mL of water for an experiment. There were 530 mL of water in a beaker. She added 380 mL of water. Does she have enough water for the experiment?

26. Maria surveyed 1,000 people before an election. The most popular candidate received 638 votes. What part of the people surveyed did not choose the most popular candidate? Express the number as a decimal.

Place Value

You will learn to read and write numbers from thousands to thousandths.

Why learn this? You can read decimal numbers such as a measure of distance.

A science magazine reported that the Concorde, an airplane built by the English and the French, can travel 2,125.348 kilometers per hour.

You can use a place-value chart to show the value of each digit in 2,125.348.

Thousands	Hundreds	Tens	Ones	Tenths	Hundredths	Thousandths
2	1	2	5	3	4	8
2 × 1,000 = 2,000	1 × 100 = 100	2 × 10 = 20	5 × 1 = 5	3 × 0.1 = 0.3	4 × 0.01 = 0.04	8 × 0.001 = 0.008

Standard Form: 2,125.348
Expanded Form: 2,000 + 100 + 20 + 5 + 0.3 + 0.04 + 0.008
Written Form: two thousand, one hundred twenty-five and three hundred forty-eight thousandths

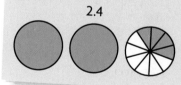

> **REMEMBER:**
> A *mixed decimal* is a number that is made up of a whole number and a decimal.
>
> 2.4

Talk About It

- Which part of the number is the whole-number part?

- Which part of the number is the decimal part?

- What is used to separate the whole-number part from the decimal part of the number?

💡 **CRITICAL THINKING** What part of a mixed decimal names a number greater than 1 and what part names number less than 1?

Check Your Understanding

For Problems 1–6, use the number 4,605.271.

1. Write the number in expanded form.

2. Write the value of the digit 7.

3. Name the place-value position of the 5.

4. Write the written form of the number.

5. Write the value of the digit 2.

6. Name the place-value position of the digit 1.

PRACTICE

Write in standard form.

7. 4,000 + 200 + 50 + 6 + 0.1 + 0.03 + 0.005

8. one thousand, two hundred five and three hundred six thousandths

9. 2,000 + 500 + 0 + 8 + 0.3 + 0.07 + 0.009

10. three thousand, seventeen and one hundred fifteen thousandths

One last lap to go!

Write the value of the digit 3 in each number.

11. 2,467.138   **12.** 3,108.657

13. 1,942.673   **14.** 4,508.305

Mixed Applications

For Problems 15–18, use the table.

15. Write the speed record for 1965 in written form.

16. Write the speed record for 1983 in expanded form.

17. Name the place-value position of the digit 9 in the 1933 speed record.

19. What number has 5 in the thousands and thousandths place, 6 in the hundreds and hundredths place, 7 in the tens and tenths place, and 9 in the ones place?

AUTO RACING ONE-MILE SPEED RECORD		
Driver	**Year**	**Miles per hour**
Milon	1920	155.046
Campbell	1933	272.109
Breedlove	1965	600.601
Noble	1983	633.468

18. How many years after 1920 did the speed record increase more than 475 miles per hour?

20.  **Write a problem** using a number from thousands to thousandths.

Mixed Review

Write the related number sentence. Find the sum or difference.
(pages 18–19)

21. $137 - 68 = n$ **22.** $125 - 49 = n$ **23.** $45 + n = 82$

Write the expanded numbers in standard form. (pages 6–7)

24. 300,000 + 20,000 + 8,000 + 0 + 60 + 5   **25.** 700,000 + 0 + 0 + 500 + 30 + 2

26. 400,000 + 0 + 4,000 + 400 + 40 + 4   **27.** 80,000 + 3,000 + 0 + 40 + 3

Equivalent Decimals

You will learn to identify equivalent decimals.	Why learn this? You can use equivalent decimals when you are measuring something or making change.	WORD POWER
		equivalent decimal

Numbers can have many names.

Here are some ways you can express the number 35.

3 tens 5 ones   35 ones   thirty-five $30 + 5$

5×7 $40 - 5$ $70 \div 2$ 35.00

Equivalent decimals are different names for the same number or amount.

You can use base-ten blocks to model equivalent decimals.

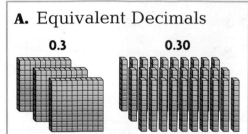

A. Equivalent Decimals	B. Not Equivalent Decimals
0.3 0.30	0.02 0.002

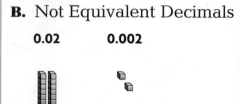

Talk About It

- In Example A, how do the blocks show that 0.3 and 0.30 are equivalent?

- In Example B, what happens to the size of the blocks when an additional zero is placed to the *left* of the digit?

- Are 0.4 and 0.40 equivalent decimals? Explain how you know.

Science Link

Giraffes are the tallest animals living in Africa. Newborn giraffes are about 1.8 m tall, and adult giraffes are from 4.25 m to 5.5 m tall.

Write an equivalent decimal for 1.8 and 5.5.

Check Your Understanding 💡 CRITICAL THINKING

Write *equivalent* or *not equivalent* to describe each set of decimals.

1. 0.04 and 0.004

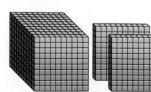

2. 1.2 and 1.20

PRACTICE

Write *equivalent* or *not equivalent* to describe each set of decimals.

3. 0.06 and 0.006   **4.** 1.3 and 1.30

  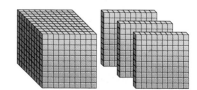

5. 1.052 and 1.025

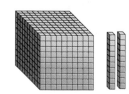

Write an equivalent decimal for each.

6. 0.01   **7.** 0.4   **8.** 0.53   **9.** 1.3   **10.** 0.600

11. 2.45   **12.** 0.070   **13.** 4.20   **14.** 3.300   **15.** 5.550

Mixed Applications

16. At a long-jump competition, Phoebe jumped 96.2 inches. Write an equivalent decimal for the length of Phoebe's jump.

17. Danny stopped at the gas station to buy gas. Write an equivalent decimal for the number of gallons Danny bought.

18. ✏️ **Write a problem** about the change Danny receives from a $10 bill when he buys gasoline.

Mixed Review

Find the difference. (pages 22–23)

19.	**20.**	**21.**	**22.**
800	4,000	15,000	40,000
−267	−1,976	− 7,542	−32,618

Choose a method and estimate each sum. (pages 26–27)

23.	**24.**	**25.**	**26.**	**27.**
12	58	125	489	523
25	24	340	187	795
19	39	209	293	645
+38	+82	+387	+337	+495

Comparing and Ordering

| You will learn to compare and order decimals. | Why learn this? You can compare scores at a sports event. |

At the gymnastics meet, Melanie scored 8.69 on the balance beam, and Cindy scored 8.85. Whose score was higher?

You can use a number line to compare decimals.

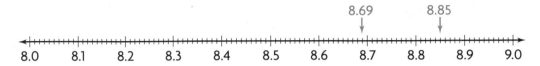

The number 8.85 is to the right of 8.69. This means that 8.85 is greater than 8.69. So, since 8.85 > 8.69, or 8.69 < 8.85, Cindy's score was higher.

Compare 3.452 and 3.456. Look for the first place where the digits are different.

◗ Step 1	◗ Step 2	◗ Step 3	◗ Step 4
Begin at the left. Compare the ones.	Compare the tenths.	Compare the hundredths.	Compare the thousandths.
3.452 ↓ 3.456 same number of ones	3.452 ↓ 3.456 same number of tenths	3.452 ↓ 3.456 same number of hundredths	3.452 ↓ 3.456 6 > 2, or 2 < 6

So, 3.456 > 3.452, or 3.452 < 3.456.

You can order numbers by comparing them in the same way. Order these numbers from least to greatest: 4.37, 4.42, 4.21

◗ Step 1	◗ Step 2	◗ Step 3	◗ Step 4
Begin at the left. Compare the ones.	Compare the tenths.	Order the digits.	Order the numbers.
4.37 ↓ 4.42 ↓ 4.21 same number of ones	4.37 ↓ 4.42 ↓ 4.21	2 < 3 < 4	4.21 < 4.37 < 4.42

• How can you order the numbers from greatest to least?

PRACTICE

Write in standard form.

7. 4,000 + 200 + 50 + 6 + 0.1 + 0.03 + 0.005

8. one thousand, two hundred five and three hundred six thousandths

9. 2,000 + 500 + 0 + 8 + 0.3 + 0.07 + 0.009

10. three thousand, seventeen and one hundred fifteen thousandths

Write the value of the digit 3 in each number.

11. 2,467.138   **12.** 3,108.657

13. 1,942.673   **14.** 4,508.305

One last lap to go!

Mixed Applications

For Problems 15–18, use the table.

15. Write the speed record for 1965 in written form.

16. Write the speed record for 1983 in expanded form.

17. Name the place-value position of the digit 9 in the 1933 speed record.

19. What number has 5 in the thousands and thousandths place, 6 in the hundreds and hundredths place, 7 in the tens and tenths place, and 9 in the ones place?

AUTO RACING ONE-MILE SPEED RECORD		
Driver	Year	Miles per hour
Milon	1920	155.046
Campbell	1933	272.109
Breedlove	1965	600.601
Noble	1983	633.468

18. How many years after 1920 did the speed record increase more than 475 miles per hour?

20. ✏️ **Write a problem** using a number from thousands to thousandths.

Mixed Review

Write the related number sentence. Find the sum or difference.
(pages 18–19)

21. 137 − 68 = n   **22.** 125 − 49 = n   **23.** 45 + n = 82

Write the expanded numbers in standard form. (pages 6–7)

24. 300,000 + 20,000 + 8,000 + 0 + 60 + 5   **25.** 700,000 + 0 + 0 + 500 + 30 + 2

26. 400,000 + 0 + 4,000 + 400 + 40 + 4   **27.** 80,000 + 3,000 + 0 + 40 + 3

Equivalent Decimals

You will learn to identify equivalent decimals.

Why learn this? You can use equivalent decimals when you are measuring something or making change.

WORD POWER

equivalent
decimal

Numbers can have many names.

Here are some ways you can express the number 35.

3 tens 5 ones	35 ones	thirty-five	30 + 5
5 × 7	40 − 5	70 ÷ 2	35.00

Equivalent decimals are different names for the same number or amount.

You can use base-ten blocks to model equivalent decimals.

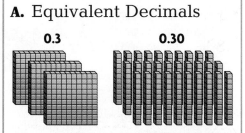

A. Equivalent Decimals

0.3   0.30

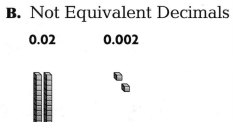

B. Not Equivalent Decimals

0.02   0.002

Talk About It

- In Example A, how do the blocks show that 0.3 and 0.30 are equivalent?

- In Example B, what happens to the size of the blocks when an additional zero is placed to the *left* of the digit?

- Are 0.4 and 0.40 equivalent decimals? Explain how you know.

Science Link

Giraffes are the tallest animals living in Africa. Newborn giraffes are about 1.8 m tall, and adult giraffes are from 4.25 m to 5.5 m tall.

Write an equivalent decimal for 1.8 and 5.5.

Check Your Understanding

 **CRITICAL THINKING**

Write *equivalent* or *not equivalent* to describe each set of decimals.

1. 0.04 and 0.004   **2.** 1.2 and 1.20

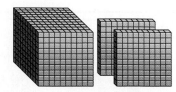

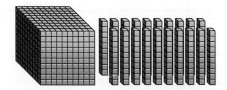

PRACTICE

Write *equivalent* or *not equivalent* to describe each set of decimals.

3. 0.06 and 0.006   **4.** 1.3 and 1.30

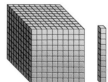   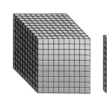 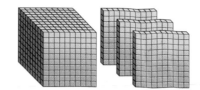

5. 1.052 and 1.025

Write an equivalent decimal for each.

6. 0.01   **7.** 0.4   **8.** 0.53   **9.** 1.3   **10.** 0.600

11. 2.45   **12.** 0.070   **13.** 4.20   **14.** 3.300   **15.** 5.550

Mixed Applications

16. At a long-jump competition, Phoebe jumped 96.2 inches. Write an equivalent decimal for the length of Phoebe's jump.

17. Danny stopped at the gas station to buy gas. Write an equivalent decimal for the number of gallons Danny bought.

18.  **Write a problem** about the change Danny receives from a $10 bill when he buys gasoline.

Mixed Review

Find the difference. (pages 22–23)

19. 800
       −267

20. 4,000
       −1,976

21. 15,000
       − 7,542

22. 40,000
       −32,618

Choose a method and estimate each sum. (pages 26–27)

23. 12
        25
        19
       +38

24. 58
        24
        39
       +82

25. 125
        340
        209
       +387

26. 489
        187
        293
       +337

27. 523
        795
        645
       +495

MORE PRACTICE Student Handbook page H75

1 Comparing and Ordering

You will learn to compare and order decimals.

Why learn this? You can compare scores at a sports event.

At the gymnastics meet, Melanie scored 8.69 on the balance beam, and Cindy scored 8.85. Whose score was higher?

You can use a number line to compare decimals.

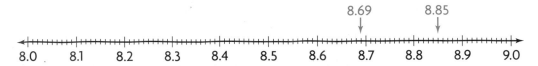

8.69   8.85

8.0 8.1 8.2 8.3 8.4 8.5 8.6 8.7 8.8 8.9 9.0

The number 8.85 is to the right of 8.69. This means that 8.85 is greater than 8.69. So, since 8.85 > 8.69, or 8.69 < 8.85, Cindy's score was higher.

Compare 3.452 and 3.456. Look for the first place where the digits are different.

▶ Step 1	▶ Step 2	▶ Step 3	▶ Step 4
Begin at the left. Compare the ones.	Compare the tenths.	Compare the hundredths.	Compare the thousandths.
3.452 ↓ 3.456 same number of ones	3.452 ↓ 3.456 same number of tenths	3.452 ↓ 3.456 same number of hundredths	3.452 ↓ 3.456 6 > 2, or 2 < 6

So, 3.456 > 3.452, or 3.452 < 3.456.

You can order numbers by comparing them in the same way. Order these numbers from least to greatest: 4.37, 4.42, 4.21

▶ Step 1	▶ Step 2	▶ Step 3	▶ Step 4
Begin at the left. Compare the ones.	Compare the tenths.	Order the digits.	Order the numbers.
4.37 ↓ 4.42 ↓ 4.21 same number of ones	4.37 ↓ 4.42 ↓ 4.21	2 < 3 < 4	4.21 < 4.37 < 4.42

• How can you order the numbers from greatest to least?

PRACTICE

Use the number line to compare the decimals. Write <, >, or = for each ●.

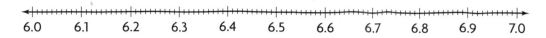

```
6.0   6.1   6.2   6.3   6.4   6.5   6.6   6.7   6.8   6.9   7.0
```

1. 6.52 ● 6.25   **2.** 6.4 ● 6.39   **3.** 6.02 ● 6.10

4. 6.09 ● 6.90   **5.** 6.60 ● 6.6   **6.** 6.76 ● 6.67

Write <, >, or = for each ●.

7. 0.65 ● 0.63   **8.** 4.25 ● 4.52   **9.** 35.83 ● 35.85

10. 1.04 ● 1.040   **11.** 132.94 ● 132.49   **12.** 156.938 ● 156.839

13. 229.035 ● 229.305   **14.** 12.7 ● 12.700   **15.** 999.989 ● 999.998

16. 13.07 ● 13.707   **17.** 210.946 ● 210.946 **18.** 435.691 ● 435.961

Order from least to greatest.

19. 4.13, 4.05, 4.09   **20.** 15.49, 15.36, 15.63   **21.** 8.010, 8.001, 8.100

22. 21.025, 20.250, 20.052   **23.** 6.783, 6.387, 6.873, 6.837

Mixed Applications

For Problems 24–28, use the menu.

24. Write the salads in order from the least expensive to the most expensive.

25. Which soup costs more than the tomato soup?

26. Which item costs more than the fruit salad but less than the yogurt?

27. Which two items each cost more than the yogurt but less than the onion soup?

28. Write the soups in order from the most expensive to the least expensive.

29. The soccer team earned $300 to purchase new equipment. They spent $237 at the sports store. How much money do they have left?

30. ✏️ **WRITE ABOUT IT** Explain how you know that 1.26 is greater than 1.06.

Welcome to Betty's RESTAURANT

Lunch Menu

Bean Soup	$2.25
Onion Soup	$2.95
Tomato Soup	$2.75
Taco Salad	$1.89
Garden Salad	$1.80
Fruit Salad	$1.85
Yogurt	$1.95

LESSON
CONTINUES ▶

PART 2 · PROBLEM-SOLVING STRATEGY
Make a Table

THE PROBLEM Kendra's science fair project was to compare Fertilizers A, B, and C to see which one would produce the tallest plant. She planted 3 identical plants and used a different fertilizer on each plant. After four weeks, the plants measured 0.27 meter, 0.38 meter, and 0.31 meter. Which fertilizer produced the tallest plant?

☑ Understand

- What are you asked to do?
- What information will you use?
- Is there information you will not use? If so, what?

☑ Plan

- What strategy can you use to solve the problem?

  You can *make a table* to analyze the data.

☑ Solve

- How can a table help you solve this problem?

  You can make a table to record the measurements of the plants after they had grown for four weeks. Then you can compare the three decimal numbers to determine which fertilizer produced the tallest plant.

Math and science work together.

PLANT GROWTH AFTER FOUR WEEKS	
Fertilizer	Height
A	0.27 meter
B	0.38 meter
C	0.31 meter

$0.38 > 0.31 > 0.27$

So, Fertilizer B produced the tallest plant after four weeks of growth.

Technology Link

You can use *Graph Links* computer software to make a data table.

GRAPH LINKS

☑ Look Back

- How did the table help you find the answer?
- What other strategy could you use?

PRACTICE

Make a table to solve.

1. Sara, Tara, and Tom were at the doctor's office. Sara's temperature was 98.9°F, Tara's was 99.8°F, and Tom's was 98.7°F. Who had the highest temperature?

2. Three students were in the long-jump competition. Sam jumped 6.25 meters, Ron jumped 6.32 meters, and Vicki jumped 6.20 meters. Who made the longest jump?

3. Four friends are measuring their heights. Sharon is shorter than Bobby. Jenny is taller than Bobby but shorter than Sammy. Who is the tallest?

4. At the gymnastics competition, Brandi scored 9.925 on the vault, Wendy scored 9.950 on the vault, and Susie scored 9.910 on the vault. Which gymnast had the highest score?

Mixed Applications

Solve.

CHOOSE A STRATEGY

• Draw a Diagram   • Make a Table •   Work Backward   • Guess and Check   • Write a Number Sentence

5. The map shows five countries in Europe and their areas in square miles. Which of these European countries has the greatest area? the least area?

6. In the month of December, it rained 3.3 inches in Tampa, 2.4 inches in Miami, and 2.8 inches in Jacksonville. Which city had the greatest amount of rainfall in December?

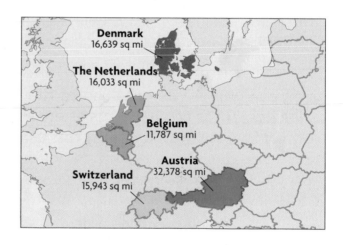

7. Jack now has $435 in a savings account. He deposited $125 after his birthday in March. In August he deposited the $230 he earned over the summer. How much money did Jack have before the two deposits?

8. The Millers bought a new car for $14,589. If they paid a total of $17,438, including $925 for tax and tag, $819 for shipping, and payment for accessories, how much were the accessories?

9. Two numbers have a sum of 18 and a product of 56. What are the two numbers?

10. Jane's car gets 28 miles to a gallon of gasoline. Its tank holds 12 gallons of gasoline. How far can the car be driven on one tank of gas?

MATH FUN!

How Many Blues?

PURPOSE To model hundredths of a sample

YOU WILL NEED 100 M&M® candies

Did you know that when your parents were your age, there were no blue M&Ms? Use math to find out what part of your sample is blue.

Count the number of each color in your sample of 100 M&Ms.

Write each as a decimal and compare them.

Which color represents the greatest decimal?

How Many Blues?

28 blue = $\frac{28}{100}$ = 0.28

16 red = $\frac{16}{100}$ = 0.16

HUMAN CALCULATOR GAME

PURPOSE To practice making decimals from fractions

YOU WILL NEED index cards, calculator

Make game cards. Write a fraction showing tenths, hundredths, or thousandths on the front of the card. On the back, write its decimal form.

$\frac{3}{100}$ 0.03

After your teacher has checked the cards, have one player read the fraction and the other player enter the decimal on the calculator. Check the answer on the card.

Take turns tallying correct decimals.

YOUR RADIO BAND

PURPOSE To compare and order decimals

YOU WILL NEED crayons, markers, or colored pencils

Your group will make a chart of favorite radio stations.

Make a list of the radio stations (AM or FM) and their frequencies (the number on the dial).

Ask people to choose their favorite station, and record their choices.

Place all the stations on a chart organized with the lower frequencies on the left and higher ones on the right, like a number line. Use frequency intervals of one tenth.

 HOME NOTE Ask family members of all ages what radio stations they listen to.

92.1   96.4   100.5   102.7   104.9

✓ CHECK UNDERSTANDING

VOCABULARY

1. The base-ten block that this model represents is one __?__. (page 36)

2. __?__ decimals are different names for the same number or amount. (page 40)

Write the decimal for each model. (pages 34–37)

3.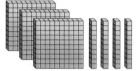

4.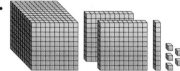

5.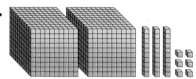

✓ CHECK SKILLS

Write the value of each underlined digit as a decimal and as a fraction. (pages 34–39)

6. 0.2<u>1</u>

7. 4.8<u>3</u>

8. <u>5</u>.904

9. 1.90<u>2</u>

10. 2.7<u>1</u>2

Write the decimal for each. (pages 34–39)

11. five tenths

12. $\frac{26}{100}$

13. one and two hundredths

14. four and thirteen hundredths

15. 5 + 0.7 + 0 + 0.002

16. $\frac{3}{1,000}$

17. 12 + 0 + 0.06

18. six and nine thousandths

19. $7\frac{46}{100}$

Write an equivalent decimal for each. (pages 40–41)

20. 0.06

21. 0.30

22. 0.720

23. 1.60

24. 0.900

✓ CHECK PROBLEM SOLVING

Solve. (pages 44–45)

CHOOSE A STRATEGY

• Work Backward   • Act It Out   • Make a Table   • Draw a Diagram

25. Roxanne knitted three scarves. The blue one is 0.75 meter, the red one is 0.85 meter, and the green one is 0.80 meter. Which scarf is the shortest?

26. What number has 8 in the thousands and thousandths places, 6 in the hundreds and hundredths places, 3 in the tens and tenths place, and 0 in the ones place?

CHAPTER 4

ADDING AND SUBTRACTING DECIMALS

HOW TO PLAY PANNING FOR GOLD

Try your luck. Take turns for six turns. Toss two number cubes to find out how much you earned each week.

If you toss:

two ones: sick with fever, no gold

two twos: a dull week, earn $1.50

two threes: a lucky week, earn $103.50

two fours or two fives: better luck yet, earn $198.25

two sixes: your claim is jumped! lose $50

non-doubles: an average week, earn $96.00

Keep track of your finances after each turn.

DID YOU KNOW...

People went to California, from 1848–1850 to mine gold. With so many people competing for supplies, prices rose dramatically. A pair of boots that cost $2.50 back home might cost from $12 to $16 in the mining towns.

Team-Up Time

Try Your Luck at Mining

Suppose it is mid-March in 1850. You have just arrived in California and plan to pan for gold. The miner's store will give you credit to buy food and supplies. You will start on April 1 and will try 8 weeks of panning for gold. On May 27, you will decide if you want to go on.

YOU WILL NEED: The Miner's Shopping List, calculators, number cubes

Work with a group. Your job is to

- make a shopping list of 100 pounds of food and the Miner's Tool Pack. Show the total cost.

- "pan for gold" with number cubes.

- make a chart showing how much you spent and earned.

- decide whether to continue to mine gold.

Miner's Shopping List
Food prices per pound:

ham	$ 0.45
beans	$ 0.07
lard	$ 0.30
cheese	$ 0.35
cornmeal	$ 0.10
rice	$ 0.12
beef jerky	$ 0.75
dried apples	$ 0.62
coffee	$ 0.12
tea	$ 1.00
brown sugar	$ 0.12
molasses	$ 1.50 per gallon
flour	$ 8.00/hundred pounds

Miner's Tool Pack $ 145.95

DID YOU

☑ make a shopping list and calculate the amount you owe the store?

☑ play Panning for Gold?

☑ make a chart to track your spending and earning?

☑ decide whether to continue?

GENERAL LEDGER

SUPPLY STORE EXPENSE

ACCT. NO.

Explanation	Debit	Credit	Balance
			-388
		96 00	-292
I owe the Supply Store			-292
Toss 1: earn $96.00			
Toss 2: sick with fever, no earnings I still owe		1 50	-29
Toss 3: earn $1.50			
I still owe		198 25	-9
Toss 4: earn $198.25			
I still owe		96 00	
Toss 5: earn $96.00			
I cleared			
Toss 6: claim was jumped lose $50.00			

HANDS ON

COOPERATIVE LEARNING

Adding Decimals

You will investigate adding decimals in tenths, hundredths, and thousandths.

Why learn this? You can add decimals, such as distances measured to the thousandths of a mile and amounts of money.

You can use base-ten blocks to find decimal sums.

Explore

Find $1.62 + 0.53 = n$.

MATERIALS: base-ten blocks

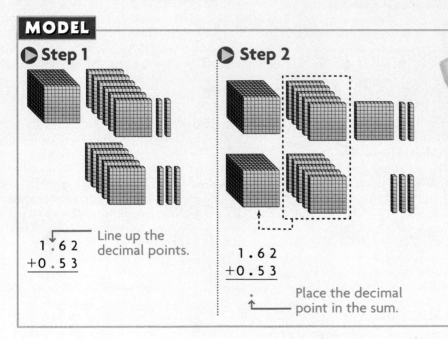

MODEL

▶ **Step 1**

$$\begin{array}{r} 1.62 \\ +0.53 \end{array}$$

Line up the decimal points.

▶ **Step 2**

$$\begin{array}{r} 1.62 \\ +0.53 \end{array}$$

Place the decimal point in the sum.

• When adding decimals, how do you know when to regroup?

Record

Use a place-value chart to record the problem and the answer. Explain how you found the sum.

Now, investigate adding decimals to thousandths.

Try This

Find $0.582 + 1.431 = n$. Model the problem with base-ten blocks. Record on a place-value chart.

TALK ABOUT IT How does the Order or Commutative Property apply to adding decimals?

Nuggets	Price
1.	$259
2.	$1050

REMEMBER:

The addition properties for whole numbers apply to decimals.

Order or Commutative Property Addends can be added in any order. The sum is always the same.

$2.67 + 1.32 = 3.99$ or
$1.32 + 2.67 = 3.99$

Zero Property When zero is added to any addend, the sum is the other addend.

$3.45 + 0 = 3.45$ or
$0 + 3.45 = 3.45$

Grouping or Associative Property Addends can be grouped differently. The sum is always the same.

$(1.2 + 3.6) + 2.0 = 6.8$ or
$1.2 + (3.6 + 2.0) = 6.8$

Technology Link

E–Lab • Activity 4 Available on CD-ROM and the Internet at http://www.hbschool.com/elab

✏️ **WRITE ABOUT IT** How is adding decimals like adding whole numbers?

HANDS-ON PRACTICE

Use base-ten blocks to model. Record the sum on a place-value chart.

1.	0.1 $+0.7$	**2.**	0.3 $+0.9$	**3.**	1.15 $+0.62$
4.	0.57 $+1.07$	**5.**	1.525 $+0.795$	**6.**	1.032 $+0.451$

Applying What You Learned

Find the sum.

7. 2.1 $+1.7$	**8.** 3.6 $+4.3$	**9.** 2.45 $+0.63$	**10.** 5.08 $+4.18$	**11.** 1.21 $+1.73$
12. 3.41 $+2.54$	**13.** 1.746 $+0.243$	**14.** 6.037 $+1.547$	**15.** 3.985 $+1.125$	**16.** 2.505 $+1.449$

17. $2.3 + 1.2 = n$ **18.** $3.95 + 2.19 = n$ **19.** $5.31 + 2.24 = n$

20. $1.84 + 1.92 = n$ **21.** $1.347 + 4.616 = n$ **22.** $2.095 + 1.294 = n$

23. $8.67 + 7.55 = n$ **24.** $6.224 + 2.478 = n$ **25.** $9.007 + 4.773 = n$

Mixed Applications

26. At Pacific High School's stadium, there were 293 fans in the upper seats and 332 fans in the lower seats. Atlantic High School's stadium had 221 fans in each of the upper and lower seats. Which school had more fans?

27. The weather forecaster says the temperature will drop 20 degrees by Monday. The thermometer shows Sunday's temperature. What is the temperature expected to be on Monday?

28. Steven went to the soccer game. He paid $9.45 for a ticket and $3.75 for snacks. How much money did Steven spend?

29. ✏️ **Write a problem** about temperature, using the thermometer at the right.

MORE PRACTICE Student Handbook page H76

More About Adding Decimals

You will learn how to use equivalent decimals to find sums.

Why learn this? You can add money amounts with different place values.

Suppose you wanted to add decimal amounts with different place values?

You can use equivalent decimals to write addition problems.

Find the sum of 25.8 and 56.75.

```
        1 1          Line up the decimal points.
  25.8  →   25.80  ← Place a zero to show equivalent
+56.75 → +56.75      decimals.
          82.55  ← Place the decimal point in the sum.
```

So, the sum of 25.8 and 56.75 is 82.55.

REMEMBER:

Equivalent decimals name the same number or amount.

$0.1 = 0.10$

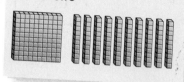

EXAMPLES

A.
```
           1 1
   0.27  →   0.270
 +1.893 → +1.893
             2.163
```

B.
```
              1
  31.37 →   31.37
 +42.8  → +42.80
            74.17
```

C.
```
   4     →   4.000
+2.089 → +2.089
           6.089
```

D.
```
  $5    →   $5.00
+ 2.98 → + 2.98
           $7.98
```

Talk About It CRITICAL THINKING

- Why is it helpful to show equivalent decimals when adding?

- In Example A, how do you know that $0.27 = 0.270$?

- Explain how the Zero Property is used in Example C.

Check Your Understanding

Find the sum.

1. $1.08 + 0.236 = n$

2. $7.355 + 9.2 = n$

3. $0.286 + 2.27 = n$

4. $3.54 + 1.2 = n$

5. $2.06 + 1.179 = n$

6. $9.153 + 7.368 = n$

7. $3.7 + 2.014 = n$

8. $5.602 + 2 = n$

In **Mighty Math Calculating Crew**, the game *Superhero Superstore* challenges you to add and subtract decimals.

PRACTICE

Use an equivalent decimal to find the sum.

9. $2.16 + 0.289 = n$ **10.** $1.603 + 5.1 = n$ **11.** $1.35 + 4.767 = n$

12. $4.69 + 7 = n$ **13.** $23.9 + 18.289 = n$ **14.** $41.69 + 5.897 = n$

15.
$$\begin{array}{r} 4 \\ +0.5 \\ \hline \end{array}$$

16.
$$\begin{array}{r} 3.8 \\ +2.37 \\ \hline \end{array}$$

17.
$$\begin{array}{r} 2.05 \\ +0.975 \\ \hline \end{array}$$

18.
$$\begin{array}{r} 5 \\ +9.18 \\ \hline \end{array}$$

19.
$$\begin{array}{r} 5.255 \\ +0.44 \\ \hline \end{array}$$

20.
$$\begin{array}{r} 2.8 \\ +3.54 \\ \hline \end{array}$$

21.
$$\begin{array}{r} 6.74 \\ +0.846 \\ \hline \end{array}$$

22.
$$\begin{array}{r} 9.6 \\ +7.457 \\ \hline \end{array}$$

23.
$$\begin{array}{r} 8.359 \\ +1.2 \\ \hline \end{array}$$

24.
$$\begin{array}{r} 12.1 \\ +\ 9.01 \\ \hline \end{array}$$

Mixed Applications

25. Carlos ran 0.75 mile on his first day of training camp, 0.95 mile on the second day, and 1.25 miles on the third day. How many total miles did he run at training camp?

26. Mrs. Hall used 35.350 gallons of gas in August, 21.098 gallons in September, and 29.567 gallons in October. How much gas did she use in the three months?

27. Bob bought a tennis racket cover for $9.98, 2 cans of balls for $2.98 each, and wristbands for $1.89. How much did Bob spend for all of his purchases?

28. ✏️ **WRITE ABOUT IT** Explain how writing equivalent decimals helps you find sums.

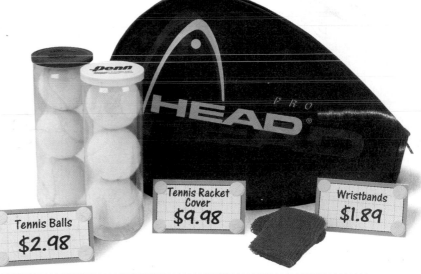

Tennis Racket Cover $9.98

Wristbands $1.89

Tennis Balls $2.98

Mixed Review

Solve. Use the inverse operation to check each problem.
(pages 18–19)

29.
$$\begin{array}{r} 20 \\ -13 \\ \hline \end{array}$$

30.
$$\begin{array}{r} 46 \\ +37 \\ \hline \end{array}$$

31.
$$\begin{array}{r} 96 \\ -75 \\ \hline \end{array}$$

32.
$$\begin{array}{r} 87 \\ +58 \\ \hline \end{array}$$

Find the difference. (pages 22–23)

33.
$$\begin{array}{r} 200 \\ -134 \\ \hline \end{array}$$

34.
$$\begin{array}{r} 4{,}000 \\ -2{,}999 \\ \hline \end{array}$$

35.
$$\begin{array}{r} 8{,}000 \\ -6{,}982 \\ \hline \end{array}$$

36.
$$\begin{array}{r} 50{,}000 \\ -36{,}159 \\ \hline \end{array}$$

37.
$$\begin{array}{r} 90{,}000 \\ -73{,}248 \\ \hline \end{array}$$

Subtracting Decimals

You will learn to subtract decimals to thousandths.

Why learn this? You can compare two distances to find how much farther you have to go.

Arcenio's mom is driving him to baseball practice. They live 1.252 miles from the baseball field. They stopped to pick up a teammate who lives 1.135 miles from Arcenio. How much farther do they have to drive to get to the baseball field?

MODEL

Find $1.252 - 1.135 = n$.

▶ **Step 1**

Record:

Line up the decimal points.

```
  1.252
 -1.135
```

▶ **Step 2**

Record:

```
     4 12
  1.2 5 2
 -1.1 3 5
 ─────────
  0.1 1 7
```

Decide whether to regroup. 5 > 2.

Regroup 5 hundredths as 4 hundredths 10 thousandths.

Subtract.

Place a decimal point in the difference.

So, they have 0.117 miles farther to drive to the baseball field.

• How can you find how much more 3.0 is than 1.987?

EXAMPLES

A.
```
    8 10
  2.9 0
 -0.7 4
 ───────
  2.1 6
```

B.
```
     5 10
  1.6 0 3
 -0.3 4 2
 ─────────
  1.2 6 1
```

C.
```
   9    14
  1 0.4 7 8
 -  9.5 3 1
 ──────────
    0.9 4 7
```

D.
```
     5 10
  0.1 6 0
 -0.0 4 7
 ─────────
  0.1 1 3
```

💡 **CRITICAL THINKING** In Example C, why is it necessary to regroup in the tens place?

Check Your Understanding

Find the difference.

1. $3.25 - 0.856 = n$ **2.** $5.1 - 4.932 = n$ **3.** $0.6 - 0.099 = n$

4.
```
  2.08
 -0.79
```

5.
```
  4.2
 -2.148
```

6.
```
  12.311
 - 9.635
```

7.
```
  3.17
 -0.456
```

PRACTICE

Find the difference.

8.	9.	10.	11.	12.
1.3 −0.7	2.6 −2.3	3.05 −2.6	5.7 −4.8	4.2 −1.02

13.	14.	15.	16.	17.
4.43 −2.12	2.5 −1.646	6.832 −3.98	11.537 − 9.125	18.349 −10.24

18. $2.45 - 1.39 = n$ **19.** $1.4 - 0.422 = n$ **20.** $2.1 - 1.2 = n$

21. $5.95 - 1.994 = n$ **22.** $4.7 - 1.616 = n$ **23.** $5.31 - 2.264 = n$

Mixed Applications

For Problems 24–26, use the table.

24. Tim and William ran the 50-meter dash. Which boy won the race? How much faster was his time?

25. Tonya and Jennifer ran the same race as Tim and William. How much slower was Jennifer's time than Tonya's time?

26. How much faster was the fastest runner's time than the slowest runner's time?

50-Meter Dash	
Tim	9.345 seconds
Tonya	8.483 seconds
William	8.300 seconds
Jennifer	10.293 seconds

The 50-meter dash

27. Mary walked 0.85 mile the first day, 1.25 miles the second day, and 2.90 miles the third day. How many miles did Mary walk in all?

28. ✏️ **Write a problem** using subtraction and the following information: Jeff is 1.325 meters tall, and Maria is 1.245 meters tall.

Mixed Review

Order from least to greatest. (pages 10–11)

29. 245, 524, 452

30. 1,539; 1,935; 1,395

31. 798, 987, 789

32. 2,634; 4,326; 2,364

Write the related number sentence. Find the sum or difference. (pages 18–19)

33. $23 + n = 42$ **34.** $132 - 56 = n$ **35.** $206 + n = 311$ **36.** $124 - 89 = n$

37. $212 - 19 = n$ **38.** $89 + n = 167$ **39.** $521 - n = 286$ **40.** $359 + n = 380$

Estimating Sums and Differences

You will learn to estimate decimal sums and differences.

Why learn this? You can round to estimate times in a race.

Kim ran the race in 35.71 seconds. Ashley ran it in 33.59 seconds. To the nearest tenth of a second, how much faster was Ashley's time?

You can estimate by rounding to the nearest tenth.

$$3\,5.7\,1 \rightarrow 3\,5.7$$
$$-3\,3.5\,9 \rightarrow 3\,3.6$$
$$\overline{2.1}$$

- Line up the decimal points.
- If the digit in the hundredths place is 5 or more, round to the next higher tenths digit.
- If the digit in the hundredths place is less than 5, the tenths digit stays the same.

So, Ashley's time was about 2.1 seconds faster.

- Rounded to the nearest whole second, how much faster was Ashley's time?

_____

At the gymnastics meet, Kathy scored 7.872 on uneven parallel bars, 8.749 on floor exercise, 8.645 on balance beam, and 9.024 on vault. To the nearest hundredth, what was her total score for the meet?

You can estimate by rounding to the nearest hundredth.

$$7.8\,7\,2 \rightarrow 7.8\,7$$
$$8.7\,4\,9 \rightarrow 8.7\,5$$
$$8.6\,4\,5 \rightarrow 8.6\,5$$
$$+9.0\,2\,4 \rightarrow 9.0\,2$$
$$\overline{3\,4.2\,9}$$

- Line up the decimal points.
- If the digit in the thousandths place is 5 or more, round to the next-higher hundredths digit.
- If the digit in the thousandths place is less than 5, the hundredths digit stays the same.

So, to the nearest hundredth, Kathy's score for the meet was 34.29.

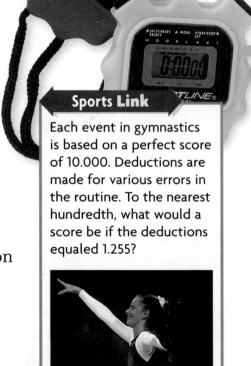

Sports Link

Each event in gymnastics is based on a perfect score of 10.000. Deductions are made for various errors in the routine. To the nearest hundredth, what would a score be if the deductions equaled 1.255?

Check Your Understanding

Estimate the sum to the nearest tenth.

1. 0.41
    +1.79

2. 3.62
    +5.25

Estimate the difference to the nearest hundredth.

3. 1.649
    −0.233

4. 2.026
    −1.163

PRACTICE

Estimate the sum or difference to the nearest tenth.

5. 5.59 −1.73	**6.** 6.61 −2.34	**7.** 9.87 +4.63	**8.** 25.08 +14.85	**9.** 39.25 −11.02

Estimate the sum or difference to the nearest hundredth.

10. 1.345 +0.744	**11.** 4.651 +9.349	**12.** 3.050 −2.363	**13.** 5.751 −3.845	**14.** 2.645 +0.244

Estimate the sum or difference and compare. Write $<$ or $>$ for each ●.

15. 8.14 − 4.89 ● 7.45 − 2.37

16. 3.82 + 5.46 ● 6.45 + 2.09

17. 7.925 + 5.392 ● 6.401 + 7.396

18. 22.45 − 12.57 ● 42.45 − 31.59

19. 35.24 + 24.76 ● 45.54 + 13.99

20. 68.98 + 46.97 ● 54.29 + 58.09

21. 8.075 − 6.395 ● 2.450 − 1.392

22. 9.269 − 1.423 ● 5.857 − 2.419

Mixed Applications

23. Leslie bought a CD for $9.99. One week later the same CD was on sale for $6.89. How much money would Leslie have saved if she had bought the CD on sale?

24. Mike watched two movies. The first movie was 115 minutes long. The second movie was 127 minutes long. Write the length of each as hours and minutes.

25. Sandy skated the first of two laps in 25.19 seconds. She skated the second lap in 24.89 seconds. She estimates her total time to be about 50 seconds. Is this a good estimate?

26. ◁▭▷ **WRITE ABOUT IT** How is estimating decimals like estimating whole numbers?

Mixed Review

Write the value of the digit 8 in each number. (pages 6–7)

27. 2,398   **28.** 3,830   **29.** 8,309   **30.** 380,254

Write $<$ or $>$ for each ●. (pages 10–11)

31. 433 ● 343   **32.** 1,593 ● 1,395   **33.** 5,565 ● 5,655   **34.** 9,797 ● 9,779

35. 8,006 ● 8,060   **36.** 896 ● 869   **37.** 2,117 ● 2,711   **38.** 19,782 ● 19,872

PART 1 Choosing Addition or Subtraction

You will learn to choose addition or subtraction by analyzing the problem.	**Why learn this?** You will know whether to add or subtract to solve problems, such as comparing the costs of two items.

You can analyze a problem to decide which operation to use.

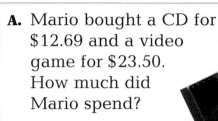

A. Mario bought a CD for $12.69 and a video game for $23.50. How much did Mario spend?

$$
\begin{array}{r}
1 \\
\$1\,2\,.\,6\,9 \\
+\ 2\,3\,.\,5\,0 \\
\hline
\$3\,6\,.\,1\,9
\end{array}
$$

Add if the problem asks you to *join groups.*

So, Mario spent $36.19.

B. Sara ran the race in 47.09 seconds. Mandy ran it in 39.15 seconds. How much faster was Mandy's time?

$$
\begin{array}{r}
{\scriptstyle 3\ 16\ 10} \\
4\,7\,.\,\cancel{0}\,9 \\
-\,3\,9\,.\,1\,5 \\
\hline
7\,.\,9\,4
\end{array}
$$

Subtract if the problem asks you to *take away* part of the group or to *compare* two groups.

So, Mandy's time was 7.94 seconds faster.

- What would happen if you didn't line up the decimal points to subtract?

_____

You can use a calculator to add and subtract decimals.

Add. 17.643 + 2.5 = n

Press: 1 7 . 6 4 3 + 2 . 5 =   = 20.143

Subtract. 71.3 − 68.755 = n

Press: 7 1 . 3 − 6 8 . 7 5 5 =   = 2.545

- Do you need to place zeros to show equivalent decimals when you use a calculator? Explain.

Check Your Understanding CRITICAL THINKING

Choose and name the operation. Solve.

1. Jerry had $10. He bought a CD for $8.98. How much does he have left?

2. Ann drove 126.75 miles on Monday and 95.25 miles on Tuesday. How far did she drive in the two days?

PRACTICE

Choose and name the operation. Solve.

3. Eduardo ran 0.52 mile the first day, 0.75 mile the second day, and 1.25 miles the third day. How many total miles did Eduardo run?

4. Scott paid $25.89 for a new video movie at Best Movies. John paid $27.75 for the same movie at another store. How much more did John pay for the movie?

5. Latoya is driving 94.2 miles to see her uncle. She has already traveled 58.7 miles. How many miles does Latoya have left to go?

6. Jose timed a race car doing laps around a race track. The times for three laps were 45.675, 46.849, and 43.439 seconds. How many seconds did it take for all three laps?

For Problems 7–10 and 14, use the items shown below.

7. James bought 1 folder, 1 pen and pencil set, and 2 spiral notebooks. How much money did James spend in all?

8. James paid for these school supplies with a $10 bill. How much change did he receive?

9. The school bookstore held a sale on school supplies. Markers were on sale for $0.50 off. What was the sale price of the markers?

10. Cindy received $3.71 in change from the bookstore. She bought 1 folder. How much money did Cindy have to start with?

Mixed Applications

11. Jill counted 245 flowers on a nature walk. Tracy counted 442 flowers. How many more flowers did Tracy count?

12. Side A of Jason's new tape played for 21.5 minutes. Side B played for 19.8 minutes. How much longer did Side A play?

13. Carl is enclosing a rectangular field with fencing. The field is 120 feet long and 50 feet wide. How much fencing does he need to enclose the field?

14.  **Write a problem** that requires addition or subtraction. Use items from the picture above.

LESSON CONTINUES ▶

PROBLEM-SOLVING STRATEGY
Write a Number Sentence

THE PROBLEM Mrs. McKay wants to write a check for $74.97 to the electric company. The bank charges a fee if a customer writes checks for more money than is in the account. Does she have enough money in her checking account to write the check to the electric company?

REMEMBER:

☑ Understand
☑ Plan
☑ Solve
☑ Look Back

☑ Understand

- What are you asked to do?

- What information will you use?

- Is there information you will not use? If so, what?

☑ Plan

- How can you solve the problem?

  You can *write number sentences* to show the transactions in Mrs. McKay's checkbook.

Check Number	Date	Description	Amount of Check	Amount of Deposit	Balance
					$282.76
725	2/16	Hall's Food Store	$25.78		$256.98
726	2/18	Kenny Shoe Store	$32.36		$224.62
727	2/19	Grogin's Book Shop	$12.63		
	2/20	rebate		$23.50	
728	2/22	Bell Phone Co.	$49.82		
	2/24	paycheck		$50.00	
729	2/24	Bank-a-Card	$150.00		

☑ Solve

- Write number sentences for the checks and deposits. Begin each number sentence with the previous balance. Subtract the amount of each check, and add the amount of each deposit as it is made. You may wish to use a calculator.

So, Mrs. McKay has $85.67 in her account. This is enough to write the check for $74.97.

Balance

$224.62 − $12.63 = $211.99
$211.99 + $23.50 = $235.49
$235.49 − $49.82 = $185.67
$185.67 + $50.00 = $235.67
$235.67 − $150.00 = $85.67

☑ Look Back

- How does writing a number sentence help you find the answer?

- What other strategy could you use?

PRACTICE

Write a number sentence to solve.

1. Sara's checking account had a starting balance of $98.29. She wrote checks for $23.84, $52.39, and $14.45. She made deposits of $25.50 and $95.00. What is her balance? Does Sara have enough to write a check for $112.93?

2. Paul received his bank statement in the mail. He had a starting balance of $45.96. The statement shows deposits of $59.90 and $199.28. He wrote checks for $54.29 and $89.48. What is Paul's current balance?

3. At baseball practice, Justin caught 36 fly balls. Brad caught 41 fly balls. Kevin caught 10 fewer than Justin and Brad combined. How many fly balls did Kevin catch?

4. The four girls on the 400-meter relay team each ran 100 meters. Their times were 15.2 seconds, 14.7 seconds, 14.4 seconds, and 15.5 seconds. What was their combined time?

Mixed Applications

Solve.

CHOOSE A STRATEGY

• Draw a Diagram   • Use a Table   • Write a Number Sentence   • Work Backward

5. Janine's car can get 210 miles to a tank of gas. About how many tanks of gas does she need to drive from Chicago to Boston?

6. Sandy drove from Chicago to Atlanta, back to Chicago, and then to Denver. How many miles did she drive in all?

7. Candace wants 2 pairs of running shoes that cost $39.98 a pair. When she buys them, she gets $8 off the price of the second pair. What will Candace pay for the 2 pairs of shoes?

8. The soccer coach had 24 students try out for his team, and the tennis coach had 18 students try out. The basketball coach had 8 more students try out than for soccer and tennis combined. How many students tried out for the basketball team?

Road Mileage from Chicago	
Boston	963
Atlanta	674
New York	802
Denver	996

Technology Link

You can use *Data ToolKit* computer software to display data in a spreadsheet.

CULTURAL CONNECTION

Atlanta, Home of the 1996 Olympics

Jasmine lives near Atlanta, Georgia, the site of the 1996 Centennial Olympic Games. Her cousins traveled from New York City to see some Olympic events. Jasmine lives 7.87 miles from Stone Mountain, where the cycling events were held. How far did she and her cousins ride their bikes to see the cycling events round trip?

Work Together

1. Jasmine saw Michael Johnson win the 200-meter race with a time of 19.32 seconds. In the trials to qualify for the Olympics, his time was 19.66 seconds. What was the difference between the two times? Round the answer to the nearest tenth of a second.

2. Frank Fredericks is from Namibia. He earned the silver medal in the 200-meter race with a time of 19.86 seconds. What is the difference between his time and Michael Johnson's time?

3. Alto Boldon from Trinidad received the bronze medal in the 200-meter race. He crossed the finish line 0.12 second behind Frank Fredericks. What was his time? What is the difference between his time and Michael Johnson's time?

4. Jasmine measured on a map the distances between event locations to see if she and her cousins could walk to some events. From the track and field events in Olympic Stadium to the field hockey events at Clark Atlanta University, she measured about 2.6 miles. From field hockey to the basketball games at Morehouse College was about 0.7 mile farther. About how far would they have to walk if they went from a track event to field hockey to a basketball game and back?

> **CULTURAL LINK**
>
> Atlanta, Georgia was the birthplace of Martin Luther King, Jr. The Sweet Auburn neighborhood where he lived is now part of a 23.5-acre National Historic site. Special films and programs can be seen at the Martin Luther King, Jr., Center for Non-Violent Change.

✓ CHECK UNDERSTANDING

Find the sum or difference. You may use base-ten blocks. (pages 50–51)

1. $\begin{array}{r} 1.3 \\ +0.5 \\ \hline \end{array}$	**2.** $\begin{array}{r} 3.7 \\ +2.8 \\ \hline \end{array}$	**3.** $\begin{array}{r} 5.15 \\ -0.97 \\ \hline \end{array}$	**4.** $\begin{array}{r} 4.09 \\ +6.13 \\ \hline \end{array}$	**5.** $\begin{array}{r} 9.736 \\ -7.524 \\ \hline \end{array}$

Use an equivalent decimal to find the sum or difference. (pages 52–55)

6. $2.32 + 0.287 = n$ **7.** $1.03 - 0.987 = n$ **8.** $0.286 + 2.27 = n$

9. $11.754 - 8.6 = n$ **10.** $5.384 + 8.1 = n$ **11.** $3.1 - 0.985 = n$

✓ CHECK SKILLS

Find the sum or difference. (pages 50–55)

12. $\begin{array}{r} 2.4 \\ -1.9 \\ \hline \end{array}$	**13.** $\begin{array}{r} 1.76 \\ +4.02 \\ \hline \end{array}$	**14.** $\begin{array}{r} 2.905 \\ +1.973 \\ \hline \end{array}$	**15.** $\begin{array}{r} 6.011 \\ -4.842 \\ \hline \end{array}$	**16.** $\begin{array}{r} 8.254 \\ -6.087 \\ \hline \end{array}$

17. $6.27 + 3.098 = n$ **18.** $4.748 - 2.01 = n$ **19.** $8.009 + 2.91 = n$

Estimate the sum to the nearest tenth. (pages 56–57)

20. $\begin{array}{r} 1.52 \\ +0.24 \\ \hline \end{array}$	**21.** $\begin{array}{r} 4.03 \\ +1.26 \\ \hline \end{array}$

Estimate the difference to the nearest hundredth. (pages 56–57)

22. $\begin{array}{r} 2.753 \\ -0.627 \\ \hline \end{array}$	**23.** $\begin{array}{r} 6.074 \\ -4.255 \\ \hline \end{array}$

Choose and name the operation. Solve. (pages 58–59)

24. Jodie had $39 in savings. She bought a CD for $14.69. How much does she have left?

25. Ted rode his bicycle 1.5 miles to school and then returned. Later he rode 0.8 mile to the store and then returned. How far did Ted ride?

✓ CHECK PROBLEM SOLVING

Solve. (pages 60–61)

CHOOSE A STRATEGY

• Write a Number Sentence   • Act It Out   • Guess and Check   • Work Backward

26. Ken had $49.61 in his bank account. He deposited $52.50 and wrote checks for $12.89 and $29.99. How much is left in his account?

27. In a tennis tournament, Jenna won 2 matches more than Shandra. Ann won 1 match more than Shandra. Ann won 4 matches. Who won the tournament?

STUDY GUIDE & REVIEW

VOCABULARY CHECK

Choose a term from the box to complete each sentence.

WORD BANK
benchmark
equivalent
inverse

1. A ? is a point of reference. (page 4)

2. When one operation undoes another, they are ? operations. (page 18)

3. Decimals that are different names for the same number or amount are ? . (page 40)

STUDY AND SOLVE

CHAPTER 1

EXAMPLE

Write the value of the underlined digit.

5̲16,214,890

500,000,000, or
5 hundred millions

The 5 is in the hundred millions place.

Tell whether each number is expressed as *cardinal, ordinal,* or *nominal.* (pages 2–3)

4. 621 Lynn St. 5. 260,898

6. ninety-fifth 7. 65 mi

Write the value of the underlined digit. (pages 6–9)

8. 5̲6,784,091 9. 541,09̲6,327

Write two other forms for each number. (pages 8–9)

10. 6,453,211

11. three hundred one million, twenty-four thousand, six hundred fifteen

Write < , > , or = for each ●. (pages 10–11)

12. 5,478 ● 5,480

13. 11,000 ● 10,998

For Problems 14–15, use the table. (pages 12–13)

1990 POPULATIONS OF OHIO CITIES	
City	**Population**
Cincinnati	364,114
Columbus	632,945
Cleveland	505,616

14. List the cities from the one with the least population to the one with the greatest population.

15. How many more people live in Columbus than in Cincinnati?

CHAPTER 2

EXAMPLE

Find the difference.

$$\begin{array}{r} {\scriptstyle 3\ 9\ 9\ 10} \\ 4{,}000 \\ -2{,}482 \\ \hline 1{,}518 \end{array}$$

Regroup 400 tens as 399 tens 10 ones.
Subtract from right to left.

Solve. Use the inverse operation to check each problem. (pages 18–19)

16. $\begin{array}{r} 45 \\ +64 \\ \hline \end{array}$ **17.** $\begin{array}{r} 754 \\ -548 \\ \hline \end{array}$

Show how you regrouped for each problem. Solve. (pages 22–23)

18. $\begin{array}{r} 3{,}000 \\ -1{,}321 \\ \hline \end{array}$ **19.** $\begin{array}{r} 19{,}000 \\ -\ 7{,}942 \\ \hline \end{array}$

Choose and name the operation. Solve. (pages 24–25)

20. Lia spent $68. She gave the clerk $100. What is Lia's change?

Estimate each sum. (pages 26–27)

21. $\begin{array}{r} 289 \\ 111 \\ 395 \\ +205 \\ \hline \end{array}$ **22.** $\begin{array}{r} 298 \\ 184 \\ 305 \\ +413 \\ \hline \end{array}$

CHAPTER 3

EXAMPLE

Write a decimal and a fraction.

two and five hundredths

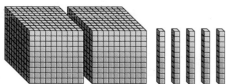

decimal: 2.05   fraction: $2\frac{5}{100}$

Write each as a decimal. (pages 34–39)

23. ten and five tenths   **24.** $2 + 0 + 0.04$

25. six and one thousandth   **26.** $8\frac{33}{100}$

Write the value of the underlined digit as a decimal and as a fraction. (pages 34–39)

27. 0.3<u>2</u>   **28.** 6.50<u>6</u>

Write an equivalent decimal for each. (pages 40–41)

29. 0.80   **30.** 1.83

CHAPTER 4

EXAMPLE

Find the sum.

$$\begin{array}{r} {\scriptstyle 1\ 1\ 1} \\ 3.765 \\ +2.347 \\ \hline 6.112 \end{array}$$

Line up the decimal points.
Add as with whole numbers.
Place the decimal point in the sum.

Find the sum or difference. (pages 50–55)

31. $\begin{array}{r} 3.846 \\ +1.404 \\ \hline \end{array}$ **32.** $\begin{array}{r} 6.015 \\ -3.766 \\ \hline \end{array}$

Estimate the sum or difference to the nearest hundredth. (pages 56–57)

33. $\begin{array}{r} 2.561 \\ +4.675 \\ \hline \end{array}$ **34.** $\begin{array}{r} 3.458 \\ -\ 2.379 \\ \hline \end{array}$

Choose and name the operation. Solve. (pages 58–59)

35. Blake had $49.50. He earned $15.75 more. How much money does he have in all?

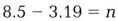 WRITE ABOUT IT

1. Explain how to use place value to order 5,608, 5,860, 5,806 from the least to the greatest. Then write the numbers in order. (pages 10–13)

2. Show and explain each step as you find the difference. (pages 22–23)

$$\begin{array}{r} 6{,}080 \\ -1{,}245 \\ \hline \end{array}$$

3. Write an equivalent decimal for each. Explain how you know the decimals are equivalent. (pages 40–41)

0.5; 0.360; 1.22

4. Show and explain each step as you solve the problem. (pages 52–55)

$2.51 + 6.208 = n$

$8.5 - 3.19 = n$

✓ PERFORMANCE ASSESSMENT

Solve. Explain your method.

CHOOSE A STRATEGY

- Use a Table
- Act It Out
- Make a Model
- Make a Table
- Write a Number Sentence

5. How many computers were sold in 1995? What conclusion can you draw from this data? (pages 12–13)

Year	Computers Sold
1993	5,085,000
1994	6,725,000
1995	8,225,000
1996	9,525,000

6. A class is buying books for $49.95, computer software for $28.89, and science equipment for $41.25. They have about $125.00. Estimate. Do they have enough money? (pages 28–29)

7. In the Daytona 500 car race, average winning speeds in 3 different years were 160.627 mph for Driver A; 160.875 mph for Driver B; and 159.730 mph for Driver C. Show the speeds from fastest to slowest. (pages 44–45)

8. Jon's allowance is $15.00 a week. His lunches cost $9.45 a week. He earned $8.75 raking leaves, but he spent $6.50 for a movie and $4.30 for a book. Does he have enough money for another movie? (pages 60–61)

CUMULATIVE REVIEW

Solve the problem. Then write the letter of the correct answer.

1. *Seventy-eighth* is a(n) _?_ number.

A. cardinal   **B.** measurement
C. nominal   **D.** ordinal

(pages 2–3)

2. What is the value of the underlined digit? (pages 6–9)
3<u>4</u>2,461,980

A. 400,000, or 4 hundred thousands   **B.** 4,000,000, or 4 millions

C. 40,000,000, or 4 ten millions   **D.** 400,000,000, or 4 hundred millions

3. What is the standard form for four hundred two million, three hundred sixty thousand, nineteen? (pages 8–9)

A. 402,360,190   **B.** 402,360,019
C. 402,036,019   **D.** 42,360,019

4. Compare. 109,989 ⬤ 110,000

A. +   **B.** =
C. >   **D.** <   (pages 10–11)

5. Find the difference.

$$\begin{array}{r} 4,000 \\ -2,436 \\ \hline \end{array}$$

A. 1,564
B. 2,436
C. 2,674
D. 6,436   (pages 22–23)

6. Estimate the sum.

$$\begin{array}{r} 288 \\ 112 \\ +396 \\ \hline \end{array}$$

A. 1,100   **B.** 800
C. 900   **D.** 700

(pages 26–27)

7. Which fraction has the same value as the underlined digit?
5.73<u>2</u>

A. $\frac{2}{1}$ **B.** $\frac{2}{10}$

C. $\frac{2}{100}$ **D.** $\frac{2}{1,000}$ (pages 34–37)

8. What is the standard form for ten and six thousandths?

A. 10.006   **B.** 10.06
C. 10.6   **D.** 6,010   (pages 34–37)

9. Which decimal is equivalent to 1.070?

A. 1.007   **B.** 1.07
C. 1.7   **D.** 1.70   (pages 40–41)

10. $4.25 + 3.078 = n$

A. 1.172   **B.** 3.503
C. 7.228   **D.** 7.328   (pages 50–53)

11. $7.008 - 3.04 = n$

A. 3.968   **B.** 4.048
C. 6.704   **D.** 10.048   (pages 54–55)

12. Decide whether to estimate or to find the exact answer. Solve.

Alex had $100 to spend on clothes. He paid $34.99 for a sweater and $29.95 for a pair of jeans. Will he be able to buy a pair of shoes for $49.75?

A. exact answer; no
B. exact answer; yes
C. estimate; no
D. estimate; yes   (pages 28–29)

CHAPTER 5

MULTIPLYING BY ONE-DIGIT NUMBERS

HEARTBEATS PER MINUTE	
Mouse	650
Newborn baby	120
Child	90
Woman	75
Man	70
Olympic swimmer	40
Marathon runner	35
Hibernating groundhog	3

DID YOU KNOW . . .

Small creatures have faster heartbeats than large creatures, if they are not hibernating.

Feel the Beat

Have you ever wondered how much your heart speeds up with exercise? With your group, you will take 1-minute pulse readings at rest, after you have walked, and after you have done the exercise of your choice. Then you will decide which exercise makes your pulse beat fastest.

YOU WILL NEED: stopwatch, or clock with a second hand

Work with a partner. Your job is to

- record each person's pulse at rest.
- go for a 2-minute walk, and record each person's pulse immediately afterward.
- do a 2-minute workout such as running in place, jumping rope, or doing jumping jacks. Record your pulses again.
- make a chart showing each person's pulse rate at rest, after walking, and after a workout.

CHECK YOUR PULSE

Wherever an artery is just below the skin, you can feel it pulse. Using three fingers, and a little patience, feel the beat in these spots. Be sure not to press hard!

WHERE THE CHIN MEETS THE NECK, ABOUT AN INCH BELOW THE EAR

ON THE UNDERSIDE OF THE WRIST

INSTEP OF THE FOOT

Count the number of pulses in 20 seconds; multiply by three. That's your pulse rate. Take it at rest, walking and exercising.

DID YOU

☑ measure and record your pulses at rest, after walking, and after a workout?

☑ make a chart?

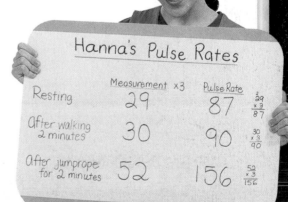

Hanna's Pulse Rates

	Measurement ×3	Pulse Rate	
Resting	29	87	29 ×3 = 87
After walking 2 minutes	30	90	30 ×3 = 90
After jumprope for 2 minutes	52	156	52 ×3 = 156

69

Using Multiplication Properties

You will learn to identify and use multiplication properties.

Why learn this? Multiplication properties help when you use mental math.

WORD POWER

Commutative
  Property of
  Multiplication
Associative
  Property of
  Multiplication
Property of One
Zero Property for
  Multiplication

Stacy has 8 shelves. She has 5 CDs on each shelf. Bjorn has 5 shelves. He has 8 CDs on each shelf. Who has more CDs?

COMMUTATIVE PROPERTY OF MULTIPLICATION

You can multiply numbers in any order. The product is always the same.

Example $8 \times 5 = 40$ $5 \times 8 = 40$

factors product   factors product

So, Stacy and Bjorn have the same number of CDs.

More Properties

ASSOCIATIVE PROPERTY OF MULTIPLICATION

You can group factors differently. The product is always the same.

Example $(4 \times 4) \times 2 = 4 \times (4 \times 2)$

16    $\times 2 = 4 \times$ 8

$32 = 32$

PROPERTY OF ONE

When one of the factors is 1, the product equals the other number.

Example $8 \times 1 = 8$ $1 \times 8 = 8$

ZERO PROPERTY FOR MULTIPLICATION

When one factor is 0, the product is 0.

Example $6 \times 0 = 0$ $0 \times 6 = 0$

Talk About It

- How is the Commutative Property different from the Associative Property?

 Calculator Activities page H61

- How can the Associative Property of Multiplication help when you use mental math?

PRACTICE

Write the name of the multiplication property used in each number sentence.

1. $2 \times (4 \times 3) = (2 \times 4) \times 3$ **2.** $5 \times 4 = 4 \times 5$ **3.** $6 \times 1 = 6$

4. $8 \times 6 = 6 \times 8$ **5.** $0 \times 7 = 0$ **6.** $(7 \times 3) \times 8 = 7 \times (3 \times 8)$

Copy and complete the equation. Identify the property used.

7. $5 \times \blacksquare = 5$ **8.** $4 \times (8 \times 3) = (\blacksquare \times 8) \times 3$ **9.** $9 \times 0 = \blacksquare$

10. $4 \times 6 = 6 \times \blacksquare$ **11.** $(8 \times 2) \times 5 = 8 \times (\blacksquare \times 5)$ **12.** $\blacksquare \times 7 = 7 \times 4$

13. $1 \times 3 = \blacksquare$ **14.** $8 \times \blacksquare = 0$ **15.** $5 \times (4 \times 6) = (5 \times \blacksquare) \times 6$

Show two ways to group by using parentheses. Find the product.

16. $3 \times 2 \times 4 = n$ **17.** $2 \times 6 \times 3 = n$ **18.** $7 \times 2 \times 4 = n$

19. $6 \times 3 \times 5 = n$ **20.** $7 \times 5 \times 6 = n$ **21.** $8 \times 4 \times 9 = n$

Mixed Applications

22. Karl has 4 dimes in each of 2 rows. Sue has 3 dimes in each of 3 rows. Who has more money?

23. Tracy took her pulse for 20 seconds. She counted 29 heartbeats. How many beats per minute is that?

24. Darius drove 232.5 miles last week. He drove 147.8 miles this week. How far did Darius drive in the two weeks?

25. ✏️ **Write a problem** in which you multiply three numbers. Write the steps you would follow to solve the problem using the Associative Property of Multiplication.

Mixed Review

Write the value of the blue digit. (pages 6–7)

26. 126,374   **27.** 506,923   **28.** 437,948   **29.** 842,042

Order from least to greatest. (pages 42–43)

30. 3.52, 3.25, 2.35   **31.** 9.64, 6.94, 9.46   **32.** 17.01, 17.10, 17.11

Recording Multiplication

You will learn to use counters to multiply whole numbers by one-digit numbers.

Why learn this? You can model multiplication problems, such as the total distance traveled on a trip.

Mr. Ruiz drives 215 miles each week. How many miles does he drive in 5 weeks?

Use four colors of counters to make a model.

Let ● = 1,000, ● = 100, ● = 10, and ○ = 1.

MODEL

How can you use colored counters to model this problem?

▶ Step 1

Model the problem by making 5 groups of 215.

$$215 \times 5$$

▶ Step 2

Group all counters by color or place value.

$$
\begin{array}{r}
215 \\
\times \quad 5 \\
\hline
25 \leftarrow 5 \times 5 \\
50 \leftarrow 5 \times 10 \\
1{,}000 \leftarrow 5 \times 200 \\
\end{array}
$$

Hundreds	Tens	Ones

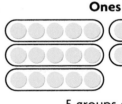

5 groups of 2 hundreds, or 10 hundreds

5 groups of 1 ten, or 5 tens

5 groups of 5 ones, or 25 ones

▶ Step 3

Regroup. Start with the ones. Record.

Thousands **Hundreds** **Tens** **Ones**

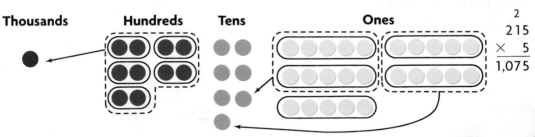

$$
\begin{array}{r}
2 \\
215 \\
\times \quad 5 \\
\hline
1{,}075 \\
\end{array}
$$

1   0   7   5

So, Mr. Ruiz drives 1,075 miles in 5 weeks.

• How were the counters representing ones and hundreds regrouped?

- In Step 3 of the model, why is a zero recorded in the hundreds place?

PRACTICE

Explain how you would model with colored counters.

1. $\begin{array}{r} 400 \\ \times\ \ 3 \\ \hline \end{array}$	**2.** $\begin{array}{r} 285 \\ \times\ \ 5 \\ \hline \end{array}$	**3.** $\begin{array}{r} 593 \\ \times\ \ 6 \\ \hline \end{array}$	**4.** $\begin{array}{r} 602 \\ \times\ \ 7 \\ \hline \end{array}$

Solve by using colored counters.

5. $2 \times 134 = n$ **6.** $4 \times 360 = n$ **7.** $3 \times 728 = n$ **8.** $5 \times 501 = n$

9. $6 \times 199 = n$ **10.** $7 \times 263 = n$ **11.** $4 \times 672 = n$ **12.** $6 \times 390 = n$

13. $3 \times 270 = n$ **14.** $5 \times 432 = n$ **15.** $7 \times 391 = n$ **16.** $2 \times 512 = n$

Mixed Applications

For Problems 20–21, use the table.

17. There are 463,000 people living in Douglas and 657,000 people living in Limon. There are 1,200,000 people living in Youngsville. Which has more people—Youngsville, or Douglas and Limon combined?

18. Paulo arrived at soccer practice at 10:00 A.M. and stayed for 2 hours. It took him 20 minutes to get home, 10 minutes to shower, and 30 minutes to eat lunch. What time was it when he finished eating lunch?

19. Mrs. Roger drove 25 miles each day for 5 days. Mrs. Blake drove 21 miles each day for 6 days. Who drove a greater distance? How many more miles did she drive?

20. Sabrina and Donald went to the movies 2 Friday nights in a row. They each bought a ticket, a popcorn, and a drink both nights. How much did they spend in all?

21. ✐ **Write a problem** using the information from the Movie Prices table.

Movie Prices	
Tickets	$ 5.00
Popcorn	$ 2.25
Cold Drink	$ 1.75
Candy	$ 1.50

Mixed Review

Write $<$, $>$, or $=$ for each ●. (pages 10–11)

22. 475 ● 457   **23.** 6,120 ● 6,210   **24.** 8,093 ● 8,093   **25.** 9,907 ● 9,709

Write the decimal for each. (pages 34–35)

26. $1 + 0.7 + 0.03$ **27.** $6 + 0.4 + 0.09$ **28.** seven and two hundredths

Practicing Multiplication

You will learn more about multiplying by one-digit numbers.

Why learn this? You can find out how many items you need, such as cups for a picnic.

A lightning flash can be 8 kilometers long!

Vanessa sees a flash of lightning. She hears thunder 7 seconds later. Vanessa knows that sound travels at about 350 meters per second. About how far away is the lightning from Vanessa?

MODEL

What is 7 × 350?

▶ Step 1

Multiply the ones.
7 × 0 ones = 0 ones

```
  350
×   7
────
    0
```

▶ Step 2

Multiply the tens.
7 × 5 tens = 35 tens.
Regroup.

```
   3
  350
×   7
────
   50
```

▶ Step 3

Multiply the hundreds.
7 × 3 hundreds = 21 hundreds
Add the regrouped hundreds.

```
   3
  350
×   7
────
2,450
```

So, the lightning is about 2,450 meters away from Vanessa.

Talk About It

• Why should you multiply in the ones place first?

• How are 35 tens recorded in Step 2?

In *Mighty Math Calculating Crew*, the game *Intergalactic Trader* challenges you to multiply by one-digit numbers.

EXAMPLES

A.
```
   1
  241
×   4
────
  964
```

B.
```
    1
  380
×   2
────
  760
```

C.
```
  3 2
  576
×   4
────
2,304
```

Check Your Understanding ⚡ CRITICAL THINKING

Tell which place-value position must be regrouped. Find the product.

1.
```
  307
×   3
```

2.
```
  219
×   4
```

3.
```
  126
×   7
```

4.
```
  137
×   9
```

Find the product.

5. $526 \times 6 = n$

6. $322 \times 8 = n$

7. $624 \times 5 = n$

8. $810 \times 3 = n$

Calculator Activities page H60

PRACTICE

Find the product.

9. 212 × 4	**10.** 246 × 5	**11.** 293 × 7	**12.** 250 × 9
13. 303 × 2	**14.** 324 × 4	**15.** 351 × 6	**16.** 390 × 6
17. 419 × 7	**18.** 725 × 3	**19.** 506 × 6	**20.** 331 × 9

21. $368 \times 7 = n$　　**22.** $452 \times 5 = n$　　**23.** $501 \times 8 = n$　　**24.** $562 \times 8 = n$

25. $528 \times 6 = n$　　**26.** $536 \times 7 = n$　　**27.** $572 \times 8 = n$　　**28.** $579 \times 9 = n$

29. $190 \times 9 = n$　　**30.** $303 \times 4 = n$　　**31.** $241 \times 8 = n$　　**32.** $953 \times 2 = n$

Mixed Applications

33. Monique sees lightning, counts 5 seconds, and then hears thunder. She knows that sound travels at about 350 meters per second. About how far away is the lightning from Monique?

34. Navin collects baseball cards. He had $11.00 at the beginning of the day. He bought 3 cards for $3.50 each. He sold 2 cards for $4.00 each and 4 for $1.25 each. How much money did Navin have at the end of the day?

35. Jake has 520 points. He earned the following scores on his first five tests: 86, 79, 99, 92, and 83 points. What score did he earn on his sixth test?

36. ✏ **WRITE ABOUT IT** Explain the steps you follow to multiply by a one-digit number.

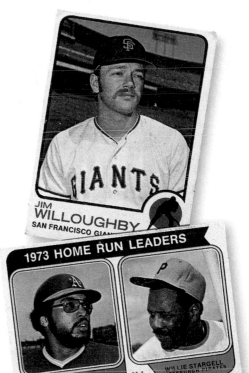

Mixed Review

Find the difference. (pages 22–23)

37. 200 −126	**38.** 700 −357	**39.** 2,000 − 579	**40.** 7,000 −6,451	**41.** 15,000 − 9,630

Write an equivalent decimal for each. (pages 40–41)

42. 0.02　　　**43.** 0.65　　　**44.** 2.9　　　**45.** 0.800

MORE PRACTICE Student Handbook page H78

Finding Volume

You will investigate finding volumes of rectangular prisms.	**Why learn this?** You can figure out how many items a box will hold.	**WORD POWER** volume cubic units

Area is the number of square units needed to cover a surface. Area is measured in square units. **Volume** is the measure of the space a solid figure occupies. Volume is measured in **cubic units**.

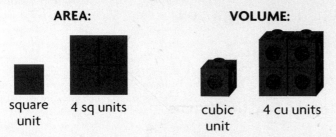

AREA:

square unit   4 sq units

VOLUME:

cubic unit   4 cu units

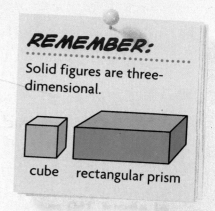

REMEMBER:

Solid figures are three-dimensional.

cube   rectangular prism

You can use unit cubes to help you think about volume.

Liam uses unit cubes to build a rectangular prism. Each layer of the prism is 3 cubes long and 2 cubes wide. There are 2 layers in the prism.

Explore

MATERIALS: unit cubes

Build a rectangular prism like the one Liam made. Let each unit cube represent 1 cubic unit. Find how many rectangular prisms you can make with the same volume.

TALK ABOUT IT Is a 2 × 1 × 2 rectangular prism the same as a 2 × 2 × 1 rectangular prism? Explain.

Record

Record the volume of the rectangular prism in cubic units. Record the number of prisms you can make with the same volume. Write the measurements for each prism.

Now, investigate finding the volumes for different rectangular prisms.

Technology Link

E–Lab • Activity 5 Available on CD-ROM and the Internet at http://www.hbschool.com/elab

Try This

Use unit cubes to build each prism. Copy and complete the table.

Length of Base	Width of Base	Height (number of layers)	Volume (cubic units)
8 cubes	4 cubes	4 cubes	?
9 cubes	8 cubes	3 cubes	?
7 cubes	5 cubes	4 cubes	?
6 cubes	6 cubes	5 cubes	?

✏️ **WRITE ABOUT IT** What operation can you use to find the volume of a rectangular prism? How do you use the operation to compute volume?

HANDS-ON PRACTICE

Use unit cubes to build each rectangular prism. Find the volume.

1. 6 cubes long
3 cubes wide
3 layers high

2. 5 cubes long
3 cubes wide
2 layers high

3. 4 cubes long
5 cubes wide
3 layers high

4. 6 cubes long
4 cubes wide
4 layers high

5. 7 cubes long
2 cubes wide
5 layers high

6. 8 cubes long
4 cubes wide
6 layers high

Use unit cubes to build each prism. Copy and complete the table.

	Length of Base	Width of Base	Height	Volume
7.	8 cubes	3 cubes	4 cubes	?
8.	5 cubes	? 3	3 cubes	45 cu units
9.	6 cubes	2 cubes	?	60 cu units
10.	?	4 cubes	2 cubes	64 cu units

Mixed Applications

11. Matt has the two rectangular prisms shown. He wants to use the prism with the larger volume. Which prism should Matt choose?

12. How many ways can you build a rectangular prism with a volume of 6 cubic units? What are they?

13. Daniel's mom gives him $2.75 for every room he cleans and $1.25 for every bush he trims. If he cleans 3 rooms and trims 5 bushes, how much money will he earn?

A.

B.

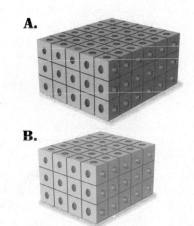

PART 1 Finding Area and Volume

You will learn to use a formula to find area and volume.	Why learn this? You use area and volume when you build things.	**WORD POWER** formula

Will wants to build a dog pen. Which pen has the greatest area?

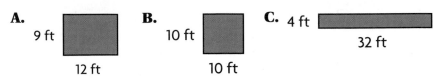

A. 9 ft / 12 ft   B. 10 ft / 10 ft   C. 4 ft / 32 ft

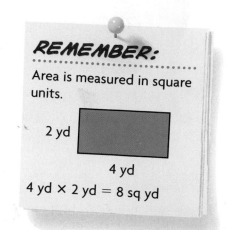

REMEMBER:

Area is measured in square units.

2 yd / 4 yd

4 yd × 2 yd = 8 sq yd

You can use a formula to find the area of each dog pen. A **formula** is a set of symbols that expresses a mathematical rule. Here is the formula for area.

Area = length × width, or $A = l \times w$

Use the formula to find the area of each dog pen.

A	B	C
$A = l \times w$ $A = 12 \times 9$ $A = 108$ sq ft	$A = l \times w$ $A = 10 \times 10$ $A = 100$ sq ft	$A = l \times w$ $A = 32 \times 4$ $A = 128$ sq ft

So, Dog Pen C has the greatest area.

Will wants to build a dog house. Which dog house has the greatest volume?

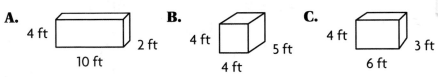

A. 4 ft / 2 ft / 10 ft   B. 4 ft / 5 ft / 4 ft   C. 4 ft / 3 ft / 6 ft

Max and Will

Here is the formula for volume.

Volume = length × width × height, or $V = l \times w \times h$

Use the formula to find the volume of each dog house.

A	B	C
$V = l \times w \times h$ $V = 10 \times 2 \times 4$ $V = 80$ cu ft	$V = l \times w \times h$ $V = 4 \times 5 \times 4$ $V = 80$ cu ft	$V = l \times w \times h$ $V = 6 \times 3 \times 4$ $V = 72$ cu ft

So, Dog Houses A and B have the greatest volume.

💡 **CRITICAL THINKING** Which multiplication property can help you compute volume? Explain.

PRACTICE

Find the area.

1.
8 in.
12 in.

2. 5 yd
23 yd

3. 6 yd
27 yd

4. 7 in.
18 in.

5. $l = 14$ cm
$w = 4$ cm
$A = \blacksquare$ sq cm

6. $l = 35$ in.
$w = 3$ in.
$A = \blacksquare$ sq in.

7. $l = 27$ ft
$w = 4$ ft
$A = \blacksquare$ sq ft

8. $l = 38$ m
$w = 5$ m
$A = \blacksquare$ sq m

Find the volume.

9.
7 in.
4 in.
8 in.

10.
3 m
7 m
4 m

11.
6 ft
3 ft
5 ft

12.
3 yd
4 yd
6 yd

13. $l = 3$ m
$w = 6$ m
$h = 6$ m
$V = \blacksquare$ cu m

14. $l = 9$ ft
$w = 4$ ft
$h = 4$ ft
$V = \blacksquare$ cu ft

15. $l = 3$ cm
$w = 6$ cm
$h = 7$ cm
$V = \blacksquare$ cu cm

16. $l = 8$ in.
$w = 5$ in.
$h = 4$ in.
$V = \blacksquare$ cu in.

Mixed Applications

17. Francesca's dresser is 8 feet long, 5 feet wide, and 3 feet high. Duncan's dresser is 6 feet long, 4 feet wide, and 4 feet high. Who has the dresser with the larger volume? Explain.

18. The fifth grade is going on a field trip. Each class in the fifth grade has 22 students, 2 parent chaperones, and 1 teacher. There are 6 classes in the fifth grade. How many people are going on the field trip?

19. Mr. Schneider's new car runs 23 miles on a gallon of gasoline. The gas tank in the car holds 9 gallons. How far can Mr. Schneider drive with 1 tank of gas?

20. 📖 **WRITE ABOUT IT** Suppose you have two rectangular prisms. The area of the base of the first prism is less than the area of the base of the second prism. The volume of the first prism is greater than the volume of the second prism. How is this possible?

LESSON
CONTINUES ▶

PART 2 PROBLEM-SOLVING STRATEGY
Use a Formula

THE PROBLEM Eduardo is buying an aquarium. He has narrowed his choices to two aquariums with the same features. One measures 6 ft × 2 ft × 3 ft and costs $285. The other measures 4 ft × 3 ft × 3 ft and costs $345. Which aquarium is the better buy?

REMEMBER:
- ☑ Understand
- ☑ Plan
- ☑ Solve
- ☑ Look Back

☑ Understand

- What are you asked to find?

- What information will you use?

- Is there information you will not use? If so, what?

☑ Plan

- What strategy can you use to solve the problem?

  You can *use a formula* to find the volumes.

☑ Solve

- How can you use the strategy to solve the problem?

  Use the formula $V = l \times w \times h$ to find the volume of each aquarium. Compare each volume to each price to determine the better buy.

$285 Aquarium	$345 Aquarium
$V = l \times w \times h$	$V = l \times w \times h$
$V = 6 \times 2 \times 3$	$V = 4 \times 3 \times 3$
$V = 36$ cu ft	$V = 36$ cu ft

The two aquariums have the same volume. So, the $285 aquarium is the better buy.

☑ Look Back

- How can you determine if your answer is reasonable?

- What other strategy could you use?

PRACTICE

Use a formula to solve.

1. Marty has narrowed his choices to two aquariums with the same features. One measures 4 ft × 3 ft × 4 ft and costs $243. The other measures 6 ft × 4 ft × 2 ft and costs $212. Which aquarium is the better buy?

2. Jimet can buy a cage for her pet rabbits that measures 5 ft × 4 ft × 3 ft, or she can buy a cage that measures 4 ft × 4 ft × 5 ft. Jimet wants to get the cage with the larger volume. Which cage should she buy?

3. Tony is going to put a new carpet in his room. The floor in his room is 12 feet long and 9 feet wide. How many square feet of carpet should he buy?

4. LaPorsha is decorating the sidewalk with chalk drawings. The sidewalk is 9 feet long and 8 feet wide. What is the area of the sidewalk she is decorating?

Mixed Applications

Solve.

CHOOSE A STRATEGY

- **Draw a Diagram**   - **Write a Number Sentence**   - **Use a Table**   - **Make a Model**   - **Use a Formula**

5. Brittany and her classmates are painting scenery for a play. They need to cover a board that is 9 feet tall and 32 feet wide. What is the area of the board they are painting?

6. Kyle counted the light bulbs around a movie-theater sign that was 12 feet wide and 6 feet tall. The light bulbs were 1 foot apart. How many light bulbs were there?

7. Ms. Enriquez drinks 1 cup of coffee with breakfast. She has 2 glasses of iced tea with lunch, 1 glass of cola with dinner, and 1 cup of hot cocoa before bed. How much caffeine does she consume in one day?

AMOUNTS OF CAFFEINE	
Drink	**Amount (milligrams)**
Coffee	175
Cola	40
Hot Cocoa	10
Iced Tea	25

8. Ray is making a quilt for the arts festival. Each quilt square is divided into 4 equal parts. Each of the 4 parts is a triangle. The quilt is 2 squares long and 2 squares wide. What does it look like?

9. Paul has $20.00 to buy supplies for a project. He buys wood for $4.89 and nails for $2.79. Paint costs $5.63 per bucket. How many buckets of paint can Paul buy? How much money will he have left?

MATH FUN!

$3 \times 7 = 21$

DOMINO SNAKE

PURPOSE To practice multiplication facts

YOU WILL NEED dominoes, calculator

Playing Domino Snake will help you practice the basic multiplication facts. Place tiles face down. Say the product of the two numbers shown on the tile. If you don't know the product, let your partner tell it to you. Stand the tiles in a long row, or snake. If neither of you knows the product, find it with a calculator and place the tile back in the pile. The last person to place a tile gets to topple the snake.

Roundabout Number

PURPOSE To practice multiplying and finding patterns

YOU WILL NEED paper and pencil, calculator

Find out why the number 142,857 is called a roundabout number.

Multiply 142,857 by 2. Write the product. What do you notice?

142,857	Product	What I notice
× 2		
× 3		

Multiply 142,857 by 3, 4, 5, 6, and 7. Each time you find the product, look for a pattern.

Nick's Room

PURPOSE To practice finding area

YOU WILL NEED paper and pencil, centimeter grid paper, centimeter ruler

Nick's room is 10 feet square. His mom is helping him choose furniture for his room. Nick finds carpeting for $5 a square foot. His mom will buy him a carpet that costs $150 or less.

Draw a 10-by-10 grid like the one shown. Cut out rectangles to show Nick's furniture. Arrange the furniture and plan two rugs that will cost $150 or less.

Furniture for Nick's Room

Bed   3 squares × 6 squares
Desk   3 squares × 2 squares
Chair   2 squares × 1 square
Dresser 2 squares × 4 squares

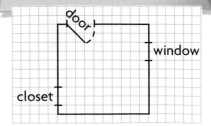

On a grid, draw a room at home. What is the area of the room?

☑ CHECK UNDERSTANDING

VOCABULARY

1. The __?__ states that when one of the factors is 1, the product equals the other number. (page 70)

2. The __?__ states that you can group factors differently. The product is always the same. (page 70)

3. The __?__ states that when one factor is 0, the product is 0. (page 70)

4. The __?__ states that you can multiply numbers in any order. The product is always the same. (page 70)

5. __?__ is the measure of the space inside a solid figure. (page 76)

6. Volume is measured in __?__ units. (page 76)

Tell which place-value position must be regrouped. Find the product. (pages 74–75)

7. 425
   × 7

8. 608
   × 6

9. 900
   × 5

10. 532
    × 3

☑ CHECK SKILLS

Find the product. (pages 74–75)

11. $243 \times 4 = n$

12. $856 \times 2 = n$

13. $710 \times 3 = n$

14. $604 \times 5 = n$

Find the area. (pages 78–79)

15. $l = 13$ ft
    $w = 8$ ft
    $A = \blacksquare$ sq ft

16. $l = 42$ in.
    $w = 5$ in.
    $A = \blacksquare$ sq in.

Find the volume. (pages 78–79)

17. $l = 9$ cm
    $w = 5$ cm
    $h = 3$ cm
    $V = \blacksquare$ cu cm

18. $l = 6$ m
    $w = 4$ m
    $h = 7$ m
    $V = \blacksquare$ cu m

☑ CHECK PROBLEM SOLVING

Solve. (pages 80–81)

CHOOSE A STRATEGY

• Draw a Diagram   • Use a Formula   • Make a Model

19. Jacob can buy one of two toolboxes with the same features. Both cost $15. One measures 12 in. × 6 in. × 6 in. The other measures 10 in. × 8 in. × 6 in. Which is the better buy?

20. Hannah glues gold stars around a picture frame that is 8 inches wide and 10 inches tall. She places the stars 2 inches apart. How many stars does she use?

CHAPTER 6

MULTIPLYING LARGER NUMBERS

DID YOU KNOW ...

A vegetable garden should be located in a spot that gets at least 6 hours of sunlight each day.

Your Critter-Proof Budget Garden

Your group has $100.00 to create a garden. Plan a fence around your garden to keep critters out. Work together to figure out costs.

YOU WILL NEED: 1-inch grid paper, colored pencils or markers, scissors, paper for group diagram

Work with a group. Your job is to

- design a 2-by-3 garden plot. Draw it on 1-inch grid paper, making 1 square inch equal 1 square foot.

- cut out your garden plot. Combine the plots of your group members in any pattern you like, as long as the sides touch.

- find out how many feet of fencing and how much soil your group needs.

- figure out how much money your group spent. If you spent more than $100.00, rearrange your plots and try again.

COSTS	
FENCING	$1.59 per ft
SOIL	$0.52 per sq ft

DID YOU

- ☑ draw a garden plot on 1-inch grid paper?
- ☑ put the plots together to make the group's garden?
- ☑ figure out how many feet of fencing and how much soil the whole garden needs?
- ☑ figure out the total cost of your garden?

Our Group Garden

Cost of Garden:
$34.98 + $9.36 = $44.34
We're under budget! ☺

Using the Distributive Property

You will investigate using the Distributive Property of Multiplication.	Why learn this? The Distributive Property helps you do mental math.	WORD POWER Distributive Property

The **Distributive Property** states that multiplying a sum by a number is the same as multiplying each addend by the number and then adding the products.

MODEL

How can you use the Distributive Property to multiply 10×15?

▶ Step 1

On grid paper, outline a rectangle that is 10 units high and 15 units wide. Think of the area as the product of 10×15.

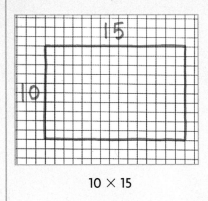

10×15

▶ Step 2

Count over 10 units from the left, and draw a line to break apart the rectangle.

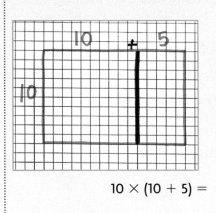

$10 \times (10 + 5) =$

▶ Step 3

Use the Distributive Property to restate the problem as a sum of two products. Multiply what is in parentheses first. Add the products.

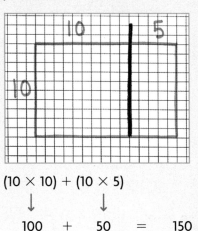

$(10 \times 10) + (10 \times 5)$
$\downarrow$ $\downarrow$
$100 + 50 = 150$

So, $10 \times 15 = 150$.

TALK ABOUT IT How was place value used to break apart the rectangle in Step 2 of the model?

✏ **WRITE ABOUT IT** Explain how the rectangle in Step 1 was broken apart in Step 3.

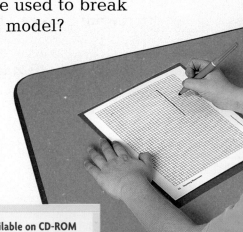

Technology Link
E–Lab • Activity 6 Available on CD-ROM and the Internet at http://www.hbschool.com/elab

Explore

MATERIALS: grid paper

Use grid paper to find $20 \times 17 = n$.

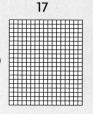

On grid paper, outline a rectangle that is 20 units high and 17 units wide.

$20 \times 17 = n$

17

20

Record

Draw your model and record the steps you used to break apart 20×17. Record the product.

- In what other way can you break apart the factors so they are easy to multiply?

Now, investigate making your own model for the Distributive Property.

Try This

Use grid paper to model $25 \times 14 = n$. Draw your model and record your method and the product.

✏️ **WRITE ABOUT IT** Why does breaking apart the numbers make it easy to compute products?

HANDS-ON PRACTICE

Use grid paper to model. Find the product.

1. $20 \times 19 = n$ **2.** $20 \times 28 = n$ **3.** $30 \times 29 = n$

Applying What You Learned

Use the Distributive Property to rewrite each equation. Find the product.

4. $14 \times 16 = n$ **5.** $20 \times 27 = n$ **6.** $30 \times 39 = n$

Mixed Applications

7. Darrell bought 24 cookies for each class. There are 4 fifth-grade classes. How many cookies did Darrell buy?

8. Eric grows carrots in his garden. He eats 5 carrot sticks each day. How many carrot sticks does he eat in 14 days?

MORE PRACTICE Student Handbook page H80

Multiplying by Two-Digit Numbers

You will learn to multiply by two-digit numbers.

Why learn this? You can find the total number of miles run in a race.

Jeanette is training for the Boalsburg Marathon. The marathon is 27 days away. On each of the 27 days, Jeanette will walk 19 miles. How many miles will she walk in all?

MODEL

What is 19×27?

▶ Step 1

Multiply by the ones.

$$
\begin{array}{r}
6 \\
27 \\
\times 19 \\
\hline
243
\end{array} \quad \leftarrow 9 \times 27
$$

▶ Step 2

Multiply by the tens.

$$
\begin{array}{r}
27 \\
\times 19 \\
\hline
243 \\
270
\end{array} \quad \leftarrow 10 \times 27
$$

↑ The zero shows there are 27 tens.

▶ Step 3

Add the products.

$$
\begin{array}{r}
27 \\
\times 19 \\
\hline
243 \\
+270 \\
\hline
513
\end{array}
$$

So, Jeanette will walk 513 miles in all.

Talk About It

• Why should you multiply by the ones before multiplying by the tens?

• In Step 2, why is it important to show the zero?

• How could you use the Distributive Property to find 19×27?

EXAMPLES

A.
$$
\begin{array}{r}
1 \\
34 \\
\times 24 \\
\hline
136 \\
+680 \\
\hline
816
\end{array}
\begin{array}{l}
\\
\\
\\
\leftarrow 4 \times 34 \\
\leftarrow 20 \times 34
\end{array}
$$

B.
$$
\begin{array}{r}
60 \\
\times 35 \\
\hline
300 \\
+1{,}800 \\
\hline
2{,}100
\end{array}
\begin{array}{l}
\\
\\
\leftarrow 5 \times 60 \\
\leftarrow 30 \times 60
\end{array}
$$

C.
$$
\begin{array}{r}
2 \\
105 \\
\times 15 \\
\hline
525 \\
+1{,}050 \\
\hline
1{,}575
\end{array}
\begin{array}{l}
\\
\\
\\
\leftarrow 5 \times 105 \\
\leftarrow 10 \times 105
\end{array}
$$

• In Example C, what happens to the regrouped digit when there is a zero in the factor?

PRACTICE

Find the product.

1. 15 $\times 14$	**2.** 17 $\times 13$	**3.** 18 $\times 16$	**4.** 19 $\times 15$
5. 21 $\times 12$	**6.** 23 $\times 14$	**7.** 26 $\times 17$	**8.** 34 $\times 19$
9. 60 $\times 25$	**10.** 70 $\times 45$	**11.** 105 $\times\ 20$	**12.** 110 $\times\ 35$
13. 26 $\times 37$	**14.** 21 $\times 42$	**15.** 47 $\times 33$	**16.** 65 $\times 30$

17. $81 \times 56 = n$ **18.** $102 \times 36 = n$ **19.** $117 \times 48 = n$

20. $110 \times 45 = n$ **21.** $124 \times 37 = n$ **22.** $131 \times 45 = n$

The first Boston Marathon was held on April 19, 1897, to honor Paul Revere's famous ride in 1775. Of the 15 runners who started the race, 8 finished. Some marathon runners run 15 to 20 miles each day. How many miles do they run in 7 days?

Mixed Applications

23. One restaurant has 27 servers. Each server can wait on 15 people at the same time. How many people can they serve in all?

24. A roller-coaster car can take 32 people on every ride. You waited for 8 rides for your turn. How many people rode the roller coaster ahead of you?

25. Kristina had $45.00. She paid $15.75 for a ticket to a football game. She bought a drink for $3.50, a shirt for $12.95, and a hat for $10.55. How much money does she have left?

26. Mr Fanning has 120 tickets to a baseball game. There are 32 students in his class. Each student wants 4 tickets. How many more tickets does Mr. Fanning need?

27. Carlos wants to buy new carpet for his bedroom. His bedroom floor is 17 feet by 12 feet. What is the area of his bedroom floor?

28. ▭▶ **WRITE ABOUT IT** How would you multiply a two-digit number by a two-digit number?

Mixed Review

Write $<$, $>$, or $=$ for each ⬤. (pages 42–43)

29. 3.46 ⬤ 3.64   **30.** 74.76 ⬤ 74.760   **31.** 124.98 ⬤ 124.89

Use an equivalent decimal to find the sum. (pages 52–53)

32. 4.21 $+0.773$	**33.** 3.05 $+5.197$	**34.** 7.65 $+9.024$	**35.** 25.044 $+18.27$

Estimating Products

You will learn to estimate products.

Why learn this? You can make decisions based on your estimate.

Ms. Russo, the art teacher, is ordering supplies for the year. She teaches 153 fifth-grade students. Each student will use about 12 slabs of clay. About how many slabs of clay should Ms. Russo order?

When you see the word "about" in a question, you can estimate the product.

MODEL

How can you estimate 12 × 153?

▶ Step 1

Round each factor to its greatest place-value position.

$$153 \rightarrow 200$$
$$\times\ 12 \rightarrow \times\ 10$$

▶ Step 2

Multiply the rounded factors.

$$
\begin{array}{r}
200 \\
\times\ 10 \\
\hline
2{,}000
\end{array}
$$

So, Ms. Russo should order about 2,000 slabs of clay.

* To which place-value position was 153 rounded? 12?

> **REMEMBER:**
>
> To round a number:
>
> * Find the digit in the place to be rounded.
> * Look at the digit to its right.
> * If that digit is *less than 5,* the digit being rounded remains the same.
> * If the digit is *5 or greater,* the digit being rounded increases by 1.

EXAMPLES

A.
$$
\begin{array}{r}
329 \rightarrow\ \ 300 \\
\times\ 55 \rightarrow \times\ 60 \\
\hline
18{,}000
\end{array}
$$

B.
$$
\begin{array}{r}
461 \rightarrow\ \ 500 \\
\times\ 42 \rightarrow \times\ 40 \\
\hline
20{,}000
\end{array}
$$

Talk About It  CRITICAL THINKING

* Which basic multiplication facts helped you find the products in Examples A and B?

* Look for a pattern of zeros in the factors and products. How can you tell how many zeros to add at the end of the product for the basic fact?

* How does estimation help you determine if your answer is reasonable?

> **CULTURAL LINK**
>
> Native people of the southwestern United States have been making pottery from the clays of the area for more than 2,000 years.

Check Your Understanding

Round each number to its greatest place-value position.

1. 495 **2.** 51 **3.** 74 **4.** 649

PRACTICE

Estimate the product by rounding each factor to its greatest place-value position.

5. 103 × 21	**6.** 110 × 35	**7.** 143 × 68	**8.** 519 × 25
9. 157 × 38	**10.** 232 × 73	**11.** 298 × 81	**12.** 428 × 49
13. 376 × 79	**14.** 423 × 93	**15.** 592 × 72	**16.** 650 × 34

17. $48 \times 602 = n$

18. $88 \times 746 = n$

19. $94 \times 864 = n$

20. $12 \times 365 = n$

21. $43 \times 421 = n$

22. $83 \times 682 = n$

23. $26 \times 883 = n$

24. $63 \times 943 = n$

25. $89 \times 896 = n$

Mixed Applications

For Problems 26 and 28, use the table.

26. Suppose that every student who collects football cards has 14 cards in his or her collection. Estimate the number of cards in all.

27. The students in Mrs. Ling's class wanted to help decorate the school. Mrs. Ling's class has 15 girls and 14 boys. Each student made 15 decorations. How many decorations did Mrs. Ling's class make in all?

FOOTBALL CARD COLLECTIONS	Have Cards	Do Not Have Cards
Boys	345	672
Girls	196	853

28. ✏️ **Write a problem** using the information in the Football Card Collections table.

Mixed Review

Write in standard form. (pages 36–37)

29. one and five thousandths

30. six and thirty-three thousandths

31. seven and one hundred six thousandths

32. four and two hundred one thousandths

33. ten and twenty-one thousandths

34. five and four thousandths

Copy and complete the equation. Identify the property used. (pages 70–71)

35. ■ × 4 = 4 × 9

36. 6 × 0 = ■

37. 3 × (7 × 8) = (3 × ■) × 8

38. 8 × ■ = 8

39. 5 × 7 = 7 × ■

40. 2 × ■ = 0

Multiplying by Three-Digit Numbers

You will learn to multiply three-digit numbers.

Why learn this? You can figure out how many people fly on airplanes each day.

One kind of jet seats 462 passengers. Suppose 135 of these jets leave an airport on one day. If each jet is full, how many passengers will leave on these jets?

Multiply. $135 \times 462 = n$

Estimate. $100 \times 500 = 50{,}000$ So, $n \approx 50{,}000$.

```
    462
  ×135
  2,310  ←  5 × 462
 13,860  ←  30 × 462
+46,200  ←  100 × 462
 62,370
```

So, 62,370 passengers will leave on the jets.

- How can you determine if your answer is reasonable?

EXAMPLE

Multiply. $406 \times 2{,}167 = n$

Estimate. $400 \times 2{,}000 = 800{,}000$ So, $n \approx 800{,}000$.

Paper and Pencil

```
   2,167
 ×   406
  13,002
  00,000  ← These zeros can
+866,800    be omitted.
 879,802
```

 Calculator

Press:

2 1 6 7 × 4 0 6 =

Display: = 879'802.

- In the example, what does 13,002 represent? 866,800?

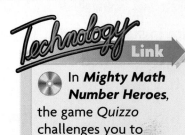
Technology Link

In **Mighty Math Number Heroes**, the game *Quizzo* challenges you to multiply three-digit numbers.

Check Your Understanding

Estimate. Then find the product.

1. $243 \times 496 = n$ **2.** $578 \times 132 = n$ **3.** $650 \times 809 = n$

PRACTICE

Estimate to the greatest place-value position. Then find the product.

4.	134 ×115	5.	167 ×122	6.	238 ×203
7.	314 ×246	8.	379 ×331	9.	448 ×401
10.	524 ×389	11.	631 ×538	12.	1,384 × 232
13.	1,637 × 402	14.	2,472 × 125	15.	2,354 × 311

16. $332 \times 479 = n$ 17. $528 \times 625 = n$ 18. $624 \times 883 = n$

19. $581 \times 1,093 = n$ 20. $1,302 \times 716 = n$ 21. $369 \times 2,278 = n$

Mixed Applications

22. Everyday last week 15 schools went to the Renaissance Fair. From each school, 210 students and 6 teachers attended. How many people attended in 7 days?

23. Noah worked for 18 hours. He earned $5.00 each hour. He bought a helmet for $15.95 and a skateboard for twice that amount. How much money did Noah have left?

24. For the past 12 years, Alfredo has brushed his teeth 3 times a day. About how many times has he brushed his teeth in that time?

25. ✏️ **WRITE ABOUT IT** Why should you estimate the product before multiplying three- and four-digit numbers?

Mixed Review

Choose a method and estimate each sum. (pages 26–27)

26.	23 35 19 +41	27.	56 53 47 +38	28.	189 501 250 +422	29.	854 408 119 +221	30.	901 249 385 +267

Find the difference. (pages 54–55)

31. $2.72 - 1.58 = n$ 32. $4.09 - 3.632 = n$ 33. $5.78 - 3.803 = n$

PART 1 Multiplying to Find Perimeter and Area

You will learn more about multiplying to solve problems.	Why learn this? You can find the perimeter and area of a rectangular object, such as your desk.

Josie built a sandbox for her younger brother. The sides of the sandbox measure 12 feet by 13 feet. What is the perimeter? What is the area?

Multiply and add to find the perimeter.

Perimeter = (2 × length) + (2 × width)
$P = (2 \times l) + (2 \times w)$
$P = (2 \times 12) + (2 \times 13) = 24 + 26 = 50$

So, the perimeter of the sandbox is 50 feet.

Multiply length times width to find the area.

$A = l \times w$
$A = 12 \times 13 = 156$

So, the area of the sandbox is 156 square feet.

REMEMBER:

Perimeter is the distance around a figure. To find the perimeter of a rectangle, multiply the length of each side by 2. Add the products.

30 in.

25 in.

Perimeter (P) =
(2 × 30) + (2 × 25) =
60 + 50 = 110 in.

EXAMPLES

A.

48 yd

54 yd

$P = (2 \times l) + (2 \times w)$
$P = (2 \times 48) + (2 \times 54)$
$P = 96 + 108 = 204$ yd

$A = l \times w$
$A = 48 \times 54 = 2{,}592$ sq yd

B.

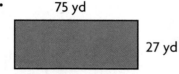

75 yd

27 yd

$P = (2 \times l) + (2 \times w)$
$P = (2 \times 75) + (2 \times 27)$
$P = 150 + 54 = 204$ yd

$A = l \times w$
$A = 75 \times 27 = 2{,}025$ sq yd

C.

51 yd

51 yd

$P = (2 \times l) + (2 \times w)$
$P = (2 \times 51) + (2 \times 51)$
$P = 102 + 102 = 204$ yd

$A = l \times w$
$A = 51 \times 51 = 2{,}601$ sq yd

Talk About It  CRITICAL THINKING

• Compare Examples A, B, and C. What do you notice about the perimeters? the areas?

• Is there a shorter number sentence that can be used to find the perimeter for Example C? Explain.

PRACTICE

Find the perimeter and area for each figure.

1.
150 in.
75 in.

2.
147 yd
118 yd

3.
188 m
282 m

4.
136 cm
213 cm

5.
202 ft
104 ft

6.
286 yd
355 yd

7.
202 cm
85 cm

8.
191 ft
147 ft

9.
253 in.
425 in.

Mixed Applications

10. Mason's yard is 107 feet by 238 feet. What are the perimeter and area of Mason's yard?

11. A factory produces 864 cars every week. How many cars does the factory produce in one year? (HINT: 1 year = 52 weeks)

12. Jerome traveled 17 miles round trip to soccer practice. He practiced 4 days. He traveled 19 miles round trip to his grandma's house on Saturday and again on Sunday. How many miles did Jerome travel in all?

13. Ariana, Cari, and Hannah play on the school basketball team. In one year, Ariana scored a total of 562 points. Cari scored 26 fewer points. Hannah scored 12 fewer points than Cari. How many points did Cari and Hannah score?

14. The fuel tank in Mr. Roja's car holds 18 gallons, and the car travels 14 miles for each gallon of gasoline. About how far can Mr. Roja expect to drive on one tank of gas?

15. ✍ **Write a problem** about a playground, using perimeter and area.

MORE PRACTICE Student Handbook page H81

PART 2 PROBLEM-SOLVING STRATEGY
Draw a Diagram

THE PROBLEM The members of the Science Club want to fence in a rectangular garden. They have 68 feet of fencing. What dimensions should the garden be so that it has the greatest area?

☑ Understand

• What are you asked to find?

• What information will you use?

• Is there information you will not use? If so, what?

☑ Plan

• What strategy can you use to solve the problem?

You can *draw a diagram*.

☑ Solve

• How can you use the strategy to solve the problem?

You can draw diagrams of different rectangles with a perimeter of 68 feet. Then multiply to find the rectangle with the greatest area.

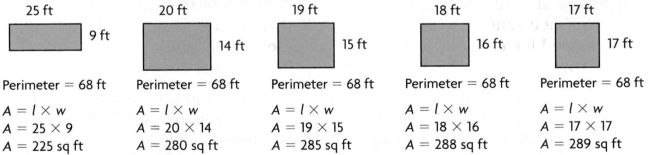

25 ft	20 ft	19 ft	18 ft	17 ft
9 ft	14 ft	15 ft	16 ft	17 ft
Perimeter = 68 ft	Perimeter = 68 ft	Perimeter = 68 ft	Perimeter = 68 ft	Perimeter = 68 ft
$A = l \times w$	$A = l \times w$	$A = l \times w$	$A = l \times w$	$A = l \times w$
$A = 25 \times 9$	$A = 20 \times 14$	$A = 19 \times 15$	$A = 18 \times 16$	$A = 17 \times 17$
$A = 225$ sq ft	$A = 280$ sq ft	$A = 285$ sq ft	$A = 288$ sq ft	$A = 289$ sq ft

So, the garden should be 17 feet long by 17 feet wide to have the greatest area.

☑ Look Back

• How can you determine if your answer is reasonable?

• What other strategy could you use?

PRACTICE

Draw a diagram to solve.

1. The Rileys want to fence in a rectangular section of their yard. They have 60 yards of fence to use. What dimensions will give the greatest possible area?

2. A school has 72 meters of wood to use to border a rectangular play area. The school wants the play area to have the greatest possible area. What dimensions should it have?

3. A bulletin board is a 36-inch square. Michael decorates the border by putting a star every 6 inches along the edge, including one in each corner. How many stars are on the bulletin board?

4. Julie uses chalk to write the numbers from 0 to 50, in order, on the sidewalk. She starts at 0 and moves forward 34 numbers, back 29, back 3, and forward 15. On what number does Julie end?

Mixed Applications

Solve.

CHOOSE A STRATEGY

• Draw a Diagram • Use a Formula • Write a Number Sentence • Make a Table • Guess and Check

5. It takes Tracy 5 minutes to plant one flower in her garden. How long will it take her to plant 16 flowers in her garden?

6. Jordan's room is 12 feet by 11 feet. Carly's room is 13 feet by 10 feet. Whose room has the greater area?

7. Ms. McKenzie has 144 feet of wire to surround a flower bed. What dimensions should the flower bed have so that it has the greatest area?

8. The Browns' home is 250 square feet larger than the Jacksons' home. The total area of both homes is 4,450 sq ft. How many square feet are in each home?

9. Jerry has baseball, football, and basketball cards. He has twice as many football as baseball cards and 3 times as many basketball as baseball cards. He has 150 cards in all. How many of each kind of card does he have?

10. There are four high schools in the district. Lincoln has 2,285 students. Oakland has 2,187, and Evans has 2,852. Orange has 1,987. Which school has the fewest students? the most students?

11. Ms. Humphrey has the two plastic containers shown. She wants to store food in the container with the greater volume. Which container should she use?

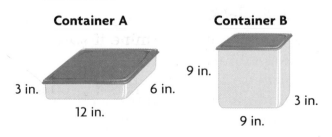

Container A   3 in.   6 in.   12 in.

Container B   9 in.   3 in.   9 in.

CULTURAL CONNECTION

A Vacation in Germany

Ute's parents came to the United States 13 years ago. The family will be returning to Germany at the end of the year. Ute is studying the German language 10 hours a week. She will be in the United States 18 more weeks. How many hours of German language study will she have during that time?

> ### CULTURAL LINK
> The Rhine (Rhein in German) is an important German river. Its source is in the Swiss Alps, and it empties into the North Sea. Melting snow and glaciers feed the river. The Rhine is about 820 miles (1,319 kilometers) long.

Work Together

1. Ute and her parents will have 23 days to travel around Germany before going to Heidelberg. They have planned a 4-day boat trip on the Rhine River. A trip to the Black Forest will take 6 days. How many vacation hours have they planned? After the two trips, how many hours of vacation will they have left?

2. Ute and her parents plan to hike in the Bavarian Alps in southern Germany. They take walks every day so that they will be ready for the hike. Last week they walked 17 kilometers. Suppose they walked the same number of kilometers each week for 18 weeks. Estimate, then find the actual distance.

3. Germany has an area of 137,823 square miles. It has an average of 590 people per square mile. Estimate the population of Germany by rounding each factor to the greatest hundred.

4. Ute has a wooden music box her grandmother sent from Germany. The lid of the box measures 14 centimeters x 24 centimeters. Find the perimeter and area of the music box lid.

✓ CHECK UNDERSTANDING

1. **VOCABULARY** The __?__ states that multiplying a sum by a number is the same as multiplying each addend by the number and then adding the products. **(page 86)**

Estimate the product by rounding each factor to its greatest place-value position. **(pages 90–91)**

2. 526
    × 29

3. 285
    × 41

4. 943
    × 72

5. 836
    × 93

✓ CHECK SKILLS

Find the product. **(pages 88–89, 92–93)**

6. 27
    ×24

7. 35
    ×90

8. 96
    ×53

9. 394
    × 33

10. 184
    × 37

11. 603
    × 11

12. 836
    ×497

13. 501
    ×420

14. 315
    ×641

15. 1,320
    × 191

16. 3,109
    × 226

17. 6,543
    × 123

Find the perimeter and area for each figure. **(pages 94–95)**

18.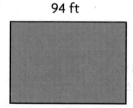
94 ft
66 ft

19.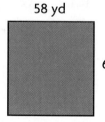
58 yd
63 yd

20.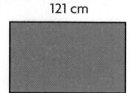
121 cm
74 cm

✓ CHECK PROBLEM SOLVING

Solve. **(pages 96–97)**

CHOOSE A STRATEGY

- **Draw a Diagram** - **Use a Formula** - **Write a Number Sentence** - **Use a Table**

21. Kasey is building a rectangular cage for her hamster. She has 52 inches of wire to use. What dimensions should the cage have so that it has the greatest area? What is the area? What is the perimeter?

22. In Oakdale, there are 73 players on hockey teams. There are twice as many players on basketball teams, and 10 more players on softball teams than on hockey teams. No player is on more than one team. How many players are there in all?

DIVIDING BY ONE-DIGIT NUMBERS

DID YOU KNOW...

There are actually about $365\frac{1}{4}$ days in a year. That's why we have a "leap year" once every 4 years.

The extra day in a leap year is February 29. If a year is divisible by 4 or 100, then it is a leap year.

Leapin' Leap Years!

Do you know anyone whose birthday is February 29? Leap year birthdays happen only once every 4 years. Suppose your birthday came around only once every 3 years or only once every 6 years. Work together to find which years are divisible by 3, 4, 5, 6 or 9.

WHAT IS DIVISIBILITY?
A number is *divisible* by another number if there is no remainder.

YOU WILL NEED: 1-inch grid paper, calculator, pencil, paper, markers

Work with a group. Your job is to

- make a chart that shows the next 40 years.

- identify all the leap years.

- invent names for years that come every 3 years, 4 years, 5 years, 6 years or 9 years. For example, "BOP" years could happen every 3 years, and "ROCKET" years could happen every 6 years.

- mark each type of year on your chart with a different symbol. Make a key showing the symbols.

- describe the patterns on your chart.

DID YOU
- ✓ make a chart that shows the next 40 years?
- ✓ find which years are divisible by 3, 4, 5, 6, or 9?
- ✓ mark each type of year on your chart with a different symbol?
- ✓ describe the patterns on your chart?

POM YEARS (÷by 3) LEAP YEARS (÷by 4) ZOOFY YEARS (÷by 5) ROCKET YEARS (÷by 6) NINERS (÷ by 9)

1988	1989	1990	1991	1992
1994	1995	1996	1997	1998
	2001	2002	2003	2004
			2009	2010
2012	2013	2014	2015	2016
2018	2019	2020	2021	2022

HANDS ON

COOPERATIVE LEARNING

Divisibility

You will investigate the rules of divisibility.

Why learn this? You will know how to round dividends to make them divisible by the divisor.

WORD POWER

divisible

A number is **divisible** by another number if the quotient is a whole number and there is a zero remainder. For example, 32 is divisible by 4 because the quotient is 8 and the remainder is zero.

Some numbers have a *rule of divisibility*. If you know the rule, you can quickly tell whether a number is divisible by that number.

Look at these examples to help you recall the rules of divisibility for 2, 5, and 10.

Numbers divisible by 2: 12, 34, 72, 84, 96, 108, 120
Numbers divisible by 5: 10, 35, 60, 110, 145, 180, 230
Numbers divisible by 10: 20, 40, 70, 100, 140, 190, 250

• What is the rule of divisibility for 2? 5? 10?

Explore

Use a calculator to discover more rules of divisibility.

MATERIALS: calculator

▶ **Step 1**	▶ **Step 2**	▶ **Step 3**
Use mental math and a calculator. Test the numbers in the second column of the chart to see if they are divisible by 3. Record the numbers that passed the divisibility test.	Read the hint. With your partner, write the rule of divisibility for 3. Then give three other examples of numbers that pass the divisibility test.	Repeat Steps 1 and 2 to discover the rule of divisibility for 9.

Number	Numbers to Test	HINT: Look at
3	15, 20, 36, 70, 105, 141	. . . the sum of the digits of the numbers.
9	63, 95, 138, 216, 531, 882	. . . the sum of the digits of the numbers.

Record

Make a table to record the divisibility rules for 3 and 9 and examples of numbers that are divisible by each.

Technology Link

E–Lab • Activity 7 Available on CD-ROM and the Internet at http://www.hbschool.com/elab

Now, investigate finding the rules of divisibility for 4 and for 6.

Try This

Use a calculator and the hint to test the numbers given. Add them to your table.

Number	Numbers to Test	HINT: Look at
4	20, 36, 75, 104, 148, 210	. . . the last two digits in the numbers.
6	35, 42, 56, 128, 132, 216	. . . whether the numbers are divisible by both 2 and 3.

Talk About It

• If a number is divisible by 10, is it also divisible by 2? Explain.

• If a number is divisible by 5, is it also divisible by 2? Explain.

• If a number is divisible by 4, is it also divisible by 2? Explain.

 **WRITE ABOUT IT** What is the least number that is divisible by 2, 3, 5, and 10? Explain.

HANDS-ON PRACTICE

Use mental math and a calculator. Test each number for divisibility by 2, 3, 4, 5, 6, 9, and 10. List the numbers that work.

1. 24   **2.** 45   **3.** 72   **4.** 130   **5.** 185

6. 297   **7.** 519   **8.** 728   **9.** 2,604   **10.** 3,750

Applying What You Learned

Mr. Allen wants to divide his science class of 36 students into equal groups for an experiment.

11. What are all the possible equal-sized groups into which he could divide them?

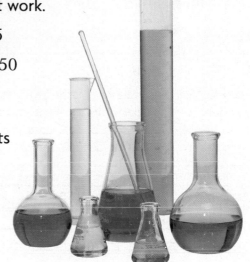

Mixed Applications

12. I am a number between 50 and 60. I am divisible by 2, 3, and 9. What number am I?

13. If 5 friends share 37 marbles equally, how many marbles does each person have? How many are left over?

Placing the First Digit

You will learn how to decide where to place the first digit in order to find the quotient.

Why learn this? You can find the number of pages filled in a photo album

Felicia bought a new photograph album. She has 142 photos. Each page of the album holds 6 photos. How many pages can she fill?

Divide. $142 \div 6 = n$ $6\overline{)142}$

First, estimate.

To estimate a quotient, you can use compatible numbers. **Compatible numbers** are numbers close to the actual numbers and can be divided evenly. Compatible numbers for 6 are numbers divisible by 6, such as 12, 18, or 24.

Estimate.   **Think:** $120 \div 6 = 20$ So, $n \approx 20$.

120 is divisible by 6 because it is divisible by 2 and by 3.

MODEL

What is $142 \div 6$?

▶ **Step 1**

Decide where to place the first digit in the quotient.

$\dfrac{x}{6\overline{)142}}$ $1 < 6$

There are not enough hundreds.

$\dfrac{x\blacksquare}{6\overline{)142}}$ $14 > 6$

Use 14 tens. Place the first digit in the tens place.

▶ **Step 2**

Divide the tens. $6\overline{)14}$

Think: $6 \times n = 12$

$\begin{array}{r} 2 \\ 6\overline{)142} \\ -12 \\ \hline 2 \end{array}$ Multiply. 6×2

Subtract. $14 - 12$

Compare. $2 < 6$

▶ **Step 3**

Bring down the ones.

Divide. $6\overline{)22}$

Think: $6 \times n = 18$

$\begin{array}{r} 23\ r4 \\ 6\overline{)142} \\ -12 \\ 22 \\ -18 \\ \hline 4 \end{array}$ Multiply. 6×3

Subtract. $22 - 18$

Compare. $4 < 6$

Since $n = 23$ r4, Felicia will fill 23 pages. The twenty-fourth page will have only 4 photos.

Talk About It

• How do compatible numbers help you estimate mentally?

LA MERE CATHERINE

- How do you know how many digits will be in the quotient?

Check Your Understanding

Copy each problem. Draw a box where the first digit in the quotient should be placed.

1. 5)519　　**2.** 3)256　　**3.** 4)745　　**4.** 6)829　　**5.** 4)330

6. 5)457　　**7.** 4)523　　**8.** 3)310　　**9.** 6)468　　**10.** 8)742

PRACTICE

Estimate the quotient.

11. $145 \div 3 \approx n$　**12.** $298 \div 9 \approx n$　**13.** $501 \div 5 \approx n$　**14.** $375 \div 6 \approx n$

15. $623 \div 3 \approx n$　**16.** $337 \div 4 \approx n$　**17.** $295 \div 7 \approx n$　**18.** $641 \div 3 \approx n$

Find the quotient.

19. 6)138　　**20.** 7)642　　**21.** 9)700　　**22.** 4)832　　**23.** 2)785

24. 5)277　　**25.** 3)343　　**26.** 7)615　　**27.** 9)569　　**28.** 8)941

Mixed Applications

29. Linda bought a 132-ounce jug of shampoo. She was able to completely refill a smaller bottle with the shampoo 8 times. How many ounces did the smaller bottle hold? How many ounces were left over?

30. Each cup of yogurt contains 225 calories. How many calories are in 4 cups of yogurt?

31. Rachel saved $282 from baby-sitting during a 6-month period. She saved the same amount of money each month. How much did she save each month?

32. ✏ **WRITE ABOUT IT** Explain why it is important to place the first digit correctly when you divide.

Mixed Review

Write the value of the blue digit. (pages 6–7)

33. 2,354　　　**34.** 54,697　　　**35.** 424,576　　　**36.** 901,627

Use an equivalent decimal to find the sum. (pages 52–53)

37. $3.12 + 0.683 = n$　　**38.** $1.492 + 7.5 = n$　　**39.** $14.69 + 1.249 = n$

Zeros in Division

You will learn to divide when there is a zero in the dividend or in the quotient.

Why learn this? You can find the number of items divided into equal groups, such as supplies for a group of stores.

Mr. Baxter owns 4 music stores. He is ordering 408 portable stereos for his stores. He wants each store to have the same number of portable stereos. How many will each store receive?

Divide. $408 \div 4 = n$ $4\overline{)408}$

Estimate.   **Think:** $400 \div 4 = 100$ So, $n \approx 100$.

MODEL

What is $408 \div 4$?

▶ Step 1

Since 4 hundreds can be divided by 4, the first digit in the quotient will be in the hundreds place. Divide the 4 hundreds.

Think: $4 \times n = 4$

$$
\begin{array}{r}
1 \\
4\overline{)408} \\
-4 \\
\hline
0
\end{array}
$$

Multiply. 4×1

Subtract. $4 - 4$

Compare. $0 < 4$

▶ Step 2

Bring down the tens. Divide the 0 tens.

Think: Since $4 > 0$, write 0 in the quotient.

$$
\begin{array}{r}
10 \\
4\overline{)408} \\
-4 \\
\hline
00 \\
-0 \\
\hline
0
\end{array}
$$

$0 \div 4 = 0$

$4 \times 0 = 0$

▶ Step 3

Bring down the ones. Divide the 8 ones.

Think: $4 \times n = 8$

$$
\begin{array}{r}
102 \\
4\overline{)408} \\
-4 \\
\hline
00 \\
-0 \\
\hline
08 \\
-8 \\
\hline
0
\end{array}
$$

Multiply. 4×2

Subtract. $8 - 8$

Compare. $0 < 4$

Since 102 is close to the estimate of 100, the answer is reasonable. So, each store will receive 102 stereos.

Talk About It  CRITICAL THINKING

- What does the zero indicate in the quotient in the problem above?

- When do you write a zero in the quotient?

- How can you use a rule of divisibility to check if the answer is reasonable?

Technology **Link**

In *Mighty Math Calculating Crew*, the game *Intergalactic Trader* challenges you to divide by one-digit numbers.

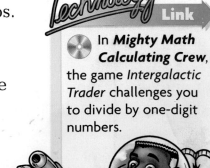

Check Your Understanding

Estimate the quotient.

1. $5\overline{)250}$ **2.** $7\overline{)734}$ **3.** $4\overline{)824}$ **4.** $6\overline{)305}$ **5.** $3\overline{)927}$

PRACTICE

Estimate the quotient.

6. $3\overline{)310}$ **7.** $7\overline{)440}$ **8.** $4\overline{)340}$ **9.** $2\overline{)419}$ **10.** $9\overline{)873}$

Find the quotient.

11. $4\overline{)816}$ **12.** $3\overline{)908}$ **13.** $6\overline{)612}$ **14.** $5\overline{)525}$ **15.** $6\overline{)624}$

16. $7\overline{)745}$ **17.** $9\overline{)980}$ **18.** $2\overline{)121}$ **19.** $5\overline{)544}$ **20.** $2\overline{)801}$

21. $3\overline{)961}$ **22.** $8\overline{)887}$ **23.** $5\overline{)454}$ **24.** $7\overline{)763}$ **25.** $3\overline{)613}$

26. $4\overline{)803}$ **27.** $2\overline{)417}$ **28.** $4\overline{)836}$ **29.** $6\overline{)965}$ **30.** $5\overline{)205}$

31. $122 \div 4 = n$ **32.** $504 \div 5 = n$ **33.** $824 \div 8 = n$ **34.** $631 \div 6 = n$

35. $340 \div 5 = n$ **36.** $130 \div 2 = n$ **37.** $907 \div 7 = n$ **38.** $400 \div 3 = n$

Mixed Applications

39. On Saturday and Sunday a total of 414 people visited a local beach. If the same number of people came each day, how many visited the beach on Saturday?

40. Bailey and his family went on a 108-mile hiking trip in the mountains. They hiked 9 miles each day. For how many days did they hike?

41. Adult tickets for the school play cost $8. Student tickets cost $5. Lisa sold 20 tickets for $136. How many adult tickets did she sell?

42. Ken saved $328 from mowing lawns over an 8-month period. He saved the same amount of money each month. How much did he save each month?

43. The county-wide math fair begins in one week. Each school will have its own display table. The tables will be placed in 15 rows of 15 tables each. How many schools are participating?

44. ▭✐ **WRITE ABOUT IT** Choose one of Exercises 11–38 in which there is no remainder. Explain how you could use a rule of divisibility to determine before dividing that there would be no remainder.

Mixed Review

Find the difference. (pages 22–23)

45. 100
       $-\ 57$

46. 500
       -176

47. $2,000$
        $-\ 786$

48. $5,000$
        $-3,067$

49. $12,000$
        $-\ 9,886$

Write an equivalent decimal for each. (pages 40–41)

50. 0.04   **51.** 0.390   **52.** 1.74   **53.** 2.800   **54.** 3.20

Practicing Division

You will learn to check division problems, using multiplication.

Why learn this? You can find out how much less something weighs on the moon than on Earth.

Earth's gravity causes things to weigh 6 times as much on Earth as they weigh on the moon. Suppose rocks taken from the moon weighed 108 pounds on Earth. How much did those rocks weigh on the moon?

Divide. $108 \div 6 = n$ $6\overline{)108}$

Estimate. **Think:** $100 \div 5 = 20$ So, $n \approx 20$.

Predict. **Think:** 108 is divisible by 6 because it is divisible by 2 and by 3.

MODEL

What is $108 \div 6$?

▶ Step 1

Decide where to place the first digit in the quotient.

$$6\overline{)108}^{\,x}$$
$1 < 6$
There are not enough hundreds.

$$6\overline{)108}^{\,x\blacksquare}$$
$10 > 6$
Use 10 tens. Place the first digit in the tens place.

▶ Step 2

Divide the tens. $6\overline{)10}$

Think: $6 \times n = 6$

$$\begin{array}{r} 1 \\ 6\overline{)108} \\ -6 \\ \hline 4 \end{array}$$

Multiply. 6×1
Subtract. $10 - 6$
Compare. $4 < 6$

▶ Step 3

Bring down the ones.

Divide. $6\overline{)48}$

Think: $6 \times n = 48$

$$\begin{array}{r} 18 \\ 6\overline{)108} \\ -6\downarrow \\ \hline 48 \\ -48 \\ \hline 0 \end{array}$$

Multiply. 6×8
Subtract. $48 - 48$
Compare. $0 < 6$

Since $n = 18$, the rocks weighed 18 pounds on the moon.

Use multiplication to check your answer to a division problem. Multiply the divisor by the quotient. If there is a remainder, add it to the product.

$$\begin{array}{r} 18 \\ \times\ 6 \\ \hline 108\ \checkmark \end{array}$$

EXAMPLES

A.
$$\begin{array}{r} 123\ \text{r}3 \\ 5\overline{)618} \\ -5\downarrow \\ \hline 11 \\ -10\downarrow \\ \hline 18 \\ -15 \\ \hline 3 \end{array}$$

Since 6 hundreds can be divided by 5, the first digit of the quotient is in the hundreds place.

Check:
$$\begin{array}{r} 123 \\ \times\ 5 \\ \hline 615 \end{array}$$
$$\begin{array}{r} 615 \\ +\ 3 \\ \hline 618 \end{array}$$

B.
$$\begin{array}{r} 330 \\ 3\overline{)990} \\ -9\downarrow \\ \hline 09 \\ -9\downarrow \\ \hline 00 \end{array}$$

Check:
$$\begin{array}{r} 330 \\ \times\ 3 \\ \hline 990 \end{array}$$

- Why is the remainder added to the product when checking the quotient?

PRACTICE

Use divisibility rules to predict if there will be a remainder.

1. $9)\overline{493}$
2. $3)\overline{472}$
3. $5)\overline{515}$
4. $4)\overline{374}$
5. $6)\overline{204}$

6. $2)\overline{221}$
7. $9)\overline{657}$
8. $4)\overline{932}$
9. $3)\overline{294}$
10. $6)\overline{188}$

Find the quotient. Check by multiplying.

11. $3)\overline{635}$
12. $7)\overline{698}$
13. $3)\overline{457}$
14. $2)\overline{164}$
15. $4)\overline{978}$

16. $6)\overline{104}$
17. $8)\overline{246}$
18. $9)\overline{288}$
19. $4)\overline{844}$
20. $5)\overline{376}$

21. $348 \div 8 = n$
22. $807 \div 9 = n$
23. $124 \div 6 = n$
24. $414 \div 2 = n$

25. $338 \div 7 = n$
26. $232 \div 4 = n$
27. $472 \div 5 = n$
28. $694 \div 3 = n$

Mixed Applications

29. Jared unpacked pencils for the school secretary. He unpacked 5 boxes that each held 125 pencils. How many pencils did he unpack?

30. Carla drove 165 miles in 3 hours. How many miles did she drive each hour?

31. Carl had $20.00 to spend at the book fair. He bought one book for $3.95 and another book for $12.95. Posters cost $1.50. How many posters can Carl buy? How much change will he get?

32. George Washington lived from 1732 to 1799. Abraham Lincoln lived from 1809 to 1865. Who lived longer? For how many years longer did he live?

33. What number has 6 in the thousands and tens places, 1 in the hundreds place, 9 in the ones and thousandths places, and 0 in the tenths and hundredths places?

34. ⬛▷ **Write a problem** about Doug's stamp collection, using division. He has 458 stamps and 5 stamp albums.

Mixed Review

Find the sum. (pages 50–51)

35. $\begin{array}{r} 1.0 \\ +5.7 \\ \hline \end{array}$

36. $\begin{array}{r} 5.30 \\ +1.56 \\ \hline \end{array}$

37. $\begin{array}{r} 2.35 \\ +7.86 \\ \hline \end{array}$

38. $\begin{array}{r} 5.982 \\ +3.067 \\ \hline \end{array}$

39. $\begin{array}{r} 12.753 \\ + 9.286 \\ \hline \end{array}$

Write in standard form. (pages 36–37)

40. one and four thousandths

41. four and eight hundredths

42. sixty-five thousandths

PART
1 Interpreting the Remainder

You will learn to interpret the remainder.	**Why learn this?** You can decide what to do with an amount left over when solving a division problem.

When there is a remainder in a division problem, look at the question. You may need to drop the remainder, round the quotient to the next greater number, or use the remainder as part of your answer.

Determine how the remainder was used to solve each of the following problems.

A. Lindsey made punch with 72 ounces of pineapple juice, 64 ounces of lemon soda, 32 ounces of cranberry juice, and 16 ounces of orange juice. How many 6-ounce servings did she make?

$$
\begin{array}{r}
30 \text{ r4} \\
6)\overline{184} \\
-18 \\
\hline
04 \\
-0 \\
\hline
4
\end{array}
$$

She made 30 six-ounce servings. The 4 ounces left over are not enough for another 6-ounce serving.

B. Mr. Webb brought in a 118-foot rope for the Boy Scouts to use to practice tying knots. He divided the rope into 3 pieces of equal length. How long was each piece of rope?

$$
\begin{array}{r}
39\frac{1}{3} \\
3)\overline{118} \\
-9 \\
\hline
28 \\
-27 \\
\hline
1
\end{array}
$$

To write the remainder as a fraction, use the remainder as the numerator and the divisor as the denominator.

When the 1-foot length is divided by 3, each part is $\frac{1}{3}$ foot. So, each piece of rope was $39\frac{1}{3}$ feet long.

C. There were 213 students and parents who signed up for the fall luncheon. There will be 5 people seated at each table. How many tables will be needed?

$$
\begin{array}{r}
42 \text{ r3} \\
5)\overline{213} \\
-20 \\
\hline
13 \\
-10 \\
\hline
3
\end{array}
$$

Since 42 tables will not be enough to seat everyone, 43 tables will be needed.

Talk About It  CRITICAL THINKING

- Explain how the remainder was used to answer each question above.

- In Example B, what does the remainder represent?

- Explain why a fractional remainder was appropriate for Problem B but not for Problems A and C.

 Calculator Activities page H62

You can use a calculator to divide.
Find the quotient $975 \div 9 = n$.

Press:

Display:

108   3

- What do Q and R in the display mean?

PRACTICE

Solve. Explain how you interpreted the remainder.

1. A group of 106 students showed up for ski lessons. There are 9 ski instructors. How many students will be in most of the groups?

2. The track for Brian's model train is 3 times as long as Mario's track. Brian's track is 245 inches long. How long is Mario's track?

3. Mrs. Pfeiffer's flower shop is running a special on roses. She is selling an arrangement of 24 roses for $19.95. She has 146 roses on hand. Can she fill 6 orders for the special?

4. The bleachers in the school gym have 148 seats. There are 8 rows with the same number of seats in all the rows except one. How many seats are in the row with the greatest number of seats?

Mixed Applications

5. Jake has 170 books to put on shelves in the store. There are 5 shelves for the books. If Jake puts an equal number of books on each shelf, how many books will be on each shelf? How many books will be left over?

6. The Future Leaders Club has 200 tickets to the school dance to sell. Each club member has 8 tickets to sell. How many members are in the club?

7. Penny practiced free throws for a week. She scored 5 on the first day, 10 on the second day, 16 on the third day, and 23 on the fourth day. If this pattern continued, what was her score on the sixth day?

8. For a crafts project, 9 students divide 537 toothpicks. How many toothpicks does each student get? How many toothpicks are left over?

9. Stuart wants to store his rock collection in boxes that each hold 18 rocks. He has only enough money to buy 4 boxes. How many rocks can he store?

10. ✐ **Write a problem** in which you divide and the remainder must be interpreted in order to answer the question. Explain how the remainder helps answer the question.

LESSON CONTINUES ➤

PART 2 PROBLEM-SOLVING STRATEGY
Guess and Check

THE PROBLEM There were 174 paintings and drawings entered in the self-portrait contest. The portraits were placed in equal groups on walls throughout the school. After the portraits were placed, 6 were left over and were placed on a wall in the main office. How many groups were formed? How many portraits were in each group?

REMEMBER:
- ☑ Understand
- ☑ Plan
- ☑ Solve
- ☑ Look Back

☑ Understand

- What are you asked to find?
- What information will you use?
- Is there information you will not use? If so, what?

☑ Plan

- What strategy can you use to solve the problem?

  You can *guess and check*.

☑ Solve

- How can you use the strategy?

  You can guess an answer and then check to see if your guess is correct.

Guess 5 groups.	Check.	Guess 6 groups.	Check.	Guess 7 groups.	Check.
$$\begin{array}{r} 34\ r\ 4 \\ 5\overline{)174} \\ -15 \\ \hline 24 \\ -20 \\ \hline 4 \end{array}$$	5 groups 34 in each group Remainder of 4 does not agree with 6 portraits left over.	$$\begin{array}{r} 29 \\ 6\overline{)174} \\ -12 \\ \hline 54 \\ -54 \\ \hline 0 \end{array}$$	6 groups 29 in each group Remainder of 0 does not agree with 6 portraits left over.	$$\begin{array}{r} 24\ r\ 6 \\ 7\overline{)174} \\ -14 \\ \hline 34 \\ -28 \\ \hline 6 \end{array}$$	7 groups 24 in each group Remainder of 6 checks.

So, one possible answer is that there were 7 groups, with 24 portraits in each group. There were 6 portraits left over.

☑ Look Back

- How can you decide if your answer is reasonable?
- What other strategy could you use?

PRACTICE

Guess and check to solve.

1. Mrs. Hewett has 217 recipe cards. She has them stored in equal groups in boxes, and has started a new box with 2 recipe cards in it. How many boxes of recipe cards does she have? How many are in each box?

2. A bridge toll is $0.50 for cars and $0.75 for trucks. In one hour, $33.50 is collected from 53 vehicles. How many cars and trucks pay the toll?

3. Spencer is 4 years old. His uncle Ralph is 6 times as old. How old will Spencer be when he is half as old as his uncle?

4. The sum of two numbers is 36. Their product is 320. What are the two numbers?

Mixed Applications

Solve.

CHOOSE A STRATEGY

• Use a Formula   • Write a Number Sentence   • Make a Table   • Guess and Check

5. What is the volume of this box?

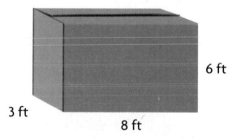

6 ft
3 ft
8 ft

6. Travel Time mailed surveys to find out where people would most like to visit. Of the people who responded, 32,589 said the beach, 32,598 said the mountains, and 32,958 said a city. What are the answers in order from greatest to least?

7. Becky and Ellen washed 9 cars one afternoon. They earned $4.25 for each car they washed. How much money did they earn?

8. A book is 38 centimeters long and 22 centimeters wide. What is the perimeter of the book? What is the area of its cover?

9. There were 412 men, women, and children on a train. There were 3 times as many men as children. There were 74 children. How many women were on the train?

10. In Glenn's city, it rained 3.2 inches in January, 2.9 inches in February, and 3.1 inches in March. In which month was there the greatest amount of rainfall?

11. For the basketball game, 468 seats were filled. For the wrestling match, 279 seats were filled. How many more seats were filled for the basketball game?

12. A cube has a volume of 125 cubic inches. What is the length of each side? What is the area of each face?

MATH FUN!

Class Camping

PURPOSE To practice division

YOU WILL NEED pencil and paper, counters

Imagine that your class is going on a camping trip. Use division and draw diagrams to make groups for the trip.

- You will have 7 vans that each holds 7 people. Make groups that are as equal as possible.

Each tent holds 8 people. The people in a tent will be all male or all female. Use division to plan the groups for the tents.

- Plan baseball teams, which will have 9 players each. Also, plan volleyball teams, with 6 players on each. In each case, how many will have to wait out?

Your Moon Weight

PURPOSE To divide and check quotients

YOU WILL NEED pencil and paper, bathroom scale

Find what your weight would be on the moon. Weigh objects around the classroom. Find the moon weight for five objects, people, or animals. Each time, check your answer by using multiplication.

Use this formula:

moon weight = Earth weight ÷ 6

HOME NOTE Find the moon weight of a large object—for example, your parents' car or your bicycle.

PERFECT NUMBERS

PURPOSE To name the numbers by which a number is divisible

YOU WILL NEED paper and pencil

A *perfect number* is one that equals the sum of all the numbers by which it is divisible. The number itself is not included. For example,

496 is divisible by 1, 2, 4, 8, 16, 31, 62, 124, 248, and 496. The sum of these numbers, not including 496, is 496. So, 496 is a perfect number.

List all the perfect numbers between 1 and 30.

CHAPTER 7 REVIEW

✓ CHECK UNDERSTANDING

VOCABULARY

1. A number is __?__ by another number if the quotient is a whole number and there is a zero remainder. (page 102)

2. __?__ are helpful when estimating because they are close to the actual numbers and can be divided evenly. (page 104)

Copy each problem. Draw a box where the first digit in the quotient should be placed. (pages 104–105)

3. $4\overline{)639}$ 4. $6\overline{)410}$ 5. $3\overline{)115}$ 6. $7\overline{)959}$ 7. $5\overline{)517}$

Estimate the quotient. (pages 104–107)

8. $3\overline{)245}$ 9. $6\overline{)551}$ 10. $8\overline{)825}$ 11. $2\overline{)608}$ 12. $4\overline{)132}$

✓ CHECK SKILLS

Test each number for divisibility by 2, 3, 4, 5, 6, 9, and 10. List the numbers that work. (pages 102–103)

13. 38   14. 64   15. 150   16. 489   17. 1,012

Find the quotient. Check by multiplying. (pages 104–109)

18. $4\overline{)624}$ 19. $7\overline{)201}$ 20. $3\overline{)513}$ 21. $8\overline{)711}$ 22. $5\overline{)476}$

23. $2\overline{)836}$ 24. $6\overline{)940}$ 25. $5\overline{)728}$ 26. $7\overline{)342}$ 27. $3\overline{)907}$

28. $815 \div 3 = n$ 29. $642 \div 5 = n$ 30. $706 \div 4 = n$ 31. $514 \div 7 = n$

✓ CHECK PROBLEM SOLVING

Solve. (pages 112–113)

CHOOSE A STRATEGY

• Use a Formula   • Write a Number Sentence   • Make a Table   • Guess and Check

32. Mr. Lehman is shopping for suitcases. He finds one that is 30 in. × 24 in. × 12 in. and another that is 27 in. × 27 in. × 12 in. Which suitcase will hold more?

33. Perry has 122 stickers. He puts an equal number of stickers on each folder. He has started a new folder with 3 stickers. How many other folders have stickers on them? How many stickers are on each?

CHAPTER 8

DIVIDING BY TWO-DIGIT NUMBERS

DID YOU KNOW...

There are many contests such as
Spelling Bees and Geography Bees,
held each year for students of all ages.

Team-Up Time

Dividing Contest Prizes

Have you ever wished there was a contest for something that you really like? Work together to plan some kind of contest. Decide what the first prize will be. Then figure out how much each student would earn if your group won first place and if your class won first place.

YOU WILL NEED: chart paper, markers

Work with a group. Your job is to

- brainstorm contest ideas.

- decide what first prize will be.

- find out what each person's share of the prize would be if your class won first prize.

- make a poster that describes your contest, the first prize, and how you would share it with your group and with your class.

Bouncing Balloons Contest

First Prize: 1,001 balloons!
Our group has
4 members.
We each get
250 balloons
with 1 left over!

```
        250 r1
      4⟌1,001
        8
        20
        20
        01
```

Our class has 26 members (including Miss Jones the teacher).

```
        38 r13
    26⟌1,001
        78
        221
        208
        13
```

Each person will have 38 balloons. There are 13 left over. We can give those to Miss Jones so she will have 51 balloons.

DID YOU

☑ plan a contest and choose a first prize?

☑ explain how to share first prize with your group and with your class?

☑ make a poster showing your contest and ways you would share first prize?

Division Patterns to Estimate

You will learn to use patterns of zeros and estimation to help you divide.

Why learn this? You can estimate to determine a car's gas mileage.

On vacation, Lindsey's family traveled 412 miles by car during two days. They used 23 gallons of gasoline. About how many miles per gallon did they average?

Estimate.

miles driven		gallons of gasoline used		miles per gallon
412	÷	23	=	n
↓		↓		↓
400	÷	20	=	20

So, they averaged about 20 miles per gallon.

- What basic fact was used to find 400 ÷ 20? What basic fact would you use to find 600 ÷ 30? 4,200 ÷ 70?

Look at these examples of division patterns.

A.
$$80 ÷ 20 = 4$$
$$800 ÷ 20 = 40$$
$$8,000 ÷ 20 = 400$$
$$80,000 ÷ 20 = 4,000$$

B.
$$120 ÷ 60 = 2$$
$$1,200 ÷ 60 = 20$$
$$12,000 ÷ 60 = 200$$
$$120,000 ÷ 60 = 2,000$$

C.
$$350 ÷ 70 = 5$$
$$3,500 ÷ 70 = 50$$
$$35,000 ÷ 70 = 500$$
$$350,000 ÷ 70 = 5,000$$

Talk About It  CRITICAL THINKING

- How does the pattern of zeros in the divisor and the dividend affect the quotient in the three examples?

- How many zeros will be in the quotient of 10,000 ÷ 10? How could you check your answer?

- How many zeros will be in the quotient of 30,000 ÷ 60? Why is this different from the pattern?

Consumer Link

The average American car got about 18 miles per gallon in 1976 and about 28 miles per gallon in 1996. About how many gallons were needed in 1976 for a 450-mile trip? in 1996?

Check Your Understanding

Complete the pattern.

1.
$$60 ÷ 20 = 3$$
$$600 ÷ 20 = 30$$
$$6,000 ÷ 20 = n$$

2.
$$700 ÷ 70 = 10$$
$$7,000 ÷ 70 = n$$
$$70,000 ÷ 70 = 1,000$$

3.
$$400 ÷ 50 = n$$
$$4,000 ÷ 50 = 80$$
$$40,000 ÷ 50 = 800$$

PRACTICE

Complete the pattern.

4. $90 \div 30 = n$
$900 \div 30 = 30$
$9,000 \div 30 = 300$

5. $100 \div 50 = 2$
$1,000 \div 50 = 20$
$10,000 \div 50 = n$

6. $450 \div 90 = 5$
$4,500 \div 90 = n$
$45,000 \div 90 = 500$

7. $420 \div 60 = 7$
$4,200 \div 60 = 70$
$42,000 \div 60 = n$

8. $240 \div 30 = 8$
$2,400 \div 30 = n$
$24,000 \div 30 = 800$

9. $150 \div 50 = n$
$1,500 \div 50 = 30$
$15,000 \div 50 = 300$

Find the quotient.

10. $90 \div 30 = n$ **11.** $40 \div 20 = n$ **12.** $160 \div 40 = n$ **13.** $360 \div 40 = n$

14. $540 \div 90 = n$ **15.** $630 \div 70 = n$ **16.** $450 \div 50 = n$ **17.** $270 \div 90 = n$

18. $60 \div 30 = n$ **19.** $80 \div 40 = n$ **20.** $180 \div 60 = n$ **21.** $250 \div 50 = n$

22. $140 \div 20 = n$ **23.** $210 \div 70 = n$ **24.** $150 \div 30 = n$ **25.** $240 \div 80 = n$

26. $280 \div 40 = n$ **27.** $3,000 \div 60 = n$ **28.** $1,000 \div 20 = n$ **29.** $3,500 \div 50 = n$

30. $7,200 \div 90 = n$ **31.** $18,000 \div 30 = n$ **32.** $5,600 \div 70 = n$ **33.** $36,000 \div 90 = n$

Mixed Applications

34. In one 30-day month, a city bus traveled a total of 6,000 miles. The bus traveled the same number of miles each day. How many miles a day did it travel?

35. Jan was in a jump-roping contest. She made 45 jumps each minute for 5 minutes. How many jumps did Jan make?

36. The seats in an auditorium are arranged in sections of 40. There are 6 sections of seats. How many seats are there in all?

37. ✏ **WRITE ABOUT IT** Explain how to determine the number of zeros in a quotient.

Mixed Review

Write the name of the multiplication property used in each number sentence. (pages 70–71)

38. $2 \times (3 \times 5) = (2 \times 3) \times 5$ **39.** $3 \times 7 = 7 \times 3$ **40.** $8 \times 1 = 8$

41. $4 \times 0 = 0$ **42.** $(9 \times 4) \times 6 = 9 \times (4 \times 6)$ **43.** $4 \times 5 = 5 \times 4$

Find the quotient. (pages 104–105)

44. $5\overline{)265}$ **45.** $4\overline{)967}$ **46.** $6\overline{)385}$ **47.** $8\overline{)982}$

48. $7\overline{)861}$ **49.** $9\overline{)296}$ **50.** $5\overline{)426}$ **51.** $3\overline{)411}$

MORE PRACTICE Student Handbook page H83

Estimating Quotients

You will learn to estimate quotients by using compatible numbers and multiples of ten.

Why learn this? You can compare your estimate with the actual quotient when you divide.

On opening night of the play, the box office took in $1,575. The tickets cost $9 each. About how many people attended the play?

Estimate. $1,575 \div 9$
                    $\downarrow$ $\downarrow$
                  $1,600 \div 10 = n$

So, $n = 160$.   **Think:** $10\overline{)1,600}$ $\quad^{160}$

So, about 160 people attended the play.

_____

Another method you can use to estimate a quotient is to think of two sets of compatible numbers. Finding more than one estimate will give you two possible quotients.

> **EXAMPLE**
>
> Estimate. $52\overline{)3,481}$ **Think:** $50\overline{)3,000}$ or $50\overline{)3,500}$

Talk About It

- What are the quotients for the two estimates?

- Are both estimates for $52\overline{)3,481}$ good estimates? Explain why or why not.

- Based on the estimates, where should the first digit be placed in $52\overline{)3,481}$? Why?

- How does finding two sets of compatible numbers help you divide?

Check Your Understanding

 **CRITICAL THINKING**

Write two pairs of compatible numbers.

1. $276 \div 42 \approx n$ **2.** $524 \div 68 \approx n$ **3.** $1,247 \div 34 \approx n$

4. $329 \div 26 \approx n$ **5.** $171 \div 34 \approx n$ **6.** $201 \div 41 \approx n$

> **Art Link**
>
> William Shakespeare is one of the most famous playwrights of all time. His theater, the Globe Theater, in England, was built in 1599. The theater seated about 1,500 people. It had a ground area and three tiers, or seating levels. If an equal number of people watched from the ground area and each tier, about how many people would be in each?

REMEMBER:

Compatible numbers are numbers that are close to the actual numbers and can be divided evenly.

Example

$2,500 \div 5 = 500$

PRACTICE

Write two pairs of compatible numbers for each.
Give two possible estimates.

7. $186 \div 62 \approx n$ **8.** $523 \div 88 \approx n$ **9.** $1,275 \div 47 \approx n$

10. $3,149 \div 36 \approx n$ **11.** $2,548 \div 65 \approx n$ **12.** $6,324 \div 76 \approx n$

Estimate the quotient.

13. $12\overline{)914}$ **14.** $42\overline{)528}$ **15.** $29\overline{)364}$ **16.** $34\overline{)279}$ **17.** $53\overline{)485}$

18. $64\overline{)532}$ **19.** $37\overline{)849}$ **20.** $73\overline{)620}$ **21.** $61\overline{)115}$ **22.** $86\overline{)743}$

23. $23\overline{)1,260}$ **24.** $47\overline{)3,524}$ **25.** $59\overline{)4,636}$ **26.** $77\overline{)8,199}$ **27.** $31\overline{)6,468}$

28. $64\overline{)4,275}$ **29.** $81\overline{)2,417}$ **30.** $36\overline{)3,384}$ **31.** $45\overline{)1,407}$ **32.** $92\overline{)5,583}$

33. $652 \div 18 \approx n$ **34.** $423 \div 27 \approx n$ **35.** $252 \div 64 \approx n$ **36.** $386 \div 48 \approx n$

37. $2,993 \div 75 \approx n$ **38.** $3,764 \div 38 \approx n$ **39.** $6,520 \div 68 \approx n$ **40.** $9,733 \div 89 \approx n$

Mixed Applications

41. A produce delivery truck delivered 21 cartons of apples and oranges to three stores. There were 1,128 apples and oranges in the delivery. About how many apples or oranges were in each carton?

42. Carla is reading a book with 316 pages. Marilyn is reading a book that has 67 more pages. How many pages are in the book Marilyn is reading?

43. Lars bought a CD for $16.95. He had only $5 bills. How many bills did he give the clerk? How much change did he get back?

44. Eva lives 28.7 miles from the airport. Jonas lives two-tenths mile farther away. How far does Jonas live from the airport?

45. Mrs. Lehr had a 34-page booklet copied. She was charged for 850 pages. About how many copies of the booklet did she have made?

46. ⏩ **WRITE ABOUT IT** Explain why using compatible numbers is a helpful way to estimate quotients.

Mixed Review

Find the quotient. Check by multiplying. (pages 108–109)

47. $256 \div 6 = n$ **48.** $734 \div 5 = n$ **49.** $659 \div 7 = n$ **50.** $875 \div 4 = n$

Estimate to the greatest place-value position.
Then find the product. (pages 92–93)

51. $325 \times 382 = n$ **52.** $584 \times 675 = n$ **53.** $490 \times 537 = n$

Placing the First Digit

You will learn to place the first digit when dividing large numbers.

Why learn this? You will know how many digits should be in the quotient.

During the two weeks the Renaissance Ensemble was in Anna's city, 1,935 people attended the performances. There were 16 performances. At each performance except for the last, the same number of people attended. How many people attended each performance?

Divide. $1,935 \div 16$ $16)\overline{1,935}$

Estimate. $1,935 \div 16 \approx n$ **Think:** $20)\overline{2,000}$ (quotient 100)

So, $n = 90$ or 100.

MODEL

What is $1,935 \div 16$?

Step 1

Decide where to place the first digit in the quotient.

$16)\overline{1,935}$ (x)   no   You *cannot* divide 1 by 16. There are not enough thousands.

$16)\overline{1,935}$ (x ▪)   yes   You *can* divide 19 by 16. There are enough hundreds.

So, place the first digit in the hundreds place.

Step 2

Divide the hundreds. $16)\overline{19}$ **Think:** $16 \times n = 16$

Write a 1 in the hundreds place in the quotient.

$$
\begin{array}{r}
1 \\
16)\overline{1,935} \\
-16 \\
\hline
3
\end{array}
$$

Multiply. 16×1
Subtract. $19 - 16$
Compare. $3 < 16$

Step 3

Divide the tens. $16)\overline{33}$ **Think:** $16 \times n = 32$

Write a 2 in the tens place.

$$
\begin{array}{r}
12 \\
16)\overline{1,935} \\
-16\downarrow \\
\hline
33 \\
-32 \\
\hline
1
\end{array}
$$

Multiply. 16×2
Subtract. $33 - 32$
Compare. $1 < 16$

Step 4

Divide the ones. $16)\overline{15}$

Think: Since $16 > 15$, write a zero in the ones place in the quotient.

$$
\begin{array}{r}
120 \text{ r}15 \\
16)\overline{1,935} \\
-16 \\
\hline
33 \\
-32\downarrow \\
\hline
15 \\
-0 \\
\hline
15
\end{array}
$$

Multiply. 16×0
Subtract. $15 - 0$

Compare. $15 < 16$

So, 120 people attended each performance, with 15 more people, or 135 people, attending on the last day.

• How does the actual quotient compare to the estimate?

PRACTICE

Estimate the quotient.

1. $3{,}152 \div 47 \approx n$ **2.** $2{,}816 \div 56 \approx n$ **3.** $3{,}974 \div 23 \approx n$ **4.** $1{,}263 \div 35 \approx n$

5. $3{,}285 \div 54 \approx n$ **6.** $5{,}690 \div 78 \approx n$ **7.** $8{,}149 \div 41 \approx n$ **8.** $1{,}067 \div 11 \approx n$

Copy each problem. Draw a box where the first digit in the quotient should be placed.

9. $14\overline{)1{,}624}$ **10.** $25\overline{)3{,}205}$ **11.** $63\overline{)1{,}824}$ **12.** $47\overline{)7{,}395}$ **13.** $68\overline{)5{,}430}$

14. $53\overline{)2{,}369}$ **15.** $71\overline{)9{,}546}$ **16.** $89\overline{)3{,}659}$ **17.** $34\overline{)3{,}525}$ **18.** $42\overline{)4{,}178}$

Find the quotient.

19. $37\overline{)4{,}801}$ **20.** $19\overline{)1{,}875}$ **21.** $62\overline{)4{,}500}$ **22.** $43\overline{)3{,}967}$ **23.** $85\overline{)1{,}056}$

24. $58\overline{)9{,}286}$ **25.** $73\overline{)5{,}841}$ **26.** $29\overline{)3{,}180}$ **27.** $26\overline{)5{,}330}$ **28.** $37\overline{)3{,}363}$

Mixed Applications

29. Each episode of *Kids in a Rocket Ship* is 26 minutes long. There are 48 episodes of the show. About how many hours is this? (HINT: Divide the total number of minutes by 60.)

30. There are 1,024 people at the Sweet Corn Festival. Each group of servers can serve 64 people at one time. How many groups of servers are needed to serve all 1,024 people?

31. A passenger train has 12 cars, each seating 44 people. How many people can be seated on the train?

32. ✏ **Write a problem** about a bird flying 1,105 miles from Washington, D.C., to Miami. Use division in the problem.

Mixed Review

Estimate the sum or difference to the nearest tenth. (pages 56–57)

33. 4.75
-1.29

34. 5.34
$+2.29$

35. 24.18
-16.09

36. 16.82
-7.48

Estimate the product by rounding each factor to its greatest place-value position. (pages 90–91)

37. $47 \times 518 = n$ **38.** $75 \times 291 = n$ **39.** $92 \times 725 = n$

40. $25 \times 608 = n$ **41.** $16 \times 351 = n$ **42.** $84 \times 535 = n$

Correcting Quotients

You will learn to correct the quotient when the estimate is too high or too low.	Why learn this? You will know how to determine if the digits you placed in the quotient are correct.

Greg collects sports cards. He has 245 cards in his collection. The cards are organized in albums that hold 32 cards each. How many sports-card albums does Greg have?

Divide. $245 \div 32$ $32\overline{)245}$

Estimate. $245 \div 32 \approx n$ **Think:** $30\overline{)210}^{\,7}$ or $30\overline{)240}^{\,8}$

So, $n = 7$ or 8.

Try 8.

$$\begin{array}{r} 8 \\ 32\overline{)245} \\ -256 \end{array}$$
Think: Since 256 > 245, this estimate is too high.

Try 7.

$$\begin{array}{r} 7\ \text{r}21 \\ 32\overline{)245} \\ -224 \\ \hline 21 \end{array}$$

So, Greg has 7 full albums and one album with only 21 cards in it. He has a total of 8 sports-card albums.

EXAMPLE

Divide. $376 \div 53$ $53\overline{)376}$

Estimate. $376 \div 53 \approx n$ **Think:** $50\overline{)300}^{\,6}$ or $50\overline{)350}^{\,7}$

So, $n = 6$ or 7.

Try 6.

$$\begin{array}{r} 6 \\ 53\overline{)376} \\ -318 \\ \hline 58 \end{array}$$
Think: Since 58 > 53, this estimate is too low.

Try 7.

$$\begin{array}{r} 7\ \text{r}5 \\ 53\overline{)376} \\ -371 \\ \hline 5 \end{array}$$

Talk About It 💡 CRITICAL THINKING

- How do you know when an estimated quotient is too high? too low?

- If you use $40\overline{)280}$ to estimate the quotient $36\overline{)295}$, will your estimate be greater than or less than the quotient? Explain.

PRACTICE

Write *too high*, *too low*, or *just right* for each estimate.

1. $25\overline{)83}$ → 4

2. $32\overline{)61}$ → 1

3. $42\overline{)321}$ → 8

4. $57\overline{)239}$ → 3

5. $64\overline{)519}$ → 8

6. $35\overline{)320}$ → 8

7. $71\overline{)403}$ → 6

8. $45\overline{)122}$ → 2

9. $29\overline{)182}$ → 7

10. $88\overline{)326}$ → 2

Choose the better estimate to use for the quotient. Write *a* or *b*.

11. $19\overline{)84}$ **a.** 3   **b.** 4

12. $34\overline{)276}$ **a.** 8   **b.** 9

13. $24\overline{)158}$ **a.** 6   **b.** 7

14. $46\overline{)463}$ **a.** 9   **b.** 10

15. $59\overline{)283}$ **a.** 3   **b.** 4

16. $28\overline{)249}$ **a.** 8   **b.** 9

17. $73\overline{)564}$ **a.** 6   **b.** 7

18. $62\overline{)506}$ **a.** 8   **b.** 9

Find the quotient.

19. $32\overline{)154}$

20. $25\overline{)278}$

21. $64\overline{)335}$

22. $15\overline{)341}$

23. $51\overline{)485}$

24. $74\overline{)525}$

25. $62\overline{)782}$

26. $35\overline{)866}$

27. $49\overline{)243}$

28. $27\overline{)487}$

29. $86\overline{)2,164}$

30. $53\overline{)4,602}$

31. $46\overline{)6,725}$

32. $91\overline{)8,095}$

33. $58\overline{)3,942}$

Mixed Applications

34. A total of 126 students signed up for the relay race. Each relay team will consist of 14 students. Each team needs 1 baton. Will 8 batons be enough?

35. **WRITE ABOUT IT** Explain how to correct an estimated quotient that is too high or too low.

Mixed Review

Estimate the sum or difference and compare. Write < or > for each ●. (pages 56–57)

36. 7.24 − 2.18 ● 6.75 − 1.44

37. 2.95 + 4.21 ● 1.85 + 4.49

Find the area. (pages 78–79)

38. $l = 12$ cm
$w = 5$ cm
$A = $ ▮ sq cm

39. $l = 25$ in.
$w = 5$ in.
$A = $ ▮ sq in.

40. $l = 18$ ft
$w = 9$ ft
$A = $ ▮ sq ft

41. $l = 12$ m
$w = 6$ m
$A = $ ▮ sq m

42. $l = 19$ yd
$w = 11$ yd
$A = $ ▮ sq yd

43. $l = 23$ m
$w = 17$ m
$A = $ ▮ sq m

44. $l = 54$ m
$w = 31$ m
$A = $ ▮ sq m

45. $l = 81$ ft
$w = 25$ ft
$A = $ ▮ sq ft

Using Division

You will learn to divide accurately. | **Why learn this?** You can find out how a number of items, such as pies, can be shared fairly.

Grandma's Oven, a pie-manufacturing company, made 2,578 pies. The company distributed the pies to 42 food stores. Each store received the same number of pies. How many pies did each store receive?

Divide.　　$2{,}578 \div 42$　　　$42\overline{)2{,}578}$

Estimate. $2{,}578 \div 42 \approx n$　　**Think:**　$\overset{60}{40\overline{)2{,}400}}$　or　$\overset{70}{40\overline{)2{,}800}}$

So, $n = 60$ or 70.

MODEL

What is $2{,}578 \div 42$?

▶ Step 1

Since the estimate is a two-digit number, divide the 257 tens.

$$\begin{array}{r} 6\phantom{{,}578} \\ 42\overline{)2{,}578} \\ -252 \\ \hline 5 \end{array}$$

Multiply.

Subtract.

Compare. $5 < 42$

▶ Step 2

Divide the 58 ones.

$$\begin{array}{r} 6\,1 \text{ r}16 \\ 42\overline{)2{,}578} \\ -252\downarrow \\ \hline 58 \\ -42 \\ \hline 16 \end{array}$$

Multiply.

Subtract.

Compare. $16 < 42$

So, each store received 61 pies. There were 16 pies left over.

In *Mighty Math Number Heroes*, the game *Quizzo* challenges you to divide by two-digit numbers.

EXAMPLES

A. Divide. $35\overline{)843}$

Think: $\overset{20}{40\overline{)800}}$　or　$\overset{30}{30\overline{)900}}$

$$\begin{array}{r} 24 \text{ r}3 \\ 35\overline{)843} \\ -70 \\ \hline 143 \\ -140 \\ \hline 3 \end{array}$$

Check by multiplying.

$$\begin{array}{r} 24 \\ \times 35 \\ \hline 120 \\ +720 \\ \hline 840 \end{array}$$

Add the remainder.

$840 + 3 = 843$

B. Divide. $28\overline{)7{,}120}$

Think: $\overset{200}{30\overline{)6{,}000}}$　or　$\overset{300}{25\overline{)7{,}500}}$

$$\begin{array}{r} 254 \text{ r}8 \\ 28\overline{)7{,}120} \\ -56 \\ \hline 152 \\ -140 \\ \hline 120 \\ -112 \\ \hline 8 \end{array}$$

Check by multiplying.

$$\begin{array}{r} 254 \\ \times\ 28 \\ \hline 2{,}032 \\ +5{,}080 \\ \hline 7{,}112 \end{array}$$

Add the remainder.

$7{,}112 + 8 = 7{,}120$

Talk About It

- How can you tell where to place the first digit in the quotient?
- How can you tell if each digit in the quotient is large enough?

PRACTICE

Divide. Check by multiplying.

1. $14\overline{)93}$
2. $32\overline{)79}$
3. $21\overline{)57}$
4. $53\overline{)98}$
5. $44\overline{)89}$

6. $54\overline{)182}$
7. $36\overline{)274}$
8. $41\overline{)619}$
9. $28\overline{)736}$
10. $65\overline{)402}$

11. $26\overline{)917}$
12. $50\overline{)643}$
13. $18\overline{)377}$
14. $45\overline{)232}$
15. $56\overline{)380}$

16. $72\overline{)463}$
17. $59\overline{)285}$
18. $34\overline{)125}$
19. $86\overline{)342}$
20. $64\overline{)875}$

21. $2,896 \div 46 = n$
22. $1,877 \div 33 = n$
23. $3,591 \div 60 = n$
24. $7,171 \div 71 = n$

25. $2,347 \div 58 = n$
26. $9,107 \div 85 = n$
27. $2,054 \div 48 = n$
28. $4,985 \div 73 = n$

Mixed Applications

29. Mr. Snyder uses 45.593 gallons of gas in his car in May, 43.236 gallons of gas in June, and 49.521 gallons in July. How many gallons does he use in the three months combined?

30. The students at Archer Middle School sold 1,700 tickets to the school carnival. Each student sold 4 tickets. How many students are at the school?

31. There are about 52 weeks in a year. Jermaine gets about 56 hours of sleep each week. About how many hours of sleep does he get in a year?

32. ▱ **Write a problem** about 1,273 baseball cards. Use division in your problem.

Mixed Review

Find the volume. (pages 78–79)

33. $l = 12$ in.
$w = 6$ in.
$h = 6$ in.
$V = \blacksquare$ cu in.

34. $l = 24$ cm
$w = 15$ cm
$h = 9$ cm
$V = \blacksquare$ cu cm

35. $l = 30$ ft
$w = 21$ ft
$h = 11$ ft
$V = \blacksquare$ cu ft

36. $l = 43$ m
$w = 22$ m
$h = 8$ m
$V = \blacksquare$ cu m

Copy and complete the equation. Identify the property used. (pages 70–71)

37. $6 \times \blacksquare = 6$
38. $2 \times (7 \times 3) = (\blacksquare \times 7) \times 3$
39. $8 \times 0 = \blacksquare$

PART 1 Choosing the Operation

You will learn how to decide whether to add, subtract, multiply, or divide to solve a problem.	Why learn this? You can choose the correct operation to solve a problem.

Before you can solve a problem, you must decide what operation to use. The chart shows situations for using each of the four operations.

Operation	Situation
Addition	• Joining groups
Subtraction	• Taking away part of a group • Comparing groups
Multiplication	• Combining equal-size groups
Division	• Separating into equal-size groups • Finding how many groups or how many in each group

Read each problem. Decide which operation should be used to solve.

A. Jeremy and his family plan to drive the 1,143 miles from Baltimore to Miami. They have traveled 659 miles. How much farther do they have to drive before reaching Miami?	**B.** Melanie has a kit for making beaded jewelry. The kit has 250 beads of each color. There are 12 colors. How many beads are in the kit?
C. There are 120 hot dogs to be shared equally by the 48 members of the East Side Boys Club. How many hot dogs will each boy get?	**D.** Ed has a stamp collection. He has 1,294 United States stamps and 2,003 foreign stamps. How many stamps does he have?

Talk About It

• What operations did you determine should be used to solve Problems A–D? Explain your reasoning for each.

• Give the solution to each problem.

PRACTICE

Tell what operation should be used to solve each problem.
Then solve.

1. On the first day of school, every student gets 25 star stickers. How many star stickers are needed for a school with 864 students?

2. A building is 432 feet high and has 36 stories. How high is each story of the building?

3. Some Girl Scout troops collected paper. Elena's troop collected 423 pounds of paper. Marta's troop collected 378 pounds. Lee's troop collected 457 pounds. How many pounds did all three troops collect?

4. Carlos earns $3,480 a month. José earns $2,975 a month. How much more money per month does Carlos earn than José?

Mixed Applications

5. Which is the longest river listed in the table? Which is the shortest? What is the difference in length between the two rivers?

WORLD RIVERS	
River	Length (miles)
Amazon	4,000
Colorado	1,450
Rio Grande	1,900
Yenisey	2,543

White-water rafting on the Colorado River

6. Mr. Stiles took his wife and three children to the movies. The cost of an adult ticket was $6.00 and the cost of a child's ticket was $3.00. How much did all the tickets cost?

7. Lightning can be as hot as 50,000°F. The surface of the sun is about 11,000°F. How much hotter can lightning be than the surface of the sun?

8. A toy company manufactured 4,644 dolls. The dolls were distributed evenly among 54 stores. How many dolls were sent to each store?

9. Bill bought a basketball for $19.78. Joe bought the same kind of basketball a week later when it went on sale for $13.88. How much more did Bill pay for his basketball?

10. Dominic needs 5 boards that are 36 inches long and 2 boards that are 63 inches long to make a bookcase. How many feet of lumber does he need? (HINT: Divide the total number of inches by 12.)

11. ✏️ **Write a problem** using the information in the table for Problem 5. At least one of the four operations must be used to solve the problem.

LESSON
CONTINUES ▶

PART 2 PROBLEM-SOLVING STRATEGY
Write a Number Sentence

THE PROBLEM Patricia's family bought furniture for their new apartment. The total cost of the furniture was $2,640. The furniture store offers a payment plan in which you may make 24 equal monthly payments. How much will Patricia's family pay per month for the furniture?

☑ **Understand**

- What are you asked to find?

- What information will you use?

- Is there information you will not use? If so, what?

☑ **Plan**

- What strategy can you use to solve the problem?

  You can *write a number sentence* to find the monthly payment amount.

☑ **Solve**

- What number sentence can you write to solve the problem?

  Since you are separating an amount into 24 equal-size groups, divide to find the monthly payment.

  Divide. $2,640 ÷ 24

  Estimate. $2,000 ÷ 20 = n

  So, n = 100.

So, the monthly payment will be $110.

$$\begin{array}{r} 110 \\ 24\overline{)2{,}640} \\ -2\,4 \\ \hline 24 \\ -24 \\ \hline 00 \end{array}$$

☑ **Look Back**

- How can you decide if your answer is reasonable?

- What other strategy could you use?

REMEMBER:

☑ Understand
☑ Plan
☑ Solve
☑ Look Back

Consumer Link

Frank Lloyd Wright was a famous architect who also designed furniture. His furniture was often designed with geometric shapes. A cube chair and a chair with a hexagon, square, and triangle are examples.

Suppose furniture costs $1,500 and is paid for in 10 monthly payments. What number sentence can you write to find out how much each payment would be?

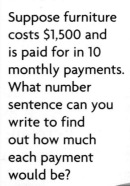

PRACTICE

Write a number sentence to solve.

1. Alice's mother bought a used car for $6,300. She will pay it off in 36 months. What will her monthly payment be?

2. Steve had 1,158 pennies in a large jar. He put them into rolls, with 50 pennies in each roll. How many rolls of pennies did he have?

3. Kim scored 12,743 on a computer game the first time she played it. She improved her score by 3,879 points the second time she played. What was her score the second time?

4. Sports Place has 22 skateboards in stock. The price of 10 of the skateboards is $13 each, and 12 of them sell for $25 each. How much money will selling all the skateboards bring in for the store?

Mixed Applications

Solve.

CHOOSE A STRATEGY

• Use a Table • Act It Out • Guess and Check • Work Backward • Write a Number Sentence

5. Lynn, Freddie, Eileen, Susan, and Nancy swim in a relay race. Susan swims before Nancy. Freddie swims before Susan but after Eileen. Lynn swims before everyone but Eileen. Who swims third?

6. A subscription to *Up and Coming* magazine is $19 a year. The magazine has 5,489 subscribers. How much money does the magazine get from its subscriptions?

7. There are 90 men, women, and children in the movie theater. There are twice as many women as men. There are three times as many children as men. How many of each are there?

8. Rodney's parents bought a car for $15,299. Three years later they sold it for $8,700. How much less was the selling price than the price they paid for the car?

9. Max spent $7 playing video games at the mall. He spent $4 for lunch, and bought a gift for $8. He had $9 when he got home. How much money did he have when he left for the mall?

10. The Hanging Gardens of Babylon were laid out on a square brick terrace that measures about 400 feet on each side. What are the perimeter and area of this terrace?

11. How much deeper is the ocean that has the greatest depth than the ocean that has the least depth?

Ocean	Average Depth (ft)
Pacific Ocean	12,925
Atlantic Ocean	11,730
Indian Ocean	12,598
Arctic Ocean	3,407

CULTURAL CONNECTION

TROPICAL MYANMAR

David and his class were making a number chart to compare countries with their state, Arizona. David looked for information about the Union of Myanmar, the country where his mother was born. It had formerly been known as Burma.

He read that Myanmar has an area of 261,228 square miles. If an equal number of people lived on each square mile, there would be about 176 people per square mile. What operation would David use to find the number of people who live in Myanmar? What estimate can he make?

> ### CULTURAL LINK
>
> Wind and rain storms, called monsoons, blow across Myanmar from May to October each year. Heavy rains, as much as 200 inches a year, pour down on the mountains and on the areas along the coast. Myanmar is a tropical country. The temperature in the lowlands does not change very much, but snow falls in the high mountains in the far north.

Work Together

1. David found that there are about 34 people per square mile in Arizona. The population is about 4,217,940. What operation can David use to find the total area of Arizona?

2. The class made a profit of $225 during the fair. An equal amount of the money was put in each of the 25 students' accounts toward a field trip to the Grand Canyon. How much was put into each account?

3. David and his classmates helped his mother prepare food for an international fair at the school. They prepared chicken with rice and curry sauce. They sold 249 cups of food to 83 people. If each person received an equal amount of food, how many cups of food did each person receive?

4. David's mother received 7,896 kyats, Myanmar's monetary unit. David wanted to know the money's value in United States dollars. He found that about 60 kyats could be traded for $10. What operations can David use to find how many dollars would equal the kyats?

✓ CHECK UNDERSTANDING

Write two pairs of compatible numbers for each.
Give two possible estimates. (pages 120–121)

1. $811 \div 24 \approx n$ **2.** $352 \div 58 \approx n$ **3.** $1,472 \div 26 \approx n$

4. $6,265 \div 86 \approx n$ **5.** $2,952 \div 41 \approx n$ **6.** $5,284 \div 63 \approx n$

Copy each problem. Draw a box where the first digit in the quotient should be placed. (pages 122–123)

7. $32\overline{)1,098}$ **8.** $56\overline{)3,374}$ **9.** $28\overline{)4,915}$ **10.** $45\overline{)2,658}$ **11.** $73\overline{)7,420}$

✓ CHECK SKILLS

Find the quotient. (pages 118–119, 122–125)

12. $90 \div 30 = n$ **13.** $280 \div 70 = n$ **14.** $4,000 \div 40 = n$ **15.** $48,000 \div 60 = n$

16. $29\overline{)87}$ **17.** $46\overline{)235}$ **18.** $51\overline{)7,866}$ **19.** $38\overline{)1,467}$ **20.** $74\overline{)2,812}$

Divide. Check by multiplying. (pages 126–127)

21. $57\overline{)74}$ **22.** $26\overline{)90}$ **23.** $38\overline{)710}$ **24.** $40\overline{)908}$ **25.** $61\overline{)795}$

26. $19\overline{)2,282}$ **27.** $39\overline{)3,140}$ **28.** $76\overline{)7,769}$ **29.** $64\overline{)9,072}$ **30.** $85\overline{)3,453}$

✓ CHECK PROBLEM SOLVING

Solve. (pages 130–131)

CHOOSE A STRATEGY

• **Make a Table**   • **Write a Number Sentence**   • **Draw a Diagram**   • **Work Backward**

31. Mr. Campbell bought a home computer system for $3,330. He will pay it off in 18 months. How much will his monthly payment be?

32. John played 12 computer games in 60 minutes. He scored about 260 points per game. About how many points did he earn per minute?

33. Monica spent $14 to get her hair cut. Then she spent $5 on lunch. After lunch, she bought a purse for $9. She had $16 when she got home. How much money did she have before she went to get her hair cut?

34. Erica saved 1,045 nickels. She put them into rolls, with 40 nickels in each roll. How many full rolls of nickels did she have? How many nickels were left over?

VOCABULARY CHECK

Choose a term from the box to complete each sentence.

WORD BANK

Associative Property
   of Multiplication
divisible
cubic
Distributive Property

1. You can group factors differently. The product is always the same. The ? states this. (page 70)

2. Volume is measured in ? units. (page 76)

3. The ? states that multiplying a sum by a number is the same as multiplying each addend by the number and then adding the products. (page 86)

4. If you divide 6 by 2, the quotient is a whole number and there is a zero remainder. This means that 6 is ? by 2. (page 102)

STUDY AND SOLVE

CHAPTER 5

EXAMPLE

```
  1 1
  654     Multiply the ones. Regroup.
×   3     Multiply the tens. Add the 1 ten you
-----     got by regrouping the ones.
1,962     Regroup. Multiply the hundreds.
          Add the 1 hundred you got by
          regrouping the tens.
```

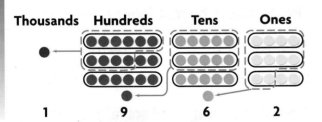

Thousands	Hundreds	Tens	Ones
1	9	6	2

Find the product. (pages 74–75)

5. $465 \times 4 = n$ 6. $328 \times 5 = n$

7. $\begin{array}{r} 806 \\ \times\ 2 \\ \hline \end{array}$ 8. $\begin{array}{r} 217 \\ \times\ 6 \\ \hline \end{array}$

Find the area. (pages 78–79)

9. $l = 15$ in.   10. $l = 33$ cm
   $w = 7$ in. $w = 8$ cm
   $A = \underline{?}$ sq in. $A = \underline{?}$ sq cm

Find the volume. (pages 78–79)

11. $l = 5$ m   12. $l = 5$ ft
    $w = 6$ m $w = 2$ ft
    $h = 4$ m $h = 7$ ft
    $V = \underline{?}$ cu m $V = \underline{?}$ cu ft

Choose a strategy and solve. (pages 80–81)

13. One rug measures 10 feet by 6 feet and costs $120. Another rug measures 12 feet by 5 feet and costs $126. Which is the better buy?

CHAPTER 6

EXAMPLE

```
    432
  ×263
  ------
  1,296     Multiply. 3 × 432
 25,920     Multiply. 60 × 432
+86,400     Multiply. 200 × 432
--------
113,616     Add the products.
```

Estimate the product by rounding each factor to its greatest place-value position. (pages 90–91)

14. 626
        × 28

15. 386
        × 51

Find the product. (pages 88–89, 92–93)

16.   36
        ×84

17. 425
        × 62

18. 403
        ×262

19. 1,423
        × 310

Find the perimeter and area for the figure. (pages 94–95)

20.

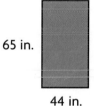

65 in.

44 in.

21.

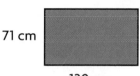

71 cm

120 cm

Choose a strategy and solve. (pages 96–97)

22. Ms. Raymer has 600 feet of fencing to surround a garden. What dimensions should the garden have so that it has the greatest area?

CHAPTER 7

EXAMPLE

Estimate the quotient.

$148 \div 5 = n$ 150 and 5 are compatible: 150 is divisible by 5 because it has a zero in the ones place.

Think: $150 \div 5 = 30$, so $n \approx 30$.

Estimate the quotient. (pages 104–107)

23. 4)420

24. 3)271

Find the quotient. Check by multiplying. (pages 104–109)

25. 2)346

26. 6)462

27. $415 \div 8 = n$

28. $525 \div 5 = n$

Choose a strategy and solve. (pages 112–113)

29. Concert tickets cost $6 each. Sellers raised $918. How many tickets did they sell?

CHAPTER 8

EXAMPLE

```
       38 r20
38)1,464
    -114
     324
    -304
      20
```

Divide the 146 tens by 38.
Estimate. $120 \div 40 = 3$
Multiply. $3 \times 38 = 114$
Subtract. $146 - 114 = 32$
Bring down the ones.
Repeat the steps.
Write 20 as the remainder.

Divide. Check by multiplying. (pages 122–127)

30. 36)144

31. 64)86

32. $8,145 \div 62 = n$ **33.** $4,104 \div 76 = n$

Choose a strategy and solve. (pages 130–131)

34. Ann borrowed $5,592 from her mother. She will pay it back in 24 months. What will her monthly payment be?

✐ WRITE ABOUT IT

1. Show and explain each step as you find the product 6×418. **(pages 74–75)**

2. Show and explain each step as you find the perimeter and area of a sandbox that is 8 feet by 10 feet. **(pages 94–95)**

3. Show and explain each step as you find the quotient $812 \div 4$. **(pages 106–109)**

4. Explain how you can use mental math and a pattern of zeros to find the quotient $6,000 \div 20 = n$. **(pages 118–119)**

✓ PERFORMANCE ASSESSMENT

Solve. Explain your method.

CHOOSE A STRATEGY

• **Use a Formula**   • **Draw a Diagram**   • **Guess and Check**   • **Write a Number Sentence**

5. Alice is buying a cage for her pet hamster. One cage measures 2 ft by 4 ft by 3 ft. The other measures 3 ft by 3 ft by 2 ft. They each cost $20.00. Which cage has the greater volume ($V = l \times w \times h$)? **(pages 80–81)**

6. Mr. Foster is building a sandbox for his daughter. He has 24 feet of wood to use as a border. He wants to build the sandbox to have the greatest area. What dimensions should he use? **(pages 96–97)**

7. Carrie took 138 pictures on her vacation. She put them in an album with an equal number on each page. The last page had only 2 pictures on it. How many pages did she use? How many pictures were on each page? **(pages 112–113)**

8. Scout troop 555 has set a goal to sell 1,500 boxes of cookies. There are 12 Scouts in the troop. How many boxes should each Scout sell to meet the troop's goal? **(pages 130–131)**

CUMULATIVE REVIEW

Solve the problem. Then write the letter of the correct answer.

1. What is standard form for three hundred four million, two hundred fifty thousand, six? (pages 8–9)

A. 34,250,006   **B.** 304,025,006
C. 304,250,006   **D.** 304,250,600

2.
$$\begin{array}{r} 534 \\ +477 \\ \hline \end{array}$$
A. 901
B. 911
C. 1,001
D. 1,011   (pages 18–19)

3. What is the value of the underlined digit?

3.0$\underline{5}$6

A. 0.005   **B.** 0.05
C. 0.5   **D.** 5   (pages 34–39)

4. $5.012 - 3.365 = n$

A. $n = 1.647$ **B.** $n = 1.746$
C. $n = 4.188$ **D.** $n = 8.377$
(pages 54–55)

5. Estimate the sum to the nearest tenth.

$$\begin{array}{r} 3.59 \\ +3.73 \\ \hline \end{array}$$
A. 6.9
B. 7.1
C. 7.3
D. 7.5   (pages 56–57)

6. Here is an example of the _?_ Property of Multiplication:
$3 \times (4 \times 2) = (3 \times 4) \times 2$

A. Commutative   **B.** Associative
C. Distributive   **D.** Zero
(pages 70–71)

7.
$$\begin{array}{r} 432 \\ \times\ \ 9 \\ \hline \end{array}$$
A. 288
B. 4,416
C. 3,888
D. 38,880 (pages 74–75)

8. Find the volume. (pages 78–79)

$l = 6$ cm, $w = 7$ cm, $h = 3$ cm

A. 16 cu cm   **B.** 42 cu cm
C. 126 cu m   **D.** 126 cu cm

9. Estimate the product by rounding each factor to its greatest place-value position.

$$\begin{array}{r} 592 \\ \times\ 43 \\ \hline \end{array}$$
A. 20,000
B. 23,600
C. 24,000
D. 30,000   (pages 90–91)

10. Find the area. (pages 94–95)

61 m
205 m

A. 144 sq m   **B.** 532 sq m
C. 1,435 sq m   **D.** 12,505 sq m

11. $4\overline{)634}$

A. 58 r2   **B.** 158
C. 158 r2   **D.** 2,536   (pages 108–109)

12. $4,050 \div 54 = n$

A. $n = 75$ **B.** $n = 76$ r46
C. $n = 79$ r14   **D.** $n = 218,700$
(pages 126–127)

ANALYZING AND GRAPHING DATA

Chicago, Illinois
Temperature °F

	highest recorded	average daily		lowest recorded
		max.	min.	
Jan	65°	32°	18°	-20°
Feb	68°	34°	20°	-21°
Mar	62°	43°	29°	-12°
Apr	91°	55°	40°	17°
May	98°	65°	56°	27°
Jun	102°	75°	60°	35°

Miami, Florida
Temperature °F

	highest recorded	average daily		lowest recorded
		max.	min.	
Jan	85°	74°	61°	29°
Feb	88°	75°	61°	27°
Mar	92°	78°	64°	34°
Apr	93°	80°	67°	45°
May	94°	84°	71°	50°
Jun	94°	86°	74°	61°

Barrow, Alaska
Temperature °F

	highest recorded	average daily		lowest recorded
		max.	min.	
Jan	33°	-9°	-22°	-53°
Feb	31°	-12°	-25°	-56°
Mar	36°	-8°	-22°	-52°
Apr	42°	7°	-8°	-42°
May	45°	24°	13°	-18°
Jun	70°	39°	29°	8°

DID YOU KNOW . . .

The national record for highest temperature is 134°F. It was recorded in 1913 in Death Valley, California. The record for lowest temperature in the United States is ⁻79.8°F. It was recorded in the Endicott Mountains of Northern Alaska.

The Worried Weather Forecaster

Suppose you are a weather forecaster. Your task is to record the high and low temperatures each day. Your supervisor tells you not to worry as long as the daily temperatures don't break any records, and their mean is close to the average temperature for the month. Make up daily temperature data that will fit the supervisor's comments.

Work with a group. Your job is to

- choose a city and a month.
- make a five-day chart of high and low temperatures that fit the supervisor's comments.
- calculate the mean for the five high and low temperatures.
- make a graph showing the five high temperatures.

DID YOU

✓ make a chart showing high and low temperatures?

✓ calculate the mean for the high and the low temperatures and check your calculations?

✓ graph the data?

Chicago Illinois in April
Average High Temperature

Highest
Lowe...

Date	3	4	5	6
High Temp	70°	72°	50°	41°

...rrow Alaska in Oct...

Highest = 40°
Average High = 22°
Average Low = 12°
Lowest = -19°

Date	Oct 15	Oct 16	Oct 17	Oct 18
High Temp.	38°	30°	32°	5°
Low Temp.	25°	21°	10°	4°

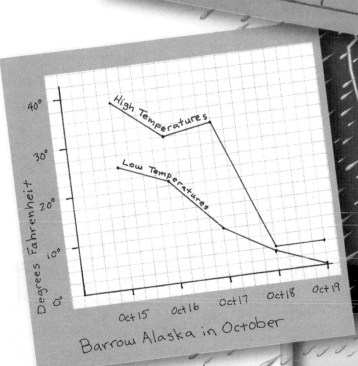

Barrow Alaska in October

HANDS ON
COOPERATIVE LEARNING

Finding the Median and Mode

You will investigate finding the median and mode of a set of data.	**Why learn this?** You can describe data using specific measures.	**WORD POWER** median mode

The coach of the Coyotes basketball team recorded the team's scores in the first 13 games. He organized these data in the table below.

COYOTES' BASKETBALL SCORES													
Game	1	2	3	4	5	6	7	8	9	10	11	12	13
Score	104	95	100	103	99	100	93	104	99	102	93	104	104

Explore

Write each score on a different index card. Use the index cards to find the median and mode.

MATERIALS: index cards

A. To find the *median*, order the scores on the cards from least to greatest.

| 93 | 93 | 95 | 99 | 99 |

Flip over the cards on each end. Keep doing this, moving toward the middle, until one card is left. The score on that card is the median.

| | | ? | | |

B. To find the *mode*, sort the cards by numbers. Find the score that occurred most often.

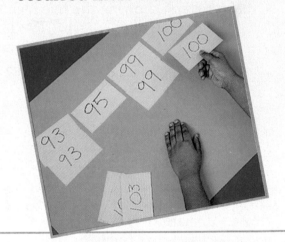

Record

Write your own definitions for *median* and *mode*. Name the median and mode for the Coyotes' basketball scores.

TALK ABOUT IT How does this activity help you find the difference between median and mode?

Technology **Link**
E–Lab • Activity 9 Available on CD-ROM and the Internet at http://www.hbschool.com/elab

Now, investigate finding the median and mode for another set of data.

Try This

Write each temperature on a different index card. Use the cards to find the median and mode for the temperatures. Record your answers.

AUGUST TEMPERATURES												
DATE	1	2	3	4	5	6	7	8	9	10	11	12	13
TEMP	96°	88°	87°	101°	94°	93°	87°	74°	91°	82°	81°	88°	73°

If you play outside when it's hot, be sure to drink plenty of water.

The **median** is the middle number in an ordered series of numbers. The **mode** is the number that occurs most often.

✏️ **WRITE ABOUT IT** For one season, the median score for one team is 88, and the mode is 87. The median score for another team is 100, and the mode is 104. Which team do you think is better? Explain.

HANDS-ON PRACTICE

Use index cards to find the median and mode for each set of data.

1.

KATIE'S TEST SCORES									
Test	1	2	3	4	5	6	7	8	9
Score	94	93	95	87	94	78	85	89	99

2.

STUDENTS' WEIGHTS					
Name	Meg	Ruth	Sara	Jon	Keith
Pounds	84	75	89	103	84

3.

BASEBALL CARD COLLECTION					
Name	Tony	Kara	Ray	Sue	Jay
Number	240	200	200	265	285

4.

PLAY TICKETS SOLD							
Week	1	2	3	4	5	6	7
Number	175	150	225	175	230	190	165

5.

MONEY SAVED IN ONE YEAR					
Initials	L.L.	S.E.	B.S.	M.D.	D.V.
Amount	$125	$150	$175	$125	$180

6.

CANS RECYCLED					
Day	Mon	Tue	Wed	Thu	Fri
Number	68	93	68	75	120

Mixed Applications

7. On each of 2 days Tony did 50 sit-ups. On each of the next 2 days he did 75. On the last 3 days he did 100 each day. What are the median and mode for the number of sit-ups Tony did?

8. There are 36 students on each of 2 buses. There are 43 students on each of 3 buses. What is the total number of students on the 5 buses?

MORE PRACTICE Student Handbook page H85

Finding the Mean

You will learn to compute the mean of a set of data.	Why learn this? You can describe data using a specific measure.

The **mean**, or average, is another way to find one number that represents all the numbers in a set of data. What is the mean for the number of tickets sold?

TICKETS SOLD	
Day	Number
Mon	6
Tue	5
Wed	9
Thu	2
Fri	3
Sat	5

MODEL

▶ **Step 1**

Use unit cubes. Make 6 stacks of cubes to model the number of tickets sold each day.

▶ **Step 2**

Arrange the stacks in order from the shortest to the tallest.

▶ **Step 3**

To find the mean, move the cubes so the 6 stacks are equal in height. The number of cubes in each stack is the mean.

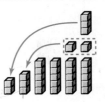

So, the mean is 5 tickets.

Talk About It

- What operation are you modeling by making 6 equal stacks?

- What information does the mean give you that the median and mode do not?

REMEMBER:
A stem-and-leaf plot shows data organized by place value.

Stem	Leaves			
1	2	4	4	7
2	1	1	1	9 9
3	0	3	5	

The tens digit is called the *stem*. The ones digits are called *leaves*.

You can read data from a stem-and-leaf plot. What is the mean for these data?

Stem	Leaves
4	6 7 8 9 9
5	0 0 1 2 4 4 4 5 5 6 7 7 7 7 8
6	1 1 4 5 8

Ages of First 25 Presidents When Sworn into Office

To compute the *mean*, add the ages of the presidents. Divide the sum by the number of presidents.

1,375 ÷ 25 = 55, so the mean is 55 years.

- What are the median and mode for these data?

CRITICAL THINKING When you are finding the mean of a set of data, what number is the dividend? the divisor? the quotient?

Stem	Leaves
7	1 3 6
8	4 7
9	5 5 6 7

Angela's Bowling Scores

PRACTICE

For Problems 1–2, use the stem-and-leaf plot.

1. Write the mean for Angela's bowling scores.

2. Write the median and mode.

For Problems 3–4, use the table.

3. What is the mean for the number of students in each grade at the school?

4. Write the median and the mode for these data.

Find the mean, median, and mode for each set of data.

FAIRVIEW ELEMENTARY SCHOOL	
Grade	**Number of Students**
First	120
Second	105
Third	120
Fourth	108
Fifth	112

5. 3, 9, 7, 7, 4   6. 20, 30, 25, 40, 20   7. 147, 116, 148, 128, 116

Mixed Applications

8. There are 5 fifth-grade classes at Duncan's school. In each of 3 classes there are 27 students. One class has 29 students, and one class has 30 students. What are the mean, median, and mode for these data?

9. Heather helped her teacher pack boxes. She packed 146 books into 8 equal-size boxes. Did Heather pack the same number of books into each box? Explain.

10. There are 4 children in Gloria's family. Gloria is 14 years old. Gloria's 3 brothers are 7, 9, and 18 years old. What is the mean for the 4 children's ages?

11. **WRITE ABOUT IT** What do the mean, median, and mode tell you about a set of data?

Mixed Review

Write in written form. (pages 36–37)

12. 0.001   13. 0.025   14. 0.306   15. 5.004

Find the sum. (pages 50–51)

16. 6.2
    +3.5

17. 4.9
    +5.7

18. 2.45
    +4.16

19. 1.273
    +2.282

20. 7.904
    +2.616

Choosing a Reasonable Scale

| **You will learn** to choose a reasonable scale for a set of data. | **Why learn this?** You can use a scale that matches the data and that makes the graph easy to read. | WORD POWER
scale
interval |

The fifth-grade students are selling magazines. They sold 35 subscriptions in Week 1, 40 in Week 2, 31 in Week 3, and 25 in Week 4. These data were organized in two different line graphs that show the same information.

Graph B

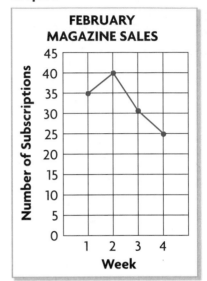

Graph A

A line graph uses a line to show how something changes over a period of time.

The **scale** is the series of numbers placed at fixed distances. A *reasonable scale* is one for which most data fall on scale lines. The **interval** is the distance between the numbers on the scale.

Notice that

⇨ Graphs A and B have different scales.

⇨ the scales have different intervals.

⇨ both graphs show an increase from Week 1 to Week 2 and a decrease from Week 2 to Week 4.

REMEMBER:

In bar and double-bar graphs, the lengths of the bars are related to the numbers in the scale.

Talk About It

• What is the interval and the scale in Graph A? in Graph B?

• Would an interval of 20 make a good scale for these data? Explain.

 **CRITICAL THINKING** In which graph do the intervals in the scale make the graph easier to read? Explain.

PRACTICE

Choose the most reasonable interval for each set of data.

a. 25	**b.** 5	**c.** 10	**d.** 1

1. 2, 5, 6, 3, 1, 4, 7

2. 10, 35, 40, 20, 30

3. 75, 25, 50, 100, 110

4. 10, 5, 20, 15, 17, 25

Choose the more reasonable scale for the set of data.

5.

FIFTH-GRADE SURVEY	
Favorite Sport	**Number of Students**
Football	20
Basketball	18
Baseball	15
Soccer	25
Other	5

6.

PLANT SALE	
Week	**Number Sold**
1	20
2	15
3	40
4	30
5	10

7.

PETS OWNED IN MS. FLOWER'S CLASS	
Pet	**Number of Students**
Dog	9
Cat	10
Fish	6
Gerbils	4

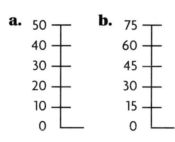

Mixed Applications

For Problems 8–11, use the table.

8. What would be an appropriate scale for these data?

9. How many students were surveyed?

10. Would an interval of 10 make a good scale for these data? Explain.

11. ✏ **Write a problem** using the information in the table.

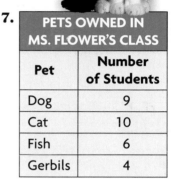

TELEVISION SURVEY	
Favorite Type of Show	Number
Comedy	25
Drama	16
Sports	15
News	5

Mixed Review

Find the product. (pages 74–75)

12. 124 × 5

13. 219 × 2

14. 918 × 3

15. 367 × 4

16. 511 × 9

Use divisibility rules to predict if there will be a remainder. (pages 108–109)

17. 9)542

18. 4)348

19. 3)129

20. 5)436

21. 6)618

Making Line Graphs

You will learn to make a line graph.	Why learn this? You can make graphs that show how data change over a period of time.	WORD POWER range

The table below shows average monthly temperatures for San Juan, Puerto Rico. You can use the table to find the **range**, or difference between the greatest and the least numbers in the set of data.

SAN JUAN AVERAGE MONTHLY TEMPERATURES						
Month	Jun	Jul	Aug	Sep	Oct	Nov
Temperature	82° F	83° F	83° F	82° F	82° F	80° F

The greatest temperature is 83°F. The least temperature is 80°F. Since 83 − 80 = 3, the range is 3.

MODEL

How can you make a line graph to show these data?

▶ Step 1

Decide on the interval and the numbers in the scale. Since the range is 3, it makes sense to use an interval of 1. The scale must be at least from 80°F to 83°F.

▶ Step 2

Scales on graphs always start at zero. Since there are no data between 0°F and 80°F, you can *break the scale* to save room. Write the temperatures along the left side of the graph.

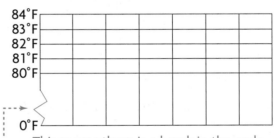

This means there is a break in the scale.

▶ Step 3

Write the names of the months along the bottom of the graph. Label the months, and then label the temperatures along the left side of the graph. Write a title for the graph.

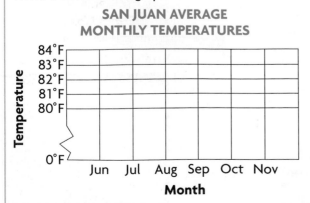

▶ Step 4

Plot the points for the data. Connect the points to show change over time.

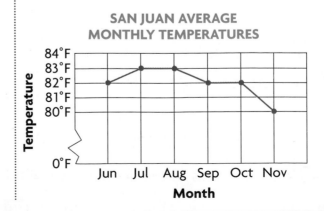

- What does the graph tell you about how the temperature in San Juan changes over time?

💡 **CRITICAL THINKING** Would it make sense to use an interval of 1 for a set of data with a range of 50? Explain.

PRACTICE

Make a line graph for each set of data.

1.
SKATING RINK ATTENDANCE					
Week	1	2	3	4	5
People	150	155	165	180	185

2.
INCHES OF RAINFALL				
Month	Jun	Jul	Aug	Sep
Inches	3	5	6	4

Mixed Applications

For Problems 3–5, use the table.

3. What would be an appropriate scale for a line graph displaying these data?

4. What would the label for the scale be?

5. Describe how the data changed each day.

6. Maria read 20 pages on Monday. On Tuesday she read twice as many pages as she did on Monday. On Friday she read 3 times as many pages as she did on Monday. What is the mean for the number of pages Maria read those 3 days?

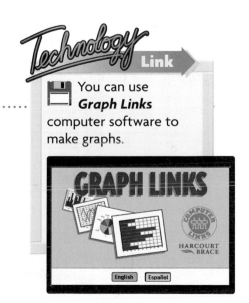

TIME MARIA SPENDS ON HOMEWORK					
Day	Mon	Tue	Wed	Thu	Fri
Time	20 min	45 min	60 min	75 min	0 min

7. ✏️ **WRITE ABOUT IT** Explain when a line graph might be a better choice to use than a bar graph.

Technology Link

💾 You can use *Graph Links* computer software to make graphs.

GRAPH LINKS

HARCOURT BRACE

English Español

ixed Review

Find the product. (pages 88–89)

8. 34
   ×15

9. 23
   ×46

10. 187
    × 16

Divide. Check by multiplying. (pages 126–127)

11. 19)616   12. 42)275   13. 31)139

PART 1 Choosing the Appropriate Graph

You will learn to choose the best graph for displaying a set of data.

Why learn this? You can use graphs to present data in different ways.

Some students used the table at the right to make graphs and plots. Whose graph or plot best displays these data?

MEAN TEMPERATURE ON APRIL 11	
City	**Temperature**
Chicago, IL	48°F
Los Angeles, CA	60°F
Miami, FL	75°F
Washington, DC	57°F

Fernando's Line Plot

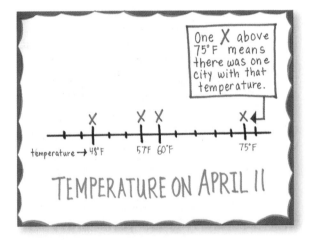

A *line plot* is used to keep track of data as they are collected. The city names are not shown. This is not the best way to display these data.

Joshua's Line Graph

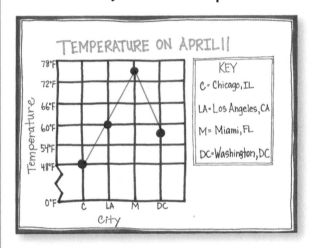

A *line graph* is used to show changes over time. So, this is not an appropriate graph to use.

Tamara's Bar Graph

A *bar graph* is used to compare facts about groups. So, this is an appropriate graph to use.

Talk About It

• Why is Tamara's graph the best for displaying these data?

• Would a stem-and-leaf plot be appropriate for displaying these data? Explain.

💡 **CRITICAL THINKING** Why is a line graph appropriate for displaying the data in the previous lesson but not in this lesson?

PRACTICE

For Problems 1–4, choose a type of graph or plot.
Explain your choice.

1. scores for a math test

2. yearbook sales over a four-week period

3. newspapers collected by five classes

4. money a business earned from January to June

Draw the graph or plot that best displays each set of data.

5.

CLASS SURVEY NUMBER OF FAMILY MEMBERS					
Number of Family Members	2	3	4	5	6
Frequency	9	7	4	2	1

6.

DISTANCE HEATHER TRAVELED ON A TRIP						
Day	1	2	3	4	5	6
Miles	250	100	0	50	100	250

7.

FAVORITE RADIO STATIONS					
Station	WRDL	WLRF	WSRS	WEMD	WWEB
Boys	24	16	12	28	20
Girls	36	22	20	4	18

> **Social Studies Link**
>
> Graphs are often used in magazines and in newspapers. The line graph below shows the population of the world. What does the graph show you about how the population of the world has changed over time?
>
> **TOTAL WORLD POPULATION**
>
> (line graph: Billions of People vs. Year, 1800–2000, with 1996 marked near top)

Mixed Applications

For Problems 8–12, use the table.

TEMPERATURE IN ORLANDO ON DECEMBER 31						
Time	6:30 A.M.	9:30 A.M.	12:30 P.M.	3:30 P.M.	6:30 P.M.	9:30 P.M.
Temperature	45°F	55°F	68°F	72°F	65°F	58°F

8. What type of graph would you use to display these data? Explain.

9. Would it be reasonable to use a scale of 1°? Explain.

10. When did the least change in temperature occur?

11. Did the temperature change more between 6:30 A.M. and 9:30 A.M. or between 9:30 A.M. and 12:30 P.M.?

12. ✏️ **Write a problem** using the data in the table.

LESSON CONTINUES ➤

PART 2 PROBLEM-SOLVING STRATEGY
Make a Graph

THE PROBLEM Carolyn surveyed the students in her class to find out what type of fund-raiser they want to have. She organized the data in the table below. What graph or plot should she use to display these data?

REMEMBER:
- ☑ Understand
- ☑ Plan
- ☑ Solve
- ☑ Look Back

FUND-RAISER CHOICES			
	Car Wash	Bake Sale	Raffle
Girls	7	3	5
Boys	10	1	4

REMEMBER:
Double-bar graphs are used to compare two sets of data in the same graph.

☑ Understand

- What are you asked to find?
- What information will you use?
- Is there information you will not use? If so, what?

☑ Plan

- What strategy can you use to solve the problem?

  You can *make a graph or plot* to organize and clearly display these data.

☑ Solve

- Which graph or plot can you make?

  You can make a double-bar graph to compare the girls' and boys' responses.

  This double-bar graph shows that the greatest number of girls and the greatest number of boys want to have a car wash for the fund-raiser.

☑ Look Back

- How do you know if this is the best graph or plot to display these data?
- What other strategy could you use?

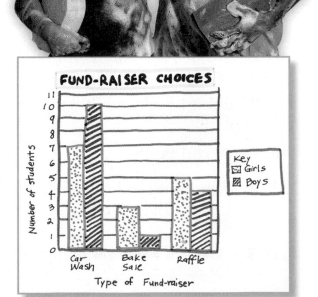

PRACTICE

Make a graph to solve.

1. Mrs. Cook, the librarian, is getting ready to order new books. She surveyed students to find out what types of books they wanted. She organized the data in the table. What graph or plot should she use to display these data? Make the graph or plot.

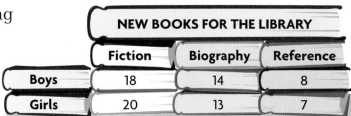

NEW BOOKS FOR THE LIBRARY			
	Fiction	Biography	Reference
Boys	18	14	8
Girls	20	13	7

2. Mrs. Mantel surveyed some students. She wanted to find ideas for the end-of-school party. She organized the data in the table. What graph or plot should she use to display these data? Make the graph or plot.

End-of-School Party Ideas			
	Carnival	Games	Sports
Number of Students	30	32	58

Mixed Applications

Solve.

CHOOSE A STRATEGY

• Make a Table   • Make a Graph   • Guess and Check   • Write a Number Sentence

3. Darien High School had five home football games. On September 13 they sold 1,018 tickets for the game. One week later they sold 650 tickets. The next week they sold 835 tickets. On October 18 they sold 1,186 tickets, and on October 25 they sold 946 tickets. What is the mean for the number of tickets sold?

4. There were 113 fifth graders at the zoo on Friday. Of the 113 students, 3 did not tour the reptile exhibit. The other students toured the reptile exhibit in equal groups. There were 5 groups of students. How many students were in each group?

5. Celeste has this money in her wallet. She bought 2 cassettes for $8.99 each and a CD for $12.95. A package of batteries costs $2.29. How many packages of batteries can Celeste buy?

6. Mr. Dow surveyed the fifth grade to find out what to buy for the spring cookout. The results are in the table. Which food choice was most popular?

SPRING COOKOUT FOOD CHOICES				
	Burgers	Hot Dogs	Chicken	Ribs
Number of Students	100	105	40	10

MATH FUN!

Three M's Game

PURPOSE To practice finding mean, mode, and median

YOU WILL NEED index cards, pencil, calculator

Label two index cards with the same number (the mode). Label the other three cards with different numbers. Find the mean and median of the numbers on your cards. Choose numbers so that the mean, median, and mode are all different. Tell a partner the mean, median, and mode for your set of numbers. Ask your partner to guess the numbers on your cards. Switch roles and play again.

Milk Math

PURPOSE To make a graph

YOU WILL NEED grid paper, pencil

If you were a child in pioneer days, milking a cow would probably be one of your daily chores. Pioneers were lucky to get 21 quarts of milk from a cow each *week*. Today, farmers get about 11 quarts from a cow each *day*.

Make a graph that shows the difference between pioneer days and now.

 Figure out how much milk your family drinks in 1 week. If you were a pioneer, would one cow give you enough milk?

Hot Potato!

PURPOSE To make a bar graph

YOU WILL NEED grid paper, ruler, pencil

Are potatoes more popular in Europe or in Asia? Use the data from the table to make a bar graph. You may want to group the data as *Europe, Asia,* or *North and South America* before you graph it.

POTATOES EATEN BY ONE PERSON IN A YEAR	
COUNTRY	POUNDS OF POTATOES
ARGENTINA	137
CHINA	35
FRANCE	161
HONG KONG	7
IRELAND	310
JAPAN	28
PHILIPPINES	3
SPAIN	226
TAIWAN	1
UNITED STATES	65
UNITED KINGDOM	249

✓ CHECK UNDERSTANDING

VOCABULARY

1. The _?_ is the middle number in an ordered series of numbers. (page 141)

2. The _?_ is the series of numbers placed at fixed distances in a graph. (page 144)

3. The _?_ is the number that occurs most often in a set of data. (page 141)

4. The _?_ is the distance between the numbers on the scale. (page 144)

5. The _?_, or average is a number that represents all the numbers in a set of data. (page 142)

6. The _?_ is the difference between the greatest and the least numbers in a set of data. (page 146)

Choose a type of graph or plot. Explain your choice. (pages 148–149)

7. favorite school subject

8. ages of students' grandparents

✓ CHECK SKILLS

Find the mean, median, and mode for each set of data. (pages 140–143)

9. 24, 14, 11, 11, 15

10. 14, 29, 36, 18, 14, 14, 36

Choose the more reasonable scale for the set of data. (pages 144–145)

11.

AREAS OF STATES	
State	Area (rounded to nearest 10,000 sq mi)
Florida	60,000
Kansas	80,000
Maine	30,000
Oregon	100,000

a.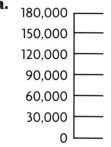

b.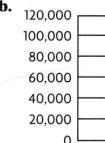

✓ CHECK PROBLEM SOLVING

Solve. (pages 150–151)

CHOOSE A STRATEGY

• Make a Graph   • Make a Table   • Guess and Check   • Write a Number Sentence

12. In April Carrie spent $100. In May she spent $120. In June she spent $80, and in July she spent $60. Between which two months did her spending change the most?

13. Miguel and his father are taking a bicycle trip. Each day, they ride 14 miles. How many miles will they ride in 14 days? How many days must they ride to complete a 294-mile trip?

CIRCLE, BAR, AND LINE GRAPHS

DID YOU KNOW...

The average person eats 60 slices of pizza a year. The most popular topping is pepperoni. The least popular topping is anchovies.

Picture Your Favorites

Your group is going to conduct its own market survey. You can ask your classmates to name their favorite pizza topping, ice-cream flavor, sport, or whatever else you can think of.

YOU WILL NEED: paper and pencil, copies of class list, 1-inch grid paper, markers or crayons, scissors, tape, ruler, posterboard

Work with a group. Your job is to

- decide on a survey topic. Each group should choose a different topic.

- make a survey with five choices, including *other*. Survey your classmates.

- color a 1-inch square for each response.

- tape or paste the squares into one long strip that you will form into a circle graph.

DID YOU

- [✓] make a survey with five choices, including *other*?

- [✓] survey everyone in your class?

- [✓] make a circle graph and label each section?

Favorite Sport to Play

28 people surveyed

football	6
soccer	12
baseball or softball	9
other	1

Cut out the strips and tape them together

Tape the strip to a circle base and color the sections

Kids who like football $\frac{6}{28}$

Kids who like other $\frac{1}{28}$

Kids who prefer soccer $\frac{12}{28}$

Kids who like baseball or softball $\frac{9}{28}$

Reading Circle Graphs

You will learn to read and interpret circle graphs.

Why learn this? You can compare data that represent parts of a whole, such as the cost of a field trip.

Miss Vier's class is taking a field trip to a museum. Of the $600 collected for the trip, $300 is for the bus, $100 is for food, and $200 is for tickets to the museum. A **circle graph** shows data as parts of a whole circle.

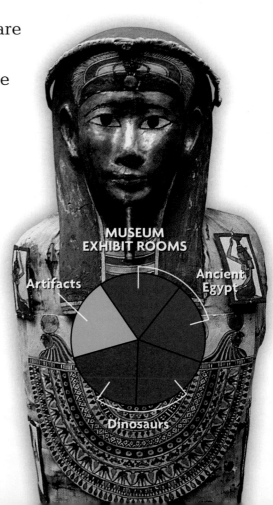

Driving to the museum

$600 COLLECTED FOR MUSEUM TRIP

$300 Bus

$100 Food

$200 Tickets

Notice that

⇨ the circle represents the whole. In this circle graph, the whole is the total amount of money collected, or $600.

⇨ one-half of the money, or $300, is for the bus.

⇨ one-sixth of the money, or $100, is for food, and two-sixths of the money, or $200, is for tickets.

Talk About It

• How does the circle graph show how the parts are related to one another?

• How would the graph change if $300 was for the bus, $300 was for tickets, and no money was collected for food?

Check Your Understanding

CRITICAL THINKING

For Problems 1–4, use the circle graph.

1. What does the whole circle represent?

2. How are the parts in the graph related to one another?

3. What fraction of the exhibit rooms are for dinosaurs? for ancient Egypt? for artifacts?

4. How would the graph change if 4 exhibit rooms were for dinosaurs and 1 was for artifacts?

MUSEUM EXHIBIT ROOMS

Artifacts

Ancient Egypt

Dinosaurs

PRACTICE

For Problems 5–7, use the circle graph.

5. What does the whole circle represent?

6. What fraction of the time Paul spent on the Internet was spent finding sports scores?

7. How many minutes did Paul spend playing games and sending e-mail?

Describe how the circle graph above would change for the data.

8. Paul spends 30 minutes playing games and 30 minutes sending e-mail.

9. Paul spends 20 minutes playing games, 20 minutes sending e-mail, and 20 minutes finding sports scores.

Mixed Applications

For Problems 11–12, use the circle graph.

10. Lucinda practiced the trumpet from 3:30 to 4:10. That night she practiced from 7:45 to 8:25. How many minutes in all did Lucinda spend practicing?

11. What fraction of the music played in band class is review? warm-up? new songs?

12. ✍ **WRITE ABOUT IT** How would the graph change if no time was spent on review, the same amount of time was spent on warm-up, and the rest of the time was spent on new songs?

Mixed Review

Find the mean, median, and mode for each set of data. (pages 142–143)

13. 5, 8, 5, 13, 14   **14.** 25, 45, 50, 45, 30   **15.** 106, 124, 116, 110, 124

16. 22, 31, 22, 32, 43   **17.** 19, 20, 16, 16, 22, 16, 10   **18.** 30, 25, 29, 31, 20, 25, 22

Make a line graph for each set of data. (pages 146–147)

19.

INCHES OF SNOWFALL			
Month	Nov	Dec	Jan	Feb
Inches	2	3	5	2

20.

LINDA'S SUMMER EARNINGS		
Month	Jun	Jul	Aug
Amount	$25	$45	$30

Making Circle Graphs

You will investigate making circle graphs.

Why learn this? You can make circle graphs to show data that you collect.

A circle graph can display data that are parts of a whole.

Explore

Fraction-circle pieces can be put together to show a whole circle. Use fraction-circle pieces to make a circle graph for the data in the table below.

MATERIALS: fraction-circle pieces, markers or crayons

32 COMMUNITY-SERVICE CLUB PROJECTS		
Project	Number	Fraction of All Projects
Cleanup	16	$\frac{1}{2}$
Planting	8	$\frac{1}{4}$
Posters	4	$\frac{1}{8}$
Painting	4	$\frac{1}{8}$

Record

Draw the circle graph by tracing each fraction-circle piece. Color each section of the graph a different color. Title the graph and label each section.

TALK ABOUT IT What does the whole circle represent? On what project does the Community-Service Club spend the most time?

Now, investigate using fraction-circle pieces to make another circle graph.

Try This

Use fraction-circle pieces to make a circle graph for the data in this table. Draw the circle graph.

TALK ABOUT IT What does the whole circle represent?

WRITE ABOUT IT Were any trees other than pine, oak, and maple planted on Arbor Day? How do you know?

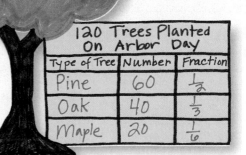

120 Trees Planted On Arbor Day		
Type of Tree	Number	Fraction
Pine	60	$\frac{1}{2}$
Oak	40	$\frac{1}{3}$
Maple	20	$\frac{1}{6}$

Technology **Link**

E-Lab · Activity 10 Available on CD-ROM and the Internet at http://www.hbschool.com/elab

💡 **CRITICAL THINKING** Suppose you make a fruit salad that is $\frac{1}{2}$ cherries, $\frac{1}{3}$ blueberries, and $\frac{1}{4}$ grapes. Can these data be shown in a circle graph? Explain, using fraction-circle pieces.

HANDS-ON PRACTICE

Use fraction-circle pieces to make a circle graph. Then draw the circle graph.

1.

TONY'S 80 CD-ROMS	
Type of CD-ROM	Fraction of All CD-ROMS
40 Games	$\frac{1}{2}$
10 Reference	$\frac{1}{8}$
30 Educational	$\frac{3}{8}$

2.

24 PICTURES JEREMY TOOK AT THE ZOO		
Animals	Number	Fraction of All Pictures
Monkeys	6	$\frac{1}{4}$
Elephants	6	$\frac{1}{4}$
Lions	6	$\frac{1}{4}$
Birds	6	$\frac{1}{4}$

3.

HOW TONY SPENT 10 HOURS AT THE THEME PARK	
Activity	Fraction of Total Time
5 hours: Rides	$\frac{1}{2}$
2 hours: Eating	$\frac{1}{5}$
3 hours: Walking	$\frac{3}{10}$

4.

LAURA'S SUMMER EARNINGS		
How Money Was Used		Fraction of Total Earnings
Savings	$100	$\frac{1}{3}$
New Clothes	$100	$\frac{1}{3}$
Entertainment	$100	$\frac{1}{3}$

Mixed Applications

5. The newspaper staff printed 325 copies of the school newspaper on Monday. They printed 150 copies on Tuesday. There are 3 pages in each newspaper. How many pages in all did they copy?

6. By Friday the newspaper staff had printed 725 newspapers. They divided the newspapers evenly among 25 classes. How many newspapers did each class receive?

7. Nicole needs 16 small triangles and 12 small squares for each large square in her quilt. There are 30 large squares in her quilt. How many small triangles and small squares does Nicole need in all?

8. Brandi earned $130 baby-sitting during the summer. She earned twice as much in August as in June. She earned $40 in July. How much did she earn in June and August?

Decimals in Circle Graphs

You will learn to organize data in circle graphs and interpret the parts as decimals.

Why learn this? You can interpret amounts in circle graphs, such as money, as fractions or decimals.

Since every fraction can be named as a decimal, all circle-graph data can be represented using decimals. Jenna has ten pencils in her desk at school. The ten pencils represent 1 whole in a circle graph. Of the whole, 0.3 are orange pencils, 0.5 are purple pencils, and 0.2 are blue pencils.

MODEL

How can you display these data in a circle graph?

▶ **Step 1**

Use a circle divided into 10 equal parts to represent tenths.

▶ **Step 2**

Shade 0.3 of the parts to represent the orange pencils. Shade 0.5 of the parts to represent the purple pencils. Shade 0.2 of the parts to represent the blue pencils.

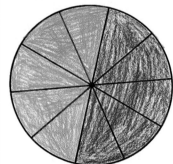

▶ **Step 3**

Label each part. Write a title for the graph.

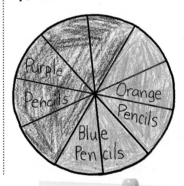

10 PENCILS IN JENNA'S DESK

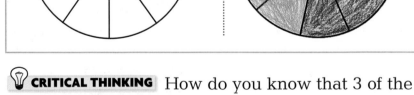

💡 **CRITICAL THINKING** How do you know that 3 of the 10 parts should be shaded to represent the orange pencils in Jenna's desk?

• What is the sum of the decimals that represent the whole, or the 10 pencils in Jenna's desk?

Check Your Understanding 💡 CRITICAL THINKING

For Problem 1, use a circle divided into 10 equal parts.

1. Of the one dollar Mika spent, 0.2 was for an eraser, 0.3 was for a pencil, and 0.5 was for a ruler. How can you display these data?

REMEMBER:

Decimals can be written as fractions.

$0.1 = \frac{1}{10}$

$0.6 = \frac{6}{10}$

Decimals can also be used to express money amounts. There are 10 dimes in $1.00. So, 1 dime is 0.1 of $1.00.

PRACTICE

For Problems 2–4, use the circle graph.

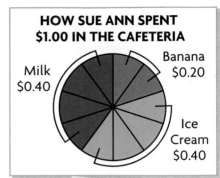

HOW SUE ANN SPENT $1.00 IN THE CAFETERIA

Milk $0.40
Banana $0.20
Ice Cream $0.40

2. Sue Ann spent $1.00 at the school cafeteria. What part of $1.00 did she spend for a banana and ice cream?

3. What fraction represents the part of the $1.00 Sue Ann spent for a banana? milk? ice cream?

4. How would the circle graph change if the banana cost $0.30, the milk cost $0.30, and the ice cream cost $0.40?

Make a circle graph for the data in the table.

5.

$1.00 SPENT AT A GARAGE SALE		
Item	Amount Spent	Decimal Part
baseball cards	$ 0.40	0.4
pen	$ 0.20	0.2
comic book	$ 0.10	0.1
toy	$ 0.30	0.3

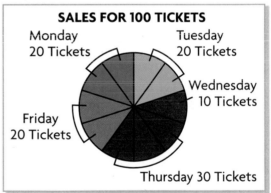

Mixed Applications

For Problems 6–9, use the circle graph.

SALES FOR 100 TICKETS

Monday 20 Tickets
Tuesday 20 Tickets
Wednesday 10 Tickets
Thursday 30 Tickets
Friday 20 Tickets

6. Write a decimal to represent the part of the 100 tickets sold on Wednesday.

7. Write a fraction to represent the part of the 100 tickets sold on Monday.

8. What combination of days represents 0.5, or $\frac{1}{2}$, of the tickets sold?

9. ✏️ **Write a problem** about the circle graph.

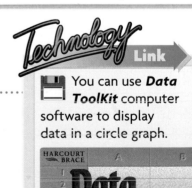

Technology Link

You can use *Data ToolKit* computer software to display data in a circle graph.

Mixed Review

Find the quotient. (pages 118–119)

10. $20)\overline{80}$ **11.** $40)\overline{240}$ **12.** $70)\overline{210}$

13. $50)\overline{250}$ **14.** $80)\overline{320}$ **15.** $90)\overline{270}$

Find the product. (pages 88–89)

16. $14 \times 239 = n$ **17.** $26 \times 391 = n$

18. $32 \times 846 = n$ **19.** $42 \times 284 = n$

Analyzing Graphs

You will learn to analyze graphs.	Why learn this? You can judge whether a graph correctly shows the given data.

When you make a graph, it is important to check your work carefully. Study the graphs below. Does each one correctly show the given data?

Line Graph

KWAN'S ABSENCES DURING ONE SCHOOL YEAR	
Marking Period	Number of Absences
First	4
Second	2
Third	2
Fourth	1

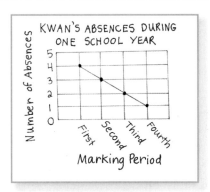

This graph is not correct. Check the plotting of each point.

Bar Graph

FAVORITE MEALS IN CLAUDIA'S CLASS	
Meal	Number of Students
Chicken	6
Ham	3
Hamburgers	6
Turkey	12

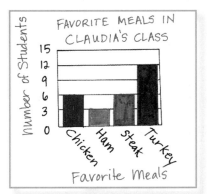

This graph is not correct. Check the labels and the title.

Circle Graph

MONEY JOE SPENT WHILE SHOPPING	
Item Bought	Decimal Part
Sunglasses	0.4
Socks	0.3
Lunch	0.2
Drink	0.1

This graph is not correct. Check how each piece of data is shown.

So, none of these graphs correctly show the given data.

Talk About It

- Why isn't the line graph correct?

- Why isn't the bar graph correct?

- Why isn't the circle graph correct?

PRACTICE

Explain why each graph does not correctly show the data.

1.

GRETA'S CD COLLECTION	
Classical	0.5
Popular	0.1
Musicals	0.1
Country	0.3

2.

GRETA'S CD COLLECTION	
Rock	4 CDs
Musicals	1 CD
Classical	2 CDs
Country	3 CDs

3.

GROWTH OF GRETA'S CD COLLECTION	
Jan	1 CD
Feb	2 CDs
Mar	5 CDs
Apr	10 CDs

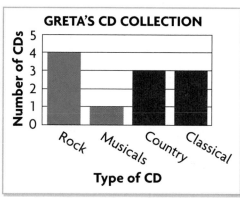

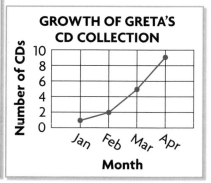

Mixed Applications

For Problems 4–6, use the circle graph.

4. What decimal represents the part of the $100 Andrew spent on a bowling ball?

5. What fraction represents the part of the $100 Andrew spent on lessons?

6. ✏️ **WRITE ABOUT IT** Andrew spends an equal part of his savings on a bowling ball, a bag, lessons, shoes, and a membership fee. Explain how the graph and parts would change.

Mixed Review

Find the product. (pages 74–75)

7. $8 \times 149 = n$
8. $3 \times 298 = n$
9. $5 \times 732 = n$

Find the quotient. (pages 106–107)

10. $237 \div 7 = n$
11. $359 \div 6 = n$
12. $542 \div 4 = n$

13. $192 \div 9 = n$
14. $486 \div 3 = n$
15. $616 \div 5 = n$

You will learn to compare different kinds of graphs.

Why learn this? You can choose the best kind of graph to use for the data you want to display.

Graphs are effective for presenting facts quickly and easily. It is often easier to interpret a graph than it is to read a written description of something.

Compare the 3 kinds of graphs shown below.

Bar graphs are used with data that can be counted. Bar graphs allow you to compare facts about groups.

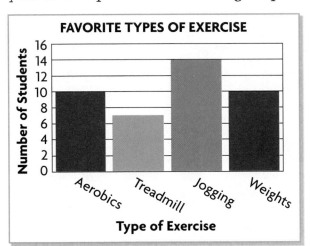

Line graphs are used to show change, or increases and decreases, over a period of time.

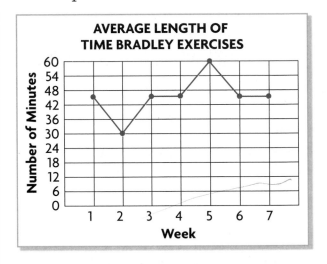

Circle graphs are used to compare parts of a group to the whole group.

Talk About It

- Which kind of graph would you use to compare students' shoe sizes?

- Which kind of graph would you use to show how you spend your time during the day?

- Which kind of graph would you use to keep track of attendance at after-school clubs for one month?

💡 **CRITICAL THINKING** Explain why each graph on this page is good for displaying its given data.

PRACTICE

Choose the best kind of graph to display the data. Explain your choice.

1. how you spend your allowance each week

2. high temperature each day for a month in your city

3. how you spend the hours in the day

4. the number of types of sports cards that you have

5.

STUDENTS PARTICIPATING IN MATH TOURNAMENT	
Class	Number of Students
Ms. Tucker	16
Mr. Rice	14
Ms. Lee	9
Ms. King	12

6.

CHANGES IN COOKIE SALES	
Week 1	$175
Week 2	$150
Week 3	$135
Week 4	$140

7.

HOW ADAM SPENT $10.00		
Item	Amount	Decimal Part
Lunch	$3.00	0.3
Movies	$4.00	0.4
Popcorn	$1.00	0.1
Drink	$2.00	0.2

8.

ALANA'S DANCE CLASSES EACH WEEK	
Type of Class	Number of Classes
Modern	2
Ballet	3
Jazz	2
Tap	1

Mixed Applications

For Problems 9–11 and 15, use the table.

9. What kind of graph would best display these data? Explain.

10. How many more miles did the Morgan family drive than the Carter family?

11. List the families in order from the one who drove the greatest number of miles in June to the one who drove the least number of miles.

MILES DRIVEN IN JUNE	
Family	Miles
Carter	1,850
Watson	1,865
Price	1,875
Morgan	1,890

12. Leona rounds a number to the nearest hundred thousand. She gets 500,000. What is the least possible number that she rounded? the greatest?

13. Mr. Janota's minivan can hold 15 passengers. He drives 75 boys to summer camp. How many trips does he need to make?

14. Denise feeds her dog 3 cups of food each day. How many cups does she feed it in 1 week? in 1 year? (HINT: 1 year = 365 days)

15. ✏ **Write a problem** using the information in the table.

LESSON CONTINUES

PROBLEM-SOLVING STRATEGY
Make a Graph

THE PROBLEM The fifth-grade students started a recycling program. They collected newspaper, glass, aluminum, and plastic. Of the 500 pounds collected, 0.2 is newspaper, 0.5 is glass, 0.2 is aluminum, and 0.1 is plastic. What graph could you make to display these data? What is the greatest part of the items to be recycled?

REMEMBER:
- ☑ Understand
- ☑ Plan
- ☑ Solve
- ☑ Look Back

☑ Understand

- What are you asked to do?

- What information will you use?

- Is there any information you will not use? If so, what?

☑ Plan

- What strategy can you use to solve the problem?

  You can *make a graph* that best shows how the parts are related to the whole.

☑ Solve

- How can you use the strategy to solve the problem?

  Use a circle divided into 10 equal parts to make a circle graph. Shade 2 parts to represent newspaper. Shade 5 parts to represent glass, 2 parts to represent aluminum, and 1 part to represent plastic. Label each shaded portion and title the graph.

  The largest portion of the circle graph is *Glass*. So, glass is the greatest part of the items to be recycled.

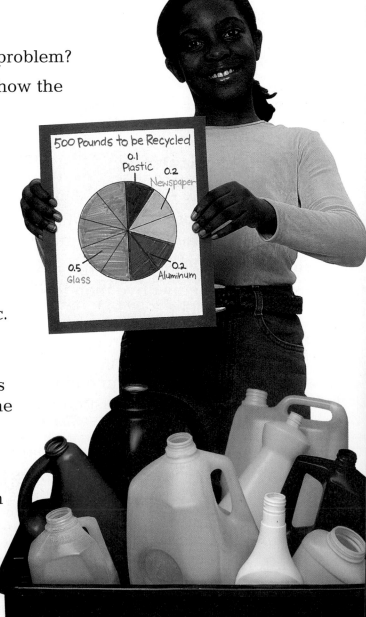

☑ Look Back

- How do you know this is the best graph to display these data?

- What other strategy could you use?

PRACTICE

Choose the best kind of graph to display the data. Then make the graph.

1. Riverside Elementary School collected items to donate to charities. Of the items they donated, 0.4 was food, 0.3 was clothing, 0.2 was toys, and 0.1 was household items. What graph could you use to display these data?

2. The fifth graders are presenting a talent show. In the talent show, 30 students act, another 45 sing, and another 25 dance. What graph could you use to display these data?

3. The Gomez family kept track of how their electric bills changed during a six-month period. They organized the data in a table. What graph could they use to display these data?

GOMEZ FAMILY ELECTRIC BILLS					
Jan	Feb	Mar	Apr	May	Jun
$212	$198	$185	$160	$165	$174

Mixed Applications

Solve.

CHOOSE A STRATEGY

• Guess and Check   • Act It Out   • Make a Graph   • Work Backward   • Draw a Diagram

4. Emily surveyed 50 families to find out ways they save energy. Of the families, 22 said they turn off lights, 9 said they hand wash dishes, 15 said they use ceiling fans, and 4 said they line dry clothes. How many more families turn off lights and use ceiling fans than hand wash dishes and line dry clothes?

5. Ashley's family has a vegetable garden. Of the 32 plants in the garden, $\frac{2}{8}$ are tomatoes and $\frac{2}{8}$ are beans. In the remaining $\frac{1}{2}$ of the garden, there are 4 lettuce plants and 12 squash plants. How does the number of lettuce plants compare with the number of tomato plants?

6. Sam had $4.96 when he returned home from the store. He had bought garden tools for $6.25 and garden plants for $14.79. How much money did he have when he left the house?

7. Bernard began working in his garden at 10:15. He worked for 1 hour and 30 minutes and then took a 45-minute break. He continued to work for 2 hours and 15 minutes. At what time did Bernard finish working?

CULTURAL CONNECTION

Traveling to India

Sanjeev and his parents live next to his grandparents. After school, Sanjeev helps his grandparents. On Thursday, Sanjeev spent $\frac{1}{2}$ hour mowing and edging the lawn, 2 hours doing his homework, and $\frac{1}{2}$ hour doing errands. Make a circle graph showing the way he spent the 3 hours at his grandparents' house. Label the graph.

CULTURAL LINK

The Taj Mahal was built in the seventeenth century as a mark of love by the emperor for his wife. It is one of the world's most beautiful buildings.

Work Together

1. Sanjeev's grandparents traveled to India. They asked Sanjeev to care for their house and birds for eight weeks, and they gave him $80 to spend. Sanjeev bought food and treats for the birds. He bought plants and supplies for the garden with the rest of the money. Make a bar graph to show the amount of money Sanjeev spent during each of the eight weeks.

Week 1	$ 7
Week 2	$12
Week 3	$14
Week 4	$ 8
Week 5	$11
Week 6	$ 7
Week 7	$ 8
Week 8	$13

2. Sanjeev spent $20 on food and treats for the birds, $20 on the garden supplies, and $40 on plants. Draw a circle graph to show how he spent his money.

3. Draw a line graph that shows the amount of time Sanjeev spent at his grandparents' house the first week they were gone: Sunday, 20 minutes; Monday, 40 minutes; Tuesday, 1 hour; Wednesday, 30 minutes; Thursday, 50 minutes; Friday, 90 minutes; Saturday, 70 minutes.

4. Sanjeev's grandparents brought him pictures of places they had visited. He received 5 pictures of the Ganges River, 12 pictures of the Taj Mahal, 3 pictures of a Hindu temple, 4 pictures of dancers, and 2 pictures of cattle decorated for the holidays. Make a graph to show the types of pictures Sanjeev received. Draw and label the graph.

✓ CHECK UNDERSTANDING

1. **VOCABULARY** A _?_ shows data as parts of a whole circle. (page 156)

For Problems 2–4, use the circle graph. (pages 156–157, 160–161)

5 HOURS OF TELEVISION WATCHED
1 hr News
2 hr Shows
2 hr Movies

2. What does the whole circle represent?

3. What fraction of the time is spent watching movies?

4. How would the graph change if 2 hours was spent watching news, 3 hours was spent watching movies, and no time was spent watching shows?

✓ CHECK SKILLS

Make a circle graph for the data in the table. (pages 160–161)

5.

FAVORITE PETS OF 10 STUDENTS	
Cat	4 students
Dog	4 students
Gerbil	1 student
Fish	1 student

6.

BARB'S 10 HOURS AT WORK	
Return messages	1 hr
Work on projects	6 hr
Lunch	1 hr
Meet with clients	2 hr

Choose the best kind of graph to display the data. Explain your choice. (pages 164–165)

7. store earnings during a month

8. flavors of doughnuts in a dozen

9. number of pull-ups done in 1 minute

✓ CHECK PROBLEM SOLVING

Solve. (pages 166–167)

CHOOSE A STRATEGY

• Work Backward   • Guess and Check   • Make a Graph   • Draw a Diagram

10. Pizza Land made 100 pizzas. Of the pizzas, 60 had onions, 30 were plain, and 10 had meat. How does the part of the pizzas that had onions compare with the part of the pizzas that were plain?

11. Todd needs $100 to buy skates. He earned $5.25 an hour cleaning houses, and worked 16 hours. How much money did Todd earn? How much more money does he need to buy the skates?

DID YOU KNOW...

Some games, like chess and Go, depend on strategy. Other games depend on luck.

A Go Gameboard

A Fair Chance of Winning?

If you like to play games, you know that sometimes winning depends on luck and sometimes it depends on skills and strategies. Try a game of Odd-Even to see if it is fair. Then work with a partner to design a game that depends on luck.

YOU WILL NEED: paper and pencil; markers; supplies for your game, such as spinners, coins, dominoes, or number cubes

Work with a partner. Your job is to

- play Odd-Even and make a chart showing who wins for 20 rounds.

- decide if Odd-Even is a fair game and why.

- design your own fair game.

- play several times to test if the game is fair.

- change the game rules to make the game unfair.

- play several times to test if the game is unfair.

ODD-EVEN A GAME FOR TWO PLAYERS

One player is *Odd* and the other is *Even*. They toss the cubes and add the numbers. Since $5+2=7$, and 7 is an odd number, Odd wins this round.

DID YOU

☑ play Odd-Even and decide if it was fair?

☑ design and play your own fair game?

☑ write new rules that make your game unfair?

"The game of **SHOOT** Basketball

When you land on a "SHOOT" space, shake 2 number cubes.

Doubles = a 2-point basket

Double 6 = a 3-point basket

First player to get 10 points wins!

Unfair Rules
1st player gets 3 points for all baskets.
2nd player gets 2 points for all baskets.

171

Certain, Impossible, Likely

You will learn how to decide if events are certain or impossible and how to predict likely events.

Why learn this? You can decide what will happen when you conduct an experiment.

WORD POWER

certain
impossible

Jerome has six tiles numbered 1–6 in a bag. He reaches in and pulls out a tile. Is it certain or impossible that Jerome will pull a one-digit number? a two-digit number?

An event is **certain** if it will always happen. An event is **impossible** if it will never happen.

So, it is *certain* that Jerome will pull a one-digit number. It is *impossible* that Jerome will pull a two-digit number.

- In the example above, what is another event that is certain? impossible?

REMEMBER:

An *event* is something that happens in an experiment that results in an outcome.

EXAMPLES

A. It is certain that December has 31 days.

It is impossible that June has 31 days.

B. It is certain that you live on Earth.

It is impossible that you live on the moon.

C. It is certain that you are a mammal.

It is impossible that you are an amphibian.

Inga has 20 yellow, 5 red, and 3 blue buttons in a bag. She reaches in and pulls out a button. What color button is Inga most likely to pull?

An event that has more chances to happen is more likely to happen. So, Inga is more likely to pull a yellow button.

It is likely that the pointer will land on purple when it is spun.

It is unlikely that the pointer will land on green when it is spun.

CULTURAL LINK

The game Parcheesi® is based on a game developed in India, in the year 600 or earlier. Before each turn, players toss 2 number cubes to determine the total number of spaces to move. What is something certain to happen when you play Parcheesi®?

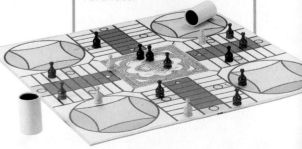

Talk About It

- Why is it likely that the pointer will land on purple when it is spun?

- If the spinner were $\frac{1}{2}$ green and $\frac{1}{2}$ purple, on which color would the pointer be more likely to land?

PRACTICE

Write *certain* or *impossible* for each event.

1. traveling backward in time

2. choosing a day with more than 5 letters from a list of weekdays

3. spinning an odd number on a spinner labeled 1, 3, 5, and 7

4. pulling a red counter from a bag containing only blue counters

5. rolling two cubes numbered 1–6 and getting a sum less than 1

6. pulling a vowel from a bag of tiles labeled **A**, **E**, **I**, **O**, and **U**

Write whether each event is *likely* or *unlikely*.

7. snow falling in July in Texas

8. being tired after running in a race

9. pulling a yellow marble from a bag of nine yellow and two green marbles

10. spinning green on a spinner with one green and eight red sections, all equal sizes

11. tossing a coin 50 times and getting all heads

12. spinning an odd number on a spinner that is numbered 1, 3, 5, 6, 7, and 9

Mixed Applications

13. Susan and her friends were bobbing for apples. Is it certain or likely that Susan will get a red apple?

14. The grocer unpacked 35 boxes of apples. There were 105 apples in each box. How many apples are there in all?

15. ✏ **WRITE ABOUT IT** Make a list of events that are certain, impossible, and likely.

Mixed Review

Find the mean, median, and mode for each set of data. (pages 142–143)

16. 2, 4, 8, 2, 14, 2, 10   **17.** 30, 20, 80, 80, 10   **18.** 109, 115, 115

Find the quotient. (pages 118–119)

19. $80 \div 20 = n$ **20.** $240 \div 30 = n$ **21.** $360 \div 90 = n$ **22.** $350 \div 50 = n$

HANDS ON
COOPERATIVE LEARNING

Probability Experiments

You will investigate and identify possible outcomes.	**Why learn this?** You can predict and record outcomes of a probability experiment.	**WORD POWER** possible outcomes

Melanie conducted an experiment by pulling color tiles from a bag of 4 yellow, 4 blue, 8 red, and 4 green tiles. She made a table of **possible outcomes**, or results that could occur. Included in her table are rows for predicted and actual frequencies.

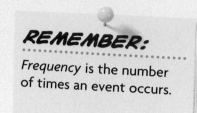

REMEMBER:

Frequency is the number of times an event occurs.

COLOR-TILE EXPERIMENT

Possible Outcomes	Yellow	Blue	Red	Green
Predicted Frequency				
Actual Frequency				

There are four possible outcomes for this experiment:

- pulling a yellow tile
- pulling a blue tile
- pulling a red tile
- pulling a green tile

TALK ABOUT IT Which outcome is most likely to occur? Why?

Explore

MATERIALS: color tiles, bag, marbles

Copy the table above. Predict the number of times each outcome will occur if you pull from the bag 10 times, replacing the tile each time before you pull again. Then test your prediction by pulling from the bag, without looking, 10 times.

Record

Use tally marks to record in your table the results for 10 pulls.

Now, investigate pulling from the bag 50 times.

Technology **Link**

E–Lab • Activity 11 Available on CD-ROM and the Internet at http://www.hbschool.com/elab

Try This

Make a new table like the one on page 174. Predict and then use tally marks to record in your table the results for 50 pulls.

TALK ABOUT IT How did your predictions compare with the results for 10 pulls? for 50 pulls?

▱ **WRITE ABOUT IT** Explain why the outcomes that are most likely to occur may not occur most often when you conduct a probability experiment.

HANDS-ON PRACTICE

For Problems 1–3, use a bag of marbles like the one shown.

1. Make a table of possible outcomes.

2. Predict and record the number of times you think each outcome will occur if you pull 10 times from the bag and replace before you pull again.

3. Pull from the bag 10 times, replacing the marble after each time. Record the results in the table.

Applying What You Learned

For Problems 4–5, use the table.

MARBLE EXPERIMENT			
Outcome	Blue	Green	Red	Yellow
Frequency	ⅢⅢⅢ Ⅱ	Ⅲ	Ⅲ	Ⅱ

4. Why do you think a blue marble was pulled so often?

5. Can you tell from the table how many of each color marble are in the bag? Explain.

Mixed Applications

6. Chris tossed a nickel 10 times. He recorded his outcomes in a table. What are the possible outcomes of this experiment?

7. David has a collection of 174 marbles. He has equal numbers of 6 colors. How many of each color does he have?

8. Samantha is counting the change in her bank. If she had 4 more nickels, she would have $4.00 in nickels. How many nickels does she have?

9. Felicia has a spinner divided into three equal sections. There are red, blue, and green sections. What would be an impossible event to happen?

PART 1 Recording Outcomes in Tree Diagrams

You will learn to make a tree diagram.	**Why learn this?** You can use a tree diagram as an organized list of choices, such as what clothes to wear.	**WORD POWER** tree diagram

Navin needs to choose a pair of pants and a shirt to wear to school. He can choose from blue, black, and tan pants. He can choose from red, white, blue, and green shirts. From how many different color combinations can Navin choose?

How many choices do I have?

You can use a **tree diagram** to show all the possible outcomes of an event.

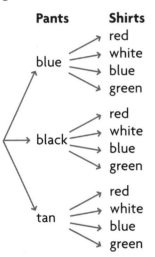

Pants	Shirts	Choices
blue	red	*blue pants with red shirt*
	white	*blue pants with white shirt*
	blue	*blue pants with blue shirt*
	green	*blue pants with green shirt*
black	red	*black pants with red shirt*
	white	*black pants with white shirt*
	blue	*black pants with blue shirt*
	green	*black pants with green shirt*
tan	red	*tan pants with red shirt*
	white	*tan pants with white shirt*
	blue	*tan pants with blue shirt*
	green	*tan pants with green shirt*

So, Navin can choose from 12 color combinations.

Talk About It

• Would the number of choices be different if you listed shirts in the first column and pants in the second? Explain.

• How many choices would Navin have if he could choose from only 3 colors of shirts?

Check Your Understanding 💡 CRITICAL THINKING

Find the number of choices by making a tree diagram.

1. Peanut Butter and Jelly Sandwiches
Peanut Butter: chunky or smooth
Jelly: grape, strawberry, or blackberry

PRACTICE

Copy and complete the tree diagram. Tell the number of choices.

2.

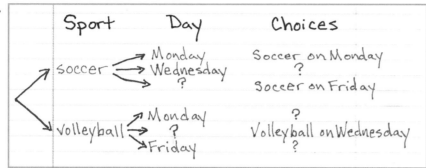

Find the number of choices by making a tree diagram.

3. Summer School Classes
Class: Foreign Language, Computer, Math, or
    Physical Education
Session: first or second

4. Room Decorating Choices
Paint: white, yellow, or blue
Window: curtains or blinds

5. Garden Choices
Type: flower, vegetable, or herb
Location: front yard, back yard, or side yard

6. New Car Choices
Size: compact, midsize, or minivan
Color: white, silver, blue, or green

Mixed Applications

For Problems 8–10, use the table.

7. Dana wants to buy a new camera. She can buy
an instant camera or a 35-mm camera. She can
buy one with or without a zoom lens. List her
choices.

8. Kyle has $25.00. List two combinations of three
accessories he has enough money to buy.

9. Jamie wants to buy one of each camera
accessory. How much will she spend?

10. ✏ **Write a problem** that can be answered by
using the information in the table.

> **Social Studies Link**
>
> A family tree is a tree
> diagram that shows an
> individual's parents,
> grandparents, great-
> grandparents, and so on.
> What does your family
> tree look like?
>
> **GEORGE WASHINGTON'S FAMILY TREE**
>
> Mary Bennett   Joseph Ball   Mildred Warner   Lawrence Washington
>
> Mary Ball   Augustine Washington
>
> George Washington

Camera Accessories

Neck Strap ▸	$ 4.29
Lens Cleaner ▸	$ 3.95
Camera Bag ▸	$14.99
Photo Album ▸	$ 6.99

LESSON
CONTINUES ▸

PART 2 PROBLEM-SOLVING STRATEGY
Make an Organized List

THE PROBLEM Kai is conducting a probability experiment. She will toss one number cube and one coin. The number cube has a different number, from 1 through 6, on each face. The coin has heads on one side and tails on the other. How many possible outcomes are there for this experiment? What are the possible outcomes?

REMEMBER:
- ☑ Understand
- ☑ Plan
- ☑ Solve
- ☑ Look Back

☑ Understand

- What are you asked to do?

- What information will you use?

- Is there any information you will not use? If so, what?

☑ Plan

- What strategy can you use to solve the problem?

  You can *make an organized list* of all the possible outcomes.

☑ Solve

- How can you use the strategy to solve the problem?

  You can make a tree diagram to organize the possible outcomes.

  So, there are 12 possible outcomes for Kai's experiment. The possible outcomes are 1 and heads, 1 and tails, 2 and heads, 2 and tails, 3 and heads, 3 and tails, 4 and heads, 4 and tails, 5 and heads, 5 and tails, 6 and heads, 6 and tails.

☑ Look Back

- How can you determine if your answer is reasonable?

- What other strategy could you use?

PRACTICE

Make an organized list to solve.

1. Diana is conducting a probability experiment with a spinner and a coin. The spinner is divided into 5 equal sections. Each section is labeled with a different number from 1 through 5. How many possible outcomes are there for this experiment? What are they?

2. Lindsey is conducting a probability experiment with a coin and a bag of marbles. There is 1 red, 1 blue, 1 yellow, and 1 green marble in the bag. She will replace the marble after each turn. How many possible outcomes are there for this experiment? What are they?

3. Marshall has 15¢. How many different combinations of coins could he have? What are they?

4. Use the digits 1, 2, and 4. List all the two-digit numbers you can make without repeating any digits in the same number.

Mixed Applications

Solve.

CHOOSE A STRATEGY

• Make an Organized List   • Use a Table   • Guess and Check   • Work Backward   • Act It Out

5. Ms. Arnold averaged her students' math grades for the semester. She organized the data in a table. How many students are in her math class?

Math Grades				
Number of Students	15	10	4	1
Grade Average	A	B	C	below C

6. Nicole has 6 coins that are dimes and quarters. She has a total of $1.05. What combination of coins does she have?

7. Alexandra has $0.30 more than Barbara. Together they have $4.50. How much money does each girl have?

8. Li was home at 5:15. It took him 35 minutes to ride his bike home from the library. He was at the library for 2 hours 10 minutes. It took him 10 minutes to get from school to the library. At what time did Li leave school?

9. Joshua can drink either orange juice or grapefruit juice for breakfast. He can eat either eggs, cereal, or waffles. From how many different breakfast combinations can Joshua choose? What are his choices?

10. There are 12 ounces in each can of orange juice. How many ounces are in a case of 24 cans?

Finding Probability

You will learn to find the probability of an event.

Why learn this? You can use probability to predict what might happen.

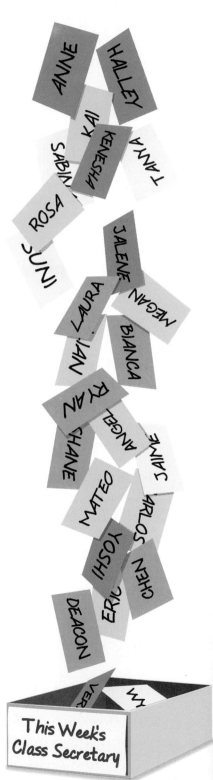

Mr. Arnaud chooses 1 new student each week to be class secretary. He writes each student's name on an index card, places the cards in a bag, and, without looking, pulls 1 name. Halley wants to be class secretary. There are 25 students in Mr. Arnaud's class. What is the probability that Halley's name will be pulled?

Probability is the chance that an event will happen.

$$\text{Probability} = \frac{\text{number of ways the event occurs}}{\text{number of ways all events can occur}} = \frac{1}{25}$$

So, the probability that Halley's name will be pulled is $\frac{1}{25}$.

Each outcome is **equally likely**, or has the same chance of happening. So, the probability of pulling any one student's name is $\frac{1}{25}$.

- What is the probability that a name other than Halley's will be pulled?

The probability of an event occurring can always be expressed as 0, 1, or a fraction between 0 and 1.

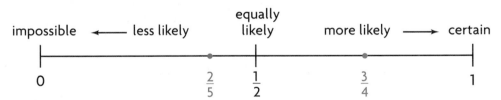

Talk About It

- Which outcome is more likely to occur, that Halley's name will be pulled or that a name other than Halley's will be pulled?

- Which is more likely to occur, an event with a probability of $\frac{2}{5}$ or an event with a probability of $\frac{3}{4}$? Why?

💡 **CRITICAL THINKING** Name two equally likely events, using the picture.

PRACTICE

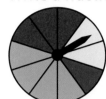

Write a fraction for the probability of pulling each color marble.

1. red   **2.** yellow   **3.** blue   **4.** purple

Write a fraction for the probability of spinning each color.

5. red	**6.** yellow	**7.** green
8. blue	**9.** red or yellow	**10.** orange

Write the probability of spinning yellow.

11.    **12.**    **13.**    **14.**

15. On which of the spinners in Exercises 11–14 is yellow most likely to occur?

16. On which of the spinners in Exercises 11–14 is yellow least likely to occur? Why?

Mixed Applications

17. There are 12 students on Ms. Taylor's basketball team. There are 8 students on Mr. Wang's team. During a game, 5 students on each team play. On which team would you have a better chance of playing?

18. Ben is one of 5 students chosen to read the morning news next week. Each day of the week a different student will have a turn. What is the probability that Ben will read the news on Monday?

19. Angelo now has $4.75. He bought a basketball ticket for $2.50. He bought a drink at the game for $0.75. He left his house with $10.00. How much money did he spend on other items?

20. ✏ **Write a problem** about a spinner with 12 sections and 3 colors.

Mixed Review

Estimate the quotient. (pages 120–121)

21. $17\overline{)163}$ **22.** $58\overline{)305}$ **23.** $27\overline{)219}$ **24.** $49\overline{)389}$ **25.** $76\overline{)560}$

Choose a type of graph or plot. Explain your choice. (pages 148–149)

26. class scores on a quiz

27. a family's bills for 6 months

Comparing Probabilities

You will learn to compare probabilities of separate events.

Why learn this? You can make decisions based on which events are more likely.

Irene and Mohammed are playing a game, using the spinner at the right. Irene earns a point when the pointer lands on red. Mohammed earns a point when the pointer lands on yellow. Which player is more likely to win the game?

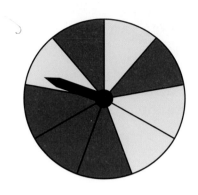

The probability that the pointer will land on red is

$$\frac{\text{number of red sections}}{\text{total number of sections}}, \text{ or } \frac{5}{9}.$$

The probability that the pointer will land on yellow is

$$\frac{\text{number of yellow sections}}{\text{total number of sections}}, \text{ or } \frac{4}{9}.$$

Since $\frac{5}{9} > \frac{4}{9}$, Irene is more likely to win the game.

Talk About It

- Is it certain that Irene will win the game? Explain.

- What is the probability that the pointer will land on blue?

- What is the probability that the pointer will land on either red or yellow?

Technology Link

In **Mighty Math Number Heroes**, the game *Probability* challenges you to predict and compare probabilities.

Check Your Understanding 💡 CRITICAL THINKING

For Problems 1–4, use the spinner. Write each probability as a fraction. Tell which outcome is more likely.

1. The pointer will land on blue; the pointer will land on red.

2. The pointer will land on either blue or green; the pointer will land on either red or yellow.

3. The pointer will land on green; the pointer will land on yellow.

4. The pointer will land on either green or yellow; the pointer will land on either blue or red.

PRACTICE

For Problems 5–10, use the bag of marbles. Write each probability as a fraction. Tell which outcome is more likely.

5. You pull a red marble; you pull a blue marble.

6. You pull a yellow marble; you pull a green marble.

7. You pull either a red or blue marble; you pull either a green or yellow marble.

8. You pull a yellow marble; you pull a purple marble.

9. You pull a marble that is not red; you pull a marble that is not yellow.

10. You pull a marble that is not blue; you pull a marble that is not green.

Mixed Applications

For Problems 11–14, use the table.

11. How many more points in all were scored by Player 1 than by Player 2?

12. Order the scores for Player 2 from the game with the most points to the game with the fewest points.

13. In which game was Player 1's score greater than 1,000 more points than Player 2?

VIDEO GAME SCORES			
Game Number	1	2	3
Player 1	3,076	3,878	2,985
Player 2	2,059	2,880	2,873

14. ✏️ **Write a problem** using the video game scores.

Mixed Review

Divide. Check by multiplying. (pages 126–127)

15. 16)80   16. 12)79   17. 13)97   18. 42)88   19. 32)66

20. 21)531   21. 19)610   22. 39)822   23. 18)757   24. 41)965

Find the product. (pages 88–89)

25. 262	26. 295	27. 173	28. 382	29. 203
× 32	× 45	× 13	× 15	× 14

30. 426	31. 361	32. 522	33. 287	34. 621
× 32	× 23	× 19	× 25	× 16

MATH FUN!

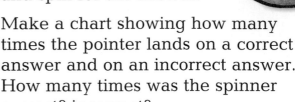

Yes or No?

PURPOSE To record outcomes of a probability experiment

YOU WILL NEED spinner, markers

In this game, you ask questions that can be answered by *yes* or *no*. Write ten questions and their answers. Five should have yes as the answer and five should have no. Make a spinner on which yes and no are equally likely.

Ask one of your questions and spin for the answer.

Make a chart showing how many times the pointer lands on a correct answer and on an incorrect answer. How many times was the spinner correct? incorrect?

Make a new spinner on which *yes* is more likely than *no*, and play again.

Disk Jockey

PURPOSE To make a tree diagram

YOU WILL NEED paper and pencil

Imagine that you are a disk jockey who can play five songs in a row.

You can play each song on CD or cassette. How many combinations can you make? Choose your five songs. Make a tree diagram showing the combinations.

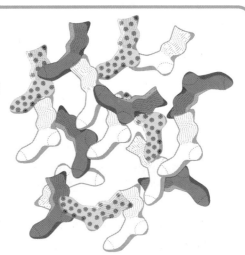

MOMI'S WILD SOCKS

PURPOSE To make an organized list

YOU WILL NEED paper and pencil

Momi has a wild-sock collection. This morning she wanted to pick out a pair of socks to wear to school. Keeping her eyes closed, she picked out 4 socks and said, "I know I have a matching pair." Is she right?

Use the picture. Make an organized list showing all the possible combinations of 4 socks that Momi could have picked out.

 Try this with three different-colored pairs of socks at home.

✓ CHECK UNDERSTANDING

VOCABULARY

1. An event is ? if it will always happen. (page 172)

2. An event is ? if it will never happen. (page 172)

3. ? are results that can occur in an experiment. (page 174)

4. ? is the chance that an event will happen. (page 180)

5. You can use a ? to show all the possible outcomes of an event. (page 176)

6. Events that are ? have the same chance of happening. (page 180)

Write *certain* or *impossible* for each event. (pages 172–173)

7. You are either a boy or a girl.

8. A dog gives birth to kittens.

Write whether each event is *likely* or *unlikely*. (pages 172–173)

9. winning a million dollars

10. having a sunny day in Florida

✓ CHECK SKILLS

Find the number of choices by making a tree diagram. (pages 176–177)

11. **Pizza Choices**
   Crust: stuffed or plain
   Toppings: cheese, meat, veggie, or combo

Write each probability as a fraction. Tell which outcome is more likely. (pages 180–183)

12. You pull a yellow cube; you pull a green cube.

13. You pull a green cube; you pull a blue cube.

✓ CHECK PROBLEM SOLVING

Solve. (pages 178–179)

CHOOSE A STRATEGY
• Make an Organized List   • Guess and Check   • Work Backward   • Act It Out

14. Regina is writing a letter. She can write on white, beige, or gray paper. She can use red, blue, or black ink. How many choices does Regina have? What are they?

15. Desmond has 18 more baseball cards than Monty. Together they have 100 baseball cards. How many baseball cards does each boy have?

VOCABULARY CHECK

Choose a term from the box to complete each sentence.

1. The middle number in an ordered series of numbers is called the __?__. (page 141)

2. One number that represents all the numbers in a set of data is that set's __?__, or average. (page 142)

3. The distance between the numbers on the scale of a graph is called the __?__. (page 144)

4. Results that could occur in an experiment are called __?__. (page 174)

5. The chance that an event will happen is that event's __?__. (page 180)

STUDY AND SOLVE

CHAPTER 9

EXAMPLE

Find the mean of the set of data.

75, 82, 85, 90   Add the numbers.
The sum is 332.   Divide this sum by
332 ÷ 4 = 83   the number of data
The mean is 83.   in the set.

Find the mean, median, mode, and range for the set of data. (pages 140–143, 146)

6. 34, 24, 21, 21, 25

7. 19, 26, 8, 4, 4, 20, 10

On a line-graph scale, what is the best interval for each set of data? (pages 144–145)

a. 2	b. 10	c. 25	d. 5

8. 50, 25, 100, 75

9. 8, 12, 6, 10, 16

Choose a graph or plot to display the set of data. Explain your choice. (pages 148–149)

10. ages of your classmates' parents

11. temperatures in several cities

Choose a graph or plot to display the data. Explain your choice. Solve. (pages 150–151)

12. Gas prices per gallon were $1.19 in May, $1.24 in June, $1.25 in July, and $1.27 in August. Tell what happened to the price of gas during these months.

13. Nadia surveyed the fifth grade to find out what food to have at the school dance. Of the students, 75 said pizza, 30 said chicken, and 45 said hamburgers. How many more students said pizza than hamburgers?

CHAPTER 10

EXAMPLE

Use the circle graph to answer the question.

What does the whole circle represent?

PAT'S ACTIVITIES FOR
6 HOURS ON SATURDAY

1 hr Watching TV
2 hr Cleaning Garage
1 hr Reading
2 hr Soccer Practice

Study the graph and read its title.

The graph shows Pat's activities for 6 hours on Saturday.

For Problems 14–16, use the circle graph above. (pages 156–157)

14. What fraction of her time did Pat spend at soccer practice?

15. Compare the amount of time Pat spent playing soccer to the time she spent reading.

16. How would the graph look if Pat spent 2 hours reading and did not watch TV?

Make a circle graph for the data in the table. (pages 160–161)

17.

$10 SPENT AT THE FAIR	
Rides	$4
Food	$3
Souvenirs	$2
Games	$1

Explain why the circle graph is not accurate. (pages 162–163)

18.

FAVORITE SUBJECTS OF 10 STUDENTS		
Subject	Number of Students	Decimal Part
Math	5	0.5
Science	3	0.3
History	2	0.2

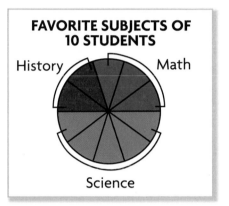

FAVORITE SUBJECTS OF
10 STUDENTS

History   Math

Science

CHAPTER 11

EXAMPLE

Use the spinner.
Write the probability
as a fraction.

You will spin yellow.

Only 1 of 10 ten sections is yellow.

The probability is $\frac{1}{10}$.

Use the spinner above. Write each probability as a fraction. Tell which outcome is more likely. (pages 180–183)

19. You spin green; you spin blue.

Make an organized list to solve.
(pages 178–179)

20. Yasmin has green and blue shoes. She has red, pink, and orange socks. How many combinations of shoes and socks can she make?

✏ WRITE ABOUT IT

1. Use connecting cubes to help you find the mean for this set of data: 3, 8, 4, 5, 5. Explain each step. (pages 142–143)

2. Explain why the graph is not accurate and how you would change the graph to make it accurate. (pages 162–163)

3. Explain each step as you make a tree diagram to show the number of different color combinations Megan has if she can choose from blue, brown, and green shorts and from white, yellow, red, and black tops. (pages 176–177)

Beth's Trophy Collection	
Soccer	4
Softball	2
Basketball	1
Swimming	3

BETH'S TROPHY COLLECTION

✔ PERFORMANCE ASSESSMENT

Solve. Explain your method.

CHOOSE A STRATEGY

• **Make an Organized List** • **Make a Model** • **Make a Graph** • **Write a Number Sentence**

4. Walter surveyed 50 boys and 50 girls to find out their favorite sports. He organized his data in the table. How can you display Walter's data? Explain. (pages 150–151)

FAVORITE SPORTS OF BOYS AND GIRLS			
	Basketball	Gymnastics	Soccer
Boys	25	10	15
Girls	10	25	15

5. Claudia surveyed 40 students about their favorite types of music. Twenty students chose rock music, 10 chose country, 5 chose jazz, and 5 chose classical. What fraction chose country? Make a graph that displays the results of the survey. (pages 166–167)

6. Ruth wants to buy a drink from a vending machine for $0.55. The machine accepts exact change only (no pennies). How many different combinations of coins could she use to buy her drink? (pages 178–179)

CUMULATIVE REVIEW

Solve the problem. Then write the letter of the correct answer.

1. Which is another name for twenty and five hundredths?

  A. 20.005   **B.** 20.05
  C. 20.5   **D.** 20,500

(pages 34–39)

2. $\begin{array}{r} 563 \\ \times\ 72 \end{array}$
  A. 1,126
  B. 4,536
  C. 39,410
  D. 40,536

(pages 88–89)

3. Estimate the quotient. (pages 104–107)

$9\overline{)449}$ $\overset{5}{}$

  A. 45   **B.** 49 r8
  C. 50   **D.** 60

4. $6{,}000 \div 50 = n$

  A. $n = 12$ **B.** $n = 100$ r10
  C. $n = 120$ **D.** $n = 300{,}000$

(pages 118–119)

5. Find the mean. (pages 142–143)

44, 34, 31, 31, 35

  A. 13   **B.** 31
  C. 34   **D.** 35

For Problems 6–7, use the circle graph.

(pages 156–157)

$8 SPENT AT FAIR
$4 Books
$2 Posters
$2 Supplies

6. What fraction of the money was spent on books?

  A. $\dfrac{1}{8}$ **B.** $\dfrac{2}{8}$, or $\dfrac{1}{4}$

  C. $\dfrac{2}{4}$, or $\dfrac{1}{2}$ **D.** 4

(pages 156–157)

7. What does each $\frac{1}{4}$ of the graph represent?

  A. $1 spent   **B.** $2 spent
  C. $4 spent   **D.** $8 spent

(pages 156–157)

For Problems 8–10, use the spinner.

(pages 172–173, 180–183)

8. What is the probability of spinning 6?

  A. $\dfrac{1}{10}$ **B.** $\dfrac{2}{10}$, or $\dfrac{1}{5}$

  C. $\dfrac{5}{10}$, or $\dfrac{1}{2}$ **D.** $\dfrac{6}{10}$, or $\dfrac{3}{5}$

9. It is _?_ that you will spin an even number.

  A. certain   **B.** impossible
  C. likely   **D.** unlikely

(pages 172–173)

10. The probability of spinning 4 is _?_ the probability of spinning 5.

  A. equal to
  B. more likely than
  C. less likely than
  D. impossible, and so is

(pages 182–183)

MULTIPLYING DECIMALS

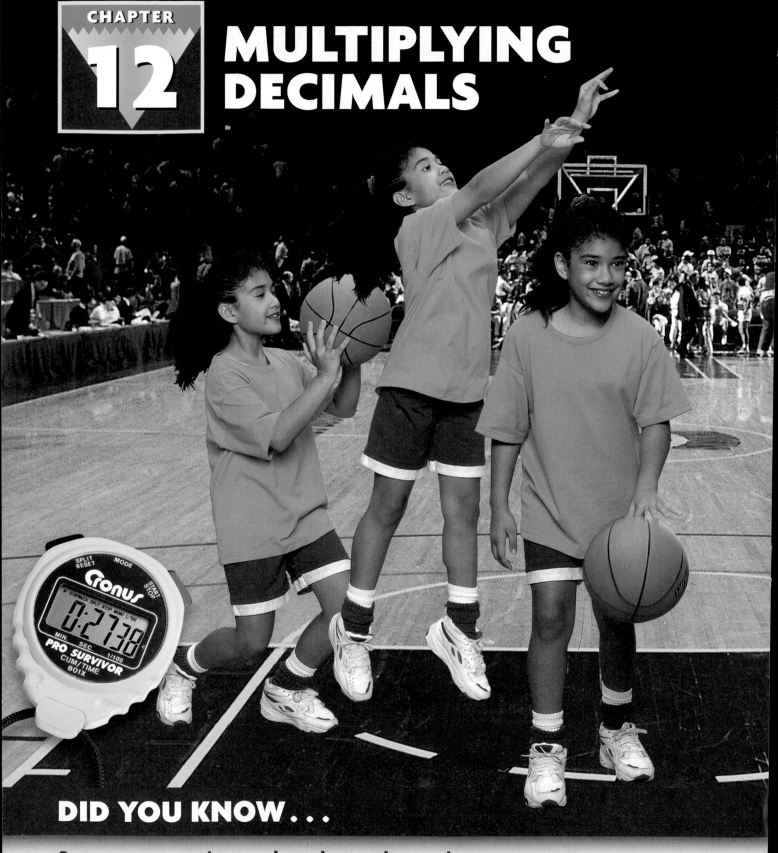

DID YOU KNOW...

Some sports equipment has changed over the years. Basketball was invented in 1891. Players shot the ball into a closed-bottom peach basket, which gave the new sport its name.

A Matter of Dollars and Sense

Suppose your fifth-grade class has been given $100 to buy new sports equipment, such as basketballs, a stopwatch, and badminton sets.

Work together to plan a budget. Make a chart showing your budget. Tell how you decided what your class should buy.

Work with a group. Your job is to

- list the sports your class likes to play.
- list the equipment needed for each.
- decide how many of each item you need and the total cost.
- choose the equipment your group recommends based on the budget of $100.

DID YOU

☑ list your class's favorite sports?

☑ decide what equipment and how many of each item your class needs?

☑ find the total cost of the purchases?

☑ make choices based on the budget limit of $100?

SPORT	VOTES
basketball	~~卌~~ 卌 II
baseball	卌 III
badminton	III
soccer	卌 I
hockey	IIII

Budget

Qty	Item	Total Cost
3	basketballs	$44.88
2	basketball nets	$ 3.90
2	baseballs	$ 7.88
3	baseball bats	$
4	badminton sets	$
6	birdies	$
3	soccer balls	$
2	goal nets	$
2	safety pad sets	$
	hockey sticks	$
	hockey pucks	$
	stopwatch	$

Multiplying Decimals and Whole Numbers

You will investigate how the factors and the product are related when you multiply a decimal and a whole number.

Why learn this? You can find the total cost when buying several items or when keeping score at a sports event.

Explore

Make models that show how to multiply 2 × 0.9 and 2 × 0.09.

MATERIALS: tenths and hundredths decimal models, markers, scissors, and tape or paste

Pencils
$0.90 each

MODEL

What is 2 × 0.9?

▶ **Step 1**
Shade 0.9 of each of the two models.

▶ **Step 2**
Combine the shaded areas of the two models.

REMEMBER:

This model represents a whole divided into tenths. Each part is $\frac{1}{10}$, or 0.1.

This model represents a whole divided into hundredths. Each part is $\frac{1}{100}$, or 0.01.

Record

Tape or paste your models to a piece of paper. Record a multiplication number sentence for each of your models.

Now investigate how the product of a whole number and a decimal is related to the whole number factor.

Try This

Make models to show the products of 2 × 0.3 and 2 × 0.30; 3 × 0.5 and 3 × 0.50. Record number sentences for each of your models.

E–Lab • Activity 12 Available on CD-ROM and the Internet at http://www.hbschool.com/elab

HANDS-ON

TALK ABOUT IT Look at your models and products. How does the product of a decimal less than one and a whole number relate to the whole number factor?

📝 **WRITE ABOUT IT** Explain how to draw a model to find the product 6 × 0.35.

PRACTICE

Make a model to find each product.

1. $2 \times 0.7 = n$ **2.** $3 \times 0.5 = n$ **3.** $4 \times 0.26 = n$

Applying What You Learned

Marcia is shopping at the school store. For Problems 4–9, use the picture.

4. 3 pencils, 1 eraser

5. 2 erasers, 2 pens

6. 3 notebooks

7. 1 pencil, 4 erasers, 2 rulers

8. 8 erasers, 2 notebooks, 3 pencils

9. 3 pens, 1 notebook

Mixed Applications

For Problems 10–11, use the picture.

10. Laura is shopping at the school store. Which is more—3 pens, or 2 pens and a notebook? 3 rulers, or 2 notebooks and a pen?

11. Nat spent $2.48 to buy four items from the school store. Which items did he buy?

12. Jason is ordering a cheese pizza for $9.99. Additional toppings cost $0.55 each. If he wants 3 extra toppings on the pizza, how much will he pay for the order?

13. Carol has $0.75. She has 5 coins. What are the coins?

14. Suppose Babs wants to buy 3 pens for $0.90 each. She has $3.00. Does she have enough to make the purchase? Explain.

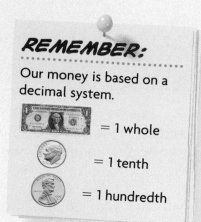

Erasers $0.25 each

Notebooks $0.99 each

Pens $0.90 each

Pencils $0.20 each

Rulers $0.85 each

Consumer Link

When you buy more than one item, you multiply a decimal times a whole number.

If these notebooks cost $2.94, what decimal and what whole number were multiplied to get the total amount owed?

Patterns in Decimal Factors and Products

You will learn that multiplying a whole number by another whole number, a tenth, or a hundredth shows a pattern.

Why learn this? You can figure out how dollars relate to dimes and pennies.

Another way to find products is to look for patterns.

MODEL

What happens when you multiply 2 by 1, by 1 tenth, and by 1 hundredth?

Ones	Tenths	Hundredths	Record
			$2 \times 1 = 2$
			$2 \times 0.1 = 0.2$
			$2 \times 0.01 = 0.02$

Talk About It

- What happens to the size of the block as you multiply by ones, by tenths, and by hundredths?

- What pattern do you notice in the placement of the decimal point and the number of zeros in the products?

You can use mental math to find patterns in products. Look for patterns in the placement of the decimal point.

$10 \times 1 = 10$	$20 \times 1 = 20$	$1 \times 25 = 25$
$10 \times 0.1 = 1.0$	$20 \times 0.1 = 2.0$	$0.1 \times 25 = 2.5$
$10 \times 0.01 = 0.10$	$20 \times 0.01 = 0.20$	$0.01 \times 25 = 0.25$

💡 **CRITICAL THINKING** How can you use the pattern to place the decimal point in the product?

> **Science Link**
>
> Numerous patterns can be found in nature. The chambered nautilus, for example, has a pattern that decreases in size. How is that pattern similar to the pattern shown in the model?

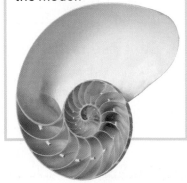

PRACTICE

Record the decimal multiplication sentences for each.

1.

Ones	Tenths	Hundredths
(3 flats)		
	(3 rods/flats)	
		(3 units)

Draw models to find each product.

2. $1 \times 5 = n$
$0.1 \times 5 = n$
$0.01 \times 5 = n$

3. $2 \times 3 = n$
$2 \times 0.3 = n$
$2 \times 0.03 = n$

4. $4 \times 2 = n$
$4 \times 0.2 = n$
$4 \times 0.02 = n$

5. $3 \times 3 = n$
$3 \times 0.3 = n$
$3 \times 0.03 = n$

Use mental math to complete the pattern.

6. $1 \times 8 = 8$
$0.1 \times 8 = 0.8$
$0.01 \times 8 = n$

7. $1 \times 40 = 40$
$0.1 \times 40 = n$
$0.01 \times 40 = 0.4$

8. $1 \times 85 = 85$
$0.1 \times 85 = n$
$0.01 \times 85 = n$

9. $18 \times 1 = 18$
$18 \times 0.1 = n$
$18 \times 0.01 = n$

10. $19 \times 1 = n$
$19 \times 0.1 = n$
$19 \times 0.01 = n$

11. $50 \times 1 = n$
$50 \times 0.1 = n$
$50 \times 0.01 = n$

12. $102 \times 1 = n$
$102 \times 0.1 = n$
$102 \times 0.01 = n$

13. $210 \times 1 = n$
$210 \times 0.1 = n$
$210 \times 0.01 = n$

Mixed Applications

14. A penny is 0.01 of a dollar. How much is a roll of 50 pennies? two rolls of 50 pennies?

15. A dime is 0.10 and a nickel is 0.05 of a dollar. How much is a roll of 50 dimes? a roll of 40 nickels?

Mixed Review

Write $<$, $>$, or $=$ for each ●. (pages 42–43)

16. 5.00 ● 5.05   **17.** 0.07 ● 0.007   **18.** 6.72 ● 6.27   **19.** 1.20 ● 1.2

Find the sum. (pages 50–51)

20. 2.3
    +3.2

21. 1.7
    +8.9

22. 2.14
    +3.95

23. 8.934
    +1.885

24. 0.795
    +4.073

MORE PRACTICE Student Handbook page H92

PART 1 Multiplying a Decimal by a Decimal

You will learn to use a decimal model to find a decimal product.

Why learn this? You can understand what a part of a part really is.

Suppose you baked a pan of brownies. You give 0.5 of the brownies to your grandparents and save 0.5 for you and your own family. If you eat 0.5 of the saved brownies, how much is left for your family?

MODEL

What is 0.5 of 0.5?

▶ **Step 1**

Divide the square into 10 equal columns. Shade **5 of the columns, or 0.5.**

▶ **Step 2**

Divide the square into 10 equal rows, or 100 equal parts. Shade **5 of the rows, or 0.5.**

▶ **Step 3**

The area in which the shading overlaps shows the product, or 0.5 of 0.5.

Record: **0.5 × 0.5 = 0.25**, or 25 hundredths.

So, 0.25, or $\frac{1}{4}$ of the brownies, are left for your family.

Check Your Understanding 💡 CRITICAL THINKING

1. Jill and Jon made models to show 0.6 × 0.8. How are their models different? How are they alike?

2. Make a table like the one below. Make up three other decimal multiplication problems with factors less than 1.

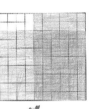

Jill's work   **Jon's work**

factors less than 1	Product	Is the product less than 1?	Is the product less than each factor?
0.6×0.8	0.48	yes	yes

3. What relationship between the decimal factors and the products do you see?

PRACTICE

Complete the multiplication number sentence for each drawing.

4.

$0.5 \times 0.7 = n$

5.

$n \times 0.9 = 0.18$

6.

$n \times 0.8 = 0.24$

7.

$0.2 \times n = 0.10$

Multiply. Write each product.

8. $0.7 \times 0.2 = n$ **9.** $0.8 \times 0.8 = n$ **10.** $0.9 \times 0.5 = n$

11. $0.6 \times 0.7 = n$ **12.** $0.5 \times 0.8 = n$ **13.** $0.3 \times 0.9 = n$

14. $0.1 \times 0.3 = n$ **15.** $0.4 \times 0.6 = n$ **16.** $0.6 \times 0.5 = n$

17. $0.4 \times 0.8 = n$ **18.** $0.9 \times 0.8 = n$ **19.** $0.8 \times 0.7 = n$

20. ✏️ **WRITE ABOUT IT** When you multiply tenths times tenths, why does the model show the product as hundredths?

Mixed Applications

21. Suppose you order a ten-slice pizza. You want 0.5 of the pizza with olives and 0.5 with mushrooms. If you want 0.8 of the mushroom part to include pepperoni, what part of the pizza has pepperoni and mushrooms?

22. Suppose you may eat 0.4 of the 0.5 brownies that are left. How much can you eat?

23. Teresa earns $18.75 each day at her job. How much does she earn in 10 days?

24. Mrs. Sander's new car can travel 34.6 miles for each gallon of gas used. How far can she travel on 9 gallons of gas?

25. Felipe likes to collect postcards. He pays $1.00 for each set of 4 postcards and $0.30 for each additional postcard. How much will Felipe pay for 15 postcards?

LESSON CONTINUES

PART 2 PROBLEM-SOLVING STRATEGY
Make a Model

THE PROBLEM Suppose you cut a pan of brownies into ten equal pieces to share with 4 of your friends. You put chocolate icing on 0.5, or $\frac{1}{2}$, of the brownies. You put pecans on 0.2 of the iced brownies. What part of the brownies have icing and pecans on them?

REMEMBER:
- ☑ Understand
- ☑ Plan
- ☑ Solve
- ☑ Look Back

☑ Understand

- What are you asked to find?
- What information did you use?
- Was there information you did not use? If so, what?

☑ Plan

- What strategy can you use to solve the problem?

  You can *make a model* to find the part of the brownies that has icing and pecans on them.

☑ Solve

- How can you solve the problem?

  You can make a model to find 0.2×0.5.

- Shade 0.5 ($\frac{5}{10}$), or $\frac{1}{2}$, of the columns.
- Then shade 0.2 ($\frac{2}{10}$), or $\frac{1}{5}$, of the rows.
- The product, 0.10, or $\frac{10}{100}$ ($\frac{1}{10}$), is represented by the overlap.

So, 0.10, or $\frac{1}{10}$, of the brownies have icing and pecans on them.

☑ Look Back

- How did you determine if your answer is reasonable?
- What other strategy could you use?

PRACTICE

Make a model to solve.

1. Suppose you cut a loaf of bread into 10 slices. You put jelly on 0.8 of the slices and peanut butter on 0.5 of the jelly slices. What part of the loaf has peanut butter and jelly?

2. Lee sold school newspapers. She collected $2.50 in coins. If she had 3 nickels, twice as many dimes as nickels, and the rest in quarters, how many of each coin did she have?

3. If 2 projects can be displayed on each side of a square table, how many projects can be displayed on 12 square tables that are pushed together end to end to form a rectangle?

4. The five planets closest to the sun are Earth, Venus, Mars, Mercury, and Jupiter. Earth is between Venus and Mars. Mercury is between Venus and the sun. Which of these planets is next to Jupiter?

Mixed Applications

Solve.

CHOOSE A STRATEGY

- Work Backward   • Make a Table   • Find a Pattern   • Make a Model
- Write a Number Sentence

5. Marta iced 0.6 of the cake with vanilla icing. She put sprinkles on 0.5 of the iced cake. What part of the cake has sprinkles on the icing?

6. If 0.35 pound of trash is recycled per person per day, how many pounds of trash are recycled in a week for a family of 3?

7. Sammy has 140 papers to deliver. If he can deliver 10 papers in 5 minutes, how long will it take him to deliver all the papers?

8. Ralph buys a package of meat that weighs 4 pounds and costs $2.65 per pound. How much change will he receive from $20.00?

9. Look at the diagram. Each cube is equal to the product of the two cubes directly below it. What are the values for yellow, purple, and orange?

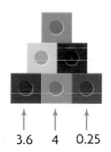

3.6   4   0.25

10. Paco recorded money spent for meals on his weekend trip. On Friday, he spent $5.35, $5.89, and $6.75. On Saturday, he spent $2.98, $6.27, and $7.94. On Sunday, he spent $3.00, $4.58, and $7.75. On which day did he spend the most for meals?

11. Pearl earned $38.50 per week for 3 weeks. She put $22.00 a week in her savings account. How much did she keep to spend?

Placing the Decimal Point

You will learn that finding decimal products is similar to finding whole number products. Placement of the decimal point can be determined by using estimation or patterns.

Why learn this? You can decide whether your answers make sense.

Is it reasonable that the mass of water in a pumpkin is 4.32 kg?

Suppose you have a pumpkin that has a mass of 4.8 kg. You know that almost 0.9 of its mass is water. How much of the pumpkin's mass is water?

You can estimate the product of 4.8×0.9 to decide about how much of the pumpkin's mass is water.

Estimate. $5 \times 1 = 5$.

Talk About It

• How can estimation help you solve the problem?

• Is the mass of water in the pumpkin 4.32 kg or 43.2 kg? How do you know?

• What strategy did you use to determine where to place the decimal point?

Estimation or patterns can help you place the decimal point in a product.

MODEL

Use estimation to find 0.6×26.

▶ Step 1

Estimate the product. First, decide whether 0.6 is closer to 0, $\frac{1}{2}$, or 1.

$$0.6 \times 26$$
$$\downarrow \qquad \downarrow$$
$$\frac{1}{2} \times 26 = 13$$

▶ Step 2

Multiply as with whole numbers.

```
   3
  2 6
×0.6
-----
  156
```

▶ Step 3

Use the estimate to place the decimal point in the product.

```
   3
  2 6
×0.6
-----
 15.6
   ↑__ the product.
```

Since the estimate is 13, place the decimal point so there is a whole number 15 in the product.

REMEMBER:

A number line can help you estimate by rounding to 0, $\frac{1}{2}$, or 1.

Example:

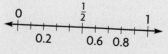

0.2 rounds to 0.

0.6 rounds to $\frac{1}{2}$.

0.8 rounds to 1.

💡 **CRITICAL THINKING** How does the estimate help you place the decimal point in the product?

A. Find $65 \times \$0.90$.

One possible estimate: $65 \times \$1 = \$65$.

$$
\begin{array}{r}
\$0.90 \\
\times\quad 65 \\
\hline
450 \\
+5400 \\
\hline
\$58.50
\end{array}
$$

Since the estimate is 65, place the decimal point so there is a whole number 58.

B. Find 21×0.48.

One possible estimate: $20 \times 0.5 = 10$.

$$
\begin{array}{r}
0.48 \\
\times\quad 21 \\
\hline
48 \\
+960 \\
\hline
10.08
\end{array}
$$

Since the estimate is 10, place the decimal point so there is a whole number 10.

Look for a pattern in the placement of the decimal point in each product. A decimal such as 0.0001 is called one ten-thousandth. It is $\frac{1}{10}$ of one thousandth.

Number Sentence	Factors	Product
$0.6 \times 0.3 = 0.18$	tenths $\times$ tenths	hundredths
$0.6 \times 0.03 = 0.018$	tenths $\times$ hundredths	thousandths
$0.06 \times 0.03 = 0.0018$	hundredths $\times$ hundredths	ten-thousandths
$0.6 \times 0.003 = 0.0018$	tenths $\times$ thousandths	ten-thousandths

WRITE ABOUT IT What relationship do you see between the number of decimal places in the product and the total number of decimal places in the factors?

Health Link

Did you know that you should drink about eight glasses of water a day to keep your body working as it should? How much water do you think you get from the fruits and vegetables you eat?

PRACTICE

Choose the best estimate. Write *a*, *b*, or *c*.

1. $21 \times 0.2 = n$ **a.** 4   **b.** 40   **c.** 45

2. $48 \times 0.5 = n$ **a.** 5   **b.** 25   **c.** 50

3. $\$0.92 \times 9 = n$ **a.** $0.90   **b.** $9.00   **c.** $90.00

Use estimation and patterns to place the decimal point in each product.

4. $2.7 \times 6 = 162$ **5.** $0.27 \times 6 = 162$ **6.** $27 \times 6 = 162$ **7.** $27 \times 0.06 = 162$

8. $27 \times 0.6 = 162$ **9.** $2.7 \times 0.6 = 162$ **10.** $0.27 \times 0.6 = 162$ **11.** $2.7 \times 0.06 = 162$

Mixed Applications

12. Isabel wants to buy 3 tapes that cost $4.39 each. If she earns $2.25 an hour, about how many hours will it take her to be able to make the purchase?

13. George earns $23.50 a week delivering papers. About how much money does he earn in 12 weeks?

LESSON CONTINUES

PART 2 More About Placing the Decimal Point

Sometimes when you multiply with decimals, there are zeros in the product.

A. Find 0.005×16.

```
      16
  ×0.005
  0.080
    ↑
```
Since 3 decimal places are needed in the product, write a zero for this place.

B. Find $0.06 \times \$0.90$.

```
    $0.90
  ×  0.06
  $0.0540
      ↑
```
Since 4 decimal places are needed, write a zero in this place.

Talk About It

- In Example A, how do you know how many decimal places are needed in the product?

- In Example B, what is the product to the nearest cent?

_____

When you use a calculator to multiply decimals, there can be a surprising result.

 Use a calculator to check the written solutions. Record each calculator answer.

REMEMBER:
. . . .
Equivalent decimals name the same number.

$0.6 = 0.60$

A calculator ignores zeros that do not change the value.

$0.50 = \boxed{0.5}$

Paper and pencil computation	Calculator keys

A.
```
   0.8
 × 0.7
  0.56
```
`0` `.` `7` `×` `0` `.` `8` `=` `[ ? ]`

B.
```
   0.15
 ×    6
   0.90
```
`6` `×` `0` `.` `1` `5` `=` `[ ? ]`

C.
```
   0.25
 ×    2
   0.50
```
`2` `×` `0` `.` `2` `5` `=` `[ ? ]`

 CRITICAL THINKING Compare the paper and pencil answer to the calculator answer for each problem. How are they alike? How are they different?

 Calculator Activities page H68

PRACTICE

Estimate each product.

1. 8×0.18 **2.** 9×0.3 **3.** 0.94×61 **4.** 84×0.6

5. 0.76×12 **6.** 29×0.02 **7.** 0.16×98 **8.** 56×0.3

9. Copy and complete the table.

Number Sentence	Factors	Product
$0.5 \times 0.8 = 0.40$	tenths × tenths	?
$0.5 \times ? = 0.040$	tenths × ?	?
$? \times ? = 0.0040$	?	?
$? \times 0.008 = ?$	?	?

Estimate to place the decimal point. Then find the product.

10. $\$5.25 \times 4 = n$ **11.** $1.6 \times 12 = n$ **12.** $0.9 \times 8.9 = n$ **13.** $2.68 \times 57 = n$

14. $\quad \$5.40$
$\quad \underline{\times \quad 3}$

15. $\quad 0.75$
$\quad \underline{\times 0.06}$

16. $\quad 0.54$
$\quad \underline{\times \quad 16}$

17. $\quad 1.74$
$\quad \underline{\times \quad 43}$

18. $\quad \$82.19$
$\quad \underline{\times \quad 7}$

19. $\quad 0.09$
$\quad \underline{\times \ 0.7}$

20. $\quad 0.29$
$\quad \underline{\times \ 1.8}$

21. $\quad 6.07$
$\quad \underline{\times \quad 17}$

22. If Evan bought 2 dozen eggs at $\$0.79$ a dozen and a loaf of bread at $\$0.99$, about how much did he spend?

23. Suppose you have a watermelon that has a mass of 6.5 kg. If 0.92 of its mass is water, how much of the watermelon's mass is water? How much is not water?

24. Which costs more—grapefruit at $\$0.89$ each, or 3 for $\$2.50$? 4 melons for $\$3.00$, or melons for $\$0.85$ each?

25. ✎ **Write a problem** including this information: The mass of a whole, unpeeled apple is 0.55 kg, and 0.84 of its mass is water.

Mixed Review

Write $<$, $>$, or $=$ for each ●. (pages 42–43)

26. $0.6 \ ● \ 0.600$ **27.** $0.72 \ ● \ 0.072$ **28.** $5.86 \ ● \ 5.68$ **29.** $69.34 \ ● \ 69.54$

30. $4.083 \ ● \ 4.308$ **31.** $12.05 \ ● \ 12.50$ **32.** $72.601 \ ● \ 72.610$ **33.** $1.26 \ ● \ 12.6$

Estimate. Then find the product. (pages 92–93)

34. $19 \times 3 = n$ **35.** $206 \times 4 = n$ **36.** $403 \times 61 = n$ **37.** $295 \times 45 = n$

38. $50 \times 29 = n$ **39.** $262 \times 32 = n$ **40.** $4,059 \times 8 = n$ **41.** $905 \times 423 = n$

MORE PRACTICE Student Handbook page H93

Multiplying Mixed Decimals

You will learn to multiply decimal factors greater than one.	Why learn this? When you are shopping, it helps you to decide if you are being charged a reasonable amount.	**WORD POWER** mixed decimal

A **mixed decimal** has a whole number part and a decimal part in the number.

You can find mixed decimal products without making models.

MODEL

What is the product of 1.4 × 2.3?
Multiply. 1.4 × 2.3 = n   Estimate. 1.5 × 2 = 3.0

▶ **Step 1**
Multiply by the tenths.

Think:
0.4 × 2.3

$$\begin{array}{r} 1 \\ 2.3 \\ \times 1.4 \\ \hline 92 \end{array}$$

▶ **Step 2**
Multiply by the ones. Add.

Think:
1.0 × 2.3

$$\begin{array}{r} 1 \\ 2.3 \\ \times 1.4 \\ \hline 92 \\ +230 \end{array}$$
Remember to
← place a zero here.

▶ **Step 3**
Use the estimate of 3.0 to place the decimal point in the product.

$$\begin{array}{r} 1 \\ 2.3 \\ \times 1.4 \\ \hline 92 \\ +230 \\ \hline 3.22 \end{array}$$

• How does the product compare to the estimate?

EXAMPLES

A. Use estimation to find 3.4 × 1.7.

Estimate: 3 × 2 = 6

$$\begin{array}{r} 3.4 \\ \times 1.7 \\ \hline 238 \\ +340 \\ \hline 5.78 \end{array}$$

Since the estimate is 6, place the decimal point so there is a whole number 5.

B. Use estimation or count the number of decimal places to place the decimal point in the product. Find 5.8 × 0.40.

Estimate: 6 × 0.40 = 2.40.

$$\begin{array}{r} 0.40 \\ \times\ 5.8 \\ \hline 320 \\ +2000 \\ \hline 2.320 \end{array}$$
← 2 decimal places
← 1 decimal place

← 3 decimal places

Talk About It

• In Examples A and B, what relationship do you see between the number of decimal places in the product and the total number of decimal places in the factors?

• How does using estimation help you place the decimal point?

PRACTICE

Find the product.

| 1. | 7.89 × 4.2 | 2. | 32.5 ×0.95 | 3. | $87.68 × 4.8 | 4. | 856.4 × 0.84 | 5. | 602.74 × 2.7 |

| 6. | 46.2 ×9.07 | 7. | 29.9 × 7.6 | 8. | $14.34 × 5.2 | 9. | 37.3 ×4.06 | 10. | 1.008 × 5.5 |

11. $2.4 \times 1.3 = n$ **12.** $1.9 \times 1.8 = n$ **13.** $3.2 \times 4.3 = n$ **14.** $3.7 \times 2.6 = n$

Solve. Use the table for Exercises 15–17.

15. How much are 3 tapes at The Music Store?

16. What is the total cost of 2 CDs at Music Town, including a sales tax of $0.06 on each dollar?

17. ✐ **WRITE ABOUT IT**   If you buy both tapes and CDs, at which store should you shop? Explain.

MUSIC STORE PRICES		
Store	Tape	Compact Disc
The Music Store	$8.99	$14.99
Music Town	$8.49	$11.99
Discount Music	$7.90	$12.98
Record City	$10.49	$15.99

Mixed Applications

18. Paula bought a record cleaner for $0.69. If she paid a sales tax of $0.06 on each dollar, what did she spend on the record cleaner?

19. Bill made a phone call that cost $2.00 for the first minute and $0.45 for each additional minute. If he was on the phone for 5 minutes, what was the cost of the phone call?

When you are shopping, you are using decimals to solve problems.

Mixed Review

Write the decimal for each. (pages 34–35)

20. four and two tenths   **21.** sixteen hundredths   **22.** one and five hundredths

Find the product. (pages 88–89)

| 23. | 15 ×13 | 24. | 116 × 82 | 25. | 206 × 48 | 26. | 324 × 33 |

CULTURAL CONNECTION

NATIVE AMERICAN MONEY

Megan's class is studying Native American tribes. The students are learning about such things as the clothing they wore, the houses they lived in, how they prepared their food, and about their trading customs. Megan found out that some Native Americans used an early form of money called dentalia, which means "teeth." Dentalia shells were curved, toothlike shells that were used not only as money but also as decorations on clothes and jewelry throughout the western part of North America.

> **CULTURAL LINK**
>
> Trading and money were very important to Native Americans. Some evidence shows that people of North America may have used a system of trading more than 3,000 years ago.

For a project, Megan made a necklace using toothlike shells. She bought 14 shells to make the necklace. Each shell cost $0.39. How much did it cost her to make the necklace?

Work Together

1. Each shell on Megan's necklace weighs 2.5 ounces. The string weighs 0.5 ounces. How much does the necklace weigh?

2. The store where Megan bought the shells had larger toothlike shells that sold for $1.19 each. How much more would the necklace Megan made have cost if she had used the larger shells instead?

3. Two of Megan's classmates asked her to make them a necklace like the one she made for her project. It took her 1.2 hours to make each necklace. How much time did she spend making all three necklaces?

4. Megan bought a variety of other shells to decorate a T-shirt. She bought 18 shells that cost $0.17 each, 7 shells that cost $0.24 each, and 4 shells that cost $0.41 each. How much money did Megan spend on the shells for her T-shirt?

✓ CHECK UNDERSTANDING

VOCABULARY

1. A __?__ has a whole number and a decimal part in the number. (page 204)

Use mental math to complete the pattern. (pages 194–195)

2. $14 \times 1 = n$
   $14 \times 0.1 = n$
   $14 \times 0.01 = n$

3. $85 \times 1 = n$
   $85 \times 0.1 = n$
   $85 \times 0.01 = n$

4. $205 \times 1 = n$
   $205 \times 0.1 = n$
   $205 \times 0.01 = n$

✓ CHECK SKILLS

Find the product. (pages 196–205)

5. 0.7×6

6. 0.15×8

7. 0.9×0.4

8. 0.3×0.7

9. $\$8.29 \times 5$

10. 1.8×4

11. 6.94×7

12. 4.52×3

13. 3.67×0.5

14. 7.62×8

15. 2.58×0.6

16. 5.99×0.12

17. 0.7×0.9

18. 1.6×0.2

19. 0.83×0.9

20. $\$2.95 \times 0.6$

21. $\$4.56 \times 0.7$

22. 17.6×0.4

✓ CHECK PROBLEM SOLVING

Solve. (pages 198–199)

CHOOSE A STRATEGY

- Find a Pattern
- Work Backward
- Write a Number Sentence
- Make a Model
- Guess and Check
- Solve a Simpler Problem

23. Comic books are $1.59 each and you want 7 of them. You have $15.00. Is that enough? How much will you pay?

24. Tami is paid $0.28 a pound for recycling aluminum. How much will she receive for 75.5 pounds of aluminum?

25. Tom collected $3.10 in coins to buy a gift for his teacher. If he had 8 dimes, twice as many nickels as dimes, and the rest in quarters, how many of each coin did he have?

26. Tom colored 0.8 of his book cover blue. He put stickers on 0.5 of the blue part. What part of the book cover has stickers on the blue background?

DIVIDING DECIMALS

SMOOTHIE INGREDIENTS

Frozen Fruits (sold in bags only)		
Strawberries	$ 4	3-pound bag
Raspberries	$ 6	2-pound bag
Blueberries	$ 7	3-pound bag
Fresh Fruits (you can buy these by the pound)		
Bananas	$ 0.50	1-pound
Honeydew	$ 1	1-pound
Juices (sold in jugs)		
Apple juice	$ 4	8-pound jug
Orange juice	$ 3	6-pound jug

DID YOU KNOW . . .

Blueberries, raspberries, and strawberries provide Vitamin C, iron, and fiber. That's why berries make a "berry" good snack.

Smoothie Fundraiser

Suppose your class is having a smoothie fundraiser. You will have $20 to spend on ingredients. Your group will create and name your smoothie recipe. You will decide how many people it will serve, what to charge for the drinks, and how much profit you will make.

To make a yummy smoothie, you take frozen fruit, fresh fruit, fruit juice, and mix it up!

YOU WILL NEED: recipe ingredients, calculator

Work with a group. Your job is to

- make up a smoothie recipe and figure out how many people you can serve.

- decide how much to charge for one smoothie.

- predict how much profit you will make.

- present your calculations in an easy-to-read report.

DID YOU

☑ make a recipe and calculate how many people it will serve?

☑ decide how much to charge and figure your profit?

☑ write a report explaining your calculations?

Our Sensational Strawberry Smoothie

Ingredients		
$8	strawberries	6 lbs
$4	apple juice	8
$5	bananas	
$3	honeydew melon	1
$20	TOTAL	27

How many people can we serve? Allow 1 pound drink per person (A pint is a pound.)

How much does it cost for 1 smoothie? $\frac{$20}{27}$

How much will we charge for it? We will charge about twice the cost of ingredients, but we will round the number.

If our recipe is chosen as the smoothie fundraiser, we will charge $1.50. We will sell 27 smoothies. 27 × We will pay $20 for ingredients, will be $20.50.

PART 1 Patterns in Decimal Division

You will learn to use a pattern to determine a decimal quotient.	Why learn this? You can find quotients by using mental math.

One way to find quotients is to look for patterns. You can use the patterns from quotients you know to find quotients you do not know.

Look for the pattern in these quotients to find $1 \div 5$.

$1,000 \div 5 =$ 200

$100 \div 5 =$ 20

$10 \div 5 =$ 2

$1 \div 5 =$ 0.2

Notice that

⇨ $1 \div 5$ results in a quotient that is a decimal.

> **REMEMBER:**
> Use a place-value chart to place the decimal point.
>
> | Tens | Ones | Tenths |
> |---|---|---|
> | 2 | 0 | 0 |
> | | 2 | 0 |
> | | 0 | 2 |

EXAMPLES

A. $1,000 \div 2 =$ 500
       $100 \div 2 =$ 50
       $10 \div 2 =$ 5
       $1 \div 2 =$ 0.5

B. $10,000 \div 4 = 2,500$
       $1,000 \div 4 = 250$
       $100 \div 4 = 25$
       $10 \div 4 = 2.5$

Talk About It

- How does the number of zeros in the dividend change in each example?

- What happens to the position of the decimal point in the quotient in each example?

💡 **CRITICAL THINKING** How does the pattern in each example above show that $1 \div 5$, $1 \div 2$, and $10 \div 4$ have quotients that are decimals?

Check Your Understanding

Copy and complete each pattern.

1. $1,000 \div 2 = n$
     $100 \div 2 = n$
      $10 \div 2 = n$
       $1 \div 2 = n$

2. $4,000 \div 8 = n$
     $400 \div 8 = n$
      $40 \div 8 = n$
       $4 \div 8 = n$

3. $5,000 \div 2 = n$
     $500 \div 2 = n$
      $50 \div 2 = n$
       $5 \div 2 = n$

> ◄ **Art Link** ►
>
> M.C. Escher was a Dutch artist. He is famous for his drawings of repeating patterns. In *Ascending and Descending*, which means "up and down," people are walking up stairs and down stairs, but each person will end up in the same place he or she started. What patterns can you find in the picture?

M.C. Escher's "Ascending and Descending"
© 1997 Cordon Art - Baarn-Holland. All rights reserved.

PRACTICE

Copy and complete each pattern.

4. $3{,}000 \div 5 = n$
$300 \div 5 = n$
$30 \div 5 = n$
$3 \div 5 = n$

5. $2{,}000 \div 4 = n$
$200 \div 4 = n$
$20 \div 4 = n$
$2 \div 4 = n$

6. $15{,}000 \div 6 = n$
$1{,}500 \div 6 = n$
$150 \div 6 = n$
$15 \div 6 = n$

7. $2{,}000 \div 5 = n$
$200 \div 5 = n$
$20 \div 5 = n$
$2 \div 5 = n$

8. $20{,}000 \div 8 = n$
$2{,}000 \div 8 = n$
$200 \div 8 = n$
$20 \div 8 = n$

9. $7{,}000 \div 4 = n$
$700 \div 4 = n$
$70 \div 4 = n$
$7 \div 4 = n$

10. $10{,}000 \div 8 = n$
$1{,}000 \div 8 = n$
$100 \div 8 = n$
$10 \div 8 = n$

11. $6{,}000 \div 5 = n$
$600 \div 5 = n$
$60 \div 5 = n$
$6 \div 5 = n$

12. $4{,}000 \div 5 = n$
$400 \div 5 = n$
$40 \div 5 = n$
$4 \div 5 = n$

Mixed Applications

13. Sammy has a newspaper route. He has 140 papers to deliver. He can deliver 7 papers in 5 minutes. How long will it take him to deliver all the papers?

14. Jamie's group used a recipe that makes 68 ounces of smoothies. If each serving is 8 ounces, how many servings can they make?

15. Albert has collected 1,372 pennies. How much money does he have in dollars and cents?

16. Joanne makes $80 a week. She works 4 hours each week. How much does she make per hour?

For Problems 17–19, use the information at the right.

17. Paco recorded the amount of money he spent on each meal during his vacation. On which day did he spend the most?

18. On which day did Paco spend the least?

19. How much more did Paco spend for meals on Friday than he did on Saturday?

20. ✏️ **WRITE ABOUT IT** Explain how a pattern beginning with $300 \div 6 = 50$ leads to a decimal quotient of 0.5.

LESSON
CONTINUES ▶

PART 2 PROBLEM-SOLVING STRATEGY
Write a Number Sentence

THE PROBLEM Ramona wants to buy a stereo system for $400. She wants to save enough money to buy it before the price goes up after 8 weeks. How much does she need to save each week?

☑ Understand

- What are you asked to find?

- What information will you use?

- Is there information you will not use? If so, what?

☑ Plan

- What strategy can you use to solve the problem?

  You can *write a number sentence* to find the amount Ramona needs to save each week.

☑ Solve

- What number sentence can you write to solve the problem?

  Divide to find the amount she needs to save.

  Use mental math to find the quotient.

  $$\$400 \div 8 = \$50$$

  So, Ramona needs to save $50 each week.

☑ Look Back

- How can you determine if your answer is reasonable?

- What other strategy can you use?

> **REMEMBER:**
> ☑ Understand
> ☑ Plan
> ☑ Solve
> ☑ Look Back

> **Consumer Link**
>
> In 1897 a guitar cost about $16, and a ten-hole harmonica cost $0.45. Today a beginner's guitar costs about $200. A ten-hole harmonica costs about $20.
>
> About how many guitars could you have bought for $200 in 1897? About how many harmonicas could you have bought for $20 in 1897?

PRACTICE

Write a number sentence to solve.

1. Joan and 3 classmates bought some food to share. The bill was $40.00. They shared the bill equally. How much did each owe?

2. James has deposited $555 in his savings account. He made 5 equal deposits. How much was each deposit?

3. Each week Nina saves $9.75 from her allowance. In 12 weeks, how much money will she have saved?

4. Samuel and Adam worked together on a school project. Adam spent $4.60 on supplies. Samuel spent $3.90. How much did they spend together?

Mixed Applications

Solve.

CHOOSE A STRATEGY

• Make a Table   • Guess and Check   • Write a Number Sentence

5. Dennis wants to buy 2 new baseballs. At Joe's Sports Store, he saw a baseball for $3.95, a bat for $5.95, and a glove for $32.95. At Max's Sports Store, he saw a package of 2 baseballs for $7.95. At which store will he get a better buy on baseballs?

6. Sara Ann wants to buy 2 new video games. At a store 4.5 miles from her house, she can buy 2 games for $39.98. At a store 2 miles from her house, the games are $21.95 each. What is the difference in the cost for one video game?

7. Jared and his brother have been saving baseball cards for 4 years. Jared has 1,123 cards, and his brother has 792 cards. If they continue to save at the same rate during the next 4 years, about how many cards will they have together?

8. Nancy made a phone call that cost $2.00 for the first minute and $0.45 for each additional minute. She was on the phone for 5 minutes. What was the cost of the phone call?

9. Laura needs $130 to buy a coat. She has $45. If she saves $5 each week, how many weeks will it take her to save enough money to buy the coat?

10. Ralph bought the salad shown at the right. How much change will he receive from $5.00?

FRESH GARDEN SALAD
NET WT.   PRICE PER LB.
1.20 $ 2.25
TOTAL PRICE
$

11. What is the smallest 4-digit number that can be divided by 50 with a remainder of 17?

Decimal Division

You will investigate how to divide decimals by using decimal models.

Why learn this? You can find the cost of each item in a package, such as the cost of each pencil in a package of 5 pencils.

Explore

Make models to show how to divide 1.5 by 3.

MATERIALS: tenths and hundredths decimal models, markers, scissors, and tape or paste

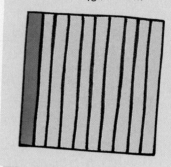

REMEMBER:

Division is separating into equal groups.

This model represents a whole divided into tenths. Each part is $\frac{1}{10}$, or 0.1.

MODEL

▶ Step 1

Show 1.5 by shading two decimal models.

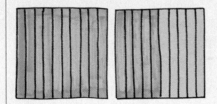

▶ Step 2

Cut each model to show the tenths.

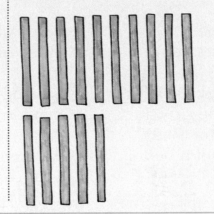

Record

Divide the tenths into three groups of the same size. Tape or paste your model on a piece of paper. Record a division number sentence for your model.

Talk About It

*   Look at your model and quotient. What happened to the 1 whole?

*   How can you use the pattern at the right to show that your quotient is correct?

$$150 \div 3 = 50$$
$$15 \div 3 = 5$$
$$1.5 \div 3 = \underline{\ ?\ }$$

 Link

E–Lab • Activity 13 Available on CD-ROM and the Internet at http://www.hbschool.com/elab

Now, investigate dividing hundredths by a whole number.

Try This

Make models to show $0.09 \div 3$ and $0.24 \div 2$. Record number sentences for each of your models.

HANDS-ON PRACTICE

Make a model and find the quotient.

1. $1.2 \div 4 = \underline{\ ?\ }$ 2. $0.12 \div 4 = \underline{\ ?\ }$ 3. $3.5 \div 5 = \underline{\ ?\ }$

4. $6.4 \div 8 = \underline{\ ?\ }$ 5. $0.64 \div 8 = \underline{\ ?\ }$ 6. $0.69 \div 3 = \underline{\ ?\ }$

7. $0.44 \div 2 = \underline{\ ?\ }$ 8. $0.18 \div 9 = \underline{\ ?\ }$ 9. $2.08 \div 2 = \underline{\ ?\ }$

Applying What You Learned

Use the model to complete the number sentence.

10.

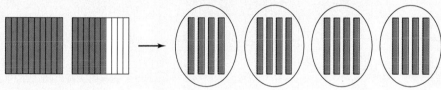

$1.6 \div 4 = \underline{\ ?\ }$

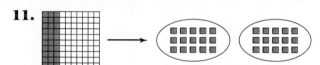

11. $0.30 \div 2 = \underline{\ ?\ }$ 12. $0.12 \div 3 = \underline{\ ?\ }$

Mixed Applications

13. Mark is building a doll house for his little sister. For the trim around the roof, he bought 4 pieces of wood for a total of $7.16. How much was each piece of wood?

14. Mr. Wu is organizing a field day for his fifth-grade class. He wants to make 3 award ribbons for each of 3 events. He has a ribbon that is 1.8 meters long. How long can each award ribbon be?

15. Four friends are playing a game. They have $39.52 in play money. If each player gets the same amount to begin the game, how much will each player get?

16. ✏️ **WRITE ABOUT IT** Explain how to draw a model to find the quotient $0.10 \div 5$.

Dividing Decimals by Whole Numbers

You will learn that dividing decimals by whole numbers is like dividing whole numbers.

Why learn this? You can find equal parts of a decimal.

You can use models and what you know about dividing whole numbers to divide a decimal by a whole number. The model below shows how to find $3.8 \div 2$.

"Dividing decimals is like dividing with whole numbers."

MODEL

Find $3.8 \div 2$.

▶ Step 1

Show 3.8.

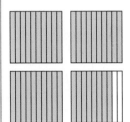

$2\overline{)3.8}$

▶ Step 2

Divide as with whole numbers. Begin with the whole number.

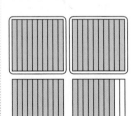

There are 3 ones to divide into 2 groups.

$$\begin{array}{r} 1 \\ 2\overline{)3.8} \\ -2 \\ \hline 1 \end{array}$$

$3 \div 2 = 1$ with 1 whole left over.

▶ Step 3

Rename the 1 whole that is left over as 10 tenths. There are 18 tenths to divide into 2 groups.

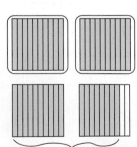

$$\begin{array}{r} 1 \\ 2\overline{)3.8} \\ -2\downarrow \\ \hline 18 \end{array}$$

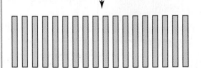

▶ Step 4

Divide the tenths.

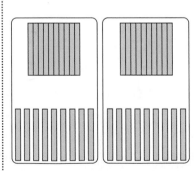

$$\begin{array}{r} 1.9 \\ 2\overline{)3.8} \\ -2\downarrow \\ \hline 18 \\ -18 \\ \hline 0 \end{array}$$

$18 \div 2 = 9$ with 0 left over.

Place a decimal point between the whole and the tenths.

So, $3.8 \div 2 = 1.9$.

A.
```
   1.35
4)5.40
  -4
   14
  -12
   20
  -20
    0
```
Divide the whole number 5 by 4.

Divide 14 tenths by 4.

Divide 20 hundredths by 4.

Check:
```
   1.35
×     4
   5.40
```

B.
```
   4.3
5)21.5
 -20
   15
  -15
    0
```

Check:
```
   4.3
×    5
  21.5
```

- How can a pattern help you decide if the answer in Example B is reasonable?

💡 **CRITICAL THINKING** How is division with decimals like division with whole numbers? How is it different?

PRACTICE

Find the quotient. Check by multiplying.

1. 7)6.3

2. 4)8.08

3. 8)6.00

4. 5)4.05

5. 8)74.4

6. 3)27.9

7. 5)55.5

8. 2)19.6

9. 24.6 ÷ 6 = _?_

10. 2.46 ÷ 6 = _?_

11. 0.93 ÷ 3 = _?_

Mixed Applications

12. Kevin is building a doghouse. He bought 4 pieces of wood to trim the roof. The 4 pieces cost $6.52. How much did each piece cost?

13. At Marie's Market, strawberries cost $4.98 for 2 pounds. How much does 1 pound cost?

STRAWBERRIES
2 pounds
$4.98

Mixed Review

Write the decimal for each model. (pages 34–35)

14.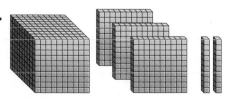

15.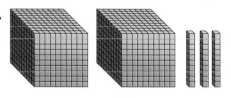

Write an equivalent decimal for each. (pages 40–41)

16. 0.03

17. 5.20

18. 0.500

19. 3.75

20. 1.4

Placing the Decimal Point

You will learn how to use estimation or a pattern to place the decimal point when dividing decimals by whole numbers.

Why learn this? Changing the position of the decimal point changes the value of the digits, so the placement is important.

Natalia walked 3 miles in 4 days. What average distance did she walk each day?

Estimate 3 ÷ 4 to help solve the problem.

Since 3 ÷ 4 is less than 1, add a decimal point and zeros to divide.

4)3 can be written as 4)3.0 or 4)3.00.

REMEMBER:

3 is equivalent to 3.0 or 3.00.

MODEL

▶ Step 1

Since 3 ÷ 4 is less than 1, place a 0 in the ones place. Then place a decimal point.

```
   0.
4)3.00
```

▶ Step 2

Divide as with whole numbers.

```
   0.75
4)3.00
  −28
   20
  −20
    0
```

▶ Step 3

Check by multiplying.

```
  0.75
×    4
 3.00
```

Notice that

⇨ the decimal point in the quotient goes directly above the decimal point in the dividend.

So, Natalia walked an average of 0.75 mile each day.

Since 0.75 is less than 1, the quotient is reasonable.

Talk About It

- In Step 1, how many zeros can you write after the decimal point and not change the value of the 3?

- How can you use the pattern below to help place the decimal point?

  $300 \div 4 = 75$
  $30 \div 4 = 7.5$
  $3 \div 4 = n$

- What basic division facts did you use to solve the problem?

EXAMPLES

A.

$$\begin{array}{r} 60.5 \\ 7\overline{)423.5} \\ -42 \\ \hline 03 \\ -00 \\ \hline 35 \\ -35 \\ \hline 0 \end{array}$$

Use estimation to place the decimal point.

$420 \div 7 = 60$

So, place the decimal point so there is a whole number 60 in the quotient.

B.

$$\begin{array}{r} 0.73 \\ 2\overline{)1.46} \\ -14 \\ \hline 06 \\ -6 \\ \hline 0 \end{array}$$

Use estimation and a pattern to place the decimal point.

$140 \div 2 = 70$
$14 \div 2 = 7$
$1.4 \div 2 = 0.7$

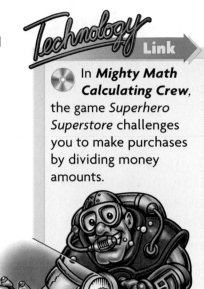

Technology Link

In *Mighty Math Calculating Crew*, the game *Superhero Superstore* challenges you to make purchases by dividing money amounts.

💡 **CRITICAL THINKING** In Example A, why is the quotient 60.5, not 6.05? In Example B, why is the quotient 0.73, not 7.3?

PRACTICE

Use estimation or patterns to place the decimal point.
Then find the quotient.

1. $3\overline{)1.8}$ **2.** $4\overline{)2.0}$ **3.** $6\overline{)0.24}$ **4.** $5\overline{)3.5}$

5. $7\overline{)1.47}$ **6.** $3\overline{)3.69}$ **7.** $9\overline{)83.7}$ **8.** $4\overline{)44.8}$

9. $8\overline{)56.8}$ **10.** $6\overline{)54.48}$ **11.** $2\overline{)19.62}$ **12.** $5\overline{)19.75}$

Mixed Applications

For Problems 13–16, use the price list.

13. Estimate the cost of 1 pound of potatoes.

14. Evan bought a dozen eggs and 2 loaves of bread. How much did he spend?

15. Suppose you need to buy 1 gallon of milk. Would you buy 2 half-gallon containers of milk or 1 one-gallon container of milk? Why?

16. ✏️ **Write a problem** that can be solved by dividing. Use the price list.

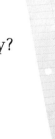

Price List
5-pound bag potatoes $2.39
half-gallon milk $1.35
gallon milk $2.39
dozen eggs $0.99
bread $1.19

Mixed Review

Use an equivalent decimal to find the sum. (pages 52–53)

17. $1.25 + 0.786 = n$ **18.** $2.30 + 8.604 = n$ **19.** $12.35 + 1.459 = n$

Estimate the quotient. (pages 106–107)

20. $58 \div 6 \approx n$ **21.** $430 \div 6 \approx n$ **22.** $209 \div 7 \approx n$ **23.** $355 \div 6 \approx n$

MORE PRACTICE Student Handbook page H94

Choosing the Operation

You will learn how to use multiplication and division of decimals to solve problems.	Why learn this? You can decide which operation you should use to solve a problem.

Mr. Regan shared the seafood that he bought at the market with 3 of his neighbors. His purchases are listed in the table at the right. If they shared each kind of seafood equally, how many pounds of salmon was each person's share?

The table shows that Mr. Regan bought 16.8 pounds of salmon. Since he and his 3 neighbors are sharing equally, you can divide 16.8 by 4 to find the answer.

$$\begin{array}{r} 4.2 \\ 4\overline{)16.8} \\ -16 \\ \hline 08 \\ -8 \\ \hline 0 \end{array}$$

So, each person's share was 4.2 pounds of salmon.

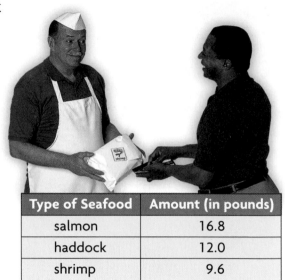

Type of Seafood	Amount (in pounds)
salmon	16.8
haddock	12.0
shrimp	9.6

Suppose Mr. Fu bought 22.8 pounds of seafood 5 weeks in a row for his restaurant. How many pounds of seafood did he buy in all?

Since he bought the same amount 5 weeks in a row, you need to multiply to find the answer.

$$\begin{array}{r} 22.8 \\ \times 5 \\ \hline 114.0 \end{array}$$

So, Mr. Fu bought 114 pounds of seafood.

Talk About It

- How do you know when to divide?
- How do you know when to multiply?

Check Your Understanding  CRITICAL THINKING

Choose the operation and solve.

1. Sam, Joe, and Bob share 14.4 pounds of shrimp equally. How much is Bob's share?

2. If Bob buys the same amount of shrimp for 4 weeks in a row, how much shrimp will he buy in all?

> **Science Link**
>
> Chinook salmon live along the Pacific coast. They spend from one to five years in the ocean and then return to lay eggs in the stream of their origin. Large female salmon usually lay between 2,000 and 3,000 eggs. How many salmon from one female survive if 0.10 of her eggs survive and grow? if 0.01 of her eggs survive and grow?

Calculator Activities page H67

PRACTICE

For Problems 3–6, use the table on page 220. Choose the operation and solve.

3. How much haddock did Mr. Regan have after sharing with his neighbors?

4. How much shrimp did Mr. Regan and each of his neighbors get?

5. Mr. Regan bought the same amount of shrimp 4 weeks in a row. How many pounds of shrimp did he buy?

6. Mr. Regan bought the same amount of salmon 3 weeks in a row. How many pounds of salmon did he buy?

7. Carl receives an allowance of $3.75 a week. If Carl saves all his allowance, how much will he have in 4 weeks?

8. Lola wants to buy a touring bike for $599.94. She agrees to pay off the total cost of the bike in 9 months. How much does she have to pay each month?

Mixed Applications

9. Amy is comparing breakfast cereals. A box of Brand A weighs 13 ounces and sells for $2.08. A box of Brand B weighs 14 ounces and sells for $2.10. Which cereal costs less per ounce?

10. Janell bought 2 shirts for $11.98 each, a sweater for $18.95, and 3 pairs of socks for $3.05 a pair. About how much did all these items cost?

11. Each week for 6 weeks, Harry deposited his check of $74.28 into his bank account. During that time he also deposited $25.00 he received as a gift. How much did Harry deposit during the 6 weeks?

12. ⬛▷ **Write a problem** that can be solved by dividing a decimal.

Mixed Review

Find the area. (pages 78–79)

13. $l = 12$ ft
$w = 4$ ft
$A = \blacksquare$ sq ft

14. $l = 23$ ft
$w = 3$ ft
$A = \blacksquare$ sq ft

15. $l = 48$ ft
$w = 7$ ft
$A = \blacksquare$ sq ft

16. $l = 18$ ft
$w = 5$ ft
$A = \blacksquare$ sq ft

Divide. Check by multiplying. (pages 126–127)

17. $1,089 \div 37 = n$ **18.** $6,156 \div 18 = n$ **19.** $7,956 \div 43 = n$ **20.** $5,172 \div 25 = n$

MATH FUN!

The Found Kitten

PURPOSE To see patterns in dividing 10.00

YOU WILL NEED calculator

Your kitten is missing, and your family is offering a $10 reward if someone finds it. Great news! You hear that your kitten has been found—by more than one person.

How will you divide the reward between 2 people? 3 people? up to 10 people? Make a chart of the amount per person. Which numbers will not come out evenly?

Number of People	Amount per Person
1	$10.00
2	
3	

ON TARGET?

PURPOSE To estimate whether a quotient is more or less than one

YOU WILL NEED calculator

Write a division problem in which the dividend (number to be divided) is a decimal.

Your partner will estimate whether the quotient (answer) will be more or less than one or equal to one.

Check the division with a calculator. Is the estimate on target?

Switch. Play at least three rounds with large and small numbers.

$2\overline{)9.9}$

$5\overline{)0.85}$

You Can Make Money Recycling

PURPOSE To use multiplication and division to solve problems

YOU WILL NEED calculator

Your group can choose the goal and be the brains behind your class recycling project.

Find out how much is paid for cans and state a goal in dollars.

Calculate how many pounds of cans you would need to turn in to meet your goal.

CITY RECYCLING CENTER
It CAN Pay to Recycle!

Pounds of Aluminum Cans	Price per Pound
1-25	$0.75/lb
26-50	$0.80/lb
51-100	$0.95/lb

Do you think your class could reasonably recycle that many cans in 4 weeks? Why or why not?

 Collect aluminum drink cans at home, and see how many of them it takes to make one pound.

✓ CHECK UNDERSTANDING

Copy and complete each pattern. (pages 210–211)

1. $3,000 \div 6 = n$
$300 \div 6 = n$
$30 \div 6 = n$
$3 \div 6 = n$

2. $8,000 \div 5 = n$
$800 \div 5 = n$
$80 \div 5 = n$
$8 \div 5 = n$

3. $7,000 \div 2 = n$
$700 \div 2 = n$
$70 \div 2 = n$
$7 \div 2 = n$

4. $9,000 \div 5 = n$
$900 \div 5 = n$
$90 \div 5 = n$
$9 \div 5 = n$

Use the model to complete the number sentence. (pages 214–215)

5.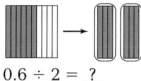

$0.6 \div 2 = \underline{?}$

6.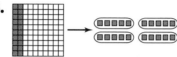

$0.20 \div 4 = \underline{?}$

Use estimation or patterns to place the decimal point.
Then find the quotient. (pages 218–219)

7. $2\overline{)18.2}$ **8.** $5\overline{)9.5}$ **9.** $4\overline{)0.24}$ **10.** $4\overline{)2.4}$

✓ CHECK SKILLS

Find the quotient. Check by multiplying. (pages 216–217)

11. $9\overline{)1.8}$ **12.** $5\overline{)2.5}$ **13.** $6\overline{)0.42}$ **14.** $8\overline{)3.2}$

15. $6\overline{)28.8}$ **16.** $3\overline{)2.13}$ **17.** $2\overline{)2.44}$ **18.** $6\overline{)37.2}$

Choose the operation and solve. (pages 220–221)

19. Bobbie bought 2 cans of tennis balls at $3.95 for each can. How much did the tennis balls cost?

20. Jarod paid $150 to attend 8 computer classes. How much did he pay per class?

✓ CHECK PROBLEM SOLVING

Solve. (pages 212–213)

CHOOSE A STRATEGY

• Make a Table   • Guess and Check   • Write a Number Sentence

21. Ed bought 4 magazines for $3.00 each. He paid a sales tax of $0.06 on each dollar of his purchase. How much sales tax did he pay?

22. From Monday through Friday, Hillary drove 4.8 miles to and from work each day. How many miles did she drive for the week?

CHAPTER 14
MEASUREMENT: METRIC UNITS

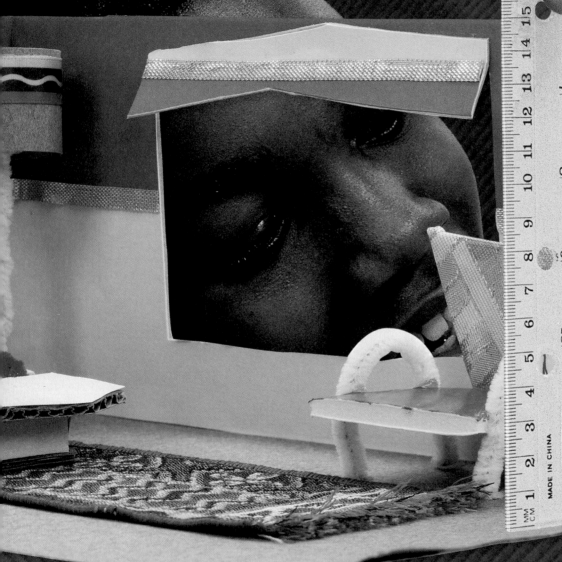

DID YOU KNOW....

Though the U.S. has not officially adopted the metric system, by 1990 all U.S. automobiles were being designed to metric specifications.

Make a Miniature Metric Room

Tiny action figures need places to live, too. Work together to create a unique environment for the action figure of your choice. When all the rooms are finished, present them in a mini-metric room tour.

YOU WILL NEED: an action figure, a cardboard box, paper and fabric scraps, small boxes, spools and so on, scissors, glue, and a cm ruler

Work with a group. Your job is to

- measure an action figure and a box.

- divide the tasks of making and measuring furniture, doors, windows, rugs, or any other furnishings.

- make a chart with the dimensions of the room and each item in it.

- present your room at a mini-metric room tour.

A Room for Max: Dimensions

Max is 7cm tall
His room (box) is
$29\frac{1}{2}$ cm × 13 cm
and 10cm tall

Things We Made

Kira — rug
27cm × 13cm

Steve — table
a circle 7cm across
and 3cm high

Jessica — window
5cm × 7cm.

DID YOU

☑ measure the action figure, the box, and all the furnishings in centimeters?

☑ make a chart with all measurements?

☑ present your room at a mini-metric room tour?

CRAFT GLUE

Final Project
How long are the rooms end to
How many cm? How many m?

Max	Ozzie	Penny	Frank	Poca
$29\frac{1}{2}$ cm	33cm	28cm	40cm	30cm

Total: $160\frac{1}{2}$ centimeters = 160.5cm
In meters: 1.605 meters

Linear Units

You will learn how to measure length in metric units.

Why learn this? You can choose which metric units to use to measure objects.

The objects shown below will help you understand some metric units that are used to measure length.

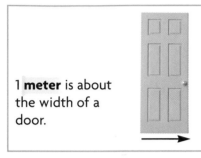

1 **meter** is about the width of a door.

1 **centimeter** is about the width of a large paper clip.

1 **millimeter** is about the thickness of a dime.

Kara and Luke want to use metric units to measure the length of the action figure's car. They made the list at the right to help them decide which unit to use.

Units of Length

1,000 millimeters (mm) = 1 meter (m)
100 centimeters (cm) = 1 meter (m)
10 decimeters (dm) = 1 meter (m)
1 kilometer (km) = 1,000 meters (m)

The length of the car is shorter than a meter. Centimeters can usually be used to measure objects shorter than a meter. Kara and Luke decided to use centimeters to measure the action figure's car.

> The action figure's car is 16 cm long.

Talk About It

- Which units are shorter than a meter? longer than a meter?

- Which unit would you use to measure the height of your desk? Explain why your choice is reasonable.

- What objects in your classroom would you measure in meters? Explain why your choices are reasonable.

💡 **CRITICAL THINKING** Is an object with a length of 10 centimeters longer than an object with a length of 2 meters? Explain how you know.

PRACTICE

Choose the most reasonable unit of measure.
Write *mm, cm, dm, m,* or *km.*

1. thickness of paper
2. distance to the next state
3. length of a bulletin board
4. thickness of a dime
5. height of a chalkboard
6. distance around a baseball field
7. distance from Earth to the moon
8. length of a pencil
9. length of a truck
10. distance from your home to school

Write the measurements in order from shortest to longest.

11. 10 m, 10 km, 10 dm
12. 8 mm, 8 dm, 8 cm
13. 4 km, 4 m, 4 cm
14. 12 m, 12 mm, 12 cm

Mixed Applications

15. Lani's house is 2 km from the library. How many meters is Lani's house from the library?

16. Fran has a piece of ribbon 14 cm long. Ken has a piece of ribbon 2 dm long. Whose ribbon is longer? How much longer?

17. Mary used 3 pieces of ribbon for her project. They were 9.5 cm, 12.7 cm, and 5.3 cm in length. How many cm of ribbon did Mary use?

18. Cameron drove 10.7 km to get to the museum. Jon drove twice as far. How far did Jon drive?

19. Greg and Malita measured the length of the chalkboard. Greg said it measured 3 dm long. Malita said it measured 3 m long. Whose measurement is more reasonable?

20. **Write a problem** about using m, dm, or cm to measure something in your house.

ixed Review

Multiply. Write each product. (pages 196–197)

21. $0.8 \times 0.3 = n$
22. $0.2 \times 0.9 = n$
23. $0.4 \times 0.4 = n$
24. $0.5 \times 0.7 = n$

Use mental math to complete the pattern. (pages 194–195)

25. $1 \times 5 = 5$
$0.1 \times 5 = 0.5$
$0.01 \times 5 = n$

26. $1 \times 3 = 3$
$0.1 \times 3 = n$
$0.01 \times 3 = 0.03$

27. $16 \times 1 = 16$
$16 \times 0.1 = 1.6$
$16 \times 0.01 = n$

28. $84 \times 1 = 84$
$84 \times 0.1 = n$
$84 \times 0.01 = n$

29. $24 \times 1 = 24$
$24 \times 0.1 = 2.4$
$24 \times 0.01 = n$

30. $1 \times 7 = 7$
$0.1 \times 7 = n$
$0.01 \times 7 = 0.07$

31. $39 \times 1 = 39$
$39 \times 0.1 = n$
$39 \times 0.01 = n$

32. $12 \times 1 = n$
$12 \times 0.1 = n$
$12 \times 0.01 = n$

Units of Mass

You will learn how to use metric units to measure the mass of objects.	Why learn this? You can choose which metric unit to use to find the mass of an object.	**WORD POWER** gram (g) kilogram (kg) milligram (mg)

Marti wants to use metric units to find the mass of a quarter and a book. She knows that the mass of a large paper clip is about 1 gram. She can estimate the mass of each object by comparing it with the mass of a paper clip.

Units of Mass

1,000 milligrams (mg) = 1 gram (g)

1,000 grams (g) = 1 kilogram (kg)

It takes about 5 large paper clips to balance a quarter. So, a quarter has a mass of about 5 grams.

It takes about 1,000 paper clips to balance this book. So, this book has a mass of about 1,000 grams, or 1 kilogram.

Talk About It

• Which unit is less than a gram? more than a gram?

• Which objects in your classroom would you measure the mass of in kilograms? in grams? Explain how to put these items in order from the least mass to the greatest mass.

💡 **CRITICAL THINKING** You know the mass of a pencil and you have a box of pencils. How can you use the pencils to find the mass of another object?

Check Your Understanding

Choose the most reasonable unit. Write *kg, g,* or *mg.*

1. a computer

2. a loaf of bread

3. a grain of rice

4. a full box of cereal

PRACTICE

Choose the most reasonable unit. Write *kg*, *g*, or *mg*.

5. stamp

6. a large dog

7. a bagel

8. a snowflake

9. a bag of apples

10. a full suitcase

Choose the more reasonable measurement.

11. 225 g or 225 kg

12. 175 mg or 175 g

13. 5 g or 5 kg

14.  450 mg or 450 kg

15. 30 g or 30 kg

16. 4 mg or 4 g

17. 15 g or 15 kg

18. 35 mg or 35 g

Mixed Applications

19. One cereal bar has a mass of 37 g. What is the mass of 6 cereal bars? Is that more than or less than 1 kg?

20. Larry needs 1 kg of potting soil for his plants. He has 750 g. How much more soil does he need?

21. Wanda needs to move 110 kg of rocks. She can carry 10 kg each trip. How many trips must she make?

22. Brian ran a 100-meter dash in 10.45 seconds. Chris ran the race in 9.98 seconds. How much faster was Brian's time?

23. Stephanie is using a recipe that makes 1 dozen cookies. Would the mass of the cookies be greater than or less than a kilogram?

24. **Write a problem** about the mass of an item in your kitchen.

Mixed Review

Use estimation and patterns to place the decimal point in each product. (pages 200–201)

25. $1.6 \times 4 = 64$ **26.** $1.6 \times 0.4 = 64$ **27.** $1.6 \times 0.04 = 64$ **28.** $0.16 \times 4 = 64$

Copy and complete each pattern. (pages 210–211)

29. $200 \div 5 = n$
$20 \div 5 = n$
$2 \div 5 = n$

30. $300 \div 6 = n$
$30 \div 6 = n$
$3 \div 6 = n$

31. $100 \div 4 = n$
$10 \div 4 = n$
$1 \div 4 = n$

32. $600 \div 5 = n$
$60 \div 5 = n$
$6 \div 5 = n$

Units of Capacity and Volume

You will investigate estimating and measuring with metric units of capacity.

Why learn this? You can choose which metric units to use to measure liquids and to find volume.

WORD POWER

capacity
kiloliter (kL)
liter (L)
milliliter (mL)

The **capacity** of a container measures the amount the container will hold. The metric units of capacity are listed at the right.

In the metric system, volume and capacity are related. A volume of 1 cubic centimeter (cc) can hold 1 milliliter (mL) of water.

Units of Capacity
1,000 milliliters (mL) = 1 liter (L)
1,000 liters (L) = 1 kiloliter (kL)
1 metric cup = 250 milliliters (mL)
4 metric cups = 1 liter (L)

1mL   1cm
1cm

Explore

MATERIALS: 5 empty containers of different sizes, water, metric measuring cup marked with mL and cc units

• Label each container with a different letter from *A* to *E*.

• Use metric units of capacity to estimate how much liquid each container can hold.

• Fill each container with water. Pour the water from the container into the measuring cup to find the capacity and volume of each container.

REMEMBER:

Volume is measured by length × width × height. It is expressed in cubic units.

Record

Copy the table and use it to record your measurements.

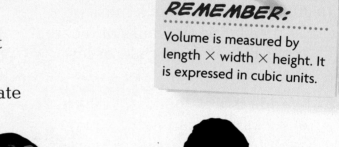

Container	A	B	C	D	E
Estimated Capacity					
Measured Capacity (mL)					
Volume (cc)					

Talk About It

- How can the shape of a container make estimating its capacity difficult?

- How did you find the volume of the container once you knew its capacity?

- How would you determine which unusual shape container has the greatest capacity?

Now, investigate the capacity of objects in your classroom or school.

Try This

Choose two containers, such as a paper cup and a coffee can. Estimate the capacity of each. Then use a metric measuring cup to find the capacity and volume of each container.

✏️ WRITE ABOUT IT What do you notice about the size of each object and its capacity?

Health Link

Water plays an important role in helping our bodies work well. It helps keep our temperature constant. Young people need to drink about 1 to $1\frac{1}{2}$ liters of water each day. About how many milliliters of water do you need to drink each day to keep your body healthy?

Applying What You Learned

Choose the reasonable unit. Write *mL, L,* or *kL.*

1.
2.
3.
4.

Choose the more reasonable measurement.

5.
6.
7.
8.

250 mL or 250 L   4 mL or 4 L   50 mL or 50 L   50 mL or 50 kL

Mixed Applications

9. Travis found an old recipe for pancakes. He cannot read some of it. The recipe makes 12 to 14 pancakes. Would the amount of milk be 300 mL or 30 L?

10. ✏️ **Write a problem** using this information. A carton holds 1 L of orange juice.

Relating Metric Units

You will learn how units of metric measurement are related.

Why learn this? You can understand the prefixes and know which units are very small and which are very large.

You have seen how metric units can be used to measure length, capacity, and mass. Metric units use a *prefix* and a *base unit.*

Length	Capacity	Mass
millimeter	milliliter	milligram
centimeter		
decimeter		
meter	liter	gram
kilometer	kiloliter	kilogram

Metric units are related to place value. The prefix determines the value of the unit.

Tuolumne Meadows   13 km
Crane Flat   76 km
Yosemite Village   101 km

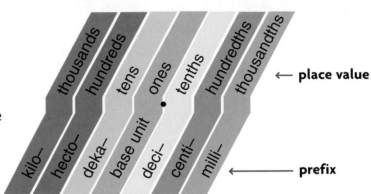

← place value

← prefix

You can write measurements by using the base unit.

7 kilograms = _?_ grams	3 milliliters = _?_ liter
Think: 1 kilogram = 1,000 grams	**Think:** 1 milliliter = 0.001 liter
7 × 1,000 = 7,000	3 × 0.001 = 0.003
7 kilograms = 7,000 grams	3 milliliters = 0.003 liter

Talk About It

- Which prefixes indicate units smaller than the base units?

- Which prefix indicates a unit 1,000 times as great as the base unit?

Check Your Understanding

Write the equivalent measurement.

1. 4 centimeters = _?_ meter

2. 5 milligrams = _?_ gram

PRACTICE

Choose the smaller unit of measure. Write *a* or *b*. Use the prefix to help you.

3. a. kilometer
   b. meter

4. a. milliliter
   b. liter

5. a. gram
   b. milligram

Choose the larger unit of measure. Write *a* or *b*. Use the prefix to help you.

6. a. kiloliter
   b. liter

7. a. gram
   b. kilogram

8. a. decimeter
   b. centimeter

Write the equivalent measurement.

9. 5 decimeters = __?__ meter

10. 4 milliliters = __?__ liter

11. 8 grams = __?__ milligrams

12. 9 milligrams = __?__ gram

13. 2 milliliters = __?__ liter

14. 6 kilograms = __?__ grams

15. 4 centimeters = __?__ meter

16. 12 milligrams = __?__ gram

Mixed Applications

17. Suzanne has a piece of ribbon 2.2 dm long. Joel has a piece of ribbon 22 cm long. Whose ribbon is longer?

18. Rita is painting a mural in her classroom. She needs 1.5 L of paint to complete the mural. She has only 0.25 L of paint. How much more paint does she need?

19. Conner and Kelly need string for their art projects. Conner needs 3.5 m of string, and Kelly needs 4.2 m of string. How much string do they need in all?

20. Dustin used a piece of wire that was 4.5 m long. He cut the wire into 5 equal pieces. Was each piece of wire greater than or less than 1 m?

21. Carl has an object with a mass of 1 kg. Mark has an object with a mass of 1 mg. Who has the object with a smaller mass?

22. ▱▶ **WRITE ABOUT IT** Explain how to decide if the capacity of a container should be measured in milliliters or liters.

Mixed Review

Find the quotient. Check by multiplying. (pages 216–217)

23. $9\overline{)3.6}$
  24. $7\overline{)4.9}$
  25. $9\overline{)8.1}$
  26. $3\overline{)3.3}$
  27. $2\overline{)4.04}$

Find the product. (pages 204–205)

28. $2.5 \times 1.8 = n$
  29. $3.9 \times 4.6 = n$
  30. $1.6 \times 7.3 = n$
  31. $2.05 \times 9.9 = n$

MORE PRACTICE Student Handbook page H96

PART 1 Changing Units

You will learn how to change units of measure by multiplying or dividing.

Why learn this? You can change large units of measure to smaller units and small units to larger units.

Changing units in the metric system is like moving from one place-value position to another.

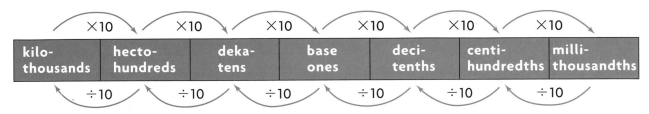

kilo- thousands	hecto- hundreds	deka- tens	base ones	deci- tenths	centi- hundredths	milli- thousandths

$\times 10$ across the top, $\div 10$ across the bottom

A. To change units to smaller units, multiply.

5 m = ? cm

Hint: Meters are longer than centimeters.

So, 5 m = 500 cm.

To change base unit meter to centimeters, move two places to the right.

Multiply by 10 × 10, or 100.

5 × 100 = 500

m ones	dm tenths	cm hundredths

$\times 10$, $\times 10$

B. To change units to larger units, divide.

4,000 L = ? kL

Hint: Liters are less than kiloliters.

So, 4,000 L = 4 kL.

To change base unit liters to kiloliters, move three places to the left.

Divide by 10 × 10 × 10, or 1,000.

4,000 ÷ 1,000 = 4

kL thousands	hL hundreds	daL tens	L ones

$\div 10$, $\div 10$, $\div 10$

Talk About It

- If you change 7 meters to centimeters, does the number become larger or smaller? Explain how you know.

- Why do you multiply to change 7 kilograms to grams?

- Why do you divide to change 8 mL to liters?

💡 **CRITICAL THINKING** If you get fewer units when you change from one unit to another, did you start with a larger or smaller unit?

PRACTICE

Write the missing unit.

1. 4 kg = 4,000 _?_
2. 60 km = 60,000 _?_
3. 9 m = 900 _?_
4. 8.136 L = 8,136 _?_
5. 9.373 kg = 9,373 _?_
6. 800 mm = 80 _?_
7. 5.9 m = 590 _?_
8. 5,560 mm = 5.56 _?_
9. 2,000 mL = 2 _?_
10. 30 m = 300 _?_
11. 6,800 g = 6.8 _?_
12. 7 kg = 7,000 _?_

Write *multiply* or *divide*. Then write the equivalent measurement.

13. 2.5 cm = _?_ mm
14. 70 mm = _?_ cm
15. 5 cm = _?_ dm
16. 12 L = _?_ mL
17. 8,000 mg = _?_ g
18. 6,000 g = _?_ kg
19. 34,000 mL = _?_ L
20. 6.25 g = _?_ mg
21. 8.8 L = _?_ mL
22. 3.75 m = _?_ cm
23. 50 mm = _?_ dm
24. 1,600 mL = _?_ L
25. 0.005 m = _?_ mm
26. 7,700 mg = _?_ g
27. 9 g = _?_ kg

Mixed Applications

28. Tara poured 0.5 L of water into a beaker. During an experiment, she added 200 mL of water. How much water was in the beaker at the end of the experiment?

29. While he was doing a science experiment, Todd learned that weather balloons burst at an altitude of 27 km. What is this altitude in meters?

30. Janis had a piece of string for her string-art project that was 2.7 m long. She cut the string into 3 equal pieces. Was each piece of string longer than or shorter than 1 m?

31. ✏️ **WRITE ABOUT IT** Explain how to decide when to multiply and when to divide when changing units.

LESSON CONTINUES ▶

PART 2 PROBLEM-SOLVING STRATEGY
Draw a Diagram

THE PROBLEM Sammy, Jamal, and Enrique skate 6 days each week. They skate 2.3 km each day. How many meters do they skate each day?

☑ Understand
- What are you asked to find?
- What information will you use?
- Is there information you will not use? If so, what?

☑ Plan
- What strategy can you use to solve this problem?

  You can *draw a diagram* to find how many meters Sammy, Jamal, and Enrique skate.

☑ Solve
- What diagram can you draw to solve the problem?

You can use the diagram shown below.

2.3 km = <u>?</u> m   Multiply by 10 × 10 × 10, or 1,000.

2.3 km = 2,300 m   2.3 x 1,000 = 2,300

kilo-	hecto-	deka-	base
thousands	hundreds	tens	ones
2.3 km	23 hm	230 dam	2,300 m

So, Sammy, Jamal, and Enrique each skate 2,300 m each day.

☑ Look Back
- How can you decide if your answer is reasonable?
- What other strategy can you use?

PRACTICE

Draw a diagram to solve.

1. Darla found that her Spanish book has a mass of 0.650 kg. What is the mass of Darla's Spanish book in grams?

2. Gary's height is 1.5 m. Rick is 1 dm taller than Gary. How tall is Rick in meters?

3. Derrick poured 0.4 L of milk into a pitcher. Then his dad poured 0.23 L of milk into the pitcher. How many milliliters of milk are in the pitcher?

4. A dog run will be 6 yd long and 3 yd wide. One side that is 6 yd long will be formed by a garage. The other three sides will be made of fencing. How much fencing is needed?

Mixed Applications

Solve.

CHOOSE A STRATEGY

• Work Backward   • Find a Pattern   • Draw a Diagram
• Make an Organized List   • Write a Number Sentence

5. Ken will do a science project on either electricity, sea life, space, or weather. He can work on the project either alone or with a partner. What are the choices Ken has for doing the science project?

6. During a rainstorm, a rain barrel contained 1.5 in. of water at 4:00 P.M. By 5:00 P.M. it held 3 in. of water. At 6:00 P.M. there were 4.5 in. of water. If rain continues to fall at this rate, how many inches of water will the barrel contain at 9:00 P.M.?

7. Nicki can juggle up to 5 pounds of juggling balls, regardless of the number of balls. If she wants to juggle 10 balls of equal weight, what is the most each ball can weigh?

8. Sara poured 0.2 L of orange juice into each of 3 glasses. How many millimeters of orange juice did Sara use?

9. Christa spent half her weekly allowance on materials for her art project. Then she spent half of what was left on colored pencils. Part of her receipt is shown at the right. How much is her weekly allowance?

CHANGE $2.50

Thank You
For Shopping With Us

CULTURAL CONNECTION

THE ARIZONA HOPI

Louise brought traditional Hopi foods, jewelry, and pottery to school to share with her new classmates in Phoenix, Arizona. She wanted to tell the other students about her Hopi village in northeastern Arizona. She drew a map and made a scale to show the 525-kilometer distance between her village and Phoenix. The scale she used was 1 cm = 100 km. How many centimeters apart did she draw Phoenix and her village?

CULTURAL LINK

To make piki bread, spread a thin layer of cornmeal batter on a hot greased rock or skillet. When the batter is cooked, remove it and spread a second layer of batter on the skillet. The first paper-thin layer is set on top of the sizzling batter. Make four layers, stack together, and roll them up so they are shaped like a cylinder.

Work Together

1. Louise brought the following items to school: a basket of blue corn, silver earrings, a silver and turquoise necklace, a small Kachina doll, and a pottery bowl. Make a table with two columns. Write Kilogram on one side and Gram on the other. List each item under the metric unit that would best represent its mass.

2. The students in Louise's class visited the cultural museum and saw a model of a traditional Hopi house. They estimated that the height of the walls was $2\frac{5}{10}$ meters. How many ways can you write this height, using metric terms?

3. Louise and her mother made piki bread on an electric griddle in the classroom. They poured 20 metric cups of the batter into a container to make enough bread for all the students. How many liters of the cornmeal mixture did they have in the container?

4. If a basket filled with piki bread has a mass of 3 kilograms, what is its mass in grams? in milligrams?

✓ CHECK UNDERSTANDING

VOCABULARY

1. The __?__ of a container measures the amount the container can hold. (page 230)

2. The width of a large paper clip is about a __?__ . (page 226)

3. The width of a doorway is about 1 __?__ . (page 226)

4. The thickness of a dime is about a __?__ . (page 226)

5. A __?__ is equivalent to 1,000 mg. (page 228)

6. A unit of mass that is 1,000 as much as a gram is a __?__ . (page 228)

7. A capacity of 1,000 mL is equivalent to 1 __?__ . (page 230)

8. A __?__ is equivalent to 1,000 L. (page 230)

Choose the more reasonable measurement. (pages 226–231)

9.

17 cm or 17 dm

10.

10 kg or 10 g

11.

200 g or 200 mg

12.

2 L or 2 mL

✓ CHECK SKILLS

Write the equivalent measurement. (pages 232–235)

13. 6 m = __?__ mm

14. 2,000 mg = __?__ g

15. 4 L = __?__ kL

16. 77 cm = __?__ dm

17. 4.2 g = __?__ mg

18. 35 mL = __?__ L

19. 5 kg = __?__ g

20. 0.008 L = __?__ mL

21. 0.7 m = __?__ dm

✓ CHECK PROBLEM SOLVING

Solve. (pages 236–237)

CHOOSE A STRATEGY

• Find a Pattern   • Draw a Diagram   • Make an Organized List

22. Jason can buy either a blue, red, green, or black bike. It can be either a 10-speed or a 12-speed bike. What choices does Jason have?

23. Jackie and each of her 3 friends had a glass of juice at their picnic. There were 300 mL of juice in each glass. How many liters of juice did Jackie and her friends drink?

VOCABULARY CHECK

Choose a term from the box to complete each sentence.

WORD BANK
gram
centi-
liter
meter
mixed decimal
capacity

1. A number with a whole number part and a decimal part is a __?__ . (page 204)

2. There are 100 centimeters (cm) in 1 __?__ . (page 226)

3. A container's __?__ measures the amount it can hold. (page 230)

4. A mass of 1,000 milligrams (mg) is equivalent to 1 __?__ . (page 228)

5. A capacity of 1 __?__ is equivalent to 1,000 milliliters (mL). (page 230)

6. The prefix __?__ indicates a metric unit that is $\frac{1}{100}$ of the base unit. (page 232)

STUDY AND SOLVE

CHAPTER 12

EXAMPLE

Estimate to place the decimal point. Find the product.

$$\begin{array}{r} 3\ 4 \\ 2.57 \\ \times\ \ 0.6 \\ \hline 1.542 \end{array}$$

Multiply as with whole numbers. Use estimation to place the decimal point.

Think: 0.6×2.57 is about 0.5×3, or about half of 3, which is 1.5.

Use mental math to complete the pattern.
(pages 194–195)

7. $64 \times 1 = n$
$64 \times 0.1 = n$
$64 \times 0.01 = n$

8. $302 \times 1 = n$
$302 \times 0.1 = n$
$302 \times 0.01 = n$

Find the product. (pages 192–205)

9. $\begin{array}{r} 0.8 \\ \times\ 9 \\ \hline \end{array}$

10. $\begin{array}{r} 0.37 \\ \times\ \ 4 \\ \hline \end{array}$

11. $\begin{array}{r} 0.7 \\ \times 0.5 \\ \hline \end{array}$

12. $\begin{array}{r} \$6.14 \\ \times\ \ \ 6 \\ \hline \end{array}$

13. $\begin{array}{r} 1.9 \\ \times\ 3 \\ \hline \end{array}$

14. $\begin{array}{r} 5.63 \\ \times\ \ 7 \\ \hline \end{array}$

15. $\begin{array}{r} 3.42 \\ \times\ 0.8 \\ \hline \end{array}$

16. $\begin{array}{r} 2.31 \\ \times\ 0.4 \\ \hline \end{array}$

17. $\$2.98 \times 0.5 = n$ 18. $0.76 \times 2.2 = n$

Choose a strategy and solve. (pages 198–199)

19. After a party, 0.4 of a pizza was left. Al ate 0.5 of the leftover pizza. How much of a whole pizza did he eat?

CHAPTER 13

EXAMPLE

Find the quotient.

$$\begin{array}{r} 9.3 \\ 3\overline{)27.9} \end{array}$$

Divide as with whole numbers. Place the decimal point in the quotient above the decimal point in the dividend, between the ones place and the tenths place.

Copy and complete each pattern.
(pages 210–211)

20. $4{,}000 \div 5 = n$
$400 \div 5 = n$
$40 \div 5 = n$
$4 \div 5 = n$

21. $9{,}000 \div 4 = n$
$900 \div 4 = n$
$90 \div 4 = n$
$9 \div 4 = n$

Find the quotient. Check by multiplying.
(pages 216–219)

22. $7\overline{)3.5}$ **23.** $5\overline{)4.5}$

24. $6\overline{)0.36}$ **25.** $8\overline{)5.68}$

26. $3\overline{)3.69}$ **27.** $4\overline{)7.2}$

28. $2\overline{)6.08}$ **29.** $9\overline{)82.8}$

Choose a strategy and solve.

30. Vicky and Raúl went to lunch. Their bill was $23.88. They decided to split the cost. How much did each pay? (pages 212–213)

31. The market is selling chicken at $2.25 per pound. How much do 3 pounds cost? (pages 220–221)

CHAPTER 14

EXAMPLE

Write the equivalent measurement.

66 cm = _?_ dm   Since 1 dm = 10 cm, multiply by 0.1.
66 cm = 6.6 dm $66 \times 0.1 = 6.6$

Write the equivalent measurement.
(pages 232–235)

32. 5 m = _?_ cm

33. _?_ mm = 8 m

34. 4,000 g = _?_ kg

35. 3.5 g = _?_ mg

36. 9 L = _?_ kL

37. _?_ L = 55 mL

Choose the more reasonable measurement.
(pages 226–231)

38.

15 cm or 15 m

39.

8 g or 8 kg

40.   **41.**

40 g or 40 kg   2 mL or 2 L

Choose a strategy and solve. (pages 236–237)

42. Karla is 150 cm tall. Pablo is 1 dm shorter than Karla. How tall is Pablo in centimeters? in meters?

✎ WRITE ABOUT IT

1. Explain the pattern you see in the problems. Then explain how to use mental math to find the products and name the products. (pages 194–195)

$45 \times 1 = n$
$45 \times 0.1 = n$
$45 \times 0.01 = n$

2. Show and explain each step as you use patterns or estimation to place the decimal point and then find the quotient. (pages 216-219)

$8\overline{)32.8}$

3. Which metric unit of mass would you use to measure each object? Explain your choice. (pages 228-229)

- a bag of potatoes
- a stamp
- a quarter

✔ PERFORMANCE ASSESSMENT

Solve. Explain your method.

╭─────────────────────╮
│ **CHOOSE A STRATEGY** │
╰─────────────────────╯

| • Find a Pattern | • Act It Out | • Make a Model | • Make a Table | • Write a Number Sentence |

4. Suppose you recycle 10 pounds of paper. Of the paper, 0.5 is newspaper and 0.5 is computer paper. If 0.8 of the newspaper is colored pages, how much of the recycled paper is colored?

(pages 198–199)

5. Pens cost $0.59 each when purchased separately, or 5 pens for $1.99 when purchased in packages. Write a number sentence to find out which is the better buy. Explain your answer.

(pages 212–213)

6. Hector is 1.5 m tall. His dog, Pepper, is 5 dm shorter than he is. Rosa, his sister, is 3 dm taller than Pepper. How tall are Rosa and Pepper, in meters? (pages 236–237)

Solve the problem. Then write the letter of the correct answer.

1. What is the value of the blue digit?

2̲03,462,851

A. 2
B. 200,000
C. 2,000,000
D. 200,000,000   (pages 6–9)

2. Dan has $15.00 with him at the bookstore. He chooses a book for $8.95, a greeting card for $2.25, and a magazine for $1.95. Does he have enough for all three items if the sales tax is about $1.00? Estimate what he will pay at the cash register, including tax.

A. yes; about $12.00
B. yes; about $14.00
C. no; about $15.50
D. no; about $16.00   (pages 28–29)

3. $228 \times 4 = n$

A. $n = 57$ B. $n = 232$
C. $n = 912$ D. $n = 9,120$
    (pages 74–75)

4. By which numbers is 884 divisible?

A. 2, 3   B. 2, 3, 4
C. 2, 3, 5   D. 2, 4
    (pages 102–103)

5. Find the mode.

105, 110, 115, 105, 130

A. 25   B. 105
C. 110   D. 113
    (pages 140–141)

6. $3.54 \times 0.6 = n$

A. $n = 2.124$ B. $n = 4.14$
C. $n = 21.24$ D. $n = 212.4$
    (pages 196–203)

7. $4\overline{)6.84}$

A. 1.71   B. 17.1
C. 171   D. 27.36
    (pages 216–219)

8. A dime is about 1 __?__ thick.

A. centimeter
B. kiloliter
C. milligram
D. millimeter   (pages 226–231)

9. Choose the most reasonable measurement.

A. 25 mm
B. 25 cm
C. 25 m
D. 25 km
    (pages 226–227)

10. $5 \text{ kg} = $ __?__ g

A. 0.005   B. 0.5
C. 500   D. 5,000
    (pages 228–229, 232–233)

UNDERSTANDING FRACTIONS

DID YOU KNOW...

In the early 1800's, people all over the world enjoyed a Chinese puzzle called a tangram. They arranged the seven pieces of the tangram to make pictures.

Fraction Time with Tangrams

You have probably made tangram puzzles by arranging the seven pieces in different ways. But have you ever thought about why the pieces fit together? Work with a group to analyze tangram pieces as fractions of one whole. Then make a poster showing designs that add up to $\frac{1}{2}$.

YOU WILL NEED: tangram pattern, scissors, poster board, markers

Work with a group. Your job is to

- figure out which pieces make $\frac{1}{4}$, which pieces make $\frac{1}{8}$, and which pieces make $\frac{1}{16}$ of the whole square.

- write the fractions on each piece.

- use the tangram pieces to make designs that cover $\frac{1}{2}$ of the whole square.

- make a poster showing your designs.

- share your tangram poster with the class.

RULES FOR MAKING TANGRAMS THAT ADD UP TO $\frac{1}{2}$

- Pieces must add up to $\frac{1}{2}$.
- Write the fraction on each piece.
- It is all right to flip pieces over.
- It is all right to use small pieces from more than one tangram.

DID YOU

☑ figure out the fraction for each tangram piece?

☑ make designs that add up to $\frac{1}{2}$?

☑ make a poster of your designs?

☑ share your poster with the class?

Understanding Fractions

You will learn to identify, read, and write fractions.	**Why learn this?** You can use fractions to describe parts of your class.

Lita's class is making tangram designs. Of the students, $\frac{1}{2}$ make people, $\frac{1}{3}$ make animals, and $\frac{1}{4}$ make flowers. Which group is largest?

You can use fraction strips and number lines to show fractions. The fraction strips and number lines below show the fractions $\frac{1}{1}$, $\frac{1}{2}$, $\frac{1}{3}$, and $\frac{1}{4}$.

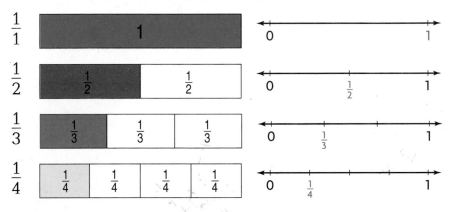

So, the group that makes people is largest.

- If the denominator increases and the numerator stays the same, what happens to the size of the part of the whole?

The fraction strips and number lines below show the fractions $\frac{1}{4}$, $\frac{2}{4}$, $\frac{3}{4}$, and $\frac{4}{4}$.

$\frac{1}{4}$ | $\frac{1}{4}$ $\frac{1}{4}$ $\frac{1}{4}$ $\frac{1}{4}$ | 0 $\frac{1}{4}$ 1

$\frac{2}{4}$ | $\frac{1}{4}$ $\frac{1}{4}$ $\frac{1}{4}$ $\frac{1}{4}$ | 0 $\frac{2}{4}$ 1

$\frac{3}{4}$ | $\frac{1}{4}$ $\frac{1}{4}$ $\frac{1}{4}$ $\frac{1}{4}$ | 0 $\frac{3}{4}$ 1

$\frac{4}{4}$ | $\frac{1}{4}$ $\frac{1}{4}$ $\frac{1}{4}$ $\frac{1}{4}$ | 0 1

- If the denominator stays the same and the numerator increases, what happens to the size of the part of the whole?

💡 **CRITICAL THINKING** Why do the parts of the whole get smaller when the denominator increases and larger when the numerator increases?

PRACTICE

Write the fraction shown.

1.

| $\frac{1}{3}$ | $\frac{1}{3}$ | $\frac{1}{3}$ |

2.

| $\frac{1}{5}$ | $\frac{1}{5}$ | $\frac{1}{5}$ | $\frac{1}{5}$ | $\frac{1}{5}$ |

3.

| $\frac{1}{5}$ | $\frac{1}{5}$ | $\frac{1}{5}$ | $\frac{1}{5}$ | $\frac{1}{5}$ |

4.

| $\frac{1}{6}$ | $\frac{1}{6}$ | $\frac{1}{6}$ | $\frac{1}{6}$ | $\frac{1}{6}$ | $\frac{1}{6}$ |

5.

| $\frac{1}{8}$ | $\frac{1}{8}$ | $\frac{1}{8}$ | $\frac{1}{8}$ | $\frac{1}{8}$ | $\frac{1}{8}$ | $\frac{1}{8}$ | $\frac{1}{8}$ |

6.

| $\frac{1}{10}$ | $\frac{1}{10}$ | $\frac{1}{10}$ | $\frac{1}{10}$ | $\frac{1}{10}$ | $\frac{1}{10}$ | $\frac{1}{10}$ | $\frac{1}{10}$ | $\frac{1}{10}$ | $\frac{1}{10}$ |

Shade a fraction strip to show the fraction.

7. $\frac{2}{3}$ **8.** $\frac{1}{6}$ **9.** $\frac{5}{8}$ **10.** $\frac{9}{10}$ **11.** $\frac{3}{4}$

12. $\frac{2}{9}$ **13.** $\frac{7}{12}$ **14.** $\frac{3}{5}$ **15.** $\frac{1}{3}$ **16.** $\frac{5}{6}$

Draw a number line. Locate the fraction.

17. $\frac{4}{5}$ **18.** $\frac{3}{6}$ **19.** $\frac{3}{10}$ **20.** $\frac{2}{3}$ **21.** $\frac{5}{6}$

Mixed Applications

22. Gina is planting 8 rows of vegetables in her garden. Today she planted 3 rows. What fraction of her garden does she have left to plant?

23. ✏️ **Write a problem** about a family sharing a pie. Use fractions in your problem.

Mixed Review

Solve. Use the inverse operation to check each problem. (pages 18–19)

24. $\begin{array}{r} 11 \\ +25 \\ \hline \end{array}$ **25.** $\begin{array}{r} 37 \\ -14 \\ \hline \end{array}$ **26.** $\begin{array}{r} 44 \\ +17 \\ \hline \end{array}$ **27.** $\begin{array}{r} 132 \\ -\ 91 \\ \hline \end{array}$

Write the value of the digit 4 in each number. (pages 38–39)

28. 4,782.513 **29.** 8,304.597 **30.** 6,926.482 **31.** 3,523.704

32. 3,406.002 **33.** 1,625.147 **34.** 5,242.198 **35.** 9,621.407

Mixed Numbers

You will learn to identify, read, and write mixed numbers and to rename fractions greater than 1 as mixed numbers.

Why learn this? You can use mixed numbers to name amounts made up of wholes and parts.

The fifth-grade soccer team had a pizza party. They ordered two rectangular pizzas that were cut into eighths. The team ate one whole pizza and three slices from the other pizza.

A **mixed number** is made up of a whole number and a fraction. Look at the fraction bars that represent the pizza the soccer team ate.

Read: one and three eighths

Write: $1\frac{3}{8}$

• How many eighths are represented by the fraction bar for 1? How many eighths are shown in all? What fraction does this name?

CRITICAL THINKING Are all mixed numbers greater than 1? Why or why not?

EXAMPLES

A. one and two fifths

$1\frac{2}{5}$

B. two and one fourth

$2\frac{1}{4}$

C. three and five sixths

$3\frac{5}{6}$

When a fraction is greater than 1, it can be renamed as a mixed number.

EXAMPLE

Rename $\frac{5}{4}$ as a mixed number.

• How can you tell if a fraction is greater than 1?

Technology **Link**

In **Mighty Math Calculating Crew**, the game *Nautical Number Line* challenges you to identify mixed numbers.

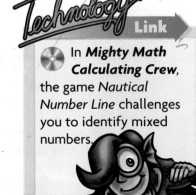

Calculator Activities page H64

You can also use a calculator to change a fraction to a mixed number.

 Press: **Display:** | 1 ⌐ 1/5 |

PRACTICE

For Problems 1–4, use the figures at the right.

1. How many whole figures are shaded?

2. Into how many parts is each figure divided?

3. How many parts of the fourth figure are shaded?

4. Write a fraction and a mixed number for the picture.

Rename each fraction as a mixed number.

5. $\dfrac{21}{8}$ 6. $\dfrac{9}{2}$ 7. $\dfrac{7}{6}$ 8. $\dfrac{13}{5}$ 9. $\dfrac{15}{4}$

Rename each mixed number as a fraction.

10. $2\dfrac{1}{2}$ 11. $3\dfrac{1}{4}$ 12. $7\dfrac{2}{3}$ 13. $1\dfrac{3}{4}$ 14. $2\dfrac{4}{5}$

Mixed Applications

15. Tina found a page from her great-grandmother's old math book. Tina wants to rename all the fractions as mixed numbers. Rename the fractions for her.

16. ✎ **WRITE ABOUT IT** Explain how to rename a mixed number as a fraction.

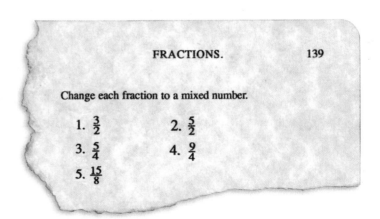

FRACTIONS.   139

Change each fraction to a mixed number.

1. $\dfrac{3}{2}$ 2. $\dfrac{5}{2}$

3. $\dfrac{5}{4}$ 4. $\dfrac{9}{4}$

5. $\dfrac{15}{8}$

Mixed Review

Write in standard form. (pages 38–39)

17. four thousand, two hundred fifty and five hundred sixty-one thousandths

18. six thousand, one hundred two and two hundred four thousandths

Use an equivalent decimal to find the sum. (pages 52–53)

19. $\begin{array}{r} 5 \\ +0.8 \\ \hline \end{array}$ 20. $\begin{array}{r} 4.7 \\ +2.96 \\ \hline \end{array}$ 21. $\begin{array}{r} 8.53 \\ +0.491 \\ \hline \end{array}$ 22. $\begin{array}{r} 17.2 \\ +\ 5.38 \\ \hline \end{array}$

MORE PRACTICE Student Handbook page H97

Multiples and Least Common Multiples

You will investigate finding the least common multiple of two numbers.

Why learn this? You can use the least common multiple to rename fractions.

WORD POWER

multiple
common
  multiples
least common
  multiple
  (LCM)

A **multiple** is the product of two or more numbers.

Multiples of one number that are also multiples of another number are called **common multiples**. The least number that is a common multiple is called the **least common multiple**, or **LCM**.

Explore

MATERIALS: red and yellow counters

Use counters to find the least common multiple of 3 and 4.

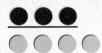

Step 1

Place 3 red counters in a row. Place 4 yellow counters in a row directly below.

● ● ●
○ ○ ○ ○

Step 2

Continue placing groups of 3 red and 4 yellow counters until both rows have the same number of counters. At that point, the number of counters in each row is the least common multiple, or LCM, of 3 and 4.

● ● ● ● ● ●
○ ○ ○ ○ ○ ○ ○ ○ ○

Complete the steps to find the least common multiple of 3 and 4. Use the same method to find the least common multiple of 4 and 5.

Record

Write the least common multiple of 3 and 4 and the least common multiple of 4 and 5. Explain how you know.

TALK ABOUT IT Can two numbers have more than one common multiple? Explain.

Technology Link ▶
E–Lab • Activity 15 Available on CD-ROM and the Internet at http://www.hbschool.com/elab

You can also find the LCM of two or more numbers by making a list or using a number line.

Multiples of 2: 2, 4, 6, 8, 10, 12
Multiples of 3: 3, 6, 9, 12, 15, 18

So, the least common multiple, or LCM, is 6.

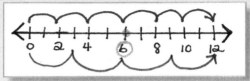

Try This

You can use the least common multiple, or LCM, to rename fractions with unlike denominators as fractions with like denominators.

EXAMPLE

Rename $\frac{1}{2}$ and $\frac{2}{3}$ so they have the same denominator.

Use the least common multiple, or LCM, of the denominators as the new denominator. The LCM of 2 and 3 is 6.

Use fraction strips to rename the fractions.

$\frac{1}{2} = \frac{3}{6}$

$\frac{2}{3} = \frac{4}{6}$

Use fraction strips and the LCM to rename $\frac{3}{4}$ and $\frac{2}{3}$ so they have the same denominator. Write the new pair of fractions.

✏ **WRITE ABOUT IT** How is the LCM used to rename fractions?

HANDS-ON PRACTICE

Use counters to name the least common multiple for each.

1. 2 and 4   **2.** 2 and 5   **3.** 4 and 6   **4.** 9 and 3   **5.** 4 and 8

Rename each pair of fractions so they have the same denominator. Use fraction strips and the LCMs from Exercises 1–5.

6. $\frac{1}{2}$ and $\frac{1}{4}$ **7.** $\frac{1}{2}$ and $\frac{2}{5}$ **8.** $\frac{1}{4}$ and $\frac{5}{6}$ **9.** $\frac{5}{9}$ and $\frac{2}{3}$ **10.** $\frac{3}{4}$ and $\frac{5}{8}$

Mixed Applications

11. Ethan rides his bike $\frac{3}{4}$ mile every day. Brad rides his bike $\frac{4}{6}$ mile. How can you rename the distances Ethan and Brad ride so that they have the same denominators?

12. Nita will use ceramic and glass beads, and she will use all the beads she buys. Ceramic beads come 5 to a pack, and glass beads come 3 to a pack. She uses the same number of each bead. What is the least number of beads she will buy?

Comparing

You will learn to compare fractions with unlike denominators.

Why learn this? You can compare fractional amounts when cooking.

To compare fractions with unlike denominators, you can use fraction strips.

$\frac{1}{6}$	$\frac{1}{6}$	$\frac{1}{6}$	$\frac{1}{6}$	$\frac{1}{6}$	$\frac{1}{6}$

$\frac{1}{8}$	$\frac{1}{8}$	$\frac{1}{8}$	$\frac{1}{8}$	$\frac{1}{8}$	$\frac{1}{8}$	$\frac{1}{8}$	$\frac{1}{8}$

$$\frac{5}{6} > \frac{6}{8}$$

REMEMBER:

To compare fractions with like denominators, compare the numerators.

Since $3 > 1$, $\frac{3}{4} > \frac{1}{4}$.

You can also rename fractions with unlike denominators, such as $\frac{1}{2}$ and $\frac{2}{3}$, so they have like denominators.

MODEL

▶ **Step 1**

Find the least common multiple, or LCM, of the denominators.

2: 2, 4, 6, 8
3: 3, 6, 9, 12

So, the LCM is 6.

▶ **Step 2**

Use 6 as a denominator. Find the missing factor to rename each denominator as 6.

$\frac{1 \times \blacksquare}{2 \times \blacksquare} = \frac{}{6}$ The missing factor is 3.

$\frac{2 \times \blacksquare}{3 \times \blacksquare} = \frac{}{6}$ The missing factor is 2.

▶ **Step 3**

Multiply the numerator and the denominator by the missing factor from Step 2. Compare the numerators of the renamed fractions.

$\frac{1 \times 3}{2 \times 3} = \frac{3}{6}$

$\frac{2 \times 2}{3 \times 2} = \frac{4}{6}$ Since $3 < 4$, $\frac{3}{6} < \frac{4}{6}$.

So, $\frac{1}{2} < \frac{2}{3}$.

EXAMPLE

Use the LCM to compare $\frac{3}{5}$ and $\frac{7}{10}$.

Find the LCM of the denominators.

5: 5, 10, 15, 20
10: 10, 20, 30, 40

Rename the fractions.

$\frac{3 \times 2}{5 \times 2} = \frac{6}{10}$

$\frac{7 \times 1}{10 \times 1} = \frac{7}{10}$

Compare.

Since $6 < 7$, $\frac{6}{10} < \frac{7}{10}$.

So, $\frac{3}{5} < \frac{7}{10}$.

- Can the least common multiple of two numbers be one of the numbers? Explain.

💡 **CRITICAL THINKING** Which pair of fractions is easier to compare, $\frac{2}{3}$ and $\frac{5}{9}$ or $\frac{2}{3}$ and $\frac{5}{7}$? Explain.

PRACTICE

Rename, using the least common multiple, and compare.
Write <, >, or = for each ⬤.

1. $\frac{5}{21}$ ⬤ $\frac{3}{7}$
2. $\frac{4}{6}$ ⬤ $\frac{2}{3}$
3. $\frac{2}{9}$ ⬤ $\frac{3}{18}$
4. $\frac{11}{15}$ ⬤ $\frac{4}{5}$

5. $\frac{3}{8}$ ⬤ $\frac{5}{16}$
6. $\frac{4}{12}$ ⬤ $\frac{1}{3}$
7. $\frac{2}{3}$ ⬤ $\frac{25}{27}$
8. $\frac{13}{20}$ ⬤ $\frac{3}{5}$

9. $\frac{5}{6}$ ⬤ $\frac{3}{4}$
10. $\frac{5}{6}$ ⬤ $\frac{3}{8}$
11. $\frac{1}{2}$ ⬤ $\frac{4}{7}$
12. $\frac{2}{3}$ ⬤ $\frac{4}{5}$

13. $\frac{3}{10}$ ⬤ $\frac{1}{4}$
14. $\frac{2}{5}$ ⬤ $\frac{3}{4}$
15. $\frac{4}{9}$ ⬤ $\frac{2}{6}$
16. $\frac{1}{3}$ ⬤ $\frac{3}{8}$

Mixed Applications

17. Jan used $\frac{2}{3}$ cup flour to make cookies. She used $\frac{3}{4}$ cup flour to make brownies. For which did she use more flour?

18. The Grocery Store sells 4 bags of rice for $16.20. The Warehouse Market sells 1 bag of rice for $4.10. The Country Store sells 6 bags of rice for $25.00. In which store is the price the least?

19. Donald runs 3.5 miles on Monday, Wednesday, and Friday. He runs 4.8 miles on Tuesday, Thursday, and Saturday. If Donald wants to run 27 miles in a week, how many miles should Donald run on Sunday?

20. Merriellen planted 5 types of flowers in her garden. Each row contains one of each type of flower. If she planted 10 rows of flowers, how many flowers did she plant?

21. Park rangers plan to move 2 alligators from one lake to another this month. For the next 5 months they will move 3 more alligators than the month before. How many alligators will they move in all?

22. ✏️ **WRITE ABOUT IT** When renaming fractions, why do you multiply the numerator by the same number by which you multiply the denominator?

Mixed Review

Order from least to greatest. (pages 42–43)

23. 3.34, 3.61, 3.01
24. 9.400, 9.004, 9.040
25. 14.43, 14.29, 14.91

Find the difference. (pages 54–55)

26. 2.6
    −0.9

27. 5.04
    −0.7

28. 7.938
    −5.21

29. 8.972
    −3.54

30. 9.512
    −2.093

You will learn to order fractions with unlike denominators.	Why learn this? You will be able to compare more than two fractional amounts.

Mr. Scott bought some supplies for the Ice Cream Dream Shop. Which item was the heaviest? Which was the lightest?

ICE CREAM DREAM SHOP

$\frac{5}{6}$ pound peanut butter chips $0.40

$\frac{1}{2}$ pound chocolate chips $0.30

$\frac{1}{4}$ pound granola $0.50

You can use fraction strips to order fractions from least to greatest.

1

| $\frac{1}{6}$ | $\frac{1}{6}$ | $\frac{1}{6}$ | $\frac{1}{6}$ | $\frac{1}{6}$ | $\frac{1}{6}$ |

| $\frac{1}{2}$ | $\frac{1}{2}$ |

| $\frac{1}{4}$ | $\frac{1}{4}$ | $\frac{1}{4}$ | $\frac{1}{4}$ |

The fraction strips show that $\frac{1}{4} < \frac{1}{2} < \frac{5}{6}$. So, the peanut butter chips were the heaviest and the granola was the lightest.

You can also rename the fractions so they have like denominators and then put them in order.

MODEL

▶ **Step 1**

Find the least common multiple, or LCM, of 2, 4, and 6.

2: 2, 4, 6, 8, 10, 12

4: 4, 8, 12

6: 6, 12

▶ **Step 2**

Rename the fractions so that the LCM is the denominator.

$$\frac{1}{4} \times \frac{3}{3} = \frac{3}{12}$$

$$\frac{1}{2} \times \frac{6}{6} = \frac{6}{12}$$

$$\frac{5}{6} \times \frac{2}{2} = \frac{10}{12}$$

▶ **Step 3**

Compare the numerators. Put them in order from least to greatest.

Since $3 < 6 < 10$,

$$\frac{3}{12} < \frac{6}{12} < \frac{10}{12}.$$

So, $\frac{1}{4} < \frac{1}{2} < \frac{5}{6}.$

Talk About It

• How would you order the fractions above from greatest to least?

• Explain how to place $\frac{1}{2}, \frac{2}{3}, \frac{1}{4},$ and $\frac{5}{6}$ in order from least to greatest.

💡 **CRITICAL THINKING** Can you compare fractions with *like* numerators and *unlike* denominators, like $\frac{2}{5}$ and $\frac{2}{3}$, without renaming or using fractions strips? Explain.

PRACTICE

Rename the fractions, using the LCM as the denominator.

1. $\frac{1}{2}, \frac{1}{4}, \frac{1}{5}$

2. $\frac{1}{8}, \frac{3}{4}, \frac{1}{2}$

3. $\frac{2}{3}, \frac{2}{5}, \frac{4}{5}$

4. $\frac{1}{6}, \frac{1}{4}, \frac{1}{8}$

5. $\frac{7}{12}, \frac{3}{4}, \frac{7}{8}$

6. $\frac{5}{6}, \frac{7}{9}, \frac{2}{3}$

Write in order from least to greatest.

7. $\frac{7}{12}, \frac{3}{4}, \frac{1}{2}$

8. $\frac{3}{5}, \frac{1}{3}, \frac{4}{15}$

9. $\frac{5}{8}, \frac{3}{4}, \frac{1}{2}$

10. $\frac{1}{10}, \frac{3}{5}, \frac{1}{2}$

11. $\frac{2}{3}, \frac{3}{4}, \frac{7}{12}$

12. $\frac{9}{14}, \frac{1}{2}, \frac{5}{7}$

Write in order from greatest to least.

13. $\frac{7}{15}, \frac{1}{5}, \frac{2}{3}$

14. $\frac{4}{5}, \frac{1}{2}, \frac{9}{10}$

15. $\frac{11}{16}, \frac{3}{4}, \frac{7}{8}$

16. $\frac{5}{6}, \frac{2}{3}, \frac{7}{9}$

17. $\frac{2}{5}, \frac{1}{2}, \frac{3}{4}$

18. $\frac{1}{2}, \frac{2}{3}, \frac{5}{9}$

Mixed Applications

19. It will cost Heath $27.50 to get into the amusement park. He wants to buy a shirt that costs $12.99. Heath earns $7.00 each week mowing lawns. How long will it take him to earn enough money to go to the amusement park and buy the shirt?

20. Aaron has already bought $\frac{1}{2}$ pound trail mix for $2.89, $\frac{1}{3}$ pound cashew nuts for $1.25, and $\frac{1}{4}$ pound raisins for $1.00. He can spend $10.00 in all. Does he have enough money to buy 1 more pound of trail mix? Explain.

21. Tara paid $2.25 for $\frac{1}{3}$ pound yogurt-covered pretzels and $2.00 for $\frac{1}{4}$ pound chocolate-covered pretzels. Which cost more per pound?

22. There are 1,200 students at South Middle School. There are the same number of students in each grade from sixth through eighth. How many students are in each grade?

23. Bernard scored 97, 88, 89, 93 and 83 on 5 spelling tests. What is his mean score?

24. Each week, Remy saves $15.95. How much money will he save in 4 weeks?

25. Stacey makes punch for her class party. She uses $\frac{1}{2}$ gallon orange juice, $\frac{2}{3}$ gallon ginger ale, and $\frac{3}{4}$ gallon pineapple juice. List the ingredients in order from greatest to least.

26. ✏️ **Write a problem** using the fractions $\frac{1}{2}, \frac{3}{4}$, and $\frac{1}{3}$.

LESSON CONTINUES ▶

PART 2 PROBLEM-SOLVING STRATEGY
Draw a Diagram

THE PROBLEM Mr. Lucas is making a fruit salad. He adds $\frac{1}{4}$ cup strawberries, $\frac{2}{3}$ cup peaches, and $\frac{1}{2}$ cup pineapple. What is the order of the fruit Mr. Lucas used from least to greatest?

☑ Understand

• What are you asked to find?

• What information will you use?

• Is there information you will not use? If so, what?

☑ Plan

• What strategy can you use to solve the problem?

You can *draw a diagram* of a number line.

☑ Solve

• How can you solve the problem?

First, find the LCM and rename the fractions.

Multiples of 4: 4, 8, (12), 16, 20, 24 $\frac{1}{4} \times \frac{3}{3} = \frac{3}{12}$ cup strawberries

Multiples of 3: 3, 6, 9, (12), 15, 18 $\frac{2}{3} \times \frac{4}{4} = \frac{8}{12}$ cup peaches

Multiples of 2: 2, 4, 6, 8, 10, (12) $\frac{1}{2} \times \frac{6}{6} = \frac{6}{12}$ cup pineapple

Next, make a number line divided into twelfths. Plot each fraction on the number line.

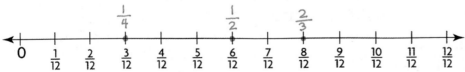

So, the order of the fruit from least to greatest is strawberries, pineapple, peaches.

☑ Look Back

• How can you decide if your answer is reasonable?

• What other strategy could you use?

PRACTICE

Draw a diagram to solve.

1. Mr. Lucas is making a dinner salad. He adds $\frac{7}{8}$ cup lettuce, $\frac{1}{4}$ cup carrots, and $\frac{1}{2}$ cup tomatoes. What is the order of the ingredients Mr. Lucas uses from least to greatest?

2. Niki has red, green, and blue balloons. She has a total of 12 balloons. If $\frac{1}{3}$ of her balloons are red and $\frac{1}{4}$ are green, how many blue balloons does she have?

3. Carla used a recipe calling for $\frac{3}{4}$ cup raisins, $\frac{2}{3}$ cup water, $\frac{1}{2}$ cup honey, and $\frac{1}{3}$ cup flour. List the ingredients in order from the greatest amount to the least amount.

4. A spinner has 10 equal sections. $\frac{1}{5}$ of the spinner is green, $\frac{1}{10}$ is yellow, $\frac{1}{2}$ is blue, and $\frac{1}{5}$ is red. How many sections make up each color?

Mixed Applications

Solve.

CHOOSE A STRATEGY

- Draw a Diagram   - Work Backward   - Write a Number Sentence   - Find a Pattern

5. Roxie spent 20 minutes in her garden on Monday, 30 minutes on Tuesday, 45 minutes on Wednesday, and 65 minutes on Thursday. If the pattern continues, how much time will she spend in her garden on Friday? on Saturday?

6. Blake has $5.40 left after going to the mall. He spent $4.95 on lunch, $3.50 on a book, and $15.95 on a CD. How much did he have when he left for the mall?

7. There are 15 bushes around a circular sidewalk. Julie picks a flower from every fourth bush. How many times will she have to walk around the sidewalk in order to pick one flower from each bush?

8. Greg is making a wood frame for a poster of his favorite music group. The poster is 72 cm long and 48 cm wide. How many centimeters of wood does Greg need to buy?

9. Mrs. Green's class asked 40 students in their school to name their favorite vegetable. The table at the right shows the results as fractions of the students surveyed. What is the most popular vegetable? the least popular vegetable?

Favorite Vegetables	
Vegetable	Students
Broccoli	$\frac{1}{10}$
Peas	$\frac{1}{8}$
Corn	$\frac{3}{8}$
Green Beans	$\frac{2}{5}$

MATH FUN!

PLAN THE PAN

PURPOSE To model fractions

YOU WILL NEED paper and pencil, crayons

You and a family member have made a pan of brownies. Before you cut them, the phone rings. Friends are coming over! You want to give each visitor a brownie.

Draw a rectangular pan for each of the three situations given. Color one brownie. Write the fraction it shows.

Three Situations

Your basketball team calls. You will need brownies for 6.

Your baseball team visits. You will need brownies for 10.

Your soccer team is coming over. You will need brownies for 12.

← $\frac{1}{25}$

Situation: My whole class is coming over! With Mom, that makes 25.

HOME NOTE Make up your own situation. Use any number you like.

Mixed-Number Match

PURPOSE To match mixed numbers and fractions

YOU WILL NEED construction paper, ruler, scissors, markers

Make a pack of 24 cards. On 12 cards, write mixed numbers. On the other 12 cards, write the mixed numbers as fractions.

Mix up the cards and place them face down in rows. Take turns. One player turns up two cards. If they match, the player keeps them and turns up two more cards. If they do not match, the player replaces them in the same place. The other player does the same. The player with more matches wins.

Fraction-Circle Collage

PURPOSE To order fractions on a number line

YOU WILL NEED fraction-circle patterns, colored pencils, markers, yarn or string, glue, scissors, poster board, ruler

Work with other students to make a collage showing a number line with fraction circles placed along it.

Cut out fraction circles. Color one section on each, and write the fraction it represents. Paste the circles along a number line, starting at zero and ending at $\frac{1}{2}$. Use yarn to connect each fraction circle to its spot on the number line.

CHAPTER 15 REVIEW

✓ CHECK UNDERSTANDING

VOCABULARY

1. A __?__ is made up of a whole number and a fraction. (page 248)

2. A __?__ is the product of two or more numbers. (page 250)

3. Multiples of one number that are also multiples of another number are called __?__. (page 250)

4. The least number that is a common multiple of two or more numbers is called the __?__. (page 250)

Write the fraction shown. (pages 246–247)

5.

$\frac{1}{5}$	$\frac{1}{5}$	$\frac{1}{5}$	$\frac{1}{5}$	$\frac{1}{5}$

6.

$\frac{1}{4}$	$\frac{1}{4}$	$\frac{1}{4}$	$\frac{1}{4}$

7.

$\frac{1}{8}$	$\frac{1}{8}$	$\frac{1}{8}$	$\frac{1}{8}$	$\frac{1}{8}$	$\frac{1}{8}$	$\frac{1}{8}$	$\frac{1}{8}$

8.

$\frac{1}{10}$	$\frac{1}{10}$	$\frac{1}{10}$	$\frac{1}{10}$	$\frac{1}{10}$	$\frac{1}{10}$	$\frac{1}{10}$	$\frac{1}{10}$	$\frac{1}{10}$	$\frac{1}{10}$

✓ CHECK SKILLS

Rename each fraction as a mixed number. (pages 248–249)

9. $\frac{5}{3}$ 10. $\frac{7}{2}$ 11. $\frac{11}{6}$ 12. $\frac{9}{5}$ 13. $\frac{19}{4}$

Rename, using the least common multiple, and compare.
Write $<$, $>$, or $=$ for each ●. (pages 252–253)

14. $\frac{2}{5}$ ● $\frac{7}{15}$ 15. $\frac{3}{8}$ ● $\frac{9}{16}$ 16. $\frac{6}{7}$ ● $\frac{1}{2}$ 17. $\frac{4}{5}$ ● $\frac{4}{8}$

Write in order from least to greatest. (pages 254–255)

18. $\frac{2}{3}, \frac{3}{4}, \frac{1}{5}$ 19. $\frac{3}{8}, \frac{1}{4}, \frac{5}{8}$ 20. $\frac{1}{3}, \frac{4}{5}, \frac{1}{2}$

✓ CHECK PROBLEM SOLVING

Solve. (pages 256–257)

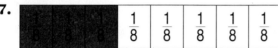

CHOOSE A STRATEGY

• Make an Organized List   • Find a Pattern   • Draw a Diagram

21. Mandy mixed $\frac{1}{3}$ cup bananas, $\frac{1}{4}$ cup pineapple juice, $\frac{1}{2}$ cup milk, and $\frac{5}{6}$ cup ice in a blender. What is the order of the ingredients she used from least to greatest?

22. Ken ran $\frac{1}{2}$ mile on Monday, 1 mile on Tuesday, 2 miles on Wednesday, and 4 miles on Thursday. If this pattern continues, how many miles will he run on Friday?

CHAPTER 16

FRACTIONS AND NUMBER THEORY

DID YOU KNOW ...

A time signature tells how many beats there are in a measure. $\frac{4}{4}$ time means there are 4 beats in a measure and a quarter note gets 1 beat.

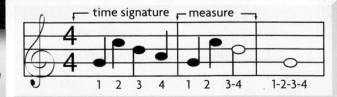

time signature — measure

4
4

1 2 3 4   1 2 3-4   1-2-3-4

Making Music in Four Beats

Music is written in measures, or sections, just like words are written in sentences. When we say that music is in $\frac{4}{4}$ time, that means there are 4 beats to a measure. We count it like this: "1, 2, 3, 4." Write measures of music by combining at least 16 notes in different ways.

Work with a partner. Your job is to

• use at least 16 notes to write some music in $\frac{4}{4}$ time.

• use each kind of note at least twice. Some notes are whole notes, half notes, quarter notes, and eighth notes.

• divide your notes so that there are four beats per measure.

• below each note, write it as a fraction.

• share your music with the class.

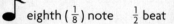

CHART OF NOTE VALUES In $\frac{4}{4}$ Time	
○ whole note	4 beats
♩ half ($\frac{1}{2}$) note	2 beats
♪ quarter ($\frac{1}{4}$) note	1 beat
♪ eighth ($\frac{1}{8}$) note	$\frac{1}{2}$ beat

DID YOU
✓ write musical notes?

✓ divide your notes into measures of $\frac{4}{4}$ time?

✓ write each note as a fraction?

✓ share your music with the class?

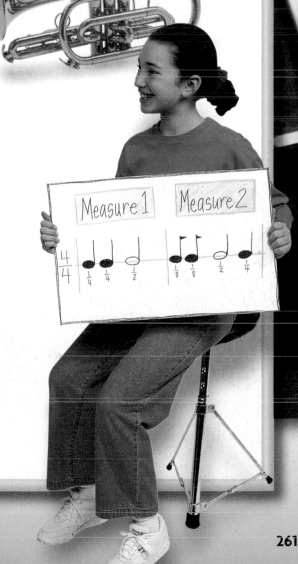

Prime and Composite Numbers

You will investigate finding factors of numbers to determine if they are prime or composite.

Why learn this? You can classify numbers as prime or composite when you know how many factors each number has.

Cara is using squares of material to design a quilt. She is going to arrange 16 squares in a rectangle. How many ways can she arrange the 16 squares?

Explore

Use square tiles to show all the ways that 16 squares can be arranged to form a rectangle.

MATERIALS: square tiles

Record

Draw a picture of each model. Record the length and the width of each rectangle. The length and width are also factors.

• How many different factors were used to show the lengths and widths?

Now, investigate prime and composite numbers.

Prime numbers have exactly two factors, 1 and the number itself. **Composite numbers** have more than two factors. The number 1 is neither prime nor composite.

Try This

Find out whether the numbers 6 and 7 are prime or composite. Use tiles to show all the ways they can be arranged to form a rectangle. Record all of the different factors for each number.

• Which number is a prime number and which number is a composite number? How do you know?

REMEMBER:

Factors are numbers multiplied together to find a product.

$$2 \times 4 = 8$$
factor factor product

The Property of One for Multiplication says the product of any number and 1 is the number.

$$6 \times 1 = 6$$

Technology Link

E-Lab • Activity 16 Available on CD-ROM and the Internet at http://www.hbschool.com/elab

Use tiles to show all the ways the numbers 2–12 can be arranged to form a rectangle. Make a table to record the length and width of each rectangle, and all of the different factors for each number.

TALK ABOUT IT How many factors did you find for the number 5? Why?

✏ **WRITE ABOUT IT** What kind of number is 16, prime or composite? How do you know?

Models	▪▪▪	▪▪▪▪	▪▪▪▪
Numbers	2	3	4
Length and Width	1 x 2 2 x 1	1 x 3 3 x 1	1 x 4 ? ?
Factors	1, 2	1, 3	?

HANDS-ON PRACTICE

Use square tiles to show all the rectangles that can be made using each number. Record the length and the width of each rectangle.

1. 13   **2.** 11   **3.** 15   **4.** 14

Applying What You Learned

Write *prime* or *composite* for each number.

5. 13   **6.** 19   **7.** 14   **8.** 21

9. 23   **10.** 15   **11.** 31   **12.** 18

Mixed Applications

13. Use the Sieve of Eratosthenes to find prime numbers. Copy the table onto grid paper. Continue the table to 100. Cross out 1. Circle 2, 3, 5, and 7. Then cross out all multiples of 2, 3, 5, and 7. Circle the remaining numbers. List all the circled numbers. What is true about all these numbers?

Sieve of Eratosthenes

1	2	3	4	5	6	7	8	9	10
11	12	13	14	15	16	17	18	19	20
21	22	23	24	25	26	27	28	29	30
31	32	33	34	35	36	37	38	39	40
41	42	43	44	45	46	47	48	49	50

14. Five students sit in the same row in math class. Nick sits in front of Carla, and Pat sits four seats behind Jordan. Carla sits in front of Tony. Who sits directly behind Jordan?

15. ✏ **WRITE ABOUT IT** You and your friend are the same age. Your age is a prime number. Your friend says that his age is a composite number. Is this possible? Explain.

Factors and Greatest Common Factors

You will learn to find factors of numbers and to find the greatest common factor of 2 or more numbers. | **Why learn this?** You can find which factors of two different numbers are the same. | **WORD POWER**

greatest common factor (GCF)

John and his mother made 12 peanut butter candies and 18 caramel candies to give as gifts. John wants to use only one size box to pack the candies. He wants the box to be as large as possible and to hold only one kind of candy. How many candies will each box hold?

John can solve this problem by finding the common factors of 12 and 18. The greatest factor that two or more numbers have in common is the **greatest common factor**, or **GCF**.

You can use yellow square tiles to model the peanut butter candies and blue square tiles to model the caramel candies.

1×12
2×6
3×4

1×18
2×9
3×6

Talk About It

• What are the factors of 12?

• What are the factors of 18?

• What factors of 12 and 18 are the same? What is the greatest factor that is the same?

So, the boxes should each hold 6 candies.

EXAMPLES

A. Find the greatest common factor of 18 and 27.

Factors of 18: **Factors of 27:**
1, 2, 3, 6, 9, 18 **1, 3, 9, 27**

The common factors of 18 and 27 are 1, 3, and 9. So, the *greatest* common factor, or GCF, is 9.

B. Find the greatest common factor of 16 and 40.

Factors of 16: **Factors of 40:**
1, 2, 4, 8, 16 **1, 2, 4, 5, 8, 10, 20, 40**

The common factors of 16 and 40 are 1, 2, 4, and 8. So, the *greatest* common factor, or GCF, is 8.

CRITICAL THINKING How can you find the GCF of two prime numbers such as 3 and 7?

PRACTICE

List the factors of each number.

1. 8	**2.** 15	**3.** 18	**4.** 21	**5.** 24
6. 28	**7.** 30	**8.** 35	**9.** 36	**10.** 42
11. 7	**12.** 16	**13.** 32	**14.** 45	**15.** 20

List the factors of each number. Write the greatest common factor for each pair of numbers.

16. 4, 8	**17.** 12, 21	**18.** 6, 15	**19.** 7, 14	**20.** 5, 20
21. 12, 20	**22.** 7, 35	**23.** 18, 45	**24.** 10, 25	**25.** 30, 50
26. 9, 15	**27.** 24, 16	**28.** 16, 28	**29.** 35, 45	**30.** 32, 24

Mixed Applications

For Problems 31–33, use the table at the right.

31. The members of the Garden Club are selling packs of plants. They want to pack the plants in boxes that hold the same number. Each box will have the same kind of plants. What is the greatest number of plants each box should hold?

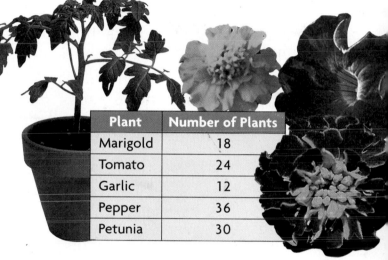

Plant	Number of Plants
Marigold	18
Tomato	24
Garlic	12
Pepper	36
Petunia	30

32. The Garden Club buys empty boxes in packages of 5. How many boxes in all are needed to pack the plants? How many packages of boxes are needed?

33. ✏️ **WRITE ABOUT IT** How can you find the greatest common factor of three numbers?

Mixed Review

Find the quotient. Check by multiplying. (pages 216–217)

34. 9)3.6	**35.** 8)6.4	**36.** 5)25.5	**37.** 7)21.07	**38.** 4)86.6
39. 2)47.5	**40.** 4)66.8	**41.** 5)60.75	**42.** 3)65.4	**43.** 6)79.62

Write the measurements in order from shortest to longest.
(pages 226–227)

44. 7 km, 7 m, 7 cm   **45.** 16 dm, 16 mm, 16 km   **46.** 18 dm, 18 cm, 18 mm

Equivalent Fractions

You will learn to name equivalent fractions.	Why learn this? You can decide whether different fractions name the same amount.	WORD POWER equivalent fractions

Mary and Mark remember from music lessons that a half note is the same time as two quarter notes. So, they name the same amount. You can write $\frac{1}{2} = \frac{2}{4}$.

Mary and Mark drew number lines that show $\frac{1}{2}$ and $\frac{2}{4}$. Fractions that name the same amount are called **equivalent fractions**.

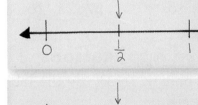

You can find equivalent fractions by multiplying or dividing.

EXAMPLES

A. You can *multiply* both the numerator and the denominator by any number.

To find an equivalent fraction to $\frac{2}{3}$, multiply both the numerator and denominator by 2.

$$\frac{2}{3} = \frac{2 \times 2}{3 \times 2} = \frac{4}{6}$$

B. You can *divide* both the numerator and the denominator by a common factor.

To find an equivalent fraction to $\frac{8}{12}$, divide both the numerator and denominator by 4.

$$\frac{8}{12} = \frac{8 \div 4}{12 \div 4} = \frac{2}{3}$$

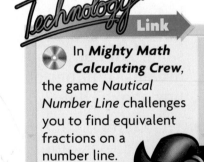

Technology Link

In **Mighty Math Calculating Crew**, the game *Nautical Number Line* challenges you to find equivalent fractions on a number line.

Talk About It

• How is using multiplication to find equivalent fractions different from using division?

• How can you use a number line to show that the fractions in Examples A and B are equivalent?

Check Your Understanding

CRITICAL THINKING

Use the number lines to name an equivalent fraction for each.

1. $\frac{3}{4}$ **2.** $\frac{2}{8}$ **3.** $\frac{2}{4}$ **4.** $\frac{6}{8}$

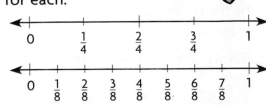

PRACTICE

Use the number lines to name an equivalent fraction for each.

5. $\frac{1}{2}$ **6.** $\frac{2}{6}$ **7.** $\frac{2}{3}$ **8.** $\frac{1}{3}$

Number line: 0, $\frac{1}{3}$, $\frac{1}{2}$, $\frac{2}{3}$, 1

Number line: 0, $\frac{1}{6}$, $\frac{2}{6}$, $\frac{3}{6}$, $\frac{4}{6}$, $\frac{5}{6}$, 1

Find an equivalent fraction. Use multiplication or division.

9. $\frac{1}{4}$ **10.** $\frac{2}{16}$ **11.** $\frac{2}{5}$ **12.** $\frac{9}{12}$ **13.** $\frac{1}{3}$ **14.** $\frac{5}{6}$

15. $\frac{4}{11}$ **16.** $\frac{5}{25}$ **17.** $\frac{7}{10}$ **18.** $\frac{3}{15}$ **19.** $\frac{7}{21}$ **20.** $\frac{7}{8}$

Which fraction is *not* equivalent to the given fraction?
Write *a*, *b*, or *c*.

21. $\frac{3}{4}$ **a.** $\frac{15}{20}$ **b.** $\frac{12}{16}$ **c.** $\frac{6}{12}$ **22.** $\frac{4}{6}$ **a.** $\frac{2}{3}$ **b.** $\frac{1}{2}$ **c.** $\frac{8}{12}$

23. $\frac{1}{2}$ **a.** $\frac{6}{12}$ **b.** $\frac{3}{7}$ **c.** $\frac{4}{8}$ **24.** $\frac{4}{12}$ **a.** $\frac{2}{3}$ **b.** $\frac{1}{3}$ **c.** $\frac{5}{15}$

Mixed Applications

25. Nick and 5 friends decide to share some pizza. Each pizza is cut into 10 pieces. How many pizzas will they have to buy in order for everyone to get 3 pieces? How many pieces will be left over?

26. Nick ordered a large pizza with 12 slices. Suppose he ate 4 pieces of pizza. Write two equivalent fractions to represent the part of the pizza Nick ate.

27. Lanni has $10.50 to spend on seeds from the garden catalog. She wants to buy 2 packages of zinnia seeds. Does she have enough to buy at least one package of each of the other types of seeds? If not, how much more does she need?

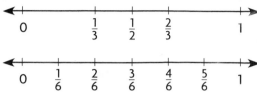

Type of Seed	Price per Package
Zinnia	$1.85
Marigold	$1.50
Ageratum	$1.90
Pansy	$1.66
Petunia	$1.98
Salvia	$2.10

28. Dave and Selena each have some leftover pansy seeds. Dave has $\frac{3}{4}$ package left and Selena has $\frac{2}{3}$ left. Who has more pansy seeds left?

29. ✏ **WRITE ABOUT IT** Explain how to use multiplication or division to find equivalent fractions.

LESSON
CONTINUES ▶

PART 2 PROBLEM-SOLVING STRATEGY
Draw a Diagram

THE PROBLEM Wanda is having a party. She is making a vegetable dip. The recipe calls for $\frac{1}{4}$ cup of yogurt, $\frac{2}{8}$ cup of grated carrots, $\frac{3}{12}$ cup of sour cream, and $\frac{4}{16}$ cup of chopped spinach. Which ingredient in the dip is there more of?

☑ Understand

- What are you asked to find?

- What information will you use?

- Is there information you will not use? If so, what?

☑ Plan

- What strategy can you use to solve the problem?

  You can *draw a diagram*, using a number line, to compare the fractional amounts.

☑ Solve

- How can you use the strategy to solve the problem?

  You can draw a number line for each fraction. Mark the location of each fraction on each of the number lines.

  The number lines show that $\frac{1}{4}$, $\frac{2}{8}$, $\frac{3}{12}$, and $\frac{4}{16}$ are equivalent fractions. So, Wanda used the same amount of each ingredient to make the dip.

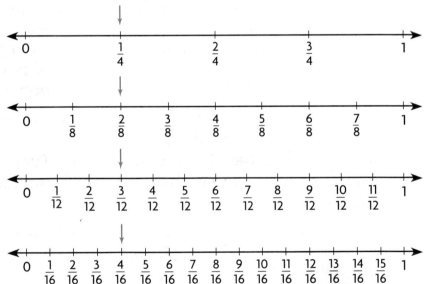

☑ Look Back

- How can you decide if your answer is reasonable?

- What other strategy could you use?

PRACTICE

Draw a diagram to solve.

1. For the party, Kevin spends $\frac{2}{16}$ of his money on favors and $\frac{3}{8}$ on food. On which item is he spending the most money? Explain how you know.

2. Shari bought 18 dishes, 8 of which are plates. Ned said that $\frac{4}{9}$ of the dishes she bought are plates. Is Ned right? Explain.

3. Tori has equal numbers of red, black, and blue pencils. She has a total of 21 pencils. Write two equivalent fractions to describe the fraction of the pencils that are red.

4. Mr. Frank had a package containing 10 cans of juice. He gave 3 cans to Greg and 5 to Margaret. Write two equivalent fractions to describe the fraction of the package of juice that is left.

Mixed Applications

Solve.

CHOOSE A STRATEGY

- Draw a Diagram   - Write a Number Sentence   - Guess and Check   - Make a Model

5. Anita had 16 rosebushes to sell. She sold 12 rosebushes. What fraction of the rosebushes did she sell?

6. A garden store sells 3 packs of seeds for $5.25. A catalog sells each pack for $1.49. What is the difference in the price per pack between the stores?

7. There are 53 people in the hotel. Today 8 people checked out and 4 times that number checked in. How many people are in the hotel now?

8. Corey ran $\frac{4}{5}$ of a mile on Monday, and $\frac{8}{10}$ of a mile on Tuesday. Which day did Corey run farther?

9. Casey's garden has 5 rows of strawberry plants with 10 plants in each row. She picks about 10 strawberries from each plant. About how many strawberries does she pick?

10. Josh, Leslie, and Rob saved $57 to buy flowers for their mother for Mother's Day. Josh saved $17, and Leslie saved $8 less than Rob. How much money did Rob save?

11. ✏️ **Write a problem** about the basket of apples that uses fractions.

Simplest Form

You will learn to use fraction bars to find an equivalent fraction in simplest form.

Why learn this? You can recognize that fractional amounts modeled in simplest form use larger fraction pieces.

A fraction is in simplest form when it matches the largest fraction bar possible.

To find $\frac{6}{12}$ in simplest form, start with the fraction bars for $\frac{6}{12}$. Line up fraction bars to find equivalent fractions for $\frac{6}{12}$. Look for the fraction that uses the largest fraction bar possible.

So, $\frac{6}{12}$ in simplest form is $\frac{1}{2}$.

Talk About It

• What is the relationship among the fractions shown by the fraction bars above?

• What is the simplest form of $\frac{2}{3}$?

• How do you know when you have found the simplest form of a fraction?

EXAMPLES

A. $\frac{3}{6}$

$\frac{3}{6}$ in simplest form is $\frac{1}{2}$.

B. $\frac{6}{8}$

$\frac{6}{8}$ in simplest form is $\frac{3}{4}$.

C. $\frac{3}{5}$

Since no other fraction bars line up with $\frac{3}{5}$, it is in simplest form.

Check Your Understanding

💡 **CRITICAL THINKING**

Use fraction bars. Write each fraction in simplest form.

1. $\frac{4}{8}$

2. $\frac{3}{12}$

3. $\frac{4}{12}$ **4.** $\frac{3}{6}$ **5.** $\frac{3}{4}$ **6.** $\frac{3}{12}$ **7.** $\frac{8}{10}$

 Calculator Activities page H63

PRACTICE

Is the fraction in simplest form? Write *yes* or *no*.

8. $\frac{2}{3}$ **9.** $\frac{4}{8}$ **10.** $\frac{6}{12}$ **11.** $\frac{3}{8}$ **12.** $\frac{6}{9}$

Use fraction bars. Write the fraction in simplest form.

13. $\frac{2}{10}$ | $\frac{1}{10}$ | $\frac{1}{10}$ |

| $\frac{1}{5}$ |

14. $\frac{8}{12}$ | $\frac{1}{12}$ | $\frac{1}{12}$ | $\frac{1}{12}$ | $\frac{1}{12}$ | $\frac{1}{12}$ | $\frac{1}{12}$ | $\frac{1}{12}$ | $\frac{1}{12}$ |

| $\frac{1}{3}$ | $\frac{1}{3}$ |

15. $\frac{5}{6}$ | $\frac{1}{6}$ | $\frac{1}{6}$ | $\frac{1}{6}$ | $\frac{1}{6}$ | $\frac{1}{6}$ |

| ? |

Write each fraction in simplest form.

16. $\frac{1}{2}$ **17.** $\frac{3}{12}$ **18.** $\frac{9}{12}$ **19.** $\frac{2}{10}$ **20.** $\frac{7}{8}$

21. $\frac{9}{15}$ **22.** $\frac{4}{5}$ **23.** $\frac{4}{12}$ **24.** $\frac{6}{10}$ **25.** $\frac{5}{15}$

26. $\frac{8}{12}$ **27.** $\frac{3}{21}$ **28.** $\frac{4}{16}$ **29.** $\frac{6}{18}$ **30.** $\frac{7}{14}$

Mixed Applications

31. Hannah used $\frac{1}{2}$ cup sugar, $\frac{2}{3}$ cup cornmeal, and $\frac{3}{4}$ cup flour in her corn muffin recipe. Of these ingredients, which was used the most? How do you know?

32. Gary bought 5 T-shirts on Monday. He now has 30 T-shirts. What fraction of his T-shirts did he buy on Monday? Write your answer in simplest form.

33. Victor has 12 pencils. He gives 2 pencils to his friends, accidentally breaks three times that many, and trades 1 pencil for a marker with his teacher. How many pencils does Victor have now?

34. ✏️ **Write a problem** using fractions about Andrea and Joey dividing the lemon cake their mom baked for them.

Mixed Review

Copy and complete each pattern. (pages 210–211)

35. $800 \div 4 = n$
$80 \div 4 = n$
$8 \div 4 = n$

36. $2,500 \div 5 = n$
$250 \div 5 = n$
$25 \div 5 = n$

37. $1,200 \div 3 = n$
$120 \div 3 = n$
$12 \div 3 = n$

Use estimation or patterns to place the decimal point.
Then find the quotient. (pages 218–219)

38. $11\overline{)5.5}$ **39.** $5\overline{)7.65}$ **40.** $8\overline{)88.8}$ **41.** $25\overline{)19.75}$ **42.** $5\overline{)49.55}$

More About Simplest Form

<table>
<tr><td>**You will learn** to use the greatest common factor to find an equivalent fraction in simplest form.</td><td>**Why learn this?** Fractional amounts expressed in simplest form are usually easier to understand.</td><td>**WORD POWER**

simplest form</td></tr>
</table>

A fraction is in **simplest form** when the greatest common factor, or GCF, of the numerator and denominator is 1. Since the numerator and denominator of $\frac{18}{24}$ do not have a GCF of 1, the fraction is not in simplest form. To write $\frac{18}{24}$ in simplest form, follow these steps.

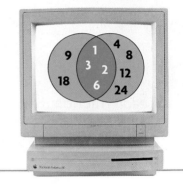

▶ Step 1	▶ Step 2
Find the greatest common factor of 18 and 24. Factors of 18: 1, 2, 3, 6, 9, 18 Factors of 24: 1, 2, 3, 4, 6, 8, 12, 24 The GCF is 6.	Divide the numerator and the denominator by the GCF. $\dfrac{18 \div 6}{24 \div 6} = \dfrac{3}{4}$ Since the GCF of 3 and 4 is 1, $\frac{3}{4}$ is in simplest form.

So, $\frac{18}{24}$ in simplest form is $\frac{3}{4}$.

Another way to change a fraction to simplest form is to divide the numerator and denominator by any common factor. Continue to divide by common factors until the GCF of the numerator and denominator is 1.

$$\frac{12}{18} = \frac{12 \div 2}{18 \div 2} = \frac{6 \div 3}{9 \div 3} = \frac{2}{3}$$

So, the simplest form of $\frac{12}{18}$ is $\frac{2}{3}$.

Talk About It

- Which way would you use to write $\frac{10}{15}$ in simplest form?

💡 **CRITICAL THINKING** If a fraction is not in simplest form, can the greatest common factor of the numerator and denominator be 1? Explain.

📱 **Calculator Activities page H66**

Talk About It

• How are the two methods for writing fractions in simplest form different?

• When is it easier to use the method of repeated division to write a fraction in simplest form?

PRACTICE

Is the fraction in simplest form? Write *yes* or *no*. If it is not in simplest form, write it in simplest form.

1. $\frac{4}{12}$

2. $\frac{4}{5}$

3. $\frac{9}{12}$

4. $\frac{2}{8}$

5. $\frac{5}{14}$

Write each fraction in simplest form.

6. $\frac{3}{15}$

7. $\frac{3}{4}$

8. $\frac{12}{36}$

9. $\frac{15}{25}$

10. $\frac{15}{18}$

11. $\frac{14}{21}$

12. $\frac{18}{30}$

13. $\frac{15}{40}$

14. $\frac{6}{16}$

15. $\frac{18}{45}$

Mixed Applications

16. Stan's class is doing a science project. He brought 8 plants to school for this project. His class brought 36 plants in all. Write in simplest form the fraction of plants Stan brought.

17. Sasha receives $12 a week for baby-sitting. She puts $8 of that money in her savings account. Write in simplest form the fraction of her earnings that Sasha saves.

18. Chris works 10 minutes in her garden on Monday, 20 minutes on Tuesday, 35 minutes on Wednesday, and 55 minutes on Thursday. If the pattern continues, how long will she work in the garden on Saturday?

19. WRITE ABOUT IT Explain how you know that a fraction such as $\frac{3}{4}$ is in simplest form.

Mixed Review

Choose the smaller unit of measure. Write *a* or *b*.
Use the prefix to help you. (pages 232–233)

20. **a.** kilometer
    b. decimeter

21. **a.** liter
    b. milliliter

22. **a.** gram
    b. kilogram

Write the missing unit. (pages 234–235)

23. 4 L = 4,000 __?__

24. 500 mm = 50 __?__

25. 60 g = 60,000 __?__

Visitors from Jordan

Basma and Hassan live in Jordan. Every summer they visit their cousins in the United States. On this visit they will bring a Bedouin rug for their aunt. It covers an area of 36 square feet. Use tiles to find how many different rectangles can be formed that equal 36 square feet. Let each tile represent 1 square foot. List the factors of 36, circle the prime numbers, and underline the composite numbers.

CULTURAL LINK

Many traditional arts have been handed down for centuries in Jordan. They include pottery and ceramics, embroidery, mosaic art, and Bedouin Rugs. The geometric designs in many of these rugs made today are based on patterns made centuries ago by migrating tribes of the region or people who settled in communities at the edge of Jordan's desert.

Work Together

1. Basma and Hassan have 12 models of Arabian horses and 18 models of camels as gifts for their cousins. They want to pack the models so that each box contains only horses or camels. They also want to put the same number of animals in each box. How many animals can they put into each box? Why?

2. Basma and Hassan's grandfather gave them each a box of almonds for the trip. After they ate some, Basma had $\frac{3}{4}$ box left, and Hassan had $\frac{9}{12}$ box left. Who had more almonds? Explain.

3. Hassan told his cousins about his trip to the Dead Sea, which borders Israel and Jordan. The sea is about $\frac{1}{3}$ mineral salts. Write two equivalent fractions for $\frac{1}{3}$.

4. Basma and Hassan's cousins live in Utah. Together they visited the Great Salt Lake near Salt Lake City. It is a little less than $\frac{25}{1,000}$ parts mineral salts. Find the simplest form of this fraction.

✓ CHECK UNDERSTANDING

VOCABULARY

1. Fractions that name the same amount are called ___?___ . (page 266)

2. The greatest factor that two or more numbers have in common is called the ___?___ . (page 264)

3. Numbers that have exactly two factors, 1 and the number itself, are called ___?___ . (page 262)

4. Numbers that have more than two factors are called ___?___ . (page 262)

5. A fraction is in ___?___ when the GCF of the numerator and denominator is 1. (page 272)

Write *prime* or *composite* for each number. (pages 262–263)

6. 15   7. 2   8. 8   9. 50

✓ CHECK SKILLS

Find an equivalent fraction. Use multiplication or division. (pages 266–267)

10. $\frac{6}{18}$ 11. $\frac{2}{7}$ 12. $\frac{1}{6}$ 13. $\frac{7}{15}$ 14. $\frac{8}{18}$

List the factors of each number. Write the greatest common factor for each pair of numbers. (pages 264–265)

15. 6, 8   16. 7, 14   17. 8, 12   18. 6, 15   19. 12, 16

Write each fraction in simplest form. (pages 270–273)

20. $\frac{2}{8}$ 21. $\frac{9}{15}$ 22. $\frac{18}{20}$ 23. $\frac{15}{35}$ 24. $\frac{10}{12}$

✓ CHECK PROBLEM SOLVING

Solve. (pages 268–269)

CHOOSE A STRATEGY

• Make a Model   • Find a Pattern   • Draw a Diagram

25. Jane made 24 oatmeal cookies and 36 peanut butter cookies for the school bake sale. She wants to put the cookies in bags that contain the same number of one kind of cookie. What is the greatest number of cookies she can put into each bag?

26. Carla cut $\frac{1}{2}$ yard of blue fabric, $\frac{3}{4}$ yard of red fabric, and $\frac{4}{12}$ yard of green fabric. Of which color fabric does she have the least?

MODELING ADDITION OF FRACTIONS

REPORTINGLIVE
FROMPOETRYCITY
AUDITORIUMSITEOF
THEANNUALSCHOOL
POETRYPRESENTATIONS
WHERESTUDENTSFROM
ALLOVERTHESTATE
RECITEPOEMSTO
AUDIENCES
WORLDWIDE

DID YOU KNOW...

An announcer says about
104 words each minute during
a news broadcast.

Team-Up Time

Your Poetry Presentation

Do you ever have trouble understanding someone who talks too fast? Work with a group to plan a poetry reading.

YOU WILL NEED: clock or timer, poem books, construction paper, ruler, scissors, glue

Work with a group. Your job is to

- choose a poem for each group member.

- time each person's reading of the poem to the nearest $\frac{1}{4}$ minute. (HINT: There are 60 seconds in 1 minute. $\frac{1}{4} = \frac{?}{60}$)

- write a $\frac{1}{4}$-minute introduction for your group.

- make a different colored strip to show how long it will take to read each poem.

- make a chart that lists each title and time.

- add your group's times to find out how long your presentation will last.

HOW TO FOLD PAPER TO SHOW $\frac{1}{4}$ MINUTE

Cut a paper strip that is 6 inches long. This represents 1 minute.

Fold the paper in half. Each section represents $\frac{1}{2}$ minute.

Fold the paper in half again. Each section represents $\frac{1}{4}$ minute.

DID YOU

☑ time the reading of each poem to the nearest $\frac{1}{4}$ minute?

☑ write a $\frac{1}{4}$-minute introduction?

☑ make a strip to show how long it will take to read each poem?

☑ make a chart?

☑ find out how long your presentation will last?

Group One's Poetry Times

$\frac{1}{4} + \frac{1}{4} + \frac{1}{4} + \frac{1}{4} = 1$

$\frac{1}{4} + 1\frac{1}{4} = 1\frac{1}{2}$

$\frac{1}{4} + \frac{3}{4} = 1$

Total: $3\frac{1}{2}$ minutes

Adding Like Fractions

You will learn to add fractions that have the same denominators.

Why learn this? You can solve problems that involve finding the sum of parts, such as the parts of a pizza eaten.

Max and Gayle shared a small pizza. Max ate $\frac{3}{8}$ of the pizza. Gayle ate $\frac{1}{8}$ of the pizza. What part of the pizza did they eat together?

You can use fraction bars to show the part of the pizza each person ate.

Max ate $\frac{3}{8}$ of the pizza.

Gayle ate $\frac{1}{8}$ of the pizza.

Together, they ate
$\frac{3}{8} + \frac{1}{8} = \frac{4}{8}$, or $\frac{1}{2}$ of the pizza.

REMEMBER:

Like fractions are fractions that have the same denominators.

Example $\frac{1}{8}$ and $\frac{3}{8}$

Science Link

Time is often expressed as a fraction of an hour. For example, 15 minutes equals $\frac{1}{4}$ hour and 30 minutes equals $\frac{1}{2}$ hour. How many minutes equal $\frac{3}{4}$ hour?

Talk About It

- How do you know that the sum is $\frac{4}{8}$?

- What do you notice about the numerator of the sum of the two like fractions? What do you notice about the denominator?

- Why is $\frac{4}{8}$ written as $\frac{1}{2}$?

EXAMPLES

A. Find the sum of $\frac{2}{3}$ and $\frac{2}{3}$.

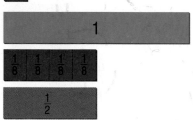

$\frac{2}{3} + \frac{2}{3} = \frac{4}{3}$, or $1\frac{1}{3}$

B. Find the sum of $\frac{3}{10}$ and $\frac{5}{10}$.

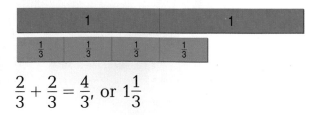

$\frac{3}{10} + \frac{5}{10} = \frac{8}{10}$

$\frac{8}{10} = \frac{4}{5}$ ← Remember to write the answer in simplest form.

- How do you know if the sum of two fractions is greater than 1?

💡 **CRITICAL THINKING** What rule can you write for adding fractions with like denominators?

PRACTICE

Write an addition sentence for each drawing.

1.
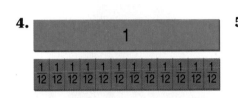

2.
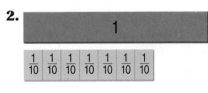

3.
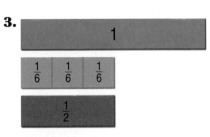

4.
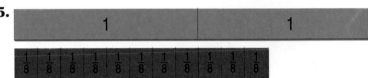

5.

Use fraction strips to find the sum. Write the answer in simplest form.

6. $\frac{1}{3} + \frac{1}{3} = n$ 7. $\frac{2}{4} + \frac{3}{4} = n$ 8. $\frac{2}{5} + \frac{4}{5} = n$ 9. $\frac{1}{9} + \frac{2}{9} = n$

10. $\frac{1}{6} + \frac{3}{6} = n$ 11. $\frac{5}{7} + \frac{4}{7} = n$ 12. $\frac{3}{8} + \frac{5}{8} = n$ 13. $\frac{1}{6} + \frac{5}{6} = n$

14. $\frac{3}{5} + \frac{4}{5} = n$ 15. $\frac{4}{9} + \frac{2}{9} = n$ 16. $\frac{2}{4} + \frac{3}{4} = n$ 17. $\frac{2}{12} + \frac{4}{12} = n$

Mixed Applications

18. Carmen had a brand-new package of construction paper. She used $\frac{4}{8}$ of the paper. Her friend used $\frac{3}{8}$ of the paper. How much of the package of paper did they use?

19. Jason was making a sign. He bought a package of 8 markers for $3.76. How much did each marker cost?

20. Mark's family walks together three times a week. They walk $\frac{1}{5}$ mile, $\frac{3}{5}$ mile, and $\frac{2}{5}$ mile. How far does Mark's family walk in all?

21. ✏️ **Write a problem** about three friends eating apple pie, using like fractions.

Mixed Review

Write *certain* or *impossible* for each event. (pages 172–173)

22. Money will grow in your garden.

23. The Earth will revolve around the sun.

Write the missing unit. (pages 234–235)

24. 700 mm = 70 ___?___   25. 6,043 mm = 6.043 ___?___   26. 5 kg = 5,000 ___?___

Adding Unlike Fractions

You will investigate using fraction bars to add fractions with unlike denominators.

Why learn this? You can add fractions with unlike denominators when measuring ingredients for a recipe.

Joyce and Renee baked two kinds of muffins for the bake sale. They used $\frac{1}{8}$ cup sugar for one kind. They used $\frac{1}{2}$ cup sugar for the other kind. How much sugar did they use in all?

Explore

Use fraction bars to add fractions with unlike denominators.

MATERIALS: fraction bars

MODEL

What is $\frac{1}{8} + \frac{1}{2}$?

▶ **Step 1**

Model with fraction bars.

1

$\frac{1}{8}$	$\frac{1}{2}$

▶ **Step 2**

Find the like fraction bars that are equivalent to $\frac{1}{8} + \frac{1}{2}$ in length.

1

	$\frac{1}{2}$

?

Record

Write a fraction for the amount of sugar Joyce and Renee used in all. Record an addition sentence for the model. Explain how you used the fraction bars to find the sum.

Now, investigate adding different unlike fractions.

Try This

Use fraction bars to find the sum of $\frac{1}{2}$ and $\frac{2}{3}$. Record by writing a number sentence.

E–Lab • Activity 17 Available on CD-ROM and the Internet at http://www.hbschool.com/elab

TALK ABOUT IT What is the least common multiple of 2 and 3? What do you notice about the LCM and the sum of $\frac{1}{2}$ and $\frac{2}{3}$?

WRITE ABOUT IT Explain how to add fractions with unlike denominators.

HANDS-ON PRACTICE

Use fraction bars to find the sum.

1.

2.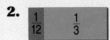

3.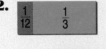

4.

5.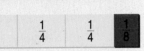

6.

7.

8.

9.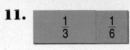

10.

11.

12.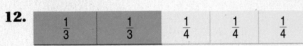

Use fraction bars to find the sum.

13. $\frac{1}{4} + \frac{1}{6} = n$

14. $\frac{1}{5} + \frac{3}{10} = n$

15. $\frac{3}{4} + \frac{5}{6} = n$

16. $\frac{2}{5} + \frac{1}{2} = n$

17. $\frac{5}{6} + \frac{1}{12} = n$

18. $\frac{1}{4} + \frac{1}{3} = n$

19. $\frac{3}{10} + \frac{1}{2} = n$

20. $\frac{1}{2} + \frac{5}{6} = n$

21. $\frac{4}{10} + \frac{1}{2} = n$

Mixed Applications

22. Frank is baking muffins for a school bake sale. Frank used $\frac{1}{3}$ cup brown sugar and $\frac{3}{4}$ cup white sugar. How much sugar did he use in all?

23. Roy has $\frac{1}{4}$ yard of ribbon. He needs $\frac{3}{8}$ yard more for the costume he is making. How much ribbon does he need in all?

24. John needs one board that is $\frac{1}{2}$ foot long and one that is $\frac{1}{4}$ foot long. He has a board that is $\frac{7}{8}$ foot long. Can John cut the shorter boards from the longer board? Explain.

25. Maria and Kevin have $25.00. They bought 3 cans of paint for $3.99 each and 2 paint brushes for $2.89 each. Posterboard costs $1.75 per sheet. How many sheets of posterboard can Maria and Kevin buy? How much change will they get?

MORE PRACTICE Student Handbook page H101

Using the Least Common Denominator to Add Fractions

You will learn to add unlike fractions by finding the least common denominator.

Why learn this? You can add unlike fractions, such as fractions of a pound.

WORD POWER

least common denominator (LCD)

Shawna took $\frac{1}{6}$ pound of aluminum cans to be recycled. Preston took $\frac{1}{4}$ pound. How many pounds of aluminum did they take in all?

To find the sum of unlike fractions, you need to rename them as like fractions. The least common multiple of two or more denominators is used to find the **least common denominator**, or **LCD**.

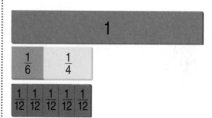

REMEMBER:

The *least common multiple*, or *LCM*, is the least number that is a common multiple of two or more numbers.

Multiples of 2: 2, 4, 6, 8
Multiples of 3: 3, 6, 9, 12
LCM: 6

MODEL

What is $\frac{1}{6} + \frac{1}{4}$?

▶ Step 1

Model with fraction bars.

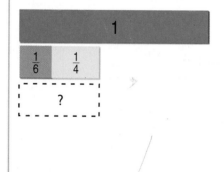

▶ Step 2

To find which fraction bars match $\frac{1}{6} + \frac{1}{4}$, find the least common denominator, or LCD.

The LCM of 6 and 4 is 12. So, the LCD of $\frac{1}{6}$ and $\frac{1}{4}$ is twelfths.

▶ Step 3

Since the LCD is twelfths, use like fraction bars to see how many twelfths equal $\frac{1}{6} + \frac{1}{4}$.

Since $\frac{2}{12} + \frac{3}{12}$ equals $\frac{1}{6} + \frac{1}{4}$ in length, $\frac{1}{6} + \frac{1}{4} = \frac{5}{12}$.

So, Shawna and Preston took $\frac{5}{12}$ pound of aluminum in all.

Talk About It

- How does knowing the least common multiple help you find the least common denominator?

- How does knowing the LCD help you find the sum?

Technology Link

In *Mighty Math Number Heroes,* the game *Fraction Fireworks* challenges you to add fractions with unlike denominators.

CRITICAL THINKING What fraction bars would you use to find the sum of $\frac{1}{6}$ and $\frac{1}{3}$? Explain.

PRACTICE

Use the LCM to name the least common denominator, or LCD, for each pair of fractions.

1. $\frac{1}{5}$ and $\frac{1}{10}$ **2.** $\frac{1}{4}$ and $\frac{1}{3}$ **3.** $\frac{1}{4}$ and $\frac{1}{8}$ **4.** $\frac{1}{3}$ and $\frac{1}{9}$

5. $\frac{1}{3}$ and $\frac{1}{2}$ **6.** $\frac{1}{4}$ and $\frac{1}{2}$ **7.** $\frac{1}{6}$ and $\frac{1}{4}$ **8.** $\frac{1}{5}$ and $\frac{1}{2}$

Use fraction strips to find the sum. Write the answer in simplest form.

9. $\frac{1}{8} + \frac{3}{4} = n$ **10.** $\frac{1}{2} + \frac{4}{5} = n$ **11.** $\frac{1}{10} + \frac{4}{5} = n$ **12.** $\frac{1}{2} + \frac{1}{12} = n$

13. $\frac{2}{3} + \frac{1}{6} = n$ **14.** $\frac{1}{4} + \frac{2}{3} = n$ **15.** $\frac{9}{10} + \frac{2}{5} = n$ **16.** $\frac{3}{8} + \frac{3}{4} = n$

17. $\frac{2}{4} + \frac{2}{3} = n$ **18.** $\frac{1}{4} + \frac{2}{8} = n$ **19.** $\frac{5}{6} + \frac{2}{3} = n$ **20.** $\frac{3}{9} + \frac{1}{3} = n$

Mixed Applications

21. Morey earns $3.25 an hour at his job. He wants to buy a puppy for his sister. A puppy costs $25.00, a collar costs $8.99, a leash costs $12.99, and a food bowl costs $1.77. How many hours will Morey have to work until he has enough money?

22. A grocery store is having a sale on apples and oranges. Which is cheaper, apples at $0.45 cents each or 3 for $1.25? 8 oranges for $3.00 or oranges for $0.36 each?

23. Jose's band has 11 members. Of the 11 members, 8 members do not play guitar. What fraction of the members play guitar?

24. **Write a problem** in which you have to add unlike fractions.

Mixed Review

Find the quotient. Check by multiplying. (pages 216–217)

25. $18.9 \div 9 = \underline{\ ?\ }$ **26.** $5.34 \div 6 = \underline{\ ?\ }$ **27.** $0.94 \div 2 = \underline{\ ?\ }$

28. $52.4 \div 4 = \underline{\ ?\ }$ **29.** $3.93 \div 3 = \underline{\ ?\ }$ **30.** $5.88 \div 7 = \underline{\ ?\ }$

Write the measurements in order from shortest to longest. (pages 226–227)

31. 2 cm, 2 km, 2 m   **32.** 5 mm, 5 dm, 5 cm   **33.** 9 m, 9 cm, 9 mm

1 Adding Three Fractions

You will learn to add three unlike fractions. | **Why learn this?** You can solve problems that involve three fractions with unlike denominators.

Miss Fox surveyed her students to find their favorite activities. Of the students, $\frac{1}{3}$ said playing sports, $\frac{1}{4}$ said reading, and $\frac{1}{6}$ said playing musical instruments. The rest of the students didn't have a preference. What fraction of Miss Fox's students have a favorite activity?

Add 3 fractions the same way you add 2 fractions.

MODEL

What is $\frac{1}{3} + \frac{1}{4} + \frac{1}{6}$?

▶ Step 1

Model with fraction bars.

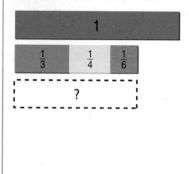

▶ Step 2

To find which fraction bars match $\frac{1}{3} + \frac{1}{4} + \frac{1}{6}$, find the least common denominator, or LCD.

The LCM of 3, 4, and 6 is 12. So, the LCD of $\frac{1}{3}$, $\frac{1}{4}$, and $\frac{1}{6}$ is twelfths.

▶ Step 3

Since the LCD is twelfths, use like fraction bars to see how many twelfths equal $\frac{1}{3} + \frac{1}{4} + \frac{1}{6}$.

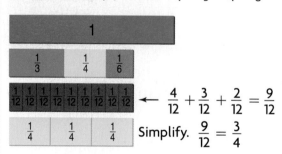

$\frac{4}{12} + \frac{3}{12} + \frac{2}{12} = \frac{9}{12}$

Simplify. $\frac{9}{12} = \frac{3}{4}$

So, $\frac{1}{3} + \frac{1}{4} + \frac{1}{6} = \frac{3}{4}$.

So, $\frac{3}{4}$ of the students have a favorite activity.

• In Step 3, why are the 3 bars for $\frac{1}{4}$ shown?

EXAMPLES

A. Find $\frac{1}{4} + \frac{1}{2} + \frac{3}{8}$.

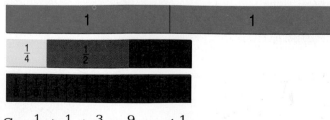

So, $\frac{1}{4} + \frac{1}{2} + \frac{3}{8} = \frac{9}{8}$, or $1\frac{1}{8}$.

B. Find $\frac{1}{2} + \frac{1}{3} + \frac{1}{6}$.

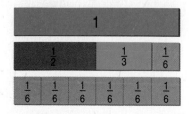

So, $\frac{1}{2} + \frac{1}{3} + \frac{1}{6} = \frac{6}{6}$, or 1.

Calculator Activities page H63

- Why is it important to compare to the fraction bar for 1?

You can use a calculator to add $\frac{1}{3} + \frac{1}{4} + \frac{1}{8}$.

Press:

| 1 | / | 3 | + | 1 | / | 4 | + | 1 | / | 8 | = |

Display: 17/24

PRACTICE

Use the LCM to name the least common denominator, or LCD, for each group of fractions.

1. $\frac{1}{5}$, $\frac{1}{10}$, and $\frac{1}{2}$

2. $\frac{1}{2}$, $\frac{1}{4}$, and $\frac{1}{6}$

3. $\frac{1}{2}$, $\frac{1}{3}$, and $\frac{1}{12}$

4. $\frac{1}{2}$, $\frac{1}{4}$, and $\frac{1}{3}$

5. $\frac{1}{6}$, $\frac{1}{2}$, and $\frac{1}{3}$

6. $\frac{1}{12}$, $\frac{1}{6}$, and $\frac{1}{3}$

Use fraction strips to find the sum. Write the answer in simplest form.

7. $\frac{3}{4} + \frac{1}{2} + \frac{1}{4} = n$

8. $\frac{1}{6} + \frac{1}{2} + \frac{1}{3} = n$

9. $\frac{1}{5} + \frac{2}{5} + \frac{7}{10} = n$

10. $\frac{1}{5} + \frac{3}{10} + \frac{1}{2} = n$

11. $\frac{1}{4} + \frac{2}{3} + \frac{1}{6} = n$

12. $\frac{1}{4} + \frac{1}{3} + \frac{1}{12} = n$

13. $\frac{1}{8} + \frac{3}{8} + \frac{1}{4} = n$

14. $\frac{5}{6} + \frac{1}{3} + \frac{1}{4} = n$

15. $\frac{7}{8} + \frac{3}{4} + \frac{1}{2} = n$

16. $\frac{2}{5} + \frac{1}{2} + \frac{1}{5} = n$

17. $\frac{2}{4} + \frac{1}{3} + \frac{1}{2} = n$

18. $\frac{1}{6} + \frac{1}{2} + \frac{1}{12} = n$

Mixed Applications

19. Mountain National Park rangers wanted to relocate 60 wolves. The first month, they relocated 4 wolves. Each month after that, they relocated twice as many wolves as the month before. How many months did it take?

20. Brianna brought 140 cookies for the fifth grade. There are 6 classes, and each class has the same number of people. How many cookies did she give to each class? Did she have any cookies left over?

21. Ray has two equal-size cans of nuts. One can is $\frac{1}{3}$ full and one is $\frac{1}{9}$ full. He puts the nuts from both cans into one can. How full is the combined can?

22. ▣ **WRITE ABOUT IT** How does adding three fractions with unlike denominators differ from adding two fractions with unlike denominators?

An adult timber wolf can measure up to $6\frac{1}{2}$ feet long.

LESSON
CONTINUES ▶

PROBLEM-SOLVING STRATEGY
Make a Model

THE PROBLEM Tara bought a tomato plant for $0.75. On Monday it had grown $\frac{1}{8}$ inch. On Wednesday it had grown another $\frac{1}{4}$ inch, and on Friday it had grown $\frac{1}{2}$ inch more. How much did the tomato plant grow?

REMEMBER:
- ☑ Understand
- ☑ Plan
- ☑ Solve
- ☑ Look Back

☑ Understand
- What are you asked to find?
- What information will you use?
- Is there information you will not use? If so, what?

☑ Plan
- What strategy can you use to solve this problem?

  You can *make a model* with fraction strips.

☑ Solve
- What model can you make?

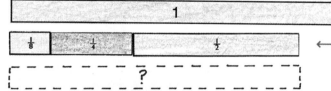

← The LCM of 8, 4, and 2 is 8. So, the LCD is eighths.

Since the LCD is eighths, use like fraction bars to see how many eighths equal $\frac{1}{8} + \frac{1}{4} + \frac{1}{2}$.

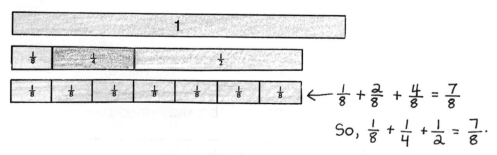

$\leftarrow \frac{1}{8} + \frac{2}{8} + \frac{4}{8} = \frac{7}{8}$

So, $\frac{1}{8} + \frac{1}{4} + \frac{1}{2} = \frac{7}{8}$.

So, the tomato plant grew $\frac{7}{8}$ inch that week.

☑ Look Back
- How can you decide if your answer is reasonable?
- What other strategy can you use?

PRACTICE

Make a model to solve.

1. Jan planted vegetables in $\frac{2}{3}$ of her garden, flowers in $\frac{1}{6}$ of her garden, and herbs in $\frac{1}{6}$ of her garden. How much of Jan's garden was planted?

2. Every day that Jerry walks home from school, he walks $\frac{1}{2}$ mile. He walked home from school 3 days in a row. How far did he walk?

3. Anita made a 3×3 square design with 1 white, 4 red, 2 blue, and 2 yellow squares. She glued a red square in each corner. She glued the white square in the middle, a blue square above and below the white square, and a yellow square in the two remaining spaces. What does Anita's design look like?

4. At Jones Elementary School, $\frac{1}{3}$ of the students have one pet, $\frac{1}{4}$ have two pets, and $\frac{1}{6}$ have three or more pets. The rest of the students do not have any pets. What part of the school has pets?

Mixed Applications

Solve.

CHOOSE A STRATEGY

• Make an Organized List • Work Backward • Guess and Check • Use a Table • Make a Model

5. Cara had 40 pencils. She gave some of her pencils to Ed and Sarah. She gave twice as many pencils to Ed as she gave to Sarah. Cara has 22 pencils left. How many pencils did she give to Ed? to Sarah?

6. Brett is playing a game. On his last turn he earned 12 points, lost 5 points, and earned 3 more points. Now he has 32 points. How many points did Brett have before his last turn?

7. Maya can wear a red or orange shirt. She can wear black, blue, or white pants. How many choices does she have? What are they?

8. Rita, Kyle, and Kira shared a pizza. Rita ate $\frac{1}{3}$ of the pizza, Kyle ate $\frac{1}{3}$, and Kira ate $\frac{1}{4}$. What part of the pizza did they eat?

9. George and Kerry are allowed to go to a movie if they clean their rooms for more than 2 hours each week. The table shows how long they cleaned every day. Will George be allowed to go to the movie? Will Kerry? Explain.

MINUTES SPENT CLEANING					
	Mon	Tue	Wed	Thu	Fri
George	20 min	20 min	40 min	30 min	30 min
Kerry	50 min	50 min	15 min	15 min	5 min

MATH FUN!

EGYPTIAN FRACTIONS

PURPOSE To practice adding unlike fractions

YOU WILL NEED pencil and paper, fraction strips

The ancient Egyptians wrote all fractions as sums of unit fractions with different denominators. Unit fractions have 1 as the numerator. For example, to show $\frac{3}{4}$, they wrote $\frac{1}{2} + \frac{1}{4}$.

$\triangleright \frac{1}{2}$ $\circ \frac{1}{4}$ $\diagup \frac{1}{8}$ $\triangle \frac{1}{16}$

Write each of the following fractions as the sum of unit fractions: $\frac{3}{8}$, $\frac{5}{8}$, $\frac{3}{16}$, and $\frac{11}{16}$. Make up two other fractions and write them as the sum of unit fractions.

HOME NOTE Teach your family how to write Egyptian fractions.

Fraction Flags

PURPOSE To add unlike fractions

YOU WILL NEED centimeter grid paper, ruler, pencil, colored pencils or markers

You and a partner are each going to design a flag, using the same main color.

Indonesia   Mexico   Lithuania

Of one person's flag, $\frac{1}{4}$, $\frac{1}{2}$, or $\frac{3}{4}$ should be the main color. Of the other person's flag, $\frac{1}{3}$ or $\frac{2}{3}$ should be the main color.

Which of the flags are about $\frac{1}{3}$ red?

Sports Fractions

PURPOSE To write word problems involving fractions

YOU WILL NEED pencil and paper

Choose a sport from the table. Fold a strip of paper into thirds or fourths, depending on which game you choose, to make a time line for the game. Mark each period on the time line. Then answer the questions that apply to the sport you chose.

baseball game	9 innings
football game	4 quarters, each 15 minutes
basketball game	4 quarters, each 12 minutes
soccer game	2 periods, each 45 minutes
hockey game	3 periods, each 20 minutes

At what point is the game

- one-third over?
- one-half over?
- two-thirds over?
- three-fourths over?

✓ CHECK UNDERSTANDING

1. VOCABULARY The least common multiple of two or more denominators is used to find the __?__. (page 282)

Use the LCM to name the least common denominator, or LCD, for each group of fractions. (pages 282–285)

2. $\frac{2}{3}$ and $\frac{2}{9}$

3. $\frac{1}{2}$ and $\frac{1}{3}$

4. $\frac{3}{10}$ and $\frac{2}{5}$

5. $\frac{1}{3}$, $\frac{3}{4}$, and $\frac{2}{3}$

6. $\frac{1}{8}$, $\frac{1}{4}$, and $\frac{1}{2}$

7. $\frac{2}{3}$, $\frac{1}{2}$, and $\frac{5}{6}$

✓ CHECK SKILLS

Use fraction strips to find the sum. Write the answer in simplest form. (pages 282–285)

8. $\frac{3}{10} + \frac{3}{5} = n$

9. $\frac{1}{4} + \frac{4}{8} = n$

10. $\frac{5}{6} + \frac{1}{3} = n$

11. $\frac{4}{5} + \frac{2}{10} = n$

12. $\frac{2}{3} + \frac{5}{9} = n$

13. $\frac{2}{8} + \frac{1}{2} = n$

14. $\frac{1}{3} + \frac{1}{4} + \frac{2}{3} = n$

15. $\frac{3}{8} + \frac{3}{4} + \frac{1}{2} = n$

16. $\frac{1}{5} + \frac{1}{10} + \frac{1}{2} = n$

✓ CHECK PROBLEM SOLVING

Solve. (pages 286–287)

CHOOSE A STRATEGY

• Work Backward   • Make a Model   • Write a Number Sentence   • Act It Out

17. Brent harvested $\frac{1}{4}$ of his garden in September, $\frac{3}{8}$ in October, and $\frac{1}{8}$ in November. What part of his garden did Brent harvest in those three months?

18. Kalin has 216 photos in an album with 36 pages. The album is full, and each page has an equal number of photos. How many photos are on each page?

19. Devon has 11 quarters. She has twice as many dimes as quarters and 5 fewer nickels than dimes. She has the same number of pennies as the other coins combined. How many of each coin does Devon have? How much money is that?

20. Trevor just came home from the mall. He has $17.04. While he was at the mall, he bought a T-shirt for $9.95 and lunch for $3.01. Then his sister gave him $5.00. How much money did Trevor begin with?

CHAPTER 18

MODELING SUBTRACTION OF FRACTIONS

DID YOU KNOW...

To make house frames, builders use "two by fours," or boards that measure 2 in. by 4 in. These boards shrink when the wood dries. A "two by four" actually measures only $1\frac{1}{2}$ in. by $3\frac{1}{2}$ in.

Designing Fraction Bars

Work with a group to design a fraction-bar kit that includes halves, thirds, fourths, sixths, and eighths. Then compare and measure the fraction bars.

YOU WILL NEED: construction paper in five colors, scissors, ruler, pencil, calculator

Work together. Your job is to

- choose the length that will represent 1 whole. All of the bars you start with to make your kit will have to be the same length.

- make bars for each denominator.

- compare and measure the different pieces. What is the difference in their lengths?

- make a poster to display your results.

FRACTION BARS COLOR KEY

$\frac{1}{2}$ tan	
$\frac{1}{3}$ green	
$\frac{1}{4}$ yellow	
$\frac{1}{6}$ gold	
$\frac{1}{8}$ red	

DID YOU

- ✓ choose the length to represent 1 whole?

- ✓ make fraction bars for each denominator?

- ✓ compare and measure the pieces?

- ✓ make a poster to display your results?

- ✓ report your results?

We used 9-inch

Each half measures
inches.

Each third measur
inches.

Each fourth measu
$2\frac{1}{4}$ inches.

Each sixth measu
$1\frac{1}{2}$ inches.

Each eighth mea s
$1\frac{1}{8}$ inches.

Subtracting Like Fractions

You will learn to subtract fractions with like denominators.

Why learn this? You can solve problems that involve finding the difference of parts.

Mona had $\frac{5}{8}$ pound of ground beef. She used $\frac{2}{8}$ pound to make a hamburger. How much meat is left?

One way to use fraction bars to subtract like fractions is to take away bars.

MODEL

TAKE AWAY: What is $\frac{5}{8} - \frac{2}{8}$?

▶ **Step 1**

Model $\frac{5}{8}$ with fraction bars.

| $\frac{1}{8}$ | $\frac{1}{8}$ | $\frac{1}{8}$ | $\frac{1}{8}$ | $\frac{1}{8}$ | $\frac{5}{8}$ |

▶ **Step 2**

Take away 2 bars, or $\frac{2}{8}$.

| $\frac{1}{8}$ | $\frac{1}{8}$ | $\frac{1}{8}$ | $\frac{1}{8}$ | $\frac{1}{8}$ | $\frac{5}{8} - \frac{2}{8}$ |

▶ **Step 3**

Count the bars left.

| $\frac{1}{8}$ | $\frac{1}{8}$ | $\frac{1}{8}$ | So, $\frac{5}{8} - \frac{2}{8} = \frac{3}{8}$.

So, there is $\frac{3}{8}$ pound of ground beef left.

Franco has $\frac{3}{6}$ yard of gift wrap. James has $\frac{1}{6}$ yard of gift wrap. How many more yards does Franco have?

Another way to use fraction bars to subtract like fractions is to compare bars.

REMEMBER:

A fraction is in *simplest form* when the greatest common factor, or GCF, of the numerator and denominator is 1.

MODEL

COMPARISON: What is $\frac{3}{6} - \frac{1}{6}$?

▶ **Step 1**

Model $\frac{3}{6}$ and $\frac{1}{6}$ with fraction bars.

▶ **Step 2**

Compare the bars for $\frac{3}{6}$ with the bar for $\frac{1}{6}$. Find the difference.

▶ **Step 3**

Find the largest bar or bars of the same length to write the answer in simplest form.

So, Franco has $\frac{1}{3}$ yard more.

• How are the two models alike? How are they different?

CRITICAL THINKING What rule can you write for subtracting like fractions with fraction bars?

PRACTICE

Use fraction strips to find the difference.

1. $\frac{4}{5} - \frac{3}{5} = n$ 2. $\frac{7}{10} - \frac{4}{10} = n$ 3. $\frac{8}{9} - \frac{4}{9} = n$

4. $\frac{7}{12} - \frac{1}{12} = n$ 5. $\frac{4}{8} - \frac{3}{8} = n$ 6. $\frac{4}{6} - \frac{3}{6} = n$

Use fraction strips to find the difference. Write the answer in simplest form.

7. $\frac{9}{10} - \frac{3}{10} = n$ 8. $\frac{7}{12} - \frac{1}{12} = n$ 9. $\frac{7}{8} - \frac{1}{8} = n$

10. $\frac{5}{12} - \frac{1}{12} = n$ 11. $\frac{3}{4} - \frac{1}{4} = n$ 12. $\frac{5}{10} - \frac{3}{10} = n$

13. $\frac{5}{6} - \frac{3}{6} = n$ 14. $\frac{5}{6} - \frac{1}{6} = n$ 15. $\frac{10}{12} - \frac{7}{12} = n$

Mixed Applications

16. Rich pulls a marble from a bag of 10 black, 5 red, 5 blue, and 2 green marbles. Which outcome is most likely? least likely? Are any outcomes equally likely?

17. Tara got 5 letters in the mail on Monday. Of the letters, 3 were from friends. What fraction of the letters was *not* from friends?

18. When Max arrived at the class party, there was $\frac{7}{8}$ of a pizza left. He ate $\frac{4}{8}$ of the pizza. How much of the pizza was left after Max ate?

19. **WRITE ABOUT IT** How can you use the comparison model to show $\frac{7}{8} - \frac{3}{8}$?

Mixed Review

Choose the most reasonable unit of measure. Write *mm, cm, dm, m*, or *km*. (pages 226–227)

20. length of a paper clip

21. height of your desk

22. distance from your home to the mall

Find the number of choices by making a tree diagram. (pages 176–177)

23. Breakfast Choices
    Food: cereal or eggs
    Drink: orange juice, milk, tomato juice, or apple juice

Subtracting Unlike Fractions

You will investigate using fraction bars to subtract fractions with unlike denominators.

Why learn this? You can solve problems that involve subtracting fractions with unlike denominators.

You can use the comparison model to subtract fractions with unlike denominators.

Explore

Use fraction bars to subtract fractions with unlike denominators.

MATERIALS: fraction bars

MODEL

What is $\frac{2}{3} - \frac{1}{6}$?

▶ **Step 1**

Model $\frac{2}{3}$ and $\frac{1}{6}$ with fraction bars.

| $\frac{1}{3}$ | $\frac{1}{3}$ | $\frac{2}{3}$ |

| $\frac{1}{6}$ | $\frac{1}{6}$ |

▶ **Step 2**

Compare the bars. Find the like fraction bars that fit exactly across. This is the difference.

| $\frac{1}{3}$ | $\frac{1}{3}$ |

| $\frac{1}{6}$ | ? |

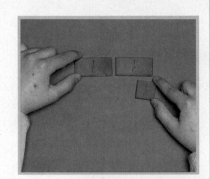

Record

Record a subtraction sentence for the model. Describe how you found the missing part.

TALK ABOUT IT How did you decide what fraction bars to try? Did more than one size fit? Why?

Now investigate finding the difference of other unlike fractions.

Try This

Find the difference of $\frac{3}{4} - \frac{1}{2}$. Explain how you used fraction bars to find the difference. Record a number sentence.

TALK ABOUT IT How is finding the difference with like fractions different from finding the difference with unlike fractions?

Technology **Link**
E-Lab • Activity 18 Available on CD-ROM and the Internet at http://www.hbschool.com/elab

✎ **WRITE ABOUT IT** Explain how to subtract fractions with unlike denominators.

HANDS-ON PRACTICE

Use fraction bars to find the difference.

1.
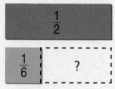

2.

3.

4.
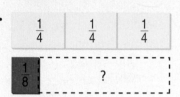

5.
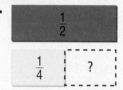

6.

7.
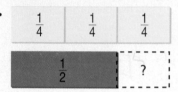

8.
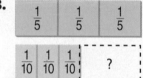

9.
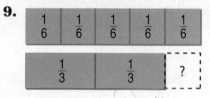

10. $\dfrac{3}{4} - \dfrac{3}{8} = n$

11. $\dfrac{5}{6} - \dfrac{1}{12} = n$

12. $\dfrac{4}{6} - \dfrac{1}{3} = n$

13. $\dfrac{7}{10} - \dfrac{1}{2} = n$

14. $\dfrac{6}{8} - \dfrac{1}{4} = n$

15. $\dfrac{5}{6} - \dfrac{1}{3} = n$

16. $\dfrac{1}{2} - \dfrac{1}{10} = n$

17. $\dfrac{7}{8} - \dfrac{3}{4} = n$

18. $\dfrac{2}{3} - \dfrac{1}{12} = n$

Mixed Applications

19. Carl worked outside for $\frac{5}{6}$ hour. He tilled his garden for $\frac{1}{2}$ hour, planted seeds for $\frac{1}{6}$ hour, and watered for the rest of the time. For what part of an hour did he water?

20. Doug and Lisa invited 25 friends to a cookout. Doug, Lisa, and each friend will eat 2 hot dogs. Hot dogs come 8 to a pack. How many packs should Doug and Lisa buy?

21. The Wegners drove from Akron to Indianapolis. They drove for 5 hours and traveled 292.5 miles in all. They did not make any stops. How fast did they drive?

22. There are 60 seconds in a minute. Pam can run 1 lap around the track in 45 seconds. How many seconds will it take Pam to run 12 laps around the track at that speed? How many minutes is that?

Using the Least Common Denominator to Subtract Fractions

You will learn more about subtracting fractions with unlike denominators.

Why learn this? You can subtract fractions, such as parts of a gallon of paint, to find the amount left over.

Lloyd and Kishi had $\frac{3}{4}$ gallon of paint for the set they are making for the play. They used $\frac{1}{3}$ gallon to paint the background scenery. How much paint do they have left?

You can use the least common denominator, or LCD, to help you subtract unlike fractions.

MODEL

What is $\frac{3}{4} - \frac{1}{3}$?

▶ **Step 1**

Model with fraction bars.

| $\frac{1}{4}$ | $\frac{1}{4}$ | $\frac{1}{4}$ |

| $\frac{1}{3}$ | ? |

▶ **Step 2**

Find the least common denominator, or LCD.

The LCM of 4 and 3 is 12, so the LCD of $\frac{3}{4}$ and $\frac{1}{3}$ is twelfths.

▶ **Step 3**

Since the LCD is twelfths, use like fraction bars to see how many twelfths fit exactly across. This is the difference.

| $\frac{1}{4}$ | $\frac{1}{4}$ | $\frac{1}{4}$ |

| $\frac{1}{3}$ | $\frac{1}{12}$ $\frac{1}{12}$ $\frac{1}{12}$ $\frac{1}{12}$ $\frac{1}{12}$ |

So, $\frac{3}{4} - \frac{1}{3} = \frac{5}{12}$.

So, Lloyd and Kishi have $\frac{5}{12}$ gallon of paint left.

EXAMPLE

What is $\frac{1}{2} - \frac{2}{5}$?

Model with fraction bars.

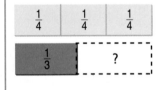

Find the LCD.

The LCM of 2 and 5 is 10, so the LCD of $\frac{1}{2}$ and $\frac{2}{5}$ is tenths.

Find the difference.

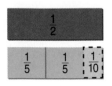

So, $\frac{1}{2} - \frac{2}{5} = \frac{1}{10}$.

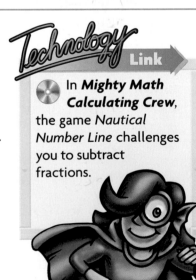

Technology Link

In **Mighty Math Calculating Crew**, the game *Nautical Number Line* challenges you to subtract fractions.

• How does using the LCD help you model this problem?

PRACTICE

Name the least common denominator, or LCD, for each pair of fractions.

1. $\frac{1}{2}$ and $\frac{1}{3}$
2. $\frac{1}{5}$ and $\frac{1}{2}$
3. $\frac{1}{3}$ and $\frac{1}{4}$

4. $\frac{1}{9}$ and $\frac{1}{3}$
5. $\frac{1}{4}$ and $\frac{1}{8}$
6. $\frac{1}{2}$ and $\frac{1}{4}$

7. $\frac{1}{6}$ and $\frac{1}{4}$
8. $\frac{1}{4}$ and $\frac{1}{10}$
9. $\frac{1}{6}$ and $\frac{1}{8}$

Use fraction strips to find the difference. Write the answer in simplest form.

10. $\frac{5}{6} - \frac{3}{4} = n$
11. $\frac{3}{5} - \frac{1}{2} = n$
12. $\frac{7}{8} - \frac{3}{4} = n$

13. $\frac{2}{3} - \frac{1}{9} = n$
14. $\frac{7}{8} - \frac{1}{2} = n$
15. $\frac{11}{12} - \frac{1}{6} = n$

16. $\frac{5}{6} - \frac{1}{2} = n$
17. $\frac{11}{12} - \frac{2}{3} = n$
18. $\frac{4}{5} - \frac{3}{10} = n$

Mixed Applications

19. Dan wrote a report for history. He found $\frac{1}{8}$ of the information for the report on the Internet and $\frac{1}{2}$ of the information at the library. How much information did he get from sources other than the Internet and the library?

20. Ms. Aquil bought a box of 144 pencils. She gave an equal number of pencils to each of her 24 students. How many pencils did each student get?

21. Mandy spent $\frac{7}{8}$ of the weekend practicing for the school play. Linda spent $\frac{1}{2}$ of the weekend practicing for the play. How much longer did Mandy spend practicing?

22. ✏️ **Write a problem** in which you subtract unlike fractions.

Mixed Review

Multiply. Write each product. **(pages 196–197)**

23. $0.7 \times 0.9 = n$
24. $0.8 \times 0.6 = n$
25. $0.4 \times 0.5 = n$
26. $0.9 \times 0.8 = n$

Find the quotient. Check by multiplying. **(pages 216–217)**

27. $6\overline{)1.08}$
28. $9\overline{)2.25}$
29. $4\overline{)3.92}$
30. $7\overline{)3.78}$
31. $8\overline{)5.84}$

32. $3\overline{)2.67}$
33. $6\overline{)1.74}$
34. $4\overline{)2.72}$
35. $7\overline{)1.12}$
36. $8\overline{)5.76}$

Subtracting Fractions Using a Ruler

You will learn to subtract fractions of an inch on a ruler.	**Why learn this?** You can compare measurements that are less than an inch, such as plant growth.

On Monday a bean plant was $\frac{1}{2}$ inch tall. On Friday the plant was $\frac{5}{8}$ inch tall. How much did the plant grow from Monday to Friday?

You can compare and subtract unlike fractions on a ruler the same way you compare and subtract unlike fractions with fraction bars.

What is $\frac{5}{8} - \frac{1}{2}$?

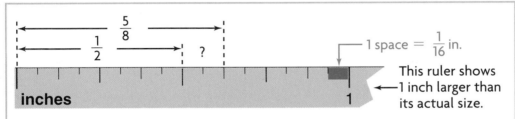

On this ruler, each space equals $\frac{1}{16}$ inch. Every 2 spaces equals $\frac{1}{8}$ inch, every 4 spaces equals $\frac{1}{4}$ inch, and every 8 spaces equals $\frac{1}{2}$ inch. The difference between $\frac{5}{8}$ inch and $\frac{1}{2}$ inch is 2 spaces, or $\frac{1}{8}$ inch.

So, the plant grew $\frac{1}{8}$ inch from Monday to Friday.

Talk About It

- How is subtracting unlike fractions on a ruler like using fraction bars to subtract?

- How is subtracting unlike fractions on a ruler different from using fraction bars?

Check Your Understanding

CRITICAL THINKING

Use the ruler to find the difference.

1. $\frac{1}{4}$ in. $- \frac{3}{16}$ in. $= \underline{\ ?\ }$

Social Studies Link

The common bean is grown in all parts of the world. It is an important source of protein in the diets of more than 50 million people. Some families get about $\frac{2}{3}$ of the protein they need from beans and the rest from beef and milk. What fraction of their protein comes from beef and milk?

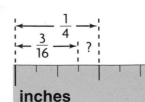

PRACTICE

Use the ruler to find the difference.

2. $\frac{15}{16}$ in. $- \frac{7}{16}$ in. $= \underline{\ ?\ }$

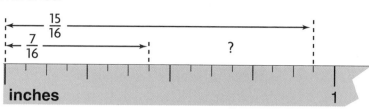

3. $\frac{1}{2}$ in. $- \frac{3}{8}$ in. $= \underline{\ ?\ }$

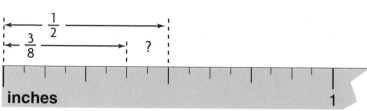

4. $\frac{3}{4}$ in. $- \frac{1}{8}$ in. $= \underline{\ ?\ }$

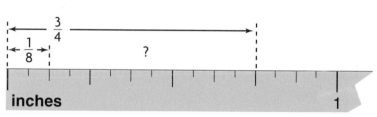

5. $\frac{1}{2}$ in. $- \frac{3}{16}$ in. $= \underline{\ ?\ }$ **6.** $\frac{7}{8}$ in. $- \frac{1}{2}$ in. $= \underline{\ ?\ }$ **7.** $\frac{7}{16}$ in. $- \frac{3}{8}$ in. $= \underline{\ ?\ }$

8. $\frac{5}{8}$ in. $- \frac{1}{4}$ in. $= \underline{\ ?\ }$ **9.** $\frac{11}{16}$ in. $- \frac{1}{2}$ in. $= \underline{\ ?\ }$ **10.** 1 in. $- \frac{1}{4}$ in. $= \underline{\ ?\ }$

Mixed Applications

For Problems 11–14, use a ruler to solve.

11. Rudy's longest fingernail is $\frac{5}{8}$ inch long. Her shortest fingernail is $\frac{5}{16}$ inch long. What is the difference in length between the two fingernails?

12. Terry is $\frac{1}{2}$ inch taller than Lisa. Rodelin is $\frac{3}{4}$ inch taller than Lisa. How much taller is Rodelin than Terry?

13. On Monday, a potato plant was $\frac{1}{4}$ inch tall. On Friday, it was $\frac{7}{16}$ inch tall. How much did the potato plant grow from Monday to Friday?

14. Dawn is sewing a shirt. She makes a buttonhole that is 1 inch wide to fit a button that is $\frac{5}{8}$ inch wide. How much wider is the buttonhole than the button?

15. Bernie, a fifth-grade student, is 1.5 meters tall. He grew 5 cm during his fourth-grade year. He grew 8 cm during his third-grade year. How tall was Bernie at the beginning of third grade? (HINT: 1 cm = 0.01 m)

16. ✏️ **Write a problem** that you could solve by subtracting fractions on a ruler.

LESSON
CONTINUES ▶

PART 2 PROBLEM-SOLVING STRATEGY
Work Backward

THE PROBLEM The students in Alana's class planted seeds. They worked in groups of three students to measure the sprouts. On Friday, Alana's sprout was $\frac{7}{8}$ inch tall. It had grown $\frac{1}{4}$ inch from Wednesday to Friday. It had grown $\frac{1}{2}$ inch from Monday to Wednesday. How tall was Alana's sprout on Monday?

☑ Understand

- What are you asked to find?
- What information will you use?
- Is there information you will not use? If so, what?

☑ Plan

- What strategy can you use to solve this problem?

  You can *work backward* to find out how tall the sprout was on Monday.

☑ Solve

- How can you work backward to solve?

  Use a ruler. Start at $\frac{7}{8}$ inch. Subtract the $\frac{1}{4}$ inch the sprout grew from Wednesday to Friday. Then subtract the $\frac{1}{2}$ inch the sprout grew from Monday to Wednesday. The answer is the height the sprout was on Monday.

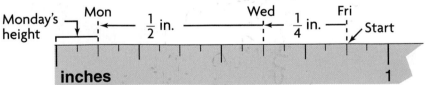

So, Alana's sprout was $\frac{1}{8}$ inch tall on Monday.

☑ Look Back

- How can you determine if your answer is reasonable?
- What other strategy can you use?

PRACTICE

Work backward to solve.

1. Len is in Alana's class. On Friday his sprout was $\frac{3}{4}$ inch tall. It had grown $\frac{1}{8}$ inch from Wednesday to Friday. It had grown $\frac{3}{8}$ inch from Monday to Wednesday. How tall was Len's sprout on Monday?

2. Maria planted a marigold seed. On Friday the marigold sprout was $\frac{5}{8}$ inch tall. It had grown $\frac{1}{4}$ inch from Wednesday to Friday. It had grown $\frac{1}{4}$ inch from Monday to Wednesday. How tall was Maria's marigold on Monday?

3. Brian came home from a baseball game with $7.26. At the game he spent $7.50 for a ticket, $2.25 for lunch, and $3.99 for a souvenir. Then he won $1.00 because he was sitting in the prize seat. How much money did Brian have before the game?

4. Faye's puppy is 8 months old. It is 0.31 meters tall. The puppy grew 4 cm from when it was 7 months to 8 months old. It grew 2 cm from when it was 6 months to 7 months old. How tall was Faye's puppy when it was 6 months old?

Mixed Applications

Solve.

CHOOSE A STRATEGY

• Work Backward   • Write a Number Sentence   • Guess and Check   • Make an Organized List

5. Micah's school has assemblies on Mondays and Fridays. Monday assemblies last 1 hour. Friday assemblies last 2 hours. How many hours of assemblies are there in 4 weeks?

6. Charity gave 12 baseball cards to Rhonda and 18 to James. Then she traded 5 of her cards for 3 of Andy's cards. Charity now has 48 cards. How many cards did she have to begin with?

7. Carlotta bought 9 packages of lemonade for $1.10 each and 2 packages of cups for $1.09 each. She sold 23 cups of lemonade every hour for 4 hours at $0.40 per cup. How much more money did Carlotta earn than she spent on supplies?

8. Sherwood earned $35 last week. He earned twice as much for baby-sitting as he did for cleaning the bathrooms. He earned twice as much for cleaning the bathrooms as he did for mowing the lawn. How much did Sherwood earn for each job?

9. Leon goes to Camp Jewell. How many combinations of food can he eat at dinner? What are they?

CAMP JEWELL DINNER CHOICES
Main Dish: Hamburger Hot Dog Rice & Beans
Dessert: Fruit Pie Ice Cream Cake

CULTURAL CONNECTION

Farming in Zambia, Africa

Matt lives on a farm in Iowa. His father volunteered to go to Zambia for 8 weeks to show farmers new ways to grow corn and wheat. Matt's dad spent 4 weeks helping farmers plant wheat and 2 weeks teaching a class about growing corn. Write a fraction to show the number of weeks he helped farmers with wheat and another fraction to show the number of weeks he taught about corn.

CULTURAL LINK

Visitors to Zambia can take safaris in Luangwa Valley National Park and Kafue National Park to see the many African animals that live in these preserves. Kafue National Park covers 8,687 square miles, which is about the size of the states of Connecticut and Delaware together.

Work Together

1. Change the fractions $\frac{4}{8}$ and $\frac{2}{8}$ to fourths. Subtract the smaller fraction from the larger fraction.

2. Matt's father spent the last 2 weeks of his trip visiting farms in Zambia and showing farmers ways to improve production of vegetables and corn. Find three ways to write the fraction of time he spent visiting farms.

3. Matt's father brought him a set of wood carvings of wild animals from Zambia. Of the animals, $\frac{1}{3}$ were elephants, and $\frac{2}{9}$ were lions. Find the least common denominator for the two fractions. What is the difference between the part of animals that was elephants and the part that was lions?

4. Use the circle graph. Write the fraction for each animal. Tell which fraction can be written in simplest form.

ANIMAL CARVINGS
lions   hippos
zebra
elephants   giraffe

✓ CHECK UNDERSTANDING

Use fraction strips to find the difference. (pages 294–295)

1.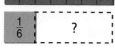

2.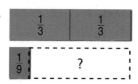

3.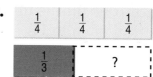

Name the least common denominator, or LCD, for each pair of fractions. (pages 296–297)

4. $\frac{2}{3}$ and $\frac{1}{6}$

5. $\frac{3}{4}$ and $\frac{3}{8}$

6. $\frac{2}{3}$ and $\frac{1}{4}$

7. $\frac{3}{4}$ and $\frac{1}{2}$

8. $\frac{3}{10}$ and $\frac{1}{5}$

9. $\frac{7}{9}$ and $\frac{2}{3}$

✓ CHECK SKILLS

Use fraction strips to find the difference. Write the answer in simplest form. (pages 292–293, 296–297)

10. $\frac{5}{8} - \frac{3}{8} = n$

11. $\frac{11}{12} - \frac{5}{12} = n$

12. $\frac{8}{9} - \frac{5}{9} = n$

13. $\frac{3}{4} - \frac{1}{2} = n$

14. $\frac{5}{8} - \frac{1}{2} = n$

15. $\frac{1}{3} - \frac{1}{12} = n$

16. $\frac{7}{10} - \frac{1}{2} = n$

17. $\frac{4}{5} - \frac{2}{10} = n$

18. $\frac{3}{4} - \frac{3}{8} = n$

19. $\frac{3}{4} - \frac{2}{3} = n$

20. $\frac{5}{8} - \frac{1}{4} = n$

21. $\frac{2}{3} - \frac{1}{6} = n$

✓ CHECK PROBLEM SOLVING

Solve. (pages 300–301)

> **CHOOSE A STRATEGY**
> • Work Backward • Write a Number Sentence • Guess and Check

22. Art planted a lima bean. On Friday the sprout was $\frac{7}{8}$ inch tall. It had grown $\frac{3}{8}$ inch from Wednesday to Friday. It had grown $\frac{1}{4}$ inch from Monday to Wednesday. How tall was the sprout on Monday?

23. Brenda gave away 21 stickers. She gave half as many stickers to her brother as she gave to her teacher. She gave twice as many to her best friend as she gave to her teacher. How many stickers did Brenda give to each person?

VOCABULARY CHECK

Choose a term from the box to complete each sentence.

WORD BANK

prime
equivalent
least common
   denominator, or LCD
least common
   multiple, or LCM
mixed number
simplest form

1. A number that is made up of a whole number and a fraction is called a __?__. (page 248)

2. The least number that is a common multiple of two or more numbers is called the __?__. (page 250)

3. A number that has exactly two factors, 1 and the number itself, is called a __?__ number. (page 262)

4. Fractions that name the same amount are __?__. (page 266)

5. When the greatest common factor of a fraction's numerator and denominator is 1, that fraction is in __?__. (page 272)

6. The least common multiple of two or more denominators is used to find the __?__. (page 282)

STUDY AND SOLVE

CHAPTER 15

EXAMPLE

Rename, using the least common multiple, and compare. Write $<$, $>$, or $=$ for the ●.

$\dfrac{2}{3}$ ● $\dfrac{3}{4}$ The LCM of 3 and 4 is 12.

$\dfrac{2}{3} \times \dfrac{4}{4} = \dfrac{8}{12}$

$\dfrac{3}{4} \times \dfrac{3}{3} = \dfrac{9}{12}$ Multiply each fraction so that the renamed fractions both have denominators of 12.

$\dfrac{8}{12}$ ● $\dfrac{9}{12}$ Compare the numerators. Since $8 < 9$, $\frac{8}{12} < \frac{9}{12}$. So, $\frac{2}{3} < \frac{3}{4}$.

$\dfrac{8}{12} < \dfrac{9}{12}$

Rename each fraction as a mixed number. (pages 248–249)

7. $\dfrac{9}{7}$

8. $\dfrac{19}{5}$

Rename, using the least common multiple, and compare. Write $<$, $>$, or $=$ for each ●. (pages 252–253)

9. $\dfrac{6}{12}$ ● $\dfrac{1}{2}$

10. $\dfrac{5}{8}$ ● $\dfrac{4}{5}$

Write in order from least to greatest. (pages 254–255)

11. $\dfrac{2}{3}, \dfrac{1}{2}, \dfrac{3}{4}$

12. $\dfrac{7}{8}, \dfrac{1}{4}, \dfrac{5}{16}$

Choose a strategy and solve. (pages 256–257)

13. Julie swam $\frac{1}{4}$ mile on Monday, $\frac{1}{2}$ mile on Tuesday, and $\frac{6}{8}$ mile on Wednesday. If this pattern continues, how far will she swim on Thursday?

CHAPTER 16

EXAMPLE

Write in simplest form.

$\dfrac{15}{20}$

Find the GCF of 15 and 20.
Factors of 15: 1, 3, 5, 15
Factors of 20: 1, 2, 4, 5, 10, 20

$\dfrac{15}{20} \div \dfrac{5}{5} = \dfrac{3}{4}$

The GCF is 5. Divide the numerator and the denominator by 5.
So, $\dfrac{15}{20}$ in simplest form is $\dfrac{3}{4}$.

Write the greatest common factor for each pair of numbers. (pages 264–265)

14. 6, 9 **15.** 4, 16

Find an equivalent fraction. Use multiplication or division. (pages 266–267)

16. $\dfrac{3}{8}$ **17.** $\dfrac{4}{12}$

Write each fraction in simplest form. (pages 270–273)

18. $\dfrac{3}{9}$ **19.** $\dfrac{16}{20}$

20. $\dfrac{12}{15}$ **21.** $\dfrac{8}{24}$

Choose a strategy and solve. (pages 268–269)

22. Quentin ate 3 slices of a pizza that was cut into sixths. Lynn said he had eaten $\frac{1}{2}$ of the pizza. Was she right? Explain.

CHAPTER 17

EXAMPLE

Use fraction strips to find the sum.

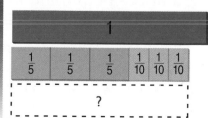

$\dfrac{3}{5} + \dfrac{3}{10} = \dfrac{9}{10}$

Use fraction strips to find the sum. Write the answer in simplest form. (pages 278–285)

23. $\dfrac{1}{8} + \dfrac{3}{8} = n$ **24.** $\dfrac{3}{5} + \dfrac{7}{10} = n$

Name the least common denominator for each group of fractions. (pages 282–285)

25. $\dfrac{2}{3}$ and $\dfrac{1}{2}$ **26.** $\dfrac{1}{2}, \dfrac{3}{4},$ and $\dfrac{5}{6}$

Choose a strategy and solve. (pages 286–287)

27. Danny used $\frac{1}{2}$ cup of flour, $\frac{1}{3}$ cup of cornmeal, and $\frac{1}{4}$ cup of sugar in a muffin recipe. How many cups of ingredients was this?

CHAPTER 18

EXAMPLE

Use fraction strips to find the difference.

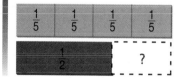

$\dfrac{4}{5} - \dfrac{1}{2} = \dfrac{3}{10}$

Use fraction strips to find the difference. Write the answer in simplest form. (pages 292–297)

28. $\dfrac{5}{6} - \dfrac{1}{3} = n$ **29.** $\dfrac{3}{4} - \dfrac{2}{3} = n$

Choose a strategy and solve. (pages 300–301)

30. Lupe used $\frac{3}{4}$ inch of ribbon. She had $\frac{2}{8}$ inch left. How much ribbon did she have to start with?

WHAT DID I LEARN?

✏️ WRITE ABOUT IT

1. Explain how you would name a fraction and a mixed number for the shaded part. (pages 248–249)

2. Explain how to use fraction bars to help you write $\frac{8}{12}$ in simplest form. (pages 270–273)

3. Show and explain each step as you use fraction strips and the least common denominator to find the sum $\frac{1}{2} + \frac{2}{5} + \frac{3}{10}$. Write the sum in simplest form. Draw a picture of what you did. (pages 282–285)

4. Show and explain each step as you use a ruler to find the difference: $\frac{1}{2}$ in. $- \frac{1}{8}$ in. $= n$. Draw a picture to show what you did. (pages 298–299)

✔️ PERFORMANCE ASSESSMENT

Solve. Explain your method.

CHOOSE A STRATEGY

- Work Backward
- Make a Model
- Draw a Diagram
- Write a Number Sentence

5. Sara is putting together a gift box of 12 decorated eggs. She wants $\frac{1}{3}$ of the eggs to be blue, $\frac{1}{4}$ to be yellow, and $\frac{5}{12}$ to be green. How many eggs will she have for each color? Show the order from least to greatest. (pages 256–257)

6. Cam spent $\frac{4}{12}$ of her allowance on clothes, $\frac{1}{4}$ on books, and $\frac{3}{6}$ on a software program. What did she spend most of her money on? (pages 268–269)

7. In Thelma's class, $\frac{1}{4}$ of the students watch TV after school, $\frac{1}{2}$ do homework, $\frac{1}{6}$ play outside, and the rest eat a snack. What part of the class eats a snack? (pages 286–287)

8. Anna was $52\frac{1}{8}$ in. tall in July. She had grown $\frac{1}{2}$ in. since June. From May to June she grew $\frac{1}{4}$ in. How tall was Anna at the beginning of May? (pages 300–301)

CUMULATIVE REVIEW

Solve the problem. Then write the letter of the correct answer.

1. Robyn had $205.16 in her bank account. She deposited $56.47 and wrote checks for $120.08 and $113.99. How much was left in her account?

   A. $27.56　　**B.** $141.55
   C. $261.63　**D.** $382.76　(pages 60–61)

2. Find the perimeter.

   55 m
   137 m

   A. 192 m　　**B.** 247 m
   C. 384 m　　**D.** 7,535 m　(pages 94–95)

3. What would be the best type of graph or plot to display data on students' and teachers' favorite colors?

   A. double-bar graph
   B. circle graph
   C. line graph
   D. stem-and-leaf plot　(pages 148–149)

4. It is __?__ that you will see a live dinosaur.

   A. certain　　**B.** impossible
   C. likely　　**D.** unlikely (pages 172–173)

5. 　0.35
   × 0.7
   　　　　A. 0.215
   　　　　B. 0.245
   　　　　C. 0.5
   　　　　D. 24.5　(pages 196–203)

6. $7\overline{)0.49}$

   A. 0.07　　**B.** 0.7
   C. 3.43　　**D.** 7　(pages 216–219)

7. A doorway is about 1 __?__ wide.

   A. centimeter　**B.** gram
   C. liter　　　　**D.** meter　(page 226–231)

8. Rename, using the least common multiple, and compare.

   $\dfrac{2}{3} \bullet \dfrac{3}{7}$　　**A.** $<$　　**B.** $>$
   　　　　　　C. $=$　　**D.** $+$
   　　　　　　　　(pages 252–253)

9. What is the greatest common factor for 9 and 12?

   A. 3　　**B.** 6
   C. 12　　**D.** 108　(pages 264–265)

For Problems 10–11, use fraction strips to solve. Choose the correct answer that is in simplest form. (pages 280–285, 292–293)

10. $\dfrac{3}{4} + \dfrac{2}{3} = n$

   A. $n = \dfrac{5}{12}$　　**B.** $n = \dfrac{5}{7}$

   C. $n = \dfrac{4}{3}$　　**D.** $n = 1\dfrac{5}{12}$

11. $\dfrac{7}{8} - \dfrac{5}{8} = n$

   A. $n = 2$　　**B.** $n = \dfrac{12}{16}$

   C. $n = \dfrac{1}{4}$　　**D.** $n = \dfrac{2}{8}$

19
ADDING AND SUBTRACTING FRACTIONS

DID YOU KNOW . . .

Beads have been used since ancient times to decorate clothing. Beads are made from materials such as shells, seeds, and minerals. Archaeologists have found evidence of beads that date back as far as 1,600 B.C.

Bead Fractions

Have you ever wanted to go on a dig? Archaeologists find beads and necklaces that are thousands of years old. Work together to make modern-day beads from colorful paper.

YOU WILL NEED: colorful magazine pages, scissors, paint brushes, white glue, yarn

Work with a partner. Your job is to

- choose paper in three colors or tones (dark, medium, light).

- follow the steps for How to Make a Bead.

- create a necklace in a pattern that uses 24 paper beads in at least three different colors.

- draw a diagram of your necklace, and find out what fraction of your necklace is in each color.

- write a fraction equation to describe your necklace.

HOW TO MAKE A BEAD

Cut a strip of magazine paper.

Roll the strip over a small paint brush or pencil.

Add glue, then roll over the glued surface. Remove pencil.

Set aside to dry.

DID YOU

- ✓ make a necklace in a pattern that uses at least 24 paper beads in different colors?

- ✓ draw a diagram of your necklace?

- ✓ find out what fraction of your necklace is in each color?

- ✓ write an equation with fractions to describe your necklace?

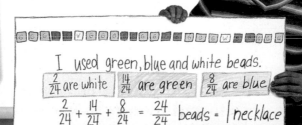

I used green, blue and white beads.
$\frac{2}{24}$ are white $\frac{14}{24}$ are green $\frac{8}{24}$ are blue
$\frac{2}{24} + \frac{14}{24} + \frac{8}{24} = \frac{24}{24}$ beads = 1 necklace

Estimating Sums and Differences

You will learn to estimate fractions and to estimate sums and differences.

Why learn this? You can estimate when an exact answer is not needed or check that your answer is reasonable.

You can use a number line to estimate fractions.

Is $\frac{3}{8}$ closer to 0, $\frac{1}{2}$ or 1?

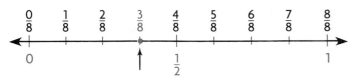

So, $\frac{3}{8}$ is closer to $\frac{1}{2}$.

Talk About It

- How do you know when a fraction is close to zero?

- What can you say about the numerator and denominator when a fraction is close to $\frac{1}{2}$? to 1?

Rounding fractions to 0, $\frac{1}{2}$, or 1 on a number line can help you estimate sums and differences.

EXAMPLES

A. Estimate the sum of $\frac{2}{3} + \frac{4}{5}$.

$\frac{2}{3}$ is close to $\frac{1}{2}$.

$\frac{4}{5}$ is close to 1. $\frac{1}{2} + 1 = 1\frac{1}{2}$

So, $\frac{2}{3} + \frac{4}{5}$ is about $1\frac{1}{2}$.

B. Estimate the difference of $\frac{5}{8} - \frac{1}{6}$.

$\frac{5}{8}$ is close to $\frac{1}{2}$.

$\frac{1}{6}$ is close to 0. $\frac{1}{2} - 0 = \frac{1}{2}$

So, $\frac{5}{8} - \frac{1}{6}$ is about $\frac{1}{2}$.

💡 **CRITICAL THINKING** If the estimated sum of two fractions is close to $\frac{1}{2}$, what do you know about the addends?

PRACTICE

Use the number lines to estimate if the fraction is closer to 0, $\frac{1}{2}$, or 1.

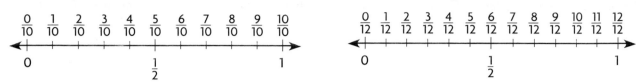

1. $\frac{7}{10}$

2. $\frac{1}{12}$

3. $\frac{3}{10}$

4. $\frac{5}{12}$

5. $\frac{9}{10}$

6. $\frac{2}{12}$

Write whether the fraction is closer to 0, $\frac{1}{2}$, or 1. You may use a number line.

7. $\frac{8}{9}$

8. $\frac{1}{3}$

9. $\frac{4}{5}$

10. $\frac{4}{7}$

11. $\frac{2}{9}$

12. $\frac{3}{11}$

Estimate each sum or difference.

13. $\frac{1}{9} + \frac{5}{6}$

14. $\frac{2}{3} + \frac{5}{6}$

15. $\frac{3}{8} - \frac{1}{5}$

16. $\frac{9}{10} - \frac{3}{8}$

17. $\frac{7}{12} + \frac{1}{7}$

18. $\frac{7}{10} - \frac{2}{3}$

19. $\frac{6}{7} + \frac{1}{5}$

20. $\frac{14}{15} - \frac{2}{3}$

21. $\frac{7}{8} + \frac{2}{3}$

22. $\frac{4}{9} + \frac{1}{5}$

23. $\frac{4}{9} - \frac{1}{8}$

24. $\frac{3}{5} + \frac{8}{9}$

25. $\frac{5}{6} + \frac{1}{10}$

26. $\frac{5}{8} - \frac{3}{15}$

27. $\frac{6}{11} + \frac{5}{12}$

Mixed Applications

28. Art practiced playing the piano for about $\frac{9}{10}$ hour on Monday, about $\frac{4}{5}$ hour on Tuesday, and about $\frac{5}{6}$ hour on Wednesday. About how long did he practice during those three days?

29. Micah used 12 beads to make a necklace. She used 3 white beads, 2 blue beads, and 7 red beads. Which color beads make up about $\frac{1}{2}$ of the necklace?

30. Karla and 11 of her friends formed a computer club. There are 8 boys in the club. What fraction of the club is girls?

31.  **WRITE ABOUT IT** Describe how to round $\frac{3}{5}$ and $\frac{1}{10}$ so you can estimate the sum.

Mixed Review

Write *prime* or *composite* for each number. (pages 262–263)

32. 25

33. 61

34. 76

35. 43

List the factors of each number. (pages 264–265)

36. 6

37. 15

38. 18

39. 20

40. 25

Adding and Subtracting Like Fractions

You will learn to add and subtract fractions with the same denominators.

Why learn this? You can find the total amount of time spent on an activity, such as practicing a favorite sport.

Christa practiced playing basketball for $\frac{3}{8}$ hour on Monday and $\frac{5}{8}$ hour on Tuesday. How long did Christa practice on Monday and Tuesday?

Add. $\frac{3}{8} + \frac{5}{8} = n$ Estimate. $\frac{1}{2} + \frac{1}{2} = 1$ So, $n \approx 1$.

MODEL

▶ **Step 1**

Compare the denominators. They are the same.

$\frac{3}{8}$

$+\frac{5}{8}$

▶ **Step 2**

Add the numerators.

$\frac{3}{8}$ ← 3 eighths

$+\frac{5}{8}$ ← 5 eighths

Think: $3 + 5 = 8$

▶ **Step 3**

Write the sum over the denominator. Write the sum in simplest form.

$\frac{3}{8}$

$+\frac{5}{8}$

$\frac{8}{8} = 1$ So, $n = 1$.

So, Christa practiced for 1 hour on Monday and Tuesday.

How much longer did Christa practice on Tuesday than on Monday?

Subtract. $\frac{5}{8} - \frac{3}{8} = n$ Estimate. $\frac{1}{2} - \frac{1}{2} = 0$ So, $n \approx 0$.

MODEL

▶ **Step 1**

Compare the denominators. They are the same.

$\frac{5}{8}$

$-\frac{3}{8}$

▶ **Step 2**

Subtract the numerators.

$\frac{5}{8}$ ← 5 eighths

$-\frac{3}{8}$ ← 3 eighths

Think: $5 - 3 = 2$

▶ **Step 3**

Write the difference over the denominator. Write the difference in simplest form.

$\frac{5}{8}$

$-\frac{3}{8}$

$\frac{2}{8} = \frac{1}{4}$ So, $n = \frac{1}{4}$.

So, Christa practiced $\frac{1}{4}$ hour longer on Tuesday than on Monday.

💡 **CRITICAL THINKING**   What is the *difference* between adding and subtracting like fractions? What is the *same*?

PRACTICE

Find the sum. Write the answer in simplest form.

1. $\dfrac{2}{3} + \dfrac{1}{3} = n$ **2.** $\dfrac{1}{4} + \dfrac{2}{4} = n$ **3.** $\dfrac{5}{10} + \dfrac{2}{10} = n$

4. $\dfrac{1}{6} + \dfrac{3}{6} = n$ **5.** $\dfrac{5}{7} + \dfrac{1}{7} = n$ **6.** $\dfrac{5}{8} + \dfrac{7}{8} = n$

7. $\dfrac{4}{5} + \dfrac{1}{5} = n$ **8.** $\dfrac{7}{12} + \dfrac{1}{12} = n$ **9.** $\dfrac{4}{9} + \dfrac{1}{9} = n$

10. $\dfrac{2}{11} + \dfrac{7}{11} = n$ **11.** $\dfrac{3}{8} + \dfrac{1}{8} = n$ **12.** $\dfrac{4}{6} + \dfrac{2}{6} = n$

Find the difference. Write the answer in simplest form.

13. $\dfrac{2}{3} - \dfrac{1}{3} = n$ **14.** $\dfrac{7}{8} - \dfrac{1}{8} = n$ **15.** $\dfrac{5}{6} - \dfrac{2}{6} = n$

16. $\dfrac{3}{10} - \dfrac{1}{10} = n$ **17.** $\dfrac{5}{7} - \dfrac{1}{7} = n$ **18.** $\dfrac{5}{10} - \dfrac{4}{10} = n$

19. $\dfrac{7}{8} - \dfrac{2}{8} = n$ **20.** $\dfrac{8}{9} - \dfrac{2}{9} = n$ **21.** $\dfrac{10}{12} - \dfrac{6}{12} = n$

22. $\dfrac{3}{4} - \dfrac{1}{4} = n$ **23.** $\dfrac{8}{12} - \dfrac{6}{12} = n$ **24.** $\dfrac{4}{5} - \dfrac{3}{5} = n$

Sports Link

Basketball games are played in four quarters, each lasting $\frac{1}{5}$ hour, or 12 minutes. What part of an hour does the actual playing time of a basketball game take up?

Mixed Applications

25. Rick read for $\frac{5}{6}$ hour on Saturday and $\frac{2}{6}$ hour on Sunday. How much longer did he read on Saturday than on Sunday?

26. Fran has $\frac{3}{5}$ of her stamp collection in a special album. What part of her collection is not in the album?

27. Donald can ride his bike 10 times as fast as he can walk. If he can walk 2.7 kilometers in the morning, how far could he ride his bike in that time?

28. **WRITE ABOUT IT** When adding or subtracting two like fractions, when will the answer be a fraction with a different denominator?

Mixed Review

Find an equivalent fraction. Use multiplication or division.
(pages 266–267)

29. $\dfrac{3}{8}$ **30.** $\dfrac{4}{7}$ **31.** $\dfrac{2}{12}$ **32.** $\dfrac{1}{2}$ **33.** $\dfrac{3}{4}$ **34.** $\dfrac{5}{15}$

Name the least common denominator, or LCD, for each pair of fractions. (pages 266–267)

35. $\dfrac{1}{3}$ and $\dfrac{1}{2}$ **36.** $\dfrac{1}{4}$ and $\dfrac{1}{2}$ **37.** $\dfrac{1}{3}$ and $\dfrac{1}{5}$ **38.** $\dfrac{1}{4}$ and $\dfrac{1}{3}$

MORE PRACTICE Student Handbook page H103

Adding and Subtracting Unlike Fractions

You will learn to add and subtract fractions with unlike denominators.	Why learn this? You can solve problems such as finding the total number of yards of material needed to make a costume.

Lisa and Tim were making costumes for the play. For each costume, they needed $\frac{1}{2}$ yard of brown fabric and $\frac{1}{6}$ yard of yellow fabric. How much fabric is needed for the costume?

Add. $\frac{1}{6} + \frac{1}{2} = n$ Estimate. $0 + \frac{1}{2} = \frac{1}{2}$ So, $n \approx \frac{1}{2}$.

REMEMBER:

The least common denominator (LCD) is the least common multiple (LCM) of the denominators.

Example

$\frac{1}{2}$ and $\frac{3}{8}$

The least common multiple of 2 and 8 is 8. So, the LCD is eighths.

MODEL

▶ Step 1

The LCM of 6 and 2 is 6. So, the LCD of $\frac{1}{6}$ and $\frac{1}{2}$ is sixths. Use the LCD to change the fractions to like fractions.

$$\frac{1}{6} = \frac{1}{6}$$
$$+\frac{1}{2} = \frac{1 \times 3}{2 \times 3} = \frac{3}{6}$$

▶ Step 2

Add the fractions. Write the answer in simplest form.

$$\begin{array}{r} \frac{1}{6} \\ +\frac{3}{6} \\ \hline \frac{4}{6}, \text{ or } \frac{2}{3} \end{array} \quad \text{So, } n = \frac{2}{3}.$$

So, $\frac{2}{3}$ yard of fabric is needed for the costume.

• Why didn't $\frac{1}{6}$ change?

Subtract. $\frac{3}{4} - \frac{1}{6} = n$ Estimate. $\frac{1}{2} - 0 \approx \frac{1}{2}$

MODEL

▶ Step 1

The LCM of 4 and 6 is 12. So, the LCD of $\frac{3}{4}$ and $\frac{1}{6}$ is twelfths. Use the LCD to change the fractions to like fractions.

$$\frac{3}{4} = \frac{3 \times 3}{4 \times 3} = \frac{9}{12}$$
$$-\frac{1}{6} = \frac{1 \times 2}{6 \times 2} = \frac{2}{12}$$

▶ Step 2

Subtract the fractions. Write the answer in simplest form.

$$\begin{array}{r} \frac{9}{12} \\ -\frac{2}{12} \\ \hline \frac{7}{12} \end{array}$$

$\frac{7}{12}$ is in simplest form. So, $n = \frac{7}{12}$.

Talk About It

- Why was 3 used to change $\frac{3}{4}$ to $\frac{9}{12}$?

- How do you know the difference, $\frac{7}{12}$, is in simplest form?

PRACTICE

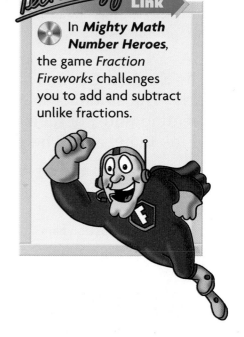

Technology **Link**

In *Mighty Math Number Heroes*, the game *Fraction Fireworks* challenges you to add and subtract unlike fractions.

Find the sum or difference. Write the answer in simplest form.

1. $\frac{2}{3} + \frac{1}{4} = n$ **2.** $\frac{1}{5} + \frac{1}{2} = n$ **3.** $\frac{7}{10} - \frac{2}{5} = n$

4. $\frac{2}{3} - \frac{1}{2} = n$ **5.** $\frac{5}{6} + \frac{1}{3} = n$ **6.** $\frac{5}{9} - \frac{1}{6} = n$

7. $\frac{2}{9} + \frac{2}{3} = n$ **8.** $\frac{3}{8} - \frac{1}{16} = n$ **9.** $\frac{1}{15} + \frac{4}{5} = n$

10. $\frac{3}{7} + \frac{1}{2} = n$ **11.** $\frac{5}{6} - \frac{2}{3} = n$ **12.** $\frac{5}{12} + \frac{1}{6} = n$

13. $\frac{5}{12} - \frac{1}{6} = n$ **14.** $\frac{1}{2} - \frac{3}{20} = n$ **15.** $\frac{3}{4} - \frac{1}{12} = n$

16. $\frac{7}{8} - \frac{1}{2} = n$ **17.** $\frac{4}{5} + \frac{3}{10} = n$ **18.** $\frac{5}{6} - \frac{7}{12} = n$

19. $\frac{2}{3} - \frac{1}{9} = n$ **20.** $\frac{7}{8} + \frac{1}{4} = n$ **21.** $\frac{7}{10} - \frac{1}{5} = n$

Mixed Applications

22. John and Jack both made a book shelf from the same board. John said he used $\frac{3}{8}$ of the board. Jack said he used $\frac{3}{4}$ of the board. Is this possible? Why or why not?

23. Eve rides $\frac{1}{2}$ mile on her way to school. She always goes to a friend's house after school, so she rides $\frac{3}{4}$ mile on her way home. How far does Eve ride her bike in all?

24. To decide which day students will present a book report, each student draws the name of a day of the school week from a hat. What is the probability of drawing a day that begins with T?

25. ✏ **WRITE ABOUT IT** Explain how to add or subtract unlike fractions.

Mixed Review

Is the fraction in simplest form? Write *yes* or *no*. (pages 270–271)

26. $\frac{2}{3}$ **27.** $\frac{3}{9}$ **28.** $\frac{2}{12}$ **29.** $\frac{4}{16}$ **30.** $\frac{7}{8}$

Write the missing unit. (pages 234–235)

31. 3 kg = 3,000 _?_ **32.** 10 km = 10,000 _?_ **33.** 7 m = 700 _?_

MORE PRACTICE Student Handbook page H104

Practicing Addition and Subtraction

You will learn to add and subtract both like and unlike fractions.

Why learn this? You can add or subtract fractions such as finding how many tickets have been sold and the fraction of the tickets that are left.

The Student Council is selling tickets to the school play. The students sold $\frac{1}{8}$ of the tickets at the PTA meeting and $\frac{3}{4}$ of them at Open House. How many of the tickets have been sold so far?

James, Leslie, and Drew are each solving the problem.

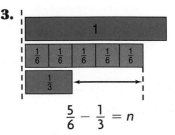

EXAMPLES

James used fraction bars.

Leslie used a ruler.

Drew used paper and pencil.

Find $\frac{1}{8} + \frac{3}{4}$.

The LCM of 8 and 4 is 8.

So, the LCD of $\frac{1}{8}$ and $\frac{3}{4}$ is eighths. Use the LCD of 8 to write like fractions. Then add.

$$\frac{1}{8} = \frac{1}{8}$$
$$+\frac{3}{4} = \frac{3 \times 2}{4 \times 2} = \frac{6}{8}$$
$$\frac{7}{8}$$

So, $\frac{7}{8}$ of the tickets have been sold so far.

Talk About It

- How do the bars and the ruler help you find the sum?

- Which method would you use to solve the problem? Why?

Check Your Understanding

💡 **CRITICAL THINKING**

Add or subtract. Write the answer in simplest form.

1.

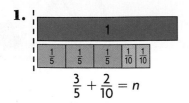

$$\frac{3}{5} + \frac{2}{10} = n$$

2.

$$\frac{1}{2} + \frac{1}{4} = n$$

3.

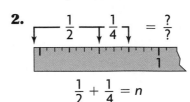

$$\frac{5}{6} - \frac{1}{3} = n$$

4. $\frac{4}{5} - \frac{1}{5} = n$ **5.** $\frac{7}{10} + \frac{1}{10} = n$ **6.** $\frac{5}{6} + \frac{1}{6} = n$ **7.** $\frac{7}{12} - \frac{5}{12} = n$

PRACTICE

Find the sum or difference. Write each answer in simplest form.

8. $\dfrac{1}{3} + \dfrac{2}{3} = n$ 9. $\dfrac{1}{3} + \dfrac{1}{6} = n$ 10. $\dfrac{5}{6} - \dfrac{1}{6} = n$

11. $\dfrac{5}{6} + \dfrac{1}{2} = n$ 12. $\dfrac{3}{7} - \dfrac{1}{4} = n$ 13. $\dfrac{7}{8} - \dfrac{1}{8} = n$

14. $\dfrac{2}{3} + \dfrac{3}{4} = n$ 15. $\dfrac{3}{10} - \dfrac{1}{10} = n$ 16. $\dfrac{7}{15} + \dfrac{1}{3} = n$

17. $\dfrac{9}{10} - \dfrac{3}{10} = n$ 18. $\dfrac{3}{4} - \dfrac{1}{5} = n$ 19. $\dfrac{6}{7} + \dfrac{1}{4} = n$

Mixed Applications

20. Tami used $\dfrac{2}{3}$ of her stamps to mail letters to friends and $\dfrac{1}{6}$ of her stamps to mail letters to relatives. What fraction of her stamps did she use?

21. Sarah invited 20 friends to her party on Saturday. Then 4 of the friends she invited could not come. What fraction of the friends Sarah invited came to her party?

22. David had $\dfrac{3}{8}$ package of notebook paper left. He gave $\dfrac{1}{8}$ package to his sister. What part of the package is left?

23. Patrick had $\dfrac{3}{4}$ box of candles to sell. He sold $\dfrac{1}{3}$ of the candles to his neighbors. What fraction of the box of candles does he have left?

24. A Girl Scout troop had 6 more 11-year-old girls than 12-year-old girls. There were 24 girls in the troop. How many of the girls were 12 years old?

25. The cast included 10 students. If there were 4 boys in the cast, what fraction of the cast were girls?

26. Jane mailed 198 flyers on Monday, 356 on Tuesday, and 219 on Wednesday. By the end of the week, Jane must mail 1,000 flyers. How many flyers are left to be mailed?

27. ✏️ **Write a problem** in which you have to add and subtract unlike fractions.

Mixed Review

Rename each fraction as a mixed number. (pages 248–249)

28. $\dfrac{9}{2}$ 29. $\dfrac{14}{5}$ 30. $\dfrac{13}{3}$ 31. $\dfrac{20}{3}$ 32. $\dfrac{19}{4}$

Find the difference. (pages 54–55)

33. $3.59 - 1.27 = n$ 34. $8.02 - 7.65 = n$ 35. $12.15 - 9.79 = n$

36. $10.05 - 7.97 = n$ 37. $21.15 - 18.38 = n$ 38. $40.08 - 25.19 = n$

MORE PRACTICE Student Handbook page H104

1 Choosing Addition or Subtraction

You will learn how to determine whether to use addition or subtraction to solve a problem. | **Why learn this?** You will know whether to add or subtract to solve problems such as comparing two fractional amounts.

You can use addition when you are joining groups. You can use subtraction when you are comparing groups or finding how many are left in a group.

Decide whether to add or subtract the fractions to solve these problems.

A. Julio rode $\frac{1}{3}$ mile to school, $\frac{5}{12}$ mile to the store, and then $\frac{3}{4}$ mile home. How far did Julio ride?

B. Evelyn has $\frac{3}{8}$ yard of material. She needs $\frac{3}{4}$ yard to make a costume for her class play. How much more material does she need for the costume?

C. Mrs. Chen had $\frac{5}{6}$ of a box of pancake mix. She used $\frac{1}{3}$ of the box to make pancakes for breakfast. How much of the box of pancake mix was left?

D. Jason completed $\frac{1}{4}$ of his homework before soccer practice, and $\frac{1}{3}$ after practice. How much of his homework did Jason complete?

Talk About It

• In which examples might you add to solve the problem? Why?

• In which examples might you subtract to solve the problem? Why?

• In each problem what helped you decide whether to add or subtract?

Check Your Understanding 💡 CRITICAL THINKING

Good pass!

Tell whether you would add or subtract to solve the problem. Solve.

1. Julianne uses $\frac{1}{4}$ cup of pecans to make nut bread and $\frac{3}{8}$ cup to make muffins. How many cups of pecans does she use in all?

2. Alex had $\frac{3}{4}$ pitcher of orange juice. He drank $\frac{1}{3}$ of the juice. How much orange juice was left?

PRACTICE

Tell whether you would add or subtract to solve the problem. Solve.

3. Mark wrote $\frac{1}{2}$ of his science report on Monday and $\frac{2}{5}$ of it on Tuesday. What part of his science report did he write on Monday and Tuesday?

4. Carla had $\frac{2}{3}$ cup of flour. She used $\frac{1}{2}$ cup to make biscuits. How much flour does she have left?

5. Raul lives $\frac{1}{2}$ mile from Luke. Tonya lives $\frac{3}{4}$ mile from Raul. Raul lives between Luke and Tonya. How far does Luke live from Tonya?

6. Jason practiced piano for $\frac{7}{8}$ hour on Thursday and $\frac{1}{2}$ hour on Friday. How much longer did he practice on Thursday?

Mixed Applications

7. Corey memorized $\frac{1}{6}$ of his lines for the play on Monday and $\frac{1}{4}$ of his lines on Tuesday. What part of his lines did he memorize on Monday and Tuesday?

8. The cast for the school play includes actors and dancers. There are 6 dancers and 24 actors in the play. What part of the cast for the play are the dancers?

9. Ms. Wright teaches a music class of 3rd, 4th, and 5th grade students. The 4th graders make up $\frac{1}{4}$ of the class and the 5th graders make up $\frac{1}{3}$ of the class. What part of the class are 3rd graders?

10. The students at Bay School collected 3,240 pennies for the Lucky Penny charity. They already had collected $47.89 so far this year. How much does the Lucky Penny charity have altogether?

11. Ted took $\frac{3}{4}$ of his allowance to the amusement park. He spent $\frac{1}{6}$ on food and $\frac{1}{4}$ on souvenirs. How much of his allowance did Ted have left after he bought food and souvenirs?

12. A blueberry-nut muffin recipe calls for $\frac{3}{4}$ cup of whole-wheat flour. If Tyra has $\frac{1}{2}$ cup whole-wheat flour, how much more does she need?

13. Brady is making her costume for the play. She needs $\frac{1}{3}$ yd of red fabric, $\frac{1}{2}$ yd of blue fabric, and $\frac{3}{4}$ yd of white fabric. How much fabric does Brady need?

14. Amal mixed together $3\frac{2}{5}$ gallons of white paint and $4\frac{3}{10}$ gallons of red paint. How much paint did Amal mix?

15. ✐ **Write a problem** that you would solve by subtracting two unlike fractions.

LESSON CONTINUES ▶

PROBLEM-SOLVING STRATEGY
Draw a Diagram

THE PROBLEM The fifth graders can enroll in after-school programs. They can enroll in the music program, the athletics program, or the acting program. Of the fifth graders enrolled in these programs, $\frac{1}{3}$ are in music, $\frac{1}{2}$ are in athletics, and $\frac{1}{6}$ are in acting. There are 4 fifth graders in the acting program. How many students are enrolled in each of the other programs? How many are enrolled in all three programs?

> **REMEMBER:**
> ☑ Understand
> ☑ Plan
> ☑ Solve
> ☑ Look Back

☑ Understand

- What are you asked to find?

- What information will you use?

- Is there information you will not use? If so, what?

☑ Plan

- What strategy can you use to solve this problem?

  You can *draw a diagram* to find out how many fifth graders are enrolled in music and athletics.

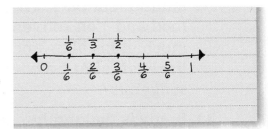

Try-outs for the school play.

☑ Solve

- How can you draw a diagram to solve?

  Use a number line to model the problem. The whole number line represents the total number of students.

  $\frac{1}{6}$ = 4 students in acting

  $\frac{1}{3}$, or $\frac{2}{6}$ = 2 × 4, or 8. So, there are 8 students in music.

  $\frac{1}{2}$, or $\frac{3}{6}$ = 3 × 4, or 12. So, there are 12 students in athletics.

  4 + 8 + 12 = 24. So, there are 24 fifth graders enrolled in the after-school programs.

☑ Look Back

- How can you determine if your answer is reasonable?

- What other strategy can you use?

PRACTICE

Draw a diagram to solve.

1. Students at three schools are giving a concert. Of the students participating, $\frac{1}{4}$ are from Rhodes Elementary School, $\frac{1}{2}$ are from South Elementary School, and $\frac{1}{4}$ are from West Elementary School. There are 36 students from Rhodes. How many students are participating in the concert?

2. Ms. Smith asked the students in her class whether they prefer to watch movies, television, or plays. Of her students, $\frac{5}{8}$ chose movies, $\frac{1}{4}$ chose television, and $\frac{1}{8}$ chose plays. There were 3 students who chose plays. How many students are in Ms. Smith's class?

3. Andrea walks a certain number of miles every week. She walks $\frac{1}{3}$ the total weekly distance on Monday, $\frac{2}{5}$ on Wednesday, and $\frac{4}{15}$ on Friday. She walks 5 miles on Monday. How many miles does Andrea walk every week?

4. Nina, Debbie, and Peter are comparing their heights. At 54 inches, Nina is 6 inches taller than Peter. Peter is 3 inches shorter than Debbie. How tall is Debbie?

Mixed Applications

Solve.

CHOOSE A STRATEGY

• Draw a Diagram   • Use a Table   • Write a Number Sentence   • Guess and Check

5. Beth's class is going to see a play. There are 150 students in her class. How many buses will be needed if each bus can hold 40 students?

6. Eric is 5 years old. His Uncle Tim is 7 times as old. How old will Eric be when he is one third as old as his uncle?

7. Lee counted 50 instruments in the orchestra. What fraction of the orchestra is percussion?

ORCHESTRA	
Section	Number
Woodwinds	12
Percussion	5
Strings	25
Brass	8

8. The members of the choir scheduled an extra practice for their concert. The vote showed that $\frac{2}{3}$ of the members preferred Monday evening. There were 20 members who voted for Monday evening. How many students are in the choir?

9. A bridge toll is $0.75 for a car and $1.25 for a truck. In 30 minutes, $26.25 was collected from 27 vehicles. How many cars and trucks paid the toll?

10. One store sells 6 cans of juice for $3.90. Another store sells each can for $0.69. What is the difference in price per can at the two stores?

MATH FUN!

$\dfrac{1}{6}$ $\dfrac{1}{3}$ $\dfrac{1}{2}$

GO FISH FOR ONE

PURPOSE To practice adding and subtracting like and unlike fractions

YOU WILL NEED index cards

Make a set of fraction cards. The objective of the game is to find cards that add up to 1. Each player takes four cards. The rest are face down. Take turns asking for a card by its denominator or numerator. "Go fish" from the pile if you do not receive it. When you have a group of fractions that add up to 1, place those cards down for everyone to check.

The Counting Game of Ding Dong

PURPOSE To practice finding least common multiples of two numbers

YOU WILL NEED paper and pencil

Play this game in a group of four. Choose a number from 2 to 9. Take turns counting until a multiple of the number comes up. Say "Ding!" instead of the number and write the number down. Do this until you have written five numbers. Switch to another number from 2 to 9. When it is your turn to say a multiple, say "Dong!" instead. If it is a common multiple of the numbers chosen for game 1 and 2, say "Ding Dong!"

Number: 3
1, 2, Ding, 4, 5, Ding, 7, 8, Ding, 10, 11, Ding

Number: 5
1, 2, 3, 4, Dong, 6, 7, 8, 9, Dong, 11, 12, 13, 14, Ding Dong!, 16, 17, 18, 19, Dong

Your Joke is How Long?

PURPOSE To change seconds to fractions of a minute

YOU WILL NEED books of jokes, timer, pencils, markers

Play this game in a small group. Each person will tell or read aloud a joke and record the time to tell it in seconds. Figure out what fraction of a minute your joke takes. With your group, add all the fractions to find how long the joke show lasts.

Do the jokes add up to more than a minute? Then decide: Is the funniest joke the longest one?

 HOME NOTE Ask parents or other adults if they remember any jokes from when they were kids. You might be surprised at how funny they are!

"Did you know that 15 seconds is $\frac{1}{4}$ minute and 20 seconds is $\frac{1}{3}$ minute? I wonder what 30 seconds is?"

"A long time to tell a joke!"

✓ CHECK UNDERSTANDING

Estimate the sum or difference. (pages 310–311)

1. $\dfrac{2}{3} + \dfrac{1}{6}$

2. $\dfrac{3}{8} - \dfrac{1}{10}$

3. $\dfrac{1}{6} + \dfrac{1}{10}$

4. $\dfrac{9}{10} - \dfrac{3}{5}$

5. $\dfrac{7}{9} - \dfrac{3}{5}$

6. $\dfrac{7}{8} + \dfrac{4}{5}$

7. $\dfrac{8}{9} - \dfrac{1}{6}$

8. $\dfrac{2}{5} + \dfrac{7}{12}$

✓ CHECK SKILLS

Find the sum or difference. Write the answer in simplest form.

(pages 312–317)

9. $\dfrac{3}{4} + \dfrac{1}{4} = n$

10. $\dfrac{3}{4} - \dfrac{1}{4} = n$

11. $\dfrac{5}{7} + \dfrac{1}{7} = n$

12. $\dfrac{11}{12} - \dfrac{3}{4} = n$

13. $\dfrac{1}{2} + \dfrac{1}{8} = n$

14. $\dfrac{4}{5} - \dfrac{1}{2} = n$

15. $\dfrac{4}{5} + \dfrac{1}{3} = n$

16. $\dfrac{1}{4} + \dfrac{7}{8} = n$

17. $\dfrac{7}{10} - \dfrac{2}{5} = n$

18. $\dfrac{5}{6} + \dfrac{1}{3} = n$

19. $\dfrac{3}{4} - \dfrac{1}{6} = n$

20. $\dfrac{3}{8} + \dfrac{5}{12} = n$

21. $\dfrac{5}{8} - \dfrac{1}{4} = n$

22. $\dfrac{9}{10} + \dfrac{2}{5} = n$

23. $\dfrac{5}{6} - \dfrac{1}{3} = n$

24. $\dfrac{1}{3} + \dfrac{2}{9} = n$

Tell whether you would add or subtract to solve the problem.
Solve. (pages 318–319)

25. Valeska made two cakes for her party. She used $\frac{3}{4}$ cup flour for one cake and $\frac{2}{3}$ cup flour for the other cake. How much flour did she use for both cakes?

26. Mr. Danko spent $\frac{3}{4}$ hour shopping and $\frac{1}{2}$ hour cooking. How much more time did he spend shopping than cooking?

✓ CHECK PROBLEM SOLVING

Solve. (pages 320–321)

CHOOSE A STRATEGY

• Draw a Diagram   • Act it Out   • Guess and Check   • Work Backward

27. Tickets to the concert sold for $10, $12, and $15. Of the tickets sold, $\frac{1}{10}$ were $15 tickets, $\frac{1}{5}$ were $12 tickets, and $\frac{7}{10}$ were $10 tickets. There were one hundred $15 tickets sold. How many tickets were sold to the concert?

28. Ashley had 60 calendars to sell. She sold 20 calendars to friends and 25 calendars to neighbors. What fraction of the calendars does she have left to sell?

ADDING AND SUBTRACTING MIXED NUMBERS

DID YOU KNOW...

An English game of bowls involves rolling a ball closest to the target ball known as the jack and represented by a dot. See who can get closest to the dot.

Bill – 8½ in. from the dot

Jenna – 4¼ in. from the dot

Try a Game of Bowls

Play the game of Bowls with your group. This game is usually played outside. Use subtraction to compare distances between rolls.

YOU WILL NEED: one tennis ball per group, a dot, tape, a yardstick

Work with a group. Your job is to

- Play three rounds of Bowls.

- Measure and record your distances.

- Find the difference between your best roll and your worst.

- Share results and game strategies.

DID YOU

- ☑ play three rounds of Bowls as a team?

- ☑ measure the distance for each roll?

- ☑ find the difference between your best roll and your worst?

- ☑ share your results with the class?

HOW TO PLAY BOWLS

- Each player kneels behind the starter's tape and gently rolls the ball, trying to get it to stop as near to the dot as possible.

- Any ball that stops more than three feet away from the dot can be rolled again.

- A teammate measures the distance from the ball to the dot.

- Record distance to the nearest 1/4 of an inch.

- After three rolls, each player finds the difference between his or her best roll and worst roll.

TO MEASURE A DISTANCE

- Place a piece of tape where your ball touches the floor. Then measure between the tape and the dot.

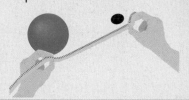

$18\frac{1}{2}$
$17\frac{3}{4}$
$\left(11\frac{1}{4}\right)$

$18\frac{1}{2} - 11\frac{1}{4} = 7\frac{1}{4}$ inches

Jack's scores

$16\frac{1}{4}$
$\left(13\frac{3}{4}\right)$
$14\frac{1}{8}$

$16\frac{1}{4} - 14\frac{1}{8} = 2\frac{1}{8}$ inches

Ramon's scores

Estimating Sums and Differences

You will learn how to estimate sums and differences of mixed numbers.	**Why learn this?** You can estimate distances when playing a game.

You can use a number line to estimate mixed numbers.

Is $2\frac{1}{8}$ closer to $1\frac{1}{2}$, 2, or $2\frac{1}{2}$?

So, $2\frac{1}{8}$ is closer to 2.

Talk About It

REMEMBER:

You can round fractions to the nearest 0, $\frac{1}{2}$, or 1.

$\frac{2}{3}$ is close to $\frac{1}{2}$.

- What can you say about the mixed number when the numerator and denominator of the fraction are about the same?

- Is $1\frac{5}{8}$ closer to $1\frac{1}{2}$, 2, or $2\frac{1}{2}$? Explain how you know.

Rounding mixed numbers to the nearest whole number or one half on a number line can help you estimate sums and differences of mixed numbers.

EXAMPLES

A. Estimate the sum of $2\frac{2}{3} + 1\frac{1}{6}$.

$2\frac{2}{3}$ is close to $2\frac{1}{2}$.

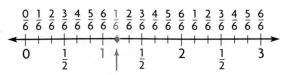

$1\frac{1}{6}$ is close to 1. $2\frac{1}{2} + 1 = 3\frac{1}{2}$

So, $2\frac{2}{3} + 1\frac{1}{6}$ is about $3\frac{1}{2}$.

B. Estimate the difference of $2 - 1\frac{3}{5}$.

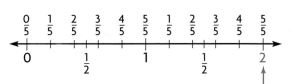

2 is equal to 2.

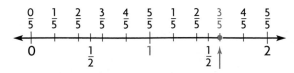

$1\frac{3}{5}$ is close to $1\frac{1}{2}$. $2 - 1\frac{1}{2} = \frac{1}{2}$

So, $2 - 1\frac{3}{5}$ is about $\frac{1}{2}$.

💡 **CRITICAL THINKING** How could you use a ruler to estimate the sum of $1\frac{1}{8}$ in. and $2\frac{3}{16}$ in.?

PRACTICE

Round the mixed number to the nearest $\frac{1}{2}$ or whole number.
You may use a number line or a ruler.

1. $4\frac{7}{8}$
2. $2\frac{5}{6}$
3. $1\frac{7}{8}$
4. $3\frac{3}{5}$
5. $6\frac{1}{12}$
6. $8\frac{4}{9}$

7. $1\frac{1}{8}$
8. $9\frac{6}{8}$
9. $3\frac{1}{4}$
10. $7\frac{1}{16}$
11. $4\frac{7}{12}$
12. $6\frac{2}{3}$

Estimate the sum or difference.

13. $2\frac{1}{8} + 4\frac{15}{16}$
14. $3\frac{7}{8} - 2\frac{1}{2}$
15. $1\frac{9}{16} + 1\frac{5}{8}$

16. $6\frac{9}{10} - 4\frac{4}{5}$
17. $9\frac{1}{8} + 1\frac{10}{12}$
18. $6\frac{4}{9} + 7\frac{1}{5}$

19. $9\frac{4}{9} - 6\frac{1}{8}$
20. $9\frac{5}{8} - 3\frac{14}{16}$
21. $7\frac{5}{12} + 1\frac{5}{6}$

Mixed Applications

22. Janis read her book for $\frac{3}{4}$ hour in the morning. After school, she read for another $\frac{1}{4}$ hour. She read for $\frac{1}{3}$ hour just before bedtime. What is the total amount of time she spent reading?

23. Seth needs $6\frac{3}{4}$ feet of wallpaper border for his kitchen. He needs $10\frac{3}{8}$ feet of the same wallpaper border for his dining room. About how many feet of wallpaper border does he need?

24. Kelli used $2\frac{7}{8}$ yards of fabric for her craft project. She started with $4\frac{1}{8}$ yards of fabric. About how much fabric does she have left?

25. **WRITE ABOUT IT** How is estimating the sum or difference of mixed numbers like estimating the sum or difference of fractions?

Mixed Review

Draw a number line. Locate the fraction. (pages 246–247)

26. $\frac{3}{5}$
27. $\frac{2}{6}$
28. $\frac{5}{10}$
29. $\frac{7}{8}$
30. $\frac{1}{3}$

31. $\frac{1}{4}$
32. $\frac{3}{8}$
33. $\frac{5}{12}$
34. $\frac{2}{3}$
35. $\frac{1}{5}$

Name the least common denominator, or LCD, for each pair of fractions. (pages 296–297)

36. $\frac{1}{4}$ and $\frac{1}{8}$
37. $\frac{1}{2}$ and $\frac{1}{6}$
38. $\frac{1}{4}$ and $\frac{1}{3}$

39. $\frac{1}{3}$ and $\frac{1}{6}$
40. $\frac{1}{5}$ and $\frac{1}{10}$
41. $\frac{1}{9}$ and $\frac{1}{3}$

Adding Mixed Numbers

You will learn to add mixed numbers.	**Why learn this?** You can find the sum of two amounts, such as two measurements.

The Boy Scouts are having their annual Pinewood Derby. Juwan is making a banner for the finish line. He needs $2\frac{1}{8}$ yards of black fabric and $1\frac{1}{4}$ yards of white fabric to make the checkered banner. How many yards of fabric does Juwan need for the banner?

MODEL

Add $2\frac{1}{8}$ and $1\frac{1}{4}$. Estimate. $2 + 1 = 3$

▶ **Step 1**

The fractions are unlike. Use the LCD to change the fractions to like fractions. Add the fractions.

$$2\frac{1}{8} = 2\frac{1}{8}$$
$$+1\frac{1}{4} = 1\frac{2}{8}$$
$$\overline{\quad\quad\quad \frac{3}{8}}$$

▶ **Step 2**

Then add the whole numbers.

$$2\frac{1}{8} = 2\frac{1}{8}$$
$$+1\frac{1}{4} = 1\frac{2}{8}$$
$$\overline{\quad\quad\quad 3\frac{3}{8}}$$

So, Juwan needs $3\frac{3}{8}$ yards of fabric for the banner.

Talk About It

- How did you add the fractions?

- How did you add the whole numbers?

- How does your solution compare to your estimate?

EXAMPLES

A.
$$1\frac{1}{3} = 1\frac{2}{6}$$
$$+3\frac{4}{6} = 3\frac{4}{6}$$
$$\overline{\quad\quad 4\frac{6}{6} \text{ or } 5}$$

or

B.
$$2\frac{5}{8} = 2\frac{5}{8}$$
$$+2\frac{1}{2} = 2\frac{4}{8}$$
$$\overline{\quad\quad 4\frac{9}{8} \text{ or } 5\frac{1}{8}}$$

or

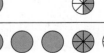

- How are Examples A and B different from the model?

PRACTICE

Find the sum. You may wish to draw a picture.
Write the answer in simplest form.

1. $1\frac{1}{4}$
$+2\frac{1}{2}$

2. $1\frac{1}{5}$
$+3\frac{2}{5}$

3. $5\frac{1}{3}$
$+2\frac{1}{6}$

4. $2\frac{5}{6}$
$+1\frac{1}{3}$

5. $4\frac{2}{3}$
$+2\frac{4}{9}$

6. $5\frac{2}{5}$
$+1\frac{4}{10}$

7. $4\frac{5}{8}$
$+2\frac{1}{4}$

8. $4\frac{3}{4}$
$+3\frac{3}{12}$

9. $9\frac{10}{12} + 1\frac{5}{6} = n$

10. $3\frac{1}{3} + 3\frac{7}{12} = n$

11. $6\frac{3}{8} + 2\frac{1}{8} = n$

12. $4\frac{3}{4} + 2\frac{3}{8} = n$

13. $3\frac{3}{4} + 1\frac{1}{8} = n$

14. $3\frac{1}{2} + 5\frac{3}{4} = n$

15. $3\frac{1}{10} + 2\frac{3}{5} = n$

16. $3\frac{2}{3} + 4\frac{1}{6} = n$

17. $3\frac{5}{6} + \frac{2}{3} = n$

Science Link

The Pinewood Derby is a Boy Scout event. Each Scout makes a small car out of a block of wood and plastic wheels. The cars race by gravity down an inclined track that is 32 ft long. If one car used $3\frac{1}{4}$ in. of decal tape and a second car used $4\frac{1}{2}$ in. of tape, how much tape would be needed in all?

Mixed Applications

18. The dancers will form 5 equal rows for the grand finale of the recital. There are 65 dancers in the recital. How many will be in each row?

19. Kendall recorded music for $1\frac{5}{6}$ hours on Monday and $2\frac{1}{3}$ hours on Tuesday. How much time did he spend recording the music on Monday and Tuesday?

20. Rachel and Jamie are making hair ribbons for the dance recital. Rachel has $4\frac{1}{2}$ yards of pink ribbon and Jamie has $3\frac{1}{3}$ yards of white ribbon. How much ribbon do they have in all?

21. **WRITE ABOUT IT** Explain how adding mixed numbers is the same as adding fractions.

Mixed Review

Find the sum. Write the answer in simplest form. (pages 314–315)

22. $\frac{7}{8} + \frac{1}{4} = n$

23. $\frac{5}{6} + \frac{7}{12} = n$

24. $\frac{2}{3} + \frac{1}{4} = n$

25. $\frac{2}{3} + \frac{2}{9} = n$

Find an equivalent fraction. Use multiplication or division.
(pages 266–267)

26. $\frac{4}{16}$

27. $\frac{1}{3}$

28. $\frac{8}{24}$

29. $\frac{1}{5}$

30. $\frac{9}{12}$

1 Subtracting Mixed Numbers

You will learn how to subtract mixed numbers.	**Why learn this?** You can find how much is left, such as how much paper is left after part of a package is used.

Louis had $2\frac{3}{4}$ packages of paper for his computer printer. He placed $1\frac{1}{2}$ packages into the printer. How much paper was left?

MODEL

Subtract $2\frac{3}{4}$ and $1\frac{1}{2}$. Estimate. $3 - 1\frac{1}{2} = 1\frac{1}{2}$

▶ Step 1

The fractions are unlike. Use the LCD to change the fractions to like fractions. Subtract the fractions.

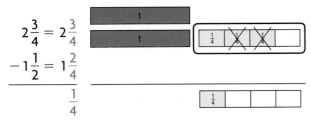

$$2\frac{3}{4} = 2\frac{3}{4}$$
$$-1\frac{1}{2} = 1\frac{2}{4}$$
$$\overline{\qquad\quad \frac{1}{4}}$$

▶ Step 2

Then subtract the whole numbers.

$$2\frac{3}{4} = 2\frac{3}{4}$$
$$-1\frac{1}{2} = 1\frac{2}{4}$$
$$\overline{\qquad\quad 1\frac{1}{4}}$$

So, Louis has $1\frac{1}{4}$ packages of paper left.

Talk About It

• How does subtraction of mixed numbers compare to addition of mixed numbers?

• How can you check your subtraction?

EXAMPLES

A.
$$3\frac{1}{2} = 3\frac{3}{6}$$
$$-1\frac{1}{3} = 1\frac{2}{6}$$
$$\overline{\qquad\quad 2\frac{1}{6}}$$

B.
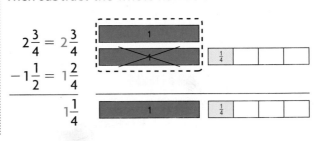
$$4\frac{3}{4} = 4\frac{3}{4}$$
$$-2\frac{1}{2} = 2\frac{2}{4}$$
$$\overline{\qquad\quad 2\frac{1}{4}}$$

 CRITICAL THINKING How do you know you must rename the fractions when you subtract two mixed numbers?

Calculator Activities page H65

PRACTICE

Subtract. Write the answer in simplest form.

1.
$$4\frac{2}{3} = 4\frac{4}{6}$$
$$-1\frac{1}{6} = 1\frac{1}{6}$$

2.
$$4\frac{5}{6} = 4\frac{5}{6}$$
$$-2\frac{2}{3} = 2\frac{4}{6}$$

3.
$$9\frac{1}{2} = 9\frac{4}{8}$$
$$-8\frac{1}{4} = 8\frac{2}{8}$$

4.
$$9\frac{4}{5} = 9\frac{8}{10}$$
$$-2\frac{3}{10} = 2\frac{3}{10}$$

5.
$$3\frac{1}{2} = 3\frac{2}{4}$$
$$-1\frac{1}{4} = 1\frac{1}{4}$$

6.
$$5\frac{7}{9} = 5\frac{7}{9}$$
$$-3\frac{1}{3} = 3\frac{3}{9}$$

7.
$$7\frac{3}{4} = 7\frac{9}{12}$$
$$-4\frac{7}{12} = 4\frac{7}{12}$$

8.
$$5\frac{5}{8} = 5\frac{5}{8}$$
$$-2\frac{1}{4} = 2\frac{2}{8}$$

9.
$$6\frac{1}{3} = 6\frac{4}{12}$$
$$-3\frac{3}{12} = 3\frac{3}{12}$$

10. $5\frac{11}{12} - 2\frac{1}{4} = n$

11. $8\frac{5}{6} - 3\frac{1}{3} = n$

12. $4\frac{8}{10} - 1\frac{2}{5} = n$

13. $6\frac{7}{8} - 2\frac{1}{2} = n$

14. $9\frac{4}{5} - 1\frac{3}{10} = n$

15. $2\frac{7}{12} - \frac{2}{6} = n$

16. $3\frac{7}{8} - 2\frac{1}{2} = n$

17. $4\frac{7}{8} - 3\frac{1}{4} = n$

18. $3\frac{9}{10} - \frac{7}{10} = n$

Mixed Applications

For Problems 19–20, use the table.

19. Amanda made the table to help keep track of the gift-wrapping paper in stock. She found that some numbers she needs were not recorded. Copy and complete the table.

20. At the end of the week, Amanda wanted to reorder the same amount of red and white paper that she had to start with. How many yards of paper should she reorder?

21. Arlo worked $2\frac{1}{4}$ hours on Monday and $3\frac{2}{3}$ hours on Tuesday. How many hours did he work on Monday and Tuesday?

22. ✏️ **Write a problem** that can be solved by adding or subtracting mixed numbers. Use the information in the table.

Color of Paper	Yards Started with	Yards Used	Yards Left
Red	$16\frac{3}{4}$	$3\frac{1}{2}$	?
White	$20\frac{3}{4}$	?	$10\frac{1}{3}$
Blue	?	$5\frac{7}{12}$	$10\frac{1}{12}$
Yellow	$21\frac{2}{3}$	$14\frac{7}{12}$	?

MORE PRACTICE Student Handbook page H105

PROBLEM-SOLVING STRATEGY
Work Backward

THE PROBLEM Mrs. Miller drives a school bus. She leaves the garage and drives to the first bus stop. Then she drives $3\frac{1}{10}$ miles to the second bus stop, $1\frac{3}{10}$ miles to the third bus stop, $2\frac{2}{10}$ miles to the fourth bus stop, and then $2\frac{3}{10}$ miles to the school. If Mrs. Miller drives a total of 10 miles, what is the distance from the bus garage to the first bus stop?

REMEMBER:
- ☑ Understand
- ☑ Plan
- ☑ Solve
- ☑ Look Back

☑ Understand

- What are you asked to find?
- What information will you use?
- Is there information you will not use? If so, what?

☑ Plan

- What strategy can you use to solve this problem?

  You can *work backward* to find the distance from the bus garage to the first bus stop.

☑ Solve

- How can you work backward to solve the problem?

  First, show what you know and what you need to find.

Miles to the first stop	Miles from the first stop to the second stop	Miles from the second stop to the third stop	Miles from the third stop to the fourth stop	Miles from the fourth stop to the school	Total miles
? →	$+3\frac{1}{10}$ →	$+1\frac{3}{10}$ →	$+2\frac{2}{10}$ →	$+2\frac{3}{10}$ →	10 →
? =	← $-3\frac{1}{10}$	← $-1\frac{3}{10}$	← $-2\frac{2}{10}$	← $-2\frac{3}{10}$	← 10
$1\frac{1}{10}$	$1\frac{1}{10}$	$4\frac{2}{10}$	$5\frac{5}{10}$	$7\frac{7}{10}$	10

So, the distance from the bus garage to the first bus stop is $1\frac{1}{10}$ miles.

☑ Look Back

- How can you determine if your answer is reasonable?
- What other strategy can you use?

PRACTICE

Work backward to solve.

1. Terri used some ribbon to decorate a hat. She used $2\frac{3}{8}$ yards of ribbon to decorate a T-shirt, and $3\frac{1}{8}$ yards of ribbon to make a costume. She had 3 yards of ribbon left. How much ribbon did she have to start with?

2. Mr. Wills returned home after running errands for $2\frac{1}{2}$ hours. During that time he spent $\frac{3}{4}$ hour at the mall, $\frac{1}{2}$ hour at the grocery store, and the rest of the time driving. How much time did Mr. Wills spend driving?

3. Cindy and Jake played a number game. Cindy told Jake to choose a number. Then she told him to multiply it by 4, add 6, divide by 2, and subtract 5. When Jake said his number was 6, Cindy told him what number he chose to begin with. What was Jake's starting number?

4. Dana went shopping for birthday gifts. He spent $16 on his brother's gift and $12 on his sister's gift. He returned an item to the sports store and got a refund of $5. He had $13 left. How much did he have to start with?

Mixed Applications

Solve.

CHOOSE A STRATEGY

- **Work Backward**   - **Draw a Diagram**   - **Act It Out**   - **Write a Number Sentence**

5. When Gail paid for groceries, she received $8.88 in change. She bought items that cost $1.89, $5.70, $3.39, and $0.89. She turned in a coupon worth $0.75. How much did Gail give the clerk to pay for the groceries?

6. Theo spent $\frac{1}{4}$ of his free time on Saturday playing basketball at the park. He spent $\frac{1}{2}$ of his free time watching a movie. If he played basketball for 1 hour, how much free time did he have on Saturday?

7. Lucia's parents bought new carpet for her bedroom. Her bedroom is 10 feet wide and 12 feet long. They had 10 square feet of carpet left over after carpeting her bedroom. How many square feet of carpeting did they buy?

8. Randy is looking at his sports cards. Of the cards, $\frac{1}{3}$ are baseball cards, $\frac{1}{2}$ are football cards, and $\frac{1}{6}$ are basketball cards. If he has 10 baseball cards, how many total cards does he have?

9. Christopher saved $4.50 of his allowance each week for 7 weeks. Which computer program does he have enough money to buy?

More About Subtracting Mixed Numbers

You will investigate renaming to subtract mixed numbers.

Why learn this? You can find the difference of two amounts, such as two measurements.

You can use the fraction bars to rename mixed numbers so you can subtract.

Explore

Use fraction bars to model the problem and to rename the mixed number so you can subtract.

MATERIALS: fraction bars

MODEL

What is $1\frac{1}{6} - \frac{2}{3}$?

▶ **Step 1**

Model $1\frac{1}{6}$ with fraction bars.

 $1\frac{1}{6}$

▶ **Step 2**

Subtract $\frac{2}{3}$ from $1\frac{1}{6}$. Since the LCD is sixths, change $\frac{2}{3}$ to sixths.

Think: $\frac{2}{3} = \frac{4}{6}$

▶ **Step 3**

Before you can take $\frac{4}{6}$ away from $1\frac{1}{6}$, you have to rename $1\frac{1}{6}$.

$1\frac{1}{6}$

$\downarrow$

$\frac{7}{6}$

▶ **Step 4**

Now, take $\frac{4}{6}$ away from $\frac{7}{6}$. Write the answer in simplest form.

Record

Record a subtraction sentence for the model. Explain how you can take-away fraction bars to subtract mixed numbers.

Now, investigate subtracting other mixed numbers.

In **Mighty Math Calculating Crew**, the game *Nautical Number Line* challenges you to add and subtract mixed numbers.

Try This

Find the difference of $2\frac{1}{2} - 1\frac{3}{4}$. Make a model and record by writing a number sentence.

TALK ABOUT IT How did you rename $2\frac{1}{2}$ so you could subtract?

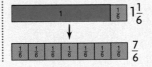

E-Lab · Activity 20 Available on CD-ROM and the Internet at http://www.hbschool.com/elab

✏️ **WRITE ABOUT IT** How do you know when to rename one of the whole numbers to fractions?

HANDS-ON PRACTICE

Match the mixed number with the fraction bars.

1. $2\frac{2}{5}$

2. $3\frac{2}{3}$

3. $4\frac{1}{5}$

a.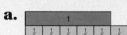

b.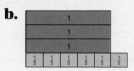

c.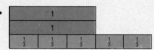

Applying What You Learned

Use fraction bars to find the difference.

4. $\begin{array}{r} 2\frac{3}{4} \\ -\ \ \frac{1}{2} \\ \hline \end{array}$

5. $\begin{array}{r} 6\frac{3}{5} \\ -4\frac{9}{10} \\ \hline \end{array}$

6. $\begin{array}{r} 5\frac{3}{4} \\ -2\frac{7}{8} \\ \hline \end{array}$

7. $\begin{array}{r} 8\frac{1}{6} \\ -2\frac{2}{3} \\ \hline \end{array}$

8. $\begin{array}{r} 7\frac{1}{8} \\ -1\frac{3}{4} \\ \hline \end{array}$

9. $\begin{array}{r} 9\frac{1}{3} \\ -4\frac{1}{2} \\ \hline \end{array}$

10. $\begin{array}{r} 6\frac{3}{4} \\ -4\frac{7}{8} \\ \hline \end{array}$

11. $\begin{array}{r} 10\frac{1}{6} \\ -\ 3\frac{2}{3} \\ \hline \end{array}$

12. $8\frac{7}{10} - 4\frac{1}{2} = n$

13. $6\frac{1}{2} - 2\frac{7}{8} = n$

14. $8\frac{1}{3} - 4\frac{5}{6} = n$

15. $6\frac{1}{2} - 1\frac{7}{10} = n$

16. $9\frac{1}{4} - 4\frac{5}{8} = n$

17. $6\frac{1}{3} - 5\frac{5}{12} = n$

Mixed Applications

18. Sean bought $2\frac{1}{2}$ gallons of orange juice for his party. He had $\frac{1}{4}$ gallon left after the party. How much orange juice did Sean serve at his party?

19. Tara spent $1\frac{3}{4}$ hours exercising on Saturday. She spent $\frac{1}{2}$ hour exercising on Sunday. How many hours did she exercise this weekend?

20. On Saturday Ms. Rowe spent $4 on lunch and $15 on dinner. This is half the amount of money she started with. How much money did Ms. Rowe have to start with?

21. Alonzo teaches an exercise class for $1\frac{2}{3}$ hour on Monday, Wednesday, and Friday of each week. How much time does Alonzo spend teaching his classes each week?

22. ✏️ **Write a problem** about subtracting two mixed numbers.

MORE PRACTICE Student Handbook page H106

CULTURAL CONNECTION

Native American Games and Crafts

Mr. Thomas, a member of the Arapaho Nation, visits schools to talk about Native Americans. His daughter, Emily, helps him sort beads for an art project. Each student needs $2\frac{1}{4}$ packages of yellow beads and $1\frac{1}{6}$ packages of red beads. Add the mixed numbers to find how many packages of beads each student will use.

Work Together

1. Emily cut 2 cords that were $7\frac{3}{8}$ inches long from a cord that was $17\frac{7}{8}$ inches long. How much cord was left over?

2. In the morning, the class worked on bead projects and listened to Native American music for $1\frac{1}{4}$ hours. In the afternoon, they listened to Indian legends for $1\frac{1}{3}$ hours while they painted. Which session lasted longer? What was the difference?

3. Every Friday Emily and her brothers ride their bicycles $2\frac{1}{2}$ miles to get fry bread. Then they ride $1\frac{3}{4}$ miles to baseball practice. After practice, they bicycle $\frac{3}{4}$ mile home. How far do they ride their bicycles on Friday?

4. Emily did $1\frac{1}{2}$ hours of homework on Wednesday and $2\frac{3}{4}$ hours of homework on Thursday. How much longer did she work on Thursday? How much time in all did she spend doing homework in the two days?

CULTURAL LINK

Native American children made their own games. One game was like a board game you might play today. To play, place 40 rocks in a circle. Leave spaces between every 10 rocks to represent a river. Find a squarish rock and mark it with dots like a number cube. Each player starts out in one of the rivers. Players move their markers the number of spaces they roll on the rock. If a player lands on a rock that already has a marker, he or she returns to his or her river. Players keep moving around the circle until one player goes around the circle and returns to his or her river.

✓ CHECK UNDERSTANDING

Round the mixed number to the nearest $\frac{1}{2}$ or whole number. You may use a number line or a ruler. (pages 326–327)

1. $2\frac{7}{8}$ **2.** $1\frac{1}{6}$ **3.** $4\frac{3}{8}$ **4.** $5\frac{4}{5}$ **5.** $7\frac{1}{10}$ **6.** $3\frac{5}{9}$

Match the mixed number with the fraction bars. (pages 334–335)

7. $3\frac{2}{5}$

8. $2\frac{1}{6}$

9. $5\frac{3}{5}$

a.

b.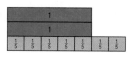

c.

✓ CHECK SKILLS

Estimate the sum or difference. (pages 326–327)

10. $1\frac{3}{8} + 3\frac{11}{12}$ **11.** $4\frac{1}{8} - 2\frac{3}{4}$ **12.** $2\frac{8}{9} + 1\frac{1}{3}$

Find the sum. (pages 328–329)

13. $1\frac{1}{4} + 4\frac{1}{2} = n$ **14.** $3\frac{1}{3} + 1\frac{1}{6} = n$ **15.** $2\frac{5}{8} + 1\frac{3}{4} = n$

Find the difference. (pages 330–331)

16. $8\frac{3}{4} - 4\frac{1}{2} = n$ **17.** $5\frac{2}{3} - 4\frac{1}{6} = n$ **18.** $6\frac{5}{8} - 2\frac{1}{2} = n$

Add or subtract. Write the answer in simplest form. (pages 328–335)

19. $6\frac{2}{3} + 1\frac{5}{6} = n$ **20.** $8\frac{2}{5} - 4\frac{3}{10} = n$ **21.** $6\frac{1}{4} + 2\frac{7}{8} = n$

✓ CHECK PROBLEM SOLVING

Solve. (pages 332–333)

CHOOSE A STRATEGY

• Work Backward   • Draw a Diagram   • Act It Out   • Write a Number Sentence

22. Kim used $9\frac{1}{2}$ in. of lace for a white dress and $6\frac{1}{2}$ in. for a blue dress. She had 8 in. of lace left. How much lace did Kim have to start with?

23. Last week Ned ran 1 mile on Monday, 2 miles on Tuesday, 5 miles on Wednesday, and 3 miles on Thursday. He ran a total of 15 miles last week. How many miles did he run on Friday?

CHAPTER 21

MEASUREMENT: CUSTOMARY UNITS

DID YOU KNOW...

Very, very small objects cannot be measured with a ruler. A tool called a micrometer caliper can measure thickness of objects to $\frac{1}{1,000}$ of an inch.

Your Closest Call

How precisely can you measure with a ruler? How many teaspoons are in a cup? You can experiment to see how precise your measurements will be.

YOU WILL NEED: ruler, 3 objects to measure, salt, teaspoon, tablespoon, a measuring cup

Work with a group. Your job is to

- choose three objects to measure with a ruler.

- measure the length, width, and height of each object and record your measurements.

- fill a cup by using tablespoons and then by using teaspoons. Record your findings.

- compare your group's most precise measurements with other groups' measurements.

DID YOU

✔ choose three objects to measure precisely, and record your findings?

✔ measure the capacity of a cup by using tablespoons and teaspoons, and record your measurements?

✔ compare your measurements with those of other groups?

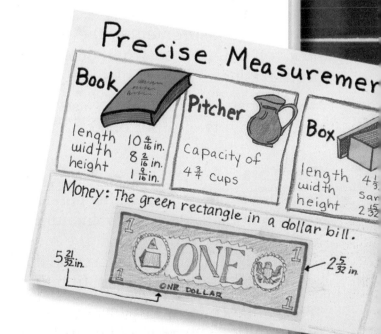

Precise Measurement

Book
length 10 4/16 in.
width 8 2/16 in.
height 1 9/16 in.

Pitcher
Capacity of 4 3/4 cups

Box
length 4 1/...
width Sar...
height 2 15/32...

Money: The green rectangle in a dollar bill.

5 21/32 in.

2 5/32 in.

ONE DOLLAR

Precise Measurements

You will investigate how to use a ruler to measure length to the nearest $\frac{1}{16}$ of an inch.	**Why learn this?** You can find the exact measurement of an object to see if it will fit inside a container.	**WORD POWER** precise

Sometimes you need a more precise measurement. **Precise** means finding a unit that measures nearest to the actual length of an object. The smaller the unit, the more precise the measurement will be.

Explore

Jeremy wants his new pen to fit inside his school-supply box which is $5\frac{1}{4}$ inches long. Use a customary ruler to measure the pen to the nearest $\frac{1}{16}$ inch.

MATERIALS: customary ruler with $\frac{1}{16}$ marks

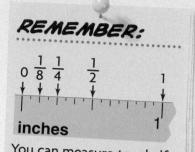

REMEMBER:

$0 \quad \frac{1}{8} \quad \frac{1}{4} \quad \frac{1}{2} \qquad 1$

inches

You can measure to a half inch, a quarter inch, or an eighth inch.

inches 1 2 3 4 5 6

$\frac{1}{16}$ in. mark

?

Record

Write the measurement of the pen. Explain how you determined whether the pen would fit inside Jeremy's school-supply box.

Now investigate finding precise measurements of other objects.

Try This

Measure three of your pens, pencils, or crayons to the nearest $\frac{1}{16}$ inch. Be sure to line up the object with the left end of the ruler. Record the measurements. Draw the length of each item. Describe the smallest school supply box that they all will fit into.

TALK ABOUT IT How is measuring to the nearest inch different from measuring to the nearest $\frac{1}{16}$ inch?

Link

E-Lab • Activity 21 Available on CD-ROM and the Internet at http://www.hbschool.com/elab

 **WRITE ABOUT IT** Choose an object and explain how you would measure it to the nearest $\frac{1}{16}$ inch.

HANDS-ON PRACTICE

For Problems 1–4, use a customary ruler.

1. Measure the length of the paper clip to the nearest $\frac{1}{4}$ inch.

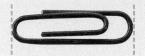

2. Measure the length of the chalk to the nearest $\frac{1}{16}$ inch.

3. Measure the length of the eraser to the nearest $\frac{1}{8}$ inch.

4. Measure the length of the sticker to the nearest $\frac{1}{16}$ inch.

Applying What You Learned

Draw a line segment to the given length.

5. $2\frac{1}{4}$ inch

6. $3\frac{3}{16}$ inch

7. $4\frac{7}{16}$ inch

8. $1\frac{3}{8}$ inch

9. $2\frac{11}{16}$ inch

10. $5\frac{5}{8}$ inch

Use a ruler to compare the measurements. Write $<$, $>$, or $=$ for each ⬤.

11. $3\frac{1}{16}$ in. ⬤ $2\frac{11}{16}$ in.

12. $1\frac{3}{16}$ in. ⬤ $1\frac{5}{16}$ in.

13. $5\frac{1}{4}$ in. ⬤ $5\frac{2}{8}$ in.

14. $6\frac{3}{4}$ in. ⬤ $6\frac{3}{16}$ in.

Mixed Applications

15. Measure the two leaves. How much longer is the yellow leaf than the green leaf?

16. LaToya wants to sew two ribbons together to make one long ribbon. Her seam will take $\frac{1}{4}$ inch from each ribbon. One ribbon is $5\frac{1}{4}$ inches long. The other is $6\frac{3}{4}$ inches long. How long will her finished ribbon be?

17.  **Write a problem** about the lengths of two objects that are between 5 and 6 inches long.

| **You will learn** how to change and compute units of measurement. | **Why learn this?** You may need to change small units of measure to large units, or large units to small units in order to compare measurements. |

The fifth-grade class is making costumes for the school play. Each costume requires 5 feet of fabric. A local store has donated 25 yards of fabric for the costumes. How many feet of fabric do the students have?

Customary Units for Linear Measure
12 inches (in.) = 1 foot (ft)
3 feet = 1 yard (yd)
5,280 feet = 1 mile (mi)
1,760 yards = 1 mile

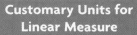

When you change larger units to smaller units, you multiply. Since you are changing yards to feet, multiply by 3.

number of yards		number of feet in 1 yard		total feet
25	×	3	=	?

Since 25 × 3 = 75, the students have 75 ft of fabric.

• How can you find the number of costumes the students can make?

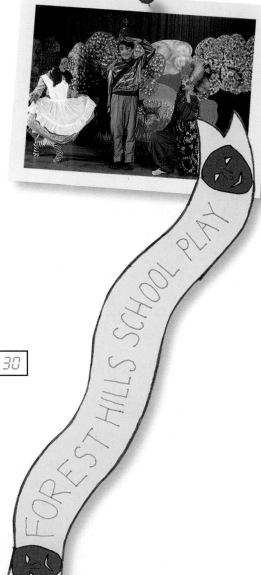

The students made a green banner to stretch across the stage. It was 360 inches long. How many feet long was the banner?

You can use a calculator when changing units.

When you change smaller units to larger units, you divide. Since you are changing inches to feet, divide by 12.

number of inches		number of inches in 1 foot		total feet
360	÷	12	=	?

          30

Since 360 ÷ 12 = 30, the banner is 30 feet long.

Talk About It

• When a change is made from feet to inches, will there be more inches or fewer inches? Explain.

• When a change is made from feet to yards, will there be more yards or fewer yards?

PRACTICE

Write *multiply* or *divide* to tell how to change the unit.

1. yards to feet   **2.** yards to miles   **3.** inches to feet   **4.** miles to feet

Change the unit. You may use a calculator.

5. 12 ft = _?_ yd   **6.** 48 in. = _?_ ft   **7.** 50 yd = _?_ ft

8. 2 mi = _?_ ft   **9.** 6 ft = _?_ in.   **10.** 30 ft = _?_ yd

Write *more* or *fewer*.

11. When I change miles to feet, I expect to have _?_ feet.

12. When I change feet to yards, I expect to have _?_ yards.

13. When I change feet to miles, I expect to have _?_ miles.

Write *multiply* or *divide*. Solve.

14. How many feet are in 120 inches?

15. How many feet are in 3 miles?

Change the unit. You may use a calculator.

16. 60 yd = _?_ ft   **17.** 5 ft = _?_ in.   **18.** 1,760 yd = _?_ mi

19. 33 ft = _?_ yd   **20.** 300 ft = _?_ yd   **21.** 2,640 ft = _?_ mi

Mixed Applications

For Problems 22–23, use the picture.

22. The student committee is getting ready for the fifth-grade talent show. They are measuring the width of the stage. How many feet wide is the stage?

23. The committee needs an extension cord for the talent show that will reach across the stage. Extension cords come in 10-ft, 25-ft, or 50-ft lengths. Which should they choose?

24. James needs 16 sheets of plywood to make the sets for the play. Each sheet costs $12.69. How much will James pay for the plywood?

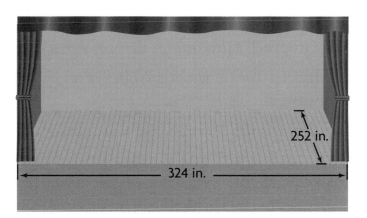

252 in.

324 in.

25. **WRITE ABOUT IT** Explain when to multiply and when to divide to change linear units.

LESSON
CONTINUES

PART 2 Computing Customary Units

Alison works at the school publishing center. She makes book covers for books the students have written. She has 2 feet 10 inches of ribbon to use as a border on the bookcovers. The teacher gave her 3 feet 9 inches more ribbon. How much ribbon does Alison have?

You may need to change units when adding or subtracting measurements.

MODEL

Add 2 ft 10 in. and 3 ft 9 in.

▶ **Step 1**

Add each kind of unit.

```
  2 ft 10 in.
+ 3 ft  9 in.
  5 ft 19 in.
```

▶ **Step 2**

Since 19 in. is more than 1 ft, rename 19 in. as 1 ft 7 in.

Think: 12 in. = 1 ft

```
  2 ft 10 in.
+ 3 ft  9 in.
  5 ft 19 in. =
  5 ft + (1 ft + 7 in.)
```

▶ **Step 3**

Combine like units.

```
  2 ft 10 in.
+ 3 ft  9 in.
  5 ft 19 in. =
  (5 ft + 1 ft) + 7 in. = 6 ft 7 in.
```

So, Alison has 6 ft 7 in. of ribbon.

Alison used 1 foot 9 inches of ribbon on the first book she covered. How much ribbon does she have left?

Subtract 1 foot 9 inches from 6 feet 7 inches.

MODEL

▶ **Step 1**

Decide whether to rename. Since 9 in. > 7 in., rename 6 ft 7 in.

```
  5 ft 19 in.    Think: 1 ft = 12 in.
  6̸ ft  7̸ in.           5 ft + 12 in. + 7 in.
- 1 ft  9 in.
```

▶ **Step 2**

Subtract the inches. Subtract the feet.

```
  5 ft 19 in.
  6̸ ft  7̸ in.
- 1 ft  9 in.
  4 ft 10 in.
```

So, Alison has 4 ft 10 in. of ribbon left.

💡 **CRITICAL THINKING** When must you rename units to add measurements? When must you rename units to subtract measurements?

PRACTICE

Rename the measurements.

1. 30 in. = _?_ ft _?_ in.　**2.** 10 ft = _?_ yd _?_ ft　**3.** 27 in. = _?_ ft _?_ in.

4. 4 ft 5 in. = 3 ft _?_ in.　**5.** 3 ft 16 in. = 4 ft _?_ in.　**6.** 5 ft 6 in. = 4 ft _?_ in.

7. 12 yd 1 ft = 11 yd _?_ ft　**8.** 14 yd = 13 yd _?_ ft　**9.** 20 yd 2 ft = 19 yd _?_ ft

Find the sum or difference.

10.   8 ft   4 in.
    +2 ft 10 in.

11.   6 ft 3 in.
    −1 ft 8 in.

12.   5 yd 2 ft
    +2 yd 2 ft

13.   9 yd 1 ft
    −7 yd 2 ft

14.   7 yd 4 ft
    −3 yd 5 ft

15.   11 yd 9 ft
    +10 yd 2 ft

16.   12 ft
    −10 ft 8 in.

17.   20 ft 11 in.
    +17 ft 10 in.

18.   18 ft 6 in.
    +17 ft 9 in.

19.   23 ft   5 in.
    +29 ft 11 in.

20.   26 yd 7 ft
    +19 yd 6 ft

21.   13 yd
    −10 yd 2 ft

Mixed Applications

For Problems 25–28, use the picture.

22. Brenda is buying lace to trim the perimeter of a tablecloth that is 80 inches long and 40 inches wide. Will she need to buy more or less than 6 yards of lace? Explain.

23. Brooke spent $7.75 on material, $2.98 for a pattern, and $3.79 for buttons. Does she have enough money left over from $15.00 to buy thread for $0.79?

24. Mary has 4 ceramic cats in her collection. Their heights are 10.2 in., 8.4 in., 7.9 in., and 8.3 in. What is the average height of the cats in her collection?

25. How much taller is Sara than Michael?

26. If Kristen grows 6 inches by the time she is in tenth grade, how tall will she be?

27. Michael's older sister is 5 ft 5 in. tall. How much taller is she than Michael?

28. ✏️ **Write a problem** using the information in the picture.

MORE PRACTICE Student Handbook page H107

Capacity

You will learn how to change units of capacity.

Why learn this? You can decide whether to buy ice cream by the pint or by the half gallon.

Maria made punch for the party. The recipe makes enough punch to fill a 2-gallon punch bowl. Maria wants to make sure she has enough to give a cup to each of her 24 guests. Does she have enough?

Maria needs to find out the number of cups in 2 gallons.

Step 1

First, find how many quarts are in 2 gallons.

number of gallons	number of quarts in 1 gallon	total quarts
2	× 4	= 8

So, 2 gallons equals 8 quarts.

Step 2

Now find how many cups are in 8 quarts.

number of quarts	number of cups in 1 quart	total cups
8	× 4	= 32

So, Maria has 32 cups of punch, more than enough for her 24 guests.

Customary Units of Capacity
8 fluid ounces (fl oz) = 1 cup (c)
2 cups = 1 pint (pt)
2 pints = 1 quart (qt)
4 cups = 1 quart
4 quarts = 1 gallon (gal)

Talk About It

- Why did you multiply in Step 2?

- How can you find how many fluid ounces are equal to 1 pint? Explain.

- How can you find how many gallons are equal to 16 pints? Explain.

Language Link

Some people think the word *pint* comes from the same Latin root as the word *paint*. An old English meaning for *pint* is "a container of paint." How many pints of paint make a gallon?

Check Your Understanding  CRITICAL THINKING

Write *multiply* or *divide*. Change the unit.

1. 1 qt = _?_ c   **2.** 20 qt = _?_ gal   **3.** 1 gal = _?_ fl oz   **4.** 5 c = _?_ fl oz

5. 4 c = _?_ pt   **6.** 8 pt = _?_ qt   **7.** 3 qt = _?_ c   **8.** 2 pt = _?_ fl oz

PRACTICE

Change the unit.

9. 8 c = _?_ pt   **10.** 1 gal = _?_ pt   **11.** 8 c = _?_ qt   **12.** 1 pt = _?_ fl oz

13. 3 gal = _?_ qt   **14.** 12 pt = _?_ qt   **15.** 5 pt = _?_ c   **16.** 10 c = _?_ fl oz

For Exercises 17–20, use the picture.

17. How many cups of yogurt?

18. How many quarts of milk?

19. How many fluid ounces of juice?

20. How many fluid ounces of milk?

Write <, >, or = for each ●.

21. 4 c ● 1 gal   **22.** 3 pt ● 1 qt   **23.** 16 c ● 1 gal   **24.** 36 fl oz ● 1 qt

25. 4 qt ● 8 pt   **26.** 2 gal ● 10 qt   **27.** 7 pt ● 110 oz   **28.** 32 fl oz ● 4 c

29. 2 gal ● 7 pt   **30.** 2 c ● 16 fl oz   **31.** 5 qt ● 1 gal   **32.** 48 fl oz ● 4 pt

Mixed Applications

33. Barry is filling a 10-gallon fish tank with water. He plans to use 9 gallons of water to leave a space at the top. He is using a pitcher that holds 1 quart. How many pitchers full of water does he need?

34. Yolanda is painting her room. She has one wall left that is 8 ft by 12 ft. She has a quart of paint to use that covers 350 square feet. How many more square feet will she be able to paint after she paints her wall?

35. George is helping his mom shop. His little sister wants him to buy a 6-pack of box drinks, each with 6 fl oz, for $2.16. Or George can buy a 48-oz bottle of juice for $2.20. Which is a better buy?

36. ✏️ **WRITE ABOUT IT** Explain how to find out how many pints are in 2 gallons.

Mixed Review

Find the quotient. Check by multiplying. (pages 216–217)

37. 8)7.2   **38.** 2)6.42   **39.** 3)18.9   **40.** 4)88.4

Write the missing unit. (pages 234–235)

41. 5.6 m = 560 _?_   **42.** 4,700 g = 4.7 _?_   **43.** 8 kg = 8,000 _?_

Weight

You will learn how to change units of weight.	**Why learn this?** You can compare products by their unit price to get the better buy.

Barry bought a 50-lb bag of dog food for his dog, Max. Max eats 10 oz of food each day. How many days will the bag of dog food last?

Think about the units of weight in the customary system.

A. 1 ounce   **B.** 1 pound   **C.** 1 ton

Now, find how many ounces are in 50 pounds.

When you change larger units to smaller units, you multiply. Since you are changing pounds to ounces, multiply by 16. You may use a calculator.

number of pounds		number of ounces in 1 pound		total ounces
50	×	16	=	800

Press:

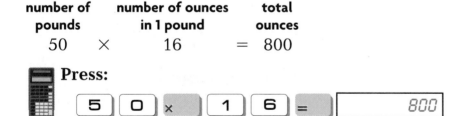

5 0 × 1 6 = 800

So, the 50-lb bag of dog food holds 800 oz.

Since Max eats 10 oz a day, you can divide to find the number of days the food will last. $800 \div 10 = n$

Press:

8 0 0 ÷ 1 0 = 80

So, $n = 80$.

So, Max has enough food for 80 days.

• How can you use a calculator to find the number of pounds equal to 144 ounces?

Sports Link

Hitting a fast-moving baseball with a bat is very difficult. Ball players have discovered that lighter bats that weigh 28 ounces or less allow them to hit with greater speed. Babe Ruth used a heavy 42-ounce bat. How does a lighter bat weighing 28 ounces compare to Babe Ruth's bat?

PRACTICE

What unit would you use to describe the weight of these objects? Write *tons, pounds,* or *ounces.*

1. a bicycle

2. a dog

3. a truckload of concrete blocks

4. a block of cheese

Write *more* or *fewer* for each statement.

5. When I change tons to pounds, I expect to have _?_ pounds.

6. When I change ounces to pounds, I expect to have _?_ pounds.

7. When I change pounds to ounces, I expect to have _?_ ounces.

8. When I change pounds to tons, I expect to have _?_ tons.

Write *multiply* or *divide.* Change the unit. You may use a calculator.

9. 32 oz = _?_ lb **10.** 40 lb = _?_ oz **11.** 2 T = _?_ lb **12.** 8,000 lb = _?_ T

13. 6,000 lb = _?_ T **14.** 15 lb = _?_ oz **15.** 10 T = _?_ lb **16.** 10,000 lb = _?_ T

Write which one is heavier.

17. 46 oz or 3 lb **18.** 2 T or 5,000 lb **19.** $\frac{1}{2}$ T or 500 lb **20.** 100 lb or 1,000 oz

Mixed Applications

21. Each apple in this display weighs 4 ounces. Which apple is the better bargain?

Special Apple Sale!

Golden Delicious, 2 apples for $1

Gala apples, $0.79 a pound

22. A 28-ounce box of granola sells for $3.29. Granola also is sold for $1.50 a pound. Which granola is the better buy?

23. ✏ **Write a problem** comparing two items for sale in the food store. One is sold by the pound and the other is sold by the ounce.

Mixed Review

Rename each fraction as a mixed number. (pages 248–249)

24. $\frac{15}{7}$ **25.** $\frac{11}{2}$ **26.** $\frac{12}{5}$ **27.** $\frac{13}{3}$ **28.** $\frac{11}{4}$

Find the sum or difference. Write the answer in simplest form. (pages 314–315)

29. $\frac{1}{9} + \frac{1}{3} = n$ **30.** $\frac{5}{12} - \frac{1}{6} = n$ **31.** $\frac{13}{16} + \frac{4}{8} = n$

You will learn to find elapsed time.	Why learn this? You can use a schedule to find the time it will take to travel from one place to another.

A group of Scouts went on a hike. They started the hike at 9:00 A.M. They stopped for lunch at 12:15 P.M. How long were the Scouts hiking?

Units of Time
60 seconds (sec) = 1 minute (min)
60 minutes = 1 hour (hr)
24 hours = 1 day
7 days = 1 week
about 52 weeks = 1 year
365 days = 1 year
366 days = 1 leap year

start   end

To find how much time has elapsed, you can count forward on the clock from the starting time to the ending time.

So, the group was hiking for 3 hr and 15 min.

REMEMBER:
This is an analog clock.

This is a digital clock.

Suppose a hiking and camping trip starts at 7 A.M. on July 22 and finishes at 5 P.M. on July 26. How many days and hours will the trip last?

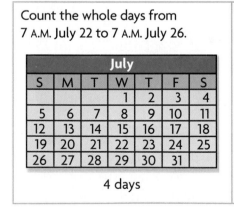

Count the whole days from 7 A.M. July 22 to 7 A.M. July 26.	Count the hours from 7 A.M. to 5 P.M.

July

S	M	T	W	T	F	S
			1	2	3	4
5	6	7	8	9	10	11
12	13	14	15	16	17	18
19	20	21	22	23	24	25
26	27	28	29	30	31	

4 days   10 hours

So, it will take 4 days and 10 hours to make the trip.

Talk About It CRITICAL THINKING

• At what time does A.M. become P.M?

• If you know the starting time and the elapsed time, how can you find the ending time?

• If you know the elapsed time and the ending time, how can you find the starting time?

PRACTICE

Write the time for each.

1. Start: 5:25 P.M.
45 min elapsed time
End: ?

2. Start: ?
2 hr 35 min elapsed time
End: 8:00 P.M.

3. Start: July 12, 6:00 A.M.
? time has elapsed
End: July 20, 8:30 A.M.

Write the elapsed time for each hike.

4.

time the hike started   time the hike finished

5.

time the hike started   time the hike finished

Look at Juanita's schedule for the day and complete the table.

	Activity	Starting Time	Ending Time	Elapsed Time
6.	School	9:10 A.M.	3:25 P.M.	?
7.	Soccer Practice	3:45 P.M.	?	1hr 55min
8.	Dinner	?	6:40 P.M.	28 min
9.	Homework	6:45 P.M.	8:12 P.M.	?

Mixed Applications

For Problems 10–13 and 15, use the following calendars.

March	April	May	June	July	August	September
S M T W Th F S	S M T W Th F S	S M T W Th F S	S M T W Th F S	S M T W Th F S	S M T W Th F S	S M T W Th F S
1 2 3 4 5 6 7	1 2 3 4	1 2	1 2 3 4 5 6	1 2 3 4	1	1 2 3 4 5
8 9 10 11 12 13 14	5 6 7 8 9 10 11	3 4 5 6 7 8 9	7 8 9 10 11 12 13	5 6 7 8 9 10 11	2 3 4 5 6 7 8	6 7 8 9 10 11 12
15 16 17 18 19 20 21	12 13 14 15 16 17 18	10 11 12 13 14 15 16	14 15 16 17 18 19 20	12 13 14 15 16 17 18	9 10 11 12 13 14 15	13 14 15 16 17 18 19
22 23 24 25 26 27 28	19 20 21 22 23 24 25	17 18 19 20 21 22 23	21 22 23 24 25 26 27	19 20 21 22 23 24 25	16 17 18 19 20 21 22	20 21 22 23 24 25 26
29 30 31	26 27 28 29 30	24/31 25 26 27 28 29 30	28 29 30	26 27 28 29 30 31	23/30 24/31 25 26 27 28 29	27 28 29 30

10. There will be a 36-hour field trip to an American history village, starting at 8 A.M. on April 21. When will the students arrive back home?

11. The fifth-grade talent show will be on April 11. The class members want to put out posters one month earlier. It takes a week to make the posters. When should they start the posters?

12. June 12 is the last day of school. School starts again on September 8. Is summer vacation 100 days long? Explain.

13. The county fair is going to be here for two weeks. They have to leave on June 3rd. On what date will the county fair open?

14. Suppose your lunch period started at 11:45 A.M., and lasted 32 minutes. At what time would your lunch period be over?

15.  **Write a problem** using the calendars.

LESSON CONTINUES

MORE PRACTICE Student Handbook page H108

PART 2 PROBLEM-SOLVING STRATEGY
Make a Table

THE PROBLEM You are helping your family plan an afternoon trip to the beach. You plan to take the earliest train out of the city and be back at 6:00 P.M. The train stops near Sandy Beach. It takes 10 minutes to walk from the train to the beach. How long can you stay at the beach?

REMEMBER:
- ☑ Understand
- ☑ Plan
- ☑ Solve
- ☑ Look Back

☑ Understand

- What are you asked to do?
- What information will you use?
- Is there information you will not use? If so, what?

☑ Plan

- What strategy can you use?

  You can use the information from the schedule to *make a table* to show the elapsed time.

Departure New York City	Arrival Sandy Beach
12:10	12:55
1:30	2:15
3:00	3:45
Sandy Beach	**New York City**
3:45	4:15
4:30	5:15
5:30	6:15

☑ Solve

- How can you solve the problem?

  You can make a table that shows the starting and ending time for each part of the trip. The earliest train leaves at 12:10 and arrives at 12:55. After the 10-minute walk, you arrive at the beach at 1:05.

Part of Trip	Start	End	Elapsed Time
Train From City	12:10 P.M.	12:55 P.M.	45 min
Walk To Beach	12:55 P.M.	1:05 P.M.	10 min
Stay At Beach	1:05 P.M.	4:20 P.M.	?
Walk To Train	4:20 P.M.	4:30 P.M.	10 min
Train To City	4:30 P.M.	5:15 P.M.	45 min

The last train that will get you home before 6:00 is the one that leaves at 4:30. You must allow 10 minutes to walk from the beach to get to the train. So, you are at the beach from 1:05 to 4:20. You can count the hours and minutes to find the elapsed time.

So, you can spend 3 hr 15 min at the beach.

☑ Look Back

- How can you decide if your answer is reasonable?
- What other strategy can you use?

PRACTICE

Make a table to solve.

1. The multipurpose room is used from 11:30 until 12:45 for lunch. For the next 50 minutes, the fifth graders practice square dancing there. Then for the next 30 minutes, the fourth graders practice their play. At what time is the room free?

2. The principal plans to give each student 5 minutes to try out for the talent show starting at 3:00. The students, in order, are Ben, Callie, Denise, Edward, and Frank. At what time does Frank start?

3. The Gibb family left on July 7th for vacation. They flew to Miami and stayed 3 days. Next, they spent 5 days in Key West, 4 days in Orlando, and returned home the following day. On what date did they arrive home?

4. Tom and Joe want to see a movie on Saturday between 4:00 and 6:15. *Starship Mars* is shown daily at 1:30, 3:45, and 6:00. *The Lost Witness* is shown Monday through Friday at 4:00 and 6:45. *Ride the Wave* is shown on weekends at 2:00, 4:10, and 6:30. Which movie will they see?

Mixed Applications

Solve.

CHOOSE A STRATEGY

• Work Backward   • Guess and Check   • Make a Table   • Write a Number Sentence

5. The school assembly began at 9:10. The principal spoke for 5 minutes. For the next 1 hour 10 minutes, the students received their awards. There was a 10-minute break and then, for the next 35 minutes, there was a guest speaker. At what time was the assembly over?

6. Nick and Lindsay are making shakes. They measure the total amount of milk needed. Nick uses 6 fluid ounces more milk than Lindsay. How many fluid ounces does each use?

7. At the school program, there were 229 students and 75 parents. The school printed only 256 programs. How many more programs should the school have printed?

8. Jack's dad is a long-distance runner. His running shoes wear out after he has run about 1,000 miles. If he runs 18 miles a week, how long will his running shoes last?

9. Rachel arrived home at 3:30. Before that she went shopping for 2 hr 20 min. Before that she spent 30 minutes eating lunch with a friend. What time did they begin eating lunch?

Temperature Changes

You will learn to read both Fahrenheit and Celsius thermometers and compare differences in degrees of temperatures.

Why learn this? You can compare two temperatures and see which is warmer.

WORD POWER

degrees
   Fahrenheit (°F)
degrees Celsius
   (°C)

Ben used a Fahrenheit thermometer to compare the high and low temperatures on Friday.

Degrees Fahrenheit (°F) are customary units for measuring temperature. This Fahrenheit thermometer shows that the room temperature was 68°F.

The low temperature was 5 degrees below zero, or ⁻5°F. The high temperature was 22°F. By how many degrees did the temperature rise?

Starting Temperature	Change in Temperature
⁻5°F	from ⁻5°F to 0° F 5° from 0°F to 22°F +22° total change 27°F

So, on Friday the temperature rose 27°F.

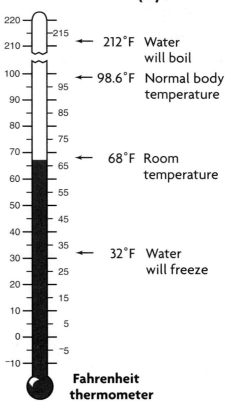

Fahrenheit thermometer

212°F   Water will boil
98.6°F   Normal body temperature
68°F   Room temperature
32°F   Water will freeze

Degrees Celsius (°C) are metric units for measuring temperature. This Celsius thermometer shows room temperature is 20°C.

On Sunday the high temperature was 10°C, and the low temperature was ⁻15°C. By how many degrees did the temperature fall?

Starting Temperature	Change in Temperature
⁺10°C	from ⁺10°C to 0°C 10° from 0°C to ⁻15°C +15 total change 25°C

So, on Sunday, the temperature fell 25°C.

Talk About It 💡 CRITICAL THINKING

- Which is warmer, 32°F or ⁻32°F?

- What is the difference between the freezing point and the boiling point of water in the Fahrenheit system? in the Celsius system?

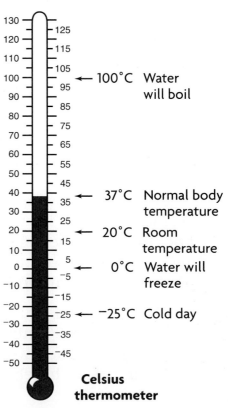

Celsius thermometer

100°C   Water will boil
37°C   Normal body temperature
20°C   Room temperature
0°C   Water will freeze
⁻25°C   Cold day

PRACTICE

Find the difference in temperature.

1. the outside temperature of 84°F and room temperature

2. a normal human body temperature and a fever of 104°F

3. the temperature at the top of a cumulus cloud, ⁻4°F, and the temperature on the ground at 60°F

4. the temperature in your classroom and the temperature outdoors

Copy and complete the table.

	Starting Temperature	Change in Temperature	Final Temperature
5.	12°C	rose 19°	?
6.	62°F	?	37°F
7.	9°C	fell 15°	?
8.	48°F	?	71°F

Mixed Applications

9. For five days Erica recorded the temperature outside in the morning. On Monday and Tuesday the temperature was 14°C. On Wednesday it was 16°C and on Thursday it was 15°C. On Friday it was 11°C. What are the mean, median, and mode temperatures for these days?

10. At sunrise the temperature was 69°F. At noon it was 24 degrees warmer. Then it was 18 degrees cooler at night. What was the temperature at night?

11. Lynn bought a jacket for $38.95, gloves for $8.99, and a scarf for $9.85. How much change did she receive from $60.00?

12. ▥▷ **WRITE ABOUT IT** Explain how to find the temperature change from 72°F to 36°F.

Mixed Review

Rename, using the least common multiple, and compare. Write < , > , or = for each ●. (pages 252–253)

13. $\frac{3}{12}$ ● $\frac{1}{4}$

14. $\frac{5}{6}$ ● $\frac{11}{12}$

15. $\frac{3}{10}$ ● $\frac{3}{4}$

16. $\frac{3}{5}$ ● $\frac{2}{7}$

Find an equivalent fraction. Use multiplication or division. (pages 266–267)

17. $\frac{3}{4}$

18. $\frac{1}{7}$

19. $\frac{2}{16}$

20. $\frac{9}{12}$

MATH FUN!

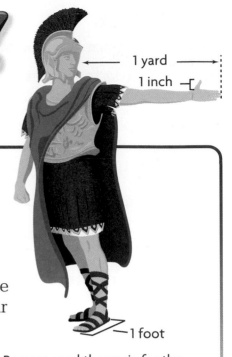

1 yard
1 inch

ROMAN MEASUREMENTS

PURPOSE To measure the ancient units that became customary linear measures

YOU WILL NEED ruler, yardstick, string

Compare customary units to the ancient Roman measures. With a partner, measure the length of your thumb, the length of your foot, and the distance from your nose to the tip of the middle finger of your outstretched arm. Record your measurements in customary units and in Roman measures.

Measure adults at home. Are any of them close to the Roman measures?

1 foot

The Romans used the uncia for the length of a thumb. The English word *inch* comes from that. Twelve uncia equals 1 foot; 3 feet made a yard. Do 12 of your uncia equal one of your feet?

Backpack Weight

PURPOSE To estimate—then verify— weight in pounds and ounces

YOU WILL NEED a full backpack, books, a scale that weighs in pounds

Have you ever felt weighed down by your studies? Weigh your backpack and see why.

First, estimate how much your backpack weighs. Then weigh it on a scale. How many pounds? How many ounces? How close was your estimate?

"IF A POUND IS 16 OUNCES, THEN HALF A POUND WOULD BE..."

Milk Carton Mystery

PURPOSE To estimate in cubic inches the volume of a half-gallon carton

YOU WILL NEED an empty half-gallon carton, a customary ruler

Imagine a cube that is one inch on all sides. That is a cubic inch. Now, figure out how many cubic inches can fit in your half-gallon container. Use a calculator to multiply the length × width × height. If a gallon holds 231 cubic inches, is your carton about the right size for a half gallon? Draw a diagram of the carton and label your measurements.

☑ CHECK UNDERSTANDING

VOCABULARY

1. Degrees _?_ are customary units for measuring temperature. (page 354)

2. A measurement using the smaller unit is a more _?_ measurement. (page 340)

3. Degrees _?_ are metric units for measuring temperature. (page 354)

Use a customary ruler to measure these lines. (pages 340–341)

4. ——————————————

5. ——————————————

6. Draw a line that is one-half foot in length.

☑ CHECK SKILLS

Change the unit. You may use a calculator. (pages 342–349)

7. 36 in. = _?_ ft

8. 72 ft = _?_ yd

9. 5 ft = _?_ in.

10. $\frac{1}{2}$ mi = _?_ ft

11. 1 pt = _?_ c

12. 2 qt = _?_ c

13. 1 gal = _?_ c

14. 1 pt = _?_ fl oz

15. 2,000 lb = _?_ T

16. 4 T = _?_ lb

17. 48 oz = _?_ lb

18. 8 oz = _?_ lb

Write the time for each. (pages 350–351)

19. Start: 2:05 P.M.
    25 min elapsed time
    End: _?_

20. Start: _?_
    2 hr 15 min elapsed time
    End: 10:45 P.M.

21. Start: May 9, 4:30 A.M.
    _?_ time has elapsed
    End: May 19, 7:40 A.M.

Find the difference in temperature. (pages 354–355)

22. high 89°F, low 62°F

23. high 14°C, low ⁻3°C

24. high 19°F, low ⁻10°F

☑ CHECK PROBLEM SOLVING

Solve. (pages 352–353)

CHOOSE A STRATEGY

• Draw a Diagram   • Use a Table   • Write a Number Sentence   • Make a Table

25. Dr. Lu does routine checkups on one day. He allows 20 min per visit. If he works from 9:00 A.M. to 4:00 P.M., and takes an hour for lunch, how many patients does he see?

26. Craig needs 2 gal of water. How many times will he need to fill an 8-oz cup to get the water he needs?

22 MULTIPLYING FRACTIONS

DID YOU KNOW . . .

A *hectare* is a metric unit for measuring area. It is approximately equal to 2.47 acres.

358

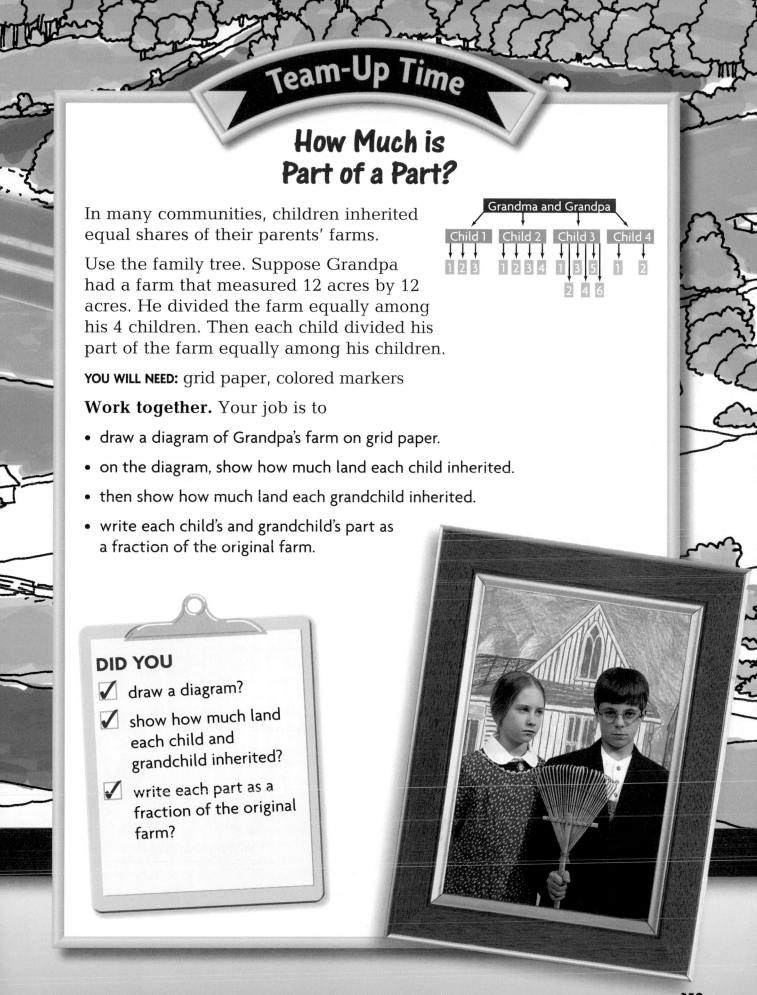

Team-Up Time

How Much is Part of a Part?

In many communities, children inherited equal shares of their parents' farms.

Use the family tree. Suppose Grandpa had a farm that measured 12 acres by 12 acres. He divided the farm equally among his 4 children. Then each child divided his part of the farm equally among his children.

Grandma and Grandpa

Child 1	Child 2	Child 3	Child 4
1 2 3	1 2 3 4	1 3 5	1 2
		2 4 6	

YOU WILL NEED: grid paper, colored markers

Work together. Your job is to

• draw a diagram of Grandpa's farm on grid paper.

• on the diagram, show how much land each child inherited.

• then show how much land each grandchild inherited.

• write each child's and grandchild's part as a fraction of the original farm.

DID YOU

☑ draw a diagram?

☑ show how much land each child and grandchild inherited?

☑ write each part as a fraction of the original farm?

359

Multiplying Fractions and Whole Numbers

You will learn how to multiply a fraction by a whole number.	**Why learn this?** You can tell how many are in part of a group.

Connie is using 16 flowers to make an arrangement. Of the 16 flowers, $\frac{3}{8}$ are roses. How many roses are in her arrangement?

$\frac{3}{8}$ of $16 = n$

MODEL

You can draw a picture to show $\frac{3}{8}$ of 16.

▶ **Step 1**

Use circles to show the total number of flowers.

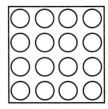

▶ **Step 2**

Separate the circles into 8 equal-size groups.

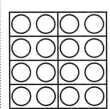

▶ **Step 3**

Shade 3 of the 8 groups, or $\frac{3}{8}$ of the total.

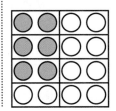

So, $n = 6$.

So, there are 6 roses in Connie's flower arrangement.

Talk About it

• Why were the circles separated into 8 groups?

• How can you use the picture to show $\frac{1}{8}$ of 16?

You can multiply fractions instead of drawing pictures.

Technology **Link**

In *Mighty Math Number Heroes*, the game *Fraction Fireworks* challenges you to multiply fractions by whole numbers.

MODEL

What is $\frac{1}{4} \times 16$?

▶ **Step 1**

Write the whole number as a fraction.

$\frac{1}{4} \times \frac{16}{1}$ **Think:** $16 = \frac{16}{1}$

▶ **Step 2**

Multiply the numerators. Multiply the denominators.

$\frac{1 \times 16}{4 \times 1} = \frac{16}{4}$

▶ **Step 3**

Write the answer in simplest form.

$\frac{16 \div 4}{4 \div 4} = \frac{4}{1} = 4$

💡 **CRITICAL THINKING** How can you rewrite the problem to show 16 groups of $\frac{1}{4}$? (HINT: Use the Commutative Property of Multiplication.)

PRACTICE

Write a number sentence for the picture.

1.

2.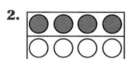

3.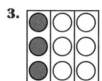

4.

5.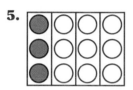

6.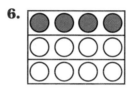

7.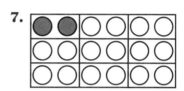

Find the product.

8. $\frac{3}{5} \times 25 = n$

9. $\frac{2}{3} \times 18 = n$

10. $\frac{2}{9} \times 18 = n$

11. $\frac{2}{3} \times 6 = n$

12. $16 \times \frac{7}{8} = n$

13. $20 \times \frac{2}{5} = n$

14. $14 \times \frac{5}{7} = n$

15. $8 \times \frac{3}{4} = n$

16. $30 \times \frac{5}{6} = n$

Mixed Applications

17. Jason has 12 pairs of pants. Of the pants, $\frac{2}{3}$ are blue jeans. How many of Jason's pants are blue jeans?

18. There are 3 crops on the Price's farm. One crop covers 11 acres. One covers 7 acres and the third covers 3 acres. What is the mean for the number of acres?

19. Anne has $\frac{5}{8}$ yard of yellow material. She needs $\frac{3}{4}$ yard for a top she is making. How much more material does she need?

20. ✏️ **Write a problem** about the 30 students in Mr. Walker's class. Multiply by a fraction to find out how many are in a group.

Mixed Review

Change the unit. (pages 346–347)

21. 10 c = __?__ pt

22. 2 gal = __?__ qt

23. 14 pt = __?__ qt

24. 1 pt = __?__ fl oz

Rename the fractions using the LCM as the denominator. (pages 254–255)

25. $\frac{1}{2}, \frac{1}{3}, \frac{1}{6}$

26. $\frac{2}{5}, \frac{4}{5}, \frac{2}{3}$

27. $\frac{3}{4}, \frac{2}{3}, \frac{5}{6}$

Multiplying a Fraction by a Fraction

You will investigate how to multiply two fractions.

Why learn this? You can find part of a part.

Dan read $\frac{2}{3}$ of his favorite author's books.

Scott has read $\frac{1}{4}$ of the books that Dan read. What part of the author's books has Scott read?

$\frac{1}{4}$ of $\frac{2}{3} = n$

Explore

Use paper folding, and color the parts to make a model of the problem. Find the product.

MATERIALS: paper, ruler, and 2 different-colored pencils or markers

MODEL

$\frac{1}{4} \times \frac{2}{3} = n$

▶ **Step 1**

Fold the paper vertically into 3 equal parts. Color 2 parts to represent $\frac{2}{3}$.

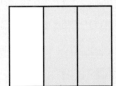

▶ **Step 2**

Fold the paper horizontally into fourths so that each of the thirds is divided into 4 equal parts.

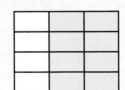

▶ **Step 3**

Use the other color to shade 1 of the fourths. The area in which the shading overlaps shows the product.

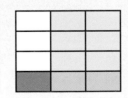

REMEMBER:
....
You can follow these steps when multiplying a decimal by a decimal:

Find 0.1×0.5.

Use a 10-by-10 grid and shade 5 of the columns to show 0.5. Then shade 1 row, or 0.1.

The area in which the shading overlaps shows the product, 0.05.

Record

Record the product, and answer the question in the problem above. How does your model show part of a part?

TALK ABOUT IT Is the product of $\frac{1}{4}$ and $\frac{2}{3}$ greater than or less than each of the factors? Explain how you know.

Technology **Link** ▶

E-Lab • Activity 22 Available on CD-ROM and the Internet at http://www.hbschool.com/elab

Try This

Make a paper-folding model to find the product of $\frac{1}{3}$ and $\frac{3}{4}$.

✏️ **WRITE ABOUT IT** How does the product of $\frac{1}{3}$ and $\frac{3}{4}$ compare with each of the factors? Why do you think this is so?

HANDS-ON PRACTICE

Make a paper-folding model to find the product.

1. $\frac{1}{5} \times \frac{1}{2} = n$ **2.** $\frac{1}{4} \times \frac{1}{3} = n$ **3.** $\frac{2}{3} \times \frac{1}{3} = n$

Applying What You Learned

Find the amount of each ingredient to cut the recipe in half.

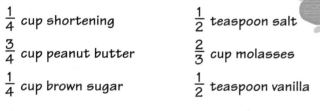

Peanut Molasses Cookies

$\frac{1}{4}$ cup shortening $\frac{1}{2}$ teaspoon salt

$\frac{3}{4}$ cup peanut butter $\frac{2}{3}$ cup molasses

$\frac{1}{4}$ cup brown sugar $\frac{1}{2}$ teaspoon vanilla

2 eggs   2 tablespoons milk

$\frac{1}{3}$ teaspoon baking soda   1 cup flour

4. shortening   **5.** peanut butter   **6.** brown sugar   **7.** egg   **8.** baking soda

9. salt   **10.** molasses   **11.** vanilla   **12.** milk   **13.** flour

Mixed Applications

14. Richard spent $\frac{2}{3}$ hour with his dog. He spent $\frac{1}{4}$ of that time walking the dog. What part of an hour did he spend walking the dog?

15. Melissa mixed $\frac{1}{4}$ gallon of blue paint, $\frac{3}{8}$ gallon of white paint, and $\frac{1}{2}$ gallon of yellow paint. How much paint did she mix?

16. Fatima bought silk fabric to make presents for her family. She used $\frac{1}{2}$ yard of silk to make a scarf, $\frac{5}{8}$ yard of silk to make a tie, and $\frac{1}{4}$ yard of silk to make a hair bow. Which item required the most silk?

17. Super Cineplex has 16 movie theaters. Each theater shows a different movie. Each movie has 7 showings per day on Saturday and Sunday. How many showings are there in one weekend?

MORE PRACTICE Student Handbook page H109

More About Multiplying a Fraction by a Fraction

You will learn to multiply two fractions, using paper and pencil.

Why learn this? You will know another way to find part of a part.

Lynn bought plants at a nursery. Of the plants, $\frac{3}{5}$ were herbs. She planted $\frac{1}{2}$ of the herbs in her backyard. What part of the plants Lynn bought were herbs that she planted in the backyard?

$$\frac{1}{2} \times \frac{3}{5} = n$$

You can use fraction squares to multiply fractions.

MODEL

▶ **Step 1**

Show fifths of the square. Shade $\frac{3}{5}$ yellow.

▶ **Step 2**

Show halves of the square.

▶ **Step 3**

Shade $\frac{1}{2}$ blue. Three of 10 parts are both yellow and blue, or green.

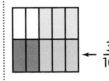 ← $\frac{3}{10}$

So, $n = \frac{3}{10}$.

So, $\frac{3}{10}$ of the plants were herbs planted in the backyard.

Talk About It

- Into how many sections did you divide the square?
- How much of the square is shaded by both colors?
- How does shading help you find the product?

You can also find the product of two fractions by multiplying the numerators and the denominators.

EXAMPLE

What is $\frac{1}{2}$ of $\frac{2}{3}$?

Think: $\frac{1}{2} \times \frac{2}{3} = n$

Multiply.

$$\frac{1}{2} \times \frac{2}{3} = \frac{1 \times 2}{2 \times 3} = \frac{2}{6}$$

Simplify.

$$\frac{2 \div 2}{6 \div 2} = \frac{1}{3}, \text{ or } n = \frac{1}{3}.$$

REMEMBER:

A fraction is in *simplest form* when the GCF of the numerator and denominator is 1.

• How does the product $\frac{1}{3}$ show that you are finding part of a part when you multiply fractions?

PRACTICE

Write a number sentence for the picture.

1.   **2.**   **3.**   **4.**

Draw fraction squares to find the product.

5. $\frac{1}{4} \times \frac{1}{3} = n$ **6.** $\frac{3}{4} \times \frac{2}{3} = n$ **7.** $\frac{2}{5} \times \frac{1}{2} = n$ **8.** $\frac{1}{3} \times \frac{2}{3} = n$

Multiply. Write the answer in simplest form.

9. $\frac{1}{4} \times \frac{1}{2} = n$ **10.** $\frac{4}{5} \times \frac{1}{5} = n$ **11.** $\frac{2}{5} \times \frac{3}{7} = n$ **12.** $\frac{3}{8} \times \frac{2}{3} = n$

13. $\frac{1}{8} \times \frac{2}{3} = n$ **14.** $\frac{1}{5} \times \frac{5}{12} = n$ **15.** $\frac{3}{4} \times \frac{3}{8} = n$ **16.** $\frac{3}{10} \times \frac{1}{6} = n$

17. $\frac{2}{9} \times \frac{3}{9} = n$ **18.** $\frac{2}{3} \times \frac{5}{6} = n$ **19.** $\frac{2}{15} \times \frac{3}{4} = n$ **20.** $\frac{3}{7} \times \frac{2}{9} = n$

Mixed Applications

21. Brian has a $\frac{7}{8}$-yard-long piece of plywood. He needs to use $\frac{1}{2}$ of the plywood for a plaque he is making. What part of a yard will he use to make the plaque?

22. Grace worked $\frac{3}{4}$ hour on her homework. Leah worked $\frac{2}{3}$ hour on hers. Who spent more time on homework?

23. A recipe calls for 2 cups milk. Marion has 12 fluid ounces of milk. How much more milk does she need for the recipe?

24. ✐ **Write a problem** in which you multiply a fraction by a fraction.

Mixed Review

Write each fraction in simplest form. (pages 270–271)

25. $\frac{9}{12}$ **26.** $\frac{10}{15}$ **27.** $\frac{6}{12}$ **28.** $\frac{15}{18}$

Find the sum. You may wish to draw a picture. Write the answer in the simplest form. (pages 328–329)

29. $1\frac{1}{2} + 3\frac{5}{6} = n$ **30.** $2\frac{1}{3} + 4\frac{1}{6} = n$ **31.** $5\frac{3}{5} + 2\frac{9}{10} = n$

PART 1 Multiplying Fractions and Mixed Numbers

You will learn to multiply a fraction by a mixed number.

Why learn this? You will be able to find a fractional part of recipe ingredients, lengths of material, and building materials such as wood.

Shelly used $1\frac{1}{3}$ yards of white felt to make a flannel board. She used $\frac{1}{4}$ as much red felt to make numbers for the flannel board. How much red felt did she use?

$\frac{1}{4} \times 1\frac{1}{3} = n$

You can use fraction squares to multiply.

MODEL

▶ Step 1

Show 2 whole squares. Divide each square into thirds. Shade 1 whole square and $\frac{1}{3}$ of the other square yellow, so that $1\frac{1}{3}$, or $\frac{4}{3}$, are shaded.

▶ Step 2

Divide the squares into fourths.

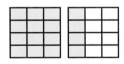

▶ Step 3

Shade $\frac{1}{4}$ of each square blue. Each whole has 12 parts. Four of the 12 parts are both yellow and blue, or green.

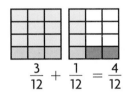

$$\frac{3}{12} + \frac{1}{12} = \frac{4}{12}$$

So, Shelly used $\frac{4}{12}$, or $\frac{1}{3}$ yard of red felt.

You can also find the product of a fraction and a mixed number by multiplying.

Multiply. $\frac{3}{4} \times 1\frac{1}{2} = n$

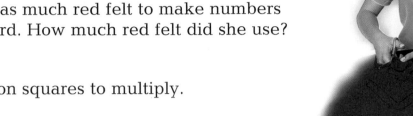

REMEMBER:
To rename a fraction greater than 1 as a mixed number, picture the parts. Then put them together.

$\frac{3}{2}$ → $1\frac{1}{2}$

MODEL

▶ Step 1

Rename the mixed number as a fraction greater than 1 by multiplying the whole number by the denominator and adding the numerator. Put the result over the denominator.

$1\frac{1}{2} = \frac{(1 \times 2) + 1}{2} = \frac{2+1}{2} = \frac{3}{2}$

So, another name for $1\frac{1}{2}$ is $\frac{3}{2}$.

▶ Step 2

Since $1\frac{1}{2} = \frac{3}{2}$, multiply $\frac{3}{4}$ by $\frac{3}{2}$. Multiply the numerators. Multiply the denominators.

$\frac{3}{4} \times \frac{3}{2} = \frac{3 \times 3}{4 \times 2} = \frac{9}{8}$

▶ Step 3

Write the product as a mixed number in simplest form.

$\frac{9}{8} = 1\frac{1}{8}$

So, $n = 1\frac{1}{8}$.

PRACTICE

Write a number sentence for the picture.

1.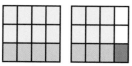
2.
3.

Draw fraction squares to help you find the product.

4. $\frac{3}{4} \times 1\frac{1}{6} = n$ 5. $\frac{2}{5} \times 3\frac{2}{3} = n$ 6. $\frac{2}{3} \times 2\frac{2}{5} = n$

7. $\frac{1}{4} \times 2\frac{1}{4} = n$ 8. $\frac{3}{5} \times 1\frac{1}{2} = n$ 9. $\frac{1}{3} \times 3\frac{2}{5} = n$

Multiply. Write the answer in simplest form.

10. $\frac{1}{4} \times 2\frac{1}{2} = n$ 11. $\frac{1}{2} \times 1\frac{1}{4} = n$ 12. $\frac{1}{2} \times 2\frac{2}{3} = n$

13. $\frac{2}{3} \times 1\frac{1}{3} = n$ 14. $\frac{1}{4} \times 1\frac{2}{3} = n$ 15. $\frac{2}{3} \times 3\frac{1}{4} = n$

16. $\frac{5}{6} \times 1\frac{1}{4} = n$ 17. $\frac{2}{5} \times 2\frac{1}{3} = n$ 18. $\frac{3}{4} \times 2\frac{1}{4} = n$

Mixed Applications

19. Holly had $3\frac{1}{2}$ pages of math homework to make up. She did $\frac{1}{3}$ of the pages before school this morning. How many pages did she do this morning?

20. Of 24 students who auditioned for the play, $\frac{2}{3}$ were chosen. How many students were chosen for the play?

21. During the weekend, Brad spent $8\frac{1}{3}$ hours helping his father in the yard. He worked $\frac{3}{5}$ of that time on Saturday. How long did he work on Saturday?

22. Lauren had $2\frac{1}{2}$ dozen apples. She used $\frac{1}{2}$ of them to make apple pies. How many dozen apples did she use in the pies?

23. Felicia has $50.00. CDs cost $13.99 each. How many CDs can Felicia buy?

24. Pang used a 3.6-meter board to make 4 shelves of equal length. How long was each shelf?

25. Carolyn used $1\frac{1}{2}$ yards of red ribbon, $2\frac{1}{4}$ yards of blue ribbon, and $1\frac{2}{3}$ yards of white ribbon for a crafts project. How many yards of ribbon did she use?

26. Lou and Leslie had $\frac{4}{5}$ package of glitter to use for their art project. They used $\frac{1}{5}$ package. How much glitter is left?

27. 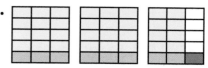 **Write a problem** in which you multiply a fraction by a mixed number.

LESSON CONTINUES

PART 2 PROBLEM-SOLVING STRATEGY
Make a Model

THE PROBLEM Barry bought a board that was $2\frac{3}{4}$ yards long to build a bookcase. He bought a board $\frac{1}{2}$ as long to build a shelf for his sports trophies. How much wood did he buy to make the shelf for his trophies?

REMEMBER:
☑ Understand
☑ Plan
☑ Solve
☑ Look Back

☑ Understand

- What are you asked to find?
- What information will you use?
- Is there information you will not use? If so, what?

☑ Plan

- What strategy can you use to solve the problem?

  You can *make a model* to find how much wood Barry bought to build the shelf.

☑ Solve

- What model will you make to solve the problem?

  You can draw fraction squares.

  Draw 3 squares, and divide them into fourths. Shade 2 whole squares and $\frac{3}{4}$ of the third square yellow. Divide the squares into halves. Shade $\frac{1}{2}$ of each square blue. Now 11 parts are shaded both blue and yellow, or green. Each whole has 8 parts. So, the total is $\frac{11}{8}$, or $1\frac{3}{8}$.

So, Barry bought $1\frac{3}{8}$ yards of wood to make the shelf.

☑ Look Back

- How can you decide if your answer is reasonable?
- What other strategy could you use?

PRACTICE

Make a model to solve.

1. Cole's dresser is $5\frac{1}{4}$ feet wide. His bookcase is $\frac{2}{3}$ as wide as his dresser. How wide is his bookcase?

2. The chickens laid $6\frac{1}{4}$ dozen eggs. The farmer sold $\frac{2}{5}$ of them. How many dozen eggs were left?

3. Meg made a square design. She colored $\frac{1}{4}$ of the square blue, $\frac{1}{8}$ yellow, and $\frac{1}{8}$ green. She left $\frac{1}{2}$ of the square white. What does her design look like?

4. Carl and some friends are in line to buy tickets to the school play. Carl is next to Bill. Sam is ahead of Carl. Bill is between Carl and Lana. Angela is before Sam. Who is last in line?

Mixed Applications

Solve.

CHOOSE A STRATEGY

• Find a Pattern • Write a Number Sentence • Guess and Check • Work Backward • Make a Model

5. Marla's pencil is 11 cm long. Chad's pencil is 1.2 dm long. Whose pencil is longer? How much longer?

6. The recycling center pays $0.28 a pound for aluminum. Neil has collected 69.5 pounds of aluminum. How much will he earn?

7. Ray had $18.79 in his wallet. He bought 2 magazines for $3.95 each and a book for $6.75. A package of pens costs $1.59. How many packages of pens can Ray buy?

8. Alice and Kyle are playing a number game. Alice asks Kyle to choose a number and multiply it by 3. Then Kyle adds 6, divides by 9, and subtracts 5. The total is 4. What number did Kyle start with?

9. Write the decimal for this model.
(HINT: 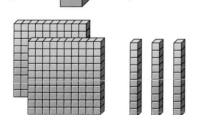 = 1)

10. Holly worked in her garden 20 minutes on Monday, 30 minutes on Tuesday, 45 minutes on Wednesday, and 65 minutes on Thursday. If the pattern continues, for how many minutes will she work in her garden on Friday? on Saturday?

11. Rachel has $4.75 in coins. She has 6 dimes and twice as many quarters. The rest are nickels. How many of each coin does she have?

CULTURAL CONNECTION

Immigrants from Luxembourg

Marie's mother gave her a family picture album with copies of photographs from 100 years ago. There were photographs of her great-great-great-grandparents, Charlotte and Charles, who had come to Illinois from Luxembourg in 1882. Next to the pictures was written the following information: "$\frac{3}{4}$ of Charlotte's brothers and sisters left Luxembourg the same year. She had 12 brothers and sisters." How many emigrated that year?

> **CULTURAL LINK**
>
> Luxembourg is a very small country, smaller than the state of Rhode Island. In the late 1800's, the farms were very small, and many farmers did not have enough land to divide among their children when they grew up. Some families sold their land and emigrated to other countries. By 1890, more than 35,000 people from Luxembourg had come to the United States to live. Many went to Illinois, Iowa, and Minnesota.

Work Together

1. Of Charles's brothers, $\frac{2}{3}$ left Luxembourg and came to the United States. Of those, $\frac{1}{2}$ went to Illinois. Find the fractional number of his brothers that went to Illinois.

2. Of the photographs in the album, $\frac{5}{8}$ were taken before 1960, and $\frac{1}{4}$ were taken before 1920. Find the fraction of photographs taken before 1920.

3. There were pictures of four generations of Marie's family in the album. Marie added pictures of herself. Her pictures filled $2\frac{1}{2}$ pages. Of her pictures, $\frac{3}{4}$ were baby pictures. What fractional part of the pages were filled with Marie's baby pictures? Write the answer in simplest form.

4. Marie made copies of some of the pictures in the album. She cut pieces of cardboard as backing for the pictures. She had a piece of cardboard that measured $1\frac{1}{3}$ yards. If she used $\frac{3}{4}$ yard of the cardboard piece, how much cardboard did she use? How much of the piece is left over?

✓ CHECK UNDERSTANDING

Write a number sentence for the picture. (pages 360–361, 364–365)

1.

2.

3.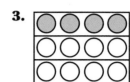

4.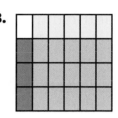

5.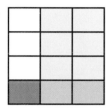

6.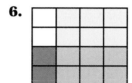

7.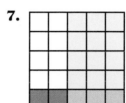

8.

✓ CHECK SKILLS

Multiply. Write the answer in simplest form. (pages 360–361, 364–367)

9. $\frac{1}{4} \times 28 = n$

10. $\frac{2}{5} \times 15 = n$

11. $21 \times \frac{2}{7} = n$

12. $16 \times \frac{5}{8} = n$

13. $\frac{1}{4} \times \frac{3}{8} = n$

14. $\frac{2}{3} \times \frac{5}{6} = n$

15. $\frac{4}{7} \times \frac{3}{8} = n$

16. $\frac{5}{9} \times \frac{4}{6} = n$

17. $\frac{1}{2} \times 1\frac{2}{3} = n$

18. $\frac{3}{4} \times 2\frac{1}{6} = n$

19. $\frac{1}{3} \times 3\frac{1}{3} = n$

20. $\frac{1}{4} \times 1\frac{1}{2} = n$

✓ CHECK PROBLEM SOLVING

Solve. (pages 368–369)

CHOOSE A STRATEGY

• Act It Out   • Make a Model   • Write a Number Sentence   • Find a Pattern   • Guess and Check

21. Paul had a board $4\frac{1}{2}$ feet long. He used $\frac{2}{3}$ of it to make a shelf. How long was the shelf?

22. Beth has $\frac{7}{8}$ yard of blue felt. She needs $\frac{2}{3}$ as much green felt. How much green felt does she need?

23. There were 70 students who wore school T-shirts on Monday. There were 75 on Tuesday and 85 on Wednesday. If this pattern continues, how many students will wear school T-shirts on Friday?

24. Buck has twice as many quarters as dimes. He has 5 fewer nickels than quarters. He has no pennies. He has 120 coins in all. How many of each coin does Buck have?

VOCABULARY CHECK

Choose a term from the box to complete each sentence.

WORD BANK
Celsius
Fahrenheit
precise

1. If you measure an object's length to the nearest sixteenth of an inch, you have made a __?__ measurement. (page 340)

2. Customary units for measuring temperature are called degrees __?__. (page 354)

3. Metric units for measuring temperature are called degrees __?__. (page 354)

STUDY AND SOLVE

CHAPTER 19

EXAMPLE

$$\frac{5}{6} - \frac{1}{3} = n$$

Use the LCD of $\frac{5}{6}$ and $\frac{1}{3}$ (sixths) to change the fractions to like fractions.

$$\frac{1}{3} \times \frac{2}{2} = \frac{2}{6}$$

Multiply by $\frac{2}{2}$.

$$\frac{5}{6} - \frac{2}{6} = \frac{3}{6}$$

Subtract.

$$n = \frac{3}{6} \div \frac{3}{3} = \frac{1}{2}$$

To write the answer in simplest form, divide the numerator and denominator by their GCF, 3.

Estimate the sum or difference.

(pages 310–311)

4. $\frac{4}{5} + \frac{2}{9}$ 5. $\frac{9}{10} - \frac{3}{5}$

Find the sum or difference. Write the answer in simplest form. (pages 312–317)

6. $\frac{3}{4} + \frac{3}{4} = n$ 7. $\frac{7}{8} - \frac{5}{8} = n$

8. $\frac{5}{8} + \frac{7}{12} = n$ 9. $\frac{5}{6} + \frac{2}{3} = n$

10. $\frac{9}{10} - \frac{2}{5} = n$ 11. $\frac{4}{5} - \frac{1}{3} = n$

Tell whether you would add or subtract to solve the problem. Solve. (pages 318–319)

12. One recipe calls for $\frac{3}{4}$ cup of flour. Another calls for $\frac{2}{3}$ cup of flour. How much more flour is needed for the first recipe?

CHAPTER 20

EXAMPLE

$$6\frac{2}{3} + 1\frac{5}{6} = n$$

The fractions are unlike. Use their LCD (sixths) to change them to like fractions.

$$\frac{2}{3} + \frac{5}{6} = \frac{4}{6} + \frac{5}{6}$$

$$\frac{4}{6} + \frac{5}{6} = \frac{9}{6}$$

Add the fractions.

$$6 + 1 = 7$$

Add the whole numbers.

$$7\frac{9}{6} = 8\frac{3}{6} = 8\frac{1}{2}$$

Write the answer in simplest form.

$$n = 8\frac{1}{2}$$

Estimate the sum or difference.

(pages 326–327)

13. $2\frac{3}{7} + 3\frac{11}{12} = n$ 14. $4\frac{1}{9} - 1\frac{7}{8} = n$

Find the sum or difference. Write the answer in simplest form. (pages 328–335)

15. $2\frac{1}{4} + 2\frac{1}{2} = n$ **16.** $2\frac{1}{3} + 3\frac{1}{6} = n$

17. $7\frac{3}{4} - 5\frac{1}{2} = n$ **18.** $4\frac{2}{3} - 3\frac{1}{6} = n$

Work backward to solve.

19. Amy's school day is 7 hours long. She spends 5 hours in class. Her lunch break is $1\frac{1}{4}$ hours long. How much time is left for other breaks?

CHAPTER 21

EXAMPLE

Change the unit.

36 in. = ___?___ ft   When you change smaller units to larger units, you divide.

36 in. = 3 ft   **Think:** 12 in. = 1 ft
Divide 36 by 12.

Use a customary ruler to measure the line. (pages 340–341)

20. _____

21. _____

Change the unit. (pages 342–349)

22. 12 ft = __?__ yd   **23.** 3 qt = __?__ c

24. 2 gal = __?__ qt   **25.** 3 lb = __?__ oz

26. 1 mi = __?__ ft   **27.** 1 T = __?__ lb

Find the sum or difference. (pages 344–345)

28. 7 ft 4 in.
   +3 ft 10 in.

29. 6 yd 1 ft
   −4 yd 2 ft

Write the time for each. (pages 350–351)

30. Start: 7:30 A.M.
   2 hr 15 min elapsed time
   End: __?__

31. Start: June 4, 5:00 P.M.
   __?__ time has elapsed
   End: June 11, 6:30 P.M.

Find the difference in temperature.
(pages 354–355)

32. high 75°F, low 56°F

33. high 12°C, low ⁻4°C

CHAPTER 22

EXAMPLE

$\frac{1}{3} \times 3\frac{1}{3}$ Rename the mixed number as a fraction greater than 1.

$\frac{1}{3} \times \frac{10}{3} = \frac{10}{9}$ Multiply the numerators and denominators.

$\frac{10}{9} = 1\frac{1}{9}$ Write the answer as a mixed number in simplest form.

Multiply. Write the answer in simplest form. (pages 360–367)

34. $16 \times \frac{3}{8} = n$ **35.** $\frac{4}{5} \times \frac{2}{3} = n$

36. $\frac{3}{4} \times \frac{8}{9} = n$ **37.** $\frac{1}{9} \times 6\frac{3}{4} = n$

Solve. (pages 368–369)

38. Ira had $5\frac{1}{2}$ pages of math homework to make up. He did $\frac{1}{2}$ of the work today. How many pages are left ?

WHAT DID I LEARN?

✏️ WRITE ABOUT IT

1. Estimate the sum or difference. Explain your methods. (pages 310–311)

$$\frac{1}{8} + \frac{5}{9} \qquad \frac{9}{10} - \frac{7}{8}$$

2. Show and explain each step as you find the sum. Write the answer in simplest form. (pages 328–329)

$$2\frac{3}{4} + 4\frac{1}{2}$$

3. Determine the elapsed time from 10:30 A.M. to 2:45 P.M. Explain your method. (pages 350-351)

4. Use fraction squares or multiply to find the product. Explain the method you use. Write the answer in simplest form. (pages 366–367)

$$\frac{1}{3} \times 3\frac{1}{4}$$

✔️ PERFORMANCE ASSESSMENT

Solve. Explain your method.

CHOOSE A STRATEGY

• Draw a Diagram • Make a Model • Make a Table • Work Backward

5. In the book club, $\frac{1}{2}$ of the students read sports books, $\frac{1}{4}$ read mysteries, $\frac{1}{8}$ read nature books, and $\frac{1}{8}$ read poetry. If 4 students read nature books, how many students are in the club? (pages 320–321)

6. David spent a total of $2\frac{1}{2}$ hours working in the yard. After raking the leaves, he spent $1\frac{1}{4}$ hours mowing, $\frac{1}{20}$ hour watering, and $\frac{1}{4}$ hour cleaning up. How much time did he spend raking? (pages 332–333)

7. Al gets home at 5:00. He plays for 45 minutes, reads for 60 minutes, helps his father cook dinner for 15 minutes, and eats dinner with his family for 30 minutes. Then he watches TV for 1 hour 30 minutes before going to bed. What time does he go to bed? (pages 352–353)

8. Todd picked $5\frac{1}{2}$ baskets of strawberries. His younger brother, Bo, picked $\frac{2}{3}$ as much as Todd. How many baskets did Bo pick? (pages 368–369)

CUMULATIVE REVIEW

Solve the problem. Then write the letter of the correct answer.

1. Compare. 209,897 ● 210,001

A. $<$ **B.** $>$
C. $=$ **D.** $-$ (pages 10–11)

---

2. 417
$\times 306$

A. 2,502
B. 15,012
C. 127,602
D. 1,276,020

(pages 92–93)

---

3. What is the best interval for this set of data?

10, 14, 8, 12, 18

A. 1   **B.** 2
C. 5   **D.** 10   (pages 144–145)

---

4. 6 cm = _?_ dm

A. 0.06   **B.** 0.6
C. 60   **D.** 600   (pages 232–235)

---

5. _?_ mL = 6 L

A. 0.006   **B.** 0.06
C. 600   **D.** 6,000   (pages 232–235)

---

6. Rename $\frac{23}{7}$ as a mixed number.

A. $\frac{7}{23}$ **B.** $1\frac{2}{7}$

C. 3   **D.** $3\frac{2}{7}$ (pages 248–249)

---

7. What is the greatest common factor of 16 and 24?

A. 2   **B.** 4
C. 8   **D.** 12

(pages 264–265)

---

8. What is the least common denominator for $\frac{2}{3}$ and $\frac{3}{4}$?

A. thirds   **B.** fourths
C. sevenths   **D.** twelfths

(pages 296–297)

For Problems 9–10, choose the correct answer that is in simplest form.

9. $\frac{1}{6} + \frac{1}{2} = n$ **A.** $n = \frac{1}{8}$ **B.** $n = \frac{1}{4}$

                 C. $n = \frac{2}{3}$ **D.** $n = \frac{4}{6}$

(pages 314–317)

---

10. $8\frac{7}{12} - 2\frac{1}{3} = n$

A. $n = 6\frac{1}{4}$ **B.** $n = 6\frac{3}{12}$

C. $n = \frac{75}{12}$ **D.** $n = 6\frac{2}{3}$

(pages 330–331)

---

11. 5 ft 6 in.
-3 ft 8 in.

A. 1 ft 4 in.
B. 1 ft 8 in.
C. 1 ft 10 in.
D. 2 ft 2 in.

(pages 344–345)

---

12. Choose the correct answer that is in simplest form.

$\frac{2}{9} \times \frac{3}{9} = n$

A. $n = \frac{2}{27}$ **B.** $n = \frac{6}{81}$

C. $n = \frac{2}{3}$ **D.** $n = \frac{81}{6}$

(pages 362–365)

PLANE FIGURES AND POLYGONS

DID YOU KNOW...

Ancient Egyptian geometers had to solve problems like accurately measuring fields after a flood. Odd-shaped fields were marked into triangles to make them easier to measure. Our word *geometry* comes from the Greek and means to "measure the earth."

Team-Up Time

Design a Geometry Game

Geometry is all about shapes and how you see them. Your group will design a game of Geometry Concentration. Use your observation skills to make picture cards and clue cards. Then play Geometry Concentration to test your visual memory.

YOU WILL NEED: 16 index cards, cut in half; triangle dot paper; scissors; glue.

Work with a group. Your job is to

- draw 16 geometric figures using triangle dot paper.

- cut out each figure and glue it to a card.

- on another set of cards, write attributes that would give someone clues about your figures.

- try out your game using the game rules, "How to Play Geometry Concentration."

- revise your game cards if you like.

- trade card sets with another group and play again.

DID YOU

- ☑ make a set of picture cards?

- ☑ make a set of clue cards?

- ☑ try out your game and revise it as needed?

- ☑ trade game cards and play again?

HOW TO PLAY GEOMETRY CONCENTRATION

Shuffle the picture cards and place them face down in a 4 by 4 array.

Shuffle the clue cards and lay them face down in a stack where all the players can reach them.

Play in groups of four. Take turns.

Each player picks a clue card. Turn up a picture card to see if it matches.

If the picture card is a match, you earn a point.

Return the picture card to its place but remember what it showed. You may want to choose it again later in the game.

The first player to earn 5 points wins the game.

I am a quadrilateral.

I have opposite sides that are parallel.

I have at least one right angle.

Line Relationships

You will learn about line relationships and geometric ideas.	Why learn this? You can identify points and line segments on maps such as those used by airline navigators, sailors, and astronauts.

WORD POWER

point
line
line segment
plane
intersecting
perpendicular
parallel

When astronauts explore space, they use geometric ideas. If they want to describe an exact location in space, they identify a geometric point. In the space around you, there are many geometric points.

A **Point** identifies a location on an object and in space. It is named by a letter.		point *B*
A **line** is a straight path in a plane. It has no end. It can be named by any two points on the line.		line *AB*, $\overleftrightarrow{AB}$ or line *BA*, $\overleftrightarrow{BA}$
A **line segment** is part of a line between two endpoints.		line segment *CA*, $\overline{CA}$ or line segment *AC*, $\overline{AC}$
A **plane** is a flat surface with no end. Planes are named by any three points in the plane.		plane *ABC*

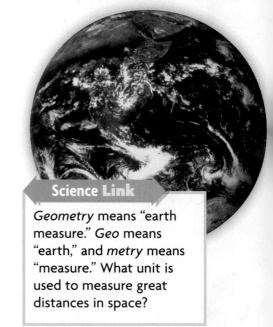

Science Link

Geometry means "earth measure." *Geo* means "earth," and *metry* means "measure." What unit is used to measure great distances in space?

Within a plane, lines can have different relationships.

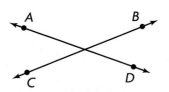

Lines that cross at one point are **intersecting** lines.

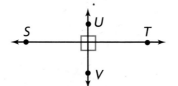

Lines that intersect to form four right angles are **perpendicular** lines.

Lines in a plane that never intersect and are the same distance apart at every point are **parallel** lines.

Talk About It  CRITICAL THINKING

- Are all intersecting lines perpendicular? Explain.

- How do you know that parallel lines will never intersect?

- What other line segments can you name that are in the plane *ABC* pictured above but are not drawn?

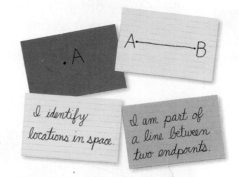

PRACTICE

For Exercises 1–4, use the figure.

1. Name the point where $\overline{AD}$ and $\overline{CD}$ intersect.

2. Name a line segment on plane ABC that is perpendicular to $\overline{DC}$.

3. Name a line segment on the plane that intersects but is not perpendicular to $\overline{AD}$.

4. Name the line segment that is parallel to $\overline{AD}$.

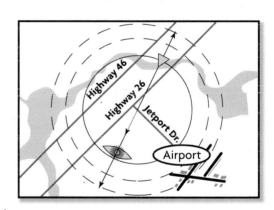

Identify each line relationship. Write *parallel, perpendicular,* or *intersecting.* Some figures may have more than one answer.

5.

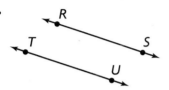

6.

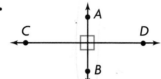

7.

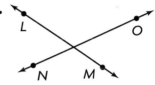

Mixed Applications

For Problems 8–9, use the flight navigation chart.

8. A pilot is using the flight navigation chart. He notices Highway 46 and Highway 26 near the airport. Describe the relationship of these two highways.

9. Describe the relationship of Jetport Dr. and Highway 26.

10. Kimberly is flying home. The flight is 320 miles. She has now flown $\frac{1}{4}$ of the trip. How many miles has she flown?

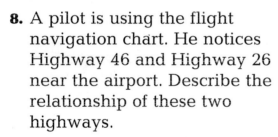

11. ✏️ **WRITE ABOUT IT** Explain what happens to two lines in the same plane that are not parallel.

Mixed Review

Change the unit. (pages 342–343)

12. 9 ft = __?__ yd

13. 2 ft = __?__ in.

14. 2 mi = __?__ yd

Find the product. (pages 362–363)

15. $\frac{1}{4} \times \frac{1}{2} = n$

16. $\frac{3}{8} \times \frac{2}{3} = n$

17. $\frac{3}{5} \times \frac{1}{5} = n$

18. $\frac{2}{3} \times \frac{1}{8} = n$

Rays and Angles

You will learn to identify different kinds of angles and line relationships.

Why learn this? You can use lines and angles when locating a point on Earth or in space.

WORD POWER

ray
angle

Scientists use rays and angles to locate points in space.

A **ray** is part of a line that has one endpoint and goes on forever in one direction. A ray is named by its endpoint and one other point on the ray.

Read: Ray *BC*
Write: $\overrightarrow{BC}$

When two rays have the same endpoint, they form an **angle**. An angle can be named by the vertex and one point on each ray, or by just the vertex.

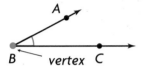

Read: angle *ABC*, or *CBA*, or angle *B* (the vertex must be the middle letter.)
Write: ∠*ABC*, ∠*CBA*, or ∠*B*

Talk About It

• Name the two rays that form angle *ABC*.

• Is a line segment part of a ray? Explain.

• Name some real things that suggest a ray.

Science Link

The National Radio Astronomy Observatory listens for sounds from outer space. The sound from an explosion that occurs in outer space reaches Earth as radio waves. Scientists use rays and angles to help them point their telescopes in the direction of the sound. How is the radio wave coming from an explosion in space like a ray?

Angles can be different sizes.

A **right** angle forms a square corner.

An **acute** angle is less than a right angle.

An **obtuse** angle is greater than a right angle.

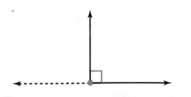
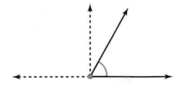
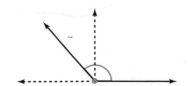

💡 **CRITICAL THINKING** Can an acute angle fit inside a right angle? Explain.

Check Your Understanding

For Exercises 1–4, use the figure.

1. Name the rays.

2. Name two acute angles.

3. Name a right angle.

4. Name an obtuse angle.

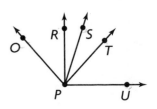

PRACTICE

Identify the angle. Write *right, acute,* or *obtuse.*

5.

6.

7.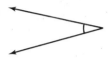

8.

9.

10.

11.

12.

For Exercises 13–20, use the figure. Identify the angle. Write *right, acute,* or *obtuse.*

13. ∠*BHE*

14. ∠*AHF*

15. ∠*DHE*

16. ∠*EHG*

17. ∠*DHA*

18. ∠*CHF*

19. ∠*CHA*

20. ∠*DHG*

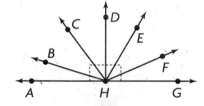

Mixed Applications

For Problems 21–22 and 24, use the drawing.

21. If the stars that make up the Little Dipper were labeled as shown, describe angle *BCD*.

22. Name an acute angle in the Little Dipper.

23. Astronomers divide the sky into 88 constellations. Kimberly has identified 11 constellations. What fraction of all constellations has she identified?

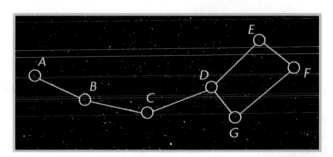

24. ▢➔ **Write a problem** using the information in the drawing of the Little Dipper.

Mixed Review

Find the sum or difference. Write the answer in simplest form. (pages 312–313)

25. $\frac{3}{5} + \frac{1}{5} = n$

26. $\frac{7}{8} - \frac{1}{8} = n$

27. $\frac{2}{9} + \frac{4}{9} = n$

Write the measurements in order from shortest to longest. (pages 226–227)

28. 10 m, 10 cm, 10 km

29. 4 dm, 4 cm, 4 mm

30. 3 km, 3 dm, 3 cm

HANDS ON

COOPERATIVE LEARNING

PART 1 Measuring Angles

You will investigate how to use a protractor to measure angles.	**Why learn this?** You can measure angles on a map or on plans when designing a room.	**WORD POWER** degree protractor

The unit used to measure an angle is called a **degree** (°). A circle is divided into 360 degrees (360°). A **protractor** is a tool for measuring the size of the opening of an angle. Its scale is marked from 0° to 180°. You can use a protractor to measure angle *ABC*.

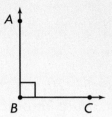

MODEL

▶ Step 1

Place the center of the protractor on the vertex of the angle.

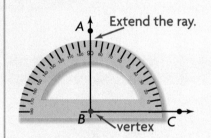

▶ Step 2

Line up the center point and the 0° mark on the protractor with one ray of the angle.

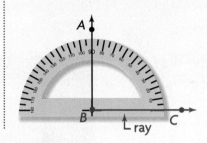

▶ Step 3

Read the measure of the angle where the other ray passes through the scale.

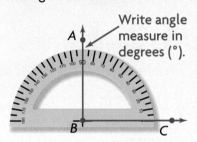

• If the rays are extended, will the angle measure change? Explain.

Explore

Use a protractor to measure angles *DEF* and *GHI*.

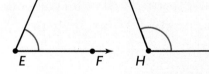

MATERIALS: protractor

Record

Trace the angles on a sheet of paper. Write the angle measurements in degrees (°). Explain how you found the measure of each angle.

Talk About It

• How many degrees are in a right angle?

• Does an acute angle measure less than or greater than 90°? an obtuse angle? Explain.

E–Lab • Activity 23 Available on CD-ROM and the Internet at http://www.hbschool.com/elab

Try This

Trace the angles below. Use a protractor to measure each angle. Record the angle measurement in degrees (°).

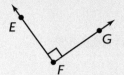
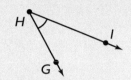
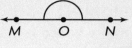

TALK ABOUT IT How many degrees are in straight angle *MON*? Why is this angle called a straight angle?

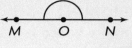

✏ WRITE ABOUT IT Explain how measuring the angles above is different from measuring the angles on page 382.

HANDS-ON PRACTICE

Trace each figure. Use a protractor to measure the angle.

1.
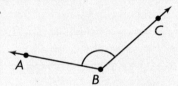

2.
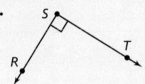

3.
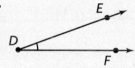

Mixed Applications

For Problems 4–6, use the airline map.

4. What is the measure of the angle formed by the airline routes with Dallas at the vertex?

5. Name the city at the vertex of an obtuse angle formed by the airline routes.

6. What is the measure of the angle from Portland to Denver to Miami?

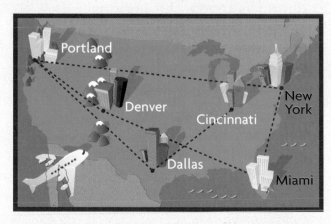

7. Andrew flew 1,238 miles from Denver to Portland. He returned to Denver, and one week later he made the same round-trip flight. How many miles did he travel on the two trips?

8. Karen started a paper route. The first week she got 1 new customer; the second week, 4; the third week, 7; the fourth week, 10. If the pattern continues, during which week will she have 40 new customers?

LESSON
CONTINUES ▶

MORE PRACTICE Student Handbook page H111

PART 2 PROBLEM-SOLVING STRATEGY
Draw a Diagram

THE PROBLEM Aunt Claire called to invite Sonia's family to her new home for the weekend. Sonia made a map from her aunt's directions. How did the map look?

REMEMBER:
☑ Understand
☑ Plan
☑ Solve
☑ Look Back

☑ Understand

- What are you asked to do?
- What information will you use?
- Is there information you will not use? If so, what?

☑ Plan

- How can you solve the problem?

  You can *draw a diagram* to make a map that will show the way to Aunt Claire's house. You will need a straightedge and a protractor.

> From your house, drive 3 blocks east. Make a 90° turn north onto Oak St. Drive 4 blocks north, and make a 90° turn west onto Elm St. Drive 1 block, and make a 45° turn onto the interstate ramp. Take the interstate north to Exit 83, and make a 45° turn onto the exit ramp. Then make a 135° turn to the west onto Ivy Lane. Drive 2 blocks to my new house.

☑ Solve

- Draw the diagram on grid paper. Mark the top of the paper as *north*, the bottom as *south*, the left as *west*, and the right as *east*. Start by drawing Sonia's house at the intersection of two lines. Follow the directions to Aunt Claire's house. At each turn, use a protractor to find the angle measure of the turn. Label the street names.

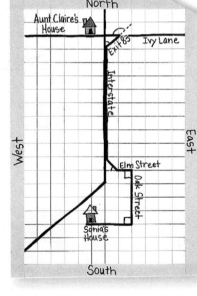

☑ Look Back

- How does drawing a diagram help you solve the problem?
- What other strategy could you use?

PRACTICE

Draw a diagram to solve.

1. Michael and Chris are making plans to watch the shuttle launch. Michael gives Chris the directions to the viewing area. Make a map of Michael's directions.

2. Donald is making a coat rack, using a piece of wood that is 3 feet long. He hammers a nail into the wood every 3 inches. He does not put nails on the ends. Use grid paper. Allow 1 space to equal 1 inch. How many nails does Donald use?

3. Michelle dug 12 holes to plant trees in a circle. If she skips 2 holes after each tree she plants, will she plant all 12 trees before coming back to the first one?

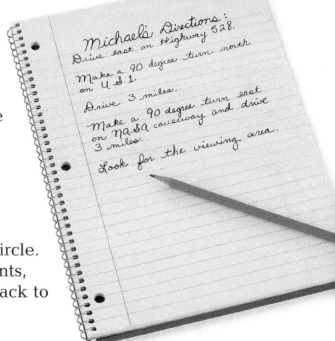

Mixed Applications

Solve.

CHOOSE A STRATEGY

• Write a Number Sentence   • Use a Schedule   • Make a Model   • Draw a Diagram

4. Mr. Levy's class went on a field trip. How long was Mr. Levy's class away from school? How much time was spent at the science center?

Activity	Starting Time	Ending Time
Travel to center	8:40	9:10
Exhibits	9:10	11:00
Planetarium	11:00	11:45
Lunch	11:45	12:30
Travel to school	12:30	1:00

5. Calculate the time that Mr. Levy's class spent traveling from school to the science center, and from the science center back to school. What was the total travel time?

6. Charmaine bought $\frac{1}{2}$ yard of red fabric, $\frac{3}{4}$ yard of white fabric, and $\frac{1}{8}$ yard of blue fabric. How much fabric did she buy altogether?

7. Nathan, Holly, and Darrell live on different floors of a 3-story apartment building. Nathan does not live on the second or third floor. Holly does not live on the first or second floor. Who lives on each floor?

8. Karl sold newspapers. He collected $4.20 in coins. He had only nickels, dimes, and quarters. He had 4 nickels and 5 times as many dimes as nickels. How many quarters did he have?

Classifying Quadrilaterals

You will learn to name and classify quadrilaterals.

Why learn this? You will be able to identify quadrilaterals in everyday objects.

WORD POWER

quadrilaterals
trapezoid
parallelogram
rhombus

Quadrilaterals are polygons with 4 sides and 4 angles. Quadrilaterals can be grouped and named by the characteristics of their sides and angles.

general quadrilateral	trapezoid	parallelogram	rectangle	rhombus	square
4 sides of any length	1 pair of parallel sides	2 pairs of congruent sides	2 pairs of congruent sides	4 congruent sides	4 congruent sides
4 angles of any size		2 pairs of parallel sides	4 right angles	2 pairs of congruent angles	4 right angles

Talk About It

• Which quadrilaterals have 4 right angles?

• Which quadrilaterals have all sides congruent?

• How are a square and a rectangle alike? How are they different?

You can use a tangram to make quadrilaterals. A tangram is an ancient Chinese puzzle.

Trace the seven pieces of the tangram. Cut out the pieces. Rearrange all seven pieces to form as many different quadrilaterals as you can. Name them.

PRACTICE

Draw and name the quadrilateral.

1. opposite sides are parallel; 2 pairs of congruent sides; 2 pairs of congruent angles

2. one pair of parallel sides

3. four sides congruent and four right angles

4. four sides congruent; 2 pairs of congruent angles

Write *true* or *false*.

5. A trapezoid has 4 sides congruent.

6. A rhombus has 4 sides congruent.

7. A square has 2 acute and 2 obtuse angles.

8. A parallelogram has 2 pairs of parallel sides.

9. A general quadrilateral can have sides of any length.

10. All 4-sided polygons are quadrilaterals.

Mixed Applications

11. The line between the bases on a softball field measures 60 feet. Rebecca hit 3 home runs in a game. She ran from home plate to each of the 3 bases and back home for each home run. What is the total number of feet she ran in the game?

12. Patricia is making a quilt. She cut fabric into 540 squares and rectangles. There are 120 more squares than rectangles. How many squares and rectangles are in the quilt?

13. Matt ran the perimeter of a field. He ran 175 feet to the west, turned 90° north, and ran 140 feet. He then turned east and ran 175 feet. He turned 90° south and ran 140 feet. How many feet did he run? What shape was the field?

14. ▱ **Write a problem** using the information that Jon's swimming pool is 30 feet long and 16 feet wide.

 ixed Review

Find the sum. (pages 282–283)

15. $\frac{1}{4} + \frac{2}{3} = n$

16. $\frac{2}{5} + \frac{3}{10} = n$

17. $\frac{1}{5} + \frac{1}{3} = n$

Write *multiply* or *divide*. Then write the equivalent measurement. (pages 234–235)

18. 80 mm = __?__ cm

19. 2.25 m = __?__ cm

20. 4,000 mg = __?__ g

Classifying Triangles

You will learn to classify triangles by the lengths of their sides.	Why learn this? You can recognize different triangular shapes by comparing the lengths of their sides.	WORD POWER isosceles scalene equilateral

Triangles can be classified according to the lengths of their sides.

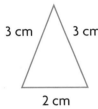

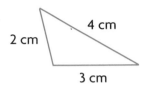

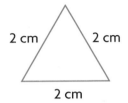

REMEMBER:
A triangle has three sides and three angles.

A triangle with two congruent sides is an **isosceles** triangle.

A triangle in which each side is a different length is a **scalene** triangle.

A triangle with all congruent sides is an **equilateral** triangle.

Talk About It

• A regular polygon has congruent sides and angles. Which triangle is a regular polygon?

• Which of the three triangles is seen most often in everyday life? Why?

Check Your Understanding 🔆 CRITICAL THINKING

Name each triangle. Write *isosceles*, *scalene*, or *equilateral*.

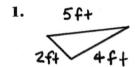

1. 5 ft 2 ft 4 ft

2. 3 yd 3 yd 3 yd

3.  1 in. 3 in. 3 in.

4. 4 ft 3 ft 2 ft

Measure the sides. Classify each triangle. Write *isosceles*, *scalene*, or *equilateral*.

5.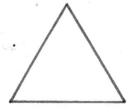

6.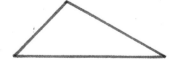

7.

PRACTICE

Name each triangle. Write *isosceles*, *scalene*, or *equilateral*.

8.
8 in.
8 in
3 in.

9.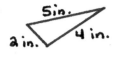
5 in.
2 in.
4 in.

10.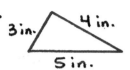
3 in.
4 in.
5 in.

11.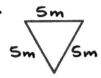
5 m
5 m
5 m

12.
4 m
4 m
2 m

13.
3 m
4 m
2 m

14.
4 ft
4 ft
2 ft

15.
4 ft
4 ft
4 ft

16.
3 ft
4 ft
1 ft

Measure the sides. Classify each triangle. Write *isosceles*, *scalene*, or *equilateral*.

17.

18.

19.

Mixed Applications

20. Margaret was tiling a kitchen wall. She counted 150 pieces in the tile design. She said $\frac{1}{2}$ of the tiles were triangles, $\frac{1}{3}$ tiles were squares, and the rest were rectangles. How many tiles were rectangles?

21. A spacecraft 200 miles high travels at a speed of 17,000 miles per hour. At 22,000 miles high, it travels at 6,900 miles per hour. What is the difference in the speeds?

22. Gwen rode her bike 1 mile north, $1\frac{1}{2}$ miles southeast, and $1\frac{1}{8}$ miles to where she started. How far did Gwen ride her bike? What shape triangle did she make?

23. Kim bought a radio that regularly sells for $129.95. She got an employee discount of $12.99. How much did Kim pay for the radio?

24. Keith drew an equilateral triangle. By drawing one more line, how can he divide the triangle into two smaller triangles that each have a right angle?

25. **Write a problem** in which you have to classify a triangle. Give the dimensions of the triangle.

LESSON CONTINUES

More About Classifying Triangles

Triangles can be classified according to the measure of their angles.

A triangle that has a right angle is a **right triangle**.

A triangle that has three acute angles is an **acute triangle**.

A triangle that has one obtuse angle is an **obtuse triangle**.

Talk About It 🔦 CRITICAL THINKING

• How can you classify a triangle as acute or obtuse without measuring the angles?

• Can a right triangle have more than 1 right angle?

• Can an obtuse triangle have more than 1 obtuse angle?

• Can an acute triangle have more than 1 acute angle?

• Why can a right triangle never be equilateral?

🔵 In *Mighty Math Number Heroes*, the game *GeoComputer* challenges you to classify triangles on the geoboard.

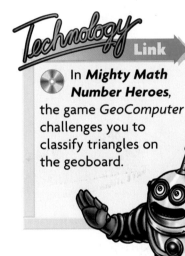

Measure the angles to determine the sum of the angles in any triangle.

A. Trace the triangle shown at the right. Label each vertex. Cut out the triangle. Tear the corners as shown. Place the angles together at a point on a straight line. What is the sum of the angle measures?

• How can you check the angle measures?

B. Trace the 3 triangles at the top of the page. Use a protractor to measure the angles in each triangle, and find the sum of the angles.

✏️ **WRITE ABOUT IT** What rule can you write about the sum of the angle measures in a triangle?

• If you did not know the measure of angle C, how could you find it?

PRACTICE

Name each triangle. Write *right*, *acute*, or *obtuse*.

1.

2.

3.

4.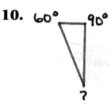

5.

6.

> **Science Link**
>
> The shape of an airplane's wing helps determine how much "lift" is needed to get the plane off the ground.
>
> What kind of triangle do the wings of this plane suggest?
>
>

Find the measure of the unknown angle in each triangle.

7.

45° 90° ?

8.

? 30° 30°

9.

60° 60° ?

10.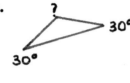

60° 90° ?

11.

95° ? 25°

12.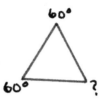

35° 110° ?

Mixed Applications

13. Isabel began working on her drawing at 9:00. She worked for 2 hours 35 minutes. Then she spent 30 minutes eating lunch and 45 minutes visiting a friend. She then spent 1 hour 15 minutes completing her drawing. At what time was she done?

14. ✏️ **WRITE ABOUT IT** Explain the difference between the three types of triangles—right triangle, acute triangle, and obtuse triangle.

Mixed Review

Copy and complete each pattern. (pages 210–211)

15. $200 \div 5 = n$
$20 \div 5 = n$
$2 \div 5 = n$

16. $800 \div 4 = n$
$80 \div 4 = n$
$8 \div 4 = n$

17. $1,500 \div 6 = n$
$150 \div 6 = n$
$15 \div 6 = n$

Choose the most reasonable unit. Write *kg*, *g*, or *mg*. (pages 228–229)

18. a cat   **19.** a bag of potatoes   **20.** a feather   **21.** a nickel

MATH FUN!

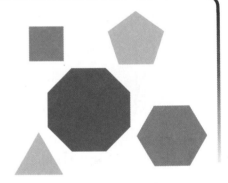

Geometry Scavenger Hunt

PURPOSE To practice classifying polygons and other plane figures

YOU WILL NEED paper and pencil

Work with your group to find examples of the figures on page H26. Look around your classroom and school. Draw the figure and describe where you found it. Is it one face of a solid object? See if your group can find all of the figures.

HOME NOTE Look for geometric shapes in furniture, buildings, and cars. What shape do you see most frequently?

PATTERNS IN POLYGONS

PURPOSE To measure angles on polygons

YOU WILL NEED protractor, ruler

These polygons have sides that are all the same lengths. Measure the angles in each polygon. Record your measurements on a chart. Describe any patterns you observe. Does the octagon have larger or smaller angles than the hexagon?

Ladders for Safe Carpenters

PURPOSE To measure the angles on a triangle

YOU WILL NEED centimeter grid paper, centimeter ruler, protractor

Did you ever notice that a ladder leaning against a wall makes a triangle? A safe ladder must be placed so the horizontal distance at the bottom is at least one fourth the length of the ladder. Make a model of an 8-ft ladder that is 8 cm long. Place this model on cm grid paper. Draw triangles showing a safe ladder and an unsafe ladder.

What angle does this ladder form with the ground? Is this ladder a safe ladder?

✓ CHECK UNDERSTANDING

VOCABULARY

1. The unit used to measure an angle is a(n) __?__. (page 382)

2. The tool for measuring the size of an angle is a(n) __?__. (page 382)

3. A triangle with all congruent sides is a(n) __?__ triangle. (page 388)

4. A triangle with two congruent sides is a(n) __?__ triangle. (page 388)

For Exercises 5–7, use the figure. (pages 378–383)

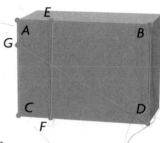

5. Name the point where $\overline{AC}$ and $\overline{AB}$ intersect.

6. Name the line segment that is parallel to $\overline{CD}$.

7. Name a line segment that intersects but is not perpendicular or parallel to $\overline{GD}$.

8. How many degrees are in the three angles of a triangle?

✓ CHECK SKILLS

Classify each figure. (pages 380–381 and 390–391)

9.

10.

11.

12.

13.

14.

 __?__ angle   __?__ angle   __?__ angle   __?__ triangle   __?__ triangle   __?__ triangle

Name the quadrilateral. Write *trapezoid, parallelogram, rectangle, rhombus,* or *square.* (pages 386–387)

15.

16.

17.

18.

✓ CHECK PROBLEM SOLVING

Solve. (pages 384–385)

CHOOSE A STRATEGY

• Write a Number Sentence   • Work Backward   • Make a Model   • Draw a Diagram

19. Eric said, "go 3 blocks east from school and make a 90° turn north. Go 4 blocks and make a 45° turn west." Draw a map to Eric's house.

20. For 24 years, Mike has eaten 3 meals a day. About how many meals has he eaten in that time?

CHAPTER 24

TRANSFORMATIONS, CONGRUENCE, AND SYMMETRY

DID YOU KNOW....

Many of the names given to quilt patterns reflect the ways families lived 150 years ago.

Pioneers heading west might have made a "Windmill" or "Mow the Lawn" quilt.

Team-Up Time

A Transformation Quilt

If you made a quilt to reflect a detail of your life, what would you call it? Quilt squares can be exciting geometric designs. They also can tell a story. Your group will design a quilt square, and create three more squares by flipping, sliding, and turning the original square.

YOU WILL NEED: grid paper, ruler, markers or colored pencils, scissors, glue

Work with a group. Your job is to

- analyze one of the designs shown. Find a line of symmetry. Look for a flip, a slide, and a turn.

- design one fourth of a quilt square on grid paper, and make three copies.

- put the four pieces together, using flips, slides, or turns.

HOW TO ORGANIZE A SQUARE

Quilt squares are organized in a 2 x 2 grid, like a tic-tac-toe board. Each square in the grid is filled with squares, rectangles, or triangles.

DID YOU

☑ analyze designs for flips, slides, and turns?

☑ design a quilt square of your own?

☑ identify flips, slides, and turns in your quilt square?

Testing for Congruence

You will learn how to test for congruence.

Why learn this? You can be sure quilt pieces or pieces of a model you are building are congruent.

Mr. Wade makes birdhouses. When he cuts out the pieces of wood, he makes sure they match his plans exactly. For example, the sides and angles of each front piece must be congruent to the sides and angles of *all* front pieces. Mr. Wade tests the pieces that he cuts out to see if they are congruent.

Here are two methods he can use to test for congruency.

Method 1	Method 2
Place the same kind of pieces on top of one another. Make sure each piece is turned the same way. 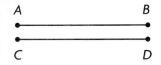	Use a ruler to measure the lengths of each side and a protractor to measure the size of each angle. 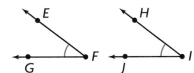

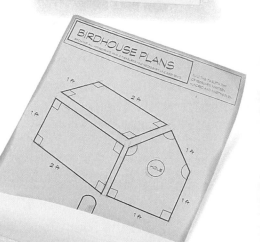

BIRDHOUSE PLANS

- When might Method 2 be used instead of Method 1? Why?

EXAMPLES

Congruent line segments

A   B

C   D

Congruent angles

E H

G F J I

Congruent figures

X Y

Check Your Understanding   💡 CRITICAL THINKING

Use a ruler and a protractor to test each pair of figures for congruency. Write *congruent* or *not congruent*.

1.

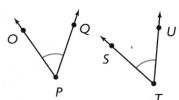

O Q U

S

P T

2.

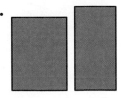

3.

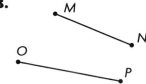

M

N

O

P

PRACTICE

Write *congruent* or *not congruent.*

4.

5.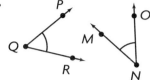

6.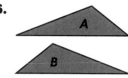

Write the letters of the two figures that are congruent.

7. a.   **b.**   **c.**

8. a. 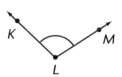   **b.**   **c.**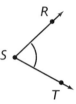

9. a. 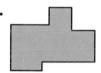   **b.**   **c.**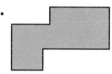

Mixed Applications

For Problems 10–13, use the drawing.

10. Mr. Dean is building a bookcase. He cut out seven pieces of wood. Name the pairs of pieces that are congruent.

11. What kind of angle is angle *EGH*?

12. What is the perimeter of the bottom piece?

13. ✏️ **Write a problem** about the relationship of line segment *EF* to line segment *GH*.

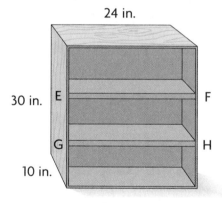

Mixed Review

Write *true* or *false.* (pages 386–387)

14. A rectangle has 2 acute angles and 2 obtuse angles.

15. A parallelogram has 2 pairs of parallel sides.

Find the quotient. Check by multiplying. (pages 216–217)

16. $5\overline{)3.55}$ **17.** $3\overline{)3.09}$ **18.** $8\overline{)2.48}$ **19.** $6\overline{)6.42}$

Congruence and Symmetry

You will learn to identify multiple lines of symmetry in a figure or an object.

Why learn this? You can recognize symmetry in nature and in designs on art, wallpaper, and fabrics.

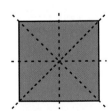

A *line of symmetry* divides a figure so that two parts of the figure are congruent.

Cindy's class is making T-shirt designs. Patterns are placed on the fold of decal paper, traced, and cut out. Then the new design is ironed onto the T-shirt. How many lines of symmetry does the butterfly have?

Place the pattern on the fold of the paper. Trace the pattern and cut it out.	Unfold the paper. Color the design.
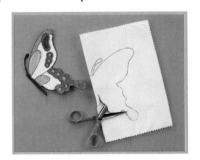	

So, the butterfly has one line of symmetry.

• How do you know that the two halves of the butterfly are congruent?

REMEMBER:

A figure has *point symmetry* if it can be turned about a central point and still look the same.

A figure has *line symmetry* if it can be folded on a line so that its two parts are congruent.

A figure can have more than one line of symmetry. Find as many lines of symmetry for a square as you can.

Fold it in half in different ways so that the two halves are congruent.

• How many lines of symmetry did you find?

Check Your Understanding 💡 CRITICAL THINKING

Trace each figure. Draw the lines of symmetry. How many lines of symmetry does each figure have?

1.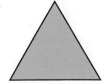

2.

3.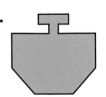

4.

PRACTICE

Tell whether the two halves of each drawing are congruent.
Write *yes* or *no*.

5.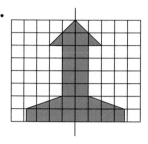

6.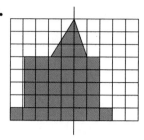

7.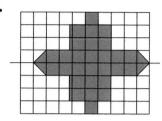

Trace each figure. Draw the lines of symmetry for each figure.

8.

9.

10.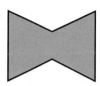

11.

Mixed Applications

For Problems 12–14, use the sign at the right.

12. Elianne likes the quilt design that has both point and line symmetry. Which design does she like better?

13. John likes the star design better. How many lines of symmetry are in the star design? the basket design?

14. Betsy has $\frac{1}{5}$ of the money she needs to buy her favorite quilt. She has $18. Which quilt is she planning to buy?

15. ✏️ **WRITE ABOUT IT** How do you find out if a figure has symmetry?

Mixed Review

Name each triangle. Write *right*, *acute*, or *obtuse*. (pages 390–391)

16.

17.

18.

Add or subtract. Write the answer in simplest form. (pages 312–313)

19. $\frac{5}{12} + \frac{3}{12} = n$

20. $\frac{7}{8} - \frac{2}{8} = n$

21. $\frac{4}{9} + \frac{2}{9} = n$

22. $\frac{9}{10} - \frac{3}{10} = n$

MORE PRACTICE Student Handbook page H113

Transformations on the Coordinate Grid

You will investigate how to transform a figure on the coordinate grid.	**Why learn this?** You can use ordered pairs to locate an object in a new position.	**WORD POWER** transformation

When you move a figure to show a translation, reflection, or rotation, it is called a **transformation**. You can transform a figure on a coordinate grid.

Explore

Use the ordered pairs, (1,2), (2,5), and (5,2), as the vertices to draw this triangle. Move the triangle to show a *translation*, a *reflection*, and a *rotation*. Name the ordered pairs that give the new location for the triangle.

MATERIALS: coordinate grids

A. Translation

Slide the figure 3 spaces to the right and 3 spaces up.

New ordered pairs: (4,5), (5,8), (?,?)

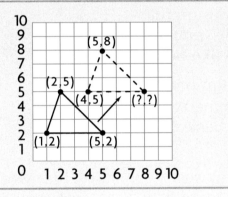

B. Reflection

Flip the figure across the line.

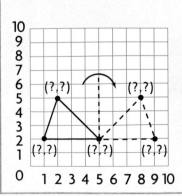

C. Rotation

Turn a figure around a point or vertex. Make the point at (1,2) end at (5,6).

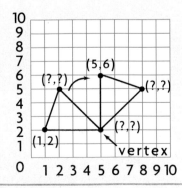

REMEMBER:

You can use two numbers to locate points on a grid. The two numbers are called an *ordered pair*.

EXAMPLE: (1,2) represents 1 space to the right of zero and 2 spaces up.

When you slide a figure, it is a *translation*.

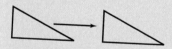

When you flip a figure over a line, it is a *reflection*.

When you turn a figure around a point, or vertex, it is a *rotation*.

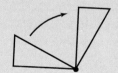

Technology **Link** ➤
E–Lab • Activity 24 Available on CD-ROM
and the Internet at http://www.hbschool.com/elab

Record

Draw the original triangle and label the ordered pairs for each point. Then draw each new figure to show a *translation*, a *reflection*, and a *rotation*. Write the new ordered pairs.

Technology Link

In *Mighty Math Number Heroes*, the game *GeoComputer* challenges you to make transformations on the geoboard.

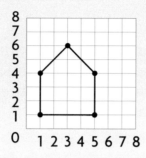

Try This

Use coordinate grids to draw the figure at the right. Label the ordered pairs for each point. Then draw a new figure to show a *translation*, a *reflection*, and a *rotation*. Label the drawings. Record the new ordered pairs.

TALK ABOUT IT How did you move the figure to show a translation? a reflection? a rotation?

WRITE ABOUT IT Explain how you found the new ordered pairs for the rotation.

HANDS-ON PRACTICE

Copy each figure on a coordinate grid. Translate, reflect, and rotate each figure. Draw the new figure. Name the ordered pairs.

1.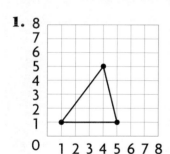

2.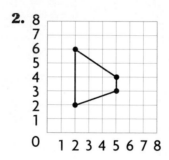

3.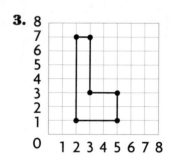

Mixed Applications

4. Kaitlin is rearranging her furniture. The new ordered pairs for the location of the couch are (6,5), (2,5), (2,6), and (6,6). Use a coordinate grid to draw the figure representing the couch in its new location. Explain how the figure was moved.

5. Jesse began studying at 10:45 A.M. He took a 25-minute break for lunch. He finished at 2:20 P.M. How long was Jesse studying?

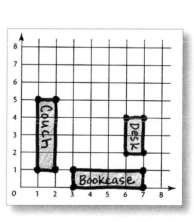

PART 1 Tessellations

You will learn to transform a figure to make a tessellation.	Why learn this? You can use tessellations to make designs such as those used on walls, floors, and fabrics.	WORD POWER tessellation

When closed figures are arranged in a repeating pattern to cover a surface that has no gaps and no overlaps, it is called a **tessellation**. Look at the examples below and name the figures.

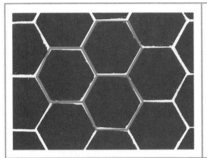

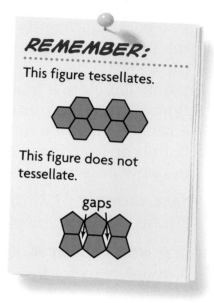

REMEMBER:
This figure tessellates.

This figure does not tessellate.

gaps

- How do you know that the figures in each example make a tessellation?

You can make a tessellation by transforming a figure. Follow these steps to make your own tessellation.

MODEL

Step 1
Draw these figures.

Step 2
Cut out the figures. Translate, reflect, or rotate the figures. Trace them to cover a surface with no gaps and no overlaps.

Step 3
Color or draw on your tessellation.

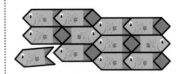

Talk About It

- What figures were used to begin the tessellation in Step 1?

- What transformations were used in Step 2?

PRACTICE

Copy each figure. Write *yes* or *no* to tell whether each figure can be arranged to tessellate.

1.

2.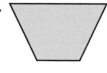

3.

4.

5.

6.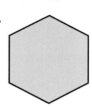

Copy each figure and translate, reflect, or rotate it to make a design that tessellates.

7.

8.

9.

10.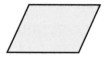

Copy the tiles and make a design that tessellates. Repeat the design 4 times to make a tessellation.

11.

12.

Mixed Applications

13. Devon is buying 12-inch square tiles for $2.35 each. He wants to cover his kitchen floor. It is 10 ft long and 8 ft wide. How many tiles will he need? What will they cost?

14. Quan bought 72 tiles. When he finished tiling the floor, $\frac{1}{6}$ of the tiles were not used. How many tiles did he have left?

15. Mandy is using square and octagonal tiles to cover her kitchen floor. Draw the design that Mandy will have on her kitchen floor.

16. ✏️ **WRITE ABOUT IT** Describe the ways that you can move a figure to make a tessellation.

LESSON CONTINUES ▶

MORE PRACTICE Student Handbook page H114

PART 2 PROBLEM-SOLVING STRATEGY
Make a Model

THE PROBLEM Matt's art class is making place mats for the Student-Parent Association Dinner. The place mats must have a mosaic design using two or more polygons. The design must cover the place mat. How can Matt determine which polygons will tessellate to make his design?

REMEMBER:
- ☑ Understand
- ☑ Plan
- ☑ Solve
- ☑ Look Back

☑ Understand

- What are you asked to do?

- What information will you use?

- Is there information you will not use? If so, what?

☑ Plan

- How can you solve the problem?

  You can *make a model* of the design to see if it will tessellate, or cover the surface. Then trace the design onto the place mat.

☑ Solve

- Use pattern blocks to make designs until you find one that tessellates. Trace the design onto the place mat. Color and decorate the design.

☑ Look Back

- How does making a model help you solve the problem?

- What other strategy could you use?

404 Chapter 24

PRACTICE

Make a model to solve.

1. Miguel is making a tile tray with a mosaic design. He can use two or more polygons. The polygons need to tessellate in order to cover the tray. Use pattern blocks to make a design that tessellates. Draw the design.

2. Rebecca has pattern blocks that are small equilateral triangles, small squares, and hexagons. Which two of these blocks will tessellate when arranged in a design? Draw the design.

3. The Harpers want to fence in a rectangular area of their yard. They have 60 meters of fence to use. What dimensions should the fence be to give the greatest possible area?

4. Of the art projects on display, $\frac{1}{4}$ were made by third-graders, $\frac{1}{2}$ were made by fourth-graders, and $\frac{1}{4}$ were made by fifth-graders. There were 16 projects made by fourth-graders. How many projects were made by fifth-graders?

Mixed Applications

Solve.

CHOOSE A STRATEGY

• **Make a Graph**   • **Write a Number Sentence**   • **Work Backward**   • **Make a Model**   • **Draw a Diagram**

5. Peggy needs a new design for a quilt she is making. She wants it to include 2 or more polygons. Use pattern blocks to make a design that tessellates for Peggy's quilt. Draw your design.

6. Mr. Jackson gave directions to the hardware store. He said to drive 5 blocks east from your house and make a 90° turn north. Drive 6 blocks north. Make a 45° turn east onto Clay Street. Go 3 blocks east, and the store is on the right. Make a map of these directions.

7. Erin spent half her money for a pair of jeans. Then she spent half of what was left for a shirt. After that, she had $8.50 left. How much did she have at the start?

8. The afghan Lana made is 4 ft $1\frac{1}{2}$ in. wide and 5 ft $3\frac{1}{2}$ in. long. What is the perimeter of the afghan?

9. Jerry kept a chart of the high temperatures each day for five days. Show a different way to display the information that is in the table. Explain your choice of display.

High Temperatures

Jan. 5	54°
Jan. 6	62°
Jan. 7	64°
Jan. 8	50°
Jan. 9	48°

CULTURAL CONNECTION

A POLISH CASTLE

Mary's grandparents immigrated to the United States from Poland 45 years ago. Mary enjoys looking through their photograph album and listening to their stories about their trips back to Poland. Look at the picture below of Wawel Castle in Kraków, Poland. Find as many congruent figures as you can.

CULTURAL LINK

Both Poland and the United States have herds of bison in national parks. Poland's bison can be seen in Bialowieza National Park. In the early 1900's, all the wild bison in Poland were killed by hungry soldiers. In 1929, zoos from other countries sent six bison to Poland to start a new herd. Today about 300 bison share the 300,000-acre park with other wild animals.

Work Together

1. Look at the picture of Wawel Castle again. Which figures have symmetry? Tell whether they have point or line symmetry or both.

2. Describe the lines of symmetry that you find in this picture of Polish dancers.

3. Use pattern blocks to make a row of six diamonds arranged like the ones on the dancer's jacket. Make a tessellation of the diamonds by using more pattern blocks. Draw your tessellation on paper.

4. Draw a diamond on a coordinate grid by using the ordered pairs (1,2), (3,4), (5,2), (3,0). Make a translation of the diamond on the grid. Record the new ordered pairs.

✓ CHECK UNDERSTANDING

VOCABULARY

1. When you move a figure to show a translation, reflection, or rotation, it is called a __?__ . (page 400)

2. When closed figures are arranged to cover a surface with no gaps and no overlaps, it is called a __?__ . (page 402)

Write *congruent* or *not congruent*. (pages 396–397)

3.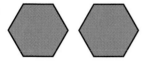

4.

5.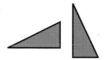

Copy each figure on a coordinate grid. Then show a translation for 6, a reflection for 7, and a rotation for 8. Name the new ordered pairs. (pages 400–401)

6.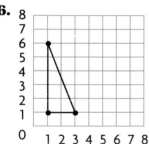

7.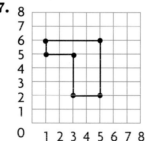

8.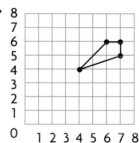

✓ CHECK SKILLS

Trace each figure. Draw the lines of symmetry for each figure. (pages 398–399)

Copy each figure. Write *yes* or *no* to tell whether each figure tessellates. (pages 402–403)

9.

10.

11.

12.

✓ CHECK PROBLEM SOLVING

Solve. (pages 404–405)

CHOOSE A STRATEGY

• Write a Number Sentence   • Work Backward   • Make a Model   • Draw a Diagram

13. Kathy is making a quilt with hexagons and triangles. Trace pattern blocks to show how her design might look.

14. Mr. Cox paid $28.95 for wood and $2.03 tax. How much change did he receive if he gave the clerk two $20 bills?

25 CIRCLES

DID YOU KNOW...

Sections of tree trunks were humans' first wheels. Heavy loads were dragged on top of tree trunks.

By 3,500 B.C., the Sumerians in the Tigris-Euphrates Valley were using carts with wheels attached to axles.

Team-Up Time

The Wondrous Wheel

Can you imagine a world without the wheel? For centuries, people have put these special cylinders to work. Work with your group to learn about wheels.

YOU WILL NEED: reference books, poster board, markers

Work with a group. Your job is to

- choose a focus area. Look at the list to the right for ideas.

- do your research. Find, and record, several interesting facts about wheels.

- decide how to present these facts to the class. Will you make a model? a poster? act it out?

- present your findings to the class.

The Wheel in Arts and crafts
potter's wheel
carpenter's lathe

The Wheel to Navigate
compass
steering wheels on ships, cars
gyroscope

Wheels in High-Tech
disk drives
CD players
knobs and dials

DID YOU

- ✓ choose a topic?
- ✓ find and record facts about wheels?
- ✓ choose a way to present your facts?
- ✓ present your facts to the class?

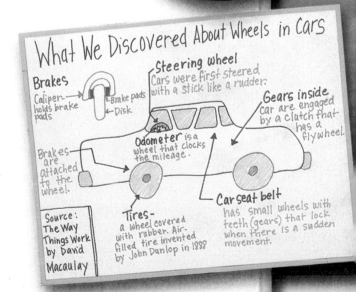

What We Discovered About Wheels in Cars

Brakes
Caliper- holds brake pads
Brake pads
Disk

Steering wheel
Cars were first steered with a stick like a rudder.

Gears inside car are engaged by a clutch that has a flywheel.

Odometer is a wheel that clocks the mileage.

Brakes are attached to the wheel.

Car seat belt has small wheels with teeth (gears) that lock when there is a sudden movement.

Source: The Way Things Work by David Macaulay

Tires- a wheel covered with rubber. Air-filled tire invented by John Dunlop in 1888

Construct a Circle

HANDS ON
COOPERATIVE LEARNING

You will investigate how to construct a circle and name its parts.	Why learn this? You can compare the sizes of bicycles by the diameter of their wheels.	**WORD POWER** circle, chord, diameter, radius, compass

A **circle** is a closed figure with all points on the circle the same distance from the center point. It has no beginning point and no ending point.

center point

Notice that

⇨ A line segment that connects any two points on the circle is called a **chord**.

⇨ A chord that passes through the center of the circle is called a **diameter**.

⇨ A line segment that connects the center with a point on the circle is called a **radius**.

Explore

A **compass** is a tool for constructing circles. Use a compass to construct a circle with a radius of 3 cm.

MATERIALS: compass, centimeter ruler

Draw a point. Place the center of the red circle of the compass over the point.	Set the compass to the length of the radius.	Hold the compass still at the center point, and move the compass to make the circle.

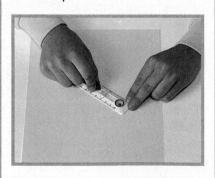 

Record

Construct the circle. Draw and label a chord, a diameter, and a radius. Write the measurement of each.

• How are a chord and a diameter alike? How are they different?

Now, investigate constructing circles of various sizes.

410 Chapter 25

Try This

Construct circles, each with radii of 3 cm, 5 cm, and 1 cm. Draw line segments to show a chord, a diameter, and a radius on each circle. Write the measurements for each.

Talk About It  CRITICAL THINKING

- Can the length of a chord be greater than a diameter? Explain.

- What relationship do you notice between a radius and a diameter of a circle?

▭ **WRITE ABOUT IT** Explain how to construct a circle with a diameter of 4 cm.

HANDS-ON PRACTICE

Use a compass to construct the circles and find the measurements.

1. Construct a circle with a radius of 4 cm. Label and measure a diameter and a chord.

2. Construct a circle with a diameter of 6 cm. Label and measure a radius and a chord.

Applying What You Learned

Write *chord, diameter,* or *radius* for each line segment.

3.   4.   5.   6.

Mixed Applications

For Problems 7–10, use the drawing.

7. Fernando knows that the diameters of the bicycles' tires are 20 in. and 24 in. What is the radius of each bicycle's tires?

8. Becky can pay for the 20-in. bike in 3 equal monthly payments. How much will each payment be?

9. If the difference in price of the two bikes is less than $20.00, Tom will buy the 24-in. bike. Which bike will Tom buy?

10. ▭ **WRITE ABOUT IT** Explain how you could draw a diagram of a bike.

HANDS ON

COOPERATIVE LEARNING

PART 1 Finding Circumference

| You will investigate how to find the circumference of a circle. | Why learn this? You can find the distance around a circular object. | WORD POWER circumference |

The perimeter of a circle is the **circumference**. Circles do not have sides, so you need to use a different method to find the distance around a circle.

REMEMBER:

Perimeter is the distance around a figure. To find the perimeter of a polygon, find the total of the lengths of the sides.

2 + 2 + 2 + 2 = 8, or 4 × 2 = 8

perimeter = 8 units

Explore

Find the circumference and diameter of a circular object such as a cup or a lid.

MATERIALS: compass, cm ruler, string, circular objects

MODEL

▶ **Step 1**

Wrap string around a circular object.

▶ **Step 2**

Use a ruler to measure the length of the string.

▶ **Step 3**

Trace the circle and measure the diameter. (HINT: Measure the greatest distance across the circle.)

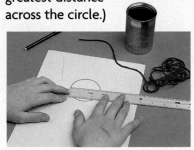

Record

Trace the circle and label it *A*. Record the circumference and the diameter to the nearest tenth of a centimeter.

Circle	Circumference (c)	Diameter (d)	c ÷ d
Example	15.7 cm	5 cm	
A			
B			

Now, investigate the relationship of the diameter to the circumference of a circle.

You may wish to use a calculator. 15.7 ÷ 5 = n

 Press:

Display:

3.14

So, n = 3.14 cm.

Technology Link
E–Lab • Activity 25 Available on CD-ROM and the Internet at http://www.hbschool.com/elab

Try This

Use the cm ruler and string to find the circumference and diameter of three other circular objects. Record both measurements in the table. Divide to find out how many times longer the circumference is than the diameter. Round each quotient to the nearest hundredth.

TALK ABOUT IT How many times longer is the circumference than the diameter of a circle?

✏️ **WRITE ABOUT IT** Explain how you could find the circumference of a circle without using the string method if you know the diameter.

> The relationship of the diameter to the circumference of a circle, $C \div d$, is *3.14* and is called *pi* (π).

HANDS-ON PRACTICE

1. Use a centimeter ruler and string to find the circumference of a pen or marker.

Use a calculator to divide the circumference of each object by its diameter. Complete the table by rounding to the nearest hundredth.

	Object	Circumference (C)	Diameter (d)	$\frac{C}{d}$
2.	Spool	9.4 cm	3 cm	?
3.	Lid	12.6 cm	4 cm	?
4.	Mug	28.3 cm	9 cm	?

Mixed Applications

For Problems 5–8, use the menu.

5. What is the perimeter of the smallest box that each pizza can fit into?

6. How much more will it cost Rosalinda to buy 3 small pizzas than to buy 2 large pizzas?

7. How much change will Darius receive from $20.00 if he buys 2 medium pizzas?

8. What is the difference in the radius of a slice from the large pizza and a slice from the medium pizza?

9. ✏️ **WRITE ABOUT IT** How would you describe to a fourth-grade student how to find the circumference of a circular object?

Momma's & Poppa's Pizza

SMALL $6.99   MEDIUM $7.99   LARGE $9.99

12 inch   14 inch   16 inch   one slice

LESSON CONTINUES ➤

PART 2   PROBLEM-SOLVING STRATEGY
Act It Out

THE PROBLEM Christy's class is making pencil holders for the crafts booth at the school fair. Everyone is bringing in cans of different sizes to be covered in brightly patterned paper. The paper must be cut to the exact size so it will fit around each can. How can Christy find out the size of the paper she needs to cover a can that is 12 cm in height?

REMEMBER:
✓ Understand
✓ Plan
✓ Solve
✓ Look Back

✓ Understand

• What are you asked to do?

• What information will you use?

• Is there information you will not use? If so, what?

✓ Plan

• What strategy can you use to solve the problem?

You can *act it out* by using string and a ruler to measure the can.

✓ Solve

• How can you solve the problem?

The surface to be covered forms a rectangle when flat, so the measurements needed are the height and circumference of the can. You know the height of the can is 12 cm. To find the circumference, wrap the string around the can and use the ruler to measure the string to the nearest tenth of a centimeter. The circumference of Christy's can measures 37.7 centimeters

So, the paper needs to be 12 cm by 37.7 cm. Now the paper can be cut out and pasted on the can.

✓ Look Back

• How does acting it out help you solve the problem?

• How else could you solve this problem?

PRACTICE

Act it out to solve.

1. Justin is making a model of a rocket for science class. He wants to cover the cylindrical part of the rocket with foil. The cylinder is 16 cm in height, and its diameter is 9 cm. What is the circumference of the cylinder? What size should Justin cut the foil to fit the cylinder exactly?

2. Melinda wants to wrap a gift that is in a cylinder container. The cylinder is 10 in. high. The diameter of the cylinder is 3 in. She has a sheet of gift-wrap paper that is 14 in. by $9\frac{1}{2}$ in. Does Melinda have enough paper? Explain.

3. Melanie, Ashley, Jenny, Sammy, and Brooke are waiting in line to buy tickets. Ashley is in front of Sammy and after Jenny. Melanie is between Jenny and Ashley. Brooke is after Sammy. Who is first in line?

4. Corey had one $20 bill, two $10 bills, two $1 bills, one quarter, two dimes, and three pennies. He spent $16 on a CD, loaned $10.25 to his sister, and saved the rest. What bills and coins does Corey have left?

Mixed Applications

Solve.

CHOOSE A STRATEGY

• Write a Number Sentence • Make a Model • Draw a Diagram • Act It Out • Work Backward

5. Abby is wrapping a cylindrical box in gift-wrap paper. It is 18 in. tall and has a diameter of 6 in. What is the circumference of the cylinder? What size paper will Abby need?

6. The diameter of Sara's white watch is $\frac{7}{8}$ in. The diameter of her brown watch is $\frac{1}{4}$ in. What is the difference in the diameters of the watches?

7. Chris withdrew $100 from his savings account to buy clothes. He bought 2 pairs of jeans, a shirt for $18.50, and a belt for $9.50. He had $23.40 when he got home. How much was each pair of jeans?

8. Ms. Ramsey's students are doing a research report. Of the students, $\frac{1}{2}$ chose to research space exploration, $\frac{1}{3}$ chose planets, and $\frac{1}{6}$ chose the sun. If 5 of the students chose to research the sun, how many students are in the class?

9. Rod wants to take the fastest train trip to New York City. Which train should he take?

TRAIN SCHEDULE	
Leave White Plains	**Arrive New York City**
7:15 A.M.	8:38 A.M.
9:36 A.M.	10:04 A.M.
11:16 A.M.	12:27 P.M.

Angles in a Circle

You will learn how to identify angle measures in a circle and to find missing angle measures.

Why learn this? You can describe parts of a circle by using the number of degrees in the angle measurement.

Angles are measured in degrees (°). A circle has 360°. Angles in a circle can measure from 0° to 360°.

One whole circle = 360°.   One-half circle = 180°.   One-quarter circle = 90°.

A.   **B.**   **C.**

Talk About It

- In Example B, how many 180° angles are formed by the diameter?

- In Example C, how many 90° angles are formed by the two diameters?

_____

If you know the measure of all but one of the angles in a circle, you can find a missing angle measure.

Find the sum of the angles that you know and subtract the sum from 360°.

$90° + 45° + 60° = 195°$

$360° - 195° = n \quad n = 165°$

So, the missing angle measure is 165°.

- Is the missing angle in the circle a right angle, an acute angle, or an obtuse angle?

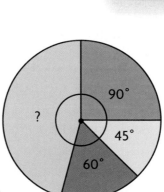

Check Your Understanding 💡 CRITICAL THINKING

Find the missing angle.

1.   **2.**   **3.**   **4.**

PRACTICE

Write *true* or *false* to describe each statement.

5. In a circle, one diameter forms two 180° angles.

6. In a circle with two radii, one angle could measure 180°.

7. If four radii form three 90° angles in a circle, the 4th angle is acute.

8. If six radii form five 60° angles in a circle, the sixth angle is obtuse.

Find the missing angle.

9.

10.

11.

Mixed Applications

For Problems 12–14, use the clocks.

12. Not including the 30 minutes Nancy spends eating lunch, how much time does she spend in school?

13. Which clock shows an acute angle?

14. How many degrees are in the angle formed by the hands of a clock at 8:20?

16. How many degrees are in the angle formed by the hands on a clock at 9:00?

15. How many degrees are in a right angle? a straight angle?

17. ✏️ **Write a problem** about the number of degrees in the angles of a sliced pie.

Mixed Review

Write *congruent* or *not congruent*. (pages 396–397)

18.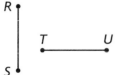

19.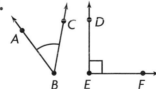

20.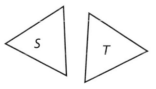

Multiply. Write the answer in simplest form. (pages 364–365)

21. $\dfrac{1}{8} \times \dfrac{2}{3}$

22. $\dfrac{1}{5} \times \dfrac{5}{12}$

23. $\dfrac{3}{4} \times \dfrac{3}{8}$

24. $\dfrac{2}{5} \times \dfrac{3}{7}$

Measuring Angles in a Circle

You will learn how to divide a circle according to given angle measurements.

Why learn this? You can make a circle graph for a given set of data.

The angles around the center point of a circle can be measured. You can use a protractor to find the number of degrees in each angle.

How many degrees are in each angle of the circle to the right?

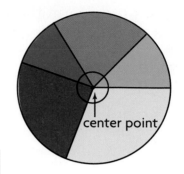
center point

MODEL

▶ Step 1

Place the center of the protractor on the center point of the circle. Line up the protractor with one side of the angle. Read the angle where the other side crosses the protractor.

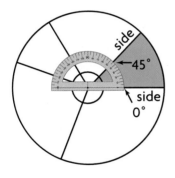

side
←45°
side
0°

▶ Step 2

To measure the second angle, rotate the protractor until it is lined up with the next side. Measure the remaining angles.

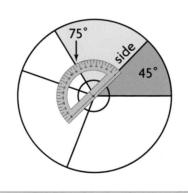

75°
side
45°

Link

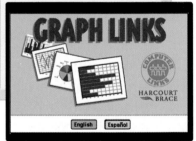

With *Graph Links* computer software, you can make graphs to display data.

So, the angles in the circle measure 45°, 110°, 90°, 40°, and 75°.

💡 **CRITICAL THINKING** How many degrees are in the sum of the angle measures of the circle? How can you find out?

Check Your Understanding

Use a protractor to find how many degrees are in each angle.

1.
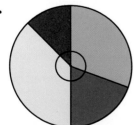

2.
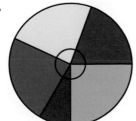

3.
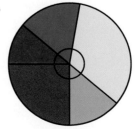

PRACTICE

Use a protractor to find the number of degrees in the angles of the circle.

4. How many degrees are in the green angle?

5. How many degrees are in the blue angle?

6. How many degrees are in the red and the yellow angles?

7. How many degrees are in the sum of the angles?

Use a compass and a protractor to draw a circle with the following angles.

8. 2 angles of 180° each

9. 2 angles of 40° each and 2 angles of 140° each

10. 2 angles of 60° each and 2 angles of 120° each

11. 3 angles of 120° each

12. 3 angles of 100° each and 1 angle of 60°

13. 4 angles of 50° each and 1 angle of 160°

Mixed Applications

14. The pizza restaurant will deliver to a house only within a 3-mile radius. To get to Lani's house from the pizza restaurant, you drive 3 miles north, make a 90° turn, and drive 3 miles east. Is her house within the 3-mile radius? Why or why not?

15. ✏️ **WRITE ABOUT IT** Dean read the time on the clock at 6:00. He said there were no angles formed by the hands on the clock. Was he correct? Explain.

Mixed Review

Trace each figure. Draw the lines of symmetry for each figure. (pages 398–399)

16.

17.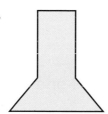

18.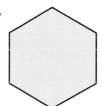

19.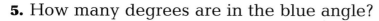

Change the unit. (pages 346–347)

20. 3 gal = _?_ qt

21. 5 pt = _?_ c

22. 16 qt = _?_ pt

23. 8 qt = _?_ gal

24. 24 pt = _?_ qt

25. 12 pt = _?_ qt

MATH FUN!

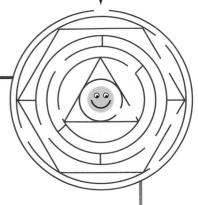

AMAZING CIRCLES

PURPOSE To draw a maze in a circle

YOU WILL NEED compass, paper and pencil

You can make amazing puzzles for your classmates to solve by using circles and polygons.

Draw a large circle. Within that circle, draw smaller circles and some polygons such as triangles, squares, hexagons and so on.

Make a pathway to the picture by making openings and drawing lines. Make several false pathways.

Place a picture at the end of the maze. Name your maze.

Anyone who solves your "Amazing Maze" keeps the picture.

PIZZA PARTY

PURPOSE To use angle measures to describe a piece of pizza

YOU WILL NEED construction paper, ruler, compass, pencil, scissors, glue, protractor

Pretend you have your own pizza company. You sell pizza by degrees! A 360° is a whole pizza, a 180° is a half pizza, and so forth. You are going to make a poster advertising different sizes by degrees! Make up prices for each size.

Draw a 12-inch pizza on red paper. Cut it out. Add toppings. Cut out sections of pizza of different sizes. Measure them using a protractor.

Make a poster advertising your special pizza. How much does a 45° piece cost?

 Ask your family members to estimate how many degrees of pizza they think they could eat.

WHEEL TEST

PURPOSE To compare wheels, their circumferences, and how far they take you

YOU WILL NEED different-size bicycles, paper and pencil, tape measure

Test each bike to see how many times you pedal it for the wheel to go around once.

That is one *revolution*.

Test 5 revolutions of the front wheels of each bike.

Measure the distance each goes.

Make a chart comparing wheel diameter, circumference, and distance covered.

✓ CHECK UNDERSTANDING

VOCABULARY

1. A ___?___ is a closed figure with all points on the circle the same distance from the center point. (page 410)

2. A line segment that connects any two points on the circle is called a ___?___. (page 410)

3. A ___?___ is a tool for constructing circles. (page 410)

4. The perimeter of a circle is the ___?___. (page 412)

Construct a circle with the given radius. Label and measure a radius, a diameter, and a chord. (pages 410–411)

5. 2 cm 6. 4 cm 7. 3 cm 8. 5 cm

✓ CHECK SKILLS

Write *true* or *false* to describe each statement. (pages 416–417)

9. There are five 60° angles in a circle.

10. There are four 90° angles in a circle.

11. A circle can have more than one obtuse angle.

12. If two of three angles in a circle each measure 120°, the third angle would be a right angle.

Find the missing angle. (pages 416–417)

Find the number of degrees in each angle. (pages 418–419)

13.

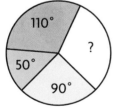

14.

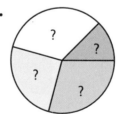

✓ CHECK PROBLEM SOLVING

Solve. (pages 414–415)

CHOOSE A STRATEGY

• Write a Number Sentence • Guess and Check • Make a Model • Act It Out

15. Heather is wrapping a cylindrical box to hold her posters. It is 20 in. tall and has a diameter of 5 in. What size paper will Heather need?

16. The sum of two numbers is 64. One of the numbers is 3 times the other number. What are the two numbers?

26 SOLID FIGURES

DID YOU KNOW....

During the 1850's and 1860's, building eight-sided houses was popular. If you live in a part of the country with buildings from that time, you may still see octagonal houses.

Team-Up Time

Your Octagonal Village

When people wanted to build octagonal houses, builders had to put on their thinking caps. Work together to make a model of an octagonal house. Then write a list of ideas to help other builders make a model of a house with more than four walls.

YOU WILL NEED: construction paper, a compass, pencil, ruler, markers, tape

Work with a group. Your job is to

- make a model of an octagonal house.
- make the roof so it will fit over an octagon.
- make a list of problems and how you solved them.
- create a class village of model octagonal houses.

DID YOU

- ☑ make a model of an octagonal house?
- ☑ make a list of problems and how you solved them?
- ☑ create a class octagonal village?

HOW TO MAKE AN OCTAGON

5 in. Draw a circle with a diameter of 5 in. or less

Fold the circle in half, three times. It will be divided into eighths. Use a ruler to draw the edges of the octagon.

Start with an octagon for a base. Figure out how to plan the walls. How many will you need?

After you cut and fold the walls, decorate them. You need doors and windows! Then tape them to the base.

If you want a pointed roof, draw a circle bigger than the house. Cut out a wedge shaped like a piece of pizza. The rest is up to you.

Building Pointers

It is hard to get the walls to fit the octagon exactly.

- You can measure each segment. Be sure to leave space for 8 (I did 6 the first time.)
- You can just mark each segment and skip measuring.
- Your wall may come out a bit too large for the floor. Just tape it anyway.
- If you want a steep roof, cut a big circle for it, then cut a big triangle out of it.
- I folded my roof into 8 parts so it would rest on the house.

Overmatter

423

Prisms and Pyramids

You will learn to name and classify prisms and pyramids by their bases.	Why learn this? You can recognize solid figures in the shapes of buildings in the world around you.	

A **prism** is a solid figure that has two congruent faces called bases. The two **bases** of a prism are congruent polygons. A prism is named by the polygons that form its bases. All other faces are rectangles.

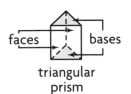

| triangular prism | rectangular prism | pentagonal prism | hexagonal prism |

REMEMBER:

Polygons are named by the number of their sides and angles.

Example: *Tri* means "three."

A triangle has three sides and three angles.

Talk About It

- What polygon determines the name of each prism above?

- All the faces of this prism are squares. Name the prism. How is it different from other kinds of prisms?

A **pyramid** is a solid figure with one base that is a polygon and three or more other faces that are triangles with a common vertex. A pyramid is named by the polygon that forms its base.

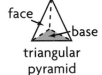

| triangular pyramid | square pyramid | pentagonal pyramid | hexagonal pyramid |

- How are a prism and a pyramid different? How are they alike?

Check Your Understanding

Write *prism* or *pyramid*. Write the polygon that names the base. Identify the solid figure.

1.
2.
3.
4.

PRACTICE

Write *prism* or *pyramid*. Write the polygon that names the base. Identify the solid figure.

5.

6.

7.

8.

Write the name of the solid figure. Make a drawing of each.

9. I have a base with 4 equal sides. My faces are 4 triangles.

10. All 6 of my faces are rectangles.

11. I have 2 congruent triangles for bases. I have 3 rectangular faces.

12. I have 4 congruent triangles.

Mixed Applications

13. April walked around the perimeter of a rectangular building. The length of the building was 118 ft and the width was 65 ft. How many yards did April walk?

14. Don bought this tent for camping. What solid figure does the tent look like?

15. A Girl Scout troop spent 48 hours on a camping trip. They spent $\frac{1}{6}$ of the time hiking on trails. How many hours did they spend hiking on trails?

16. ▭ **Write a problem** in which you identify a solid figure.

Mixed Review

Copy each figure. Write *yes* or *no* to tell whether each figure tessellates. (pages 402–403)

17.

18.

19.

20.

Write which one is heavier. (pages 348–349)

21. 35 oz or 2 lb

22. 3 T or 5,000 lb

23. 10 T or 10,000 lb

24. $\frac{1}{4}$ lb or 6 oz

Nets for Solid Figures

You will learn to recognize a two-dimensional pattern for a three-dimensional solid.

Why learn this? You can make a box or pyramid from a pattern.

WORD POWER
net

A **net** is a two-dimensional pattern for a three-dimensional solid. Use what you know about prisms and pyramids to identify nets for solid figures.

Look at the net. Analyze ways you can fold it to make a solid figure.

Talk About It

• How many faces does this net have?

• What shape is the base? What shape are the other faces?

• What solid figure can you make by folding the net?

You can make other solid figures from patterns.

Talk About It

• What solid figure can you make by folding each pattern shown at the right?

• What shape is the base of each figure?

A. 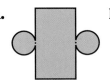   **B.**

Check Your Understanding 💡 CRITICAL THINKING

Match each solid figure with its net. Write *a, b, c,* or *d.*

1. 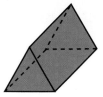   **2.**    **3.** 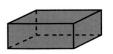   **4.**

a. 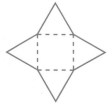   **b.** 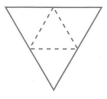   **c.** 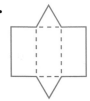   **d.**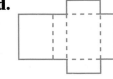

PRACTICE

Match each solid figure with its net. Write *a*, *b*, *c*, or *d*.

5. 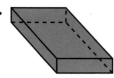   **6.**   **7.**   **8.**

a.   **b.** 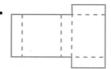   **c.** 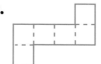   **d.**

Write the letter of the pattern that can be folded to make the figure.

9.   **a.**   **b.**   **c.**

10.   **a.**   **b.**    **c.**

11.   **a.**   **b.**   **c.**

12.   **a.**   **b.**   **c.**

Mixed Applications

13. Shelly is making six cubes for a project. How many faces will she draw?

14. The kindergarten class is sharing building blocks. There are 6 groups and 240 blocks. How many blocks does each group have?

Mixed Review

Write each fraction in simplest form. **(pages 272–273)**

15. $\frac{4}{12}$ **16.** $\frac{16}{18}$ **17.** $\frac{14}{21}$ **18.** $\frac{20}{25}$ **19.** $\frac{20}{30}$

Estimate each sum or difference. **(pages 310–311)**

20. $\frac{1}{10} + \frac{7}{8}$ **21.** $\frac{5}{8} - \frac{1}{9}$ **22.** $\frac{11}{12} + \frac{4}{10}$ **23.** $\frac{9}{10} - \frac{5}{6}$

Solid Figures from Different Views

You will investigate how to identify solid figures from different views.

Why learn this? You can use drawings to see how a solid figure will look before you build it.

A solid figure looks different when it is viewed from different positions.

Look at this figure.

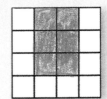

Notice that

⇨ this is a drawing of the figure viewed from the *top*.

⇨ this is a drawing of the figure viewed from the *side*.

⇨ this is a drawing of the figure viewed from the *front*.

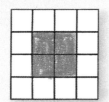

Explore

Use 18 connecting cubes to build Figure B. Move the figure to look at it from different views.

MATERIALS: connecting cubes, centimeter grid paper

Figure B

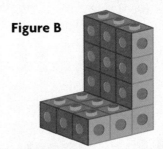

Record

Draw three pictures on grid paper to show how Figure B looks from the top, from the side, and from the front.

Now, investigate building another solid figure.

Try This

Build another figure using 24 connecting cubes. Then draw the figure on grid paper as it looks from the top, from the side, and from the front.

TALK ABOUT IT How does looking at a solid figure from different views help you identify the figure?

Technology **Link**
E-Lab • Activity 26 Available on CD-ROM
and the Internet at http://www.hbschool.com/elab

In *Mighty Math Calculating Crew*, the game *Dr. Gee's 3-D Lab* challenges you to look at solid figures from different perspectives.

WRITE ABOUT IT Suppose someone drew these views of a solid figure. Draw how you think the figure would look. Explain.

From the top	From the side	From the front
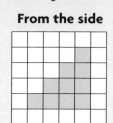	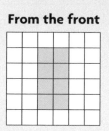	

HANDS-ON PRACTICE

Use grid paper to draw each figure from the top, the side, and the front.

1.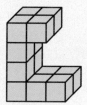

2.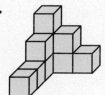

3.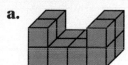

Applying What You Learned

Choose the figure that is represented by each set of three drawings.

From the top	From the side	From the front	
4. 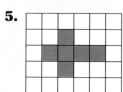	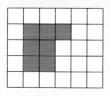	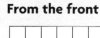	a. 
5. 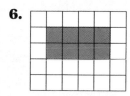	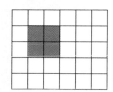	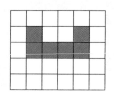	b. 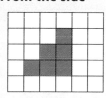
6. 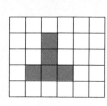	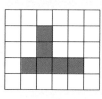	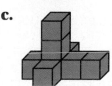	c.

Mixed Applications

7. A shoe box is completely filled with blocks. There are 6 rows with 4 blocks in each row, and 3 layers of blocks. How many blocks are in the shoe box?

8. **WRITE ABOUT IT** Name a solid figure and describe it from two views.

Algebraic Thinking: Volume

Why learn this? You can find out how tall a box is if you know its length and width and how much it can hold.

Volume is the measure of the space a three-dimensional figure occupies. You can find the volume of a rectangular prism by using its length, width, and height. If you know the length, width, and volume, how can you find the height of the figure?

Here are two methods for solving the problem.

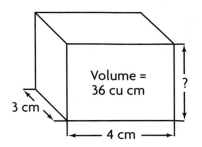

Method A	Method B
Use centimeter cubes to build a model that would fill the box. Then count the layers of cubes to find the height. 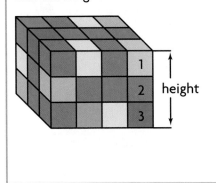	Use the mathematical formula for volume to find the height. $V = l \times w \times h$ **Think:** I know the volume is 36 cu cm, the length is 4 cm, and the width is 3 cm. *h represents the missing dimension.* So, $36 = 4 \times 3 \times h$. Since $36 = 12 \times h$, use division to find a missing factor. $36 \div 12 = 3$, or $h = 3$.

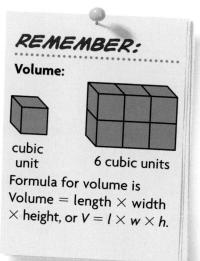

REMEMBER:

Volume:

cubic unit   6 cubic units

Formula for volume is Volume = length × width × height, or $V = l \times w \times h$.

So, the height is 3 cm.

Talk About It

• In Method A, how would you make the model?

• How did you use the formula to find the missing dimension?

You can use a calculator to find the missing dimension in a formula. $V = l \times w \times h$

So, $240 = 8 \times w \times 10$.

Press: 8 × 1 0 = [80.]

Press: 2 4 0 ÷ 8 0 = [3.]

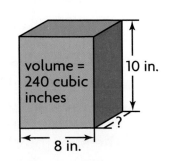

volume = 240 cubic inches

10 in.

8 in.

So, the width of the figure is 3 inches.

Calculator Activities page H60

PRACTICE

Find the missing dimension. You may use a calculator.

1.
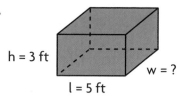
h = 3 ft
w = ?
l = 5 ft
volume = 60 cu ft

2.
h = 8 m
w = 2 m
l = ?
volume = 64 cu m

3.
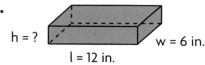
h = ?
w = 6 in.
l = 12 in.
volume = 144 cu in.

4. length = 6 yd
width = 4 yd
height = _?_
volume = 48 cu yd

5. length = 12 ft
width = 8 ft
height = 2 ft
volume = _?_

6. length = _?_
width = 7 m
height = 5 m
volume = 350 cu m

Complete the table. You may use a calculator.

	Length	Width	Height	Volume
7.	12 cm	?	5 cm	600 cu cm
8.	?	8 in.	5 in.	560 cu in.
9.	14 ft	9 ft	3 ft	?
10.	10 yd	7 yd	6 yd	?
11.	15 m	12 m	?	720 cu m

Mixed Applications

For Problems 12–14, you may use a calculator.

12. How much area will each refrigerator cover?

13. Lynn has $\frac{1}{3}$ of the money needed to buy the refrigerator that is 20 in. high. How much more money does she need?

14. Alan bought 2 small refrigerators. How many more cubic inches of volume does he have than Frank, who bought one large refrigerator?

15. ✏️ **WRITE ABOUT IT** Explain how to find the height of a solid figure when you know the length, width, and volume.

Shopping for a new refrigerator

Refrigerators for Sale

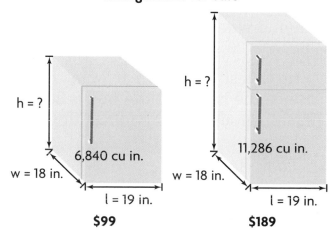
h = ?
6,840 cu in.
w = 18 in.
l = 19 in.
$99

h = ?
11,286 cu in.
w = 18 in.
l = 19 in.
$189

LESSON CONTINUES ▶

PROBLEM-SOLVING STRATEGY
Use a Formula

THE PROBLEM Amanda found a box at the grocery store that she wants to use to pack her sports trophies. She knows the box is 18 inches long and 12 inches wide. A label on the box says that it once contained tissues and can hold 4,320 cubic inches. Her tallest trophy measures 1 ft $7\frac{1}{2}$ in. Is the box tall enough for this trophy?

REMEMBER:
- ☑ Understand
- ☑ Plan
- ☑ Solve
- ☑ Look Back

☑ Understand

- What are you asked to do?

- What information will you use?

- Is there information you will not use? If so, what?

☑ Plan

- What strategy can you use to solve the problem?

  You can *use a formula* for volume and find the missing dimension.

☑ Solve

- How can you use the strategy to solve the problem?

  You can use the formula for volume. You know that $V = 4,320$ cu in., $l = 18$ in., and $w = 12$ in. The height (h) is the missing dimension in the equation. You can use a calculator to multiply 18×12, and then divide 4,320 by 216 to find the missing factor. So, $h = 20$ in.

  The tallest trophy is 1 ft $7\frac{1}{2}$ in., or $19\frac{1}{2}$ in. Since the height of the box is 20 in., the box is tall enough for the tallest trophy.

☑ Look Back

- How does using a formula help you solve the problem?

- What other strategy could you use?

PRACTICE

Use a formula to solve.

1. Yolanda is packing a suitcase that is 70 cm long and 40 cm wide and has a volume of 56,000 cu cm. She has a gift box to pack in the suitcase that is 60 cm long, 30 cm wide, and 25 cm in height. Will the gift box fit in the suitcase? Explain.

2. A toolbox is 18 in. long and 14 in. wide with a volume of 3,024 cu in. Would a cube-shaped box that has a volume of 1 cubic foot fit in the toolbox? Explain.

3. A playground area that is 66 ft long and 42 ft wide needs to be fenced. Will 75 yards of fencing be enough? Explain.

4. Rochelle's bedroom is 15 ft long and 12 ft wide. She is having wall-to-wall carpet installed. How many sq yd of carpet does she need?

Mixed Applications

Solve.

CHOOSE A STRATEGY

Draw a Diagram • Make a Table • Work Backward • Use a Formula

5. A swimming pool is 45 ft long and 20 ft wide. How many cubic feet of water will be enough to fill the pool to a depth of 6 ft?

6. Classes begin at 8:35. Each class is 55 min long and there is a 10-min break after each class. At what time is the third class over?

7. The Lopez family left on vacation on June 3. They drove for 4 days and spent 7 days with relatives. They drove 3 more days and spent 2 days visiting attractions. It took them 2 days to drive home. On what date did they arrive home?

8. Jon gave directions to his house. "From the school, go 4 blocks west and make a 90° turn south. Go 3 blocks south, make a 45° turn west, and go 2 blocks. My house is the second one on the left." Draw a map to Jon's house.

9. The thermometer shows the temperature at 6:00 P.M. The temperature has fallen 9 degrees since 3:00 P.M. The temperature had risen 12° from 9:00 A.M. to 3:00 A.M. What was the temperature at 9:00 A.M.?

First National Bank

62 °F

10. Katie's book shelf is $4\frac{2}{3}$ ft tall. Her desk is $\frac{3}{4}$ as high as the book shelf. How high is Katie's desk?

11. Of the 32 students in Andy's class, $\frac{3}{8}$ prefer watching football to other sports. How many students prefer football?

Estimating Volume

You will learn to estimate the volume of a rectangular prism in cubic units.

Why learn this? You can estimate the number of items in a box without counting them.

Oranges are shipped in a variety of boxes. Compare these two boxes to determine which can hold more oranges.

You can use a benchmark to estimate volume in cubic units. Use 1 cubic foot as a benchmark to estimate the volume of the boxes.

A.

B.

1 cu ft

Fresh oranges being shipped to the grocery store.

- What is the estimated volume of Box A? Box B?

So, based on your estimate, Box A can hold more oranges.

Talk About It

- How did you estimate the volume of the boxes?
- How many times greater than a cubic foot is a cubic yard?

Check Your Understanding 💡 **CRITICAL THINKING**

Use the benchmarks at the right to name the more reasonable unit for measuring the volume of each box. Estimate the volume.

1.

2.

3.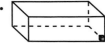

4.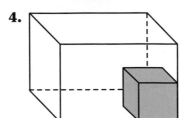

REMEMBER:

A benchmark is a point of reference and can help you determine whether an estimate is reasonable without counting.

Benchmark = (1 cu unit)
Estimated volume = 8 cu units

Benchmarks:

1 cubic centimeter (cu cm)

1 cubic decimeter (cu dm)

PRACTICE

Use the benchmarks at the right to name the more reasonable
unit for measuring the volume of each box. Estimate the volume.

5.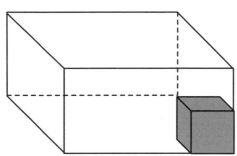

Benchmarks:

1 cubic   1 cubic
inch   foot

6. **7.**

Choose the most reasonable measure. Write *a, b,* or *c.*

8. a tissue box   **a.** 90 cu in.   **b.** 90 cu ft   **c.** 90 cu yd

9. a dresser   **a.** 10 cu in.   **b.** 10 cu ft   **c.** 10 cu yd

10. truckload of mulch   **a.** 20 cu in.   **b.** 20 cu ft   **c.** 20 cu yd

Mixed Applications

11. Erika and Karem want to make a
box large enough to hold a
basketball. Karem's box has a
volume of 1 cubic yard. Erika's
box has a volume of 1 cubic foot.
Which size is more reasonable for
a basketball?

12. Marcia's lunchbox
is 10 in. long,
7 in. wide. She
estimates the volume
as 210 cu in. Larry says the
estimated volume is 2,100 cu in.
Which estimate is more reasonable?

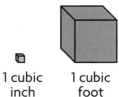

13. Mr. Beale is unpacking some
books from a box. There are 4
layers of books. Each layer has 3
rows of books with 3 books in
each row. How many books are in
the box?

14. **WRITE ABOUT IT** Explain how
to estimate volume.

Mixed Review

Write *multiply* or *divide.* Change the unit. (pages 348–349)

15. 48 oz = __?__ lb   **16.** 50 lb = __?__ oz   **17.** 4 T = __?__ lb   **18.** 16,000 lb = __?__ T

Find the quotient. Check by multiplying. (pages 216–217)

19. 34.4 ÷ 8 = __?__   **20.** 6.86 ÷ 7 = __?__   **21.** 10.68 ÷ 3 = __?__

CULTURAL CONNECTION

A TASTE OF FRANCE

Albert's family has a French bakery in Washington, D.C. The bakery made a large chocolate cake for a party. The cake was delivered in sections and put together there. The bottom layer of the cake measured 4 feet by 3 feet. Its height was 6 inches. Which of these boxes could be used to carry the bottom layer of the cake? Remember: the box must be larger than the cake.

CULTURAL LINK

The Eiffel Tower in Paris is one of the most famous structures in the world. It is 984 feet high. It was built of iron for an exhibition in 1889. Inside the tower are shops and restaurants. There are observation decks from which visitors can view the city and countryside.

A.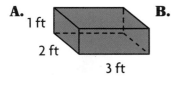
1 ft
2 ft
3 ft

B.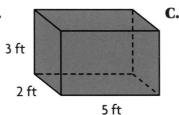
3 ft
2 ft
5 ft

C.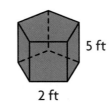
5 ft
2 ft

Work Together

1. The top of the cake was decorated with a model of the Eiffel Tower. The tower model was 2 feet tall. The base was a square with sides that measured 1 foot. Albert helped his father box the tower. Study the patterns pictured at the right. Which container could hold the tower? Name the figures.

2. Each guest at the luncheon received a model of the Eiffel Tower. Design a box that can hold the model. It has a 4-inch base and its height is 8 inches. How many faces does your box have? How many vertices? How many edges? Label an edge, a vertex, and a face on the box.

3. Small boxes with samples of French perfumes were given to the guests when they left the luncheon. The rectangular boxes were 4 inches × 3 inches. The volume of each box was 24 cubic inches. Use the formula for volume to find the height of the box.

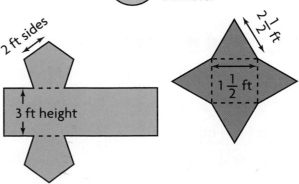

3 ft height
3 ft diameter

2 ft sides
3 ft height

2½ ft
1½ ft

✓ CHECK UNDERSTANDING

VOCABULARY

1. A solid figure that has two congruent, parallel faces called bases is a __?__. (page 424)

2. A two-dimensional pattern for a three-dimensional solid is a __?__. (page 426)

3. A solid figure with one base that is a polygon and three or more faces that are triangles with a common vertex is called a __?__. (page 424)

Write *prism* or *pyramid*. Write the polygon that names the base for each. Identify the solid figure. (pages 424–425)

4.

5.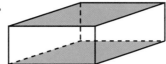

6.

✓ CHECK SKILLS

Use grid paper to draw the figure from the top, the side, and the front. (pages 428–429)

Find the missing dimension. (pages 430–431)

7.

8.

9.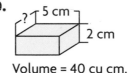
5 cm
2 cm
Volume = 40 cu cm.

10.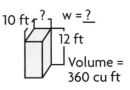
10 ft   ?   w = ?
12 ft
Volume = 360 cu ft

Choose the most reasonable measure. Write *a*, *b*, or *c*. (pages 434–435)

11. cereal box   **a.** 300 cu ft   **b.** 300 cu in.   **c.** 300 cu yd

12. washing machine   **a.** 30 cu in.   **b.** 30 cu yd   **c.** 30 cu ft

✓ CHECK PROBLEM SOLVING

Solve. (pages 432–433)

CHOOSE A STRATEGY
• Write a Number Sentence   • Guess and Check   • Make a Model   • Use a Formula

13. Sue's gift is 2 in. by 3 in. by 10 in. The box is 4 in. by 2 in. and has a volume of 88 cu in. Will the gift fit into the box? Explain.

14. Jeff is building a pen for his dog. He has 56 ft of fencing. What dimensions would give the greatest area possible?

VOCABULARY CHECK

Choose a term from the box to complete each sentence.

1. Lines in a plane that never intersect and are the same distance from each other are __?__ . (page 378)

2. When you move a figure to show a translation, reflection, or rotation, it is called a __?__ . (page 400)

3. A line segment that connects a circle's center with a point on that circle is called a __?__ . (page 410)

4. A solid figure with two bases that are congruent polygons is called a __?__ . (page 424)

STUDY AND SOLVE

CHAPTER 23

EXAMPLE

Identify the figure.

This is an angle because it is made up of two rays with the same endpoint. It is a right angle because it measures 90 degrees.

right angle

Identify the figure. Write *acute, obtuse,* or *right*. (pages 380–381, and 390–391)

5.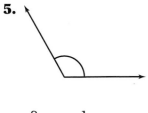

__?__ angle

6.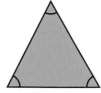

__?__ triangle

For Problems 7–8, use the figure. (pages 378–379)

7. Name a line segment that intersects *AB*, but is not perpendicular to *AB*.

8. Name a line segment that is parallel to *AB*.

Identify the figure. Write *trapezoid, parallelogram, rectangle, rhombus,* or *square*. (pages 384–385)

9.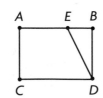

10.

CHAPTER 24

EXAMPLE

Tell how many lines of symmetry the figure has. (pages 398–399)

If you folded the square along any of the dotted lines, the halves would match exactly.

A square has 4 lines of symmetry.

Tell how many lines of symmetry. (pages 398–399)

11.

12.

Copy the figure on a coordinate grid. Translate, reflect, and rotate the figure. Name the new ordered pairs. (pages 400–401)

13.

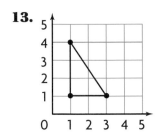

Write *yes* or *no* to tell whether the figure tessellates. (pages 402–403)

14.

15.

Use pattern blocks to solve. (pages 404–405)

16. Ken is using tiles with these figures: hexagons and triangles. Can he make a mosaic that tessellates?

CHAPTER 25

EXAMPLE

Find the missing measurement.

A circle has a total of 360°. Find the sum of the angles you know. Subtract the sum from 360°.

The missing measurement is 120°.

Construct a circle with the given radius. Label and measure a radius, a diameter, and a chord. (pages 410–411)

17. 2 cm

18. 3 cm

Find the missing measurement.
(pages 416–417)

19.

Solve. (pages 414–415)

20. Dan wants to wrap a jar in gift paper. The jar is 6 in. high. Its diameter is 5 in. Dan has a sheet of paper that is 10 in. by 10 in. Can he use it to wrap the jar? Explain.

CHAPTER 26

EXAMPLE

Choose the most reasonable measure.

a cake-mix box

a. 100 cu in. **b.** 100 cu ft **c.** 100 cu yd

Think: A cake-mix box is about 8 in. by 6 in. by 2 in. wide. 8 in. × 6 in. × 2 in. = 96 cu in., or about 100 cu in.

Write *prism* or *pyramid*. Write the polygon that names the base. Identify the solid figure. (pages 424–425)

21.

22.

Use grid paper to draw the figure from the top, the side, and the front. (pages 428–429)

23.

Choose the most reasonable measure.
(pages 434–435)

24. a clothes dryer

a. 30 cu in. **b.** 30 cu ft **c.** 30 cu yd

Solve. (pages 432–433)

25. Kim is packing a 3-in. by 5-in. by 8-in. toy. The box is 4 in. by 6 in. and has a volume of 168 cu in. Will the toy fit in the box? Explain.

✏ WRITE ABOUT IT

1. Explain your choices as you name classroom objects that remind you of intersecting lines, perpendicular lines, parallel lines, and a ray; and a right angle, an acute angle, and an obtuse angle. (pages 378–381)

2. Use a square piece of paper. Fold the paper to show as many lines of symmetry as you can. Draw a diagram to show the lines of symmetry you found. (pages 398-399)

3. Draw a pie sliced in half. Then slice one of the halves in half. Explain how to find the number of degrees in the angles of the sliced pie. (pages 416-417)

4. Use a 1-cm cube as a benchmark to estimate the volume of a paper clip box that measures 7 cm long, 5 cm wide, and 2 cm high. Explain your method. (pages 434-435)

✓ PERFORMANCE ASSESSMENT

Solve. Explain your method.

CHOOSE A STRATEGY

• Use a Formula • Act It Out • Make a Model • Draw a Diagram • Write a Number Sentence

5. A parking lot is 50 yd by 30 yd. Light poles are placed 10 yd apart. No light poles are on the edges of the lot. How many light poles are in the lot, and where they are placed? (pages 384–385)

6. Bob is designing place mats for craft class. He can use only one shape. He is trying to decide between a hexagon and an octagon. Which shape will tessellate when arranged in a design? Make a design that Bob could use. (pages 404–405)

7. Banks roll coins in wrappers. Suppose you are making a wrapper for quarters. How wide must the wrapper be to fit around the quarters with $\frac{1}{4}$-inch extra so the sides can be glued together? How did you find out? (pages 414–415)

8. Ellen found a box that is 12 in. long and 6 in. wide. The box holds 504 cubic in. Ellen wants to store her CDs in the box. The CDs are 5 in. high. Is the box big enough for Ellen's CDs? (pages 432–433)

CUMULATIVE REVIEW

Solve the problem. Then write the letter of the correct answer.

1.   5,000
       $-3,364$

A. 1,636
B. 1,746
C. 2,635
D. 8,364   (pages 22–23)

2. $67 \div 8 = n$

A. $n = 7$ r7   **B.** $n = 8$ r3
C. $n = 708$ r7   **D.** $n = 4,536$

(pages 108–109)

3. $1,000 \div 99 = n$

A. $n = 1$ r10   **B.** $n = 10$ r10
C. $n = 101$ r10   **D.** $n = 1,010$

(pages 126–127)

4. $2\overline{)8.06}$

A. 0.43   **B.** 4.03
C. 4.3   **D.** 40.3

(pages 214–217)

5. Compare. Order the numbers from least to greatest. $\frac{3}{4}, \frac{1}{6}, \frac{7}{12}$

A. $\frac{1}{6}, \frac{3}{4}, \frac{7}{12}$ **B.** $\frac{3}{4}, \frac{1}{6}, \frac{7}{12}$

C. $\frac{1}{6}, \frac{7}{12}, \frac{3}{4}$ **D.** $\frac{3}{4}, \frac{7}{12}, \frac{1}{6}$

(pages 254–255)

For Problems 6–7, choose the correct answer in simplest form.

6. $\frac{5}{6} + \frac{5}{6} = n$

A. $n = \frac{10}{12}$ **B.** $n = \frac{10}{6}$

C. $n = 1\frac{4}{6}$ **D.** $n = 1\frac{2}{3}$

(pages 278–279)

7. $\frac{5}{12} - \frac{1}{6} = n$

A. $n = \frac{1}{4}$ **B.** $n = \frac{3}{12}$

C. $n = \frac{4}{12}$ **D.** $n = \frac{2}{3}$

(pages 314–317)

8. 4 gal = __?__ qt

A. 1   **B.** 2
C. 8   **D.** 16

(pages 346–347)

9. A triangle with all congruent sides is __?__.

A. equilateral   **B.** isosceles
C. scalene   **D.** right

(pages 398–399)

For Problems 10–11, identify the figure.

10.

A. parallelogram **B.** rectangle
C. rhombus   **D.** trapezoid

(pages 386–387)

11.

A. acute triangle
B. congruent triangle
C. obtuse triangle
D. right triangle

(pages 390–391)

27 FRACTIONS AS RATIOS

DID YOU KNOW...

Some letters have small strokes, called *serifs*, at the beginning and end.

Letters without these strokes are known as *sans serif*.

Double Your Initial

Have you ever wondered how to make an enlargement of a drawing? You are going to draw one of your initials. Then you will enlarge the initial to twice as tall and twice as wide.

YOU WILL NEED: centimeter grid paper, pencil, markers

Work with a partner. Your job is to

- draw on centimeter grid paper one initial, no larger than 7 cm wide and 12 cm tall.

- enlarge your initial on another piece of centimeter grid paper. Make the enlargement twice as wide and twice as high.

- find the height, width, and area of the initial.

- make a chart that shows the ratio between measures in the small initial and the enlargement.

1. Draw a letter on grid paper. Count the number of squares across and down.

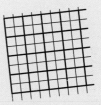

2. Darken every other grid line for the enlargement.

3. Use the dark grid lines to guide you as you draw the letter. Use pencil at first and do one big square at a time.

DID YOU

☑ make one small and one large drawing?

☑ find and record the height, width, and area of each drawing?

☑ make a chart that shows the ratio between the measures?

Understanding Ratio

You will investigate using two-color counters to show a relationship between two quantities.	**Why learn this?** You can compare two numbers of the same kind or measure.	**WORD POWER** ratio

You can use a **ratio** to compare two numbers in three ways. The kind of ratio you use depends on the problem situation.

EXAMPLE

Compare:	Ratio:	Type of Ratio:
red counters to all counters	2 to 5	part to whole
all counters to red counters	5 to 2	whole to part
red counters to yellow counters	2 to 3	part to part

Explore

You can use two-color counters to help you understand ratio.

MATERIALS: two-color counters

MODEL

There are 10 fifth-grade students in the school play. Of the students, 3 are singers and 7 are dancers. How can you find the ratio of the number of singers to the number of dancers?

▶ **Step 1**

Use the yellow side of two-color counters to represent all 10 students in the school play. Each counter represents one student.

▶ **Step 2**

Turn the red side of the counters up to represent the number of students who are singers.

So, the ratio of singers to dancers is 3 to 7.

Record

Record the type of ratio the model represents.

TALK ABOUT IT What do the yellow counters in Step 2 of the model represent?

Now, investigate finding other types of ratios.

Technology **Link** ▶

E-Lab · Activity 27 Available on CD-ROM and the Internet at http://www.hbschool.com/elab

Try This

Use two-color counters. Show the ratio of the number of singers to the number of students in the play. Then show the ratio of the number of students in the play to the number of dancers. Draw a picture of each model. Write each ratio.

TALK ABOUT IT Which types of ratios did you model for Try This? How are they alike? How are they different?

WRITE ABOUT IT Explain in your own words how to write each type of ratio.

HANDS-ON PRACTICE

Name the type of ratio and show with counters.

1. Soccer was played by 4 out of 6 students.

2. There were 3 rainy days and 7 sunny days.

3. Of 7 pets on the block, 4 are dogs.

Applying What You Learned

Use the picture to make the comparison.

4.

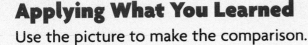

_?_ wheels to _?_ skate

5.

_?_ baseballs to _?_ players

6.

_?_ tires to _?_ bikes

Mixed Applications

7. What is the ratio of vowels to consonants in the word *MATHEMATICS*? What kind of ratio is this?

8. There are 32 students in the art club. Of the students, $\frac{3}{4}$ are in fifth grade. How many fifth-grade students are in the art club?

9. What ratio would you write to compare the sides in an octagon to the sides in a triangle?

10. Sancho is buying milk. He can buy 1 gallon for $2.69 or 1 quart for $0.75. Which is the better buy?

Expressing Ratios

You will learn to express ratios in three ways.

Why learn this? You can compare numbers in ways that help you understand their relationship.

Lauren told her brother he could have all the red gummy bears in her hand. What part of her handful is red bears compared to the whole?

You can write the ratio of red bears to the whole handful of bears in three ways.

3 to 8   3:8 $\dfrac{3}{8}$

Read each ratio "three to eight."
Find other ratios by looking at Lauren's yellow gummy bears.

part:whole	whole:part	part:part
yellow bears:all bears	all bears:yellow bears	yellow bears:red bears
5:8	8:5	5:3

Talk About It

- Is the ratio 3 to 8 the same as 8 to 3? Explain.

- Lauren ate a yellow gummy bear from her handful. Now, what is the ratio of yellow bears to the whole handful? Explain.

- Why is the order in which you write a ratio important?

Check Your Understanding   💡 CRITICAL THINKING

Write each ratio in three ways. Then write *part to whole*, *whole to part*, or *part to part* to describe the ratio.

1. circles to squares

2. all colors to red

3. circles to all shapes

4. blue to red

5. all shapes to squares

6. green to all colors

7. squares to stars

8. red to green

Health Link

The average 10-year-old needs between 9 and 12 hours of sleep each night. How many hours do you sleep at night? What is the ratio of your sleeping hours to the total hours in a day? What is the ratio of sleeping hours to waking hours?

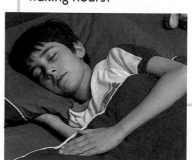

PRACTICE

Write *a* or *b* to show which fraction represents the ratio.

9. 5 to 2 **a.** $\frac{2}{5}$ **b.** $\frac{5}{2}$

10. 5:9 **a.** $\frac{9}{5}$ **b.** $\frac{5}{9}$

11. 8 to 4 **a.** $\frac{8}{4}$ **b.** $\frac{4}{8}$

12. 1:20 **a.** $\frac{1}{20}$ **b.** $\frac{20}{1}$

For Exercises 13–15, use the table. Write each ratio in three ways.

13. What is the ratio of rock CDs to country CDs?

14. What is the ratio of all CDs to show tunes?

15. What is the ratio of country CDs to all CDs?

FRANK'S CD COLLECTION	
Number of CDs	**Type**
3	Rock
4	Country
1	Show Tunes

Mixed Applications

16. All 9 players showed up for baseball practice with a mitt. What was the ratio of players to mitts?

17. Lynetta found that one-fifth of the 20 M & M® candies were green. What was the ratio of green candies to the whole?

18. Erika got a jewelry case for her birthday. The top and bottom of the case are five-sided, congruent shapes. What solid figure can you name that is the shape of the jewelry case?

19. Kurt made a circle graph that was divided into 4 sections. The angles in three sections of the graph measured 100°, 85°, and 65°. How many degrees were in the angle formed in the fourth section of the graph?

20. Some fifth-grade students caught the flu. Out of 25 students, 5 stayed home sick. What was the ratio of sick students to healthy students?

21. **WRITE ABOUT IT** How does each type of ratio help you understand the relationship between the two numbers being compared?

Mixed Review

Find the missing dimension. You may use a calculator. (pages 430–431)

22. length = 4 in.
width = 3 in.
height = 2 in.
volume = __?__

23. length = 7 ft
width = __?__
height = 6 ft
volume = 336 cu ft

24. length = 8 cm
width = 6 cm
height = __?__
volume = 144 cu cm

Identify the angle. Write *right, acute,* or *obtuse.* (pages 380–381)

25.

26.

27.

Equivalent Ratios

You will learn how to identify and make equivalent ratios.	Why learn this? You can determine if different ratios show the same relationship.	**WORD POWER** equivalent ratios

Fernando is building a kennel for his dog. His dog is 33 inches long from its nose to the tip of its tail. How long should the kennel for Fernando's dog be?

The ratio table below is given as a guide to show the relationship of dog length to kennel length.

Length of Dog from Nose to Tip of Tail (inches)	20	25	30	36	44	51
Length of Dog Kennel (inches)	40	50	60	72	88	102

You can divide or multiply both numbers of a ratio by the same number.

$$\frac{20}{40} \begin{array}{c} \div 20 \\ \\ \div 20 \end{array} = \frac{1}{2} \qquad \frac{1}{2} \begin{array}{c} \times 25 \\ \\ \times 25 \end{array} = \frac{25}{50}$$

- Simplify the other ratios in the table. To what is each equivalent?

The ratios in the table are **equivalent ratios** because they show the same relationship. No matter what size the dog is, the ratio of the length of the dog to the length of the kennel is 1 to 2.

$$\frac{1}{2} \begin{array}{c} \times 33 \\ \\ \times 33 \end{array} = \frac{33}{66} \quad \begin{array}{l} \text{length of dog} \\ \text{length of kennel} \end{array}$$

So, the kennel for Fernando's dog should be 66 inches long.

Talk About It

- Are the ratios $\frac{5}{6}$ and $\frac{15}{18}$ equivalent? Explain.

- How can you use division to find a ratio equivalent to 25:35?

CRITICAL THINKING How are equivalent ratios like equivalent fractions?

Technology Link

With *Graph Links* computer software, you can show data on a double-bar graph.

GRAPH LINKS

English   Español

REMEMBER:

Equivalent fractions name the same amount.

Examples

$\frac{2}{3} = \frac{4}{6}$ $\frac{5}{10} = \frac{1}{2}$

A fraction is in *simplest form* when the GCF of the numerator and denominator is 1.

Example $\frac{3}{7}$

Scruffy and her kennel

PRACTICE

Tell whether the ratios are equivalent. Write *yes* or *no*.

1. $\frac{2}{4}$ and $\frac{6}{12}$

2. 2:5 and 5:10

3. 4 to 12 and 1 to 3

4. $\frac{3}{4}$ and $\frac{12}{20}$

5. 5:10 and 1:2

6. 1 to 4 and 25 to 100

7. Complete the table.

Number of Apples to Make Cider	3	?	?	?
Cups of Cider	1	2	3	4

Write three ratios that are equivalent to the given ratio.

8. 3:1

9. 3:5

10. 1 to 4

11. 10 to 1

12. $\frac{2}{3}$

13. $\frac{1}{4}$

14. $\frac{1}{5}$

15. $\frac{2}{2}$

16. $\frac{9}{3}$

17. 50:100

18. 26:36

19. 100 to 1

Mixed Applications

20. Mary's brother earns $35 for 5 hours of work. How much does he earn for 3 hours of work?

21. A soccer team has 120 toes. How many players are there?

22. There are 28 canoes on the park rack. Of those, 21 are metal. What is the ratio of metal canoes to all the canoes? Write the ratio in simplest form.

23. The directions on a can of lemonade concentrate say to add 3 cans of water. What is the ratio of concentrate to water?

24. Emily baked quiche in a round pan with a diameter of 9 inches. Emily sliced the quiche into 6 equal pieces. How long is it from the tip to the edge of each piece?

25. **WRITE ABOUT IT** Explain how you can tell whether two ratios are equivalent.

Mixed Review

Write *prism* or *pyramid*. Write the polygon that names the base. Identify the solid figure. (pages 424–425)

26.

27.

28.

Multiply. Write the answer in simplest form. (pages 366–367)

29. $\frac{1}{2} \times 1\frac{2}{3} = n$

30. $\frac{2}{3} \times 2\frac{1}{2} = n$

31. $\frac{1}{4} \times 1\frac{1}{2} = n$

More About Equivalent Ratios

You will learn to use ratios to interpret map scales.

Why learn this? You can find the actual distance between two cities.

WORD POWER

map scale

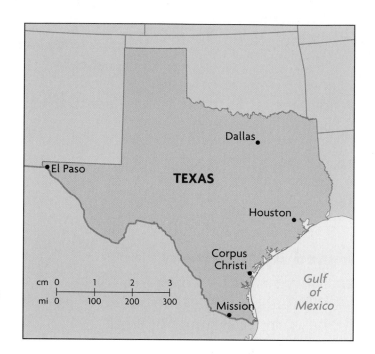

Susan lives in Dallas, Texas. She and her family are looking at a map of Texas to help them decide where to go for the weekend. How far is it from Dallas to El Paso?

Maps show great distances in a small space. A ratio that compares the distance on a map with the actual distance is a **map scale**. You can use the scale to compute the distance from Dallas to El Paso.

The distance on the map from Dallas to El Paso is 5.6 cm. The ratio of centimeters to miles is 1:100.

$$\frac{1}{100} \overset{\times\, 5.6}{\underset{\times\, 5.6}{=}} \frac{5.6}{560} \quad \begin{array}{l} \text{map distance} \\ \text{actual distance} \end{array}$$

So, it is 560 miles from Dallas to El Paso.

• Explain how equivalent ratios are used to compute actual distance on a map.

Check Your Understanding 💡 CRITICAL THINKING

Use the map and the map scale above. Copy and complete the ratio table.

	City	Distance on Map	Actual Distance
1.	Corpus Christi	?	?
	El Paso	5.6 cm	560 mi
2.	Houston	?	?
3.	Mission	?	?

PRACTICE

Copy and complete each ratio table.

4.	**Gallons of Gas Used**	1	2	?	6	?
5.	**Miles Traveled**	22	44	88	?	220

6.	**Number of Canoes**	3	6	9	?	?
7.	**Number of Passengers**	9	18	?	108	270

For Problems 8–12, use the drawing of the clubhouse.

8. What is the width of the porch in units?

9. What is the actual width of the porch?

10. What is the actual area of the meeting room? (HINT: 1 sq unit = 9 sq ft)

11. What is the perimeter of the kitchen in units? in feet?

12. What is the ratio of linear units to feet?

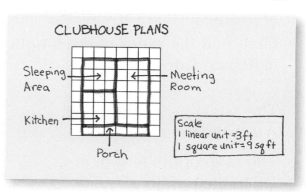

Mixed Applications

13. An architect plans to use a scale of 1 in. = 3 ft in her plan for a new playground for the school. What length will the lines be that represent 3 ft, 6 ft, 12 ft, 18 ft, and 24 ft?

14. The playground will be 48 ft long and 42 ft wide. The principal wants a fence built around the playground. Fencing costs $12 per foot. How much will it cost to fence in the playground?

15. There are 15 girls and 30 boys at Little Hands Preschool. What is the ratio of girls to boys?

16. **WRITE ABOUT IT** Explain why scale drawings are useful when making maps.

Mixed Review

Find the missing angle. (pages 416–417)

17.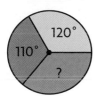

18.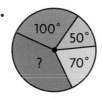

19.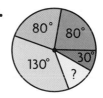

Find the sum. Write the answer in simplest form. (pages 328–329)

20. $2\frac{1}{5} + 1\frac{1}{3} = n$

21. $3\frac{2}{3} + 4\frac{3}{7} = n$

22. $6\frac{1}{8} + 4\frac{5}{6} = n$

MORE PRACTICE Student Handbook page H120

PART 1 Ratios in Similar Figures

You will learn that the matching sides of similar figures have equivalent ratios.	**Why learn this?** You can enlarge or shrink a picture.	**WORD POWER** similar

In **similar** figures, the matching angles are congruent and the sides have equivalent ratios. Similar figures do not have to be the same size.

How can you check whether the shapes of the two triangles shown are similar?

- First, find the ratios of the lengths of the matching sides.

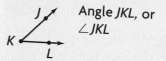

The ratio of the length of $\overline{AB}$ to the length of $\overline{AC}$ is $\frac{6}{8}$.

The ratio of the length of $\overline{DE}$ to the length of $\overline{DF}$ is $\frac{3}{4}$.

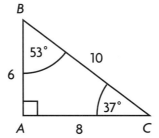

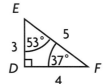

➪ Since $\frac{6}{8} \div \frac{2}{2} = \frac{3}{4}$, the ratios of the lengths of the matching sides are equivalent.

- Then, measure the matching angles.

  $\angle ABC$ measures 53°; $\angle DEF$ measures 53°.

  $\angle BCA$ measures 37°; $\angle EFD$ measures 37°.

  $\angle CAB$ measures 90°; $\angle FDE$ measures 90°.

➪ The matching angles are congruent.

So, triangle ABC and triangle DEF are similar.

REMEMBER:

When two rays have the same endpoint, they form an *angle*.

Example

Angle *JKL*, or $\angle JKL$

Talk About It

- If you rotated triangle DEF, would it still be similar to triangle ABC? Explain.

- If two shapes are congruent, are they similar? Explain.

Technology Link

In *Mighty Math Number Heroes*, the game *GeoComputer* challenges you to identify shapes that are similar to a given shape.

💡 **CRITICAL THINKING**   In the example above, how does the ratio of the length of $\overline{AB}$ to $\overline{BC}$ compare with the ratio of the length of $\overline{DE}$ to $\overline{EF}$?

PRACTICE

Write *yes* or *no* to tell whether the shapes are similar.

1.
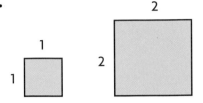

2.
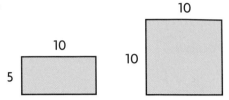

3.
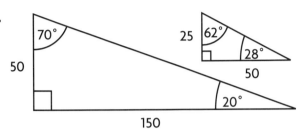

4.
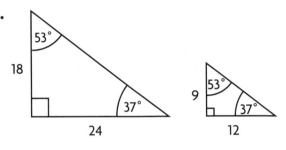

Find the length of the missing side in the similar shapes.

5.
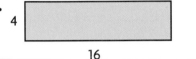

6.
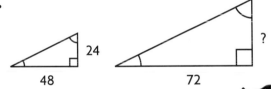

7.
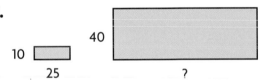

8.
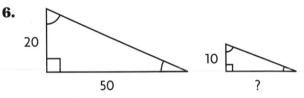

Mixed Applications

9. Laura arrived at the dance studio at 3:25. Her first class began 15 minutes later. She spent 1 hour 30 minutes in her first class and 45 minutes in her second class. She had a 10-minute break between classes. At what time did Laura's second class end?

10. The ratio of the width of a pot to the width of an African violet should be 1 to 3. What width pot should you use for a 6-inch-wide plant?

11. One pound of wax will make eight 8-inch candles. How many 4-inch candles will a pound of wax make?

12. Newscasters say it takes 1 minute to read 15 lines of news. How long does it take to read 1 line of news? (HINT: 1 min = 60 sec)

13. ✏️ **WRITE ABOUT IT** Are a 4 × 4 square and an 8 × 12 rectangle similar? Explain why or why not.

LESSON
CONTINUES ▶

PROBLEM-SOLVING STRATEGY
Write a Number Sentence

THE PROBLEM Hakeem made a sundial for his science project. In the instruction book for making the sundial it said, "Make a triangle that is similar to the one shown." What is the length of the missing side of Hakeem's triangle?

REMEMBER:
☑ Understand
☑ Plan
☑ Solve
☑ Look Back

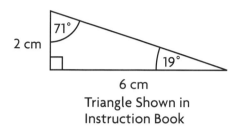

Triangle Shown in Instruction Book

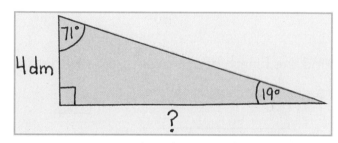

Triangle Hakeem Made

☑ Understand

• What are you asked to do?

• What information will you use?

• Is there information you will not use? If so, what?

☑ Plan

• What strategy can you use to solve the problem?

You can *write a number sentence.*

☑ Solve

• How can you use the strategy to solve the problem?

First, find the ratios of the lengths of the sides of the triangle shown in the instruction book.

The ratio is $\frac{2}{6}$, or $\frac{1}{3}$.

Since Hakeem made a triangle that was similar to the one shown, write a number sentence to form an equivalent ratio and find the missing side.

$\frac{1}{3} \times \frac{4}{4} = \frac{4}{12}$ So, the length of the missing side is 12 dm.

☑ Look Back

• How can you decide if your answer is reasonable?

• What other strategy could you use?

PRACTICE

Write a number sentence to solve.

1. Roland made a rectangular design. Then he made a similar rectangle to frame the design. What is the length of the missing side of the frame?

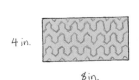

4 in.

8 in.

?

16 in.

2. Rochelle covered an $8\frac{1}{2}$-in.-tall cylinder with an $8\frac{1}{2}$ in. × 11 in. paper rectangle. What is the diameter of the base of the cylinder to the nearest half inch?

3. Chad is playing football. He and his team start at the 1-yard line. They move forward $3\frac{1}{2}$ yards on the first play. They move back $1\frac{1}{2}$ yards on the second play and forward 7 yards on the third play. On what yard line is Chad's team?

Mixed Applications

Solve.

CHOOSE A STRATEGY

• Write a Number Sentence   • Act It Out   • Work Backward   • Draw a Diagram

4. Today the mileage display on Mosi's bicycle shows 132.2 km. Yesterday he rode his bike 7.7 km. The day before yesterday he rode 5.9 km. The day before that was Friday. He rode 4.8 km. What did the mileage display show Friday morning?

5. José gave directions to get from the garage to the library. He said, "When you leave the garage, make a 90° turn east onto Elm. Walk 3 blocks, and make a 90° turn north onto Main. Walk 2 blocks and make a 90° turn east onto Magnolia. Walk 1 block to the library." Make a map of José's directions.

6. Farina poured 7.5 liters of hot water into the kitchen sink. She added 5 milliliters of liquid dishwashing soap to the hot water. How much liquid was in the sink?

7. Mr. Linnard swam 45 laps each day from Monday through Friday. He swam 66 laps each day on Saturday and Sunday. What is the mean for the number of laps he swam?

8. Eric went to a state park on Saturday. He spent $\frac{3}{5}$ of the time hiking, $\frac{1}{5}$ of the time in the park museum, and $\frac{1}{5}$ of the time taking photos. Eric hiked for 1 hour 30 minutes. How long did he spend at the park?

9. Mrs. Chung has a rectangular dining room table. She bought a rectangular tablecloth for it. Are the rectangles similar?

3 ft

6 ft

4 ft

18 ft

MATH FUN!

Are You a Square or a Rectangle?

PURPOSE To analyze two pieces of data by using a ratio

YOU WILL NEED measuring tape or yardstick, paper and pencil, calculator

Stand with your arms stretched out so that you make a T. Have a friend measure your height and your armspan, from fingertip to fingertip, in inches. Find the ratio of your height to your armspan. If the ratio is equivalent to 1, then you are a square. If the ratio is not equivalent to 1, you are a rectangle.

 HOME NOTE Do this activity with your family. Who is a square? a rectangle?

MAP IT!

PURPOSE To make a scale drawing

YOU WILL NEED grid paper, ruler, pencil

Make a scale drawing of your classroom. Use grid paper and a ruler. Be sure to include the scale you used.

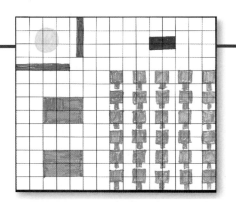

Plan a Trip

PURPOSE To use a map scale

YOU WILL NEED map, ruler, pencil

Use your knowledge of map scales to plan a trip. Find a map for a place you would like to visit. Plan a trip there. You can travel by car at 50 miles an hour or by airplane at 500 miles an hour.

Find a place on the map. Choose a way to travel there. Decide the date and time that you will leave, how many hours you want to travel, and where you will be when it's time to go to bed.

Plan the next day of your trip. Where will you be by the end of the second day?

CHAPTER 27 REVIEW

✓ CHECK UNDERSTANDING

VOCABULARY

1. You can use a __?__ to compare two numbers. (page 444)

2. __?__ show the same relationship. (page 448)

3. In __?__ figures, the matching angles are congruent and the sides have equivalent ratios. (page 452)

4. A ratio that compares the distance on a map with the actual distance is a __?__. (page 450)

Write *a* or *b* to show which fraction represents the ratio. (pages 446–447)

5. 50:1
   a. $\frac{50}{1}$ **b.** $\frac{1}{50}$

6. 9 to 5
   a. $\frac{5}{9}$ **b.** $\frac{9}{5}$

7. 12:36
   a. $\frac{36}{12}$ **b.** $\frac{12}{36}$

8. 25 to 100
   a. $\frac{25}{100}$ **b.** $\frac{100}{25}$

Write *yes* or *no* to tell whether the shapes are similar. (pages 452–453)

9.

10.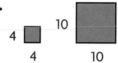

11.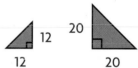

✓ CHECK SKILLS

Write three ratios that are equivalent to the given ratio. (pages 448–449)

12. 8 to 10

13. 3:7

14. 75:100

15. 12 to 6

For Problems 16 and 17, use the drawing of the garden. (pages 450–451)

16. What is the actual perimeter of the tomato section?

17. What is the actual area of the green-bean section?

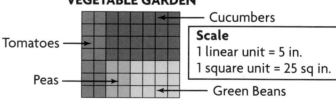

VEGETABLE GARDEN

Cucumbers

Tomatoes

Peas

Green Beans

Scale
1 linear unit = 5 in.
1 square unit = 25 sq in.

✓ CHECK PROBLEM SOLVING

Solve. (pages 454–455)

CHOOSE A STRATEGY

• **Write a Number Sentence**   • **Act It Out**   • **Work Backward**   • **Draw a Diagram**

18. Fred puts a rectangular note card in an envelope that is a similar rectangle. What is the length of the missing side of the envelope?

8 in.

3 in.

4 in.

?

DID YOU KNOW...

The Mars company in Hackettstown, New Jersey makes
M & M® candies. According to the company, this is the
color assortment: brown 30%, red 20%, yellow 20%,
green 10%, orange 10%, blue 10%.

Design a Colorful Party Product

Have you ever noticed that fun products like markers, candies, sprinkles, confetti and Post-it® notes come out in new colors all the time? If you were designing a fun product for a party, like sprinkles or party hats, what colors would you choose? How many of each color would you put in a package of 100?

YOU WILL NEED: decimal grid paper, ruler, markers or colored pencils

Work with a group: Your job is to

- Decide on a party product and create a catchy name.

- Decide on colors for your product. You should have at least three different colors in a package.

- Decide how many out of 100 will be made in each color and make a model to show the percent of each color.

A FEW IDEAS FOR COLOR SETS

- everyday colors
- last day of school colors
- birthday colors
- back to school colors
- seasonal colors
- holiday colors

Some Flavorful Ideas

- lime   - green
- kiwi fruit   - green
- mango   - orange
- watermelon   - pink
- bubble gum   - pink
- blueberry   - blue

DID YOU

✓ decide on a party product and name it?

✓ choose a set of at least three colors?

✓ decide how many out of 100 will be made in each color, and make a model to show the percent.

25% blueberry
20% strawberry
...erry

"Berry Nice C...
for late sum...

25% 25...
20% 20...
10%

Understanding Percent

You will investigate how to represent percent as part of a hundred.	**Why learn this?** Many amounts, such as your grades, sales taxes, and amount off during a sale, are expressed as percents.	**WORD POWER** percent

Did you know that "50% off" means you can buy an item for half price? **Percent** means "per hundred." The symbol for *percent* is %. 1 percent is the same as 1 out of 100.

Explore

MATERIALS: 1-inch grid paper, counters, scissors, tape

Kyle has 7 pennies. He wants to find out what percent of a dollar he has.

Use a 10 × 10 grid to represent the number of pennies in a dollar. Then use counters to show Kyle's pennies.

Record

Draw a picture of your 7 counters on the grid paper.

Write the percent of a dollar the model shows. Explain how you can use grid paper to show percent.

Talk About It

• How many pennies are in a dollar?

• How many squares do Kyle's pennies take up?

• What percent of a dollar does Kyle have in pennies?

Now, investigate showing other percent amounts on grid paper.

Try This

Place counters on the grid to show the following amounts.

Draw a picture and write the percent of each.

A. 23 campers out of 100 campers

B. 42 ducks out of 100 birds

C. 16 cents out of a dollar

> ◄ **Language Link** ►
>
> The *cent* in *percent* means "100." Use a dictionary. What other words can you find in which *cent* relates to 100?
>
> **Example**
> A *century* is 100 years.

Technology Link ►
E–Lab • **Activity 28** Available on CD-ROM
and the Internet at http://www.hbschool.com/elab

Talk About It

- Which is more, 23 percent or 42 percent?

- What does 100 percent mean?

- How is a percent like a ratio?

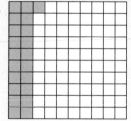

▭▷ **WRITE ABOUT IT** How could you show 100 percent on a decimal square?

HANDS-ON PRACTICE

Use counters to show the following on your 10 × 10 grid. Draw a picture and write the percent.

1. 55 dollars out of 100 dollars

2. 65 children out of 100 people at the party

3. 25 blue balloons out 100 balloons

4. 20 red M&M's® out of a bag of 100

Applying What You Learned

Look at the picture. Write the percent.

5.

6.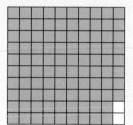

7.

For Exercises 8–9, choose the more reasonable percent. Write *a* or *b*.

8. "Almost everyone passed the test," Miss Jones exclaimed with a big smile.

    a. 99% passed **b.** 12% passed

9. "Very few children like spicy food. Out of 100 children, fewer than 5 like it," said the chef.

    a. 55% **b.** 4%

Mixed Applications

10. A few months ago, Hannah had 100 days to wait until her birthday. Now her wait is 90 percent over. How many days has she waited?

11. Rochelle bought $5\frac{1}{2}$ yards of fabric to make a new comforter for her bed. She used $\frac{3}{4}$ of the fabric she bought. How much fabric does she have left over?

12. Jim gave the ice-cream vendor $1.00 for an ice-cream sandwich. He received $0.29 in change. What percent of his dollar did he spend on the ice-cream sandwich?

13. ▭▷ **Write a problem** about percent. Mention part of 100 in your problem.

Connecting Percents and Decimals

| **You will learn** to write a percent as a decimal. | **Why learn this?** When percents are expressed as decimals, they are in a more familiar form. |

Mike surveyed 100 students on how they get to school. He showed the results on a decimal square.

Talk About It

- How many students out of 100 take the bus? What percent take the bus?

- How many students out of 100 ride bikes? What percent ride bikes?

- How many students out of 100 walk? What percent walk?

You can also write a percent as a decimal.

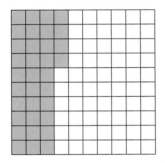

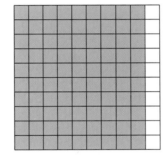

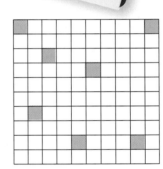

34 percent	90 percent	7 percent
Read: thirty-four hundredths	**Read:** ninety hundredths	**Read:** seven hundredths
Write: 0.34	**Write:** 0.90	**Write:** 0.07

Talk About It

- Do 0.90 and 0.09 represent the same number?

- What percent does 0.90 represent? What percent does 0.09 represent?

- Using what you know about percent as a decimal, how could you enter 78 percent into a calculator?

💡 **CRITICAL THINKING**   Explain how you know that a percent can be expressed as a decimal.

PRACTICE

For Exercises 1–3, study the shaded parts of the grid.

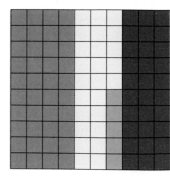

1. What percent of the squares are purple?

2. What percent of the squares are red?

3. When you add all the colors, what percent is the total?

Write the number as a percent and as a decimal.

4. fifty-one hundredths

5. eighty hundredths

6. three hundredths

7. fourteen hundredths

Write the decimal as a percent.

8. 0.75   9. 0.31   10. 0.08   11. 0.80   12. 0.15

Write the percent as a decimal.

13. 56%   14. 99%   15. 40%   16. 12%   17. 2%

Mixed Applications

For Problems 18 and 20, write the answer as a percent and as a decimal.

18. The school had a cooking contest. Out of 100 recipes, 44 were for pizza. What percent were pizza recipes?

19. During the last 24 hours, Jeremy watched 2 hours of TV. Compare his hours of watching TV to his hours of doing other things.

20. Mary planted 100 marigold seeds. She had 77 sprouts. What percent of the seeds did not sprout?

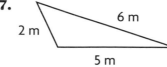

21. ✏️ **WRITE ABOUT IT** How does knowing about decimals help you understand percent? Give an example.

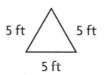ixed Review

Write *a* or *b* to show which fraction represents the ratio. (pages 446–447)

22. 6 to 2
    a. $\frac{2}{6}$ b. $\frac{6}{2}$

23. 4:8
    a. $\frac{8}{4}$ b. $\frac{4}{8}$

24. 9 to 3
    a. $\frac{9}{3}$ b. $\frac{3}{9}$

25. 1:10
    a. $\frac{1}{10}$ b. $\frac{10}{1}$

Name each triangle. Write *isosceles*, *scalene*, or *equilateral*. (pages 388–389)

26.
5 ft   5 ft
5 ft

27.
2 m   6 m
5 m

28.
6 in.   6 in.
4 in.

You will learn how to represent percents as fractions.

Why learn this? You can use a percent or a fraction, depending on which is simpler.

The Church Street Dance Club was having a square dance. There were 100 dancers. The dance did not go as planned. It turned out that 75 percent of the dancers did not know how to do-si-do! What fraction of the dancers did not know how to do-si-do?

There were 75 out of 100 dancers who did not know how to do-si-do. You can show this number on a decimal square.

You can write it as a ratio, or a fraction: $\frac{75}{100}$.

$$\frac{75}{100} = \frac{75 \div 25}{100 \div 25} = \frac{3}{4}$$

Write the fraction in simplest form.

To do-si-do, dancers pass each other right shoulder to right shoulder and circle each other back to back.

So, $\frac{3}{4}$ of the dancers did not know how to do-si-do.

• Suppose one quarter of the square dancers were wearing western outfits. What percent is that? How would you write it as a fraction?

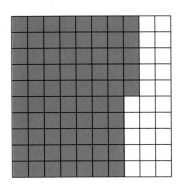

A fraction with 100 as the denominator can be written as a percent.

$$\frac{1}{100} = 1\% \qquad \frac{25}{100} = 25\% \qquad \frac{99}{100} = 99\%$$

 You can use a calculator to change a fraction to a percent. First, change it to a decimal.

Technology Link

In *Mighty Math Number Heroes,* the game *Fraction Fireworks* challenges you to change fractions to decimals.

EXAMPLE

Change $\frac{1}{100}$ to a decimal and then to a percent.

Enter the numerator first. Divide it by the denominator.

| 1 | ÷ | 1 | 0 | 0 | = | = 0.01 |

Write 0.01 as a percent: 1%.

Calculator Activities page H69

PRACTICE

Write the percent as a fraction in simplest form.

1. 20%   **2.** 35%   **3.** 50%   **4.** 48%

5. 4 percent   **6.** fifteen per hundred   **7.** thirty-seven per hundred

Write the fraction as a percent.

8. $\frac{7}{100}$ **9.** $\frac{7}{10}$ **10.** $\frac{1}{1}$ **11.** $\frac{6}{10}$

12. $\frac{2}{25}$ **13.** $\frac{3}{25}$ **14.** $\frac{16}{25}$ **15.** $\frac{6}{100}$

Write as a decimal and as a fraction in simplest form.

16. 18 percent   **17.** 25 percent   **18.** 33 percent

19. 3 percent   **20.** 30 percent   **21.** 55 percent

Mixed Applications

22. A ship went on a 100-day trip. People were ashore 25 days; the rest of the time they were at sea. What percent of time were they at sea?

23. At the spring concert, 100 fifth graders performed. Out of that group, 35 percent played the flute. How many students played the flute?

24. A cheese pizza was divided into 8 parts and an equal-size pepperoni pizza into 12 parts. Isaac ate 2 pieces from the cheese pizza. Josh ate 3 pieces from the pepperoni pizza. Who ate more?

25. Of the fifth graders, $\frac{3}{5}$ sing in the chorus and $\frac{2}{5}$ play a band instrument. Out of the 100 fifth graders, how many sing? play a band instrument?

26. The ratio of teachers to students at Pinewood Elementary School is 1 to 20. There are 8 teachers. How many students are there?

27. ⏏ **WRITE ABOUT IT** Explain how you can change a percent to a fraction and a fraction to a percent.

Mixed Review

Find the sum or difference. Write the answer in simplest form.
(pages 314–315)

28. $\frac{3}{4} + \frac{1}{3} = n$ **29.** $\frac{5}{8} - \frac{1}{3} = n$ **30.** $\frac{3}{10} + \frac{2}{5} = n$

Tell whether the ratios are equivalent. Write *yes* or *no*. (pages 448–449)

31. $\frac{1}{4}$ and $\frac{2}{8}$ **32.** 6:12 and 1:2   **33.** 4 to 12 and 1 to 4

Benchmark Percents

You will learn to estimate some commonly used percents, such as 10% and 50%.	Why learn this? You can quickly recognize a reasonable answer when estimating a percent.	

Sean's grandma has four grandchildren. She bought a jar for each of her grandchildren. Every time the children find a penny, they place it in their jar. They want to estimate how full each jar is.

You can use percents to make an estimate. A **benchmark percent** is a commonly used percent that is close to the amount you are estimating.

REMEMBER:

A *benchmark* is a point of reference you can use to make a reasonable estimate.

Examples
10; 100; 1,000

25% is a good benchmark for amounts close to one fourth.
50% is a good benchmark for amounts close to one half.
10%, 75%, and 100% are other common benchmark percents.

Talk About It

• What benchmark percent can you use to estimate each amount in the jars above?

• What benchmark percent would you use to estimate 27 pennies as a percent of a dollar? 52 pennies? 79 pennies?

Using benchmark percents can help you estimate the percent of a total other than 100.

EXAMPLES

Of the 80 students Michael surveyed, 13% said they like to cook. What is a reasonable estimate of this percent of students?

Think: 13% is close to the benchmark percent 10%.

Since 13% is a little more than 10%, a reasonable estimate would be that about 10% of the students Michael surveyed said they like to cook.

Art Link

Quilt blocks are often made with light, medium, and dark fabric. Look at the picture of a Pinwheel block. What percent is dark fabric? medium fabric? light fabric?

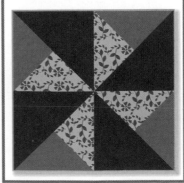

PRACTICE

For Exercises 1–4, choose from the following benchmarks:
10%, 25%, 50%, 75%, or 100%.

1. 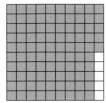   **2.** 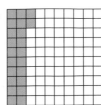   **3.** 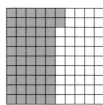   **4.**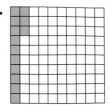

Tell what benchmark percent you would use to estimate each percent.

5. 72%   **6.** 11%   **7.** 46%   **8.** 30%   **9.** 97%

For Exercises 10–13, choose the more reasonable benchmark. Write *a* or *b*.

10. Three quarters of the class earned an A on the test.

    a. 25%   **b.** 75%

11. Very few of the children live in a house without a television.

    a. 25%   **b.** 10%

12. A quarter of the football team must lose weight.

    a. 25%   **b.** 50%

13. All of the puppies have been vaccinated.

    a. 100%   **b.** 50%

Mixed Applications

14. Mark has finished 7 out of 13 chapters of his new book. What benchmark would you use to estimate the percent of the book he has finished?

15. Lee made a scale model of his house, using a scale of 1 in. = 4 ft. The model has a 1-inch-tall fireplace. What is the actual height of the fireplace?

16. How many angles will you find in 3 triangles and 4 quadrilaterals?

17. ✏️ **Write a problem** that includes a percent that can be estimated by using a benchmark percent.

Mixed Review

Write *chord, diameter,* or *radius* for each line segment. (pages 410–411)

18.   **19.**   **20.**   **21.**

Find the sum or difference. Write the answer in simplest form. (pages 328–331)

22. $3\frac{2}{3} - 1\frac{1}{6} = n$ **23.** $4\frac{1}{8} + 2\frac{1}{4} = n$ **24.** $5\frac{4}{9} - 2\frac{1}{3} = n$

Percents in Circle Graphs

You will learn how to read percents from circle graphs.

Why learn this? You can understand circle graphs you see in newspapers and magazines.

The fifth grade held several car washes. They made $400. They decided to go to a game of their favorite baseball team.

This circle graph shows the percentage of money they spent in each category. They spent 40% of the money on the cost of a bus, 20% on tickets, 30% on food, and 10% on programs.

$400 EARNED FOR BASEBALL TRIP
10% Programs
40% Bus
30% Food
20% Tickets

Talk About It

- What decimal represents each section of the circle graph? What fraction?

- What is the sum of the percents that represent the whole, or the $400 the fifth grade made?

- If the fifth grade spent $40 on programs, how much did they spend on the cost of a bus? on tickets? on food?

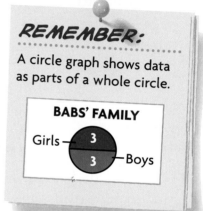

REMEMBER:
A circle graph shows data as parts of a whole circle.

BABS' FAMILY
Girls — 3
3 — Boys

Check Your Understanding  CRITICAL THINKING

For Problems 1–3, use the circle graph.

1. According to this circle graph, what fills one half of our landfills?

2. What fills one tenth of our landfills?

3. Ted saw an old toaster in the landfill. In this circle graph, under what category would it fall?

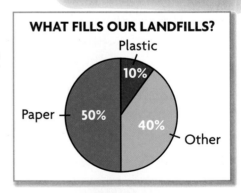

WHAT FILLS OUR LANDFILLS?
Plastic
10%
Paper — 50%
40%
Other

For Problems 4–6, use the circle graph.

4. Which group is larger, students who bring their lunch to school every day or students who buy their lunch?

5. What does the category labeled *Other* probably represent?

6. What decimal and fraction represent each section of the circle graph?

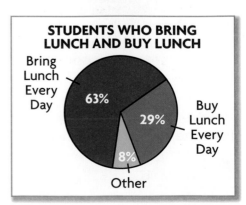

STUDENTS WHO BRING LUNCH AND BUY LUNCH
Bring Lunch Every Day
63%
29% — Buy Lunch Every Day
8%
Other

PRACTICE

For Problems 7–8, use the first circle graph.

7. Do more than half or less than half of the students surveyed get an allowance?

8. What decimal represents the students who get an allowance?

For Problems 9–11, use the second circle graph.

9. Do more students get less than $6 a week or more than $6 a week?

10. Which groups in this circle graph are the same size?

11. Which two categories cover one half of the circle graph?

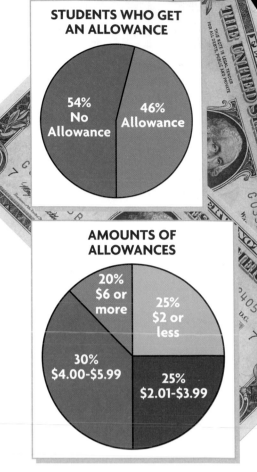

STUDENTS WHO GET AN ALLOWANCE

54% No Allowance

46% Allowance

AMOUNTS OF ALLOWANCES

20% $6 or more

25% $2 or less

30% $4.00-$5.99

25% $2.01-$3.99

Mixed Applications

For Problems 12–18, use the table.

12. What decimal and percent represent the students who chose in-line skates?

13. What decimal and percent represent the students who chose skateboards?

14. If you were to make a circle graph of these data, what would the largest section show?

15. How many times larger would the section for in-line skates be than the section for bikes?

17. What decimal represents the students who chose bikes? What percent of the students chose bikes? (HINT: 10 out of 50 chose bikes.)

Favorite Wheels	
In-line skates	30 votes
Bikes	10 votes
Skateboards	10 votes

16. Did more than half or less than half of the students choose in-line skates? bikes? skateboards?

18. ✏ **WRITE ABOUT IT** Suppose you are making a circle graph for the Favorite Wheels data, using a circle divided into ten equal sections. Explain how to represent each part of the graph using percent.

LESSON
CONTINUES ▶

PART 2 PROBLEM-SOLVING STRATEGY
Make a Graph

THE PROBLEM Glen surveyed 200 fifth-grade students in his school to find out their favorite music. He found that 30% of the students like rock music the most, 30% like pop, 20% like country, 10% like new age, and 10% like classical. Glen wants to share this information with his class. What would be the best way for Glen to display the data? Which music is the most popular?

REMEMBER:

☑ Understand
☑ Plan
☑ Solve
☑ Look Back

☑ Understand

- What are you asked to find?

- What information will you use?

- Is there information you will not use? If so, what?

☑ Plan

- What strategy can you use to solve the problem?

  You can *make a graph* to display the data, showing the percentage of students who prefer each kind of music.

What is your favorite kind of music?

☑ Solve

- What graph would be the best to make?

  Since Glen wants to show the relationship of the parts to the whole, a circle graph would be best. Use a circle divided into ten equal parts. Shade 3 sections to represent rock music, 3 sections to represent pop music, and 2 sections to represent country music. Shade 1 section to represent new age music and 1 section to represent classical music. Label and title the circle graph.

  So, rock music and pop music are the two favorite kinds of music.

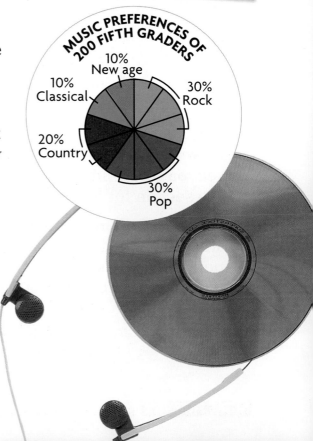

MUSIC PREFERENCES OF 200 FIFTH GRADERS

10% New age
10% Classical
30% Rock
20% Country
30% Pop

☑ Look Back

- Why is this the best way to display the data?

- What other strategy could you use?

PRACTICE

CHOOSE   Paper/Pencil Calculator Hands-on Mental Math

Make a graph to solve.

END-OF-YEAR FIELD TRIP	
Place	Percent of Votes
Planetarium	20%
Theater	10%
Water Park	40%
Museum	10%
Zoo	20%

1. Randy surveyed the fifth-grade students to find out where to go for the end-of-the-year field trip. He organized the data in the table. How can he show which two choices received 50% of the votes? What graph should he make to display these data?

MORGAN'S SAVINGS	
Month	Amount Saved
January	$10
February	$20
March	$20
April	$30
May	$20

2. Morgan has $100 that she saved from January through May. She made a table showing the amount saved each month. How can she show the two months in which she saved 50% of the $100? What graph could she make to display these data?

Mixed Applications

Solve.

CHOOSE A STRATEGY

• **Make a Graph** • **Write a Number Sentence** • **Guess and Check** • **Work Backward** • **Make a Model**

3. Daniel surveyed 40 men and women. Of the men, 5 like to read, 7 like to do yard work, and 8 like to exercise. Of the women, 7 like to read, 5 like to do yard work, and 8 like to exercise. Which activity did both men and women prefer? How can you show this?

4. Popcorn in a movie theater costs $2.55. The same amount costs $0.35 to pop at home. A movie ticket is $3.75. It costs $2.50 to rent a video. How much do you save by renting a video and popping popcorn at home?

5. What fraction multiplication sentence does this model represent? What is the product?

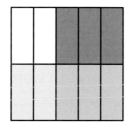

6. Mrs. Price made a long-distance phone call that cost $2.25 for the first minute and $0.30 for each additional minute. The call lasted for 18 minutes. How much did it cost?

7. There are 56 teachers at Sunridge Elementary. Of the teachers, $\frac{1}{4}$ have no children. Some teachers have 1 child, and twice as many have 2 or more children. How many have 2 or more children?

8. The Lions are ranked number 1. Since the season began they have moved up 6 places, down 2 places, down 1 place, and up 4 places. What rank were they at the beginning of the season?

CULTURAL CONNECTION

Canada's Provinces

Sara and Paul live in Boston, Massachusetts. Every summer they visit their grandparents in Halifax, Nova Scotia, in Canada. Their grandparents take them on trips to different Canadian provinces. They have visited 3 of Canada's 10 provinces. Write the percent of provinces they have visited. Change the percent to a decimal and to a fraction.

> **CULTURAL LINK**
>
> The United States and Canada are important trading partners. There is a greater exchange of products between the two countries than between any other two countries in the world. About 50% of Canada's fish products are sold to the United States. Canada supplies the world with 28% of the world's newsprint. Canada and the United States send many farm products to other countries. Canada provides 20% of the world's supply of wheat.

Fishing boats in Blue Rocks, Nova Scotia

Work Together

1. Sara and Paul made a scrapbook about the places they visited in Canada. They divided it into 5 equal sections. One section was about the cities and towns. Write this as a percent. Change the percent to a decimal and to a fraction.

2. In the city-and-town section, Sara put two photographs of Halifax, four of Toronto, three of Quebec City, and one of Montreal. Write a fraction in simplest form for each city's representation in the section. Change the fractions to decimals and to percents.

3. Next summer Sara and Paul will visit Newfoundland and New Brunswick, two more Canadian provinces. Then they will have seen 5 of the 10 provinces. Make a circle graph to show the number of provinces Sara and Paul will have visited by the end of next summer. Write the percent on the graph.

4. Make a circle graph with percents. Show that $\frac{4}{5}$ of everything that Canada exports, or sells to other countries, goes to the United States. Make a second circle graph to show that $\frac{2}{3}$ of everything that Canada imports, or buys from other countries, comes from the United States.

✓ CHECK UNDERSTANDING

VOCABULARY

1. _?_ means "per hundred."
(page 460)

2. A _?_ is a commonly used percent, such as 10%, 25%, 50%, 75%, or 100%. (page 466)

Look at the picture. Write the percent. (pages 460–461)

3.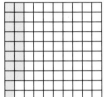

4.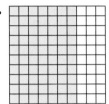

5.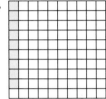

✓ CHECK SKILLS

Write the number as a percent and as a decimal. (pages 462–463)

6. eighty hundredths

7. fifteen hundredths

8. six hundredths

Write as a decimal and as a fraction in simplest form. (pages 464–465)

9. 4 percent

10. 75 percent

11. 20 percent

Tell what benchmark percent you would use to estimate each percent. (pages 466–467)

12. 27%

13. 12%

14. 53%

15. 98%

16. 74%

✓ CHECK PROBLEM SOLVING

Solve. (pages 470–471)

CHOOSE A STRATEGY

• Make a Model   • Guess and Check   • Make a Graph   • Draw a Picture

17. Nancy surveyed the fifth-grade students to find out their favorite local pizzeria. The table at the right shows the results of her survey. How can she show the class which two pizzerias received 50% of the votes?

FAVORITE PIZZERIAS	
Pizzeria	Percent of Votes
Benny's Parlor	10%
Surf's Up Pizza	40%
Pizza Palace	30%
Lotsa Pizza	20%

18. Val had 100 stickers. She gave away 22 percent of her stickers. How many stickers did she give away?

19. Jared just got a raise of $1 per week in his allowance. How much more allowance did he earn in one year?

VOCABULARY CHECK

Choose a term from the box to complete each sentence.

1. To compare two numbers, such as 3 to 1 or 5 to 7, you can use a __?__ . (page 444)

2. Ratios such as 2 to 1 and 50 to 25 show the same relationship. They are __?__ ratios. (page 448)

3. A ratio that compares the distance on a map with the actual distance is a __?__ . (page 450)

4. Figures that have matching, congruent angles and sides with equivalent ratios are called __?__ figures. (page 452)

5. "Per hundred" is another way to say the word __?__ .
(page 460)

6. A commonly used percent, such as 10%, 50%, or 100%, is called a __?__ percent. (page 466)

STUDY AND SOLVE

CHAPTER 27

EXAMPLE

Write ratios that are equivalent to the given ratio.

8 to 10

$8 \div 2 = 4$

$10 \div 2 = 5$

$8 \times 2 = 16$

$10 \times 2 = 20$

Multiply or divide both numbers by the same number to find equivalent ratios. Divide 8 by 2, and divide 10 by 2. So, 4 to 5 is equivalent to 8 to 10. Multiply 8 by 2, and multiply 10 by 2. So, 16 to 20 is equivalent to 8 to 10.

Write three ratios that are equivalent to the given ratio. (pages 448–449)

7. 6 to 10   **8.** 15:5

9. 25:100   **10.** 3 to 1

For Problems 11–13, use the diagram. Find the actual measurements. (pages 450–451)

JOHN'S APARTMENT

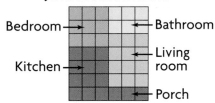

Scale:
1 linear unit = 4 ft
1 square unit = 16 sq ft

11. the perimeter of John's apartment, including the porch

12. the area of John's living room

13. the area of John's apartment, not counting the porch

Write *a* or *b* to show which fraction represents the ratio. (pages 446–447)

14. 25 to 1

   a. $\frac{25}{1}$

   b. $\frac{1}{25}$

15. 10:5

   a. $\frac{5}{10}$

   b. $\frac{10}{5}$

Write *yes* or *no* to tell whether the shapes are similar. (pages 452–453)

16. **17.**

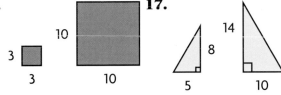

18.

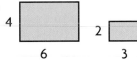

Solve. (pages 454–455)

19. Rebecca enlarged a 4-inch by 5-inch photograph. The enlarged photo is a similar rectangle 8 inches wide. How long is the enlarged photo?

CHAPTER 28

EXAMPLE

Write as a decimal and as a fraction in simplest form.

75 percent

fraction: $\frac{75}{100}$, or $\frac{3}{4}$ in simplest form

decimal: 0.75

Write 75 percent as a fraction. 75 hundredths, or $\frac{75}{100}$ To find the simplest form of $\frac{75}{100}$, divide by the GCF. The GCF of 75 and 100 is 25. $\frac{75}{100} \div \frac{25}{25} = \frac{3}{4}$ You can use a calculator to change a fraction to a decimal. $\frac{75}{100} = 75 \div 100 = 0.75$

Write as a decimal and as a fraction in simplest form. (pages 464–465)

20. 50 percent   **21.** 42%

22. 8 percent   **23.** 15%

24. 40 percent   **25.** 5%

Look at the picture. Write the percent. (pages 460–461)

26.   **27.**

Write the number as a percent and as a decimal. (pages 462–463)

28. thirty-two hundredths

29. seventy hundredths

30. eight hundredths

Tell what benchmark percent you would use to estimate each percent. (pages 466–467)

31. 9%   **32.** 54%

33. 28%   **34.** 97%

Choose the more reasonable benchmark. Write *a* or *b*. (pages 466–467)

35. <u>All</u> the kittens are tabbies.

   a. 100%   **b.** 75%

36. <u>Very few</u> of us have red hair.

   a. 25%   **b.** 10%

Choose a strategy and solve. (pages 470–471)

37. Rob earned $100. He paid 15 percent in taxes. How much money did he receive after taxes were taken out?

✏ WRITE ABOUT IT

1. Toss a handful of two-color counters. Write the ratio of red counters to yellow counters in three different ways. Explain and write other ratios for the counters. (pages 446–447)

2. Use a circle divided into 10 equal parts to make a circle graph to show the favorite school lunch choices of the fifth-grade students. Explain how you can tell from looking at the graph which lunch one half of the students liked best.

   (pages 468–469)

Favorite Lunch	
Pizza	30%
Hamburger	10%
Salad Bar	50%
Tacos	10%

✔ PERFORMANCE ASSESSMENT

Solve. Explain your method.

CHOOSE A STRATEGY

• Find a Pattern   • Act It Out   • Make a Model   • Make a Table   • Write a Number Sentence

3. Vince has a picture that is 4 in. wide and 6 in. long. He wants to put it in a larger frame that is a rectangle similar to the picture. He is considering a frame that is 8 in. wide. How long is the frame?

   (pages 454–455)

4. Rob surveyed 40 students to find out their favorite football teams. He found 20% liked the Cowboys, 30% the Jaguars, 30% the Bears, 10% the Panthers, and 10% the Falcons. Which two teams received 50%? (pages 470–471)

CUMULATIVE REVIEW

Solve the problem. Then write the letter of the correct answer. (pages 52–53)

1. $3.26 + 2.069 = n$

    A. $n = 1.191$ **B.** $n = 4.329$
    C. $n = 5.229$ **D.** $n = 5.329$

---

2.  What is the probability of pulling a green or yellow cube?

(pages 180–183)

    A. $\dfrac{1}{10}$ **B.** $\dfrac{2}{10}$, or $\dfrac{1}{5}$

    C. $\dfrac{4}{10}$, or $\dfrac{2}{5}$ **D.** $\dfrac{5}{10}$, or $\dfrac{1}{2}$

---

3. $\begin{array}{r} 2.99 \\ \times\ 0.5 \\ \hline \end{array}$ **A.** 1.045
              B. 1.495
              C. 14.95
              D. 149.5 (pages 200–203)

For Problems 4–6, choose the correct answer that is in simplest form.

4. $\dfrac{5}{6} - \dfrac{1}{3} = n$

    A. $n = \dfrac{3}{6}$ **B.** $n = \dfrac{1}{2}$

    C. $n = 1\dfrac{1}{6}$ **D.** $n = \dfrac{4}{3}$ (pages 294–297)

---

5. $5\dfrac{2}{3} + 2\dfrac{5}{6} = n$

    A. $n = 7\dfrac{7}{9}$ **B.** $n = \dfrac{51}{6}$

    C. $n = 8\dfrac{1}{2}$ **D.** $n = 8\dfrac{3}{6}$ (pages 328–329)

---

6. $\dfrac{2}{3} \times 3\dfrac{1}{4} = n$

    A. $n = \dfrac{26}{12}$ **B.** $n = 2\dfrac{1}{6}$

    C. $n = 2\dfrac{2}{12}$ **D.** $n = 2\dfrac{2}{3}$ (pages 366–367)

---

7. Find the missing measurement.

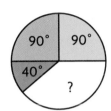

    A. $45°$
    B. $140°$
    C. $180°$
    D. $360°$ (pages 416–417)

---

8. Identify the solid figure.

    A. triangular prism
    B. rectangular pyramid
    C. hexagonal pyramid
    D. pentagonal prism (pages 424–425)

---

9. Which ratio is equivalent to 2:50?

    A. 1:25   **B.** 10:500
    C. 14:400   **D.** 25:1 (pages 448–449)

---

10. How do you write five hundredths as a percent?

    A. 0.5% **B.** 5%
    C. 50% **D.** 500% (pages 462–463)

---

11. How do you write 4% as a decimal?

    A. 0.04 **B.** 0.40
    C. 4.0 **D.** 40.0 (pages 462–465)

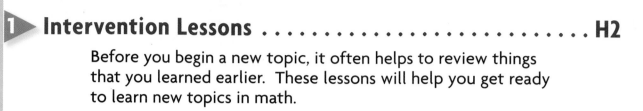

STUDENT HANDBOOK

1 Intervention Lessons H2

Before you begin a new topic, it often helps to review things that you learned earlier. These lessons will help you get ready to learn new topics in math.

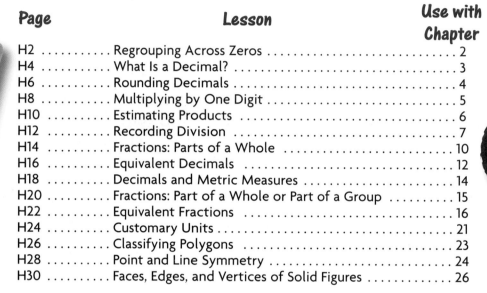

2 Extension Lessons H32

You can challenge yourself to learn new and interesting things when you try these Extension lessons.

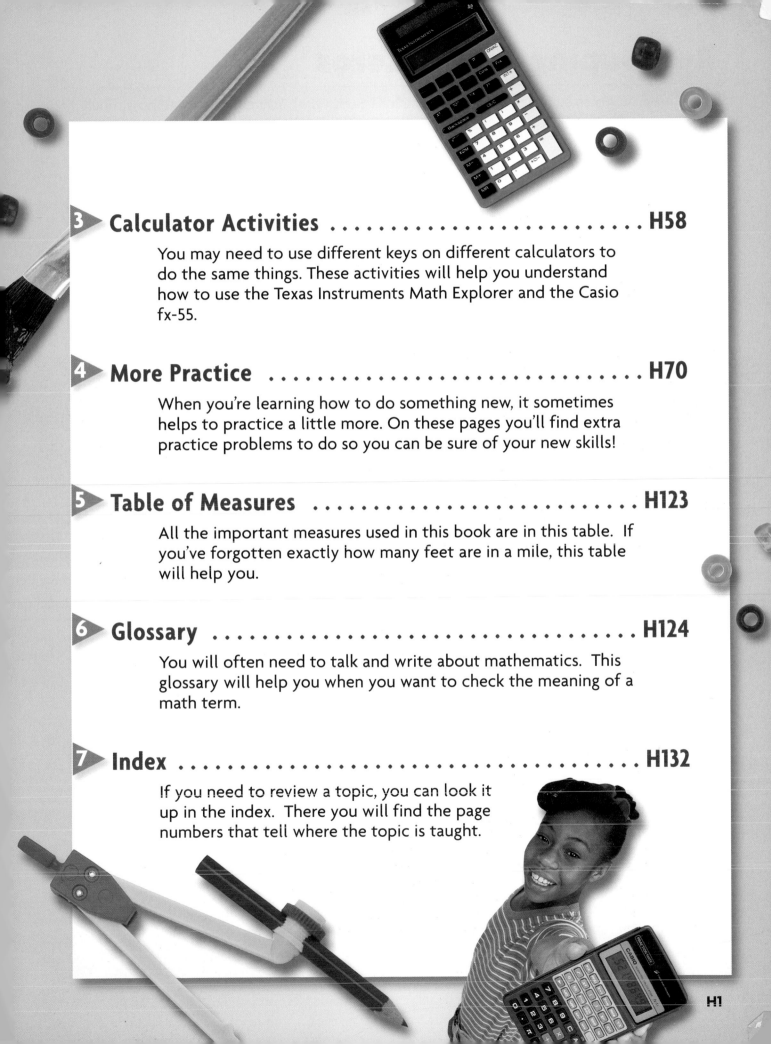

Regrouping Across Zeros

You will learn to subtract with regrouping across zeros.

Why learn this? You can compute how much money will be left after making a purchase.

While on a field trip, Horace and his class had lunch at a restaurant. Horace ordered a turkey sandwich and milk. His check was for $3.24. He gave the clerk $5.00. How much change will Horace receive?

You can subtract to find how much change Horace will receive.

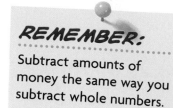

REMEMBER:
Subtract amounts of money the same way you subtract whole numbers.

MODEL

▶ Step 1

Subtract. $5.00 − $3.24 = n

Look at the ones. Since 4 > 0, regroup. There are 0 tens, so regroup 5 hundreds as 4 hundreds 10 tens.

```
  4 10
  5 0 0
− 3 2 4
```

▶ Step 2

Regroup 10 tens as 9 tens 10 ones. Subtract the ones. Subtract the tens.

```
      9
  4 10 10
  5 0 0
− 3 2 4
      7 6
```

▶ Step 3

Subtract the hundreds.

```
      9
  4 10 10
  5 0 0
− 3 2 4
  1 7 6
```
→ Place a dollar sign and decimal point in the answer. $1.76

So, Horace received $1.76 in change.

EXAMPLES

A.
```
  2 10
  3 0 0
− 2 7 0
    3 0
```

B.
```
      9
  3 10 10
  4 0 0
−   9 8
  3 0 2
```

C.
```
        9 9
  4 10 10 10
  5, 0 0 0
−     6 8 3
  4, 3 1 7
```

• When is it necessary to regroup hundreds before you can subtract in the ones place?

Check Your Understanding

Find the difference.

1. 470
   −124

2. 300
   − 79

3. 700
   −595

4. 800
   −437

5. 1,300
   − 906

6. 500
   −193

7. 600
   −487

8. 700
   − 78

9. 2,000
   − 586

10. 4,000
    −2,074

PRACTICE

Find the difference.

11. $\begin{array}{r} 200 \\ -\ 87 \\ \hline \end{array}$ 12. $\begin{array}{r} 450 \\ -145 \\ \hline \end{array}$ 13. $\begin{array}{r} \$6.00 \\ -\ 3.21 \\ \hline \end{array}$

14. $\begin{array}{r} \$5.00 \\ -\ 2.18 \\ \hline \end{array}$ 15. $\begin{array}{r} 850 \\ -546 \\ \hline \end{array}$ 16. $\begin{array}{r} 900 \\ -785 \\ \hline \end{array}$

17. $\begin{array}{r} 7,050 \\ -2,936 \\ \hline \end{array}$ 18. $\begin{array}{r} \$20.00 \\ -\ 12.45 \\ \hline \end{array}$ 19. $\begin{array}{r} \$10.00 \\ -\ 5.28 \\ \hline \end{array}$

20. $\begin{array}{r} 8,005 \\ -4,752 \\ \hline \end{array}$ 21. $\begin{array}{r} 7,400 \\ -2,196 \\ \hline \end{array}$ 22. $\begin{array}{r} \$30.05 \\ -\ 18.99 \\ \hline \end{array}$

23. $600 - 259 = n$

24. $\$8.00 - \$4.51 = n$

25. $900 - 574 = n$

26. $\$20.00 - \$12.98 = n$

27. $4,700 - 1,982 = n$

28. $7,003 - 436 = n$

29. $\$52.00 - \$16.98 = n$

30. $11,000 - 687 = n$

FOOD	GRAMS OF PROTEIN
turkey sandwich	about 21
glass of milk	about 8
carrot sticks	about 1

Mixed Applications

31. Alma bought a book for $5.95. She gave the clerk a $10.00 bill. How much change will Alma receive?

32. Larry owed his friend $7.89. Since Larry did not have the correct amount, he gave his friend a $20.00 bill. How much change will Larry receive?

33. Jenny had 200 sheets of paper. Ralph borrowed 18 sheets. How many sheets of paper does Jenny have left?

34. Randy read 317 pages of his book the first week and 239 pages the second week. How many pages did Randy read in all?

35. During a concert 389 seats were filled in an auditorium. At a pep rally 467 of the seats were filled. How many more seats were filled for the pep rally?

36. One television show was viewed in about sixty million homes. Write two different forms of the number that is one million less than sixty million.

37. In a recent year, 50,241,840 homes had cable television. If 7 million more homes were added to this number, what would be the total number of homes with cable television?

38. ▷ **Write a problem** about 600 students in a school. Use subtraction.

What Is a Decimal?

You will learn what a decimal is and how a decimal relates to a fraction.

Why learn this? You can use a decimal to name an amount of money or record a sports score.

A *decimal* is a number that uses place value and a decimal point to show a value less than one, such as tenths and hundredths.

At basketball practice, Kate made 7 out of 10 of her free throws. How can you express as a decimal the number of free throws Kate made?

You can use decimal squares to model decimals.

Model	Fraction	Decimal
	Write: $\frac{7}{10}$ **Read:** seven tenths	**Write:** 0.7 **Read:** seven tenths

So, Kate made $\frac{7}{10}$, or 0.7, of her free throws.

At the basketball game, the team made 34 out of the 100 shots they attempted. How can you express that number as a decimal?

Model	Fraction	Decimal
	Write: $\frac{34}{100}$ **Read:** thirty-four hundredths	**Write:** 0.34 **Read:** thirty-four hundredths

So, the team made $\frac{34}{100}$, or 0.34, of their shots.

REMEMBER:

You can use pennies, dimes, and dollars to model decimals.

1 dollar ($1.00) = $\frac{1}{1}$, or one dollar

1 dime ($0.10) = $\frac{1}{10}$, or 0.1 dollar

1 penny ($0.01) = $\frac{1}{100}$, or 0.01 dollar

Check Your Understanding CRITICAL THINKING

Write the decimal for the part that is shaded.

1.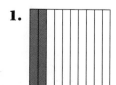

2.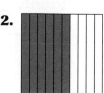

3.

4.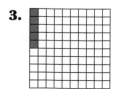

PRACTICE

Complete the table.

Model	Fraction	Decimal
5. (model)	$\frac{3}{10}$	?
6. (model)	?	0.8
7. (model)	$\frac{53}{100}$	?
8. (model)	?	0.01

Science Link

A botanist analyzes soil mixtures to see which one will grow the healthiest plants. A mixture being studied is $\frac{4}{10}$ sand, $\frac{3}{10}$ clay, and $\frac{3}{10}$ peat. Write the decimals for the sand, clay, and peat in the mixture.

Write each amount as a decimal.

9. 6 tenths   **10.** 14 hundredths   **11.** 8 tenths   **12.** 3 hundredths

Write each fraction as a decimal.

13. $\frac{1}{10}$ **14.** $\frac{1}{100}$ **15.** $\frac{5}{10}$ **16.** $\frac{51}{100}$ **17.** $\frac{99}{100}$

Mixed Applications

18. Joshua practiced serving a tennis ball. Out of 10 serves, 3 serves hit the net. Write as a decimal the number of serves that did not hit the net.

19. Felicia has 16 pennies in her wallet and 38 pennies in her drawer. Write the amount of money Felicia needs to have $1.00. Express the amount as a decimal.

20. There are about 100 nations that compete in the World Cup soccer tournament. The top 24 teams play in a three-week tournament. Express as a decimal the number of top teams.

21. ✏️ **Write a problem** using the information in the table.

BASEBALL PRACTICE		
	Number of Pitches	Number of Hits
Nick	10	7
Kyle	10	8

Rounding Decimals

You will learn to estimate decimals by rounding.

Why learn this? You can estimate distances by rounding to the nearest mile.

Jerel made a map of his community. He labeled some distances on his map. To the nearest mile, how far is it from his house to school?

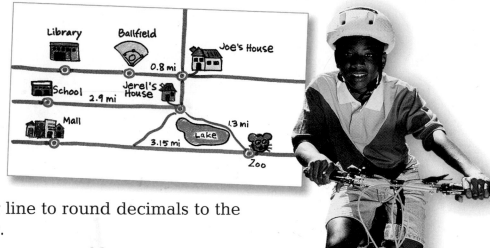

You can use a number line to round decimals to the nearest whole number.

On the number line, 2.9 is between 2 and 3 but is closer to 3. So, the school is about 3 miles from Jerel's house.

To the nearest tenth of a mile, how far is it from the mall to the zoo?

You can use a number line to round to the nearest tenth.

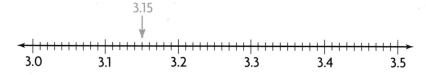

On the number line, 3.15 is between 3.1 and 3.2.

Round to the next highest tenth. So, the zoo is about 3.2 miles from the mall.

💡 **CRITICAL THINKING** How is rounding decimals like rounding whole numbers?

REMEMBER:

Rounding Whole Numbers
- If the digit to the right of the digit being rounded is 5 or more, round to the next-higher digit.
- If the digit to the right of the digit being rounded is less than 5, the digit being rounded stays the same.

12 → 10   25 → 30

43 → 40   68 → 70

Check Your Understanding

Round to the nearest whole number.

1. 2.1   **2.** 0.9   **3.** 1.6

Round to the nearest tenth.

4. 0.28   **5.** 1.45   **6.** 2.07

PRACTICE

7. Use the number line to choose the numbers from the box that round to 5.0.

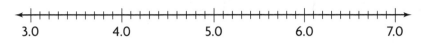

6.1	4.8	5.5	7.0
5.2	5.7	4.4	4.9

Round to the nearest whole number.

8. 2.4 **9.** 3.7 **10.** 5.5 **11.** 9.3 **12.** 8.7

13. 6.5 **14.** 7.2 **15.** 4.6 **16.** 1.8 **17.** 3.5

Round to the nearest tenth.

18. 6.49 **19.** 14.63 **20.** 35.66 **21.** 24.51 **22.** 85.50

23. 11.09 **24.** 5.97 **25.** 36.75 **26.** 19.96 **27.** 118.62

For Problems 28–32, use the table.

28. To the nearest tenth, what was Michael's score on vault?

29. To the nearest tenth, what was the highest score on floor exercise? Which gymnast received that score?

30. To the nearest tenth, in which event did Ivan score higher? How much higher?

31. To the nearest tenth, write the vault scores in order from the highest to the lowest.

32. To the nearest whole number, who scored highest in vault?

MEN'S GYMNASTICS SCORES		
	Vault	**Floor Exercise**
Ivan	9.17	9.28
Michael	9.37	9.57
Drake	8.82	9.86
Thomas	9.87	8.88
Hugh	9.76	9.12

Mixed Applications

33. Jan swam the 50-meter freestyle race in 28.25 seconds, and Sue swam the race in 27.91 seconds. To the nearest tenth of a second, what were their times?

34. Each side of a square patio is 8 feet long. Starting at one corner, there is a fence post every 2 feet. How many fence posts are around the perimeter of the patio?

35. The baseball team plays 47 games in a season. They have already played 13 games. How many games are left in the season?

36. **Write a problem** about gymnastics scores using rounding.

Multiplying by One Digit

You will learn to model and record multiplication by one-digit numbers.

Why learn this? You can figure out how many items you need in all, such as ingredients for a recipe.

The fifth-grade students are giving a spaghetti dinner. Each student brings 3 boxes of spaghetti. There are 124 fifth-grade students. How many boxes of spaghetti are there in all?

MODEL

What is 3 × 124?

▶ **Step 1**

Multiply the ones.
3 × 4 ones = 12 ones

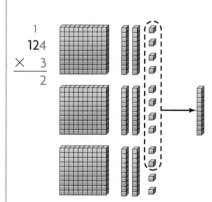

Record 12 ones. Place 2 in the ones place and 1 in the tens place.

▶ **Step 2**

Multiply the tens.
3 × 2 tens = 6 tens
Add the regrouped ten.
6 tens + 1 ten = 7 tens

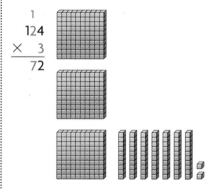

Record 7 tens.

▶ **Step 3**

Multiply the hundreds.
3 × 1 hundred = 3 hundreds

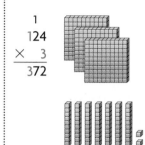

Record 3 in the hundreds place.

So, there are 372 boxes of spaghetti in all.

- In which place-value position did you need to regroup? Explain.

EXAMPLES

A.
```
  1
 164
×  2
 328
```

B.
```
   2
 209
×  3
 627
```

C.
```
    3
  361
×   5
1,805
```

- What is the greatest number of digits that will be in the product of a 1-digit number and a 3-digit number?

PRACTICE

Tell which place-value position must be regrouped.
Find the product.

1. 314
   × 3

2. 119
   × 5

3. 146
   × 5

4. 181
   × 3

Find the product.

5. 112
   × 3

6. 207
   × 4

7. 138
   × 5

8. 126
   × 3

9. 127
   × 4

10. 154
    × 3

11. 167
    × 5

12. 183
    × 3

13. 272
    × 4

14. 291
    × 3

15. 167
    × 8

16. 265
    × 5

17. 223
    × 4

18. 269
    × 4

19. 308
    × 5

20. 365
    × 6

Mixed Applications

For Problems 23–25, use the table.

21. Last month the veterinarian treated 58 dogs, 32 cats, and 10 hamsters. This month she treated 3 times as many dogs, 2 times as many cats, but no hamsters. How many more animals did she treat this month than last month?

22. There are five houses on the block. Tasha lives at one end of the block. Kristen lives at the other end, two houses away from Scott. Will lives next to Tasha, and two houses away from Benaiah. What is the order of their houses?

23. Mr. Goldberg wants to buy a volleyball and a basketball for Kevin. He wants to buy a volleyball and a football for Tammy. How much money does he need?

SPORTS EQUIPMENT PRICE LIST	
Outdoor Basketball	$15.99
Leather Football	$35.59
Hockey Stick	$13.39
Beach Volleyball	$35.99

24. Jamal earned $100.00. He wants to save half the money and spend the other half for sports equipment. He wants a leather football. What else can he buy?

25. ✏ **Write a problem** using the price list.

Estimating Products

You will learn to estimate a product that is close to the actual product.

Why learn this? You can estimate the total cost when you go shopping or the amount of supplies you need to take on a trip.

There are 56 Boy Scouts going on an overnight camp-out. Each Scout will take a half-gallon container filled with water. There are 64 ounces in a half gallon. About how many ounces will the Boy Scouts take?

Camping is an adventure!

MODEL

How can you estimate 56 × 64?

▶ **Step 1**

Estimate. Round each factor to the nearest ten.

$$64 \rightarrow 60$$
$$\underline{\times 56} \rightarrow \underline{\times 60}$$

▶ **Step 2**

Multiply.

$$60$$
$$\underline{\times 60}$$
$$3{,}600$$

So, the Boy Scouts will take about 3,600 ounces of water.

Talk About It

- How were basic facts used to estimate the product?

- When might you want to estimate a product?

REMEMBER:

To round a number:

- Find the digit in the place to be rounded.
- Look at the digit to its right.
- If that digit is *less than 5,* the digit being rounded remains the same.
- If the digit is *5 or greater,* the digit being rounded increases by 1.

EXAMPLES

A.
$$91 \rightarrow 90$$
$$\underline{\times 16} \rightarrow \underline{\times 20}$$
$$1{,}800$$

B.
$$67 \rightarrow 70$$
$$\underline{\times 33} \rightarrow \underline{\times 30}$$
$$2{,}100$$

- Why are there 2 zeros in each of the products in the examples?

Check Your Understanding

Round each factor to the nearest ten. Estimate the product.

1. 75
   $\underline{\times 25}$

2. 47
   $\underline{\times 34}$

3. 82
   $\underline{\times 65}$

4. 35
   $\underline{\times 44}$

5. 62
   $\underline{\times 73}$

PRACTICE

Round each factor to the nearest ten. Estimate the product.

6. $\begin{array}{r} 14 \\ \times 12 \\ \hline \end{array}$ 7. $\begin{array}{r} 21 \\ \times 13 \\ \hline \end{array}$ 8. $\begin{array}{r} 25 \\ \times 23 \\ \hline \end{array}$

9. $\begin{array}{r} 24 \\ \times 22 \\ \hline \end{array}$ 10. $\begin{array}{r} 28 \\ \times 13 \\ \hline \end{array}$ 11. $\begin{array}{r} 32 \\ \times 29 \\ \hline \end{array}$

12. $\begin{array}{r} 36 \\ \times 29 \\ \hline \end{array}$ 13. $\begin{array}{r} 59 \\ \times 54 \\ \hline \end{array}$ 14. $\begin{array}{r} 63 \\ \times 24 \\ \hline \end{array}$

15. $\begin{array}{r} 71 \\ \times 47 \\ \hline \end{array}$ 16. $\begin{array}{r} 84 \\ \times 79 \\ \hline \end{array}$ 17. $\begin{array}{r} 85 \\ \times 83 \\ \hline \end{array}$

18. $\begin{array}{r} 27 \\ \times 33 \\ \hline \end{array}$ 19. $\begin{array}{r} 46 \\ \times 41 \\ \hline \end{array}$ 20. $\begin{array}{r} 58 \\ \times 34 \\ \hline \end{array}$

21. $63 \times 82 = n$ 22. $69 \times 75 = n$ 23. $79 \times 84 = n$

24. $73 \times 86 = n$ 25. $81 \times 88 = n$ 26. $86 \times 92 = n$

27. $49 \times 63 = n$ 28. $52 \times 67 = n$ 29. $54 \times 81 = n$

Health Link

About half the water we lose each day can be replaced by the water content in our food, especially fruits and vegetables. Our bodies need clean drinking water to replace the remaining half. On average, a person needs about 64 ounces of water each day. About how many ounces of water does a person need in one month?

Mixed Applications

30. Dario and Mark are counting the number of seats for the band concert. Dario counted 10 rows of 14 seats. Mark counted another 16 rows of 23 seats. How many seats did they count in all?

31. Jasmine is 1 year younger than Hope. The sum of their ages is 17 years. Selena is twice as old as Jasmine. How old are Jasmine, Hope, and Selena?

32. It took Denequa 10 minutes to read 7 pages of her book. It took her 20 minutes to read the next 14 pages and 30 minutes to read the next 21 pages. If this pattern continues, how long will it take her to read the remaining 35 pages?

33. Uri wrote a 4-digit number. The number of thousands is 3 times the number of tens. There are 6 ones, and the number of ones is 2 times the number of tens. The number of hundreds is 5 more than the number of tens. What number did he write?

34. Ms. Montoya's 21 students picked up litter at a nearby park. She challenged each student to collect at least 37 pieces of trash. How many pieces of trash will they collect in all?

35. ✏️ **Write a problem** in which you estimate the product of 2 two-digit numbers.

Recording Division

You will learn to divide by one-digit numbers, using base-ten blocks.

Why learn this? You can better understand what happens when you divide, using paper and pencil.

Ms. Pearson asked 3 students to carry some books back to the library. There were 56 books to return. Each student carried the same number of books. How many books did each carry?

Divide. $56 \div 3 = n$ $3\overline{)56}$

Use base-ten blocks to model the problem. Record the numbers as you complete each step.

MODEL

What is $56 \div 3$?

▶ Step 1

Draw 3 rings. Show 56 as 5 tens and 6 ones.

Record:

$3\overline{)56}$

▶ Step 2

Place an equal number of tens into each ring.

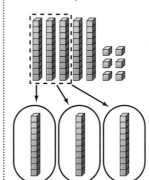

Record:

$\begin{array}{r} 1 \\ 3\overline{)56} \\ -3 \\ \hline 2 \end{array}$ ← 1 ten in each group
← 3 tens used
← 2 tens left

▶ Step 3

Regroup the 2 tens left over into ones.

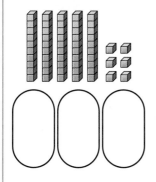

Record:

$\begin{array}{r} 1 \\ 3\overline{)56} \\ -3\downarrow \\ \hline 26 \end{array}$ Bring down the ones.

▶ Step 4

Place an equal number of ones into each ring.

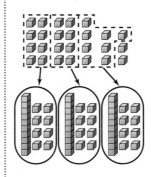

Record:

$\begin{array}{r} 18 \\ 3\overline{)56} \\ -3 \\ \hline 26 \\ -24 \\ \hline 2 \end{array}$ ← 8 ones in each group

24 ones
← used
← 2 ones left

So, $n = 18$ r2.

So, each student carried 18 books. There were 2 books left over.

• In Step 3, why did you have to regroup the 2 tens into ones?

PRACTICE

Match each division model with the correct division number sentence.

1.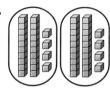

2.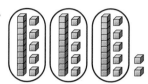

a. $45 \div 3 = 15$

b. $47 \div 3 = 15 \text{ r}2$

c. $48 \div 2 = 24$

d. $78 \div 4 = 19 \text{ r}2$

e. $53 \div 4 = 13 \text{ r}1$

f. $75 \div 3 = 25$

3.

4.

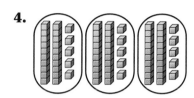

5.

6.

Use base-ten blocks to model the problem. Record the numbers as you complete each step.

7. $3\overline{)69}$ 8. $2\overline{)27}$ 9. $4\overline{)82}$ 10. $2\overline{)36}$ 11. $3\overline{)43}$

12. $2\overline{)31}$ 13. $4\overline{)55}$ 14. $5\overline{)52}$ 15. $2\overline{)54}$ 16. $3\overline{)74}$

Mixed Applications

17. Mrs. Swan bought 6 packages of colored pencils. She bought 96 colored pencils in all. How many colored pencils were in each package?

18. Suzanne guessed there were 3,100 marbles in the jar. Paul guessed there were 2,500 marbles. There were actually 2,995 marbles. Whose guess was closer?

19. Bill and Eric went to a hockey game. They each paid $10.95 for a ticket and $4.25 for snacks. How much money did they both spend?

20. Brandy made 57 cupcakes for the 2 fifth-grade classes. Both classes were the same size. How many cupcakes did each class get? Were any cupcakes left over?

21. A box is 8 feet long, 5 feet wide, and 4 feet high. What is the volume of the box?

22. ✏️ **Write a problem** about 48 videotapes. Use division in your problem.

Fractions: Parts of a Whole

You will learn to use fractions to represent parts of a whole.

Why learn this? You can share parts of a whole amount equally with friends.

The Norwalk town pool is divided into three parts of equal size. One part is the baby pool, one part is the lap area, and one part is the deep end. What fraction represents the part of the pool that is the deep end?

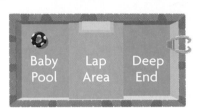

You can use a fraction to name the parts of a whole.

$$\frac{\text{numerator} \longrightarrow 1 \longleftarrow \text{number of sections named}}{\text{denominator} \longrightarrow 3 \longleftarrow \text{total number of sections}}$$

Read: one third
one out of three
one divided by three

Write: $\frac{1}{3}$

So, the deep end is $\frac{1}{3}$ of the whole pool.

- What fraction represents the part of the pool that is *not* the deep end?

EXAMPLES

A.

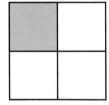

$\frac{1}{4}$ is shaded.

B.

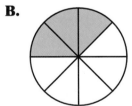

$\frac{3}{8}$ is shaded.

C.

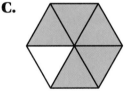

$\frac{5}{6}$ is shaded.

Talk About It

- For Examples A, B, and C, what fraction of the whole is *not* shaded?

- What fraction names the whole for each example?

- What would the figure in Example C look like if only $\frac{1}{2}$ were shaded?

Art Link

Artists use color wheels to help them understand how colors are related to one another. This basic color wheel shows the three primary colors (red, yellow, and blue) and mixtures of these colors. What fraction of the color wheel is mixtures of blue and yellow?

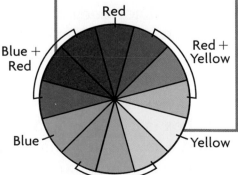

Red

Blue + Red

Red + Yellow

Blue

Yellow

Yellow + Blue

PRACTICE

Write the fraction for the part that is shaded.

1.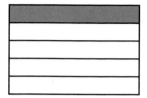

2.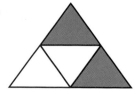

3.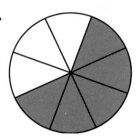

Write the fraction for the part that is not shaded.

4.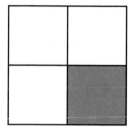

5.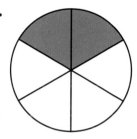

6.

For each fraction named, give the written form.

7. one third   **8.** five sixths   **9.** two fifths   **10.** three eighths

Mixed Applications

11. Preston, Joel, and Alexis shared a pizza that was divided into 8 slices. Preston ate 3 slices, Joel ate 3 slices, and Alexis ate 2 slices. Write the fraction that shows the part of the pizza that each person ate.

12. Patrick ate the first piece of his grandmother's apple pie. The pie had been cut into 6 pieces. What fraction names the amount of pie that is left?

For Problem 13, use the menu.

13. At the snack bar, Brittany ordered one slice of pizza and a small drink. How much change did she receive from $5.00?

14. There are 230 swimmers traveling on buses to the district meet. Each bus can hold 36 people. How many buses are there?

SNACK BAR MENU

Pizza	$1.25/slice
Hamburger	$1.35
Hot Dog	$0.95
Frozen Yogurt	$0.80
Drinks	$0.85/small
	$0.95/large

15. ✏️ **Write a problem** about a fraction, using this information: There are 24 swimmers on the Cobb Swim Team. Of the swimmers, 4 are on the relay team.

Equivalent Decimals

You will learn to use decimal squares to write equivalent decimals.

Why learn this? You can use equivalent decimals when you are making change for a dollar.

Equivalent decimals are different names for the same amount. Two tenths and twenty hundredths name the same amount. They are equivalent decimals.

You can use decimal squares to model equivalent decimals.

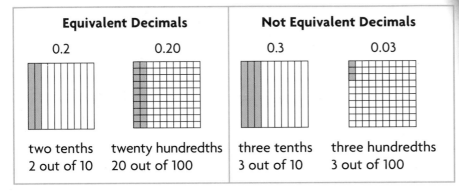

Equivalent Decimals		Not Equivalent Decimals	
0.2	0.20	0.3	0.03
two tenths 2 out of 10	twenty hundredths 20 out of 100	three tenths 3 out of 10	three hundredths 3 out of 100

Talk About It

• How do the models for 0.2 and 0.20 show that the decimals are equivalent decimals?

• How do the models for 0.3 and 0.03 show that the decimals are not equivalent decimals?

Study these models.

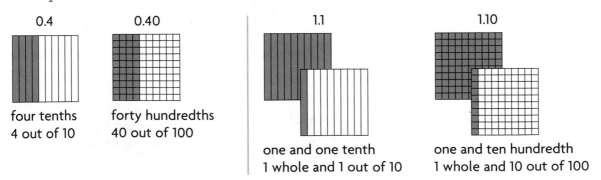

0.4 — four tenths 4 out of 10

0.40 — forty hundredths 40 out of 100

1.1 — one and one tenth 1 whole and 1 out of 10

1.10 — one and ten hundredth 1 whole and 10 out of 100

Talk About It

• Explain how you know that 0.4 and 0.40 are equivalent.

• Explain how you know that 1.1 and 1.10 are equivalent.

PRACTICE

Write two equivalent decimals for the shaded part of each model.

1.   **2.**   **3.** 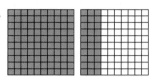   **4.**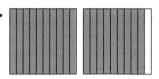

Tell whether the decimals are equivalent. Write *yes* or *no*.

5. 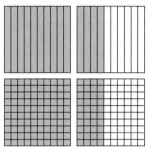   **6.** 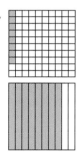   **7.**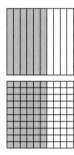

8. 15.3 and 15.03   **9.** 5.9 and 5.90   **10.** 6.20 and 6.2   **11.** 3.13 and 3.31

Write an equivalent decimal for each.

12. 0.80   **13.** 9.7   **14.** 5.60   **15.** 0.3   **16.** 2.14   **17.** 10.6

Look at the decimal squares. Write the letter of the picture that shows a decimal that is equivalent to the one shown.

18.   **a.**   **b.**   **c.**

19.   **a.**   **b.**   **c.**

Mixed Applications

20. Marion said that $0.50 is 50 hundredths of a dollar. Seth said that $0.50 is 5 tenths of a dollar. Why are both statements correct?

21. Write all the four-digit whole numbers that have only 0 and 1 as digits.

22. Use models to show how you know 1.6 and 1.60 are equivalent decimals.

Consumer Link

When you make change for a dollar, you use equivalent decimals. What amount is equivalent to three dimes?

Decimals and Metric Measures

You will learn how meters, decimeters, and centimeters are related.

Why learn this? You can use the marks on a meterstick to measure objects.

You can use a meterstick to model decimal numbers.

The *meter* is the basic unit of linear measurement in the metric system. The abbreviation for meter is *m*.

Deci- means "tenths."
There are 10 *decimeters* in a meter.
The abbreviation for decimeter is *dm*.

1 decimeter = 0.1, or $\frac{1}{10}$, meter

Centi- means "hundredths."
There are 100 *centimeters* in a meter.
The abbreviation for centimeter is *cm*.

1 centimeter = 0.01, or $\frac{1}{100}$, meter

meter
(100 centimeters)

1.0 meter

decimeter
(10 centimeters)

0.1 meter

centimeter

0.01 meter

Talk About It

- What part of a meter equals 1 dm? 1 cm?

- How can you write 0.5 m by using decimeters? centimeters? Hint: Use a meterstick to help you.

- What is another way to name 0.02 m by using decimeters? centimeters?

Check Your Understanding

 CRITICAL THINKING

Write the missing unit. You may use a meterstick.

1.

   2 dm = __?__ m

3. 5 __?__ = 50 dm

5. 20 __?__ = 200 dm

7. 0.07 m = 7 __?__

2.

   0.5 m = __?__ cm

4. 5 m = 500 __?__

6. 0.3 m = 30 __?__

8. 0.6 m = 6 __?__

> **Social Studies Link**
>
> The French created the metric system in the 1790s. The English system of measurement is an older system, and it is based on odd measurements. For example, the inch was the distance between the first and second joints of the index finger. Use your centimeter ruler and inch ruler to measure the distance between the first and second joints of your index finger.
>
>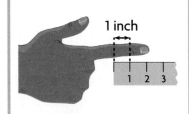
>
> 1 inch

PRACTICE

Copy the table. Fill in the missing measures.
You may use a meterstick.

	Meter	Decimeter	Centimeter
9.	?	30	?
10.	7	?	?
11.	?	?	800
12.	0.9	?	?
13.	?	4	?
14.	?	?	2
15.	?	0.9	?
16.	0.08	?	?

Write the number. You may use a meterstick.

17. 2 m = _?_ dm

18. 6 m = _?_ cm

19. 60 dm = _?_ m

20. 30 m = _?_ dm

21. 0.7 m = _?_ dm

22. 0.8 m = _?_ cm

23. 400 cm = _?_ m

24. 50 cm = _?_ m

25. 80 cm = _?_ m

26. 40 dm = _?_ m

27. 9 cm = _?_ m

28. 6 dm = _?_ m

29. 0.53 m = _?_ cm

30. 8 cm = _?_ m

Mixed Applications

31. Kelli needs 7.5 dm of string for her art project. She has a piece of string that is 35 cm long and another piece that is 40 cm long. Does she have enough string? Explain.

32. Marian and Tom are making banners for the school play. Tom's banner is 2 times as long as Marian's banner. Marian's banner is 245 cm long. How much shorter than 5 m is Tom's banner?

33. Jack's belt measures 39 cm in length. Is his belt longer or shorter than 4 dm? What is his belt's measurement in decimeters?

34. Scott cut 2 pieces of wood that are each 46 cm long. Bill cut a piece of wood that is 8 dm long. Who cut more wood?

35. Ashley cut 4 strips of colored paper for her graph. The strips were 23 cm, 16 cm, 14 cm, and 7 cm in length. How many dm of paper did she use?

36.  **WRITE ABOUT IT** Explain how to change a measurement from meters to centimeters and from decimeters to meters.

Fractions as Part of a Whole or Part of a Group

You will learn how to use fractions to represent part of a whole or part of a group, and to read and write fractions.

Why learn this? You can use fractions when you share food with someone.

Kira, Robbie, Micah, and Carmen shared a pizza and a basket of strawberries equally. What fraction of the pizza and strawberries did each person eat?

A *fraction* is a number that names a part of a whole or a part of a group.

The pizza represents 1 whole. Use fraction-circle pieces to show how 1 whole can be divided into 4 equal parts.

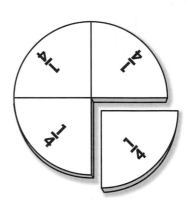

each person's part $\longrightarrow$ 1 $\longleftarrow$ numerator
total equal parts $\longrightarrow$ 4 $\longleftarrow$ denominator

So, each person ate $\frac{1}{4}$ of the pizza.

The basket of 12 strawberries represents 1 group. The picture shows how 1 group can be divided into 4 equal parts.

groups circled $\longrightarrow$ 1 $\longleftarrow$ numerator
number of equal groups $\longrightarrow$ 4 $\longleftarrow$ denominator

Read: one fourth
one out of four
one divided by four

Write: $\frac{1}{4}$

So, each person ate $\frac{1}{4}$ of the strawberries.

EXAMPLES

A.

$\frac{1}{3}$ is shaded.

B.

$\frac{5}{6}$ is shaded.

C.

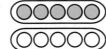

$\frac{1}{2}$ is shaded.

D.

$\frac{3}{8}$ is shaded.

Talk About It

• For each example, tell what fraction is not shaded.

• How is part of a group different from part of a whole? Explain.

PRACTICE

Copy and complete the table.

	Model	Write	Read
		$\frac{3}{4}$	three fourths; three out of four; three divided by four
1.		?	?
2.	?	?	four fifths; four out of five; four divided by five
3.	?	$\frac{6}{6}$	?
4.	○○○ ○○○	?	?
5.	○○○○○ ○○○○○ ○○○○○	?	?
6.	○○○○ ○○○○	?	?

Mixed Applications

7. Mrs. Chang has 20 students in her class. Of the students, 5 play basketball and 5 sing in the chorus. Write a fraction to describe the number of students in Mrs. Chang's class who play basketball.

8. There are 180 animals in the zoo. Each exhibit on the west side of the zoo has 8 animals. There are 15 exhibits on the west side of the zoo. Each exhibit on the east side of the zoo has 5 animals. How many exhibits are on the east side of the zoo?

9. Lyle has a box of 10 cookies, 8 of which are oatmeal. Write a fraction to describe the fraction of oatmeal cookies in the box.

10. Mr. Green traveled 5 days. Each day he spent $50 for a hotel, $30 for gas, and $25 for food. How much did Mr. Green spend in all?

11. Rafael bought 4 posters for $3.99 each. He also wants to buy a sign for $4.89. He had $20.50 to start with. Does Rafael have enough money to buy the sign? Explain.

12. ✏ **WRITE ABOUT IT** When is it possible for $\frac{1}{2}$ of your age to be less than $\frac{1}{2}$ of your friend's age?

Equivalent Fractions

You will learn to identify equivalent fractions.

Why learn this? You can decide whether different fractional parts of an object name the same amount.

Martin, Rita, and Evelyn want the same amount of granola bars. Martin has $\frac{1}{3}$ of a bar, Rita has $\frac{2}{6}$, and Evelyn has $\frac{4}{12}$. Did they all receive the same amount?

Use fraction strips to model the problem.

$$\frac{1}{3} = \frac{2}{6} = \frac{4}{12}$$

Each fraction names the same amount. They are *equivalent fractions*.

So, Martin, Rita, and Evelyn all received the same amount of a granola bar.

Talk About It

• What pattern do you see in the fractions that are the same amount as one third?

• How many sixths are equivalent to two thirds? How do you know?

• How many twelfths are equivalent to four sixths?

EXAMPLES

A.

| $\frac{1}{4}$ | $\frac{1}{4}$ | $\frac{1}{4}$ | $\frac{1}{4}$ |

| $\frac{1}{8}$ | $\frac{1}{8}$ | $\frac{1}{8}$ | $\frac{1}{8}$ | $\frac{1}{8}$ | $\frac{1}{8}$ | $\frac{1}{8}$ | $\frac{1}{8}$ |

$$\frac{1}{4} = \frac{2}{8}$$

B.

| $\frac{1}{3}$ | $\frac{1}{3}$ | $\frac{1}{3}$ |

| $\frac{1}{9}$ | $\frac{1}{9}$ | $\frac{1}{9}$ | $\frac{1}{9}$ | $\frac{1}{9}$ | $\frac{1}{9}$ | $\frac{1}{9}$ | $\frac{1}{9}$ | $\frac{1}{9}$ |

$$\frac{2}{3} = \frac{6}{9}$$

C.

| $\frac{1}{5}$ | $\frac{1}{5}$ | $\frac{1}{5}$ | $\frac{1}{5}$ | $\frac{1}{5}$ |

| $\frac{1}{10}$ | $\frac{1}{10}$ | $\frac{1}{10}$ | $\frac{1}{10}$ | $\frac{1}{10}$ | $\frac{1}{10}$ | $\frac{1}{10}$ | $\frac{1}{10}$ | $\frac{1}{10}$ | $\frac{1}{10}$ |

$$\frac{3}{5} = \frac{6}{10}$$

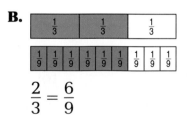

CRITICAL THINKING Explain how to use fraction strips to show whether $\frac{2}{5}$ and $\frac{3}{10}$ are equivalent.

PRACTICE

Write the equivalent fractions shown by the fraction strips.

1. | $\frac{1}{9}$ | $\frac{1}{9}$ | $\frac{1}{9}$ | $\frac{1}{9}$ | $\frac{1}{9}$ | $\frac{1}{9}$ | $\frac{1}{9}$ | $\frac{1}{9}$ | $\frac{1}{9}$ |

| $\frac{1}{3}$ | $\frac{1}{3}$ | $\frac{1}{3}$ |

2. | $\frac{1}{5}$ | $\frac{1}{5}$ | $\frac{1}{5}$ | $\frac{1}{5}$ | $\frac{1}{5}$ |

| $\frac{1}{10}$ | $\frac{1}{10}$ | $\frac{1}{10}$ | $\frac{1}{10}$ | $\frac{1}{10}$ | $\frac{1}{10}$ | $\frac{1}{10}$ | $\frac{1}{10}$ | $\frac{1}{10}$ | $\frac{1}{10}$ |

3. | $\frac{1}{4}$ | $\frac{1}{4}$ | $\frac{1}{4}$ | $\frac{1}{4}$ |

| $\frac{1}{8}$ | $\frac{1}{8}$ | $\frac{1}{8}$ | $\frac{1}{8}$ | $\frac{1}{8}$ | $\frac{1}{8}$ | $\frac{1}{8}$ | $\frac{1}{8}$ |

Use paper fraction strips to model an equivalent fraction for each. Shade part of each strip and record the fractions.

4. | $\frac{1}{5}$ | $\frac{1}{5}$ | $\frac{1}{5}$ | $\frac{1}{5}$ | $\frac{1}{5}$ |

5. | $\frac{1}{6}$ | $\frac{1}{6}$ | $\frac{1}{6}$ | $\frac{1}{6}$ | $\frac{1}{6}$ | $\frac{1}{6}$ |

6. | $\frac{1}{12}$ | $\frac{1}{12}$ | $\frac{1}{12}$ | $\frac{1}{12}$ | $\frac{1}{12}$ | $\frac{1}{12}$ | $\frac{1}{12}$ | $\frac{1}{12}$ | $\frac{1}{12}$ | $\frac{1}{12}$ | $\frac{1}{12}$ | $\frac{1}{12}$ |

Find an equivalent fraction. Use fraction strips.

7. $\frac{1}{3}$ 8. $\frac{3}{4}$ 9. $\frac{1}{6}$ 10. $\frac{4}{4}$ 11. $\frac{1}{6}$ 12. $\frac{2}{4}$

13. $\frac{3}{6}$ 14. $\frac{2}{8}$ 15. $\frac{3}{9}$ 16. $\frac{5}{5}$ 17. $\frac{4}{12}$ 18. $\frac{7}{8}$

19. $\frac{1}{4}$ 20. $\frac{6}{9}$ 21. $\frac{2}{5}$ 22. $\frac{6}{6}$ 23. $\frac{6}{12}$ 24. $\frac{1}{7}$

Mixed Applications

25. Quinn and his brother had lunch with 2 friends. They split the bill evenly. What fraction of the bill did Quinn and his brother pay?

26. Brenda folded a paper into 4 equal sections. Britton folded a paper the same size into 8 equal sections. How many sections on Britton's paper are equal to 2 sections on Brenda's paper?

27. Mrs. Blanca's class is raising money to go to the circus. They need $290.00 to pay for the bus, the tickets, and lunches. They raised $84.95 at a car wash and $63.25 at a bake sale. The P.T.O. donated $116.00. How much more money does the class need to be able to go to the circus?

28. Mike baked 12 more raisin cookies than oatmeal cookies. He baked 36 cookies altogether. What fraction of the cookies were raisin?

29. **Write a problem** about 4 friends who shared a pizza. Use equivalent fractions in your problem.

Customary Units

You will learn to choose the appropriate customary unit to measure length, capacity, and weight.

Why learn this? You can measure a package to find out how big or heavy it is, or measure a jar to see how much juice it can hold.

In the United States, many use the customary system of measurement.

Linear units measure in one direction, such as length, width, height, or distance.

Linear Customary Units
12 inches (in.) = 1 foot (ft)
3 feet = 1 yard (yd)
5,280 feet = 1 mile (mi)
1,760 yards = 1 mile

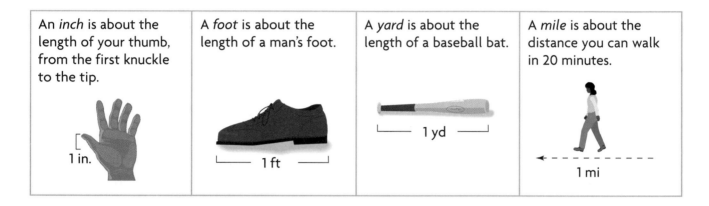

An *inch* is about the length of your thumb, from the first knuckle to the tip.

1 in.

A *foot* is about the length of a man's foot.

1 ft

A *yard* is about the length of a baseball bat.

1 yd

A *mile* is about the distance you can walk in 20 minutes.

1 mi

Units of *capacity* are used to measure the amount a container can hold when filled. Units of *weight* are used to measure how heavy an object is.

Customary Units for Measuring Liquids
2 cups (c) = 1 pint (pt)
2 pints = 1 quart (qt)
4 quarts = 1 gallon (gal)

Customary Units for Measuring Weight
16 ounces (oz) = 1 pound (lb)
2,000 pounds = 1 ton (T)

EXAMPLES

A can of soda holds a little more than a *cup*.

A large container of milk is a *gallon*.

A slice of bread weighs about an *ounce*.

A loaf of bread weighs about a *pound*.

- If you were describing the distance from home to school, would you use a linear unit, a unit of capacity, or a unit of weight? Which unit would you use?

PRACTICE

Choose the more reasonable estimate.

1.

2 oz or 2 lb

2.

2 ft or 2 yd

3.

1 gal or 1 cup

Write *length, capacity,* or *weight* for each given unit.

4. pint

5. foot

6. ounce

7. yard

8. gallon

9. mile

For Problems 10–13, choose the more reasonable estimate.

10. Teresa's brother Tommy is 2 years old. How tall is he?

32 in. or 32 ft

11. He likes to drink juice. How much might he drink at one time?

1 gal or 1 cup

12. Tommy's mom carries him from the car seat to the house. How heavy is he?

25 T or 25 lb

13. Jimmy eats about half of a hamburger. How heavy is that?

2 oz or 2 lb

Mixed Applications

14. Ralph is measuring a board to use as the base for his model plane. The model is $14\frac{1}{4}$ inches long and 13 inches wide. Ralph wants the base to be $1\frac{1}{2}$ inches longer than the plane. How long will it be?

15. Erin had a 48-ounce pitcher of lemonade. She poured 4 equal glasses of lemonade and had 8 ounces of lemonade left in the pitcher. How many ounces were in each glass?

16. The medals to be awarded at the field day events each weigh 2 oz. There are 72 medals in a box. The empty box weighs 12 oz. How much does the box weigh with the medals inside?

17. ⬛▷ **WRITE ABOUT IT** Explain the differences in a linear unit, a unit of capacity, and a unit of weight.

Classifying Polygons

You will learn to identify polygons by their sides and angles.

Why learn this? You can identify the shapes of polygons in many objects, such as a computer screen and road signs.

A *polygon* is a closed plane figure with straight sides called line segments.

Study these polygons. Name the number of sides and angles in each.

 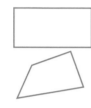   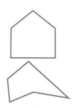

triangles　　**quadrilaterals**　　**pentagons**　　**hexagons**　　**octagons**

Talk About It ![CRITICAL THINKING]

- What relationship do you see between the number of sides and the number of angles?

- How is a polygon different from other plane figures?

- Is a circle a polygon? Explain.

Check Your Understanding

Name the polygon suggested by each road sign

1.
2.
3.
4.
5.

Name each figure.

6.
7.
8.
9.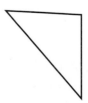
10.

PRACTICE

Copy and complete the table.

Polygon	Number of Sides	Number of Angles	Picture
11. Triangle	?	?	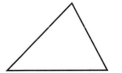
12. Quadrilateral	4	?	?
13. Pentagon	?	5	?
14. Hexagon	?	?	
15. Octagon	8	?	?

Write the letter of the figure that is a polygon.

16. a.  b.  c.

17. a.  b. c.

18. a. b.  c.

19. a.   b.   c.

Mixed Applications

20. Rafael went to see a shuttle launch. He arrived at 2:00 P.M. Describe the angle formed by the hands on a clock for this time.

21. Preston's family drove 4 hours to reach the launch site. If they drove 55 miles each hour, how many miles did they drive?

22. Stephanie is building a model sailboat. She spent $8.35 for supplies at the craft store. How much change did she received from $20.00?

23. ✏ **Write a problem** about a polygon you have noticed while on a car trip.

Point and Line Symmetry

You will learn to identify point symmetry and line symmetry in a pattern or an object.

Why learn this? You can see symmetrical objects in designs and paintings.

© Copyright The Andy Warhol Foundation for the Visual Arts/ARS, N.Y.

A figure has *point symmetry* if it can be turned about a central point and still look the same with each turn.

Shaded to show the turns

- How could you test a square to see if it has point symmetry?

A figure has *line symmetry* when it can be folded on a line so that its two parts are identical. When the figure is unfolded, one side is a reflection of the other.

Point Symmetry	Line Symmetry	Both Point and Line Symmetry
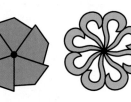	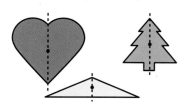	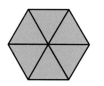

Talk About It

- How can you test a figure to see if it has line symmetry?
- Name something in everyday life with point symmetry, something with line symmetry, and something with both.

Check Your Understanding 💡 CRITICAL THINKING

Write *point*, *line*, or *both* to tell which kind of symmetry each figure represents.

1.    **2.**   **3.**    **4.**

PRACTICE

Write the letter of the figures with point symmetry.

5. a. 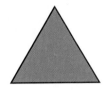   **b.**    **c.**   **d.**

Write the letter of the figures with both point and line symmetry.

6. a.   **b.**   **c.**   **d.**

Copy each drawing on grid paper. Then draw the other half of the figure to show that it has line symmetry.

7.   **8.**   **9.**

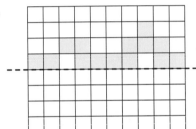   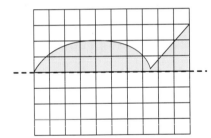   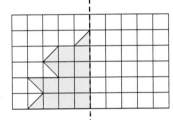

Mixed Applications

For Problems 10–11, use the pictures.

10. Which of the flowers have only line symmetry?

11. Which of the flowers have point and line symmetry?

12. Kimberly has two flower gardens. One flower garden is 8 ft wide and the other is 6 ft 6 in. wide. What is the difference in inches in their widths?

13. Mervin measured the height of a plant. It was $2\frac{5}{8}$ in. high. Two weeks later, the plant measured $4\frac{1}{2}$ in. high. How much did the plant grow in the two weeks?

buttercup

lily

orchid

daisy

14. ✏️ **WRITE ABOUT IT** Does the figure have line symmetry, point symmetry, or both? How do you know?

Faces, Edges, and Vertices of Solid Figures

You will learn to classify solid figures according to their faces, edges, and vertices.

Why learn this? You can identify the plane figures used to make a solid figure, such as the lid of a box is the face of a cube.

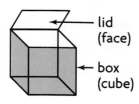
lid (face)
box (cube)

Some solid figures have faces, edges, and vertices.

Notice that

▷ a *face* is a flat surface of a solid figure.

▷ an *edge* is formed where two faces of a solid figure meet.

▷ a *vertex* is formed at the point where three or more edges of a solid figure meet.

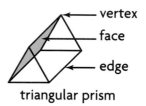
vertex
face
edge
triangular prism

Talk About It

• How many faces does a triangular prism have?

• How many edges does a triangular prism have?

• How many vertices does a triangular prism have?

• What plane figures make up a triangular prism?

Check Your Understanding 💡 CRITICAL THINKING

Copy the figure. Circle each vertex in red, outline each edge in blue, and shade one face in yellow.

The pyramids of Egypt

1.

2.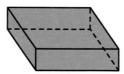

3.

Write the names of the faces and the number of each face of the solid figure.

4.

5.

6.

7.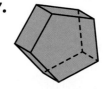

PRACTICE

Complete the table.

	Figure	Name of Figure	Number of Faces	Number of Edges	Number of Vertices
8.		?	?	?	?
9.		?	?	?	?
10.		?	?	?	?
11.		?	?	?	?
12.		?	?	?	?

Look at the pictures in the table above to answer the following. Write *a* or *b*.

13. Which figure has more faces?

  a. cube
  b. triangular pyramid

14. Which figure has more triangles as faces?

  a. triangular prism
  b. triangular pyramid

15. Which figure has more vertices?

  a. square pyramid
  b. cube

16. Which figure has more square faces?

  a. cube
  b. square pyramid

17. Which figure has the same number of faces and vertices?

  a. cube
  b. square pyramid

18. Which figure has more edges?

  a. triangular prism
  b. square pyramid

Mixed Applications

19. I am a plane figure. Every pyramid has at least 3 of me. What am I?

20. I am a solid figure. I have 4 faces. What am I?

21. I am a part of some solids. You can find me where edges meet. What am I?

22. I am a solid figure. All my faces are congruent. What am I?

23. Each of 18 students will be making a model of one cube, one triangular prism, and one triangular pyramid. What is the total number of faces that will be used by the students for their models?

24. ▥▷ **WRITE ABOUT IT** Explain the difference between a triangular prism and a square pyramid.

Powers of Ten

You will learn to express numbers as powers of ten.	Why learn this? It makes it easier to work with large numbers.

Use the chart to see the value of 1 in different place-value positions.

THOUSANDS			ONES			
Hundreds	Tens	Ones	Hundreds	Tens	Ones	
					1	
				1	0	$= 10 \times 1$
			1	0	0	$= 10 \times 10$
		1	0	0	0	$= 10 \times 10 \times 10$
	1	0	0	0	0	$= 10 \times 10 \times 10 \times 10$
1	0	0	0	0	0	$= 10 \times 10 \times 10 \times 10 \times 10$

$\$ 0.10 = 10^1$
$\$ 1.00 = 10^2$
$\$10.00 = 10^3$

- What relationship do you see between place-value positions?

_____

You can use exponents to express numbers. An *exponent* tells how many times the *base* number is used as a factor.

$$10,000 = 10 \times 10 \times 10 \times 10 = 10^4$$

exponent

4 is the exponent. It shows how many times the base is a factor.

base

10 is the base

Read: Ten to the fourth power

- How is the number of zeros in a number related to the exponent for its power of ten?

REMEMBER:

Place-value blocks help you visualize the size relationship of the digit 1 in different place-value positions.

Thousands	Hundreds	Tens	Ones
1,000	100	10	1

How many times larger is the thousands block than the tens block?

Check Your Understanding

 CRITICAL THINKING

Complete.

1. $10 \times \underline{\ ?\ } = 100$ **2.** $10^2 = \underline{\ ?\ }$ **3.** $10^{\underline{?}} = 100,000$

	Place Value	Number	Multiplication	Power of Ten
4.	tens	?	10×1	10^1
5.	hundreds	100	10×10	?
6.	thousands	1,000	?	10^3
7.	?	10,000	$10 \times 10 \times 10 \times 10$	10^4
8.	hundred thousands	100,000	$10 \times 10 \times 10 \times 10 \times 10$	?

PRACTICE

Write the base and exponent for each number.

9. 10^4 **10.** 10^2 **11.** 10^5 **12.** 10^1 **13.** 10^3

Write the exponent form for each.

14. $10 \times 10 \times 10$ **15.** $10 \times 10 \times 10 \times 10 \times 10 \times 10$

16. 10×10

Express as a power of 10, using an exponent.

17. 100,000   **18.** 1,000   **19.** 10,000   **20.** 100

Answer each question.

21. What is the exponent in 10^7?

22. What is the base in 10^6?

23. The number represented by 10^4 has how many zeros?

24. What is the number represented by 10^4?

25. What is the exponent in 10^8?

26. What is the number represented by 10^5?

Science Link

Scientists use the Richter scale to describe the strength of earthquakes. The Richter scale increases by powers of ten. An earthquake registering 2.0 is 10 times stronger than a quake registering 1.0, and a quake registering 3.0 is 10×10, or 100 times stronger. How many times stronger would a quake registering 4.0 be than one registering 1.0?

Complete.

27. $10^{\underline{?}} = 10 \times 10 \times 10$ **28.** $10^1 = \underline{\ ?\ }$

29. $10^2 = \underline{\ ?\ }$ **30.** $10 \times 10 \times 10 \times 10 = \underline{\ ?\ }$

31. $10 \times \underline{\ ?\ } = 10^2$ **32.** $10^5 = \underline{\ ?\ }$

Applications

33. There were 10 fifth graders who each volunteered 10 hours of their time to help tutor fourth graders. What is the total number of hours the students volunteered?

34. Selena earned $10 each week for 10 weeks of baby-sitting. Ricardo earned $10 each week for 10 weeks of mowing lawns. How much did they earn altogether?

35. Marshall is counting the number of people in the assembly. So far he has counted 10 rows, with 10 people in each row, in 10 different sections. How many people has he counted so far?

36. ✏ **WRITE ABOUT IT** How would you explain to a classmate that 10^5 is the same as 100,000?

Using the Calculator to Divide

| You will learn to use the memory keys on a calculator. | Why learn this? You can divide larger numbers more quickly. |

A calculator is useful when you want to divide large numbers quickly.

Divide. $19{,}295 \div 37$ $37\overline{)19{,}295}$

Estimate. $19{,}295 \div 37 \approx n$ **Think:** $40\overline{)20{,}000}^{\,500}$ or $30\overline{)18{,}000}^{\,600}$

So, $n = 500$ or 600.

Enter the problem on a calculator. Enter the dividend first.

Press: **Display:**

`1` `9` `2` `9` `5` `÷` `3` `7` `=`   `= 521.48649`

Talk About It

- What is the whole-number part of the display?

- What does the decimal part represent?

- What is one way you could find the whole-number remainder this decimal represents?

Here's another way to find the whole-number remainder represented by the decimal. Use the calculator's memory keys.

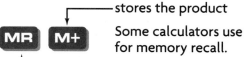

— stores the product

`MR` `M+`   Some calculators use for memory recall.   `MRC`

— recalls the product from memory

MODEL

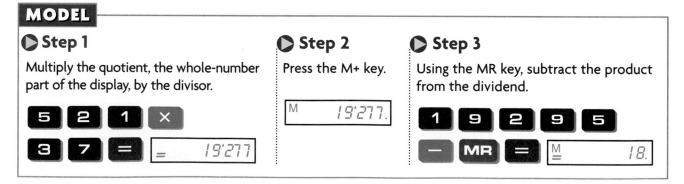

▶ **Step 1**

Multiply the quotient, the whole-number part of the display, by the divisor.

`5` `2` `1` `×`

`3` `7` `=`   `= 19'277`

▶ **Step 2**

Press the M+ key.

`M 19'277.`

▶ **Step 3**

Using the MR key, subtract the product from the dividend.

`1` `9` `2` `9` `5`

`–` `MR` `=`   `M 18.`

So, the whole-number remainder is 18.

Talk About It

- What happened when you pressed the `M+` key?

- What does the *M* on the display represent?
- What happened when you pressed the key?
- How can you check that a remainder of 18 is correct?
- What happens when you press ?

PRACTICE

Use the calculator to divide. Then find the whole-number remainder.

1. $13 \overline{)14,368}$
2. $34 \overline{)52,747}$
3. $46 \overline{)24,391}$
4. $58 \overline{)12,813}$

5. $27 \overline{)60,824}$
6. $73 \overline{)84,088}$
7. $67 \overline{)53,094}$
8. $78 \overline{)55,649}$

9. $91 \overline{)98,301}$
10. $83 \overline{)17,659}$
11. $14 \overline{)40,687}$
12. $65 \overline{)32,758}$

Applications

Use a calculator. For Problems 13–16, use the table.

13. There were 15,980 fans divided into 4 equal-size cheering sections when the Magic played the Bulls at the Orlando Arena. Of the 4 sections, 3 were filled with Magic fans. How many Magic fans were there?

NBA HOME COURTS

Team	Name	Capacity (no. of people)
Denver	McNichols Sports Arena	17,171
Houston	The Summit	16,611
Orlando	Orlando Arena	17,248
Toronto	Sky Dome	22,911

14. On opening night the Sky Dome was filled to capacity. If everyone drove to the game in groups of 3, how many cars were in the parking lot?

15. On the night Zoe went to The Summit, it was filled to capacity. T-shirts were given to every seventy-fifth person who entered. How many people got T-shirts?

16. On the night Alfonse went to McNichols Sports Arena, it was filled to capacity. The snack vendors sold 1 whole pizza for every 15 people there. How many whole pizzas did they sell?

17. Ariana has 13,574 pennies. She has been saving pennies for 11 years. Suppose Ariana saved the same number of pennies each year. How many pennies per year did she save?

18. There were $80,350 worth of tickets sold for the winter ice-skating show. Tickets cost $25 each. How many tickets were sold?

19. ✏️ **Write a problem** in which you divide using a calculator. Use the numbers 63,935 and 19.

Interpreting Histograms

You will learn to interpret a histogram.

Why learn this? You can compare data that are grouped with a range, such as ages.

A *histogram* is a bar graph that shows the number of times data occur within a certain range or interval.

Mr. Greenburg surveyed his class to find out the students' heights. Then he made a histogram.

Heights of Mr. Greenburg's Students	
Range of Heights	Number of Students
48 in. – 51 in.	2
52 in. – 55 in.	5
56 in. – 59 in.	12
60 in. – 63 in.	7
64 in. – 67 in.	1

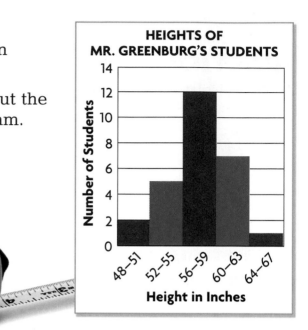

HEIGHTS OF MR. GREENBURG'S STUDENTS

Talk About It

• In which range of heights are most of Mr. Greenburg's students?

• What do you notice about the intervals for each bar in the histogram?

• How are the bars in a histogram different from the bars in a bar graph?

• How are the labels along the bottom of a histogram different from those along the bottom of a bar graph?

Check Your Understanding

 **CRITICAL THINKING**

For Problems 1–3, use the histogram.

1. During which range of months are the most cheerleaders' birthdays?

2. During which range of months do only 3 cheerleaders have birthdays?

3. How many members are there on the cheerleading squad?

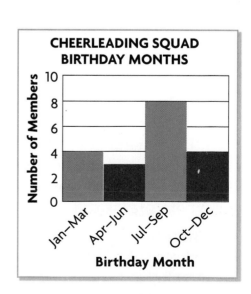

CHEERLEADING SQUAD BIRTHDAY MONTHS

PRACTICE

For Problems 4–7, use the histogram.

4. Between which ages are the greatest number of swim-club members? the least number?

5. How many swim-club members are under the age of 20?

6. How many more members are there between the ages 0–9 than between the ages 20–29?

7. How many swim-club members are there from the ages 0–39?

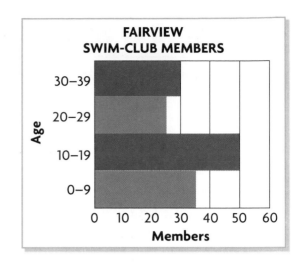

FAIRVIEW SWIM-CLUB MEMBERS

Applications

For Problems 8–16, use the histograms.

8. Between which times were the most books checked out of the media center?

9. Between which times were the least books checked out of the media center?

10. How many more books were checked out between 10:00 and 12:00 than between 8:00 and 10:00?

11. How many books were checked out between 8:00 and 4:00?

12. Between what two numbers were the most push-ups completed in one minute?

13. Between what two numbers were the least push-ups completed in one minute?

14. How many students did between 11 and 20 push-ups?

15. How many students in all did push-ups?

16. 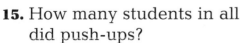 **Write a problem** using the information in one of the histograms.

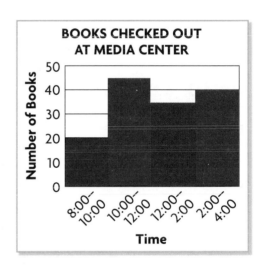

BOOKS CHECKED OUT AT MEDIA CENTER

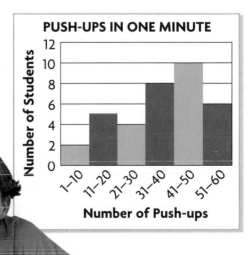

PUSH-UPS IN ONE MINUTE

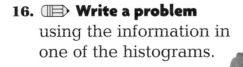

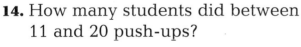

Conduct a Simulation

You will learn to simulate probability experiments.

Why learn this? You can save time and money by conducting a simulation.

Suppose LaTeisha wants to get a ring from a gumball machine. Of the 500 items in the gumball machine, 400 are gumballs, 50 are bouncing balls, and 50 are rings. How can LaTeisha design a simulation and see how many tries it might take before she gets a ring?

To conduct a *simulation* means to do something in a way that is easier than the actual experiment. The possible outcomes of the simulation have to match the possible outcomes of the real event.

You can use a spinner to simulate getting items from a gumball machine.

1. Decide how to make the spinner. Since there are 500 items in the gumball machine, you can make a spinner divided into five equal sections. Each section represents 100 items.

2. Shade four sections to represent the 400 gumballs. Shade half of one section to represent the 50 bouncing balls and the other half to represent the 50 rings.

3. Spin the pointer as many times as you want to simulate getting items from the gumball machine. Record the frequency of each outcome.

So, LaTeisha used green to stand for gumballs, blue to stand for bouncing balls, and red to stand for rings. She spun the pointer 10 times and recorded her outcomes in a table.

Talk About It

- How many spins did it take for the pointer to land on red?

- If LaTeisha spends $0.25 for each try at the gumball machine, how much money might she expect to spend to get a ring?

- If this simulation is repeated, will the results be the same? Explain.

GUMBALL-MACHINE SIMULATION		
Spin Number	Color	Item
1	green	gumball
2	blue	ball
3	green	gumball
4	green	gumball
5	green	gumball
6	green	gumball
7	blue	ball
8	red	ring
9	green	gumball
10	green	gumball

PRACTICE

Design a simulation for each situation.

1. Taylor wants to buy a concert ticket. He can't choose his seat when he buys his ticket. Of the 1,000 seats available for the concert, 200 are in Section A, 300 are in Section B, 300 are in Section C, and 200 are in Section D. What simulation can Taylor design to determine what section his ticket might be for?

2. Melissa will be assigned a band instrument to use this year. Of the 100 instruments available, 50 are clarinets, 20 are flutes, 10 are trumpets, 10 are tubas, and 10 are saxophones. What simulation can Melissa design to determine the instrument she might be assigned?

For Problem 3, design and conduct a simulation. Copy the table for recording the results of your simulation.

3. Of the 600 prizes at a carnival booth, there are 100 teddy bears, 100 games, 100 toys, and 300 goldfish. What simulation can Jenny design to determine which prize she might win?

CARNIVAL PRIZE SIMULATION			
Teddy Bear	Game	Toy	Goldfish

Which prize might Jenny win?

Applications

4. Randy is being assigned his school locker. There are 1,000 lockers. He wants to know his chances of getting a locker number from 1 through 100. What simulation can Randy design to determine what locker number he might get?

5. At Dover Elementary, there are 5 classes in each grade, kindergarten through fifth. One class will be chosen to go on a special field trip. What simulation can you design to determine the grade level of the class that will go on the trip?

6. Misty gets to choose a pencil as a prize. Of the 300 pencils in the box, 150 are red, 60 are green, and 90 are blue. What simulation can Misty design to determine which color pencil she might get?

7. ◁▷ **WRITE ABOUT IT** Do the results of a simulation tell you the exact results you would get if you conducted the actual experiment? Explain.

Estimating Quotients

You will learn to estimate quotients.

Why learn this? You can decide if your answers make sense.

Nell's basketball team is selling carnations. Each package of 8 carnations costs $5.95. About how much does each carnation cost?

Since an exact answer is not needed, estimate the quotient.

Choose a compatible number that can be divided evenly by the divisor.

$5.95 ÷ 8   **Think:** 8, 16, 24, 32, 40, 48, 56, or 64

Use a dividend of $5.60 for a compatible number.

$5.60 ÷ 8 = $0.70

So, one estimate for the cost of each carnation is $0.70.

8 CARNATIONS $5.95

Sometimes you can use more than one pair of compatible numbers. Since $6.40 is also close to $5.95 and is compatible with 8, another way to estimate the quotient is to find $6.40 ÷ 8.

$6.40 ÷ 8 = $0.80   **Think:** 8 × $0.80 = $6.40

So, another estimate for the cost of each carnation is $0.80.

Talk About It

• Are these both good estimates? Why or why not?

• Is $0.70 per carnation greater than or less than the actual quotient? How can you tell?

• Is $0.80 per carnation greater than or less than the actual quotient? How can you tell?

• If each package of 6 carnations costs $4.69, about how much does each carnation cost?

💡 **CRITICAL THINKING**   Can $1.20 be the exact cost per carnation for Nell's team? Why or why not?

> **Science Link**
>
> About 250,000 kinds of plants produce seeds. The seeds vary in size, shape, and color. Begonia flower seeds are so small that about 16 million seeds weigh about one pound. Estimate how many begonia seeds would weigh about one ounce. (**HINT:** 1 lb = 16 oz)

PRACTICE

Choose the letter of the best estimate.

1. $2\overline{)1.34}$ **a.** 0.50   **b.** 0.30   **c.** 0.60   **d.** 0.70

2. $6\overline{)5.9}$ **a.** 1.0   **b.** 10   **c.** 100   **d.** 0.1

3. $2\overline{)\$1.81}$ **a.** \$0.70   **b.** \$0.80   **c.** \$0.90   **d.** \$1.00

4. $5\overline{)\$2.63}$ **a.** \$0.50   **b.** \$5.00   **c.** \$0.05   **d.** \$50.00

5. $6\overline{)4.11}$ **a.** 0.60   **b.** 0.70   **c.** 0.80   **d.** 0.90

Estimate the quotient.

6. $3\overline{)3.6}$ **7.** $5\overline{)\$2.07}$ **8.** $8\overline{)4.90}$ **9.** $3\overline{)1.33}$

10. $4\overline{)4.03}$ **11.** $4\overline{)\$1.97}$ **12.** $8\overline{)2.50}$ **13.** $3\overline{)4.18}$

14. $3\overline{)\$6.76}$ **15.** $8\overline{)8.89}$ **16.** $6\overline{)4.9}$ **17.** $9\overline{)3.5}$

18. $7\overline{)3.6}$ **19.** $2\overline{)1.84}$ **20.** $6\overline{)3.58}$ **21.** $8\overline{)5.69}$

22. $31.8 \div 8 = n$ **23.** $\$27.75 \div 7 = n$ **24.** $16.2 \div 5 = n$

25. $\$82.20 \div 9 = n$ **26.** $35.8 \div 5 = n$ **27.** $4.21 \div 7 = n$

28. $27.9 \div 9 = n$ **29.** $0.45 \div 7 = n$ **30.** $17.5 \div 2 = n$

Applications

31. Val is transferring 237 files to diskettes. She can put 8 files on each diskette. About how many diskettes will she use?

32. A 117-minute film is recorded and divided equally onto 2 large reels. About how many minutes of film does each reel contain?

33. A theater has 240 seats. The seats are arranged in 3 sections of the same size. How many seats are in each section?

34. The 7 teacher's aides were assigned 227 tests to grade. About how many tests did each teacher's aide have to grade?

35. A group of 168 students have signed up for computer classes. If there are 8 teachers, about how many students will be with each teacher?

36. Tommy is writing a report on his computer. He wants to explain 4 topics on one page. A page has 54 lines. About how many lines should he write on each topic?

Fractions as Missing Addends

You will learn to use fraction strips to find missing addends.

Why learn this? You can find the missing amount when you know the sum and one addend.

Yesterday Josh had $\frac{1}{3}$ pound of jelly beans. Then his friend gave him some more jelly beans. Now Josh has $\frac{3}{4}$ pound of jelly beans. How many pounds of jelly beans did his friend give him?

Think: $\frac{1}{3} + \underline{\ ?\ } = \frac{3}{4}$

You can use fraction bars to find the missing addend.

MODEL

Find the missing addend for $\frac{1}{3} + \underline{\ ?\ } = \frac{3}{4}$.

▶ Step 1

Use fraction bars to model the sum.

| $\frac{1}{4}$ | $\frac{1}{4}$ | $\frac{1}{4}$ |

Use fraction bars to model the given addend.

| $\frac{1}{3}$ |

▶ Step 2

Compare the sum and the given addend to find the missing addend.

missing addend

▶ Step 3

Since the LCM of 4 and 3 is 12, the LCD is twelfths. Use fraction bars to see how many twelfths are needed for the missing addend.

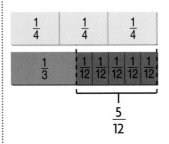

$\frac{5}{12}$

So, the missing addend is $\frac{5}{12}$.

So, Josh's friend gave him $\frac{5}{12}$ pound of jelly beans.

EXAMPLE

Find the missing addend for $\frac{3}{4} + \underline{\ ?\ } = 1\frac{1}{4}$.

Model and compare.

| 1 | $\frac{1}{4}$ |

| $\frac{1}{4}$ | $\frac{1}{4}$ | $\frac{1}{4}$ | |

Since the LCM of 4 and 4 is 4, the LCD is fourths. Use fraction bars to see how many fourths are needed for the missing addend.

| 1 | $\frac{1}{4}$ |

| $\frac{1}{4}$ | $\frac{1}{4}$ | $\frac{1}{4}$ | $\frac{1}{4}$ | $\frac{1}{4}$ |

So, the missing addend is $\frac{2}{4}$, or $\frac{1}{2}$.

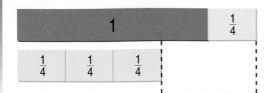
CRITICAL THINKING What other operation can you use to find a missing addend?

PRACTICE

Name the missing addend. You may wish to use fraction strips.

1. $\frac{1}{3} + \underline{\ ?\ } = \frac{5}{6}$

2. $\frac{1}{2} + \underline{\ ?\ } = \frac{3}{4}$

3. $\frac{5}{6} + \underline{\ ?\ } = \frac{11}{12}$

| $\frac{1}{12}$ | $\frac{1}{12}$ | $\frac{1}{12}$ | $\frac{1}{12}$ | $\frac{1}{12}$ | $\frac{1}{12}$ | $\frac{1}{12}$ | $\frac{1}{12}$ | $\frac{1}{12}$ | $\frac{1}{12}$ | $\frac{1}{12}$ |

| $\frac{1}{6}$ | $\frac{1}{6}$ | $\frac{1}{6}$ | $\frac{1}{6}$ | $\frac{1}{6}$ |

4. $\frac{3}{10} + \underline{\ ?\ } = \frac{4}{5}$

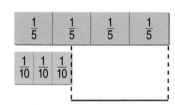

5. $\frac{1}{8} + \underline{\ ?\ } = \frac{3}{4}$

6. $\frac{1}{4} + \underline{\ ?\ } = \frac{5}{6}$

Use fraction strips to find the missing addend.

7. $\frac{1}{4} + \underline{\ ?\ } = \frac{1}{3}$

8. $\frac{7}{10} + \underline{\ ?\ } = \frac{4}{5}$

9. $\frac{1}{6} + \underline{\ ?\ } = \frac{3}{4}$

10. $\frac{1}{2} + \underline{\ ?\ } = \frac{2}{3}$

11. $\frac{1}{3} + \underline{\ ?\ } = \frac{4}{9}$

12. $\frac{1}{2} + \underline{\ ?\ } = \frac{7}{8}$

13. $\frac{4}{5} + \underline{\ ?\ } = 1\frac{3}{5}$

14. $\frac{5}{6} + \underline{\ ?\ } = 1\frac{1}{6}$

15. $\frac{5}{8} + \underline{\ ?\ } = 1\frac{3}{8}$

Applications

16. Jamie had $\frac{1}{4}$ pound peanuts. His brother gave him more peanuts. Now Jamie has $\frac{2}{3}$ pound peanuts. How many pounds of peanuts did his brother give him?

17. Paula measured the growth of her flower. On the first day, the flower grew $\frac{1}{6}$ inch. The plant grew some more on the second day. By the third day, the plant had grown $\frac{2}{3}$ inch. How much did the plant grow the second day?

18. Zach was baking a cake. The cake rose $\frac{1}{8}$ inch the first minute. The cake rose some more the second minute. Now the cake has risen $\frac{3}{4}$ inch in all. How much did the cake rise during the second minute?

19. ✏️ **WRITE ABOUT IT** Explain how you can use fraction bars to find the missing addend.

Using Fraction Circles to Subtract

You will learn to use fraction circles to subtract unlike fractions. | **Why learn this?** You can subtract to compare amounts such as those on a circle graph.

Martin surveyed his classmates to find out their favorite kind of book. Of the students, $\frac{3}{4}$ said fiction, $\frac{1}{8}$ said nonfiction, and $\frac{1}{8}$ said poetry. What is the difference between the fraction of the students who said fiction and the fraction who said poetry?

You can use fraction-circle pieces to subtract.

MODEL

What is $\frac{3}{4} - \frac{1}{8}$?

▶ **Step 1**

Model with fraction-circle pieces.

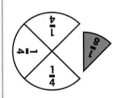

▶ **Step 2**

Stack the piece for $\frac{1}{8}$ directly on top of the pieces for $\frac{3}{4}$.

▶ **Step 3**

Find the least common denominator, or LCD.

The LCM of 4 and 8 is 8. So, the LCD of $\frac{3}{4}$ and $\frac{1}{8}$ is eighths.

▶ **Step 4**

Use like fraction-circle pieces to see how many eighths fit exactly around. This is the difference.

So, $\frac{3}{4} - \frac{1}{8} = \frac{5}{8}$.

So, $\frac{5}{8}$ more students said fiction than poetry.

MODEL

What is $\frac{2}{3} - \frac{1}{6}$?

▶ **Step 1**

Stack the piece for $\frac{1}{6}$ directly on top of the pieces for $\frac{2}{3}$.

▶ **Step 2**

Find the LCD.

The LCM of 3 and 6 is 6. So, the LCD of $\frac{2}{3}$ and $\frac{1}{6}$ is sixths.

▶ **Step 3**

Find the difference.

$\frac{2}{3} - \frac{1}{6} = \frac{3}{6}$

▶ **Step 4**

Find the largest fraction-circle piece or pieces to write the answer in simplest form.

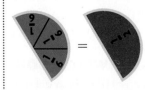

So, $\frac{2}{3} - \frac{1}{6} = \frac{1}{2}$.

💡 **CRITICAL THINKING** How is using fraction-circle pieces to subtract the same as using fraction bars? How is it different?

PRACTICE

Name the least common denominator, or LCD, for each pair of fractions.

1. $\dfrac{1}{2} - \dfrac{1}{3} = n$
  2. $\dfrac{1}{2} - \dfrac{1}{4} = n$
  3. $\dfrac{1}{2} - \dfrac{1}{8} = n$

4. $\dfrac{1}{3} - \dfrac{1}{6} = n$
  5. $\dfrac{1}{4} - \dfrac{1}{8} = n$
  6. $\dfrac{2}{3} - \dfrac{1}{2} = n$

Use fraction-circle pieces to find the difference. Write the answer in simplest form.

7. $\dfrac{1}{3} - \dfrac{1}{6} = n$
  8. $\dfrac{1}{4} - \dfrac{1}{8} = n$
  9. $\dfrac{2}{3} - \dfrac{1}{2} = n$

10. $\dfrac{3}{4} - \dfrac{1}{2} = n$
  11. $\dfrac{7}{8} - \dfrac{1}{2} = n$
  12. $\dfrac{5}{6} - \dfrac{1}{3} = n$

13. $\dfrac{3}{4} - \dfrac{3}{8} = n$
  14. $\dfrac{1}{2} - \dfrac{3}{8} = n$
  15. $\dfrac{2}{3} - \dfrac{2}{6} = n$

16. $\dfrac{6}{8} - \dfrac{1}{4} = n$
  17. $\dfrac{6}{8} - \dfrac{1}{2} = n$
  18. $\dfrac{4}{6} - \dfrac{1}{3} = n$

Applications

Use fraction-circle pieces to solve.

19. Kori and Jeananne have equal-size bags of pretzels. Kori's bag is $\frac{1}{2}$ full. Jeananne's is $\frac{1}{3}$ full. How much fuller is Kori's pretzel bag than Jeananne's?

20. Chen and Ruben collect stamps. Chen's stamp album is $\frac{7}{8}$ full. Ruben's is $\frac{1}{2}$ full. How much more of a stamp album has Chen filled?

21. The pins on Jamie's string-art design are $\frac{6}{8}$ inch apart. The pins on Nomary's design are $\frac{1}{2}$ inch apart. How much farther apart are the pins on Jamie's design?

22. Lionel has a carton of eggs that is $\frac{5}{6}$ full. Kenny has a carton of eggs that is $\frac{1}{3}$ full. How much more of a carton of eggs does Lionel have?

23. Of the students in Senn's class, $\frac{1}{2}$ take the bus home after school, $\frac{1}{4}$ ride bikes, $\frac{1}{8}$ walk, and $\frac{1}{8}$ get picked up by a parent. What is the difference between the part of the students who take the bus and the part who walk?

24. 📖 **WRITE ABOUT IT** When subtracting with fraction-circle pieces, why is it important to stack the pieces directly on top of one another?

Fractions in Music Notation

You will learn how fractions are used to write music.

Why learn this? You can understand the notes used to write music.

Composers use fractions when they write music. The musical notes they use each represent a certain number of counts, or beats.

The time signature in this musical composition is $\frac{4}{4}$. The top number of the time signature means there are 4 beats per measure. The bottom number means a quarter note gets 1 beat.

MUSICAL NOTES (in $\frac{4}{4}$ time)	
Notes	Number of beats
○ whole note	4
♩ half note	2
♩ quarter note	1
♪ eighth note	$\frac{1}{2}$

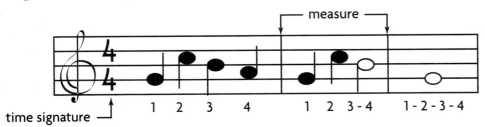

- Describe the notes and beats in each measure.

A composer must know the fractional relationship between notes.

○ = ♩♩ **1 whole** **2 half** **note** **notes**	So, a half note is held $\frac{1}{2}$ the time of a whole note.
○ = ♩♩♩♩ **1 whole** **4 quarter** **note** **notes**	So, a quarter note is held $\frac{1}{4}$ the time of a whole note.
○ = ♪♪♪♪♪♪♪♪ **1 whole** **8 eighth** **note** **notes**	So, an eighth note is held $\frac{1}{8}$ the time of a whole note.

Talk About It

- How many quarter notes equal a half note?
- How many eighth notes equal a half note?
- Describe the relationship between a quarter note and a half note.

When a dot is added to a musical note, the note is held half again as long as the original note.

$$\text{half note} \quad + \quad \text{dot} \quad = \quad \text{dotted half note}$$

half note   dot   dotted half note
(2 beats)   ($\frac{1}{2}$ of 2 = 1)   (3 beats)

2   +   1   =   3

- How many beats does a dotted quarter note have? a dotted eighth note?

PRACTICE

If the time signature is $\frac{4}{4}$, tell how many of each kind of note you can put in a measure. Then write each note as a fraction in an addition number sentence, so that the sum of each number sentence is 1.

EXAMPLES

a. half notes   2 half notes: $\frac{1}{2} + \frac{1}{2} = 1$

b. quarter notes   4 quarter notes: $\frac{1}{4} + \frac{1}{4} + \frac{1}{4} + \frac{1}{4} = 1$

1. quarter notes and half notes

2. eighth notes and half notes

3. eighth notes and quarter notes

4. eighth notes, quarter notes, and half notes

Applications

For Problems 5–6, use the music at the right.

5. How many more beats are needed in the second measure?

6. What combination of notes could you use to complete the second measure?

7. The time signature of a piece of music is $\frac{2}{4}$. How many beats are there per measure?

8. Write a short musical composition with 3 measures. Use a time signature of $\frac{4}{4}$. Write the counts for each note below each note.

9. What is the time signature of this composition?

10. ⬛▷ **WRITE ABOUT IT** Explain how musical notation and fractions are related.

Renaming Mixed Numbers

You will learn to subtract mixed numbers in which the first fraction is less than the second fraction.

Why learn this? You can subtract measurements that are expressed as mixed numbers.

The steel-manufacturing plant had $4\frac{3}{10}$ tons of steel. They sold $2\frac{4}{5}$ tons of the steel to a car-manufacturing plant. How much steel is left?

Subtract $4\frac{3}{10}$ and $2\frac{4}{5}$. Estimate. $4\frac{1}{2} - 3 = 1\frac{1}{2}$

MODEL

What is $4\frac{3}{10} - 2\frac{4}{5}$?

▶ Step 1

Rename the fractions. Since the LCD is tenths, change $\frac{4}{5}$ to tenths.

$$4\frac{3}{10} = 4\frac{3}{10}$$
$$- 2\frac{4}{5} = 2\frac{8}{10}$$

▶ Step 2

Model the mixed number from which you are subtracting. Decide if you can subtract.

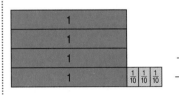

$$4\frac{3}{10}$$
$$-2\frac{8}{10}$$

▶ Step 3

Before you can subtract $\frac{8}{10}$ from $\frac{3}{10}$, you have to rename $4\frac{3}{10}$ as $3\frac{13}{10}$.

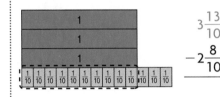

$$3\frac{13}{10}$$
$$-2\frac{8}{10}$$

▶ Step 4

Subtract the fractions. Take $\frac{8}{10}$ away from $\frac{13}{10}$.

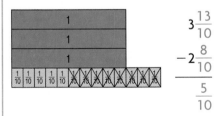

$$3\frac{13}{10}$$
$$-2\frac{8}{10}$$
$$\overline{\quad\frac{5}{10}}$$

▶ Step 5

Subtract the whole numbers. Write the answer in simplest form.

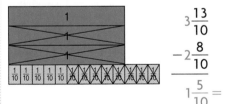

$$3\frac{13}{10}$$
$$-2\frac{8}{10}$$
$$\overline{1\frac{5}{10} = 1\frac{1}{2}}$$

So, there are $1\frac{1}{2}$ tons of steel left.

Talk About It

- Is the answer reasonable? Explain how you know.

- In Step 3, why did $4\frac{3}{10}$ have to be renamed as $3\frac{13}{10}$?

💡 **CRITICAL THINKING**   Look at Steps 1 and 3. Why must you rename twice before you can subtract mixed numbers?

Science Link

There are 2,000 pounds in 1 ton. About how many pounds are equal to $4\frac{3}{10}$ tons?

PRACTICE

Decide if you need to rename. Write *yes* or *no*.

1. $2\frac{1}{2}$
   $-1\frac{3}{4}$

2. $4\frac{1}{3}$
   $-2\frac{5}{6}$

3. $10\frac{5}{6}$
   $-6\frac{2}{12}$

4. $7\frac{4}{9}$
   $-2\frac{1}{3}$

5. $12\frac{2}{3}$
   $-3\frac{2}{9}$

6. $9\frac{3}{8}$
   $-5\frac{3}{4}$

7. $6\frac{5}{12}$
   $-5\frac{1}{2}$

8. $13\frac{4}{5}$
   $-8\frac{7}{10}$

Match the mixed number with the fraction bars.

9. $5\frac{1}{5}$

10. $5\frac{1}{3}$

11. $4\frac{4}{5}$

a.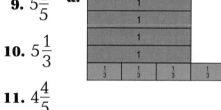

b.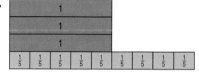

c.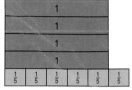

Use fraction strips to find the difference. Write the answer in simplest form.

12. $5\frac{2}{5}$
    $-1\frac{4}{5}$

13. $2\frac{1}{4}$
    $-1\frac{3}{4}$

14. $4\frac{1}{6}$
    $-2\frac{5}{6}$

15. $7\frac{1}{10}$
    $-2\frac{9}{10}$

16. $5\frac{1}{12}$
    $-2\frac{3}{4}$

17. $7\frac{3}{8}$
    $-1\frac{3}{4}$

18. $8\frac{1}{6}$
    $-3\frac{2}{3}$

19. $6\frac{2}{3}$
    $-3\frac{3}{4}$

Applications

20. Andrew had $6\frac{1}{4}$ feet of fencing. He used $3\frac{3}{4}$ feet to finish fencing in his yard. How many feet of fencing does Andrew have left over?

21. Mr. Alonzo bought $10\frac{1}{2}$ pounds of dirt to fill in around his bushes. He used $5\frac{3}{4}$ pounds of the dirt. How much dirt is left over?

22. Vivian had 2 quarts of water in a container. Today she has used $1\frac{1}{3}$ quarts. How much water is left in the container?

23. ▭ **WRITE ABOUT IT** Explain how to rename a mixed number.

Exploring Division of Fractions

You will learn to divide fractions by using fraction bars and fraction-circle pieces.

Why learn this? You will better understand division of fractions by asking the question, "How many equal parts are there?"

Sandy has a $\frac{6}{8}$-yard length of ribbon for a craft project. She must cut the ribbon into pieces that are each $\frac{2}{8}$ yard long. How many pieces of ribbon will Sandy have?

You can use fraction bars to divide fractions.

MODEL

What is $\frac{6}{8} \div \frac{2}{8}$?

▶ Step 1

Model $\frac{6}{8}$ and $\frac{2}{8}$ with fraction bars.

▶ Step 2

See how many groups of $\frac{2}{8}$ are equal in length to $\frac{6}{8}$.

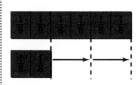

So, 3 groups of $\frac{2}{8}$ are equal in length to $\frac{6}{8}$.

▶ Step 3

Record a number sentence for the model. Divide the numerators. Divide the denominators. Write the answer in simplest form.

$\frac{6}{8} \div \frac{2}{8} = \frac{3}{1}$, or 3

So, Sandy will have 3 pieces of ribbon.

- In Step 3, what do you notice about the numerator of the quotient? the denominator?

You can also use fraction circles to divide fractions.

MODEL

What is $3 \div \frac{2}{6}$?

▶ Step 1

Rename so the denominators are the same.

$3 \div \frac{2}{6} = \frac{18}{6} \div \frac{2}{6}$

▶ Step 2

Model $\frac{18}{6}$ with fraction-circle pieces.

$\frac{6}{6} + \frac{6}{6} + \frac{6}{6} = \frac{18}{6}$, or 3

▶ Step 3

See how many groups of $\frac{2}{6}$ are equal to $\frac{18}{6}$.

So, 9 groups of $\frac{2}{6}$ are equal to $\frac{18}{6}$.

▶ Step 4

Record a number sentence for the model. Divide.

Simplify.

$\frac{18}{6} \div \frac{2}{6} = \frac{9}{1}$, or

$3 \div \frac{2}{6} = 9$

💡 **CRITICAL THINKING** What rule can you write for dividing fractions with like denominators?

PRACTICE

Record a number sentence for the picture.

1.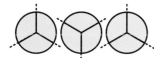

2.

3.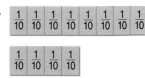

4.

| $\frac{1}{9}$ | $\frac{1}{9}$ | $\frac{1}{9}$ | $\frac{1}{9}$ | $\frac{1}{9}$ | $\frac{1}{9}$ | $\frac{1}{9}$ | $\frac{1}{9}$ |

| $\frac{1}{9}$ | $\frac{1}{9}$ |

5.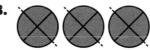

6.

| $\frac{1}{12}$ | $\frac{1}{12}$ | $\frac{1}{12}$ | $\frac{1}{12}$ | $\frac{1}{12}$ | $\frac{1}{12}$ | $\frac{1}{12}$ | $\frac{1}{12}$ | $\frac{1}{12}$ |

| $\frac{1}{12}$ | $\frac{1}{12}$ | $\frac{1}{12}$ |

7.

8.

9.

Find the quotient.

10. $\frac{3}{4} \div \frac{1}{4} = n$

11. $\frac{9}{10} \div \frac{3}{10} = n$

12. $\frac{24}{8} \div \frac{2}{8} = n$

13. $\frac{6}{9} \div \frac{2}{9} = n$

14. $\frac{6}{12} \div \frac{3}{12} = n$

15. $\frac{18}{6} \div \frac{3}{6} = n$

16. $\frac{20}{4} \div \frac{2}{4} = n$

17. $\frac{10}{2} \div \frac{1}{2} = n$

18. $\frac{16}{8} \div \frac{4}{8} = n$

Applications

19. Diane has a piece of construction paper that is $\frac{9}{10}$ meter long. She is going to divide the paper into sections that are $\frac{3}{10}$ meter long. Into how many sections will the construction paper be divided?

20. Choose one of the equations from Exercises 10–18. Draw either a fraction-bar or fraction-circle model to show the division problem.

21. Louis has a piece of wood that is $\frac{10}{12}$ yard long. He is going to cut it into pieces that are each $\frac{2}{12}$ yard long. How many pieces will he have?

22. The quotient of two fractions is 8. What are two possible division sentences for that quotient?

23. A line segment is $\frac{6}{8}$ in. long. How many $\frac{1}{8}$-in. units are there in $\frac{6}{8}$ in.?

24. 📖 **WRITE ABOUT IT** Explain how dividing fractions is like dividing whole numbers.

Angles in Circle Graphs

You will learn to read and make a circle graph.	**Why learn this?** You can display data that shows how a whole circle can be divided to show how you spend your time during the day.

Bradley is planting a vegetable garden. The table tells how much of the garden he will plant with each vegetable. Make a circle graph to display these data.

To make a circle graph, you need to find the number of degrees represented by each part. Since there are 360° about the center of a circle, multiply the fraction for each part by 360°.

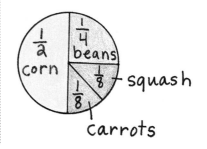

Bradley's Vegetable Garden

Vegetable	Fraction of the Garden
Corn	$\frac{1}{2}$
Beans	$\frac{1}{4}$
Squash	$\frac{1}{8}$
Carrots	$\frac{1}{8}$

MODEL

▶ Step 1

Multiply each fraction by 360°.

$\frac{1}{2} \times 360° = 180°$ (corn)

$\frac{1}{4} \times 360° = 90°$ (beans)

$\frac{1}{8} \times 360° = 45°$ (squash)

$\frac{1}{8} \times 360° = 45°$ (carrots)

▶ Step 2

Use a compass to draw a circle and a protractor to draw the angles.

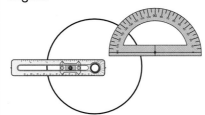

▶ Step 3

Complete and label the graph.

Talk About It

- Add the degrees for each part. What is the total number of degrees?

- Explain how the circle graph shows the data differently than the table.

Check Your Understanding 💡 CRITICAL THINKING

Find the number of degrees for the fractions in each set.

1. $\frac{1}{8}, \frac{1}{2}, \frac{1}{8}, \frac{1}{4}$

2. $\frac{1}{2}, \frac{1}{3}, \frac{1}{6}$

3. $\frac{2}{10}, \frac{3}{5}, \frac{1}{10}, \frac{1}{10}$

4. What is the sum of the fractions in Exercises 1–3?

5. What is the sum of the angles in Exercises 1–3?

PRACTICE

Find the number of degrees for the fractions in each set.
Find the sum of the angles in each set.

6. $\dfrac{1}{2}, \dfrac{1}{5}, \dfrac{3}{10}$

7. $\dfrac{1}{4}, \dfrac{2}{12}, \dfrac{1}{3}, \dfrac{3}{12}$

8. $\dfrac{1}{3}, \dfrac{1}{6}, \dfrac{1}{2}$

For Exercises 9–12, find the number of degrees for the fractions in each table. Make a circle graph to display the data.

9.

MR. FOLEY'S WORK SCHEDULE	
Activity	Fraction of Time Spent
Meetings	$\frac{3}{8}$
Telephone calls	$\frac{1}{8}$
Office work	$\frac{1}{2}$

10.

CHOICE OF FOOD FOR CLASS PARTY	
Food	Fraction of Class
Cupcakes	$\frac{1}{3}$
Cookies	$\frac{1}{3}$
Popcorn	$\frac{1}{6}$
Fruit	$\frac{1}{6}$

11.

FAVORITE BOOKS	
Books	Fraction of Class
Mystery	$\frac{4}{12}$
Humor	$\frac{1}{2}$
Biography	$\frac{1}{6}$

12.

CLASS HAIR COLORS	
Color	Fraction of Class
Brown	$\frac{2}{5}$
Red	$\frac{1}{10}$
Blond	$\frac{1}{5}$
Black	$\frac{3}{10}$

Applications

For Problems 13–17, use the circle graph.

13. Ed watched 24 television shows during the week. How many drama shows did he watch?

14. How many degrees are in the angle that represents the amount of time Ed watched drama shows?

15. Write another fraction that represents the number of sports shows that Ed watched during the week.

16. Which two angles are equal? How many degrees are in each angle?

TELEVISION SHOWS ED WATCHED IN ONE WEEK

17. ✏ **Write a problem** using the information in the circle graph.

Probability as a Ratio

You will learn how to write probability as a ratio.

Why learn this? You can analyze a game and figure out your chances of winning.

Eugene and Donna are playing a game, with the spinner shown below.

Eugene earns a point if the pointer lands on green. Donna earns a point if the pointer lands on blue. What is the probability that Eugene will earn a point when he spins?

Probability of Eugene earning

a point = $\dfrac{\text{green sections}}{\text{all sections}}$

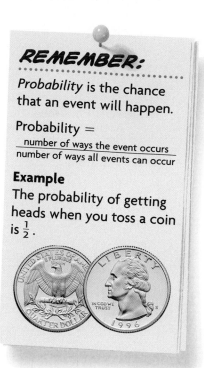

REMEMBER:

Probability is the chance that an event will happen.

Probability = $\dfrac{\text{number of ways the event occurs}}{\text{number of ways all events can occur}}$

Example

The probability of getting heads when you toss a coin is $\frac{1}{2}$.

You can write probability as a part-to-whole ratio.

The probability that Eugene will earn a point is the ratio of the number of green sections to the total number of sections.

So, the probability that Eugene will earn a point is 2 to 7, 2:7, or $\frac{2}{7}$.

Talk About It

- How would you write as a ratio the probability that Donna will not win a point when she spins?

- How is writing probability as a ratio the same as writing it as a fraction? How is it different?

Check Your Understanding CRITICAL THINKING

For Exercises 1–6, use the spinner. Write each probability as a ratio in three ways.

1. The pointer will land on red.

2. The pointer will land on yellow.

3. The pointer will not land on green.

4. The pointer will not land on blue.

5. The pointer will land on green or red.

6. The pointer will land on blue or yellow.

PRACTICE

Write the probability of each outcome as a ratio in three ways.

7. Toss a number cube and get 5.

8. Toss a coin and get tails.

9. Spin the pointer and land on the number 4.

10. Spin the pointer and land on the number 3 or higher.

11. Toss a number cube and get an odd number.

12. Spin the pointer and land on a number less than 1.

Applications

For Problems 13–16, use the spinner.

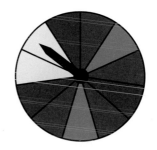

13. Franco earns a point if the pointer lands on red. Write as a ratio the probability that Franco will earn a point.

14. Sue Ellen earns a point if the pointer lands on blue. Write as a ratio the probability that Sue Ellen will earn a point.

15. Lare earns a point if the pointer does not land on blue. Write as a ratio the probability that Lare will earn a point.

16. Eda earns a point if the pointer lands on either green, yellow, or blue. Write as a ratio the probability that Eda will earn a point.

17. If you put the names of all your classmates in a hat, what is the probability that you will draw a boy's name? Write the probability as a ratio in three ways.

18. Lily rolls a number cube labeled 2, 4, 6, 8, 10, and 12. What is the probability of the cube landing on 12? Write the probability as a ratio in three ways.

19. Randy pulls a marble from a bag of 1 blue, 4 green, 3 red, and 2 yellow marbles. What is the probability as a ratio that Randy will pull a green marble?

20. **Write a problem** using the spinner above in which you find the probability and write it as a ratio.

...ing Percent of a Number

Why learn this? You can find out the price of something on sale.

You can find a percent of any number, not just 100.

Kanesha likes to find bargains. She found a $20 shirt marked "25 percent off." How much does it cost now?

What is 25 percent of $20?
25% of $20 = n

Here are two ways to find the percent of a number.

| Use decimals. | OR | Use fractions. |

Use decimals.

Write 25% as a decimal: 0.25.

To find 0.25 of $20, multiply:

$$\begin{array}{r} \$20 \\ \times 0.25 \\ \hline \$5.00 \end{array}$$ So, $n = \$5.00$.

OR

Use fractions.

Write 25% as a fraction: $\frac{25}{100} = \frac{1}{4}$.

To find $\frac{1}{4}$ of $20, multiply:

$\frac{1}{4} \times \frac{20}{1} = \frac{20}{4} = \$5$ So, $n = \$5.00$

The shirt is $5 off the regular price. $20 − $5 = $15
So, the shirt now costs $15.

_____

 You can use a calculator to find a percent of a number.

A $60 jacket is on sale for 55 percent off.
55% of $60 = n

Method 1   = 33.

Method 2   = 33.

So, $n = \$33$.
$60 − $33 = $27
So, the sale price is $27.

• Describe each method for finding the sale price.

PRACTICE

Write the percent as a decimal and as a fraction in simplest form.

1. 37%   2. 98%   3. 10%   4. 6%

5. 50%   6. 25%   7. 33%   8. 100%

Use a decimal to find the percent.

9. 37% of 150   10. 98% of 50   11. 10% of 30   12. 12% of 33

13. 16% of 175   14. 20% of 500   15. 9% of 180   16. 90% of 350

Use a fraction to find the percent.

17. 50% of 200   18. 25% of 40   19. 10% of 260   20. 75% of 180

21. 40% of 280   22. 60% of 450   23. 16% of 600   24. 30% of 280

Use a calculator. Find the value of both numbers. Which is the greater value? Write *a* or *b*.

25. **a.** 40% of 25   26. **a.** 50% of 32   27. **a.** 90% of 150
    b. 25% of 50   **b.** 50% of 30   **b.** 80% of 155

28. **a.** 50% of 400   29. **a.** 7% of $650.00   30. **a.** 75% of 53
    b. 30% of 500   **b.** 10% of $600.00   **b.** 53% of 85

Applications

31. Ted wanted to buy a $100 bat at the sporting goods sale. He waited until Wednesday to buy it. How much did he pay?

32. Nick decided to buy a $22.00 basketball. He bought it on Tuesday. How much did he pay?

33. Jamie saw a mitt that cost $39.00. She bought it on Monday. How much did she pay?

34. Tonya is stocking up on $4.50 baseballs. She bought 3 on Wednesday. What was her bill?

35. Kyle bought a belt to go with his baseball uniform. The regular price of the belt was $4.95. How much was it on Tuesday?

36. **Write a problem** about something Jody bought at the sporting goods sale.

Sporting Goods Sale

Monday   : 10% off
Tuesday   : 20% off
Wednesday : 30% off

$100.00

$39.00

$22.00 $4.95 $4.50

$5.00

$20.00

$45.00 $50.00

CALCULATOR Activities

ASTRONOMICAL NUMBERS!
Powers of 10, Exponents, and Scientific Notation

A number written in scientific notation is expressed as a product of two factors. The first factor is equal to, or greater than 1, but less than 10. The second factor is a power of 10.

The  and ▨ keys show how many times 10 is multiplied by itself. (HINT: 10^2 means 10×10, or 100.)

Standard form		Scientific notation
700,000	=	7.0×10^5
6,210,000	=	6.21×10^6

Our galaxy, the Milky Way, contains at least 9.9×10^7 stars. How can you write this number in standard form?

Using the Calculator

To find the standard form of 9.9×10^7 by using the *TI Math Explorer,* enter the following:

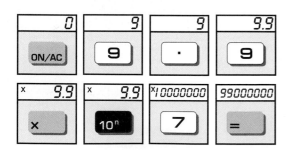

To find the standard form of 9.9×10^7 by using the *Casio fx-55,* enter the following:

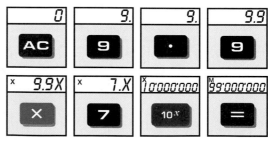

So, 9.9×10^7 written in standard form is 99,000,000.

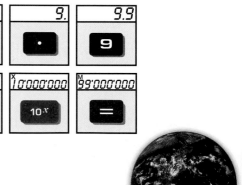

PRACTICE

Use your calculator to solve.

1. Write 3.42×10^6 in standard form.

2. Write 2.0×10^3 in standard form.

3. Write 528,000 in scientific notation.

4. Write 37,000,000 in scientific notation.

SUPER BOWL MADNESS!
Repeated Operations

It was the halftime of the Super Bowl. The Green Bay Packers were trailing the Denver Broncos by a score of 21–10. In a comeback, the Packers won the game 22–21, scoring only 3-point field goals. How many field goals did they make in the second half of the game?

Using the Calculator

To find the answer by using the *TI Math Explorer*, enter the following:

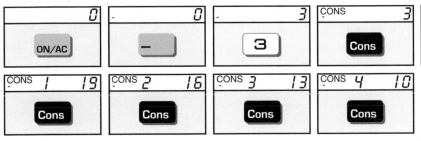

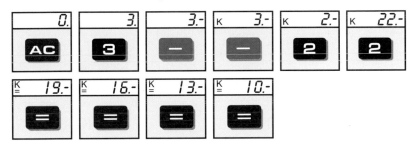

To find the answer by using the *Casio fx-55*, enter the following:

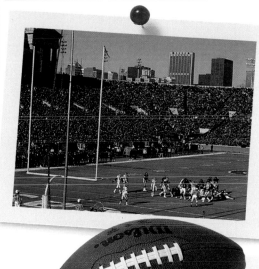

So, the Packers made 4 field goals in the second half.

PRACTICE

Use your calculator to solve.

1. Two teams were tied 21–21 going into the third quarter. If one team won with a total of 49 points, how many touchdowns, at 7 points each including the "point after," did they score?

2. The New York Giants scored only field goals in their 21–18 loss to the Chicago Bears. How many field goals did they score?

Solve by using a constant operation.

3. Start with 12. Add the same number 6 times.

4. Start with 25. Multiply the same number 3 times.

GOODNESS GROCERIES!
Multistep Problems

The memory keys are used to store numbers. The M+ key stores the product. The MR key recalls the product from memory. The MC key on the *Casio fx-55* clears the number stored.

Lucy bought 4 two-pound bags of apples. The pears she bought weighed 5 pounds. She also bought some oranges. The total weight of the fruit Lucy bought was 17 pounds. How much did the oranges weigh?

Using the Calculator

To find the answer by using the *TI Math Explorer*, enter the following:

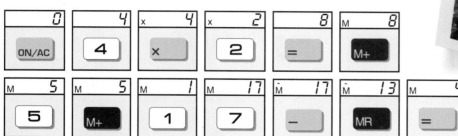

To find the answer by using the *Casio fx-55*, enter the following:

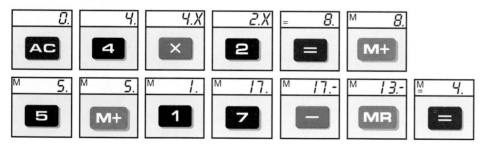

So, the oranges weighed 4 pounds.

PRACTICE

Use your calculator to solve.

1. There are 6 dozen blueberry muffins on the top shelf of the store. On the next shelf, there are 9 trays of banana muffins with 8 muffins in each tray. How many muffins are there in all?

2. A carton of apple juice holds 6 juice packs. A carton of grape juice holds 8 juice packs. There are 24 cartons of grape juice. There are 12 more cartons of apple juice than of grape juice. How many juice packs are there in all?

A BREAKFAST BONANZA!
Multiplication Properties, Order of Operations

REMEMBER:
....
Do the operation in the parentheses first when computing the answer.

$4 + (5 \times 7) - (4 \times 3) =$?
↓   ↓   ↓

$4 + \quad 35 \quad - \quad 12 \quad = 27$

Ernesto has 10 math cards from a box of cereal. To win a prize, he must order the cards in such a way that the answer is 12. Ernesto used his calculator to help him. This is the order of Ernesto's cards. Use your calculator to check whether the answer really is 12.

$36 \div (3 + 3) \times 2$

Using the Calculator

To check the answer by using the *TI Math Explorer*, enter the following:

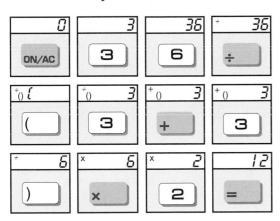

To check the answer by using the *Casio fx-55*, enter the following:

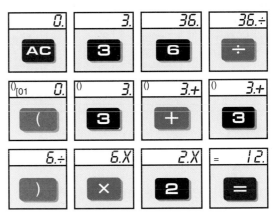

Yes, Ernesto's card arrangement results in an answer of 12.

PRACTICE

Use your calculator to solve. Check each statement.
Write *true* or *false*.

1. $(16 - 2) - 8 \div 2 = 10$

2. $62 - (12 - 10) \times 18.3 = 36.6$

Write parentheses to make the statement true.

3. $28 - 8 \div 7 - 3 = 5$

4. $4 \times 9 - 5 \div 8 = 2$

5. $6 \times 3 \div 12 + 6 = 1$

6. $3 \times 13 - 7 - 11 = 7$

7. $5 \times 6 - 3 \div 3 = 5$

8. $32 \div 2 + 2 \times 3 = 24$

VAN-TASTIC VOYAGE!
Divide with Remainders

The integer keys, [INT÷] and [÷R], allow you to show a quotient and a remainder separately.

Ms. Diaz's chess club traveled in a van for 64 days to cities hosting chess tournaments last summer. About how many weeks is that?

Using the Calculator

To find the answer by using the *TI Math Explorer*, enter the following:

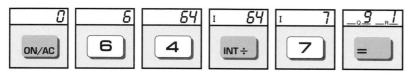

To find the answer by using the *Casio fx-55*, enter the following:

So, they traveled for about 9 weeks.

PRACTICE

Use your calculator to solve.

1. Magellan's ship returned to Spain after sailing for 155 weeks. About how many years is that? (HINT: There are about 52 weeks in a year.)

2. A hot-air balloon crossed the Atlantic Ocean in 98 hours. About how many days is that?

3. The chess tournament lasted 118 hours. About how many days is that?

Use your calculator to estimate the quotient.

4. $58 \div 6 = n$

5. $126 \div 16 = n$

6. $408 \div 32 = n$

HAVE YOUR CAKE AND EAT IT TOO!

Equivalent Fractions

Jeffrey ate 4 pieces of his birthday cake. The cake was cut into 8 equal pieces. So, Jeffrey ate $\frac{4}{8}$ of the cake. Is $\frac{4}{8}$ in simplest form, or can $\frac{4}{8}$ be renamed as an equivalent fraction? You can use your calculator to check.

Using the Calculator

To find the equivalent fraction written in simplest form by using the *TI Math Explorer*, enter the following:

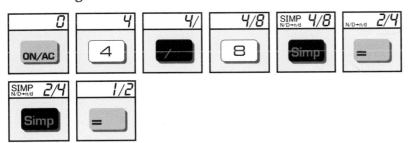

To find the equivalent fraction in simplest form by using the *Casio fx-55*, enter the following:

So, $\frac{4}{8}$ in simplest form is $\frac{1}{2}$.

PRACTICE

Use your calculator.

1. Juan was also at Jeffrey's birthday party. He ate $\frac{6}{16}$ of the cake. What is $\frac{6}{16}$ in simplest form?

2. Who ate more cake, Jeffrey or Juan?

Write the fraction in simplest form.

3. $\frac{5}{25}$ 4. $\frac{12}{48}$ 5. $\frac{26}{39}$

6. $\frac{4}{16}$ 7. $\frac{16}{32}$ 8. $\frac{28}{49}$

9. $\frac{45}{55}$ 10. $\frac{27}{36}$ 11. $\frac{10}{35}$

> **REMEMBER:**
> Equivalent fractions are fractions that name the same amount.
> $$\frac{16}{24} = \frac{8}{12} = \frac{4}{6} = \frac{2}{3}$$
> Note that $\frac{2}{3}$ cannot be simplified further. So, $\frac{16}{24}$ written in simplest form is $\frac{2}{3}$.

ALL ABOARD!

Mixed Numbers

Jim has tracks for a train set. He has 35 parts that are each $\frac{1}{4}$ of a circle. How many complete circles can he make? How many parts are left?

Using the Calculator

To find the answer by using the *TI Math Explorer*, enter the following:

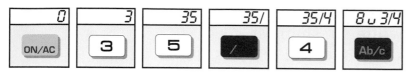

To find the answer by using the *Casio fx-55*, enter the following:

So, Jim can make 8 complete circles with 3 parts left.

PRACTICE

Use your calculator to solve.

1. If Jim buys double the amount of parts so that he has 70 parts, will the number of circles double too?

2. How many circles can Jim make if he has 70 parts?

Change these fractions to mixed numbers.

3. $\frac{23}{11} = n$

4. $\frac{307}{3} = n$

5. $\frac{73}{7} = n$

6. $\frac{50}{3} = n$

7. $\frac{87}{12} = n$

8. $\frac{746}{6} = n$

9. $\frac{124}{8} = n$

10. $\frac{29}{9} = n$

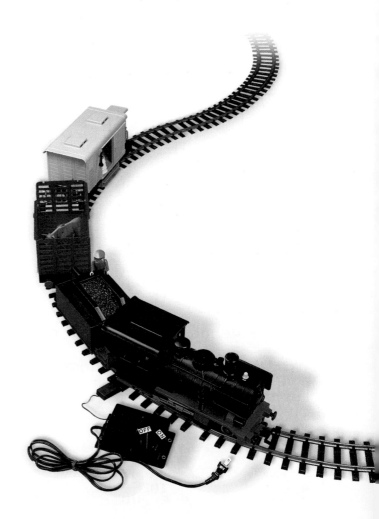

WORKING IN A WOOD-WORKING WONDERLAND!

Adding and Subtracting Mixed Numbers

Larry is helping his dad build shelves. He has a board that measures $11\frac{7}{12}$ ft. It is to be used in a spot that will be $9\frac{3}{4}$ ft. How much of the board must be cut off?

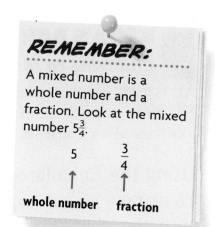

REMEMBER:

A mixed number is a whole number and a fraction. Look at the mixed number $5\frac{3}{4}$.

5 $\qquad$ $\frac{3}{4}$

↑ $\qquad$ ↑

whole number $\quad$ fraction

Using the Calculator

To find the answer by using the *TI Math Explorer*, enter the following:

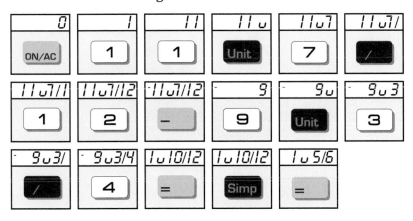

To find the answer by using the *Casio fx-55*, enter the following:

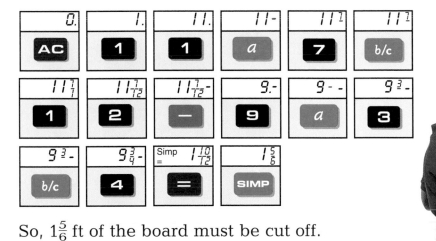

So, $1\frac{5}{6}$ ft of the board must be cut off.

PRACTICE

Use your calculator to solve.

1. $16\frac{4}{11} + 17\frac{1}{6}$

2. $19\frac{2}{3} + 39\frac{3}{4} + 67\frac{4}{9}$

BABA'S BAKERY

Changing to Mixed Numbers

Ali is helping his father in his bakery. His father uses $\frac{110}{4}$ bags of flour each week. How many bags is that expressed as a mixed number?

Using the Calculator

To find the answer by using the *TI Math Explorer*, enter the following:

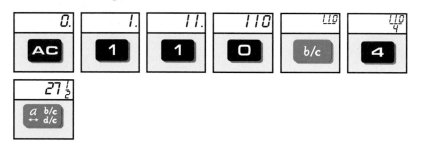

To find the answer by using the *Casio fx-55*, enter the following:

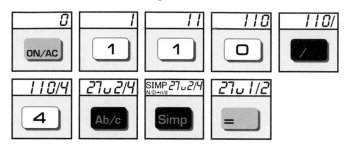

So, Ali's father uses $27\frac{1}{2}$ bags of flour each week.

PRACTICE

Use your calculator to solve.

1. If Ali needed $\frac{180}{8}$ bags, is that more than or less than $27\frac{1}{2}$ bags?

2. Express $\frac{180}{8}$ as a mixed number.

Change the fractions to mixed numbers.

3. $\frac{155}{12}$

4. $\frac{203}{24}$

5. $\frac{300}{69}$

6. $\frac{155}{45}$

BAKER'S
ENRICHED
FLOUR
XXX

 **TO THE POINT!**
Decimal Operations

Terminating decimals, such as 0.56 and 11.358, have a definite number of decimal places.

Repeating decimals, such as 0.3333... and 0.363636..., have a pattern that continues indefinitely. Repeating decimals can be written with a bar over the digit or digits that repeat.

$0.333... = 0.\overline{3}$ $0.13636... = 0.1\overline{36}$

Ed and Fred divided the number 0.4 by 9.9 on their calculators. Then they used a shortcut to write the quotient. What quotient did the calculator display? What is the shortcut that Ed and Fred used to write the quotient?

Using the Calculator

To find the quotient for 0.4 ÷ 9.9, enter the following on the *TI Math Explorer:*

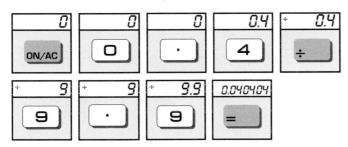

To find the quotient for 0.4 ÷ 9.9, enter the following on the *Casio fx-55:*

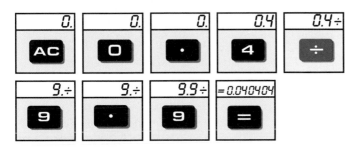

So, the calculator displayed 0.040404. Ed and Fred wrote $0.\overline{04}$.

PRACTICE

Use your calculator to solve. If the answer is a repeating decimal, write your answer with a bar over the repeating digit or digits.

1. 0.6 ÷ 9.9

2. $30.55 − $25.88

3. 7.8 × 6.1

4. $5.17 + $4.33

5. 6.3 ÷ 9.9

6. 23.8 ÷ 0.99

SHOOTING HOOPS!
Decimal Estimation

By using the fix key , you can tell the calculator how many decimal places you want to see in the answer.

After the first 30 games of the season, the standings look like this. Since Chicago has won 29 games, what decimal number shows their wins to the nearest thousandth?

Team	W	L	
I - Chicago	29	I	
I - Detroit	25	5	
I - Indiana			0.800
I - Milwaukee	16	14	
I - Atlanta			0.400

Using the Calculator

To find the answer by using the *TI Math Explorer*, enter the following:

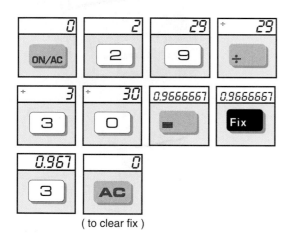

(to clear fix)

To find the answer by using the *Casio fx-55*, enter the following:

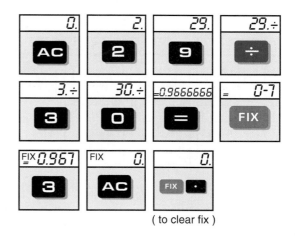

(to clear fix)

So, 0.967 shows Chicago's number of wins.

PRACTICE

Use the standings and your calculator to solve.

1. What decimal shows Detroit's wins to the nearest thousandth?

2. What decimal shows Milwaukee's wins to the nearest thousandth?

3. How many games has Indiana won so far? (HINT: Multiply by the number of games.)

4. How many games has Atlanta won so far?

HEY BATTER, BATTER!
Change Fractions to Decimals and Decimals to Fractions

Tracy has a 0.250 batting average. What fraction of her times at bat does she get a hit?

Using the Calculator

To find the answer by using the TI Math Explorer, enter the following:

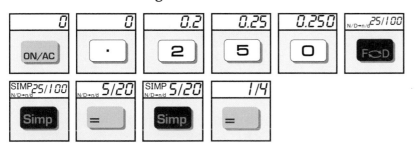

To find the answer by using the *Casio fx-55*, enter the following:

So, Tracy hits the ball $\frac{1}{4}$ of the times she is at bat.

PRACTICE

Use your calculator to solve.

1. Last year Tracy got a hit 2 out of every 5 times she batted. What decimal can you write that shows her number of hits to the nearest thousandth?

2. Her friend Joe got 1 hit out of every 3 times he batted. What decimal can you write that shows his number of hits to the nearest thousandth?

Change the following decimals to fractions.

3. 0.75   4. 0.80   5. 0.625

6. 0.45   7. 0.35   8. 0.40

9. 0.375   10. 0.25   11. 0.875

More Practice
Chapter 1

Lesson 1.1 (pages 2–3)

Tell whether the number in each picture is expressed
as *cardinal*, *ordinal*, or *nominal*.

1.

2.

5 Students

3.

1 Gallon

4.

Tell whether each number is expressed as *cardinal*, *ordinal*, or *nominal*.

5. Matthew is 1st in line.

6. Today the temperature is 56°F.

7. got home at 5 o'clock.

8. There are 33 cookies in the jar.

9. Donald is 6 feet tall.

10. I live in the 5th house on the left.

11. My address is 951 Southside Avenue.

12. There are 842 students in our school.

Lesson 1.2 (pages 4–5)

Use the benchmark number to choose the more reasonable estimate.

1. jelly beans in a jar
35 or 135

2. pretzels in a bag
20 or 200

3. marbles in a jar
50 or 250

Write *yes* or *no* to tell whether the estimate is reasonable. Explain.

4. • 12 rolls of pennies
• 50 pennies in a roll
Estimate: There is about $60.00.

5. • 90 safety pins
• 20 boxes in the store
Estimate: There are about 2,000 safety pins in the store.

6. • 30 students in a class
• 5 fifth-grade classrooms
Estimate: There are about 1,000 students in the fifth grade.

7. • 8 muffins in a box
• 20 boxes in the bakery
Estimate: There are about 200 muffins in the bakery.

Lesson 1.3 (pages 6–7)

Write the value of the blue digit.

1. 967,522   **2.** 876,534   **3.** 523,792   **4.** 117,964

5. 356,178   **6.** 692,042   **7.** 474,392   **8.** 296,574

Write the expanded numbers in standard form.

9. $90,000 + 2,000 + 0 + 40 + 6$

10. $100,000 + 70,000 + 6,000 + 300 + 90 + 6$

11. $200,000 + 90,000 + 9,000 + 400 + 0 + 4$

12. $900,000 + 0 + 0 + 0 + 40 + 6$

13. $300,000 + 40,000 + 9,000 + 0 + 30 + 7$

14. $200,000 + 90,000 + 6,000 + 100 + 40 + 0$

Lesson 1.4 (pages 8–9)

Write the value of the blue digit.

1. 38,107,692   **2.** 57,192,411   **3.** 192,096,422   **4.** 872,429,792

5. 296,172,045   **6.** 517,429,691   **7.** 781,726,019   **8.** 917,330,427

Write two other forms for each number.

9. 75,192,026

10. 529,100,845

11. $600,000,000 + 0 + 7,000,000 + 200,000 + 10,000 + 0 + 0 + 0 + 8$

12. eight hundred thirty-six million, seven hundred nine thousand, ten

Lesson 1.5 Part 1 (pages 10–11)

Write $<$, $>$, or $=$ for each ●.

1. 526 ● 562   **2.** 7,320 ● 7,302   **3.** 8,912 ● 8,912

4. 4,919 ● 4,119   **5.** 192,113 ● 192,113   **6.** 18,095 ● 18,950

Order from greatest to least.

7. 356; 536; 365   **8.** 5,912; 5,129; 9,512   **9.** 8,460; 8,406; 8,640

Order from least to greatest.

10. 17,562; 15,652; 17,265   **11.** 11,509; 11,905; 11,095   **12.** 312,962; 319,962; 312,692

Lesson 1.5 Part 2 (pages 12-13)

Use a table to solve.

ELEMENTARY SCHOOL POPULATIONS	
Elementary School	**Populations**
Sunnyside	1,020
Oakwood	900
Greenview	850
Plam	920
Greyfield	1,300
West Creek	1,100

1. This table shows some elementary schools and their student populations. Which elementary has the greatest population? the least population?

2. What is the population difference in the school with the greatest population and the school with the least population?

Chapter 2

Lesson 2.1 (pages 18–19)

For Exercises 1–5, use the data in the table.

LION'S FOOTBALL GAME SCORES 1998-99	
Game	**Score**
1	21
2	14
3	6
4	31
5	28

1. How many points were scored by the end of Game 4?

2. How many points were scored in Games 1 and 2 combined?

3. How many more points were scored in Game 4 than in Game 2?

4. How many points in all were scored during the 1998-99 season?

5. How many more points were scored in the 1998–99 season than the 79 points scored in 1997–98?

Write the related number sentence. Find the sum or difference.

6. $76 - 35 = n$ **7.** $131 - 69 = n$ **8.** $145 - 56 = n$

9. $38 + n = 79$ **10.** $46 + n = 97$ **11.** $63 + n = 165$

Solve. Use the inverse operation to check each problem.

12. $\begin{array}{r} 18 \\ +34 \\ \hline \end{array}$ **13.** $\begin{array}{r} 53 \\ -32 \\ \hline \end{array}$ **14.** $\begin{array}{r} 56 \\ +26 \\ \hline \end{array}$ **15.** $\begin{array}{r} 149 \\ -\ 58 \\ \hline \end{array}$

Lesson 2.2 (pages 20–21)

Find the difference. You may use counters.

1. $\begin{array}{r} 394 \\ -145 \\ \hline \end{array}$ **2.** $\begin{array}{r} 566 \\ -217 \\ \hline \end{array}$ **3.** $\begin{array}{r} 721 \\ -386 \\ \hline \end{array}$ **4.** $\begin{array}{r} 419 \\ -198 \\ \hline \end{array}$ **5.** $\begin{array}{r} 682 \\ -591 \\ \hline \end{array}$ **6.** $\begin{array}{r} 5,626 \\ -3,533 \\ \hline \end{array}$ **7.** $\begin{array}{r} 7,963 \\ -4,576 \\ \hline \end{array}$

Lesson 2.3 (pages 22–23)

Find the difference.

1. 100
    − 72

2. 360
    −219

3. $7.00
    − 4.17

4. 900
    −681

5. 750
    −192

6. $8.00
    − 3.16

7. $20.00
    − 13.95

8. $40.08
    − 17.76

9. 400
    −264

10. $10.00
    − 5.62

11. 6,007
    − 434

12. 40,000
    −24,916

13. 17,000
    −11,326

14. 8,000
    − 965

15. 70,000
    −49,566

16. 3,020
    −1,492

17. 54,000
    −32,782

18. 27,546
    − 8,493

19. 13,009
    − 9,148

20. 15,120
    − 6,299

Lesson 2.4 (pages 24–25)

Choose and name the operation. Solve.

1. Natalie has 48 books and Holly has 39 books. How many books do the two friends have together?

2. There were 11,561 fans at Game 1 and 15,907 fans at Game 2. How many more fans attended Game 2?

3. Charles traveled 360 miles from Springfield to Roxboro, and 576 miles from Roxboro to Brookstown. How many miles did Charles travel in all?

4. Felicia bought in-line skates for $36.50 and knee pads for 11.95. How much did Felicia spend for the two items?

Lesson 2.5 Part 1 (pages 26–27)

Choose a method and estimate each sum.

1. 15
    18
    25
    +42

2. 36
    41
    84
    +86

3. 26
    92
    41
    +36

4. 42
    39
    62
    +71

5. 29
    35
    56
    +23

6. 15
    263
    198
    +107

7. 342
    407
    569
    +186

8. 198
    206
    476
    +338

9. 426
    396
    707
    +299

10. 945
    862
    787
    +806

11. 103
    268
    214
    +327

12. 116
    110
    133
    +192

13. 205
    122
    540
    +616

14. 411
    912
    502
    +416

15. 134
    205
    897
    +343

Lesson 2.5 Part 2 (pages 28–29)

Decide whether you need to estimate, find the exact answer, or both. Solve.

1. Ron had $15.00 to spend at the movies. He spent $6.50 on the ticket, $3.79 on popcorn, and $2.35 on a drink. Does he have enough left over to spend $5.00 in the game room after the movie?

2. Sabrina had $15.00 to spend on school supplies. She bought a binder for $3.15, a box of pencils for $2.75, and a pack of notebooks for $5.99. How much did she spend on the items? How much change did she receive?

Chapter 3

Lesson 3.1 (pages 34–35)

Write the letter of the decimal that matches each model.

1. 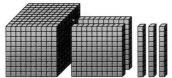   **2.**   **3.**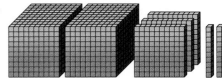

a. 2.32   **b.** 1.13   **c.** 1.23

Write the decimal.

4. one and seven tenths

5. fifteen hundredths

6. two and three hundredths

7. four hundredths

8. seven and twenty-one hundredths

9. five and five hundredths

10. 1 + 0.8

11. 3 + 0 + 0.04

12. 0.6 + 0.08

Lesson 3.2 (pages 36–37)

Write in standard form.

1. six thousandths

2. four and nine thousandths

3. one and twelve thousandths

4. forty-five thousandths

5. two hundred six thousandths

6. three and seventy-seven thousandths

7. one and one thousandth

8. nine and one hundred twenty-two thousandths

Write in written form.

9. 0.008

10. 0.063

11. 0.367

12. 2.019

Lesson 3.3 (pages 38–39)

Write in standard form.

1. $3{,}000 + 100 + 90 + 2 + 0.3 + 0.09 + 0.002$

2. five thousand, two hundred sixty-four and two hundred nine thousandths

3. $1{,}000 + 600 + 20 + 3 + 0.1 + 0.01 + 0.007$

4. four thousand, three hundred three and thirty thousandths

5. $1{,}000 + 700 + 20 + 0 + 0.3 + 0 + 0.002$

6. two thousand, three hundred six and forty-six thousandths

Write the value of the digit 5 in each number.

7. 2,356.019   8. 1,303.056   9. 2,163.516   10. 4,928.165

Lesson 3.4 (pages 40–41)

Write an equivalent decimal for each.

1. 0.08   2. 0.30   3. 0.42   4. 1.7   5. 7.650

6. 3.64   7. 0.090   8. 0.400   9. 6.30   10. 0.8

11. 7.9   12. 0.830   13. 1.09   14. 0.51   15. 4.07

Lesson 3.5 Part 1 (pages 42–43)

Write $<$, $>$, or $=$ for each ●.

1. 0.72 ● 0.73   2. 5.31 ● 5.13   3. 6.19 ● 6.190

4. 1.41 ● 14.1   5. 7.09 ● 7.090   6. 67.19 ● 67.019

7. 3.17 ● 3.170   8. 21.86 ● 2.186   9. 696.131 ● 696.113

Order from least to greatest.

10. 3.19, 3.09, 3.11   11. 14.36, 14.63, 14.29   12. 5.01, 5.011, 5.10

Lesson 3.5 Part 2 (pages 44–45)

Make a table to solve.

1. Alisha, Sandra, and Donald went to the school nurse. Alisha's temperature was 98.9° F, and Sandra's temperature was 98.6°F, and Donald's temperature was 99.1°F. Put the temperatures in order from highest to lowest.

2. Jeff ran the race in 5.39 minutes, Kevin ran in 5.37 minutes, and Darren ran in 5.49 minutes. The lowest time wins the race. Who won the race? Who came in second? third?

Chapter 4

Lesson 4.1 (pages 50–51)

Use base-ten blocks to model. Record the sum on a place-value chart.

1. $0.2 \\ +0.6$
2. $0.5 \\ +0.5$
3. $1.32 \\ +0.53$
4. $0.42 \\ +1.08$
5. $1.342 \\ +0.657$

Find the sum.

6. $3.2 \\ +1.3$
7. $4.9 \\ +5.6$
8. $2.75 \\ +0.56$
9. $5.17 \\ +4.09$
10. $1.36 \\ +1.42$

11. $6.18 \\ +3.76$
12. $1.726 \\ +0.192$
13. $3.092 \\ +1.563$
14. $7.136 \\ +2.468$
15. $2.306 \\ +1.434$

Lesson 4.2 (pages 52–53)

Use an equivalent decimal to find the sum.

1. $3.17 + 0.326 = n$
2. $1.094 + 3.2 = n$
3. $8 + 4.29 = n$
4. $7.42 + 2.163 = n$
5. $24.7 + 16.172 = n$
6. $13.92 + 4.396 = n$

7. $6 \\ +0.7$
8. $3.5 \\ +1.36$
9. $4.09 \\ +0.328$
10. $6 \\ +2.88$
11. $4.291 \\ +0.34$

12. $4.9 \\ +3.16$
13. $7.96 \\ +4.012$
14. $9.1 \\ +0.756$
15. $4.372 \\ +2.4$
16. $13.2 \\ + 6.07$

Lesson 4.3 (pages 54–55)

Find the difference.

1. $1.7 \\ -0.6$
2. $3.9 \\ -3.3$
3. $3.06 \\ -2.4$
4. $6.5 \\ -5.8$
5. $6.7 \\ -3.05$

6. $6.26 \\ -4.13$
7. $3.2 \\ -2.345$
8. $9.463 \\ -4.96$
9. $11.179 \\ -8.186$
10. $17.492 \\ -11.36$

11. $2.96 - 1.78 = n$
12. $4.9 - 1.326 = n$
13. $6.92 - 4.176 = n$

Lesson 4.4 (pages 56–57)

Estimate the sum or difference to the nearest tenth.

1. $6.78 \\ +2.83$
2. $7.82 \\ +3.79$
3. $5.69 \\ -4.25$
4. $9.67 \\ +3.85$
5. $26.39 \\ -15.46$

Estimate the sum or difference to the nearest hundredth.

6. 3.456
-2.921

7. 6.866
-5.732

8. 1.791
$+3.249$

9. 7.893
$+4.869$

10. 5.625
-2.711

Estimate the sum or difference and compare. Write $<$ or $>$ for each ●.

11. $7.24 + 6.29$ ● $10.31 + 3.42$

12. $12.19 - 6.36$ ● $10.91 - 4.13$

13. $9.62 - 3.59$ ● $12.21 - 6.67$

14. $37.82 + 29.63$ ● $39.46 + 31.49$

15. $6.54 + 3.92$ ● $5.45 + 4.62$

16. $44.92 - 23.02$ ● $66.70 - 42.85$

Lesson 4.5 Part 1 (pages 58–59)

Choose and name the operation. Solve.

1. Rob bought a CD for $15.45. He gave the cashier $20.00. How much change did he receive?

2. Nina jogged 3.25 miles on Saturday, 2.70 miles on Sunday, and 3.5 miles on Monday. How many miles did she jog on all 3 days?

3. Barbara drives 36.3 miles to get to the beach and Rick drives 25.9 miles to get to the beach. How many more miles is Barbara's trip?

4. Cassandra bought a shirt for $19.75, shorts for $16.50, and shoes for $29.25. How much did Cassandra spend on her new outfit?

Lesson 4.5 Part 2 (pages 60–61)

Write a number sentence to solve.

1. Greg's bank statement shows a starting balance of $57.95. The statement also shows he made deposits of $109.62 and $72.56. He wrote checks for $13.99 and $50.75. What is Greg's current balance?

2. At basketball practice Jeremy made 29 baskets, Josh made 35 baskets, and Austin made 25 fewer baskets than Jeremy and Josh combined. How many baskets did Austin make?

Chapter 5

Lesson 5.1 (pages 70–71)

Write the name of the multiplication property used in each number sentence.

1. $7 \times 1 = 7$

2. $6 \times 2 = 2 \times 6$

3. $(4 \times 2) \times 3 = 4 \times (2 \times 3)$

4. $9 \times 3 = 3 \times 9$

5. $2 \times 1 = 2$

6. $8 \times 0 = 0$

Copy and complete the equation. Identify the property used.

7. $9 \times 8 = \blacksquare \times 9$ **8.** $7 \times (3 \times 2) = (7 \times \blacksquare) \times 2$ **9.** $5 \times 0 = \blacksquare$

10. $(2 \times 4) \times 6 = 2 \times (\blacksquare \times 6)$ **11.** $8 \times \blacksquare = 8$ **12.** $5 \times 3 = 3 \times \blacksquare$

Show two ways to group by using parentheses. Find the product.

13. $4 \times 3 \times 2 = n$ **14.** $5 \times 9 \times 3 = n$ **15.** $6 \times 5 \times 8 = n$

16. $5 \times 4 \times 4 = n$ **17.** $7 \times 2 \times 6 = n$ **18.** $8 \times 5 \times 4 = n$

Lesson 5.2 (pages 72–73)

Explain how you would model with colored counters.
Use the colored counters shown on page 72.

1. 600	**2.** 629	**3.** 427	**4.** 632
$\times\ 6$	$\times\ 3$	$\times\ 5$	$\times\ 7$

Solve by using colored counters.

5. $4 \times 56 = n$ **6.** $5 \times 32 = n$ **7.** $3 \times 42 = n$ **8.** $9 \times 29 = n$

9. $7 \times 624 = n$ **10.** $3 \times 783 = n$ **11.** $6 \times 427 = n$ **12.** $8 \times 418 = n$

Lesson 5.3 (pages 74–75)

Find the product.

1. 159	**2.** 217	**3.** 162	**4.** 337	**5.** 495
$\times\ 5$	$\times\ 3$	$\times\ 4$	$\times\ 8$	$\times\ 6$

6. $362 \times 4 = n$ **7.** $526 \times 7 = n$ **8.** $424 \times 4 = n$ **9.** $842 \times 6 = n$

Lesson 5.4 (pages 76–77)

Use unit cubes to build each rectangular prism. Find the volume.

1. 3 cubes long
5 cubes wide
4 layers high

2. 4 cubes long
9 cubes wide
3 layers high

3. 6 cubes long
2 cubes wide
5 layers high

4. 8 cubes long
6 cubes wide
3 layers high

5. 3 cubes long
6 cubes wide
9 layers high

6. 6 cubes long
2 cubes wide
4 layers high

7. 5 cubes long
7 cubes wide
layers high

8. 7 cubes long
3 cubes wide
4 layers high

9. 8 cubes long
5 cubes wide
10 layers high

Use unit cubes to build each prism. Copy and complete the table.

	Length of Base	Width of Base	Height	Volume
10.	7 cubes	4 cubes	2 cubes	?
11.	?	2 cubes	5 cubes	50 cu units
12.	4 cubes	?	6 cubes	72 cu units
13.	6 cubes	5 cubes	?	120 cu units

Lesson 5.5 Part 1 (pages 78–79)

Find the area.

1. 15 in. / 4 in.

2. 31 yd / 4 yd

3. 25 in. / 7 in.

4. 34 yd / 6 yd

5. $l = 17$ in.
$w = 5$ in.
$A = \blacksquare$ sq in.

6. $l = 23$ m
$w = 7$ m
$A = \blacksquare$ sq m

7. $l = 32$ cm
$w = 4$ cm
$A = \blacksquare$ sq cm

8. $l = 36$ ft
$w = 8$ ft
$A = \blacksquare$ sq ft

Find the volume.

9. 7 in. / 8 in. / 3 in.

10. 8 ft / 5 ft / 8 ft

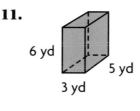

11. 6 yd / 5 yd / 3 yd

12. 6 m / 8 m / 4 m

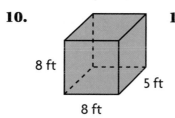

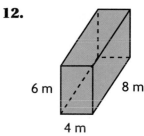

13. $l = 4$ ft
$w = 7$ ft
$h = 7$ ft
$V = \blacksquare$ cu ft

14. $l = 6$ ft
$w = 3$ ft
$h = 3$ ft
$V = \blacksquare$ cu ft

15. $l = 2$ ft
$w = 6$ ft
$h = 8$ ft
$V = \blacksquare$ cu ft

16. $l = 8$ ft
$w = 6$ ft
$h = 3$ ft
$V = \blacksquare$ cu ft

Lesson 5.5 Part 2 (pages 80–81)

Use a formula to solve.

1. Jade is tiling her kitchen floor. The floor is 15 feet long and 12 feet wide. How many square feet does Jade need to tile?

2. Nathan is choosing an aquarium for his iguana. One aquarium measures 5 feet × 4 feet × 3 feet and the other measures 6 feet × 3 feet × 3 feet. Which aquarium has the larger volume?

3. The Y.M.C.A. swimming pool measures 50 ft by 25 ft by 8 ft. What is the volume of the pool?

4. Marsha bought a new carpet that measures 9 ft by 12 ft. The carpet costs $25 per sq yard. How much did Marsha pay for the carpet?

Chapter 6

Lesson 6.1 (pages 86–87)

Use grid paper to model. Find the product.

1. $20 \times 32 = n$ **2.** $40 \times 21 = n$ **3.** $30 \times 14 = n$

Use the Distributive Property to rewrite each equation.
Find the product.

4. $17 \times 34 = n$ **5.** $30 \times 27 = n$ **6.** $11 \times 34 = n$

Lesson 6.2 (pages 88–89)

Find the product.

1. $\begin{array}{r} 17 \\ \times 12 \\ \hline \end{array}$	**2.** $\begin{array}{r} 14 \\ \times 14 \\ \hline \end{array}$	**3.** $\begin{array}{r} 23 \\ \times 18 \\ \hline \end{array}$	**4.** $\begin{array}{r} 34 \\ \times 25 \\ \hline \end{array}$
5. $\begin{array}{r} 43 \\ \times 26 \\ \hline \end{array}$	**6.** $\begin{array}{r} 137 \\ \times\ 34 \\ \hline \end{array}$	**7.** $\begin{array}{r} 67 \\ \times 43 \\ \hline \end{array}$	**8.** $\begin{array}{r} 73 \\ \times 36 \\ \hline \end{array}$

9. $82 \times 41 = n$ **10.** $109 \times 38 = n$ **11.** $76 \times 35 = n$

12. $113 \times 42 = n$ **13.** $65 \times 42 = n$ **14.** $68 \times 24 = n$

Lesson 6.3 (pages 90–91)

Estimate the product by rounding each factor to its greatest
place-value position.

1. $\begin{array}{r} 175 \\ \times\ 22 \\ \hline \end{array}$	**2.** $\begin{array}{r} 142 \\ \times\ 36 \\ \hline \end{array}$	**3.** $\begin{array}{r} 209 \\ \times\ 66 \\ \hline \end{array}$	**4.** $\begin{array}{r} 159 \\ \times\ 92 \\ \hline \end{array}$

5. $46 \times 423 = n$ **6.** $45 \times 509 = n$ **7.** $86 \times 362 = n$ **8.** $72 \times 166 = n$

Lesson 6.4 (pages 92–93)

Estimate to the greatest place-value position. Then find the product.

1. $\begin{array}{r} 123 \\ \times 116 \\ \hline \end{array}$	**2.** $\begin{array}{r} 162 \\ \times 126 \\ \hline \end{array}$	**3.** $\begin{array}{r} 216 \\ \times 153 \\ \hline \end{array}$
4. $\begin{array}{r} 324 \\ \times 276 \\ \hline \end{array}$	**5.** $\begin{array}{r} 159 \\ \times\ 92 \\ \hline \end{array}$	**6.** $\begin{array}{r} 488 \\ \times 319 \\ \hline \end{array}$

7. $346 \times 172 = n$ **8.** $526 \times 955 = n$ **9.** $421 \times 965 = n$

10. $645 \times 319 = n$ **11.** $751 \times 863 = n$ **12.** $839 \times 572 = n$

Lesson 6.5 Part 1 (pages 94–95)

Find the perimeter and area for each figure.

1.

143 in.

82 in.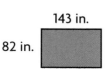

2.

96 ft

117 ft

3.

194 yd

65 yd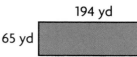

4.

139 cm

316 cm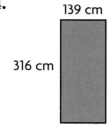

5.

157 m

227 m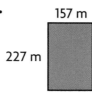

6.

253 in.

198 in.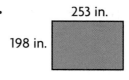

Lesson 6.5 Part 2 (pages 96–97)

Draw a diagram to solve.

1. Stephanie wants to fence in a rectangular section of her yard. She has 76 yards of fencing to use. What dimensions will give the greatest possible area?

2. Lydia has 104 feet of border to go around a flower bed. What dimensions should the flower bed have so it has the greatest area?

Chapter 7

Lesson 7.1 (pages 102–103)

Use mental math and a calculator. Test each number for divisibility by 2, 3, 4, 5, 6, 9, and 10. List the numbers that work.

1. 30   **2.** 48   **3.** 65   **4.** 114   **5.** 140

6. 210   **7.** 300   **8.** 426   **9.** 1,368   **10.** 2,728

11. 360   **12.** 73   **13.** 526   **14.** 2,000   **15.** 5,115

Lesson 7.2 (pages 104–105)

Copy each problem. Draw a box where the first digit in the quotient should be placed.

1. $4\overline{)421}$ **2.** $5\overline{)132}$ **3.** $3\overline{)417}$ **4.** $4\overline{)611}$ **5.** $7\overline{)620}$

Estimate the quotient.

6. $239 \div 6 \approx n$ **7.** $364 \div 6 \approx n$ **8.** $823 \div 4 \approx n$ **9.** $734 \div 8 \approx n$

Find the quotient.

10. $3\overline{)137}$ **11.** $5\overline{)258}$ **12.** $4\overline{)172}$ **13.** $6\overline{)193}$ **14.** $4\overline{)955}$

15. $2\overline{)762}$ **16.** $7\overline{)439}$ **17.** $8\overline{)353}$ **18.** $3\overline{)724}$ **19.** $9\overline{)642}$

Lesson 7.3 (pages 106–107)

Estimate the quotient.

1. $4\overline{)388}$ **2.** $3\overline{)879}$ **3.** $2\overline{)813}$ **4.** $7\overline{)215}$ **5.** $6\overline{)364}$

Find the quotient.

6. $4\overline{)163}$ **7.** $6\overline{)842}$ **8.** $2\overline{)617}$ **9.** $5\overline{)407}$ **10.** $8\overline{)857}$

11. $735 \div 7 = n$ **12.** $722 \div 3 = n$ **13.** $323 \div 4 = n$ **14.** $972 \div 9 = n$

Lesson 7.4 (pages 108–109)

Use divisibility rules to predict if there will be a remainder.

1. $4\overline{)142}$ **2.** $5\overline{)295}$ **3.** $9\overline{)296}$ **4.** $3\overline{)192}$ **5.** $6\overline{)329}$

Find the quotient. Check by multiplying.

6. $5\overline{)523}$ **7.** $2\overline{)628}$ **8.** $7\overline{)819}$ **9.** $9\overline{)326}$ **10.** $4\overline{)591}$

11. $723 \div 8 = n$ **12.** $486 \div 3 = n$ **13.** $721 \div 6 = n$ **14.** $438 \div 7 = n$

15. $542 \div 3 = n$ **16.** $681 \div 7 = n$ **17.** $765 \div 5 = n$ **18.** $286 \div 6 = n$

Lesson 7.5 Part 1 (pages 110–111)

Solve. Explain how you interpreted the remainder.

1. A group of 130 fifth-grade students went on a field trip to the zoo. They were put into 8 groups. How many students were in most of the groups?

2. The candy shop is selling a box of truffles for $14.75. They have 305 truffles already made. Can they fill 12 boxes of 25 truffles to sell?

Lesson 7.5 Part 2 (pages 112–113)

Guess and check to solve.

1. Sydney is 5 years old. Her cousin is 3 times as old. How old will Sydney be when she is half as old as her cousin?

2. The sum of two numbers is 29. Their product is 190. What are the two numbers?

Chapter 8

Lesson 8.1 (pages 118–119)

Complete the pattern.

1. $240 \div 60 = n$
$2,400 \div 60 = 40$
$24,000 \div 60 = 400$

2. $160 \div 40 = 4$
$1,600 \div 40 = n$
$16,000 \div 40 = 400$

3. $140 \div 20 = 7$
$1,400 \div 20 = 70$
$14,000 \div 20 = n$

Find the quotient.

4. $810 \div 90 = n$　**5.** $1,500 \div 50 = n$　**6.** $270 \div 30 = n$　**7.** $4,500 \div 50 = n$

8. $24,000 \div 80 = n$　**9.** $180 \div 20 = n$　**10.** $21,000 \div 70 = n$　**11.** $63,000 \div 90 = n$

12. $3,600 \div 40 = n$　**13.** $2,400 \div 60 = n$　**14.** $2,000 \div 40 = n$　**15.** $32,000 \div 80 = n$

16. $93,000 \div 30 = n$　**17.** $37,000 \div 20 = n$　**18.** $56,000 \div 70 = n$　**19.** $920 \div 10 = n$

Lesson 8.2 (pages 120–121)

Estimate the quotient.

1. $49\overline{)296}$　**2.** $63\overline{)431}$　**3.** $24\overline{)789}$　**4.** $62\overline{)3,592}$　**5.** $49\overline{)3,492}$

6. $147 \div 23 \approx n$　**7.** $209 \div 71 \approx n$　**8.** $8,211 \div 93 \approx n$　**9.** $242 \div 33 \approx n$

10. $3,569 \div 41 \approx n$　**11.** $1,499 \div 47 \approx n$　**12.** $8,569 \div 79 \approx n$　**13.** $2,991 \div 76 \approx n$

14. $2,482 \div 53 \approx n$　**15.** $7,205 \div 76 \approx n$　**16.** $4,539 \div 89 \approx n$　**17.** $5,592 \div 68 \approx n$

Lesson 8.3 (pages 122–123)

Copy each problem. Draw a box where the first digit in the quotient should be placed.

1. $8\overline{)2,461}$　**2.** $23\overline{)3,907}$　**3.** $49\overline{)3,149}$　**4.** $26\overline{)4,971}$　**5.** $63\overline{)4,629}$

Find the quotient.

6. $18\overline{)2,461}$　**7.** $23\overline{)3,907}$　**8.** $49\overline{)3,149}$　**9.** $26\overline{)3,971}$　**10.** $63\overline{)4,629}$

11. $24\overline{)2,342}$　**12.** $36\overline{)4,956}$　**13.** $48\overline{)1,973}$　**14.** $31\overline{)2,697}$　**15.** $64\overline{)9,107}$

Lesson 8.4 (pages 124–125)

Write *too high, too low,* or *just right* for each estimate.

1. $34\overline{)81}^{\,1}$　**2.** $29\overline{)49}^{\,1}$　**3.** $36\overline{)132}^{\,2}$　**4.** $41\overline{)219}^{\,6}$　**5.** $67\overline{)422}^{\,7}$

Choose the better estimate to use for the quotient. Write *a* or *b*.

6. $23\overline{)163}$ **a.** 7 **b.** 8   **7.** $46\overline{)286}$ **a.** 5 **b.** 6

Find the quotient.

8. $23\overline{)192}$ **9.** $41\overline{)547}$ **10.** $17\overline{)396}$ **11.** $36\overline{)408}$ **12.** $48\overline{)636}$

13. $54\overline{)6,491}$ **14.** $82\overline{)6,091}$ **15.** $66\overline{)7,276}$ **16.** $34\overline{)4,217}$ **17.** $65\overline{)7,293}$

18. $27\overline{)8,954}$ **19.** $22\overline{)1,631}$ **20.** $62\overline{)5,420}$ **21.** $31\overline{)1,742}$ **22.** $21\overline{)1,327}$

Lesson 8.5 (pages 126–127)

Divide. Check by multiplying.

1. $16\overline{)52}$ **2.** $42\overline{)255}$ **3.** $26\overline{)397}$ **4.** $31\overline{)779}$ **5.** $53\overline{)3,721}$

6. $29\overline{)1,511}$ **7.** $37\overline{)2,153}$ **8.** $64\overline{)3,078}$ **9.** $48\overline{)1,593}$ **10.** $52\overline{)4,063}$

11. $2,679 \div 33 = n$ **12.** $2,763 \div 51 = n$ **13.** $1,061 \div 27 = n$ **14.** $4,742 \div 64 = n$

15. $14,261 \div 14 = n$ **16.** $79,216 \div 58 = n$ **17.** $46,987 \div 89 = n$ **18.** $53,845 \div 52 = n$

Lesson 8.6 Part 1 (pages 128–129)

Tell what operation should be used to solve each problem. Then solve.

1. Jack was given 156 game tokens for his birthday party. He and 12 friends shared the tokens evenly. How many tokens did each person get?

2. Jack's mom ordered 6 large pizzas for $7.32 each. How much did she spend on the pizzas?

Lesson 8.6 Part 2 (pages 130–131)

Write a number sentence to solve.

1. Anne Marie bought a new stereo system for $1,265. She put down $185 and will pay off the rest in 12 months. What are her monthly payments?

2. Marcus sold 36 magazine subscriptions for his school's fund-raiser. Each subscription is $22 for one year. How much money did Marcus raise?

3. Kathy and Kevin went to baseball practice. Kathy hit 47 out of 60 pitches. Kevin hit 35 out of 60 pitches. How many more hits did Kathy get?

4. Jeff buys 2 pairs of tennis shoes for $47 a pair. He has a discount coupon for $10 off the price of one pair when you buy two pairs. How much will both pairs of shoes cost?

Chapter 9

Lesson 9.1 (pages 140–141)

Use index cards to find the median and mode for each set of data.

1.

SEA SHELL COLLECTION					
Name	Tom	Kay	Jim	June	Rick
Shells	198	250	284	250	190

2.

SIT-UPS					
Name	Joe	Kim	Roy	Meg	Jill
Number of Sit-ups	39	43	51	43	46

3.

NEWSPAPERS SOLD					
Week	1	2	3	4	5
Number	32	40	31	32	61

4.

BOOKS READ					
Name	B.J.	Pete	Kris	Sid	Carl
Number of Books	11	13	17	11	15

Lesson 9.2 (pages 142–143)

Find the mean, median, and mode for each set of data.

1. 4, 6, 9, 10, 6

2. 20, 32, 34, 52, 32

3. 14, 18, 12, 22, 14

4. 3, 9, 14, 3, 16

5. 34, 19, 21, 19, 32

6. 17, 11, 21, 15, 11

7. 41, 19, 64, 15, 41

8. 20, 43, 26, 31, 20

9. 171, 136, 171, 132, 135

10. 107, 119, 134, 119, 106

11. 99, 78, 39, 65, 39

12. 109, 141, 148, 131, 141

Lesson 9.3 (pages 144–145)

Choose the most reasonable interval for each set of data.

1. 50, 100, 75, 60, 25

2. 15, 20, 37, 35, 40

3. 3, 5, 1, 4, 7

4. 20, 40, 60, 45, 50

a. 1	**b.** 10
c. 5	**d.** 25

Choose the more reasonable scale for the set of data.

5.

FIFTH-GRADE SURVEY	
Favorite Animal	**Number of Students**
Cat	20
Dog	40
Horse	30
Bird	10
Rabbit	9

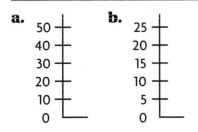

6.

CLASS SURVEY	
Favorite Color	**Number of Students**
Red	6
Blue	8
Green	2
Purple	5
Yellow	4

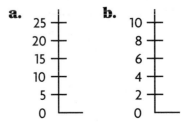

Lesson 9.4 (pages 146–147)

Make a line graph for each set of data.

1.

AVERAGE TEMPERATURE					
Month		Aug	Sep	Oct	Nov	Dec
Temperature		92	85	80	75	70

2.

INCHES OF SNOW				
Month	Dec	Jan	Feb	Mar
Inches	4	5	6	2

3.

THE ROGERS FAMILY'S ELECTRIC BILL					
Month	Jan	Feb	Mar	Apr	May
Bill	$120	$125	$115	$100	$92

4.

BOWLING ALLEY ATTENDANCE					
Week	1	2	3	4	5
People	140	90	130	100	150

Lesson 9.5 Part 1 (pages 148–149)

For Problems 1–4, choose a type of graph or plot. Explain your choice.

1. money Jenny earned baby-sitting from June to August

2. cans collected from 2 schools for canned-food drive

3. comparing boys' and girls' favorite ice cream flavors

4. Tammy's math scores for this grading period

Draw the graph or plot that best displays each set of data.

5.

FAVORITE SPORT					
Sport	Hockey	Tennis	Basketball	Golf	Soccer
Boys	5	14	22	4	12
Girls	4	20	18	2	8

6.

NUMBER OF ROCKS IN A COLLECTION								
Number of Rocks	5	6	7	8	9	10	11	12
Frequency	1	3	6	3	5	4	7	5

7.

FAVORITE COLORS				
Color	Red	Blue	Yellow	Green
Boys	11	9	0	5
Girls	8	4	6	7

8.

SOCCER TICKETS SOLD					
Day	1	2	3	4	5
Number	32	20	45	13	7

Lesson 9.5 Part 2 (pages 150–151)

Make a graph to solve.

1. Mr. Lynch surveyed his class to find out their favorite activities for Fun Friday. He organized the data in the table. What graph or plot should he use to display the data?

FUN FRIDAY ACTIVITIES				
	Board Games	Playground	Movie	Classroom Games
Boys	9	7	3	4
Girls	4	6	4	3

2. Ms. Jacob's class collected pennies for 5 weeks to raise money for the school. She organized the data in a table. What graph or plot should she use to display the data? Make the graph or plot.

PENNY COLLECTION					
Week	1	2	3	4	5
Number of Pennies	185	180	200	190	315

Chapter 10

Lesson 10.1 (pages 156–157)

For Problems 1–3, use the circle graph.

1. What does the whole circle represent?

2. What fraction of the time Craig spent doing homework was spent studying vocabulary?

3. How many minutes did Craig spend on math and reviewing spelling words?

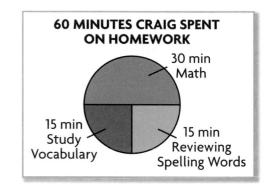

Describe how the circle graph would change for the data.

4. Craig spends 30 minutes on math and 30 minutes reviewing spelling words.

5. Craig spends 20 minutes on math, 20 minutes on vocabulary, and 20 minutes reviewing spelling words.

Lesson 10.2 (pages 158–159)

Use fraction-circle pieces to make a circle graph. Then draw the circle graph.

1.

RYAN'S BOOK COLLECTION		
Book	Number	Fraction
Fiction	25	$\frac{1}{2}$
Nonfiction	10	$\frac{1}{5}$
Humor	5	$\frac{1}{10}$
Mysteries	10	$\frac{1}{5}$

2.

MRS. POTTER'S HERBS	
Type of Herb Plant	Fraction of Plants
3 basil plants	$\frac{1}{3}$
3 oregano plants	$\frac{1}{3}$
3 dill plants	$\frac{1}{3}$

3.

TROPICAL FRUIT	
Fruit	Fraction
Strawberries	$\frac{1}{3}$
Blueberries	$\frac{1}{4}$
Pineapple	$\frac{5}{12}$

4.

8-DAY VACATION	
Activity	Fraction
Everglades	$\frac{1}{4}$
Beach	$\frac{1}{2}$
Fishing	$\frac{1}{8}$
Shopping	$\frac{1}{8}$

Lesson 10.3 (pages 160–161)

For Exercises 1–3, use the circle graph.

1. Stephen spent $1.00 at the candy store. What part of $1.00 did he spend for a candy bar and gumballs?

2. What fraction represents the part of the $1.00 Stephen spent for a candy bar? gumballs? lollipops?

3. How would the circle graph change if the candy bars cost $0.40, the gumballs cost $0.10, and the lollipops cost $0.50?

Make a circle graph for the data in the table.

4.

$1.00 SPENT IN A HARDWARE STORE		
Item	Amount Spent	Decimal Point
Nail	$0.10	0.1
Hook	$0.10	0.1
Screw	$0.30	0.3
Bolt	$0.20	0.2
Wire	$0.30	0.3

Lesson 10.4 (pages 162–163)

Explain why each graph does not correctly show the data.

1.

Duncan's Video Collection	
Animated	3
Comedy	4
Drama	1
Action	2

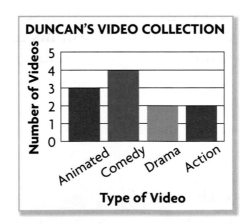

2.

Growth of Duncan's Video Collection	
Jan	1
Feb	2
Mar	4
Apr	6

3.

Duncan's Video Collection	
Animated	0.3
Comedy	0.4
Drama	0.1
Action	0.2

DUNCAN'S VIDEO COLLECTION

Animated — Drama — Westerns — Comedy

Lesson 10.5 Part 1 (pages 164–165)

Choose the best kind of graph to display the data. Explain your choice.

1. the amount of rainfall in your city each day for a month

2. the number of students' birthdays in each month

3. how you spent two hours on the Internet

4. book sales during May

5. population of 5 different cities

6. how your allowance is spent

Lesson 10.5 Part 2 (pages 166–167)

Choose the best kind of graph to display the data. Then make the graph.

1. Mr. Green's class is signing up for projects to display book reports. There are 8 students making mobiles, 16 making dioramas, and 6 making book jackets. What graph could you use to display these data?

2. On Friday Joey had baseball practice for 80 minutes. He spent $\frac{1}{8}$ of his time doing warm-up exercises, $\frac{1}{2}$ of his time running, $\frac{3}{8}$ of his time working on ball handling. What graph could you use to display the data?

Chapter 11

Lesson 11.1 (pages 172–173)

Write *certain* or *impossible* for each event.

1. that there are 60 seconds in 1 minute

2. pulling a purple counter out of a bag containing only red counters

3. rolling one cube numbered 1-6 and getting a number from 1 to 6

4. that there are 12 hours in a day

5. rolling two cubes numbered 1–6 and getting a number less than 1

6. that there are 7 days in a week

Write whether each event is *likely* or *unlikely*.

7. getting a good grade on a test if you study hard

8. 80° weather in Alaska in January

9. spinning an even number on a spinner that is numbered 1, 2, 4, 6, 8

10. rolling a 6 every time you roll a number cube

Lesson 11.2 (pages 174–175)

For Problems 1–4, use the bag of marbles.

1. Make a table of possible outcomes.

2. Predict and record the number of times you think each outcome will occur if you pull from the bag 10 times.

3. Pull from the bag 10 times, replacing the marble after each time. Record the results in the table.

4. Explain how your predictions compared with the results.

For Problems 5–6, use the table and spinner.

Spinner Experiment			
Outcome	Green	Blue	Yellow	Red
Frequency	II	II	ⅢⅠ	I

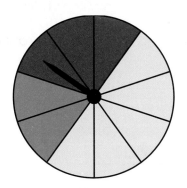

5. Why do you think yellow was spun most often?

6. Why do you think red was spun the least?

Lesson 11.3 Part 1 (pages 176–177)

Copy and complete the tree diagram. Tell the number of choices.

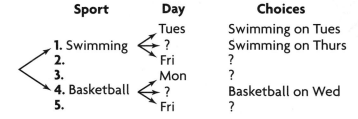

Find the number of choices by making a tree diagram.

6. Outfit Choices
Top: White, Brown, Black, Green
Pants: Blue, White, Black

7. Sandwich Choices
Bread: White, Wheat, Rye
Type: Roast Beef, Turkey, Chicken

8. Bicycle Choices
Color: Red, Black, Purple
Speed: 10-speed, 12-speed

Lesson 11.3 Part 2 (pages 178–179)

Make an organized list to solve.

1. Roland is conducting a probability experiment with a coin and a number cube numbered 1-6. How many possible outcomes are there for this experiment? What are they?

2. Use the digits 4, 5, and 6. List all the two-digit numbers you can make without repeating any digits in the same number.

Lesson 11.4 (pages 180–181)

Write a fraction for the probability of pulling each color marble.

1. blue   **2.** yellow   **3.** red   **4.** orange

Write a fraction for the probability of spinning each color.

5. blue

6. green

7. yellow or blue

8. green or red

Write the probability of spinning red.

9.    **10.**    **11.**

Lesson 11.5 (pages 182–183)

For Problems 1–6, use the spinner. Write each probability as a fraction. Tell which outcome is more likely.

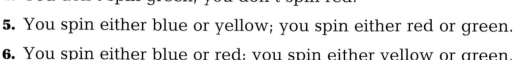

1. You spin green; you spin blue.

2. You spin red; you spin yellow.

3. You don't spin yellow; you don't spin blue.

4. You don't spin green; you don't spin red.

5. You spin either blue or yellow; you spin either red or green.

6. You spin either blue or red; you spin either yellow or green.

Chapter 12

Lesson 12.1 (pages 192–193)

Make a model to find each product.

1. $3 \times 0.6 = n$ **2.** $4 \times 0.9 = n$ **3.** $6 \times 0.19 = n$ **4.** $5 \times 0.24 = n$

5. $2 \times 0.7 = n$ **6.** $7 \times 0.31 = n$ **7.** $4 \times 0.14 = n$ **8.** $5 \times 0.31 = n$

Lesson 12.2 (pages 194–195)

Draw models to find each product.

1. $2 \times 6 = n$
$0.2 \times 6 = n$
$0.02 \times 6 = n$

2. $3 \times 8 = n$
$0.3 \times 8 = n$
$0.03 \times 8 = n$

3. $5 \times 3 = n$
$0.5 \times 3 = n$
$0.05 \times 3 = n$

4. $1 \times 7 = n$
$0.1 \times 7 = n$
$0.01 \times 7 = n$

Use mental math to complete the pattern.

5. $1 \times 4 = 4$
$0.1 \times 4 = 0.4$
$0.01 \times 4 = n$

6. $1 \times 60 = 60$
$0.1 \times 60 = n$
$0.01 \times 60 = 0.6$

7. $1 \times 37 = 37$
$0.1 \times 37 = n$
$0.01 \times 37 = n$

8. $15 \times 1 = 15$
$15 \times 0.1 = n$
$n \times 0.01 = n$

9. $14 \times 1 = n$
$14 \times 0.1 = n$
$14 \times 0.01 = n$

10. $71 \times 1 = n$
$71 \times 0.1 = n$
$71 \times 0.01 = n$

11. $1 \times 112 = n$
$0.1 \times 112 = n$
$0.01 \times 112 = n$

12. $172 \times 1 = n$
$172 \times 0.1 = n$
$172 \times 0.01 = n$

Lesson 12.3 Part 1 (pages 196–197)

Multiply. Write each product.

1. $0.5 \times 0.9 = n$ **2.** $0.2 \times 0.9 = n$ **3.** $0.3 \times 0.3 = n$ **4.** $0.7 \times 0.4 = n$

5. $0.6 \times 0.3 = n$ **6.** $0.7 \times 0.7 = n$ **7.** $0.4 \times 0.9 = n$ **8.** $0.2 \times 0.4 = n$

9. $0.6 \times 0.6 = n$ **10.** $0.8 \times 0.5 = n$ **11.** $0.8 \times 0.9 = n$ **12.** $0.8 \times 0.7 = n$

Lesson 12.3 Part 2 (pages 198–199)

Make a model to solve.

1. Rebecca has $3.35 in coins. She has 6 nickels and 3 times as many dimes as nickels. The rest are quarters. How many of each coin does she have?

2. Renee and Deon cut pizza into 10 equal pieces. They put pepperoni on 0.5 of the pizza. Then they put onions on 0.4 of the pepperoni pieces. What part of the pizza has pepperoni and onion?

Lesson 12.4 Part 1 (pages 200–201)

Choose the best estimate. Write a, b, or c.

1. $36 \times 0.6 = n$ **a.** 210   **b.** 21   **c.** 2,100

2. $42 \times 0.4 = n$ **a.** 17   **b.** 70   **c.** 170

3. $\$0.73 \times 8 = n$ **a.** $0.60   **b.** $60.00   **c.** $6.00

4. $\$0.36 \times 5 = n$ **a.** $0.20   **b.** $2.00   **c.** $20.00

Use estimation and patterns to place the decimal point in each product.

5. $3.2 \times 7 = 224$

6. $0.32 \times 7 = 224$

7. $3.2 \times 0.7 = 224$

8. $0.32 \times 0.7 = 224$

9. $32 \times 0.7 = 224$

10. $3.2 \times 0.07 = 224$

Lesson 12.4 Part 2 (pages 202–203)

Estimate each product.

1. 7×0.21 2. 6×0.33 3. 0.6×73 4. 36×0.5

5. 0.98×52 6. 49×0.04 7. 79×0.02 8. 0.17×97

Estimate to place the decimal point. Then find the product.

9. $\$7.25 \times 4$ 10. 2.8×6 11. 0.8×9.9 12. 3.79×68

Lesson 12.5 (pages 204–205)

Find the product.

1. $\begin{array}{r} 6.45 \\ \times\ 2.8 \\ \hline \end{array}$ 2. $\begin{array}{r} 23.9 \\ \times\ 4.3 \\ \hline \end{array}$ 3. $\begin{array}{r} 31.2 \\ \times\ 3.8 \\ \hline \end{array}$ 4. $\begin{array}{r} 49.76 \\ \times\ 0.36 \\ \hline \end{array}$ 5. $\begin{array}{r} 309.73 \\ \times\ 2.9 \\ \hline \end{array}$

6. $\begin{array}{r} 57.3 \\ \times\ 6.03 \\ \hline \end{array}$ 7. $\begin{array}{r} 17.9 \\ \times\ 8.2 \\ \hline \end{array}$ 8. $\begin{array}{r} 17.28 \\ \times\ 6.4 \\ \hline \end{array}$ 9. $\begin{array}{r} 42.5 \\ \times\ 6.04 \\ \hline \end{array}$ 10. $\begin{array}{r} 1.007 \\ \times\ 8.6 \\ \hline \end{array}$

11. $3.7 \times 1.4 = n$ 12. $1.7 \times 1.6 = n$ 13. $4.5 \times 3.9 = n$

Chapter 13

Lesson 13.1 Part 1 (pages 210–211)

Copy and complete each pattern.

1. $3,000 \div 6 = n$
$300 \div 6 = n$
$30 \div 6 = n$
$3 \div 6 = n$

2. $4,000 \div 8 = n$
$400 \div 8 = n$
$40 \div 8 = n$
$4 \div 8 = n$

3. $24,000 \div 5 = n$
$2,400 \div 5 = n$
$240 \div 5 = n$
$24 \div 5 = n$

4. $5,000 \div 2 = n$
$500 \div 2 = n$
$50 \div 2 = n$
$5 \div 2 = n$

5. $12,000 \div 8 = n$
$1,200 \div 8 = n$
$120 \div 8 = n$
$12 \div 8 = n$

6. $7,000 \div 4 = n$
$700 \div 4 = n$
$70 \div 4 = n$
$7 \div 4 = n$

Lesson 13.1 Part 2 (pages 212–213)

Write a number sentence to solve.

1. Courtney and 4 friends went to lunch. The bill was $35. They shared the bill equally. How much did each pay?

2. Stewart saves $14.95 from mowing lawns each week. In 9 weeks, how much will he have saved?

Lesson 13.2 (pages 214–215)

Make a model and find the quotient.

1. $800 \div 5 = $?

2. $0.21 \div 7 = $?

3. $4.5 \div 9 = $?

4. $3.6 \div 6 = $?

5. $0.18 \div 9 = $?

6. $0.8 \div 4 = $?

Lesson 13.3 (pages 216–217)

Find the quotient. Check by multiplying.

1. $8\overline{)4.8}$

2. $5\overline{)13.5}$

3. $3\overline{)6.06}$

4. $4\overline{)4.16}$

5. $7\overline{)7.28}$

6. $2\overline{)4.96}$

7. $9\overline{)27.9}$

8. $6\overline{)42.6}$

9. $6.39 \div 3 = $?

10. $20.8 \div 4 = $?

11. $18.6 \div 6 = $?

12. $15.4 \div 2 = $?

Lesson 13.4 (pages 218–219)

Use estimation or patterns to place the decimal point. Then find the quotient.

1. $3\overline{)1.5}$

2. $3\overline{)12.15}$

3. $6\overline{)0.36}$

4. $2\overline{)15.28}$

5. $4\overline{)24.8}$

6. $5\overline{)0.45}$

7. $5\overline{)17.45}$

8. $7\overline{)21.14}$

Lesson 13.5 (pages 220–221)

For Problems 1-4, use the table on page 220. Choose the operation and solve.

1. How much salmon will Mr. Regan have after sharing with 5 neighbors?

2. How many more pounds of salmon than haddock did Mr. Regan buy?

3. How many pounds of seafood did Mr. Regan buy in all?

4. Mr. Regan bought the same amount of shrimp 5 weeks in a row. How many pounds of shrimp did Mr. Regan buy?

Chapter 14

Lesson 14.1 (pages 226–227)

Choose the most reasonable unit of measure.
Write *mm, cm, dm, m,* or *km.*

1. height of a classmate

2. distance to the North Pole

3. length of a chalkboard

4. width of a paperback book

5. thickness of a dollar bill

6. distance of a marathon

Write the measurements in order from shortest to longest.

7. 9 dm   9 mm   9 cm

8. 2 km   2 dm   2 cm

9. 7 cm   7 m   7 mm

10. 13 m   13 dm   13 mm

11. 8 mm   8 cm   8 m

12. 10 cm   10 km   10 m

Lesson 14.2 (pages 228–229)

Choose the most reasonable unit. Write *kg, g,* or *mg.*

1.

2.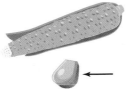

3.

Choose the more reasonable measurement.

4.

5 g or 5 kg

5.

300 g or 300 kg

6.

1 g or 1 kg

7.

7 kg or 7 mg

Lesson 14.3 (pages 230–231)

Choose the reasonable unit. Write *mL, L, or kL*.

1.
2.
3.
4.

Choose the more reasonable measurement.

5.
6.
7.
8.

240 L or 240 mL   2 L or 2 mL   120 mL or 120 L   18 mL or 18 L

Lesson 14.4 (pages 232–233)

Choose the smaller unit of measure. Write *a* or *b*. Use the prefix to help you.

1. **a.** millimeter
   b. centimeter

2. **a.** liter
   b. kiloliter

3. **a.** kilogram
   b. gram

Choose the larger unit of measure. Write *a* or *b*. Use the prefix to help you.

4. **a.** decimeter
   b. meter

5. **a.** liter
   b. milliliter

6. **a.** centimeter
   b. kilometer

Write the equivalent measurement.

7. 6 centimeters = _?_ meter

8. 9 kilograms = _?_ grams

9. 2 milligrams = _?_ gram

10. 7 grams = _?_ milligrams

11. 3 decimeters = _?_ meter

12. 5 milliliters = _?_ liter

Lesson 14.5 Part 1 (pages 234–235)

Write the missing unit.

1. 40 km = 40,000 _?_
2. 3 kg = 3,000 _?_
3. 7 m = 700 _?_
4. 3.7 m = 370 _?_
5. 5 km = 5,000 _?_
6. 9.462 L = 9,462 _?_

Write *multiply* or *divide*. Then write the equivalent measurement.

7. 4.21 g = _?_ mg
8. 2.4 m = _?_ cm
9. 50 cm = _?_ dm
10. 6,500 ml = _?_ L
11. 2,000 mg = _?_ g
12. 3,400 mm = _?_ m

Lesson 14.5 Part 2 (pages 236–237)

Draw a diagram to solve.

1. Eileen's book has a mass of 0.525 kg. Jeanne's book has a mass of 0.640 kg. What is the total mass in grams of the two books?

2. Kim has 1.9 L of lemonade in a pitcher. How many milliliters of lemonade are in the pitcher?

Chapter 15

Lesson 15.1 (pages 246–247)

Write the fraction shown.

1. | $\frac{1}{2}$ | $\frac{1}{2}$ |

2.

3.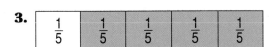

4. | $\frac{1}{4}$ | $\frac{1}{4}$ | $\frac{1}{4}$ | $\frac{1}{4}$ |

Shade a fraction strip to show the fraction.

5. $\frac{1}{10}$ 6. $\frac{1}{3}$ 7. $\frac{2}{5}$ 8. $\frac{7}{8}$ 9. $\frac{3}{10}$

Draw a number line. Locate the fraction.

10. $\frac{7}{10}$ 11. $\frac{2}{6}$ 12. $\frac{5}{8}$ 13. $\frac{5}{6}$ 14. $\frac{2}{3}$

Lesson 15.2 (pages 248–249)

Rename each fraction as a mixed number.

1. $\frac{23}{7}$ 2. $\frac{19}{4}$ 3. $\frac{8}{3}$ 4. $\frac{9}{5}$ 5. $\frac{16}{5}$

Rename each mixed number as a fraction.

6. $3\frac{1}{9}$ 7. $4\frac{2}{5}$ 8. $1\frac{3}{4}$ 9. $6\frac{2}{3}$ 10. $2\frac{3}{5}$

11. $5\frac{1}{4}$ 12. $7\frac{3}{8}$ 13. $2\frac{9}{10}$ 14. $9\frac{4}{5}$ 15. $8\frac{3}{8}$

16. $4\frac{3}{5}$ 17. $6\frac{2}{9}$ 18. $2\frac{5}{12}$ 19. $13\frac{3}{4}$ 20. $3\frac{9}{10}$

Lesson 15.3 (pages 250–251)

Use counters to name the least common multiple for each.

1. 2 and 6   2. 5 and 3   3. 7 and 2   4. 3 and 2   5. 4 and 5

6. 4 and 3   7. 8 and 4   8. 3 and 9   9. 4 and 6   10. 8 and 16

Rename each pair of fractions so they have the same denominator.
Use fraction strips and the LCM's from Exercises 1–5.

11. $\frac{1}{2} + \frac{1}{6}$ **12.** $\frac{1}{3} + \frac{2}{5}$ **13.** $\frac{2}{7} + \frac{1}{2}$ **14.** $\frac{2}{3} + \frac{1}{2}$

Lesson 15.4 (pages 252–253)

Rename, using the least common multiple, and compare.
Write $<$, $>$, or $=$ for each ⬤.

1. $\frac{1}{3}$ ⬤ $\frac{2}{9}$ **2.** $\frac{3}{4}$ ⬤ $\frac{5}{8}$ **3.** $\frac{1}{3}$ ⬤ $\frac{5}{24}$ **4.** $\frac{3}{4}$ ⬤ $\frac{11}{12}$

5. $\frac{1}{2}$ ⬤ $\frac{5}{6}$ **6.** $\frac{1}{5}$ ⬤ $\frac{3}{4}$ **7.** $\frac{4}{5}$ ⬤ $\frac{2}{3}$ **8.** $\frac{3}{15}$ ⬤ $\frac{1}{5}$

9. $\frac{2}{3}$ ⬤ $\frac{1}{4}$ **10.** $\frac{5}{6}$ ⬤ $\frac{4}{9}$ **11.** $\frac{1}{6}$ ⬤ $\frac{3}{8}$ **12.** $\frac{1}{4}$ ⬤ $\frac{5}{6}$

Lesson 15.5 Part 1 (pages 254–255)

Rename the fractions, using the LCM as the denominator.

1. $\frac{2}{3}, \frac{3}{4}, \frac{1}{2}$ **2.** $\frac{2}{3}, \frac{4}{15}, \frac{1}{5}$ **3.** $\frac{5}{6}, \frac{3}{8}, \frac{1}{4}$

Write in order from least to greatest.

4. $\frac{1}{2}, \frac{3}{4}, \frac{11}{16}$ **5.** $\frac{3}{4}, \frac{5}{6}, \frac{2}{3}$ **6.** $\frac{4}{9}, \frac{1}{3}, \frac{5}{6}$

Write in order from greatest to least.

7. $\frac{3}{4}, \frac{4}{5}, \frac{1}{2}$ **8.** $\frac{7}{12}, \frac{1}{4}, \frac{3}{8}$ **9.** $\frac{1}{2}, \frac{4}{5}, \frac{7}{10}$

10. $\frac{3}{8}, \frac{4}{16}, \frac{2}{4}$ **11.** $\frac{2}{3}, \frac{5}{9}, \frac{5}{6}$ **12.** $\frac{1}{3}, \frac{10}{15}, \frac{2}{5}$

Lesson 15.5 Part 2 (pages 256–257)

Draw a diagram to solve.

1. Lauren is making soup. She adds $\frac{2}{3}$ cup carrots, $\frac{3}{4}$ cup potatoes and $\frac{1}{2}$ cup of celery. List the ingredients in order from the least amount to the greatest amount.

2. Bert made cookies. He put in $\frac{2}{3}$ teaspoon baking soda, $\frac{1}{4}$ teaspoon salt, and $\frac{1}{3}$ teaspoon cinnamon. What is the order of ingredients from greatest to least?

3. Larry planted $\frac{1}{3}$ of his garden with carrots, $\frac{1}{4}$ with potatoes, and $\frac{5}{12}$ with radishes. List the plants in order from the one with the least area to the one with the greatest area.

4. Susan made a fruit sauce for her waffles. She used $\frac{1}{4}$ cup strawberries, and $\frac{3}{8}$ cup blueberries. Did she use more strawberries or blueberries?

Chapter 16

Lesson 16.1 (pages 262–263)

Use square tiles to show all the rectangles that can be made using each number.

1. 29   **2.** 25   **3.** 16   **4.** 7

Write *prime* or *composite* for each number.

5. 24   **6.** 36   **7.** 22   **8.** 17

9. 32   **10.** 41   **11.** 2   **12.** 37

Lesson 16.2 (pages 264–265)

List the factors of each number.

1. 12   **2.** 25   **3.** 14   **4.** 36   **5.** 16

6. 20   **7.** 15   **8.** 42   **9.** 56   **10.** 32

List the factors of each number. Write the greatest common factor for each pair of numbers.

11. 10, 35   **12.** 4, 32   **13.** 6, 16   **14.** 9, 27   **15.** 8, 20

16. 16, 20   **17.** 9, 12   **18.** 7, 28   **19.** 4, 20   **20.** 12, 30

21. 14, 21   **22.** 12, 18   **23.** 18, 36   **24.** 20, 30   **25.** 8, 24

Lesson 16.3 Part 1 (pages 266–267)

Find an equivalent fraction. Use multiplication or division.

1. $\frac{5}{15}$ **2.** $\frac{2}{3}$ **3.** $\frac{4}{12}$ **4.** $\frac{1}{5}$ **5.** $\frac{6}{30}$

6. $\frac{2}{12}$ **7.** $\frac{1}{9}$ **8.** $\frac{7}{28}$ **9.** $\frac{3}{9}$ **10.** $\frac{2}{11}$

Which fraction is *not* equivalent to the given fraction. Write *a, b,* or *c.*

11. $\frac{2}{7}$ **a.** $\frac{4}{14}$ **b.** $\frac{5}{14}$ **c.** $\frac{6}{21}$

12. $\frac{3}{15}$ **a.** $\frac{6}{30}$ **b.** $\frac{1}{5}$ **c.** $\frac{1}{3}$

13. $\frac{1}{3}$ **a.** $\frac{3}{9}$ **b.** $\frac{3}{6}$ **c.** $\frac{2}{6}$

14. $\frac{8}{12}$ **a.** $\frac{7}{10}$ **b.** $\frac{2}{3}$ **c.** $\frac{6}{9}$

Lesson 16.3 Part 2 (pages 268–269)

Draw a diagram to solve.

1. Juan has 24 sports cards, of which 6 are basketball cards. He says $\frac{1}{4}$ of his cards are basketball cards. Is he correct? Explain.

2. At the grocery store Mrs. Jewel spent $\frac{3}{8}$ of her money on fruits and $\frac{1}{4}$ of her money on meat. On which item did Mrs. Jewel spend more money? Explain how you know.

Lesson 16.4 (pages 270–271)

Write each fraction in simplest form. Use fraction bars.

1. $\frac{2}{12}$ 2. $\frac{7}{9}$ 3. $\frac{4}{14}$ 4. $\frac{6}{22}$ 5. $\frac{2}{5}$

6. $\frac{3}{18}$ 7. $\frac{6}{14}$ 8. $\frac{9}{21}$ 9. $\frac{3}{4}$ 10. $\frac{11}{88}$

11. $\frac{7}{49}$ 12. $\frac{8}{20}$ 13. $\frac{12}{15}$ 14. $\frac{14}{28}$ 15. $\frac{16}{28}$

Lesson 16.5 (pages 272–273)

Write each fraction in simplest form.

1. $\frac{2}{32}$ 2. $\frac{8}{44}$ 3. $\frac{12}{33}$ 4. $\frac{5}{45}$ 5. $\frac{2}{17}$

6. $\frac{15}{30}$ 7. $\frac{18}{39}$ 8. $\frac{42}{49}$ 9. $\frac{20}{50}$ 10. $\frac{9}{30}$

11. $\frac{27}{63}$ 12. $\frac{12}{56}$ 13. $\frac{21}{51}$ 14. $\frac{36}{45}$ 15. $\frac{16}{40}$

Chapter 17

Lesson 17.1 (pages 278–279)

Write an addition sentence for each drawing.

1.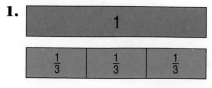

2.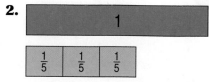

3.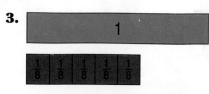

4.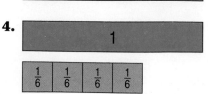

5.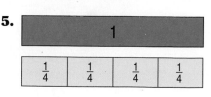

6.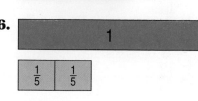

Use fraction strips to find the sum. Write the answer in simplest form.

7. $\dfrac{2}{6} + \dfrac{3}{6} = n$ **8.** $\dfrac{1}{9} + \dfrac{4}{9} = n$ **9.** $\dfrac{1}{8} + \dfrac{6}{8} = n$

10. $\dfrac{1}{4} + \dfrac{1}{4} = n$ **11.** $\dfrac{3}{5} + \dfrac{4}{5} = n$ **12.** $\dfrac{2}{3} + \dfrac{2}{3} = n$

13. $\dfrac{3}{8} + \dfrac{4}{8} = n$ **14.** $\dfrac{2}{9} + \dfrac{8}{9} = n$ **15.** $\dfrac{9}{10} + \dfrac{3}{10} = n$

Lesson 17.2 (pages 280–281)

Use fraction bars to find the sum.

1. $\dfrac{2}{3} + \dfrac{1}{4} = n$ **2.** $\dfrac{1}{2} + \dfrac{5}{8} = n$ **3.** $\dfrac{1}{6} + \dfrac{2}{3} = n$

4. $\dfrac{1}{2} + \dfrac{7}{10} = n$ **5.** $\dfrac{1}{3} + \dfrac{7}{12} = n$ **6.** $\dfrac{1}{2} + \dfrac{5}{6} = n$

7. $\dfrac{3}{4} + \dfrac{3}{8} = n$ **8.** $\dfrac{1}{6} + \dfrac{1}{3} = n$ **9.** $\dfrac{4}{5} + \dfrac{1}{2} = n$

Lesson 17.3 (pages 282–283)

Use the LCM to name the least common denominator, or LCD, for each pair of fractions.

1. $\dfrac{1}{2}$ and $\dfrac{1}{6}$ **2.** $\dfrac{1}{5}$ and $\dfrac{1}{3}$ **3.** $\dfrac{1}{8}$ and $\dfrac{1}{4}$ **4.** $\dfrac{1}{2}$ and $\dfrac{1}{10}$

Use fraction strips to find the sum. Write the answer in simplest form.

5. $\dfrac{1}{2} + \dfrac{5}{12} = n$ **6.** $\dfrac{3}{4} + \dfrac{1}{8} = n$ **7.** $\dfrac{1}{6} + \dfrac{3}{4} = n$ **8.** $\dfrac{5}{6} + \dfrac{1}{2} = n$

9. $\dfrac{1}{4} + \dfrac{3}{8} = n$ **10.** $\dfrac{1}{6} + \dfrac{2}{3} = n$ **11.** $\dfrac{2}{5} + \dfrac{1}{2} = n$ **12.** $\dfrac{1}{3} + \dfrac{4}{9} = n$

Lesson 17.4 Part 1 (pages 284–285)

Use the LCM to name the least common denominator, or LCD, for each group of fractions.

1. $\dfrac{1}{8}, \dfrac{1}{2},$ and $\dfrac{1}{4}$ **2.** $\dfrac{1}{3}, \dfrac{1}{12},$ and $\dfrac{1}{4}$ **3.** $\dfrac{1}{2}, \dfrac{1}{6},$ and $\dfrac{1}{3}$

4. $\dfrac{1}{3}, \dfrac{1}{6},$ and $\dfrac{1}{2}$ **5.** $\dfrac{1}{5}, \dfrac{1}{3},$ and $\dfrac{2}{15}$ **6.** $\dfrac{2}{3}, \dfrac{1}{12},$ and $\dfrac{1}{6}$

7. $\dfrac{1}{4}, \dfrac{1}{2},$ and $\dfrac{3}{16}$ **8.** $\dfrac{2}{3}, \dfrac{1}{9},$ and $\dfrac{1}{3}$ **9.** $\dfrac{1}{2}, \dfrac{1}{10},$ and $\dfrac{1}{5}$

Use fraction strips to find the sum. Write the answer in simplest form.

10. $\dfrac{2}{3} + \dfrac{1}{4} + \dfrac{5}{12} = n$ **11.** $\dfrac{1}{3} + \dfrac{4}{9} + \dfrac{2}{3} = n$ **12.** $\dfrac{1}{2} + \dfrac{3}{4} + \dfrac{2}{3} = n$

13. $\dfrac{1}{10} + \dfrac{2}{5} + \dfrac{3}{10} = n$ **14.** $\dfrac{1}{4} + \dfrac{1}{2} + \dfrac{5}{6} = n$ **15.** $\dfrac{5}{6} + \dfrac{1}{2} + \dfrac{1}{3} = n$

16. $\dfrac{1}{2} + \dfrac{3}{8} + \dfrac{3}{4} = n$ **17.** $\dfrac{1}{2} + \dfrac{1}{2} + \dfrac{1}{5} = n$ **18.** $\dfrac{5}{8} + \dfrac{1}{4} + \dfrac{1}{2} = n$

Lesson 17.4 Part 2 (pages 286–287)

Make a model to solve.

1. Greg plants $\dfrac{1}{3}$ of his garden with tomatoes, $\dfrac{1}{2}$ with herbs, and $\dfrac{1}{6}$ with jalapenos. What part of Greg's garden is planted?

2. Jill does aerobics for $\dfrac{1}{2}$ hour 5 times a week. How long does Jill do aerobics each week?

Chapter 18

Lesson 18.1 (pages 292–293)

Use fraction strips to find the difference. Write the answer in simplest form.

1. $\dfrac{2}{4} - \dfrac{1}{4} = n$ **2.** $\dfrac{6}{8} - \dfrac{3}{8} = n$ **3.** $\dfrac{7}{10} - \dfrac{2}{10} = n$

4. $\dfrac{9}{12} - \dfrac{7}{12} = n$ **5.** $\dfrac{7}{9} - \dfrac{4}{9} = n$ **6.** $\dfrac{4}{5} - \dfrac{1}{5} = n$

7. $\dfrac{5}{6} - \dfrac{4}{6} = n$ **8.** $\dfrac{11}{12} - \dfrac{5}{12} = n$ **9.** $\dfrac{7}{8} - \dfrac{3}{8} = n$

Lesson 18.2 (pages 294–295)

Use fraction bars to find the difference.

1. $\dfrac{6}{8} - \dfrac{1}{2} = n$ **2.** $\dfrac{3}{8} - \dfrac{1}{4} = n$ **3.** $\dfrac{1}{3} - \dfrac{1}{6} = n$

4. $\dfrac{1}{2} - \dfrac{3}{10} = n$ **5.** $\dfrac{2}{4} - \dfrac{1}{8} = n$ **6.** $\dfrac{5}{6} - \dfrac{2}{3} = n$

Lesson 18.3 (pages 296–297)

Name the least common denominator, or LCD, for each pair of fractions.

1. $\dfrac{1}{2}$ and $\dfrac{1}{8}$ **2.** $\dfrac{1}{3}$ and $\dfrac{1}{12}$ **3.** $\dfrac{1}{2}$ and $\dfrac{1}{6}$

Use fraction strips to find the difference. Write the answer in simplest form.

4. $\dfrac{1}{2} - \dfrac{3}{10} = n$ **5.** $\dfrac{4}{8} - \dfrac{1}{4} = n$ **6.** $\dfrac{1}{3} - \dfrac{1}{9} = n$

7. $\dfrac{3}{4} - \dfrac{1}{8} = n$ **8.** $\dfrac{9}{12} - \dfrac{3}{12} = n$ **9.** $\dfrac{6}{9} - \dfrac{1}{3} = n$

Lesson 18.4 Part 1 (pages 298–299)

Use a ruler to find the difference.

1. $\frac{3}{8}$ in. $- \frac{3}{16}$ in. $= n$

2. $\frac{1}{2}$ in. $- \frac{5}{16}$ in. $= n$

3. $\frac{3}{4}$ in. $- \frac{5}{8}$ in. $= n$

4. $\frac{11}{16}$ in. $- \frac{5}{8}$ in. $= n$

5. $\frac{3}{4}$ in. $- \frac{1}{16}$ in. $= n$

6. 1 in. $- \frac{3}{4}$ in. $= n$

Lesson 18.4 Part 2 (pages 300–301)

Work backward to solve.

1. Derrick's sprout is $\frac{11}{16}$ inch tall. It had grown $\frac{3}{8}$ inch from Wednesday to Friday. It had grown $\frac{1}{4}$ inch from Monday to Wednesday. How tall was Derrick's sprout on Monday?

2. Matthew's leaf is $\frac{3}{4}$ inch wide. It had grown $\frac{5}{16}$ inch from Sunday to Tuesday. How wide was Matthew's leaf on Sunday?

Chapter 19

Lesson 19.1 (pages 310–311)

Write whether the fraction is closer to 0, $\frac{1}{2}$, or 1.
You may use a number line.

1. $\frac{7}{8}$

2. $\frac{1}{9}$

3. $\frac{4}{11}$

4. $\frac{2}{7}$

5. $\frac{5}{9}$

6. $\frac{6}{10}$

Estimate each sum or difference.

7. $\frac{2}{5} + \frac{4}{9}$

8. $\frac{1}{10} + \frac{5}{8}$

9. $\frac{8}{9} - \frac{3}{7}$

10. $\frac{7}{9} + \frac{1}{5}$

11. $\frac{7}{10} - \frac{1}{12}$

12. $\frac{3}{10} - \frac{1}{12}$

Lesson 19.2 (pages 312–313)

Find the sum. Write the answer in simplest form.

1. $\frac{3}{4} + \frac{1}{4} = n$

2. $\frac{2}{5} + \frac{2}{5} = n$

3. $\frac{3}{8} + \frac{3}{8} = n$

4. $\frac{4}{7} + \frac{1}{7} = n$

5. $\frac{2}{6} + \frac{3}{6} = n$

6. $\frac{3}{12} + \frac{4}{12} = n$

Find the difference. Write the answer in simplest form.

7. $\frac{5}{8} - \frac{2}{8} = n$

8. $\frac{4}{7} - \frac{3}{7} = n$

9. $\frac{9}{11} - \frac{7}{11} = n$

10. $\frac{4}{5} - \frac{2}{5} = n$

11. $\frac{9}{10} - \frac{1}{10} = n$

12. $\frac{7}{8} - \frac{3}{8} = n$

Lesson 19.3 (pages 314–315)

Find the sum or difference. Write the answer in simplest form.

1. $\dfrac{3}{4} - \dfrac{1}{4} = n$

2. $\dfrac{1}{3} + \dfrac{4}{9} = n$

3. $\dfrac{5}{7} - \dfrac{3}{7} = n$

4. $\dfrac{2}{3} + \dfrac{3}{4} = n$

5. $\dfrac{2}{3} - \dfrac{5}{12} = n$

6. $\dfrac{5}{8} - \dfrac{1}{3} = n$

7. $\dfrac{5}{9} + \dfrac{4}{9} = n$

8. $\dfrac{5}{6} + \dfrac{1}{2} = n$

9. $\dfrac{11}{15} - \dfrac{2}{5} = n$

10. $\dfrac{1}{2} + \dfrac{2}{3} = n$

11. $\dfrac{3}{5} - \dfrac{1}{4} = n$

12. $\dfrac{2}{3} + \dfrac{3}{5} = n$

Lesson 19.4 (pages 316–317)

Find the sum or difference. Write each answer in simplest form.

1. $\dfrac{3}{10} + \dfrac{1}{2} = n$

2. $\dfrac{1}{4} + \dfrac{5}{6} = n$

3. $\dfrac{7}{9} - \dfrac{4}{9} = n$

4. $\dfrac{2}{8} + \dfrac{2}{8} = n$

5. $\dfrac{1}{2} - \dfrac{3}{7} = n$

6. $\dfrac{1}{2} - \dfrac{2}{9} = n$

7. $\dfrac{1}{3} + \dfrac{1}{4} = n$

8. $\dfrac{3}{4} - \dfrac{5}{9} = n$

9. $\dfrac{7}{10} + \dfrac{5}{10} = n$

10. $\dfrac{2}{3} - \dfrac{8}{18} = n$

11. $\dfrac{5}{7} - \dfrac{2}{3} = n$

12. $\dfrac{6}{7} + \dfrac{1}{2} = n$

Lesson 19.5 Part 1 (pages 318–319)

Tell whether you would add or subtract to solve the problem. Solve.

1. Madison practiced piano for $\frac{3}{4}$ hour on Monday and $\frac{1}{3}$ hour on Tuesday. How long did she practice on both days?

2. The Cohens had $\frac{1}{2}$ gallon of milk. They used $\frac{1}{4}$ gallon. How much milk do they have left?

Lesson 19.5 Part 2 (pages 320–321)

Draw a diagram to solve.

1. Some fifth graders took a survey asking students whether they liked mysteries, comedies, or dramas best. The survey showed that $\frac{2}{5}$ liked mysteries best, $\frac{1}{2}$ preferred comedies, and $\frac{1}{10}$ liked dramas. There were 5 students who preferred dramas. How many students took the survey?

2. Ginger, Rebecca, and Alvin are comparing the number of pages they read. Ginger read 18 pages, Rebecca read 6 pages fewer than Ginger. Alvin read 7 pages more than Rebecca. How many pages did Alvin read?

Chapter 20

Lesson 20.1 (pages 326–327)

Round the mixed number to the nearest $\frac{1}{2}$ or whole number.
You may use a number line or a ruler.

1. $6\frac{1}{6}$ **2.** $1\frac{7}{8}$ **3.** $3\frac{2}{5}$ **4.** $9\frac{5}{12}$ **5.** $4\frac{1}{3}$ **6.** $7\frac{3}{4}$

Estimate the sum or difference.

7. $2\frac{1}{8} + 3\frac{3}{4}$ **8.** $4\frac{2}{9} - 1\frac{1}{5}$ **9.** $3\frac{5}{8} + 3\frac{9}{16}$

10. $7\frac{6}{7} - 6\frac{11}{12}$ **11.** $1\frac{1}{9} + 9\frac{2}{12}$ **12.** $7\frac{1}{8} - 4\frac{4}{9}$

Lesson 20.2 (pages 328–329)

Find the sum. You may wish to draw a picture. Write the
answer in simplest form.

1. $\begin{array}{r} 2\frac{2}{7} \\ +4\frac{3}{7} \\ \hline \end{array}$ **2.** $\begin{array}{r} 4\frac{1}{2} \\ +1\frac{1}{4} \\ \hline \end{array}$ **3.** $\begin{array}{r} 7\frac{1}{6} \\ +2\frac{2}{3} \\ \hline \end{array}$ **4.** $\begin{array}{r} 5\frac{1}{3} \\ +3\frac{2}{12} \\ \hline \end{array}$

5. $7\frac{2}{7} + 2\frac{1}{2} = n$ **6.** $4\frac{1}{2} + 4\frac{1}{4} = n$ **7.** $8\frac{2}{3} + 1\frac{1}{4} = n$

8. $3\frac{4}{9} + 5\frac{2}{3} = n$ **9.** $6\frac{3}{4} + 2\frac{4}{16} = n$ **10.** $5\frac{5}{6} + 1\frac{1}{3} = n$

11. $4\frac{1}{12} + 3\frac{3}{4} = n$ **12.** $5\frac{7}{15} + 3\frac{3}{5} = n$ **13.** $6\frac{4}{9} + 7\frac{1}{3} = n$

Lesson 20.3 Part 1 (pages 330–331)

Subtract. Write the answer in simplest form.

1. $\begin{array}{r} 3\frac{2}{5} = 3\frac{6}{15} \\ -1\frac{1}{3} = 1\frac{5}{15} \\ \hline \end{array}$ **2.** $\begin{array}{r} 6\frac{7}{12} = 6\frac{7}{12} \\ -3\frac{1}{4} = 3\frac{3}{12} \\ \hline \end{array}$ **3.** $\begin{array}{r} 9\frac{3}{4} = 9\frac{3}{4} \\ -5\frac{1}{2} = 5\frac{2}{4} \\ \hline \end{array}$

4. $7\frac{7}{9} - 5\frac{2}{3} = n$ **5.** $8\frac{9}{10} - 4\frac{3}{5} = n$ **6.** $4\frac{1}{2} - 3\frac{3}{8} = n$

7. $3\frac{7}{12} - \frac{2}{6} = n$ **8.** $9\frac{7}{10} - 3\frac{1}{2} = n$ **9.** $6\frac{13}{14} - 2\frac{2}{7} = n$

10. $4\frac{3}{8} - 2\frac{1}{4} = n$ **11.** $7\frac{3}{4} - \frac{8}{16} = n$ **12.** $9\frac{3}{5} - \frac{1}{10} = n$

Lesson 20.3 Part 2 (pages 332–333)

Work backward to solve.

1. Elizabeth spent $69 on a new outfit. She spent $23 on a skirt and $18 on a blouse. How much did she spend on the new shoes?

2. Jerry worked on his homework for $1\frac{1}{2}$ hours. During that time he spent $\frac{3}{4}$ hour doing math and $\frac{1}{2}$ hour reading a science chapter. How much time did he spend reviewing vocabulary words?

Lesson 20.4 (pages 334–335)

Use fraction bars to find the difference.

1. $\begin{array}{r} 7\frac{1}{2} \\ -2\frac{1}{4} \\ \hline \end{array}$

2. $\begin{array}{r} 4\frac{2}{3} \\ -\frac{1}{6} \\ \hline \end{array}$

3. $\begin{array}{r} 9\frac{2}{3} \\ -3\frac{1}{6} \\ \hline \end{array}$

4. $\begin{array}{r} 5\frac{1}{2} \\ -\frac{1}{8} \\ \hline \end{array}$

5. $7\frac{1}{6} - 3\frac{2}{3} = n$

6. $3\frac{5}{6} - 1\frac{2}{3} = n$

7. $6\frac{2}{5} - \frac{1}{10} = n$

8. $9\frac{1}{4} - 5\frac{1}{8} = n$

9. $2\frac{1}{3} - 1\frac{8}{12} = n$

10. $4\frac{3}{8} - \frac{3}{4} = n$

Chapter 21

Lesson 21.1 (pages 340–341)

Draw a line segment to the given length.

1. $3\frac{3}{4}$ inches

2. $2\frac{1}{16}$ inches

3. $4\frac{9}{16}$ inches

4. $1\frac{1}{4}$ inches

Use a ruler to compare the measurements. Write $<$, $>$, or $=$ for each ●.

5. $4\frac{3}{16}$ ● $3\frac{3}{4}$

6. $5\frac{1}{16}$ ● $5\frac{3}{16}$

7. $6\frac{3}{4}$ ● $6\frac{1}{8}$

8. $1\frac{4}{16}$ ● $1\frac{1}{4}$

9. $1\frac{5}{8}$ ● $1\frac{3}{4}$

10. $2\frac{7}{8}$ ● $3\frac{1}{8}$

11. $2\frac{7}{16}$ ● $2\frac{1}{2}$

12. $4\frac{5}{16}$ ● $4\frac{1}{4}$

Lesson 21.2 Part 1 (pages 342–343)

Change the unit. You may use a calculator.

1. 15 ft = _?_ yd

2. 60 ft = _?_ yd

3. 62 yd = _?_ ft

4. 156 in. = _?_ ft

5. 8 ft = _?_ in.

6. 17 yd = _?_ ft

7. 3 mi = _?_ ft

8. 3,520 yd = _?_ mi

9. 252 in. = _?_ ft

Write *multiply* or *divide*. Solve.

10. How many feet are in 60 inches?　　**11.** How many inches are in 4 feet?

12. How many yards are in 7 miles?　　**13.** How many feet are in 2 miles?

14. How many feet are in 7 yards?　　**15.** How many inches are in 6 yards?

Lesson 21.2 Part 2 (pages 344–345)

Rename the measurements.

1. 39 in. = _?_ ft _?_ in.　　**2.** 17 ft = _?_ yd _?_ ft　　**3.** 64 in. = _?_ ft _?_ in.

4. 6 ft 7 in. = 5 ft _?_ in.　　**5.** 9 ft 14 in. = 10 ft _?_ in.　　**6.** 7 yd 1 ft = 6 yd _?_ ft

Find the sum or difference.

7.　7 ft 5 in.
　　+3 ft 9 in.

8.　4 yd 3 ft
　　+7 yd 2 ft

9.　13 ft 8 in.
　　− 9 ft 3 in.

10.　12 yd 1 ft
　　− 7 yd 2 ft

Lesson 21.3 (pages 346–347)

Change the unit.

1. 10 c = _?_ pt　　**2.** 7 pt = _?_ c　　**3.** 2 pt = _?_ fl oz　　**4.** 4 gal = _?_ qt

5. 40 fl oz = _?_ c　　**6.** 7 gal = _?_ qt　　**7.** 3 pt = _?_ c　　**8.** 12 c = _?_ fl oz

Write <, >, or = for each ●.

9. 2 gal ● 10 qt　　**10.** 4 c ● 2 pt　　**11.** 1 c ● 16 fl oz　　**12.** 4 pt ● 6 c

Lesson 21.4 (pages 348–349)

What unit would you use to describe the weight of these objects?
Write *tons, pounds,* or *ounces.*

1. a child　　**2.** an elephant　　**3.** a book　　**4.** a box of cereal

Write *multiply* or *divide*. Change the unit. You may use a calculator.

5.　8 T = _?_ lb　　**6.** 12,000 lb = _?_ T　　**7.** 80 oz = _?_ lb　　**8.** 50 lb = _?_ oz

Write which one is heavier.

9. 5 lb or 84 oz　　**10.** 4 T or 6,000 lb　　**11.** 130 oz or 9 lb　　**12.** 10 lb or 30 oz

Lesson 21.5 Part 1 (pages 350–351)

Write the elapsed time for each hike.

1.

Time the hike started   Time the hike finished

2.

Time the hike started   Time the hike finished

Look at Roberto's schedule for the day and complete the table.

	Activity	Starting Time	Ending Time	Elapsed Time
3.	School	8:30 A.M.	2:50 P.M.	?
4.	Swim Practice	3:35 P.M.	?	1 hr 30 min
5.	Dinner	?	6:30 P.M.	40 min
6.	Homework	7:05 P.M.	8:14 P.M.	?

Lesson 21.5 Part 2 (pages 352–353)

Make a table to solve.

1. Mrs. Winter's class members are making 5 minute presentations starting at 12:35. The students, in order, are Clara, Bobby, Renee, Pam, and Paul. At what time does Pam start her presentation?

2. Three classes are scheduled for 45 minute research time. Ms. Hodson's class begins at 9:05 and Mrs. Atwood's class begins at 9:50. What time is Mr. Bower's class scheduled?

Lesson 21.6 (pages 354–355)

Find the difference in temperature.

1. room temperature of 79°F and the outside temperature of 88°F

2. a fever of 101°F and normal human body temperature

Copy and complete the table.

	Starting Temperature	Change in Temperature	Final Temperature
3.	78°F	?	87°F
4.	13°C	rose 11°	?
5.	63°F	?	45°F
6.	7°F	fell 2°	?

Chapter 22

Lesson 22.1 (pages 360–361)

Write a number sentence for the picture.

1.

2.

3.

4.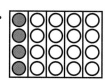

5.

6.

7.

8.

Find the product.

9. $\frac{2}{3} \times 12 = n$

10. $\frac{1}{4} \times 28 = n$

11. $\frac{3}{4} \times 12 = n$

12. $\frac{5}{6} \times 12 = n$

13. $15 \times \frac{2}{5} = n$

14. $14 \times \frac{2}{7} = n$

15. $24 \times \frac{3}{8} = n$

16. $18 \times \frac{1}{9} = n$

17. $\frac{1}{6} \times 12 = n$

18. $20 \times \frac{2}{5} = n$

19. $10 \times \frac{1}{5} = n$

20. $27 \times \frac{2}{3} = n$

Lesson 22.2 (pages 362–363)

Make a paper-folding model to find the product.

1. $\frac{1}{3} \times \frac{1}{3} = n$

2. $\frac{1}{2} \times \frac{2}{3} = n$

3. $\frac{2}{3} \times \frac{2}{9} = n$

4. $\frac{1}{4} \times \frac{3}{4} = n$

5. $\frac{3}{4} \times \frac{2}{5} = n$

6. $\frac{1}{5} \times \frac{2}{3} = n$

Lesson 22.3 (pages 364–365)

Multiply. Write the answer in simplest form.

1. $\frac{1}{6} \times \frac{1}{3} = n$

2. $\frac{3}{5} \times \frac{1}{3} = n$

3. $\frac{2}{3} \times \frac{4}{9} = n$

4. $\frac{3}{8} \times \frac{2}{5} = n$

5. $\frac{1}{7} \times \frac{1}{6} = n$

6. $\frac{3}{4} \times \frac{4}{5} = n$

7. $\frac{6}{7} \times \frac{1}{3} = n$

8. $\frac{5}{9} \times \frac{3}{4} = n$

9. $\frac{7}{8} \times \frac{3}{7} = n$

10. $\frac{4}{15} \times \frac{3}{8} = n$

11. $\frac{4}{7} \times \frac{3}{10} = n$

12. $\frac{7}{12} \times \frac{6}{7} = n$

13. $\frac{4}{7} \times \frac{2}{3} = n$

14. $\frac{3}{4} \times \frac{3}{8} = n$

15. $\frac{2}{3} \times \frac{5}{6} = n$

16. $\frac{3}{8} \times \frac{2}{3} = n$

17. $\frac{5}{8} \times \frac{3}{4} = n$

18. $\frac{2}{5} \times \frac{3}{10} = n$

19. $\frac{4}{7} \times \frac{1}{4} = n$

20. $\frac{2}{16} \times \frac{2}{2} = n$

Lesson 22.4 Part 1 (pages 366–367)

Multiply. Write the answer in simplest form.

1. $\frac{1}{2} \times 2\frac{2}{3} = n$

2. $\frac{2}{3} \times 1\frac{2}{5} = n$

3. $\frac{1}{4} \times 2\frac{1}{7} = n$

4. $\frac{3}{4} \times 1\frac{2}{3} = n$

5. $\frac{2}{5} \times 1\frac{2}{3} = n$

6. $\frac{3}{5} \times 1\frac{1}{6} = n$

7. $\frac{1}{6} \times 2\frac{2}{5} = n$

8. $\frac{3}{4} \times 3\frac{1}{3} = n$

9. $\frac{1}{5} \times 1\frac{3}{4} = n$

10. $\frac{1}{3} \times 3\frac{1}{9} = n$

11. $\frac{5}{6} \times 4\frac{3}{5} = n$

12. $\frac{2}{7} \times 3\frac{2}{4} = n$

Lesson 22.4 Part 2 (pages 368–369)

Make a model to solve.

1. Samuel had $2\frac{1}{4}$ dozen markers. After a while, $\frac{1}{3}$ of the markers dried up and he threw them away. How many dozen markers does he have left?

2. Bruce bought 3 books. He received $3.77 back in coins. He has 10 quarters, half as many dimes as quarters, 3 times as many nickels as dimes, and the rest are pennies. How many of each coin does he have?

Chapter 23

Lesson 23.1 (pages 378–379)

For Exercises 1–4, use the figure.

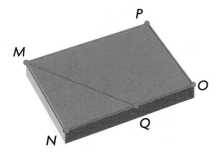

1. Name the point where *MN* and *NO* intersect.

2. Name the line segment that is parallel to *PO*.

3. Name the line segment that intersects but is not perpendicular to *NO*.

4. Name a line segment on plane *MNO* that is perpendicular to *PO*.

For Exercises 5–7, use the figure.

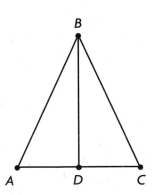

5. Name the line segment that is perpendicular to *AC*.

6. Name the point where *AC* and *BD* intersect.

7. Is line segment *AB* parallel to *BC*?

Identify each line relationship. Write *parallel, perpendicular,* or *intersecting.* Some figures may have more than one answer.

8.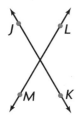

9.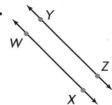

10.

Lesson 23.2 (pages 380–381)

Identify the angle. Write *right, acute,* or *obtuse.*

1.

2.

3.

4.

For Exercises 5–12, use the figure. Identify the angle. Write *right, acute,* or *obtuse.*

5. ∠IPL

6. ∠KPL

7. ∠JPI

8. ∠IPM

9. ∠NPO

10. ∠LPO

11. ∠JPN

12. ∠NPI

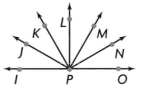

Lesson 23.3 Part 1 (pages 382–383)

Trace each figure. Use a protractor to measure the angle.

1.

2.

3.

4.

Lesson 23.3 Part 2 (pages 384–385)

Draw a diagram to solve.

1. Sandy is having a birthday party. She gave Terry directions to her house. Make a map of Sandy's directions.

2. Rex is hanging pictures in a straight line on a 6-foot wall. He hammers a nail into the wall every 9 inches. He does not put nails on the ends. How many pictures can Rex hang?

Sandy's directions:

Drive north on 34th Street. Make a 90° turn east on Riverview Blvd., and drive 2 blocks. Make a 90° turn right on Elm Street. Look for the balloons on the mailbox.

Lesson 23.4 (pages 386–387)

Draw and name the quadrilateral.

1. two pairs of congruent sides and four right angles

2. four congruent sides and 2 pairs of congruent angles

Write *true* or *false*.

3. A trapezoid has 2 pairs of parallel sides.

4. All quadrilaterals have 4 sides.

5. A square has 4 right angles.

6. A rectangle has 2 pairs of congruent sides.

Lesson 23.5 Part 1 (pages 388–389)

Name each triangle. Write *isosceles*, *scalene*, or *equilateral*.

1. 5 m, 5 m, 5 m

2. 8 cm, 2 cm, 7 cm

3. 5 cm, 6 cm, 4 cm

4. 3 ft, 3 ft, 1 ft

5. 7 in., 7 in., 7 in.

6. 2 m, 2 m, 2 m

7. 2 in., 3 in., 4 in.

8. 7 ft, 14 ft, 14 ft

9. 3 in., 4 in., 1 in.

10. 6 cm, 6 cm, 3 cm

11. 5 yd, 2 yd, 4 yd

12. 4 m, 4 m, 4 m

Lesson 23.5 Part 2 (pages 390–391)

Name each triangle. Write *right*, *acute*, or *obtuse*.

1.

2.

3.

4.

5.

6.

Find the measure of the unknown angle in each triangle.

7. 70° ? 60°

8. 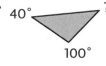 40° ? 100°

9. 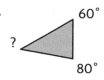 60° ? 80°

10. 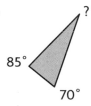 ? 85° 70°

11. 45° ? 90°

12. 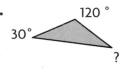 120° 30° ?

Chapter 24

Lesson 24.1 (pages 396–397)

Write *congruent* or *not congruent*.

1.

2.

3.

Write the letters of the two figures that are congruent.

4. a.
b.
c.

5. a.
b.
c.

Lesson 24.2 (pages 398–399)

Tell whether the two halves of each drawing are congruent. Write *yes* or *no*.

1.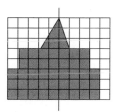

2.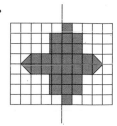

3.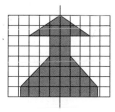

Trace each figure. Draw the lines of symmetry for each figure.

4.

5.

6.

Lesson 24.3 (pages 400–401)

Copy each figure on a coordinate grid. Translate, reflect, and rotate each figure. Draw the new figure. Name the ordered pairs.

1.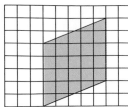

2.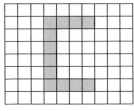

3.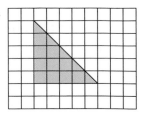

4.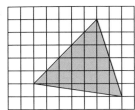

5.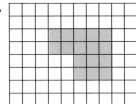

6.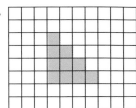

Lesson 24.4 Part 1 (pages 402–403)

Copy each figure. Write *yes* or *no* to tell whether each figure can be arranged to tessellate.

1.

2.

3.

Copy each figure and translate, reflect, or rotate it to make a design that tessellates.

4.

5.

6.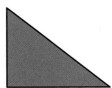

Lesson 24.4 Part 2 (pages 404–405)

Make a model to solve.

1. Cassandra is making a mosaic design. She is using trapezoids and triangles. Draw a design that may look like Cassandra's.

2. Of the hot lunches, $\frac{1}{8}$ were bought by third graders, $\frac{1}{4}$ by fourth graders, and $\frac{5}{8}$ by fifth graders. There were 30 third graders who bought hot lunches. How many fifth graders bought hot lunches?

Chapter 25

Lesson 25.1 (pages 410–411)

Use a compass to construct the circles and find the measurements.

1. Construct a circle with a radius of 5 cm. Label and measure a diameter and a chord.

2. Construct a circle with a radius of 7 cm. Label and measure a radius and a chord.

Write *chord*, *diameter*, or *radius* for each line segment.

3.   **4.**   **5.**   **6.**

Lesson 25.2 Part 1 (pages 412–413)

Use a calculator to divide the circumference of each object by its diameter. Complete the table by rounding to the nearest hundredth.

	Object	Circumference (C)	Diameter (d)	$\frac{C}{d}$
1.	ball	12.6 cm	4 cm	?
2.	jar	15.6 cm	5 cm	?
3.	vase	28.2 cm	9 cm	?
4.	glass	25.1 cm	8 cm	?
5.	roll of tape	18.9 cm	6 cm	?
6.	stick	6.28 cm	2 cm	?

Lesson 25.2 Part 2 (pages 414–415)

Act it out to solve.

1. Liza, Ian, Wade, Max, and Audrey are waiting on a bench for the school bus. Wade is on the left end, Ian is between Liza and Wade. Max is on the far right. Who is Audrey between?

2. Lakeisha had one $20 bill, one $10 bill, two $5 bills, one $1 bill, three quarters, and two dimes. She spent $21.25 on a shirt and $15.50 on a CD. What bills and coins does Lakeisha have left?

Lesson 25.3 (pages 416–417)

Write *true* or *false* to describe each statement.

1. In a circle with three radii, each of three angles could measure 120°.

2. In a circle, one diameter forms two acute angles.

3. If in a circle, four radii form three 80° angles, the fourth angle is acute.

4. If in a circle, six radii form five 60° angles, the sixth angle is acute.

Find the missing angle.

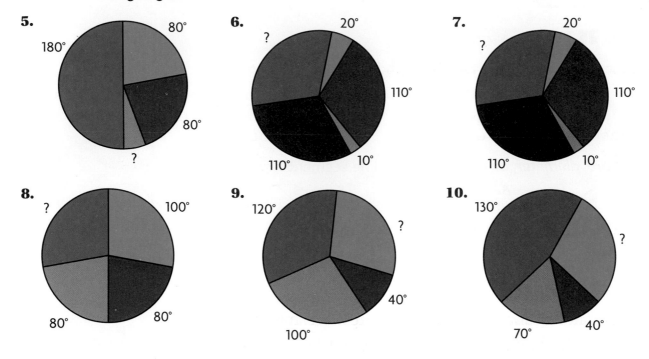

5. 180° 80° 80° ?

6. ? 20° 110° 10° 110°

7. ? 20° 110° 10° 110°

8. ? 100° 80° 80°

9. 120° ? 40° 100°

10. 130° ? 70° 40°

Lesson 25.4 (pages 418–419)

Use a protractor to find how many degrees are in each angle.

1.

2.

3.

Use a compass and a protractor to draw a circle with the following angles.

4. 4 angles of 90° each

5. 2 angles of 60° each and 2 angles of 120° each

6. 6 angles of 60° each

7. 2 angles of 110° each and 1 angle of 140°

8. 3 angles of 80° each and 1 angle of 120°

9. 4 angles of 80° each and 1 angle of 40°

10. 3 angles of 60° each, 2 angles of 45° each, and 1 angle of 90°

11. 2 angles of 90° each and 3 angles of 60° each

12. 3 angles of 25° each, 3 angles of 45° each, and 3 angles of 50° each

Chapter 26

Lesson 26.1 (pages 424–425)

Write *prism* or *pyramid.* Write the polygon that names the base. Identify the solid figure.

1.
2.
3.
4.

Write the name of the solid figure. Make a drawing of each.

5. I have 6 congruent squares.

6. I have a hexagonal base and 6 congruent triangles.

7. I have 6 rectangular faces.

8. I have an octagonal base and 8 congruent triangles.

9. I have 2 triangular faces and 3 congruent rectangles.

Lesson 26.2 (pages 426–427)

Match each solid figure with its net. Write *a, b, c,* or *d.*

1.
2.
3.
4.

a.
b.
c.
d.

Lesson 26.3 (pages 428–429)

Use grid paper to draw each figure from the top, the side, and the front.

1.
2.
3.

Lesson 26.4 Part 1 (pages 430–431)

Find the missing dimension. You may use a calculator.

1.
7 yd
4 yd
volume = 168 cu yd

2.
2 in.
7 in.
volume = 154 cu in.

3.
8 ft
3 ft
volume = 288 cu ft

4. length = 7 ft
width = __?__
height = 2 ft
volume = 84 cu ft

5. length = 15 in.
width = 9 in.
height = 4 in.
volume = __?__

6. length = __?__
width = 11 cm
height = 8 cm
volume = 352 cu cm

Complete the table. You may use a calculator.

	Length	Width	Height	Volume
7.	9 in.	5 in.	8 in.	?
8.	9 cm	10 cm	7 cm	?
9.	12 ft	4 ft	3 ft	?
10.	6 yd	15 yd	11 yd	?

Lesson 26.4 Part 2 (pages 432–433)

Use a formula to solve.

1. A pencil box is 13 in. long and 6 in. wide. It has a volume of 234 cu in. What is the height of the pencil box?

2. Trevor is putting down linoleum in his kitchen. His kitchen is 16 ft wide and 24 ft long. How many square feet of linoleum does Trevor need?

Lesson 26.5 (pages 434–435)

Use the benchmarks at the right to name the more reasonable unit for measuring the volume of each box. Estimate the volume.

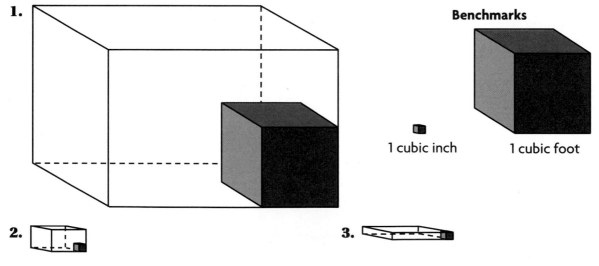

1.

Benchmarks

1 cubic inch   1 cubic foot

2.

3.

Choose the most reasonable measure. Write *a, b,* or *c.*

4. a suitcase   **a.** 1 cu in.   **b.** 1 cu ft   **c.** 1 cu yd

5. a shoe box   **a.** 110 cu in.   **b.** 110 cu ft   **c.** 110 cu yd

6. a refrigerator   **a.** 80 cu in.   **b.** 80 cu ft   **c.** 80 cu yd

Chapter 27

Lesson 27.1 (pages 444–445)

Name the type of ratio and show with counters.

1. Of the 8 books on a shelf, 5 are fiction.

2. There were 7 boys and 10 girls.

3. During vacation, 3 of the 7 days were rainy.

4. There are 6 roses and 7 daisies.

5. Of the 9 students, 2 are sick.

6. Homework was finished by 9 out of 11 students.

Lesson 27.2 (pages 446–447)

Write a or b to show which fraction represents the ratio.

1. 2 to 5
   a. $\frac{2}{5}$ b. $\frac{5}{2}$

2. 1:10
   a. $\frac{1}{10}$ b. $\frac{10}{1}$

3. 3:11
   a. $\frac{11}{3}$ b. $\frac{3}{11}$

4. 6 to 5
   a. $\frac{5}{6}$ b. $\frac{6}{5}$

For Exercises 5–8, use the table. Write each ratio in three ways.

5. What is the ratio of non-fiction books to fiction books?

6. What is the ratio of mystery books to non-fiction books?

7. What is the ratio of all books to comedy books?

8. What is the ratio of fiction books to all books?

SHELBY'S BOOK COLLECTION	
Number of Books	Type
4	Comedy
9	Fiction
7	Non-Fiction
3	Mystery

Lesson 27.3 (pages 448–449)

Tell whether the ratios are equivalent. Write yes or no.

1. 3:4 and 9:12

2. $\frac{1}{3}$ and $\frac{6}{9}$

3. 3 to 10 and 6 to 7

4. 1:2 and 2:3

5. $\frac{2}{5}$ and $\frac{4}{10}$

6. 4 to 9 and 2 to 6

Write three ratios that are equivalent to the given ratio.

7. $\frac{2}{3}$

8. $\frac{3}{5}$

9. 1 to 5

10. 6 to 1

11. 15:30

12. 20:60

13. $\frac{4}{5}$

14. 8 to 1

15. 3:21

16. 10 to 1

17. 12:36

18. $\frac{3}{4}$

Lesson 27.4 (pages 450–451)

Copy and complete the ratio table.

1.	**Number of Cars**	2	5	?	11	?
2.	**Number of Passengers**	10	25	40	?	75

3.	**Number of Buses**	1	6	12	?	?
4.	**Number of Passengers**	9	54	?	153	189

5.	**Number of Boxes**	1	4	?	8	?
6.	**Number of Cookies**	12	48	72	?	120

Lesson 27.5 Part 1 (pages 452–453)

Write *yes* or *no* to tell whether the shapes are similar.

1.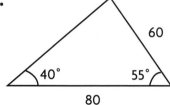

2.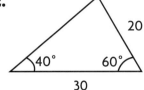

3.

4.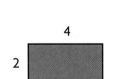

Find the length of the missing side in the similar shapes.

5.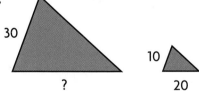

6.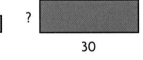

Lesson 27.5 Part 2 (pages 454–455)

Write a number sentence to solve.

1. Josie has a framed picture of her family that measures 8 in. by 10 in. She has a similar framed picture of her best friend that measures 4 in. on one side. What is the length of the other side of the frame?

2. Shakira has a vase with a 14-inch circumference. What is the diameter of Shakira's vase to the nearest half inch?

Chapter 28

Lesson 28.1 (pages 460–461)

Use counters to show the following on your 10-by-10 grid.
Draw a picture and write the percent.

1. 25 books out of 100 on a shelf

2. 42 women out of 100 people

3. 4 dogs out of 100 animals

4. 12 parrots out of 100 birds

Look at the picture. Write the percent.

5.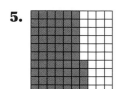

6.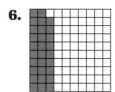

7.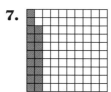

8.

For Exercises 9-10, choose the more reasonable percent. Write *a* or *b*.

9. "Very few people like anchovies. Out of 100 people, fewer than 12 like anchovies," said the pizza man.
a. 10%   **b.** 80%

10. "Almost every member of the team placed in at least one event," said the coach.
a. 15%   **b.** 98%

Lesson 28.2 (pages 462–463)

Write the number as a percent and a decimal.

1. forty-six hundredths

2. eight hundredths

3. twenty-one hundredths

4. twelve hundredths

Write the decimal as a percent.

5. 0.93   **6.** 0.41   **7.** 0.06   **8.** 0.50   **9.** 0.24

Write the percent as a decimal.

10. 92%   **11.** 17%   **12.** 3%   **13.** 70%   **14.** 37%

Lesson 28.3 (pages 464–465)

Write the percent as a fraction in simplest form.

1. 65%   **2.** 25%   **3.** ten percent   **4.** thirty per hundred

Write the fraction as a percent.

5. $\frac{9}{100}$ **6.** $\frac{8}{10}$ **7.** $\frac{3}{3}$ **8.** $\frac{4}{25}$

Write as a decimal and as a fraction in simplest form.

9. 13 percent   **10.** 77 percent   **11.** 40 percent   **12.** 70 percent

Lesson 28.4 (pages 466–467)

For Exercises 1–4, choose from the following benchmarks:
10%, 25%, 50%, 75%, or 100%.

1.   **2.**   **3.**   **4.**

Tell what benchmark percent you would use to estimate each percent.

5. 89%   **6.** 33%   **7.** 76%   **8.** 9%   **9.** 48%

10. 66%   **11.** 53%   **12.** 13%   **13.** 94%   **14.** 19%

Lesson 28.5 Part 1 (pages 468–469)

For Problems 1-2, use the circle graph.

1. Do more than half or less than half of the students surveyed have a pet?

2. What decimal shows the students who have a pet? who don't have a pet?

For Problems 3–5, use the circle graph.

3. Do more students have a cat or a dog?

4. What decimal represents the students who have a dog? a cat? a bird? a fish?

5. Which two categories cover one half of the circle graph?

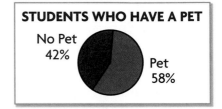

Lesson 28.5 Part 2 (pages 470–471)

Make a graph to solve.

1. The fifth graders voted for class president. They organized the data in the table. How can they show which two students received 50% of the votes? What graph should they make to display these data?

2. Tina saved $100 in 5 weeks from baby-sitting. She made a table showing the amount she saved each week. In which two weeks did she save 50% of the $100? What graph could she make to display these data?

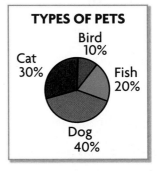

CLASS PRESIDENT ELECTION	
Student	Percent of Votes
Brett	20%
Carla	30%
Owen	40%
Kay	10%

TINA'S SAVINGS	
Week	Amount Saved
1	$30
2	$10
3	$20
4	$25
5	$15

TABLE OF MEASURES

METRIC	CUSTOMARY

Length

1,000 millimeters (mm) = 1 meter (m)	12 inches (in.) = 1 foot (ft)
100 centimeters (cm) = 1 meter	36 in., or 3 ft = 1 yard (yd)
10 decimeters (dm) = 1 meter	5,280 ft, or 1,760 yd = 1 mile (mi)
1 kilometer (km) = 1,000 meters	

Capacity

1,000 milliliters (mL) = 1 liter (L)	1 tablespoon (tbsp) = 3 teaspoons (tsp)
250 milliliters = 1 metric cup	8 fluid ounces (fl oz) = 1 cup (c)
	2 c = 1 pint (pt)
	2 pt = 1 quart (qt)
	4 qt = 1 gallon (gal)

Mass/Weight

1,000 milligrams (mg) = 1 gram (g)	16 ounces (oz) = 1 pound (lb)
1,000 grams = 1 kilogram (kg)	2,000 lb = 1 ton (T)

TIME	SYMBOLS

TIME

60 seconds (sec) = 1 minute (min)
60 minutes = 1 hour (hr)
24 hours = 1 day
7 days = 1 week (wk)
52 weeks = 1 year (yr)
12 months (mo) = 1 year
365 days = 1 year
366 days = 1 leap year

SYMBOLS

$=$	is equal to
$>$	is greater than
$<$	is less than
$\approx$	is approximately equal to
1:3	ratio of 1 to 3
$\overrightarrow{AB}$	ray AB
$\overleftrightarrow{AB}$	line AB
$\overline{AB}$	line segment AB
$\angle ABC$	angle ABC
$\triangle ABC$	triangle ABC
π	pi (3.14)
$\circ$	degree
°C	degree Celsius
°F	degree Fahrenheit
(2,3)	ordered pair 2,3

FORMULA

Perimeter of rectangle	$P = (2 \times l) + (2 \times w)$
Perimeter of square	$P = 4 \times s$
Circumference	$C = \pi \times d$
Area of Rectangle	$A = l \times w$
Volume of prism	$V = l \times w \times h$

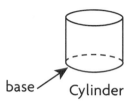

GLOSSARY

A

acute angle An angle that measures less than a right angle *(page 380)*

acute triangle A triangle that has three acute angles *(page 390)*
Example:

angle A figure formed by two rays that meet at a common endpoint *(page 380)*

area The number of square units needed to cover a surface *(page 78)*

Associative Property of Multiplication The property which states that when multiplying three or more factors, any two of the factors can be multiplied, and the remaining factors may then be multiplied without changing the total product *(page 70)*
Example: $(3 \times 4) \times 5 = 3 \times (4 \times 5)$
$$12 \times 5 = 3 \times 20$$
$$60 = 60$$

average The number found by dividing the sum of a set of numbers by the number of addends *(page 142)*

axes (of a graph) The horizontal and vertical number lines used in a rectangular graph or coordinate grid *(page 400)*

B

bar graph A graph that compares facts about groups *(page 148)*

base A face of a solid figure by which the figure is measured or named *(page 424)*
Example:

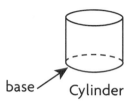

base — Cylinder

benchmark Numbers like 10, 25, 50, or 100 that are used to help make estimates *(page 4)*

benchmark percent A commonly used percent that is close to the amount you are estimating *(page 466)*

C

capacity The amount of liquid a container can hold *(page 230)*

cardinal Numbers that tell how many *(page 2)*
Examples: 4 puppies
93 cents

centimeter (cm) A unit for measuring length in the metric system *(page 226)*
0.01 meter = 1 centimeter

certain Something that will always happen *(page 172)*

chord A line segment with endpoints on a circle *(page 410)*
Example:

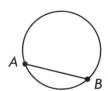

A
B

circle A closed figure with all points on the figure the same distance from the center point *(page 410)*
Example:

center point

circle graph A graph in the shape of a circle that shows fractions, percents, or decimals as parts of a whole *(page 156)*

circumference The perimeter of a circle *(page 412)*
Example:

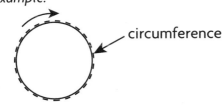

circumference

common factor A number that is a factor of two or more numbers *(page 264)*
Example: The common factors of 6 and 12 are 1, 2, 3, and 6.

common multiple A number that is a multiple of two or more numbers *(page 250)*
Example: A common multiple of 2, 3, 4, and 6 is 24.

Commutative Property of Multiplication The property which states that when the order of two factors is changed, the product is the same *(page 70)*
Example: $5 \times 7 = 7 \times 5$
$35 = 35$

compass A tool used to construct circles *(page 410)*

compatible numbers Pairs of numbers that are easy to compute mentally *(pages 26, 104)*

composite numbers Numbers that have more than two factors *(page 262)*
Example: 6 is a composite number since its factors are 1, 2, 3, and 6.

cone A solid figure with a circular base and one vertex *(page 426)*
Example:

congruent figures Figures that have the same size and shape *(page 396)*
Example:

cube A solid figure with six congruent square faces *(page 424)*

cubic units The number of cubes with dimensions of 1 unit × 1 unit × 1 unit that can fit inside a solid figure, that gives the volume *(page 76)*

cylinder A solid figure with two parallel bases that are congruent circles *(page 426)*
Example:

D

decimal A number that uses place value and a decimal point to show values less than one, such as tenths and hundredths *(page 34)*

decimeter (dm) A unit for measuring length in the metric system *(page 226)*
10 centimeters = 1 decimeter

degree (°) A unit for measuring angles and for measuring temperature *(page 382)*

degree Celsius (°C) A metric unit for measuring temperature *(page 354)*

degree Fahrenheit (°F) A unit of the customary system for measuring temperature *(page 354)*

diameter A line segment that passes through the center of a circle and has its endpoints on the circle *(page 410)*
Example:

direct measure Obtaining the measure of an object by using measuring devices *(page 340)*

Distributive Property of Multiplication The property which states that multiplying a sum by a number is the same as multiplying each addend by the number and then adding the products *(page 86)*
Example:
$$3 \times (4 + 2) = (3 \times 4) + (3 \times 2)$$
$$3 \times 6 = 12 + 6$$
$$18 = 18$$

divisible A number is divisible by another number if the result of the division is a whole number and the remainder is zero *(page 102)*
Example: 18 is divisible by 3.

edge An edge is formed when two faces of a solid figure meet *(page H30)*

equally likely Outcomes that have the same chance of occurring *(page 180)*

equilateral triangle A triangle with three congruent sides *(page 388)*
Example:

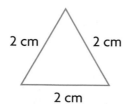

equivalent decimals Decimals that name the same number or amount *(page 40)*
Example: 0.5 = 0.50 = 0.500

equivalent fractions Fractions that name the same number or amount *(page 266)*
Example: $\dfrac{3}{4} = \dfrac{6}{8}$

equivalent ratios Ratios that name the same comparisons *(page 448)*

expanded form A way to write numbers by showing the value of each digit *(page 6)*
Example: 635 = 600 + 30 + 5

exponent A number that tells how many times the base is used as a factor *(page H32)*

exponent
↓
Example: $10^3 = 10 \times 10 \times 10$
10 is the base.

expression A collection of numbers, operation signs, and sometimes, variables that names a number *(page 40)*
Examples: 7 + 3   3 × (2 + n)

extrapolate To estimate or predict a value or quantity beyond the known range *(pages 148-149)*

face A flat surface of a solid figure *(page 424)*
Example:

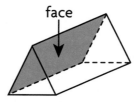

face

factor A number multiplied by another number to find a product *(page 262)*

formula A set of symbols that expresses a mathematical rule *(page 78)*
Example: $A = l \times w$

frequency The number of times an event occurs *(page 174)*

function The relationship between two sets *(page 448)*

G

gram (g) A unit for measuring mass in the metric system *(page 228)*
1,000 milligrams = 1 gram

greatest common factor (GCF) The greatest factor that two or more numbers have in common *(page 264)*
Example: 6 is the GCF of 18 and 30.

H

histogram A bar graph that shows the number of times data occur within a certain range or interval *(page H36)*

impossible Something that will never happen *(page 172)*

inequality A mathematical sentence that shows that two expressions do not represent the same quantity *(page 10)*
Example: $3 + 2 > 4 - 1$

intersecting lines Two lines that cross at exactly one point *(page 378)*
Example:

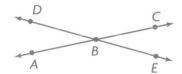

interval The distance between the numbers on the scale of a graph *(page 144)*

inverse operations Opposite operations that undo each other; addition and subtraction or multiplication and division are inverse operations. *(page 18)*

isosceles triangle A triangle with at least two congruent sides and two congruent angles *(page 388)*
Example:

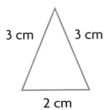

3 cm   3 cm

2 cm

K

kilogram (kg) A unit for measuring mass in the metric system *(page 228)*
1,000 grams = 1 kilogram

kiloliter (kL) A unit for measuring capacity in the metric system *(page 230)*
1,000 L = 1 kiloliter

kilometer (km) A unit for measuring length in the metric system *(page 226)*
1,000 meters = 1 kilometer

L

least common denominator (LCD) The least common multiple of two or more denominators *(page 282)*
Example:
The LCD for $\frac{1}{4}$ and $\frac{5}{6}$ is twelfths.

least common multiple (LCM) The least number other than zero that is a multiple of two or more given numbers *(page 250)*
Example: The LCM of 6 and 9 is 18.

like fractions Fractions that have the same denominator *(page 278)*
Example: $\frac{1}{8}$ and $\frac{5}{8}$

line A straight path extending in both directions with no endpoints *(page 378)*
Example:

line graph A graph that shows how data change over time *(page 148)*
Example:

line of symmetry A line that divides a figure so that the two parts of the figure are congruent *(page 398)*
Example:

line plot A diagram that shows the frequency of data *(page 148)*

line segment Part of a line between two endpoints *(page 378)*
Example:

M   N

line symmetry When a figure can be folded on a line so that its two parts are congruent *(page 398)*

liter (L) A unit for measuring capacity in the metric system *(page 230)*
1,000 milliliters = 1 liter

map scale A ratio that compares the distance on a map with the actual distance *(page 450)*

mass The measure of the quantity of matter of an object *(page 228)*

mean One way to find a number that represents all the numbers in a set *(page 142)*

median The middle number in an ordered series of numbers *(page 140)*
Example:
The median of 1, 3, 4, 6, and 7 is 4.

memory key A key on the computer keyboard that is used to store numbers *(page H60)*

meter (m) A unit for measuring length in the metric system *(page 226)*
100 centimeters = 1 meter

milligram A unit for measuring mass in the metric system *(page 228)*
1,000 milligrams = 1 gram

milliliter (mL) A unit for measuring capacity in the metric system *(page 230)*
0.001 L = 1 milliliter

millimeter (mm) A unit for measuring length in the metric system *(page 226)*
1,000 millimeters = 1 meter

mixed number A number that is made up of a whole number and a fraction or a whole number and a decimal *(pages 204, 248)*

Examples: $2\frac{1}{2}$ or 2.5

mode The number that occurs most often in a list of data *(page 140)*
Example: The mode of 1, 3, 4, 4, and 6 is 4.

multiple A number that is the product of a given number and another whole number *(page 250)*

multistep problems Problems that require more than one step to solve *(page H60)*

N

net A two-dimensional pattern for a three-dimensional solid *(page 426)*

nominal A number that names a thing *(page 2)*
Examples: 337 Havana St.
Hank is number 44 on his team.

O

obtuse angle An angle that measures greater than a right angle *(page 380)*
Example:

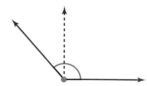

obtuse triangle A triangle that has one obtuse angle *(page 390)*
Example:

order of operations The correct order in which operations are done within an expression *(page H61)*

ordered pair A pair of numbers used to locate a point on a grid *(page 400)*
Example: (5,3)

ordinal Numbers that tell position or order *(page 2)*
Examples: Jon won first place.
Jean is 4th in line.

parallel lines Lines in a plane that stay exactly the same distance apart *(page 378)*
Example:

parallelogram A quadrilateral with opposite sides parallel and congruent *(page 386)*

percent A ratio of some number to 100 *(page 460)*

perimeter The distance around a figure *(page 412)*

period Each group of three digits in a number *(page 8)*

perpendicular lines Two lines that intersect to form right angles *(page 378)*
Example:

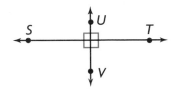

pi (π) The ratio of the circumference of a circle to the length of its diameter (π = 3.14) *(page 413)*

plane A flat surface that extends without end in all directions *(page 378)*

point An exact location in space *(page 378)*

point symmetry When a figure can be turned about a central point and still look the same *(page 398)*
Example:

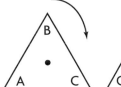

possible outcomes Something that has a chance of happening in an experiment *(page 174)*

precise Finding a unit that measures nearest to the actual length of an object *(page 340)*

prime numbers Numbers that have only two factors, 1 and the number itself *(page 262)*
Example: 5, 7, 11, 13, 17, and 19 are prime numbers.

prism A solid figure whose ends are congruent, parallel polygons, and whose sides are rectangles *(page 424)*
Example:

pentagonal
prism

probability The chance of an event happening *(page 180)*

$$P = \frac{\text{number of ways the event occurs}}{\text{number of ways all events can occur}}$$

Property of One for Multiplication The property which states that the product of any number and 1 is that number *(page 70)*
Examples: 5 × 1 = 5
16 × 1 = 16

protractor A tool for measuring the size of the opening of an angle *(page 382)*

pyramid A solid figure with a base that is a polygon and three or more faces that are triangles with a common vertex *(page 424)*
Example:

 Q

quadrilateral A polygon with four angles and four sides *(page 386)*

R

radius A line segment with one endpoint at the center of a circle and the other endpoint on the circle *(page 410)*
Example:

range The difference between the greatest and least numbers in a set of data *(page 146)*

ratio A comparison of two numbers *(page 444)*

ray A part of a line that begins at one endpoint and extends forever in only one direction *(page 380)*

reflection When a figure is flipped across a line *(page 400)*

relative size The size of one number in comparison to the size of another number or numbers *(page 42)*

rhombus A parallelogram with four congruent sides whose opposite angles are congruent *(page 386)*
Example:

rhombus

right angle An angle that forms a square corner and measures 90° *(page 380)*
Example:

right triangle A triangle with one right angle *(page 390)*
Example:

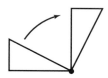

rotation When a figure is turned around a point or vertex *(page 400)*
Example:

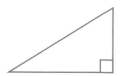

S

scale The series of numbers placed at fixed distances on a graph *(page 144)*

scalene triangle A triangle with three unequal angles and sides that are not congruent *(page 388)*
Example:

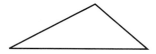

scientific notation A method of expressing a number between 1 and 10 as a power of 10 *(page H58)*
Example: $7.0 \times 10^5 = 700,000$

similar figures Figures that have the same shape but may not have the same size *(page 452)*
Example:

simplest form A fraction that has 1 as the greatest common factor of the numerator and denominator *(page 272)*

simulation To do something in a way that is easier than the actual experiment, or to match possible outcomes of a real event *(page H38)*

slope The incline of a line *(page 163)*

standard form A way to write numbers using the digits 0–9, with each digit having a place value *(page 8)*

survey To ask questions to find the most frequent choice of a group *(page 150)*

T

terminating decimal A decimal that ends; a decimal for which the division operation results in a remainder of zero *(page H67)*

Example: $\frac{1}{2} = 0.5$

tessellation A repeating pattern of closed figures that covers a surface with no gaps and no overlaps *(page 402)*
Example:

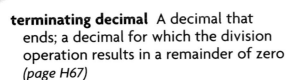

thousandth One part of 1,000 equal parts *(page 36)*

transformation The movement of a figure, either a translation, rotation, or reflection *(page 400)*

translation When a figure slides in any direction *(page 400)*
Example:

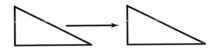

trapezoid A quadrilateral with only one pair of sides parallel *(page 386)*
Example:

trapezoid

tree diagram An organized list that shows all possible outcomes of an event *(page 176)*

U

unlike fractions Fractions that have different denominators *(pages 280, 294)*

Example: $\frac{3}{4}$ and $\frac{2}{3}$

V

Venn diagram A diagram that uses geometric shapes to show relationships *(page 272)*
Example:

Numbers Divisible by Two or Three

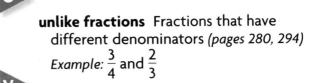

vertex The point where two rays of an angle, two sides of a polygon, or three or more edges of a solid figure meet *(pages 380, 424)*
Example:

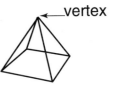
vertex

volume The measure of the space a solid figure occupies *(page 76)*

Z

Zero Property for Multiplication The property which states that the product of zero and any number is zero *(page 70)*
Examples: $13 \times 0 = 0$
$0 \times 7 = 0$

INDEX

practice with, 225, 227, 229, 231, 233, 235, 339,
341, 343, 345, 347, 349, 351, 353, 355, 356,
383, H19, H25
precision in, 338–339, 340–341
renaming units to add or subtract, 344–345,
350–351
Roman, 356
temperature, 2, 354–355
units of area, 78, 358
units of capacity or volume
customary, 2, 78, 80, 339, 346–347, 356,
H24–H25
metric, 36, 230–231, 232
units of length
customary, 2, 340–341, 342–343,
344–345, H24–H25
metric, 34, 225, 226–227, 232, 238,
H18–H19
units of mass or weight
customary, 2, 348–349, 356, H24–H25,
H48
metric, 228–229, 232, 238
units of time, 322, 350–351
using rulers to measure length, 224–225,
338–339, 340–341
using scale to weigh, 2, 356
using thermometers, 354–355
See also Customary units; Metric system;
Rulers
Median, 140–141, 142–143, 152
Memory keys, H34–H35, H60
Mental math
addition, 26–27, 56–57
division, 102–103, 104–105, 106–107,
108–109, 120–121, 122–123, 124–125,
126–127
multiplication, 86–87, 90–91, 200–201, 203,
204–205, H10–H11
practice with, 19, 27, 57, 87, 91, 103, 105, 107,
109, 121, 123, 125, 127, 201, 203, 205, 327
subtraction, 18–19, 56–57, 326–327
See also Estimation; Rounding
Meters, 34, 225, 226–227, 234–235, 238,
H18–H19
Metric system
analyzing units with prefixes and base units,
232–233, 234–235, H18–H19
millimeter, 226–227, 232, 235
relating metric units, 34, 226–227, 228–229,
230–231, 232–233, 234–235, H18–H19
units of area, hectare, 358
units of capacity and volume, 36, 230–231,
232–233
units of length, 34, 226–227, 232–233, 238,
H18–H19
units of mass, 228–229, 232–233
units of temperature, 354–355
Micrometer caliper, 338
Miles, 342–343, H24–H25
Milligrams, 228–229, 232–233
Milliliters, 36, 230–231, 232–233
Millimeters, 226–227, 232, 235
Minutes, 322, 350–351, 352–353
Mirror images. See Symmetry
Mixed Applications. See Problem solving
Mixed numbers
adding, 326–327, 328–329, 332–333, 336
decimals, 38, 204–205
defined, 248
estimating, 326–327, 328, 330
modeling with fraction bars, 328, 330,
334–335, H48–H49
multiplying by decimals, 204–205
multiplying by fractions, 366–367, 368–369
practice with, 205, 327, 329, 331, 333, 335, 367,
369, H49

renaming, 248–249, H48–H49
rounding, 326–327
subtracting, 326–327, 330–331, 332–333,
334–335, 336
Mixed Review. See Assessment
Mode, 140–141, 142–143, 152
Modeling
addition
of decimals, 50–51
of like fractions, 278–279, 316–317
of unlike fractions, 280–281, 282–283,
284–285, 286–287, 310–311, 316–317
decimals, 33, 34–35, 36–37, 40–41, 42–43, 46,
50–51, 192–193, 194–195, 196–197, 198–199,
200, 214–215, 216–217, 362–363, H4–H5,
H16–H17
Distributive Property, 86–87
division, 114, 214–215, 216–217, H12–H13
equivalent decimals with decimal squares,
H16–H17
equivalent fractions, 266–267, 268–269,
270–271, H22–H23
factors with an array, 262, 264
fractions
beads, 309, 311
drawings, 258, 262, 329, 359, 360, 387
folded paper, 362–363
fraction bars, 270–271, 278–279,
280–281, 282–283, 284–285, 291,
292–293, 294–295, 296–297, 316, 328,
330, 334–335, H42–H43, H48–H49,
H50–H51
fraction circles, 158–159, 160–161,
H44–H45, H50–H51
fraction squares, 364–365, 366–367,
368–369
fraction strips, 246–247, 251, 252, 254,
288
musical notes, 260–261, H46–H47
number lines, 246–247, 251, 266–267,
268–269, 310–311, 326
a ruler, 298–299, 300, 316
geometric solids, 423, 426–427, 428–429,
430–431
least common multiples using
counters, 250–251
a number line, 251
mean of data, 142–143
multiplication, 72–73, 192–193, 194–195,
196–197, 198–199, 364–365, 366–367,
368–369, H8–H9
percent using decimal grid, 459, 460–461,
462–463, 464, 467
place value, 34–35, 36–37, H16–H17, H32
practice with, 37, 51, 73, 77, 87, 97, 193, 199,
215, 237, 247, 258, 263, 269, 279, 281, 283,
285, 287, 293, 295, 297, 299, 321, 363, 365,
367, 369, 385, 387, 405, 427, 429, 445, 447,
H13, H15, H17, H21, H23, H43, H45
probability experiments, H38–H39
quadrilaterals with tangrams, 386
ratios using counters, 444–445
subtraction
of like fractions, 292–293
of mixed numbers, 330–331, 332–333,
334–335, 336
of unlike fractions, 294–295, 296–297,
298–299
subtraction with counters, 20–21
volume of a prism, 76–77
Money
adding, 28–29, 49, 52–53, 57, 58–59, 191
balancing a checkbook, 60–61
decimal system and, 41, 50, 52–53, 60–61,
193, H4
dimes, 462, H4, H17

dividing, 209, 217, 222
dollars, 460, 462, H4, H16–H17
making a budget, 49, 85, 191
multiplying, 201, 202–203, 204–205, 206,
209, 221
pennies, 25, 195, 460, 462, H4
sales tax, 205
See also Connections, Consumer
Months, 138, 350–351
More Practice, H70–H122
Multicultural Connections. See Connections,
Cultural
Multiples
common, 250–251, 252–253, 254–255,
256–257, 292, 296
defined, 250
least common, 250–251, 252–253, 254–255,
256, 296, 314–315, 316
of ten, 120–121
Multiplication
Associative Property of, 70–71
with calculators, 92–93, 202–203, 342–343,
348–349
to change units in measurement, 234–235,
236–237, H18–H19
Commutative Property of, 70–71
of decimals, 192–193, 194–195, 196–197,
198–199, 200–201, 202–203, 204–205,
220–221, 236–237, 362
Distributive Property of, 86–87
and division, 108–109, 112–113, 120–121,
122–123, 124–125, 126–127, 132, 217,
218–219, 220–221
estimating products, 90–91, 200–201,
202–203, 204–205, H10–H11
factors, 262–263, 264–265
to find equivalent fractions, 266–267
to find perimeter and area, 82, 94–95,
96–97
to find sales tax, 204–205
to find volume, 76–77, 78–79, 80–81, 230,
430–431, 432–433, 434–435
of fractions, 252–253, 266–267, 360–361,
362–363, 364–365, 366–367, 368–369, 370
mental math, 86–87, 90–91, 200–201, 203,
204–205, H10–H11
modeling, 72–73, 86–87, 192–193, 194–195,
196–197, 198–199, 364–365, 366–367,
368–369
of money amounts, 201, 202–203, 205, 206,
221
by one digit, 70–71, 72–73, 74–75, 76–77,
78–79, H8–H9
practice with, 73, 75, 77, 79, 81, 82, 87, 89, 91,
93, 95, 125, 127, 131, 193, 195, 197, 201, 203,
205, 213, 217, 235, 343, 347, 349, 361, 363,
365, 367, H9, H11
properties of, 70–71
Property of One, 70–71, 262
recording, 72–73, 192–193, 194–195, H8–H9
by three-digit numbers, 92–93, 95
by two-digit numbers, 86–87, 88–89, 90–91,
94–95, 96–97, H10–H11
of whole numbers, 69, 70–71, 72–73, 74–75,
76–77, 78–79, 80–81, 82, 85, 86–87, 88–89,
90–91, 92–93, 94–95, 96–97, 98
Zero Property for, 70–71
Multistep problems, H60

N

Nets, 426–427, 436
Nominal numbers, 2–3
Number lines
comparing numbers on, 10, 42–43
decimals on, 42–43, 200, H6–H7
finding sums and differences on, 310–311

fractions on, 246–247, 256, 258, 266–267, 268, 310–311
least common multiples on, 251
probability of an event on, 180
using to round, H6
Number sense. *See* Estimation; Mental math; Rounding
Number theory, 262–263, 264–265, 266–267, 268–269, 270–271, 272–273
Numbers
cardinal, 2–3
compatible, 26, 104, 120–121, H40
composite, 262–263
even or odd, 171
expanded form of, 6–7, 8–9, 34–35, 36–37, 38–39
nominal, 2–3
order of, 10–11, 42–43, 140–141
ordered pairs, 400–401
ordinal, 2–3
perfect, 114
periods, 6, 8
pi, 413
prime, 262–263
standard form of, 8–9, 34–35, 36–37, 38–39
in words, 8–9, 34–35, 36–37, 38–39
See also Decimals; Fractions; Mixed numbers; Place value; Whole numbers
Numerators, 246, 278, H14, H20

O

Obtuse angles, 380–381, 390–391, 416
Obtuse triangles, 390–391
Octagon, 423, 425, H26–H27
Ones place, 6, 8, 20–21, 22, 194–195, 210, 234, H32
Operations
choosing, 24–25, 30, 58–59, 128–129, 132, 168, 220–221, 222, 234–235, 318–319, 342–343, 348–349
inverse, 18–19, 128–129, 220–221, 222
See also Addition; Division; Multiplication; Subtraction
Order
of addends, 50
of decimals, 42–43
of fractions, 246–247, 256, 258, 266–267, 268, 310–311
of operations, H61
of whole numbers, 10–11, 140–141
Order Property, 50
Ordered pairs, 400–401
Ordinal numbers, 2–3
Organized list, 176–177, 178–179, 184
Ounces
fluid, 346–347
unit of weight, 348–349, H24–H25
Outcomes, 172–173
See also Possible outcomes
Overestimates, 28

P

Parallel lines, 378–379
Parallelograms, 386–387
Patterns
in division, 118–119, 210–211, 214–215, 217, 218–219, 222
finding, 82, 210–211
functions and, 82, 102–103, 118–119, 194–195, 210–211, 214–215, 217, 218–219, 443, 444–445, 446–447, 448–449, 450–451, 452–453, 454–455, H54–H55
in multiplication, 82, 194–195
in polygons, 392, 398–399, H28–H29
tessellations in, 402–403, 404–405

Pennies, 25, 195, 460, 462, H4
Pentagon, H26–H27
Pentagonal prisms, 424–425, 427, H30
Pentagonal pyramids, 424–425, 427, H30
Percent
benchmark, 466–467
in a circle graph, 468–469, 470–471, 472
as a decimal, 462–463, 464–465, 472, H56–H57
defined, 460
finding with a calculator, 464–465, H56–H57
as a fraction, 464–465, 472, H56–H57
modeling on decimal squares, 459, 460–461, 462–463, 464, 467
Perfect numbers, 114
Performance. *See* Assessment
Perimeter
of a circle (circumference), 412–413, 420
of polygons, 412
of rectangles, 85, 94–95
of squares, 94
Periods, 6, 8
Perpendicular lines, 378–379
Pi, 413
Pints, 346–347, H24–H25
Place value
base-ten blocks and, 34–35, 36–37, 40–41, 50–51, 194–195, H8, H12–H13, H32
charts, 6, 8, 34, 36–37, 38, 50, 210, 232, 236, H32
of decimals, 34–35, 36–37, 38–39, 50–51, 52–53, 54–55, 56–57, 194–195, 210–211, 214–215, 216–217, 462–463, 464–465, H16–H17
to hundred millions place, 8–9
to hundred thousands place, 6–7, H32–H33
hundredths, 34–35, 36–37, 38–39, 42–43, 45, 50–51, 52–53, 54–55, 56–57, 194–195, 459, 462–463, 464–465, H16–H17
in metric units, 232–233, 234–235, 236–237
multiples of ten and, 120–121
ones, 194–195
periods, 6, 8
powers of ten and, H32
practice with, 7, 9, 37, 51, 91, 93, 195, 463, 465, H17, H33
stem-and-leaf plots and, 142–143, 148–149
tens, 6–7, 8, 38–39, H32
tenths, 34–35, 36–37, 38–39, 50–51, 56–57, 194–195, 214, 216–217, H6–H7, H16–H17
thousandths, 36–37, 50–51, 54–55, 56–57
of whole numbers, 6–7, 8–9, 10–11
Plane figures
area of, 76, 78–79
circles, 409, 410–411, 412–413, 414–415, 416–417, 418–419, 420, H52–H53
congruent, 396–397
perimeter of, 85, 94–95, 412–413
polygons, 377, 386–387, 388–389, 390–391, 392, 423, H26–H27
similar, 452–453
symmetry in, 398–399, H28–H29
transforming on a coordinate grid, 400–401
Planes, 378–379
Plotting data
line plot, 148–149
stem-and-leaf plot, 142–143, 148–149
P.M., 149, 350–351, 352
Point
coordinates on a grid, 400–401
defined, 378
endpoint, 380
of intersection, 378–379
symmetry, 398–399, H28–H29
vertex, 380, 390, H30–H31
See also Decimal points

Polygons
identifying, 377, 386–387, H26–H27
making octagons, 423
naming, 377, 424
parallelograms, 386–387
quadrilaterals, 386–387
rectangles, 76, 78, 94–95, 96–97
rhombus, 386–387
squares, 94, 96–97, 386–387
trapezoids, 386–387
triangles, 388–389, 390–391, 392
See also Plane figures
Possible outcomes, 172–173, 174–175, 176–177, 178–179, 180–181, 182–183, 184, H38–H39, H54–H55
Pounds, 2, 348–349, H24–H25
Powers of ten, H32–H33
Precision in measurement, 338–339, 340–341
Predicting outcomes, 172–173, 174–175, 176–177, 178–179, 180–181, 182–183, H54–H55
Prime numbers, 262–263
Prism
bases of, 424–425, H30–H31
classifying, 424–425, H30–H31
modeling with nets, 423, 426–427
volume of, 76–77, 78–79, 80–81, 430–431, 432–433, 434–435, 436
Probability
certain events, 172–173
equally likely outcomes, 180–181
experiments with, 172–173, 174–175, 178–179, 180–181, 184, H38–H39
fair and unfair games, 171
as a fraction, 180–181, 182–183, H54–H55
impossible events, 172–173
practice with, 173, 175, 177, 179, 181, H39, H55
predicting outcomes, 172–173, 174–175, 176–177, 178–179, 180–181, 182–183, H54–H55
as a ratio, H54–H55
recording outcomes, 171, 174–175, 176–177, 184, H38–H39
simulations, H38–H39
tree diagrams, 176–177, 178–179, 184
Problem solving
applications. *Provided in every lesson*
choose the method of computation, 13, 29, 45, 61, 81, 97, 113, 131, 151, 167, 179, 199, 213, 237, 257, 269, 287, 301, 321, 333, 353, 369, 385, 405, 415, 433, 455, 471
choose the operation, 24–25, 30, 58–59, 128–129, 132, 168, 220–221, 234–235, 318–319, 342–343, 348–349
choose a strategy, 13, 15, 29, 31, 45, 47, 61, 63, 66, 81, 83, 97, 99, 113, 115, 131, 133, 136, 151, 153, 167, 169, 179, 185, 188, 199, 207, 213, 223, 237, 239, 242, 257, 259, 269, 275, 287, 289, 301, 303, 306, 321, 323, 333, 337, 353, 357, 369, 371, 374, 385, 393, 405, 407, 415, 421, 433, 437, 440, 455, 457, 471, 473, 476
conduct a simulation, H38–H39
estimate or exact answer, 28–29
relevant/irrelevant information, 12, 28, 44, 60, 96, 112, 130, 150, 166, 178, 198, 212, 236, 256, 268, 286, 300, 320, 332, 352, 368, 384, 404, 414, 432, 454, 470
use a schedule, 352–353
See also Critical Thinking
Problem-solving strategies
act it out, 414–415
draw a diagram, 96–97, 236–237, 256–257, 268–269, 320–321, 384–385
guess and check, 112–113
make a graph, 150–151, 166–167, 470–471
make a model, 198–199, 286–287, 368–369, 404–405

make an organized list, 178–179
make a table, 44–45, 352–353
use estimation, 28–29
use a formula, 80–81, 432–433
use a table, 12–13
work backward, 300–301, 332–333
write a number sentence, 60–61, 130–131,
212–213, 454–455

Products
checking, 202–203
defined, 262
estimating, 90–91, 92–93, H10–H11
zeros in, 70, 90–91, 202–203

Projects. *See* Team-Up Time Projects

Properties
of addition, 50
Associative, 50, 70–71, 79
Commutative, 50, 70–71, 361
Distributive, 86–87
Grouping, 50
of multiplication, 70–71, 79, 86–87, 361
of One, 70–71, 262
Order, 50
practice with, 71, 87, 131
Zero, 50, 52, 70–71

Protractors, 382–383, 390–391, 396–397,
418–419, H52–H53

Puzzles, tangrams, 244–245, 386–387

Pyramid
base of, 424–425
defined, 424
modeling with nets, 426–427
types of, 424–425, H30–H31

Q

Quadrilaterals
defined, 386–387, H26–H27
parallelograms, 386–387
rectangles, 76, 78, 94–95, 96–97, 386–387
rhombus, 386–387
squares, 386–387
trapezoids, 386–387

Quarts, 152, 346–347, H24–H25

Quotients. *See* Division

R

Radius (plural: radii), 410–411

Range of data, H36

Ratios
equivalent, 448–449, 450–451, 452–453, 456
expressing three ways, 446–447
in similar figures, 443, 452–453, 454–455
map scale, 450–451, 456
modeling, 444–445, 456
percents, 464–465, 468–469, 472, H56–H57
probability, 180–181, 182–183, H54–H55
used to make an enlargement, 443

Rays, 380–381

Reasoning. *See* Critical Thinking

Rectangles
area of, 78–79, 82
perimeter of, 85, 94–95, 96–97
squares, 82, 94, 96–97

Rectangular prism
cubic units of, 76, 230, 430
defined, 424–425
estimating volume of, 434–435
volume of, 76–77, 78–79, 80–81, 230,
430–431, 432–433, 434–435

Rectangular pyramid, 424–425, 426–427

Reflection, 395, 400–401

Regrouping
in addition, 24–25, 50–51, 52–53
in division, H12–H13

in multiplication, 72–73, 74–75, 88–89,
H8–H9
in subtraction, 20–21, 22–23, 24–25, 54–55,
H2–H3, H48–H49

Relative size, 42

Remainders
divisibility and, 102–103
interpreting, 110–111, 112
ways to write, 110–111

Renaming
fractions, 248–249, 250–251, 252–253,
254–255, 256–257, 258, 266–267, 268–269,
366
measurement units, 344–345, 350–351
mixed numbers, 248–249, H48–H49

Review. *See* Assessment

Rhombus, 386–387

Richter scale, H33

Right angle, 378–379, 380–381, 390–391, 416

Right triangle, 390–391

Rotation, 395, 400–401

Rounding
decimals, 56–57, 200, H6–H7
factors, 90–91, H10–H11
fractions, 310–311
mixed numbers, 326–327
percent, 466–467
practice with, 91, 311, 327, 467, H7, H11
rules for, 26, 56, 90, H6, H10
whole numbers, 26–27, 90–91, H6, H10–H11

Rulers
customary, 2, 277, 298–299, 300, 338–339,
340–341
metric, 224–225
used to measure, 2, 225, 277, 339, 340–341
used to model fractions, 298–299, 300, 316

S

Scale drawings, 443, 450–451, 456

Scalene triangle, 388–389

Scales
choosing for graphs, 144–145
intervals, 144–145
map, 450–451, 456
weight, 2, 114, 356

Schedules, 352–353

School-Home Connections. *See* Home Note

Science Connections. *See* Connections

Scientific notation, H58

Seconds, 277, 322, 350–351,

Sieve of Eratosthenes, 263

Similar figures, 452–453, 454–455

Simplest form of fractions, 270–271, 272–273,
278, 284, 292, 302, 312–313, 314–315, 316–317,
364, 366, 464–465, H44–H45, H57

Simulations, H38–H39

Slides, 395, 400–401

Slope, 163

Social Studies Connections. *See* Connections

Solid figures
cone, 426–427
cylinder, 408–409, 426–427
prism, 76–77, 78–79, 80–81, 423, 424–425,
426–427, 430–431, 432–433, 434–435, 436,
H30–H31
pyramid, 424–425, 426–427, H30–H31
volume of, 76–77, 78–79, 80–81, 230–231,
430–431, 432–433, 434–435

Sports Connections. *See* Connections

Square pyramids, 424–425, 426–427, H30–H31

Square units, 76, 78–79, 82

Squares
identifying, 386–387
perimeter of, 94, 96–97

Standard form
of decimals, 34, 36, 38
of whole numbers, 6, 8, H58

Statistics. *See* Data; Graphs; Tables and Charts

Stem-and-leaf plot, 142–143, 148–149

Study Guide and Review. *See* Assessment

Subtraction
addition and, 18–19, 24–25, 128–129, 316–317,
318–319, 326–327
with calculators, 24–25, 58
checking differences, 18–19
of decimals, 54–55, 56–57, 58–59, 60–61, 62,
206
estimating differences, 56–57, 326–327
of fractions, 292–293, 294–295, 296–297,
298–299, 300–301, 310–311, 312–313,
314–315, 316–317, 318–319, H44–H45
of mixed numbers, 326–327, 330–331,
332–333, 334–335, H48–H49
modeling, 20–21, 54, 292–293
of money, 60–61, H2
practice with, 19, 21, 23, 55, 59, 61, 129, 293,
295, 297, 299, 301, 311, 313, 315, 317, 319, 321,
331, 335, 345, 351, 355
recording, 54, 334
regrouping in, 20–21, 22–23, 24–25, 54–55,
H2–H3, H48–H49
of three-digit numbers, 18–19, 20–21, 22–23,
24–25
of two-digit numbers, 18–19
with units of measure, 344–345, 350–351
of whole numbers, 18–19, 20–21, 22–23,
24–25
across zeros, 22–23, H2–H3

Sums. *See* Addition

Surveys, 17, 150, 155

Symbols
angle, 380
degree, 382
is approximately equal to, 26, 92, 106
less than and greater than, 11, 43, 57, 73, 89,
125, 253
line, 380
line segment, 378
ray, 380

Symmetry, 398–399, H28–H29

T

Tables and Charts
analyzing data from, 9, 11, 12–13, 15, 19, 25,
26–27, 29, 39, 43, 55, 81, 103, 129, 140–141,
143, 144–145, 146–147, 148–149, 150–151,
152, 158–159, 165, 175, 183, 205, 208–209,
211, 220, 225, 230–231, 257, 265, 267, 287,
321, 385, 413, 415, 420, 447, 450, 469, 471,
H5, H7, H35, H38
making, 44–45, 69, 102–103, 139, 155, 171,
174–175, 352–353, 392, 420, 443
practice with, 45, 103, 175, 351, 353, 449, 451,
H5, H19
relating units of measure, 226, 228, 230, 232,
234, 236, 342, 346, 348, 350, H24
schedules, 352–353
tally, 174–175
using. *See* analyzing data from
See also Place value, charts

Talk About It, 4, 6, 8, 21, 22, 34, 37, 38, 40, 50,
52, 70, 74, 76, 86, 88, 90, 94, 103, 104, 106,
110, 118, 120, 124, 127, 128, 140, 142, 144, 156,
158, 162, 172, 174, 175, 176, 180, 182, 193, 194,
200, 202, 204, 210, 214, 218, 220, 226, 228,
231, 232, 234, 250, 254, 263, 264, 266, 270,
272, 273, 278, 281, 282, 294, 298, 310, 315, 316,
317, 318, 326, 328, 330, 334, 340, 342, 346, 350,
354, 360, 362, 364, 378, 380, 382, 383, 386,

ART CREDITS

Ortelius Design 10, 21, 45, 450; Raymond Smith 8; All other art not listed by The Quarasan Group, Inc.

PHOTO CREDITS

Page Placement Key: (t)-top (c)-center (b)-bottom (r)-right (l)-left

Chapter 1 Harcourt Brace & Company 3 (tl), (tc), (c); 4 (tr); 14 (br); xviii-1 (l), 3 (tr) ASG Sherman Graphics, Inc.; 4 (c), (cr) Rich Franco; 4 (bl), (bc) ASG Sherman Graphics, Inc.; 7 (r), 12 (r) Allan Landau; 14 (tr) ASG Sherman Graphics, Inc. **Other** xviii-1 (bkg) James Martin/Tony Stone Worldwide; xviii-1 (tr) Corel Co.; xviii-1 (c) ; xviii-1 (c) Corel Co.; xviii-1 (cr) SuperStock, Inc; xviii-1 (cr) Corel Co.; 1 (tr) Stuart Westmorland/Tony Stone Worldwide; 5 (br) John Lei/Stock•Boston; 6 (tr) NASA; 6 (b) NASA; 8 (tr) Everett Collection; 9 (r) Uniphoto; 11 (r) Chris Noble/Tony Stone Worldwide. **Chapter 2 Harcourt Brace & Company** 29 (r); 16 (c), 17 (r), 18 (t), 25 (br) ASG Sherman Graphics, Inc.; 26 (c) Allan Landau; 27 (cr), 28 (c) ASG Sherman Graphics, Inc. **Other** 18 (br) PhotoDisc; 19 (tr) David Young-Wolff/PhotoEdit; 20 (tc) PhotoDisc; 20 (tr) Mark Lewis/Tony Stone Worldwide; 23 (r) SuperStock, Inc; 24 (t) PhotoDisc; 24 (r) John Lei/Stock•Boston; 25 (cr) Stephen Dunn/Allsport U.S.A.; 28 (b) SuperStock, Inc; 30 (c) Michele & Tom Grimm/Tony Stone Worldwide; 30 (cr) Gary Retherford/Photo Researchers, Inc. **Chapter 3 Harcourt Brace & Company;** 37 (r); 46 (cr); 32 (c), (r), (br), 33 (br), 34 (r), 36 (cr) ASG Sherman Graphics, Inc.; 44 (cr) Rich Franco; 46 (tr) Eric Camden; 46 (br) ASG Sherman Graphics, Inc. **Other** 32 (c) Chia Pet® is a registered trademark and is used with permission by Joseph Enterprises, Inc.; 32-33 (bkg) SuperStock, Inc; 35 (cr) Focus on Sports; 36 (tr) Dennis O'Clair/Tony Stone Worldwide; 38 (t) Benjamin Rondel/The Stock Market; 39 (t) Thomas Zimmerman/Tony Stone Worldwide; 39 (c) Tony Stone Worldwide; 40 (r) The Stock Market; 42 (r) Doug Pensinger/Allsport U.S.A.; 43 (b) PhotoDisc. **Chapter 4 Harcourt Brace & Company** 61 (c); 48 (c), (c), 50 (tr) ASG Sherman Graphics, Inc.; 51 (t) Allan Landau; 53 (c) ASG Sherman Graphics, Inc.; 54 (tr) Allan Landau; 56 (tr), 58 (tc), 59 (c) ASG Sherman Graphics, Inc.; 60 (b) Weronica Ankarorn; 61 (r) ASG Sherman Graphics, Inc. **Other** 48-49 (bkg) Thomas Styczynski/Tony Stone Worldwide; 49 (b) Corel Co.; 55 (cr) Bob Daemmrich/Stock•Boston; 56 (cr) Jon Feingersh/The Stock Market; 57 (r) David Young-Wolff/PhotoEdit; 62 (tr) John Elk III/Bruce Coleman, Inc.; 66 (cr) greg Crisp/Uniphoto. **Chapter 5 Harcourt Brace & Company** 73 (tr); 75 (cr); 80 (br); 68 (c), (c), (c), (c), 69 (br), 70 (r), 71 (cr) ASG Sherman Graphics, Inc.; 76 (b) Weronica Ankarorn; 77 (tr) ASG Sherman Graphics, Inc.; 78 (br) Ed McDonald; 80 (cr) Allan Landau; 81 (b), 82 (tc), (tr) ASG Sherman Graphics, Inc. **Other** 68 (br) SuperStock, Inc; 68-69 (bkg) Jim Millay/Panoramic Images; 71 (c) James Blank/Stock•Boston; 72 (t) Alan Levenson/Tony Stone Worldwide; 72 (b) Metatools; 74 (tr) A. & J. Verkaik/The Stock Market; 78 (cr) Julie Houck/Stock•Boston. **Chapter 6 Harcourt Brace & Company** 96 (cr); 96 (br); 96 (br); 84 (l) Allan Landau; 84 (c), (cr), 84-85 (bkg), 85 (tr), (br) ASG Sherman Graphics, Inc.; 86 (b) Allan Landau; 87 (t), 88 (r) Weronica Ankarorn; 90 (tr) ASG Sherman Graphics, Inc.; 93 (cr) Rich Franco. **Other** 84 (br) PhotoDisc; 84-85 (bkg) Bruce Coleman, Inc.; 89 (tr) Bettmann Archive; 90 (br) The Lowe Art Museum, The University of Miami/SuperStock, Inc; 92 (c) SuperStock, Inc; 94 (br) Metatools; 98 (c) D. & J. Heaton/Stock•Boston. **Chapter 7 Harcourt Brace & Company** 109 (cr); 100 (c), 100-101 (bkg), 101 (cr) ASG Sherman Graphics, Inc.; 103 (t), 104 (tr) Allan Landau; 105 (cr) ASG Sherman Graphics, Inc.; 106 (tr) Weronica Ankarorn; 109 (cr) Metropolitan Museum of Art, Rogers Fund ; 110 (tr) Allan Landau; 110 (br), 111 (r) ASG Sherman Graphics, Inc. **Other** 100-101 (bkg) Tony Stone Worldwide; 103 (br) PhotoDisc; 104 (b) Julie Bendel; 108 (tr) NASA. **Chapter 8 Harcourt Brace & Company** 121 (tc); 121 (tr); 123 (cr); 116 (tl), (c), (r), 116-117 (bkg), 117 (br), 124 (cr) ASG Sherman Graphics, Inc.; 124 (b) Allan Landau; 126 (tr) Weronica Ankarorn; 128 (c) Allan Landau; 128 (r) ASG Sherman Graphics, Inc. **Other** 118 (tr) SuperStock, Inc; 118 (bc) John Lei/Stock•Boston; 118 (br) The Stock Market; 119 (cr) PhotoDisc; 120 (cr) Bettmann Archive; 122 (tr) Rob Crandall/Stock•Boston; 129 (cr) Mark Gamba/The Stock Market; 130 (cr) Hans Neleman/Image Bank; 130 (br) David Austen/Stock•Boston; 132 (c) Owen Franken/Stock•Boston; 136 (cl), (c), (cr) Corel Co. **Chapter 9 Harcourt Brace & Company** 143 (tr); 138 (cl), (c), (cr), 140 (tr) ASG Sherman Graphics, Inc.; 140 (cr) Allan Landau; 143 (cr) Sheri O'Neal; 144 (b), 150 (cr) Rich Franco. **Other** 141 (tr) David Young-Wolff/PhotoEdit; 145 (tr) PhotoDisc; 146 (r) Thomas R. Fletcher/Stock•Boston; 147 (cr) Lawrence Migdale/Photo Researchers, Inc.; 150 (tc) PhotoDisc. **Chapter 10 Harcourt Brace & Company** 156 (tr); 158 (c); 162 (tr); 163 (cr); 154 (t), (c) Allan Landau; 154-155 (bkg) ASG Sherman Graphics, Inc.; 158 (cr) Allan Landau; 160 (tr), 161 (tr) ASG Sherman Graphics, Inc.; 162 (br) Allan Landau; 165 (l) Metatools; 166 (r) Allan Landau; 167 (cr) ASG Sherman Graphics, Inc. **Other** 154-155 (bkg) PhotoDisc; 156 (br) D.P. Hershkowitz/Bruce Coleman, Inc.; 159 (tr), (cr) Corel Co.; 159 (br) Catherine Ursillo/Photo Researchers, Inc.; 166 (b) Chuck Keeler/Tony Stone Worldwide; 167 (bl), (br) Metatools; 168 (c) Corel Co. **Chapter 11 Harcourt Brace & Company** 170 (c); 170 (cr); 178 (tc); 178 (tr); 170 (tr), (cl), (cr), 172 (tr), (br) ASG Sherman Graphics, Inc.; 173 (cr), 174 (r), 176 (r) Allan Landau; 177 (br) Weronica Ankarorn; 178 (r) Allan Landau; 183 (c) ASG Sherman Graphics, Inc. **Other** 170 (tl), (c), (bl) Corel Co.; 171 (tr), (bl) Corel Co.; 175 (r) Tony Stone Worldwide; 179 (br) Eleanor Thompson/The Stock Market; 184 (cr) PhotoDisc; 188 (bl) David Young/Wolff/PhotoEdit. **Chapter 12 Harcourt Brace & Company** 190 (cl); 190-191 (bkg) Anthony Neste; 194 (cr); 195 (cr); 199 (cr); 201 (cr); 201 (cr); 203 (tr); 204 (tr); 190 (bkg), 191 (r) Allan Landau; 191 (bc), 192 (t) ASG Sherman Graphics, Inc.; 192 (b) Allan Landau; 193 (cr), (b) ASG Sherman Graphics, Inc.; 196 (tr), 197 (cr), 198 (b), 202 (tr) Allan Landau. **Other** 200 (tr) Vincent Merritt/PhotoEdit; 201 (cr) Metatools; 205 (cr) Mary Kate Denny/PhotoEdit. **Chapter 13 Harcourt Brace & Company** 208 (cl) Allan Landau; 208 (c) ASG Sherman Graphics, Inc.; 208 (cr) Allan Landau; 208-209 (bkg), 209 (br), 211 (cr), (b) ASG Sherman Graphics, Inc.; 212 (b) Allan Landau; 213 (br) ASG Sherman Graphics, Inc.; 215 (br), 216 (tr) Allan Landau; 217 (cr) ASG Sherman Graphics, Inc.; 218 (r) Allan Landau; 219 (cr) ASG Sherman Graphics, Inc.; 210 (br) © 1981 M. C. Escher Heirs, c/o Beeldrecht, Amsterdam Published in 1983 by Harry Abrams, Incorporated, New York; 212 (cr) Sears Roebuck & Co.; 220 (t) Allan Landau; 221 (cr) ASG Sherman Graphics, Inc. **Other** 220 (br) Gary Vestal/Tony Stone Worldwide; 222 (tr) PhotoDisc. **Chapter 14 Harcourt Brace & Company** 226 (tc); 226 (tr); 229 (tr); 229 (cr); 224 (bkg), 224-225 (c), 225 (br) ASG Sherman Graphics, Inc.; 226 (b) Allan Landau; 227 (r), 228 (cl) ASG Sherman Graphics, Inc.; 228 (cr) Sheri O'Neal; 228 (b) Rich Franco; 230 (c) Allan Landau; 231 (tr), 233 (r), 234 (b), 235 (r), 237 (br) ASG Sherman Graphics, Inc. **Other** 224 (br) SuperStock, Inc; 226 (tl) Metatools; 229 (tl) PhotoDisc; 231 (c) David Young-Wolff/PhotoEdit; 231 (cr) Metatools; 231 (bl) Mark C. Burnett/Stock•Boston; 232 (tr) Doug Armand/Tony Stone Worldwide; 236 (c) Myrleen Ferguson/PhotoEdit; 238 (c) David Weintraub/Stock•Boston; 238 (br) Lawrence Migdale/Stock•Boston. **Chapter 15 Harcourt Brace & Company** 251 (r); 252 (br); 257 (tr); 244 (r), 245 (br) ASG Sherman Graphics, Inc.; 246 (r), 248 (tr) Allan Landau; 248 (tr) ASG Sherman Graphics, Inc.; 250 (t) Allan Landau; 253 (c), 254 (r), 255 (tr) ASG Sherman Graphics, Inc.; 256 (r) Allan Landau. **Other** 244-245 (b), 246 (tr), 247 (cr), 253 (r) PhotoDisc. **Chapter 16 Harcourt Brace & Company** 265 (c); 271 (cr); 272 (tr); 260 (cl), (c), 261 (br) ASG Sherman Graphics, Inc.; 262 (r) Allan Landau; 262 (b) ASG Sherman Graphics, Inc.; 264 (tr) Rich Franco; 267 (br) ASG Sherman Graphics, Inc.; 268 (br) Weronica Ankarorn; 269 (br) ASG Sherman Graphics, Inc.; 272 (b) Rich Franco. **Other** 260-261 (bkg) David Binder/Stock•Boston; 261 (cr) PhotoDisc; 265 (cr) Corel Co.; 270 (br) Diane Graham-Henry/Tony Stone Worldwide; 274 (c) Michele Burgess/Stock•Boston. **Chapter 17 Harcourt Brace & Company** 279 (r); 281 (tr); 283 (cr); 287 (cr); 276 (cl) ASG Sherman Graphics, Inc.; 276 (c) Allan Landau; 276-277 (bkg), 277 (br) ASG Sherman Graphics, Inc.; 280 (r) Allan Landau; 286 (r) Sheri O'Neal. **Other** 276 (l) Tony Stone Worldwide; 284 (tr) Bob Daemmrich/Stock•Boston; 285 (cr) Tom Tietz/Tony Stone Worldwide; 287 (tr) PhotoDisc. **Chapter 18 Harcourt Brace & Company** 292 (tr); 294 (r); 299 (r); 290 (cl), (cr) ASG Sherman Graphics, Inc.; 290-291 (bkg), 291 (cr) Allan Landau; 291 (bc) ASG Sherman Graphics, Inc.; 294 (cr) Allan Landau; 297 (r), 298 (tr) ASG Sherman Graphics, Inc.; 300 (r) Sheri O'Neal. **Other** 295 (cr) Eleanor Thompson/The Stock Market; 298 (br), 301 (cr) PhotoDisc; 302 (c) Ian Murphy/Tony Stone Worldwide; 302 (cr) Tony Stone Worldwide; 306 (bl) Roberto Valladares/Image Bank. **Chapter 19 Harcourt Brace & Company** 308 (l) Allan Landau; 308 (br), 309 (c), (b) ASG Sherman Graphics, Inc.; 310 (tr) Allan Landau; 311 (cr), 316 (tr) ASG Sherman Graphics, Inc.; 316 (cl), (c), (cr) Eric Camden; 317 (tr), 318 (tr), 319 (tr) ASG Sherman Graphics, Inc. **Other** 308-309 (bkg) Ben Simmons/The Stock Market; 312 (tr) Michelle Bridwell/PhotoEdit; 312 (r) Mark Burnett/Stock•Boston; 313 (tr) Richard Pasley/Stock•Boston; 314 (br) Tony Freeman/PhotoEdit; 315 (cr) Pete Saloutos/The Stock Market; 318 (br) SuperStock, Inc; 320 (tr) Frank Siteman/PhotoEdit. **Chapter 20 Harcourt Brace & Company** 324 (tl), (cl), (c), (cr), 324-325 (bkg), (bkg), 326 (tr), 327 (cr) ASG Sherman Graphics, Inc.; 328 (tr) Allan Landau; 328 (cr) Weronica Ankarorn; 330 (t) ASG Sherman Graphics, Inc.; 333 (br) Weronica Ankarorn; 334 (t) Allan Landau; 335 (br) ASG Sherman Graphics, Inc. Other 329 (cr) Gilbert R. Boucher II/Daily Herald; 332 (cr) Richard Hutchings/PhotoEdit; 333 (tr) PhotoDisc; 336 (b) Bruce Hands/Stock•Boston. **Chapter 21 Harcourt Brace & Company** 343 (tr); 352 (br); 338 (cl), (c), (cr), 338-339 (bkg), 339 (tr) ASG Sherman Graphics, Inc.; 340 (c), (br) Sheri O'Neal; 341 (tl), (tc), (cl), (c) ASG Sherman Graphics, Inc.; 344 (r) Allan Landau; 345 (br) Rich Franco; 346 (tr) Allan Landau; 346 (br) Rich Franco; 348 (tl) Allan Landau; 350 (cl), (cr), (cr), 355 (r) ASG Sherman Graphics, Inc. **Other** 338 (br) PhotoDisc; 342 (cr) Lawrence Migdale/Tony Stone Worldwide; 348 (br) David Madison/Bruce Coleman, Inc. **Chapter 22 Harcourt Brace & Company** 358 (l), (c), (r), 358-359 (c), 359 (br) ASG Sherman Graphics, Inc.; 360 (tr) Allan Landau; 363 (tr) ASG Sherman Graphics, Inc.; 364 (tr) Weronica Ankarorn; 366 (tr), 368 (r) Allan Landau; 369 (br) Weronica Ankarorn. **Other** 359 (br) Metatools; 361 (cr) Dennis McDonald/PhotoEdit; 362 (cr) David Young-Wolff/PhotoEdit; 367 (tr) Elaine Rebman/Photo Researchers, Inc.; 370 (cl), (c) Hulton Getty/Tony Stone Worldwide; 374 (tr) SuperStock,Inc. **Chapter 23 Harcourt Brace & Company** 392 (tr); 376 (c), (r), 377 (r) ASG Sherman Graphics, Inc.; 382 (br), 384 (b) Allan Landau; 385 (tr), 387 (cr) ASG Sherman Graphics, Inc. **Other** 376-377 (bkg), 378 (cr) NASA; 380 (tr) SuperStock, Inc; 381 (cr) James Lowenthal/Bruce Coleman, Inc.; 383 (t) Stephen Kline/Bruce Coleman, Inc.; 388 (cr) PhotoDisc; 391 (tr) Corel Co. **Chapter 24 Harcourt Brace & Company** 404 (cr); 394 (c), 395 (br) ASG Sherman Graphics, Inc.; 396 (cl), (c) Rich Franco; 396 (cr), 398 (tr), (cl), (c) ASG Sherman Graphics, Inc.; 399 (cr) Rich Franco; 402 (tl) Weronica Ankarorn; 402 (c) Rich Franco; 402 (r) Allan Landau; 403 (r), (bc) Rich Franco; 404 (b) Allan Landau; 405 (br) ASG Sherman Graphics, Inc. **Other** 394 (bkg) Maggio Kalish/The Stock Market; 406 (cl) Robert Herko/Tony Stone Worldwide; 406 (cr) Kenneth W. Fink/Bruce Coleman, Inc.; 406 (br) SuperStock, Inc. **Chapter 25 Harcourt Brace & Company** 408 (tl), (tr), (c), 409 (br) ASG Sherman Graphics, Inc.; 410 (cr), (bl), (bc), (br) Rich Franco; 412 (cl), (c), (cr), 413 (cr) Allan Landau; 414 (cr) ASG Sherman Graphics, Inc.; 414 (r) Allan Landau; 417 (c), (cr) Rich Franco; 419 (cr) ASG Sherman Graphics, Inc.; 420 (br) Allan Landau. **Other** 408-409 (bkg) PhotoDisc; 411 (tr) Photo Researchers, Inc.; 415 (br) SuperStock, Inc. **Chapter 26 Harcourt Brace & Company** 434 (br); 422 (c), (cr), 422-423 (bkg), 423 (tr) ASG Sherman Graphics, Inc.; 426 (c) Allan Landau; 427 (r) ASG Sherman Graphics, Inc.; 432 (cr) Allan Landau; 432 (br), 433 (tr), 435 (cr) ASG Sherman Graphics, Inc. **Other** 425 (tr) SuperStock, Inc; 431 (cr) Bob Daemmrich/Stock•Boston; 434 (tr) John Elk III/Stock•Boston; 436 (cr) Corel Co.; 440 (cr) S.L. Craig Jr./Bruce Coleman, Inc. **Chapter 27 Harcourt Brace & Company** 446 (br); 454 (cr); 442 (c) Allan Landau; 442 (cr), 443 (br) ASG Sherman Graphics, Inc.; 444 (tr), (br), 446 (tr) Allan Landau; 447 (tr), 449 (cr) ASG Sherman Graphics, Inc.; 450 (b), 456 (tr) Allan Landau; 456 (br) ASG Sherman Graphics, Inc. **Other** 442-443 (bkg) Panoramic Images; 442-443 (c) Westlight; 448 (tr) Frank Siteman/Stock•Boston; 451 (tr) SuperStock, Inc; 453 (cr) David Young-Wolff/PhotoEdit. **Chapter 28 Harcourt Brace & Company** 458 (br); 461 (tr); 471 (cr); 458 (tr), (c), (cr), 458-459 (bkg), 459 (bc) ASG Sherman Graphics, Inc.; 460 (r), (br) Allan Landau; 462 (tr), 466 (cl), 470 (br) ASG Sherman Graphics, Inc. **Other** 463 (bc) Mark E. Gibson/The Stock Market; 464 (tr) Jim Pickerell/Tony Stone Worldwide; 465 (tr) David Young-Wolff/PhotoEdit; 467 (cr) PhotoDisc; 470 (cr) David Young-Wolff/PhotoEdit; 472 (cl) John Neubauer/SuperStock, Inc; 472 (c) John Neubauer/PhotoEdit; **Student Handbook Harcourt Brace & Company** H08 (b); H11 (tr); H23 (br); H24 (bc); H24 (br); H26 (tr); H42 (r); H02 (c) ASG Sherman Graphics, Inc.; H05 (bc) Victoria Bowen; H12 (tr) Sheri O'Neal; H19 (r) Rich Franco; H20 (c) ASG Sherman Graphics, Inc.; H22 (cl) Rich Franco; H24 (bl), (bc), H28 (bc) ASG Sherman Graphics, Inc.; H34 (tr) Weronica Ankarorn; H36 (c) ASG Sherman Graphics, Inc.; H37 (b) Rich Franco; H38 (r), H40 (tr) ASG Sherman Graphics, Inc.; H40 (br) Rich Franco; H44 (tr) Allan Landau; H50 (r) ASG Sherman Graphics, Inc.; H53 (tr) Metatools; H56 (br) ASG Sherman Graphics, Inc. **Other** H4 (tr) Anthony Edgeworth, Inc./The Stock Market; H5 (tr) Tony Stone Worldwide; H6 (tr) Chip Henderson/Tony Stone Worldwide; H7 (cr) Doug Pensinger/Allsport U.S.A.; H8 (br) StockFood America; H10 (tr) E. Foster/Bruce Coleman, Inc.; H13 (br) PhotoDisc; H14 (tr) Keith Wood/Tony Stone Worldwide; H16 (tr) Tony Freeman/PhotoEdit; H21 (r) Art Wolfe/Tony Stone Worldwide; H25 (cr) The Stock Market; H26 (bl) Philip Jon Bailey/Stock•Boston; H26 (bl) PhotoDisc; H26 (bc), (br) Metatools; H27 (r) NASA; H28 (tr) Art Resource, Inc.; H28 (bl) Metatools; H28 (bc) Peter Steiner/The Stock Market; H28 (br) PhotoDisc; H29 (c) Richard Parker/Photo Researchers, Inc.; H29 (cr) Metatools; H29 (bc) SuperStock, Inc; H29 (br), H30 (cr) PhotoDisc; H33 (cr) David Weintraub/Photo Researchers, Inc.; H39 (cr) Bob Daemmrich/Tony Stone Worldwide; H43 (r) PhotoDisc; H47 (cr) Bruno De Hogues/Tony Stone Worldwide; H48 (tr) Geoffrey Clifford/The Stock Market; H48 (br) Kevin Horan/Stock•Boston; H56 (tr) Michael Newman/PhotoEdit; H66 (br) Dennis M. Gottlieb/The Stock Market; H69 (cr) Don Smetzer/Tony Stone Worldwide.

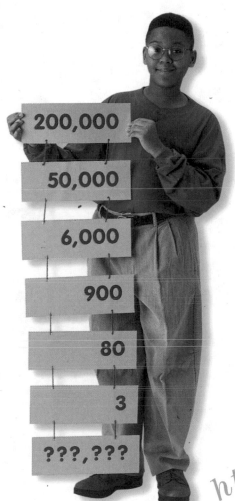

200,000

50,000

6,000

900

80

3

???,???

200,000

50,000

6,000

900

80

3

???,???

http://www.hbschool.com